Defect

Detect

School of Security

.NET
Memory Dump Analysis
Accelerated

Seventh Edition

Dmitry Vostokov
Software Diagnostics Services

Accelerated .NET Memory Dump Analysis: Training Course Transcript with WinDbg and LLDB Practice Exercises, Seventh Edition

Published by OpenTask, Republic of Ireland

OpenTask books are available through booksellers and distributors worldwide. For further information or comments, send requests to press@opentask.com.

A CIP catalog record for this book is available from the British Library.

ISBN-13: 978-1-912636-87-7 (Paperback)

Revision 7.02 (May 2025)

Contents

About the Author

Dmitry Vostokov is an internationally recognized expert, speaker, educator, scientist, inventor, and author. He founded the pattern-oriented software diagnostics, forensics, and prognostics discipline (Systematic Software Diagnostics) and Software Diagnostics and Observability Institute (DA+TA: DumpAnalysis.org + TraceAnalysis.org). Vostokov has also authored over 50 books on software diagnostics, anomaly detection and analysis, software and memory forensics, root cause analysis and problem solving, memory dump analysis, debugging, software trace and log analysis, reverse engineering, and malware analysis. He has over 30 years of experience in software architecture, design, development, and maintenance in various industries, including leadership, technical, and people management roles. Dmitry founded OpenTask Iterative and Incremental Publishing (OpenTask.com) and Software Diagnostics Technology and Services (former Memory Dump Analysis Services) PatternDiagnostics.com. In his spare time, he explores Software Narratology and Quantum Software Diagnostics. His interest areas are theoretical software diagnostics and its mathematical and computer science foundations, application of formal logic, semiotics, artificial intelligence, machine learning, and data mining to diagnostics and anomaly detection, software diagnostics engineering and diagnostics-driven development, diagnostics workflow and interaction. Recent interest areas also include functional programming, cloud native computing, monitoring, observability, visualization, security, automation, applications of category theory to software diagnostics, development and big data, and diagnostics of artificial intelligence.

Introduction

.NET
Memory Dump Analysis
Accelerated

Version 7.0

Dmitry Vostokov
Software Diagnostics Services

Hello Everyone, my name is Dmitry Vostokov, and I teach this training course.

Course Versions

◉ Accelerated .NET Memory Dump Analysis
Versions 1 – 3 (.NET Framework)

◉ Accelerated .NET Memory Dump Analysis
Version 4 (.NET Framework + .NET Core)

◉ Accelerated .NET Core Memory Dump Analysis
Versions 1 – Revised (.NET Core + .NET)

◉ Accelerated .NET Memory Dump Analysis
Version 7 (.NET)

Prerequisites

WinDbg Commands	LLDB Commands
We use these boxes to introduce some WinDbg commands used in practice exercises	We use these boxes to introduce some LLDB commands used in practice exercises

Basic .NET programming and debugging

You need to have software development and debugging experience in .NET or the previous .NET Core and .NET Framework versions. I suppose you know C#, although this is not strictly necessary. The ability to read unmanaged assembly language has some advantages but is not necessary for this training and we also review the relevant disassembly basics. I also assume you already know what .NET is, its basic architecture and vocabulary such as assemblies, CLR, managed code, classes, and objects. Familiarity with stack traces is essential, too.

Training Goals

⊙ Review fundamentals

⊙ Learn how to analyze process dumps

⊙ Learn necessary commands in context

Our primary goal is to learn .NET memory dump analysis in an accelerated fashion. So, first, we review the absolutely essential fundamentals necessary for memory dump analysis. Then we go through several process memory dumps with the goal to learn the most useful WinDbg and its debugging extension commands in the context of real-life-like examples where multiple threads are modeling different patterns of abnormal software behavior. We cover CoreCLR for .NET 9.

Training Principles

- ◉ Talk only about what I can show

- ◉ Lots of pictures

- ◉ Lots of examples

- ◉ Original content

There were many training formats to consider, and I decided that the best way is to concentrate on exercises. Specifically, for this training, I developed more than 15 of them.

What's New in Version 7

- ⊙ .NET 9

- ⊙ x64 Linux

- ⊙ LLDB

- ⊙ Relevant x64 disassembly review

- ⊙ Basics of IL disassembly

- ⊙ Mechanism analysis patterns

- ⊙ Memory dump collection methods

What We Do Not Cover

- ARM64

- macOS

We promise to include these topics in the next edition

Fundamentals (Windows)

Memory Space (x86)

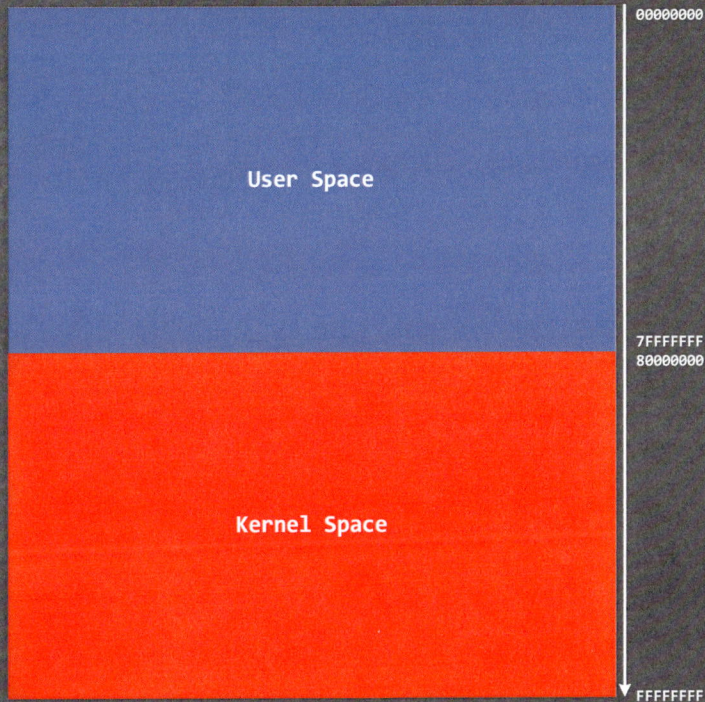

User Space

`00000000`

`7FFFFFFF`
`80000000`

Kernel Space

`FFFFFFFF`

Now I show you some pictures. We use x64 examples in this training course. .NET exercises are x64, with one x86 exercise showing the difference. Most of the time, fundamentals do not change when we move to the x86 Windows platform, and the analysis process (including WinDbg commands) is the same. However, there may be slight differences.

Every Windows process memory range is divided into kernel space part and user space part. I follow the long tradition of using red color for kernel and blue color for user part. This uniform memory space is called virtual process space because it is an abstraction that allows us to analyze memory dumps without thinking about how it is all organized in physical memory. In this training, we are concerned with the user space only.

Memory Space (x64)

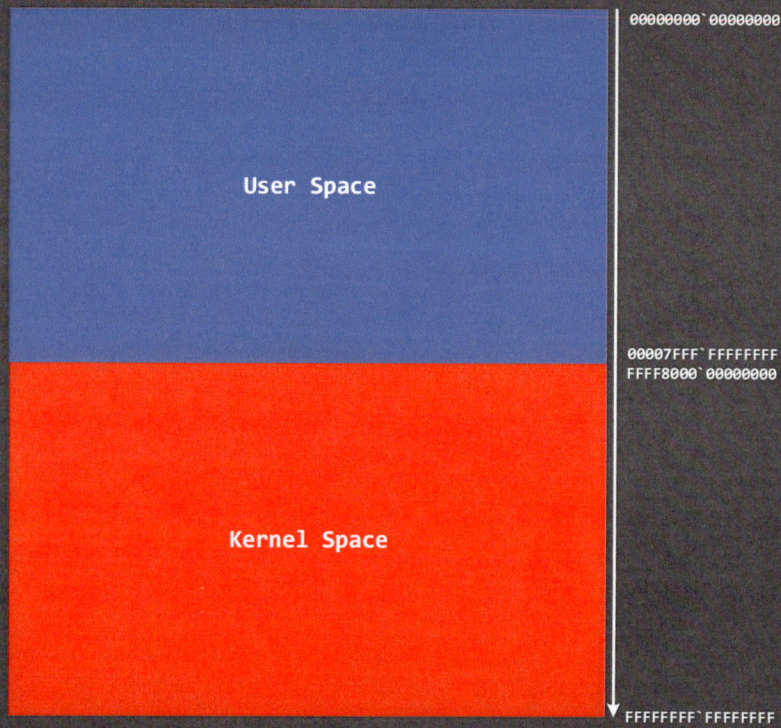

User Space

`00000000`00000000`

`00007FFF`FFFFFFFF`
`FFFF8000`00000000`

Kernel Space

`FFFFFFFF`FFFFFFFF`

Further slides assume x64 virtual process memory space.

User/Managed Space

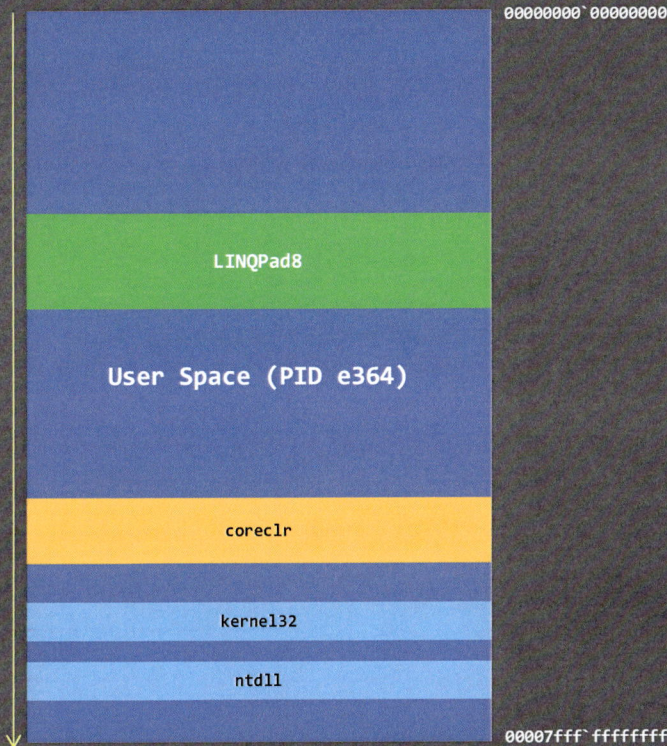

```
00000000`00000000
```

LINQPad8

User Space (PID e364)

coreclr

kernel32

ntdll

```
00007fff`ffffffff
```

WinDbg Commands

lmv command lists all loaded modules (EXE and DLLs)

When an application is loaded, all modules (an executable image on a disk and associated DLLs) are organized sequentially in memory space. Some modules can also be loaded twice at different memory locations. A process is then set up for running, and a process ID is assigned to it. If you run another such process, it has a different memory space (it could be the same in layout, but most recent Windows versions put modules in a different order). Note that **coreclr** is just another module in a process address space, and so are all supporting modules from .NET. All subsequent slides assume .NET. Managed space is also an abstraction that refers to managed code, its IL assembly language, and associated managed stack traces during hardware-independent execution. .NET CLR translates managed code to code running in unmanaged user space on particular hardware.

Types/Assemblies/Modules

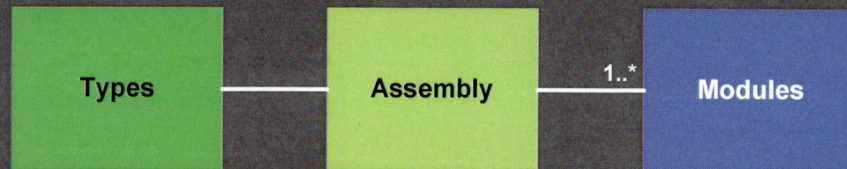

Remember that all assembly types (classes) can be spread through several modules like DLLs. Three commands listed in a box allow you to see which module corresponds to a code address from an unmanaged stack trace. I will show you an example in one of the following slides.

Process Threads

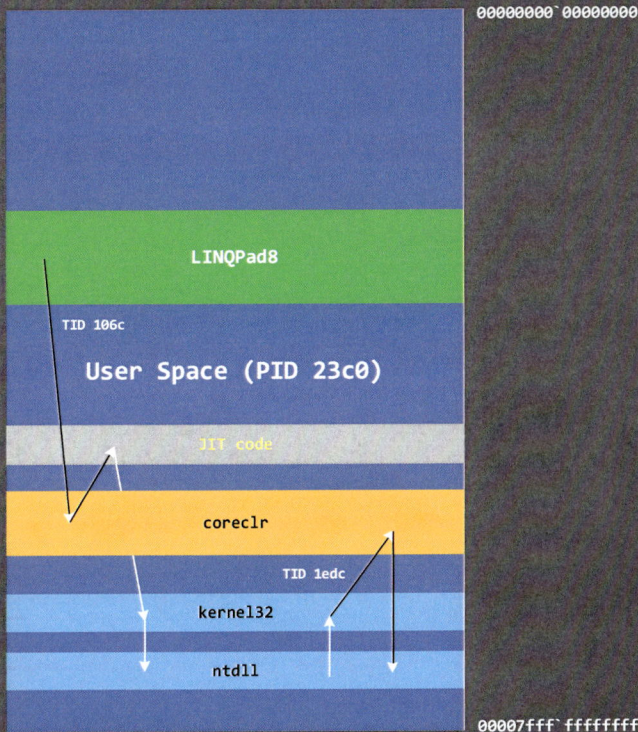

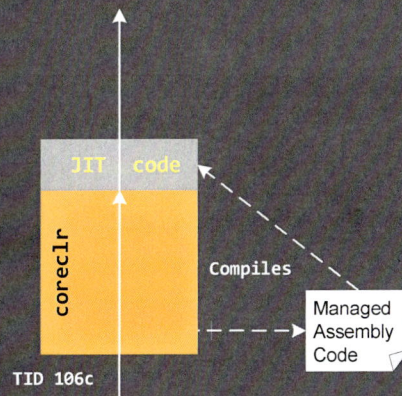

Now, we come to another important fundamental concept in Windows memory dump analysis: a thread. It is a unit of execution, and there can be many threads in a given process. When a thread executes managed code, it is compiled into memory: the so-called JIT code. We need to load a WinDbg SOS extension to analyze it. It is named **sos.dll**. For .NET, it is included with the latest WinDbg or Debugging Tools for Windows we use in this training. If it is not automatically loaded on demand or the wrong version is loaded, we show how to load the required version.

Thread Stack Raw Data

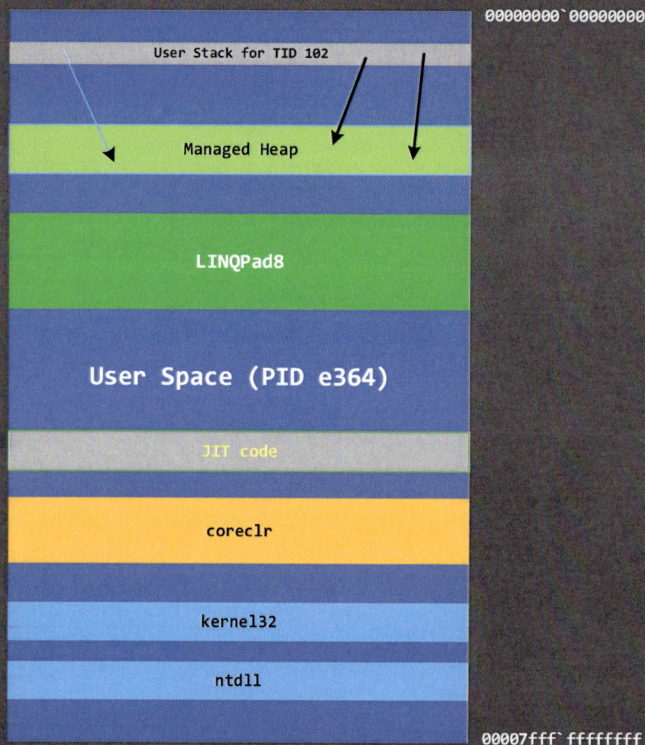

Every thread also needs a temporary memory region to store its execution history and temporary data. This region is called the **thread stack**. Please note that the stack region is just any other memory region, and you can use any WinDbg data dumping commands there. We also learn how to get the thread stack region address range. Examining raw stack data can hint at the past system behavior: the so-called **Execution Residue** pattern. Because managed code (an abstraction) is JIT-translated to unmanaged machine code, raw stack data also contains object references, and you can dump them using **!DumpStackObjects (!dso)** command.

Thread Stack Trace

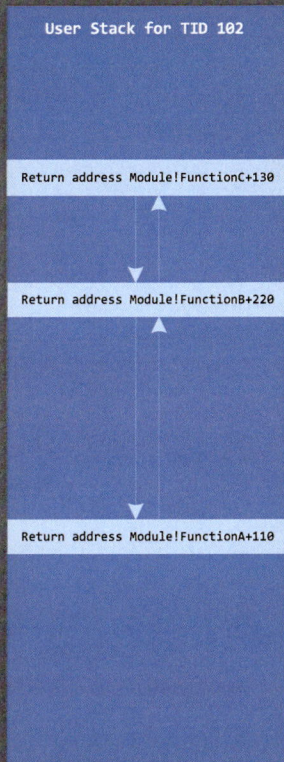

```
FunctionA()
{
  ...
  FunctionB();
  ...
}
FunctionB()
{
  ...
  FunctionC();
  ...
}
FunctionC()
{
  ...
  FunctionD();
  ...
}
```

User Stack for TID 102

Return address Module!FunctionC+130

Return address Module!FunctionB+220

Return address Module!FunctionA+110

Module!FunctionA

Resumes from address   Saves return address
Module!FunctionA+110   Module!FunctionA+110

Module!FunctionB

Resumes from address   Saves return address
Module!FunctionB+220   Module!FunctionB+220

Module!FunctionC

Resumes from address   Saves return address
Module!FunctionC+130   Module!FunctionC+130

Module!FunctionD

WinDbg Commands

```
0:000> k
Module!FunctionD
Module!FunctionC+130
Module!FunctionB+220
Module!FunctionA+110
```

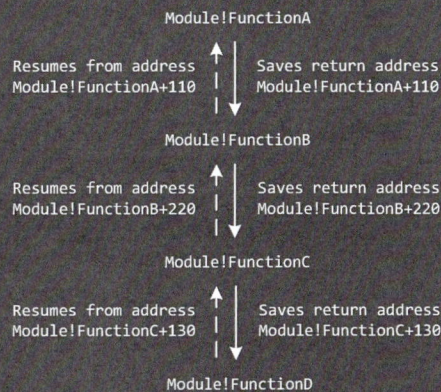

Now, we explain thread stack traces in unmanaged user space. Suppose we have source code where *FunctionA* calls *FunctionB* at some point, and *FunctionB* calls *FunctionC,* and so on. This is a thread of execution. If *FunctionA* calls *FunctionB*, you expect the execution thread to return to the same place where it left and then resume from there. This is achieved by saving a return address in the thread stack region. So every return address is saved and then restored during the course of thread execution. Although the memory addresses grow from top to bottom in this picture, return addresses are saved from bottom to top. This might seem counter-intuitive to all previous pictures, but this is how you would see the output from WinDbg commands. What WinDbg does when you instruct it to dump a stack trace from a given thread is to analyze thread raw stack data and figure out return addresses, map them to symbolic form according to symbol files, and show them from top to bottom. Note that *FunctionD* is not present in the raw stack data on the left because the thread is currently executing the function *FunctionD* called from *FunctionC*. However, *FunctionC* called *FunctionD,* and the return address of *FunctionC* was saved. In the gray box on the right, we see the results of the WinDbg command.

Thread Stack Trace (no PDB)

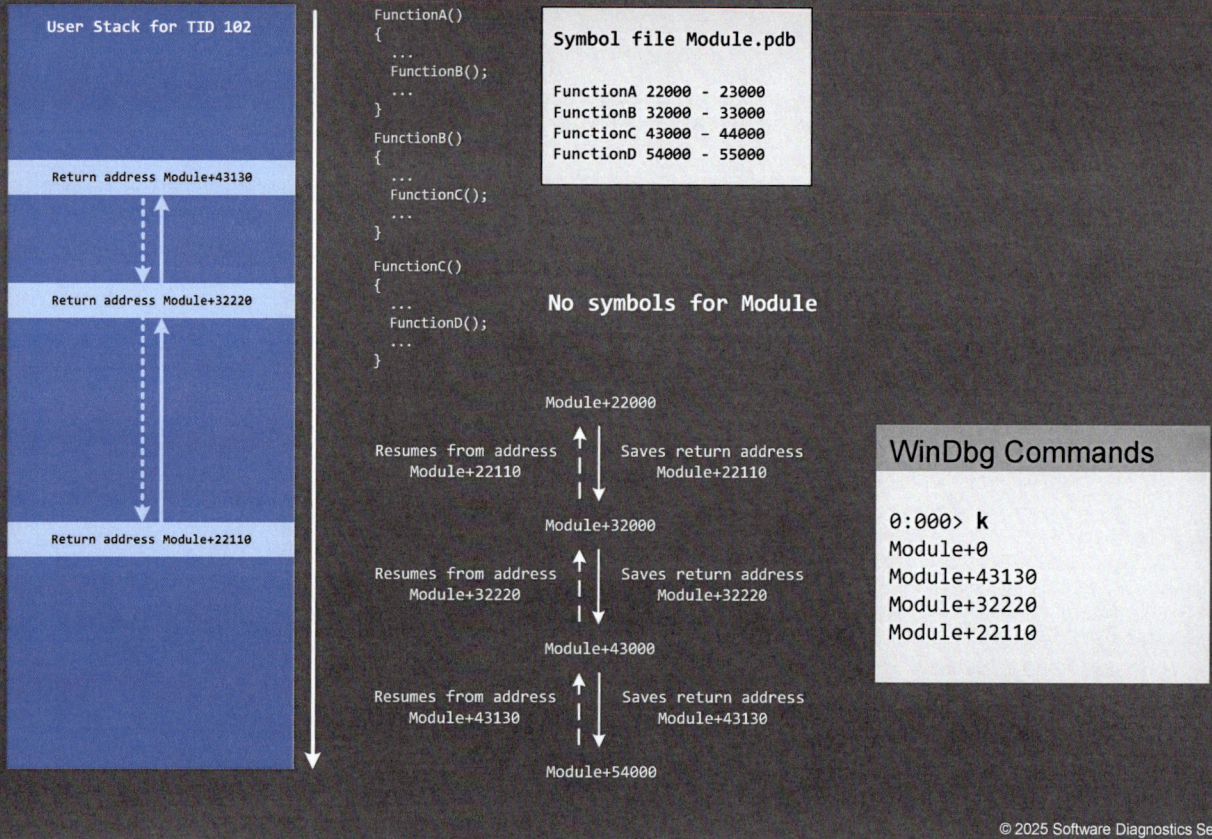

User Stack for TID 102

Return address Module+43130

Return address Module+32220

Return address Module+22110

```
FunctionA()
{
  ...
  FunctionB();
  ...
}
FunctionB()
{
  ...
  FunctionC();
  ...
}
FunctionC()
{
  ...
  FunctionD();
  ...
}
```

```
Symbol file Module.pdb

FunctionA 22000 - 23000
FunctionB 32000 - 33000
FunctionC 43000 - 44000
FunctionD 54000 - 55000
```

No symbols for Module

Module+22000

Resumes from address
Module+22110 → Saves return address Module+22110

Module+32000

Resumes from address
Module+32220 → Saves return address Module+32220

Module+43000

Resumes from address
Module+43130 → Saves return address Module+43130

Module+54000

WinDbg Commands

```
0:000> k
Module+0
Module+43130
Module+32220
Module+22110
```

© 2025 Software Diagnostics Services

Here, I'd like to show you why symbol files are important and what stack traces from unmanaged user space you get without them. Symbol files just provide mappings between memory address ranges and associated symbols, like a table of contents in a book. So, in the absence of symbols, we are left with bare module names that are saved in a dump. Dumps with .NET code are much better because .NET assembly modules usually include full code description inside, and the managed stack trace has full function names.

Thread Stack Trace (JIT Code)

Similar stack trace actions occur in the case of JIT code with the difference that we may not have symbolic names, only plain addresses. The recent SOS extensions for Windows can show the symbolic names.

Unmanaged Stack Trace

```
0:000> kL
 # Child-SP          RetAddr           Call Site
00 000000af`59afdf38 00007ffc`d7ef6434 win32u!NtUserWaitMessage+0x14
01 000000af`59afdf40 00007ffd`06a7ee79 System_Windows_Forms_Primitives!Windows.Win32.PInvoke.WaitMessage+0x74
02 000000af`59afdff0 00007ffd`06a81194 System_Windows_Forms!System.Windows.Forms.Application.ComponentManager.Microsoft...+0x2e9
03 000000af`59afe100 00007ffd`06a80e75 System_Windows_Forms!System.Windows.Forms.Application.ThreadContext...+0x2d4
04 000000af`59afe180 00007ffc`d4c59c08 System_Windows_Forms!System.Windows.Forms.Application.ThreadContext.RunMessageLoop+0x45
05 000000af`59afe1e0 00007ffc`d4c01931 LINQPad_GUI!LINQPad.UIProgram.Run+0xbb8
06 000000af`59afe4d0 00007ffc`d4bf7f93 LINQPad_GUI!LINQPad.UIProgram.Go+0x9f1
07 000000af`59afe800 00007ffc`d4bf6c6f LINQPad_GUI!LINQPad.UIProgram.Start+0x63
08 000000af`59afe860 00007ffc`d4bf61d0 LINQPad_GUI!LINQPad.UI.UILoader.Start+0x31f
09 000000af`59afe980 00007ffd`34769f43 LINQPad_GUI!LINQPad.UI.TestHarness.ContinueWithHostContext+0x80
0a 000000af`59afe9d0 00007ffd`346d24ba coreclr!CallDescrWorkerInternal+0x83
0b 000000af`59afea10 00007ffd`15c33a02 coreclr!RuntimeMethodHandle::InvokeMethod+0x37a
0c 000000af`59afed40 00007ffd`15c3339a System_Private_CoreLib!System.Reflection.MethodBaseInvoker.InvokeDirectByRefWithFewArgs+0xa2
0d 000000af`59afedc0 00007ffd`15c32953 System_Private_CoreLib!System.Reflection.MethodBaseInvoker.InvokeWithOneArg+0x25a
0e 000000af`59afeea0 00007ffc`d4bf2bc4 System_Private_CoreLib!System.Reflection.MethodBase.Invoke+0x23
0f 000000af`59afeee0 00007ffc`d4bf24ea LINQPad_GUI!
10 000000af`59afef90 00007ffc`d4bf230f LINQPad_GUI!
11 000000af`59aff060 00007ff7`be1c513b System_Private_CoreLib!ILStubClass.IL_STUB_ReversePInvoke(Int64, Int32)+0x4f
12 000000af`59aff0c0 00007ff7`be1c7df3 LINQPad8+0x1513b
13 000000af`59aff250 00007ff7`be1d5a72 LINQPad8+0x17df3
14 000000af`59affba0 00007ffd`eb2be8d7 LINQPad8+0x25a72
15 000000af`59affbe0 00007ffd`ec8714fc kernel32!BaseThreadInitThunk+0x17
16 000000af`59affc10 00000000`00000000 ntdll!RtlUserThreadStart+0x2c
```

```
0:000> !IP2MD 00007ffc`d4bf24ea
MethodDesc:        00007ffcd4d85db8
Method Name:       LINQPad.UI.TestHarness.Test(IntPtr, Int32)
Class:             00007ffcd4de6dc0
MethodTable:       00007ffcd4d85e18
mdToken:           0000000006000D1E
Module:            00007ffcd4d81740
IsJitted:          yes
Current CodeAddr:  00007ffcd4bf2370
Version History:
  ILCodeVersion:     0000000000000000
  ReJIT ID:          0
  IL Addr:           000002890c0d58ac
    CodeAddr:          00007ffcd4bf2370 (MinOptJitted)
    NativeCodeVersion: 0000000000000000
```

```
0:000> !DumpModule 00007ffcd4d81740
Name: C:\Program Files\LINQPad8\LINQPad.GUI.dll
Attributes:              PEFile
TransientFlags:          00209011
Assembly:                0000024875466540
BaseAddress:             000002890C050000
LoaderHeap:              00007FFD34A9B618
TypeDefToMethodTableMap: 00007FFCD4DA0000
TypeRefToMethodTableMap: 00007FFCD4DA2240
MethodDefToDescMap:      00007FFCD4DB3118
FieldDefToDescMap:       00007FFCD4DC2F88
MemberRefToDescMap:      00007FFCD4DA5308
FileReferencesMap:       0000000000000000
AssemblyReferencesMap:   00007FFCD4DD01B8
MetaData start address:  000002890C137CE4 (1142556 bytes)
```

I suppose that you know that all .NET managed code is translated to machine code (the so-called JIT). Then **coreclr** calls it. You see this continuity when you look at a stack trace. This JIT code is shown in yellow. To reiterate: IL and managed space are abstractions translated to unmanaged user space. The debugger output shows you how to manually get a JIT-compiled address's module name, class, and method from an unmanaged stack trace.

Fundamentals (Linux)

Memory Space (x64)

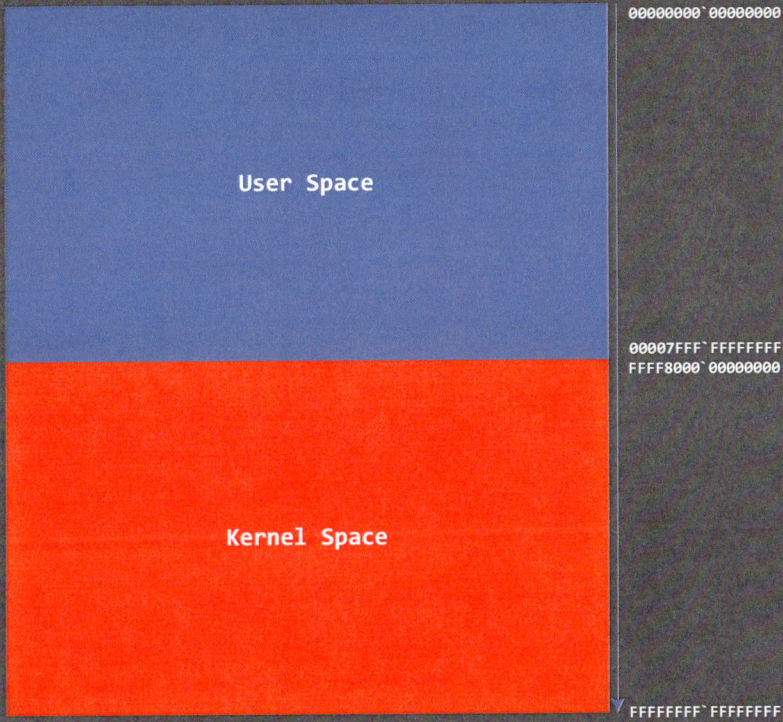

User Space

`00000000`00000000`

`00007FFF`FFFFFFFF`
`FFFF8000`00000000`

Kernel Space

`FFFFFFFF`FFFFFFFF`

© 2025 Software Diagnostics Services

The x64 memory space division for Linux is similar to the Windows one, if not identical.

User/Managed Space

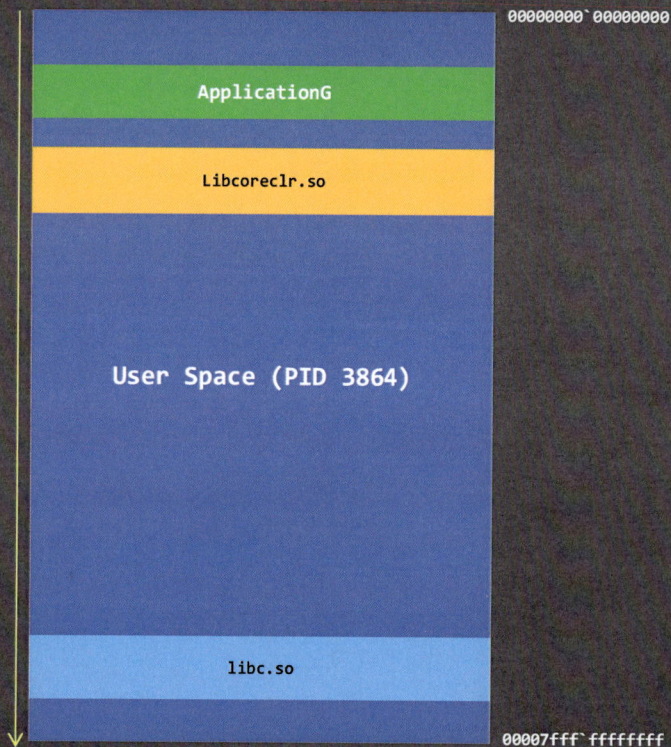

```
00000000`00000000
```

ApplicationG

Libcoreclr.so

User Space (PID 3864)

libc.so

```
00007fff`ffffffff
```

LLDB Commands

image list -p -f lists all loaded shared libraries

When an application is loaded, all modules (an executable image on a disk and associated shared libraries) are organized sequentially in memory space.

Process Threads

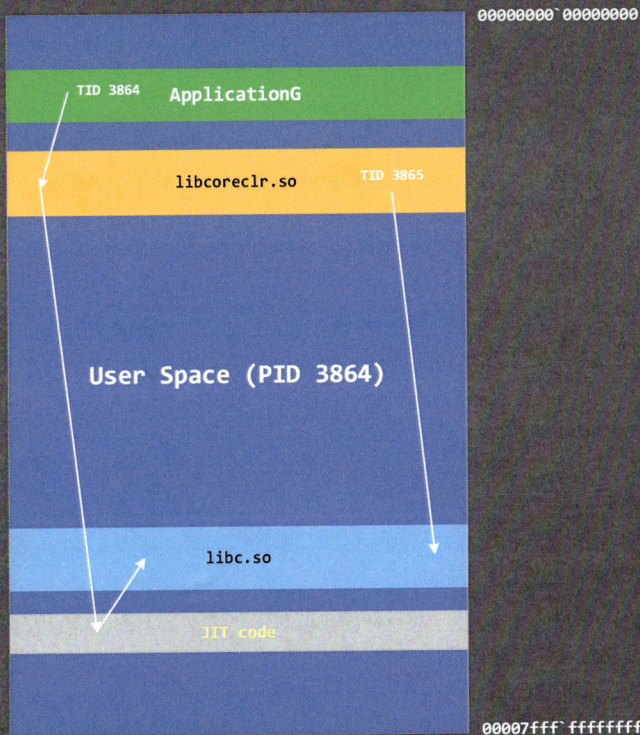

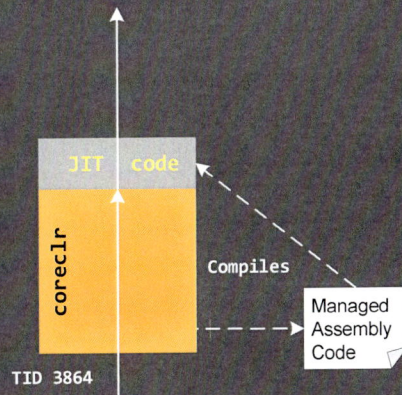

There can be many threads (lightweight processes) sharing the same process space. When a thread executes managed code, it is compiled into memory: the so-called JIT code.

WinDbg vs. LLDB

WinDbg Commands

```
0:000> k
00 00007fe9676bf300 Module!FunctionD+offset
01 00000000004005ca Module!FunctionC+130
02 00000000004005da AppA!FunctionB+220
03 0000000000000000 AppA!FunctionA+110
```

LLDB Commands

```
(lldb) bt
frame #0: 0x000000020328982a Module`FunctionD + offset
frame #1: 0x0000000203288a9c Module`FunctionC + 130
frame #2: 0x0000000104da3ea9 AppA`FunctionB + 220
frame #3: 0x0000000104da3edb AppA`FunctionA + 110
```

The difference from WinDbg here is that, in LLDB, the return address is on the same line for the function to return (except for *FunctionD*, where the address is the next instruction to execute), whereas in WinDbg, it is for the function on the next line.

Thread Stack Raw Data

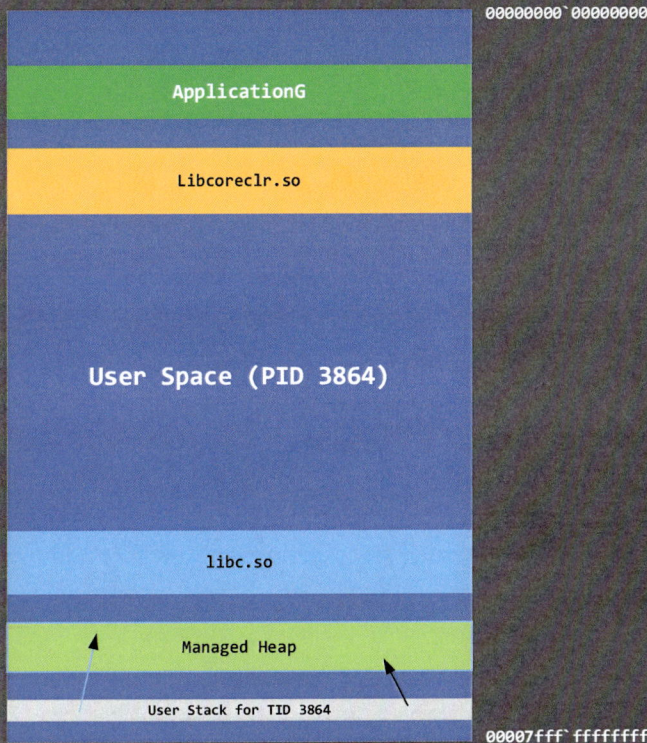

`00000000`00000000`

ApplicationG

Libcoreclr.so

User Space (PID 3864)

libc.so

Managed Heap

User Stack for TID 3864

`00007fff`ffffffff`

LLDB Commands

Get the stack range:
memory region $rsp

Dump raw data with symbols:
x/<num>a

Dump managed references:
dso

Every thread also needs a temporary memory region to store its execution history and temporary data. This region is called the **thread stack**. Please note that the stack region is just any other memory region, and you can use any LLDB data dumping commands there. We also learn how to get the thread stack region address range. Examining raw stack data can hint at the past system behavior: the so-called **Execution Residue** pattern. Because managed code (an abstraction) is JIT-translated to unmanaged machine code, raw stack data also contains object references, and you can dump them using the **dso** command.

Unmanaged Stack Trace

```
(lldb) bt
* thread #1, name = 'ApplicationG', stop reason = signal SIGABRT
  * frame #0: 0x00007f7251ffd0ca libpthread.so.0`__waitpid(pid=3872, stat_loc=0x00007ffd8a21c684, options=0) at waitpid.c:30
    frame #1: 0x00007f7251971d97 libcoreclr.so`PROCCreateCrashDump(std::vector<char const*, std::allocator<char const*> >&, char*, int,
bool) + 647
    frame #2: 0x00007f725197324b libcoreclr.so`PROCCreateCrashDumpIfEnabled + 3227
    frame #3: 0x00007f725197097d libcoreclr.so`PROCAbort + 45
    frame #4: 0x00007f72519708a9 libcoreclr.so`TerminateProcess + 137
...
    frame #10: 0x00007f72516f1749 libcoreclr.so`HandleHardwareException(PAL_SEHException*) + 921
    frame #11: 0x00007f725194445c libcoreclr.so`SEHProcessException(PAL_SEHException*) + 316
    frame #12: 0x00007f7251946000 libcoreclr.so`common_signal_handler(int, siginfo_t*, void*, int, ...) + 656
    frame #13: 0x00007f7251945d06 libcoreclr.so`signal_handler_worker + 118
    frame #14: 0x00007f7251976cb2 libcoreclr.so`CallSignalHandlerWrapper0 + 6
    frame #15: 0x00007f71d32f188a
    frame #16: 0x00007f72517c1e04 libcoreclr.so`CallDescrWorkerInternal + 124
...
    frame #27: 0x000056055d57921b ApplicationG`exe_start(int, char const**) + 1131
    frame #28: 0x000056055d57953f ApplicationG`main + 175
    frame #29: 0x00007f7251b2e09b libc.so.6`__libc_start_main(main=(ApplicationG`main), argc=1, argv=0x00007ffd8a222318,
init=<unavailable>, fini=<unavailable>, rtld_fini=<unavailable>, stack_end=0x00007ffd8a222308) at libc-start.c:308
    frame #30: 0x000056055d578399 ApplicationG`_start + 41
```

```
(lldb) ip2md 0x00007f71d32f188a
MMethodDesc:       00007f71d3399728
Method Name:            Program.Main()
Class:                  00007f71d3399760
MethodTable:            00007f71d3399760
mdToken:                0000000006000001
Module:                 00007f71d3397038
IsJitted:               yes
Current CodeAddr:       00007f71d32f1860
Version History:
  ILCodeVersion:        0000000000000000
  ReJIT ID:             0
  IL Addr:              00007f724cf42250
    CodeAddr:              00007f71d32f1860  (QuickJitted)
    NativeCodeVersion:  0000000000000000
Source file:  /mnt/c/ANETMDA-Examples/ApplicationG/Program.cs @ 12
```

```
(lldb) dumpmodule 00007f71d3397038
Name: /mnt/c/ANETMDA-
Examples/ApplicationG/bin/Release/net9.0/ApplicationG.dll
Attributes:               PEFile IsFileLayout
TransientFlags:           00008811
Assembly:                 0000560573b31a50
BaseAddress:              00007F724CF42000
LoaderHeap:               00007F7251A0F1B0
TypeDefToMethodTableMap:  00007F71D33778D0
TypeRefToMethodTableMap:  00007F71D33778E8
MethodDefToDescMap:       00007F71D33779F8
FieldDefToDescMap:        00007F71D3377A18
MemberRefToDescMap:       00007F71D3377978
FileReferencesMap:        0000000000000000
AssemblyReferencesMap:    00007F71D3377A28
MetaData start address:   00007F724CF42278 (1692 bytes)
```

I suppose that you know that all .NET managed code is translated to machine code (the so-called JIT). Then **libcoreclr** calls it. You see this continuity when you look at a stack trace. This JIT code is shown in yellow. To reiterate: IL and managed space are abstractions translated to unmanaged user space. The debugger output shows you how to manually get a JIT-compiled address's module name, class, and method from an unmanaged stack trace.

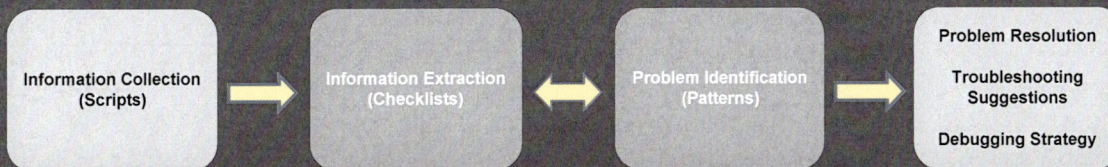

Pattern-Oriented Diagnostic Analysis

Diagnostic Pattern: a common recurrent identifiable problem together with a set of recommendations and possible solutions to apply in a specific context.

Diagnostic Problem: a set of indicators (symptoms, signs) describing a problem.

Diagnostic Analysis Pattern: a common recurrent analysis technique and method of diagnostic pattern identification in a specific context.

Diagnostics Pattern Language: common names of diagnostic and diagnostic analysis patterns. The same language for any operating system: Windows, macOS, Linux, ...

Information Collection (Scripts) → Information Extraction (Checklists) ↔ Problem Identification (Patterns) → Problem Resolution / Troubleshooting Suggestions / Debugging Strategy

Checklist: http://www.dumpanalysis.org/windows-memory-analysis-checklist

© 2025 Software Diagnostics Services

Checklist: http://www.dumpanalysis.org/windows-memory-analysis-checklist
Patterns: http://www.dumpanalysis.org/blog/index.php/crash-dump-analysis-patterns/ (also available in Memory Dump Analysis Anthology volumes or Encyclopedia of Crash Dump Analysis Patterns, see the **References** slide)
.NET Patterns: http://www.dumpanalysis.org/blog/index.php/2011/04/22/net-clr-managed-space-patterns/ (also available in Memory Dump Analysis Anthology volumes or Encyclopedia of Crash Dump Analysis Patterns, see the **Pattern Links** slide)

A few words about logs, checklists, and patterns: memory dump analysis is usually an analysis of a text for the presence of patterns. We run commands, and they output text; then, we look at that textual output, and when we find something suspicious, we execute more commands. Here, checklists can be very useful. One such checklist is provided as a link. I recently expanded it to include .NET process memory dumps. In some cases, it is beneficial to collect information into one log file by running several commands at once (like a script) and then doing the first-order analysis.

x64 Disassembly Review

WinDbg

x64 CPU Registers

- **RAX** ⊃ **EAX** ⊃ **AX** ⊇ **{AH, AL}** | **RAX 64-bit** | **EAX 32-bit** |

- ALU: **RAX**, **RDX**

- Counter: **RCX**

- Memory copy: **RSI** (src), **RDI** (dst)

- Stack: **RSP**

- Frame Pointer: **RSP**, **RBP**

- Next instruction: **RIP**

- New: **R8** – **R15**, **Rx(D|W|B)**

© 2025 Software Diagnostics Services

There are familiar 32-bit CPU register names, such as **EAX,** that are extended to 64-bit names, such as **RAX**. Most of them are traditionally specialized, such as ALU, counter, and memory copy registers. Although now they all can be used as general-purpose registers. There is, of course, a stack pointer, **RSP**, and it also takes the role of a frame pointer, which is also used to address local variables and saved parameters. In some compiler code generation implementations, **RBP** is also used as a general-purpose register, with **RSP** taking the role of a frame pointer. Together, they can be used for stack reconstruction. An instruction pointer **RIP** is saved in the stack memory region with every function call, then restored on return from the called function. In addition, the x64 platform features another eight general-purpose registers, from **R8** to **R15**.

Instructions and Registers

- Opcode DST, SRC

- Examples:

```
mov    rax, 10h        ; RAX ← 0x10
mov    r13, rdx        ; R13 ← RDX
add    r10, 10h        ; R10 ← R10 + 0x10
imul   edx, ecx        ; EDX ← EDX * ECX
call   rdx             ; RDX already contains
                       ;     the address of func (&func)
                       ; PUSH RIP; RIP ← &func
sub    rsp, 30h        ; RSP ← RSP-0x30
                       ; make room for local variables
```

This slide shows a few examples of CPU instructions involving operations with registers, such as moving a value and doing arithmetic. The direction of operands is opposite to the AT&T x64 disassembly flavor if you are accustomed to default GDB disassembly on Linux.

Memory and Stack Addressing

Lower addresses		Values
RSP-0x20 →		[RSP-0x20]
RSP-0x18 →		[RSP-0x18]
RSP-0x10 →		[RSP-0x10]
RSP-0x8 →		[RSP-0x8]
RSP →		[RSP]
RSP+0x8 →		[RSP+0x8]
RSP+0x10 →		[RSP+0x10]
RSP+0x18 →		[RSP+0x18]
RSP+0x20 →		[RSP+0x20]

Stack grows

Higher addresses

Before we look at operations with memory, let's look at a graphical representation of memory addressing where for simplicity, I use 64-bit (or 8-byte) memory cells. A thread stack is just any other memory region, so instead of **RSP,** any other register can be used. Please note that the stack grows towards lower addresses, so to access the previously pushed values, you need to use positive offsets from **RSP**.

Memory Cell Sizes

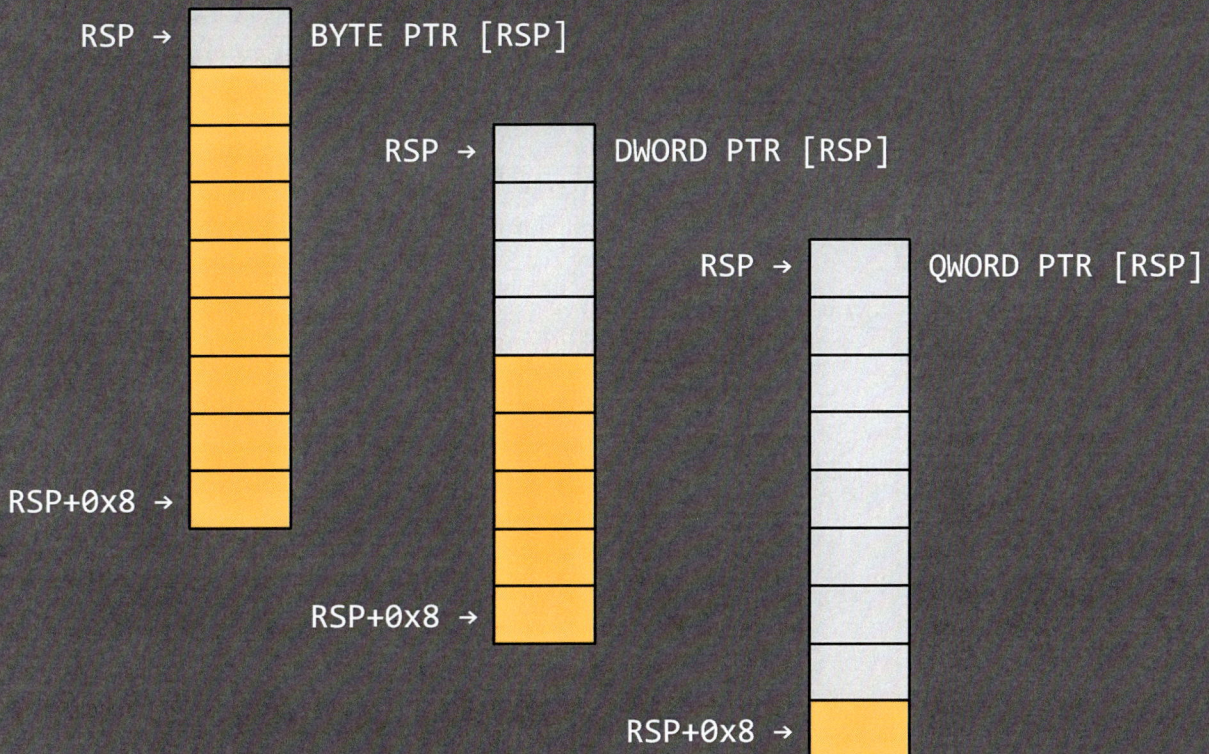

© 2025 Software Diagnostics Services

Here, each memory cell is 8-bit (or one byte). When we have a register pointing to memory, and we want to work with the value at that address, we need to specify the size of memory cells to work with, for example, **BYTE PTR** if we want to work with a byte, **DWORD PTR** if we want to work with 32-bit double words, and **QWORD PTR** if we want to work with 64-bit quad words. There's also **WORD PTR** for 16-bit values. This notation is different from Linux LLDB, where we have bytes, half-words, words, and double words.

Memory Load Instructions

- Opcode DST, PTR [SRC+Offset]

- Opcode DST

- Examples:

```
mov    rax, qword ptr [rsp+10h] ; RAX ←
                                ; 64-bit value at address RSP+0x10
mov    ecx, dword ptr [20]      ; ECX ←
                                ; 32-bit value at address 0x20
pop    rdi                      ; RDI ← value at address RSP
                                ; RSP ← RSP + 8
lea    r8, [rsp+20h]            ; R8 ← address RSP+0x20
```

Constants are encoded in instructions, but if we need arbitrary values, we must get them from memory. Square brackets show memory access relative to an address stored in a register.

Memory Store Instructions

- Opcode PTR [DST+Offset], SRC

- Opcode DST|SRC

- Examples:

```
mov   qword ptr [rbp-20h], rcx ; 64-bit value at address RBP-0x20
                               ;    ← RCX
mov   byte ptr [0], 1          ; 8-bit value at address 0 ← 1
push  rsi                      ; RSP ← RSP - 8
                               ; value at address RSP ← RSI
inc   dword ptr [rcx]          ; 32-bit value at address RCX ←
                               ;    1 + 32-bit value at address RCX
```

Storing is similar to loading.

Flow Instructions

- Opcode DST

- Opcode PTR [DST]

- Examples:

```
jmp    00007ff6`9ef2f008      ; RIP ← 0x7ff69ef2f008
                              ; ("goto" 0x7ff69ef2f008)
jmp    qword ptr [rax+10h]    ; RIP ← value at address RAX+0x10
call   00007ff6`9ef21400      ; RSP ← RSP - 8
00007ff6`9ef21057:            ; value at address RSP ← 0x7ff69ef21057
                              ; RIP ← 0x7ff69ef21400
                              ; ("goto" 0x7ff69ef21400)
```

Goto (an unconditional jump) is implemented via the **JMP** instruction. Function calls are implemented via **CALL** instruction. For conditional branches, please look at the official Intel documentation. We don't use these instructions in our exercises.

LLDB

x64 CPU Registers

- RAX ⊃ **EAX** ⊃ AX ⊇ {AH, AL} | RAX 64-bit | EAX 32-bit |

- ALU: **RAX**, **RDX**

- Counter: **RCX**

- Memory copy: **RSI** (src), **RDI** (dst)

- Stack: **RSP**, **RBP**

- Next instruction: **RIP**

- New: **R8** – **R15**, Rx(D|W|L)

There are familiar 32-bit CPU register names, such as **EAX,** that are extended to 64-bit names, such as **RAX**. Most of them are traditionally specialized, such as ALU, counter, and memory copy registers. Although, now they all can be used as general-purpose registers. There is, of course, a stack pointer, **RSP**, and, additionally, a frame pointer, **RBP**, that is used to address local variables and saved parameters. It can be used for backtrace reconstruction. In some compiler code generation implementations, **RBP** is also used as a general-purpose register, with **RSP** taking the role of a frame pointer. An instruction pointer RIP is saved in the stack memory region with every function call, then restored on return from the called function. In addition, the x64 platform features another eight general-purpose registers, from **R8** to **R15**.

x64 Instructions and Registers

- Opcode SRC, DST # default AT&T flavour

- Examples:

```
mov    $0x10, %rax        # 0x10 → RAX
mov    %rsp, %rbp         # RSP → RBP
add    $0x10, %r10        # R10 + 0x10 → R10
imul   %ecx, %edx         # ECX * EDX → EDX
callq  *%rdx              # RDX already contains
                         #    the address of func (&func)
                         # PUSH RIP; &func → RIP
sub    $0x30, %rsp        # RSP-0x30 → RSP
                         # make room for local variables
```

This slide shows a few examples of CPU instructions involving operations with registers, such as moving a value and doing arithmetic. The direction of operands is opposite to the Intel x64 disassembly flavor if you are accustomed to WinDbg on Windows.

Memory and Stack Addressing

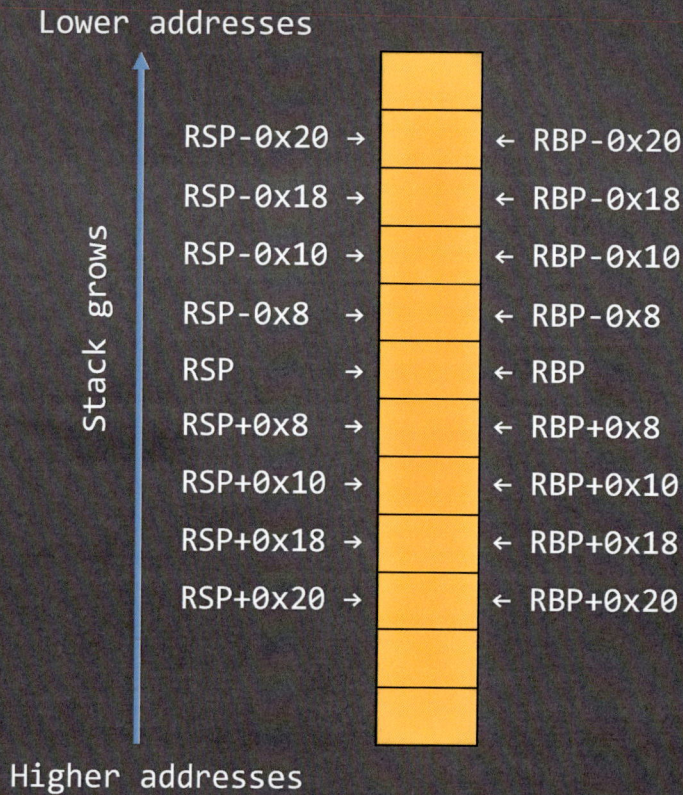

Before we look at operations with memory, let's look at a graphical representation of memory addressing. A thread stack is just any other memory region, so instead of **RSP** and **RBP,** any other register can be used. Please note that the stack grows towards lower addresses, so to access the previously pushed values, you need to use positive offsets from **RSP**.

x64 Memory Load Instructions

- Opcode Offset(SRC), DST

- Opcode DST

- Examples:

```
mov    0x10(%rsp), %rax        # value at address RSP+0x10 → RAX
mov    -0x10(%rbp), %rcx       # value at address RBP-0x10 → RCX
add    (%rax), %rdx            # RDX + value at address RAX → RDX
pop    %rdi                    # value at address RSP → RDI
                               # RSP + 8 → RSP
lea    0x20(%rbp), %r8         # address RBP+0x20 → R8
```

Constants are encoded in instructions, but if we need arbitrary values, we must get them from memory. Round brackets show memory access relative to an address stored in some register.

x64 Memory Store Instructions

- Opcode SRC, Offset(DST)

- Opcode SRC|DST

- Examples:

```
mov    %rcx, -0x20(%rbp)        # RCX → value at address RBP-0x20
addl   $1, (%rax)               # 1 + 32-bit value at address RAX →
                                #       32-bit value at address RAX
push   %rsi                     # RSP - 8 → RSP
                                # RSI → value at address RSP
inc    (%rcx)                   # 1 + value at address RCX →
                                #       value at address RCX
```

Storing is similar to loading.

x64 Flow Instructions

- Opcode DST

- Examples:

```
jmpq    0x10493fc1c        # 0x10493fc1c → RIP
                           # ("goto" 0x10493fc1c)


jmpq    *0x100(%rip)       # value at address RIP+0x100 → RIP


callq   0x10493ff74        # RSP – 8 → RSP
0x10493fc14:               # 0x10493fc14 → value at address RSP
                           # 0x10493ff74 → RIP
                           # ("goto" 0x10493ff74)
```

Goto (an unconditional jump) is implemented via the **JMP** instruction. Function calls are implemented via **CALL** instruction. For conditional branches, please look at the official Intel documentation.

IL Disassembly Basics

Part 3: IL Disassembly Basics

Stack-Based Architecture

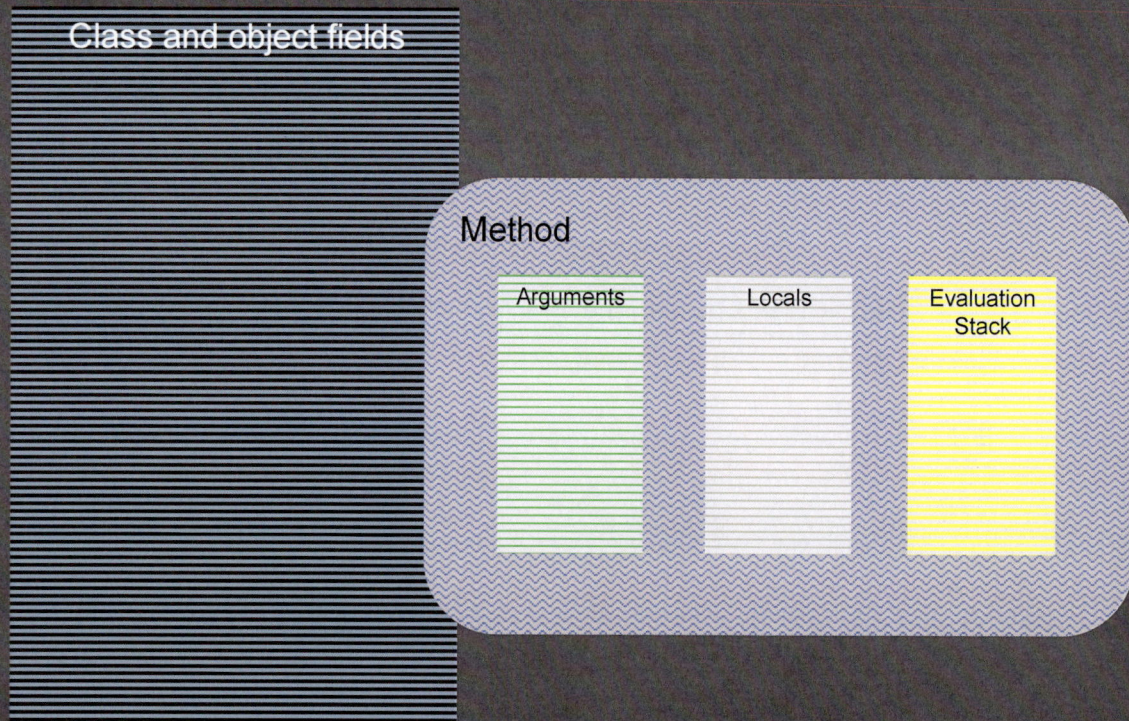

Class and object fields

Method

Arguments | Locals | Evaluation Stack

Compared to x64 architecture, IL architecture is stack-based, where instruction operands are pushed onto the evaluation stack and replaced with the execution result.

Execution Flow Example

```
IL_0000: br.s IL_0008
IL_0002: ldarg.0                          // pushes this
IL_0003: call void ClassMain::DoWork()    // pops this
IL_0008: ldarg.0                          // pushes this
IL_0009: ldfld ClassMain::time2stop       // pops this and pushes the field value
IL_000e: brfalse.s IL_0002
IL_0010: ret
```

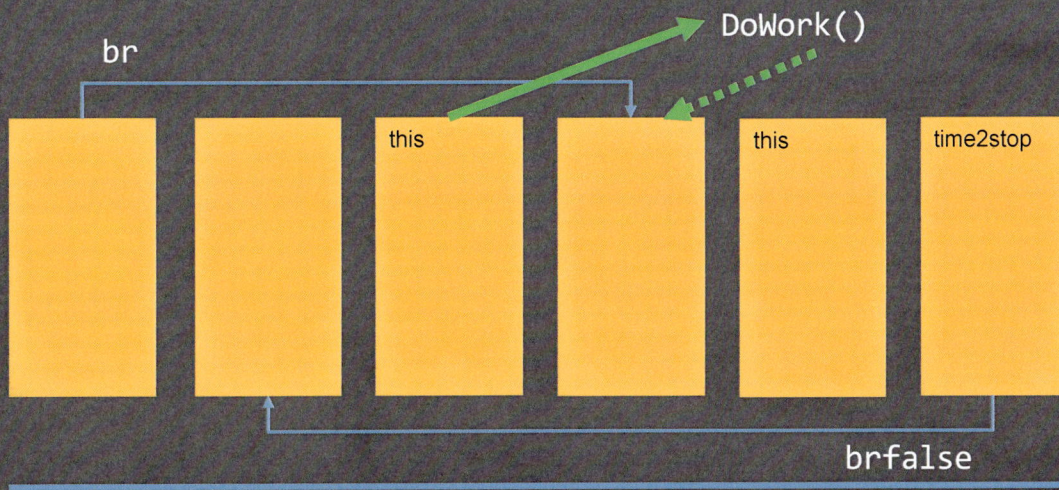

© 2025 Software Diagnostics Services

Instead of surveying instructions, I show the execution flow and corresponding evaluation stack changes on this and the next slide for *LinqB* and *ApplicationH* source code.

Stack Evaluation Example

```
IL_0000: nop
IL_0001: ldarg.0                          // pushes this
IL_0002: ldarg.0                          // pushes this
IL_0003: volatile.
IL_0005: ldfld ClassMain::outSensor       // pops this and pushes the field value
IL_000a: ldarg.0                          // pushes this
IL_000b: volatile.
IL_000d: ldfld ClassMain::inSensor        // pops this and pushes the field value
IL_0012: xor                              // pops two values and pushes the result
IL_0013: volatile.
IL_0015: stfld ClassMain::outSensor       // pops this and the result
IL_001a: ret
```

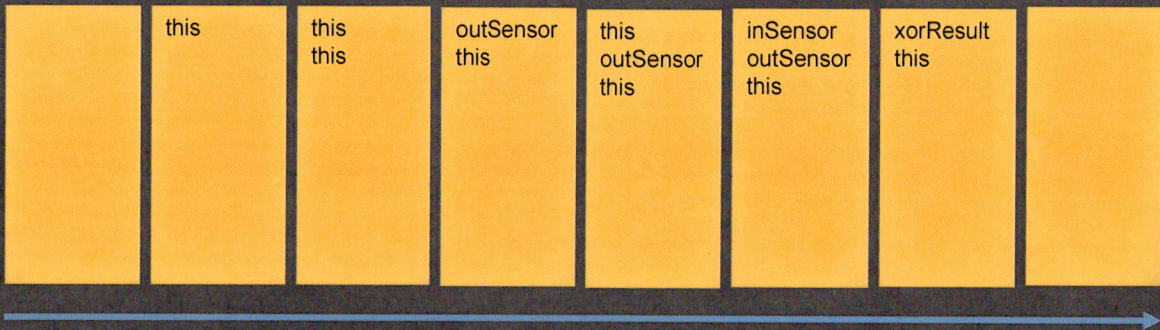

	this	this	outSensor	this	inSensor	xorResult	
		this	this	outSensor	outSensor	this	
				this	this		

Memory Dump Generation

Windows

- ◉ Crash or Hang / Leak / Spike? PID in Task Manager

- ◉ Crash: LocalDumps

- ◉ Hang / Leak / Spike: Task Manager, procdump –ma

- ◉ 32-bit processes: 32-bit Task Manager (SysWOW64)

Linux

- **Enabling:**

```
$ export DOTNET_DbgEnableMiniDump=1
$ export DOTNET_DbgMiniDumpType=4     # full process dump
```

- **Location:**

```
$ export DOTNET_DbgMiniDumpName=./core.%e.%p.dmp
$ # default: /tmp/core.pid
```

- **Hang / Leak / Spike:**

```
$ /usr/share/dotnet/shared/Microsoft.NETCore.App/9.0.4/createdump
```

- **Symbols:**

```
$ dotnet-symbol install <corefilename>
$ dotnet-symbol install <exefilename>
```

Practice Exercises

Links

◉ **.NET 9 SDK**

https://dotnet.microsoft.com/en-us/download/dotnet/9.0

◉ **Memory dumps and source code:**

Included in Exercise PN0

◉ **Exercise transcripts:**

Included in this book

Now, we have come to practice. The goal is to show you important commands and how their output helps recognize patterns of abnormal software structure and behavior.

SDK and Runtime Info

```
C:\Windows\System32>dotnet --info
.NET SDK:
 Version:           9.0.203
 Commit:            dc7acfa194
 Workload version:  9.0.200-manifests.12d79ccf
 MSBuild version:   17.13.20+a4ef1e90f

Runtime Environment:
 OS Name:     Windows
 OS Version:  10.0.26100
 OS Platform: Windows
 RID:         win-x64
 Base Path:   C:\Program Files\dotnet\sdk\9.0.203\

...

Host:
 Version:      9.0.4
 Architecture: x64
 Commit:       f57e6dc747

.NET SDKs installed:
 8.0.408 [C:\Program Files\dotnet\sdk]
 9.0.203 [C:\Program Files\dotnet\sdk]

.NET runtimes installed:
...
Microsoft.WindowsDesktop.App 8.0.15 [C:\Program Files\dotnet\shared\Microsoft.WindowsDesktop.App]
Microsoft.WindowsDesktop.App 9.0.4 [C:\Program Files\dotnet\shared\Microsoft.WindowsDesktop.App]
```

SOS Setup (Default .NET)

```
C:\Windows\System32>dotnet tool install --global dotnet-sos

C:\Windows\System32>dotnet-sos install
Installing SOS to C:\Users\dmitr\.dotnet\sos
Creating installation directory...
Copying files from C:\Users\dmitr\.dotnet\tools\.store\dotnet-sos\9.0.621003\dotnet-
    sos\9.0.621003\tools\net8.0\any\win-x64
Copying files from C:\Users\dmitr\.dotnet\tools\.store\dotnet-sos\9.0.621003\dotnet-
    sos\9.0.621003\tools\net8.0\any\lib
Execute '.load C:\Users\dmitr\.dotnet\sos\sos.dll' to load SOS in your Windows debugger.
SOS install succeeded
```

SOS Setup (Specific .NET)

```
C:\Windows\System32>dotnet tool install --global dotnet-sos --version 8.*
The requested version 8.0.547301 is lower than existing version 9.0.621003.

C:\Windows\System32>dotnet tool uninstall --global dotnet-sos
Tool 'dotnet-sos' (version '9.0.621003') was successfully uninstalled.

C:\Windows\System32>dotnet tool install --global dotnet-sos --version 8.*
You can invoke the tool using the following command: dotnet-sos
Tool 'dotnet-sos' (version '8.0.547301') was successfully installed.

C:\Windows\System32>dotnet-sos uninstall
Uninstalling SOS from C:\Users\dmitr\.dotnet\sos
SOS uninstall succeeded

C:\Windows\System32>dotnet-sos install
Installing SOS to C:\Users\dmitr\.dotnet\sos
Creating installation directory...
Copying files from C:\Users\dmitr\.dotnet\tools\.store\dotnet-sos\8.0.547301\dotnet-
    sos\8.0.547301\tools\net6.0\any\win-x64
Copying files from C:\Users\dmitr\.dotnet\tools\.store\dotnet-sos\8.0.547301\dotnet-
    sos\8.0.547301\tools\net6.0\any\lib
Execute '.load C:\Users\dmitr\.dotnet\sos\sos.dll' to load SOS in your Windows debugger.
Cleaning up...
SOS install succeeded
```

Supportability (Windows)

- Save PDB files

- Save the SOS extension folder

Supportability (Linux)

- Save PDB files

- Save the .NET version .pdb, .so, and .so.dbg files from the production environment

- Save the loaded C and C++ runtime libs from the production environment

Exercise PN0 (Windows)

- **Goal:** Install WinDbg or Debugging Tools for Windows and check that symbols are set up correctly

- **Patterns:** Stack Trace; Incorrect Stack Trace; Truncated Stack Trace

- **Commands:** k

- \ANETMDA-Dumps\Exercise-PN0-Windows.pdf

Exercise PN0 (WinDbg)

Goal: Install WinDbg or Debugging Tools for Windows and check that symbols are set up correctly.

Patterns: Stack Trace; Incorrect Stack Trace; Truncated Stack Trace.

1.   Download memory dump files if you haven't done that already and unpack the archive:

https://www.patterndiagnostics.com/Downloads/Training/ANETMDA/ANETMDA-Dumps.zip

2.   Install WinDbg (or upgrade existing WinDbg Preview) from https://learn.microsoft.com/en-gb/windows-hardware/drivers/debugger. Run WinDbg.

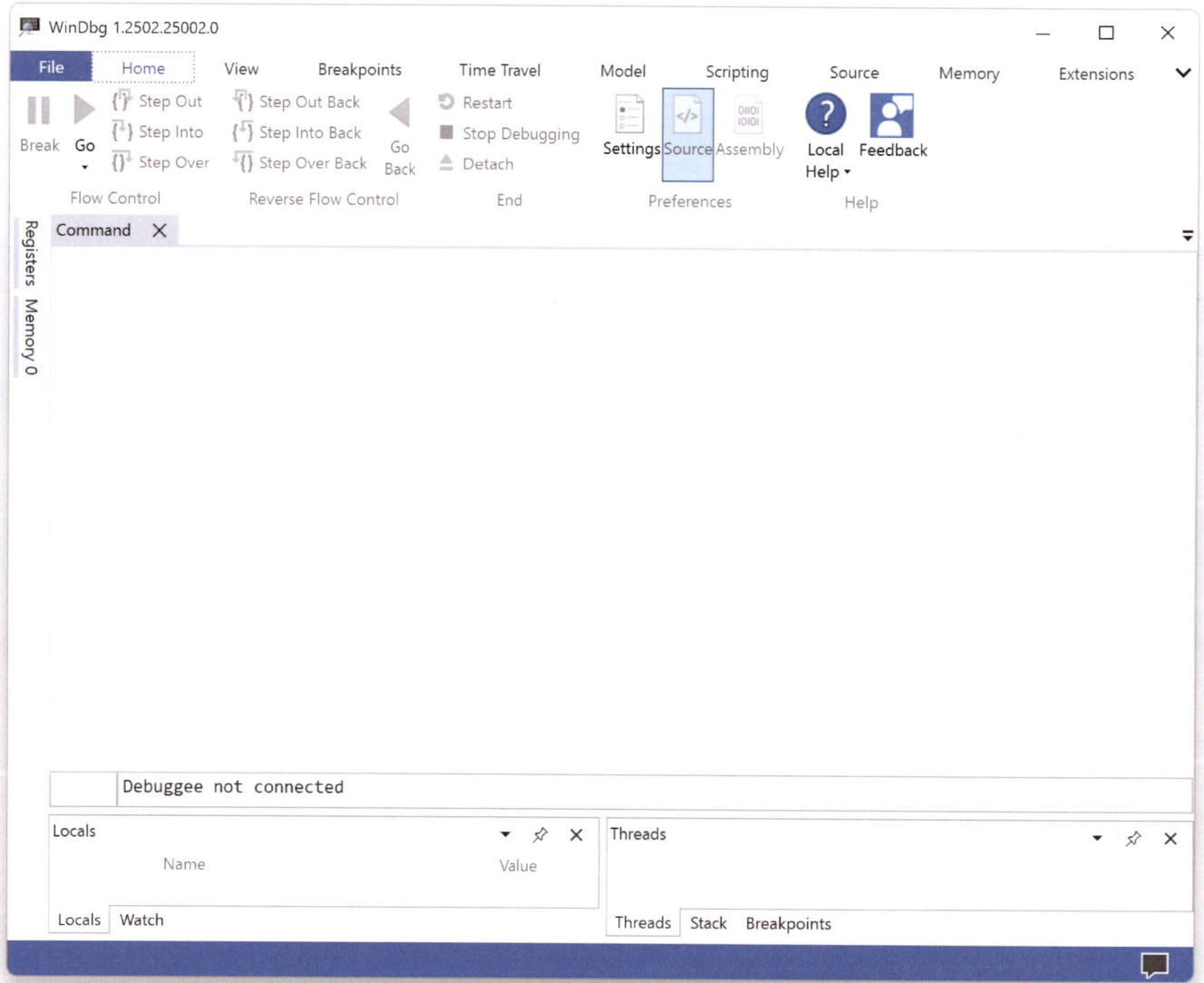

3.   Open \ANETMDA-Dumps\Windows\wordpad.DMP:

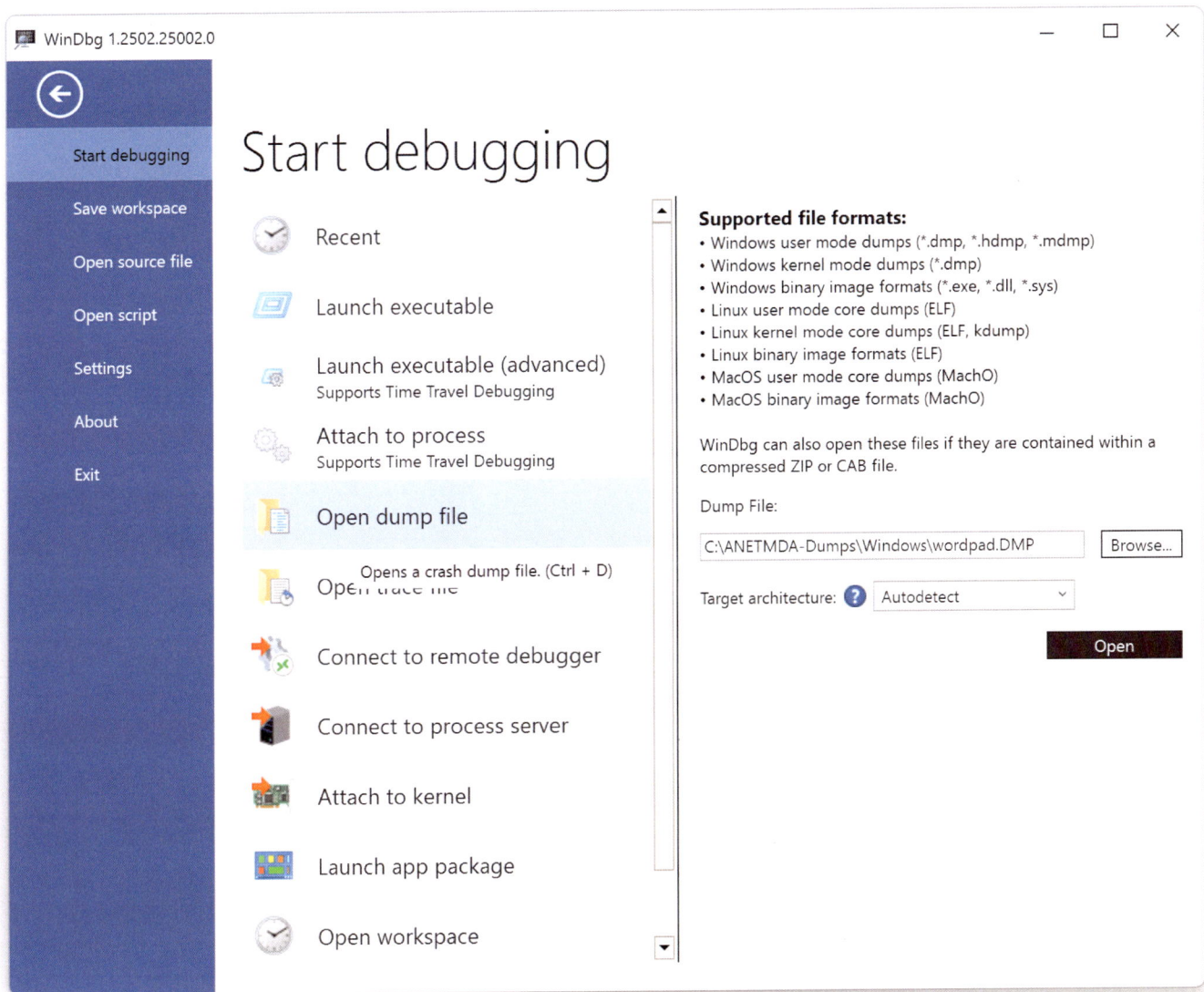

4.   We get the dump file loaded:

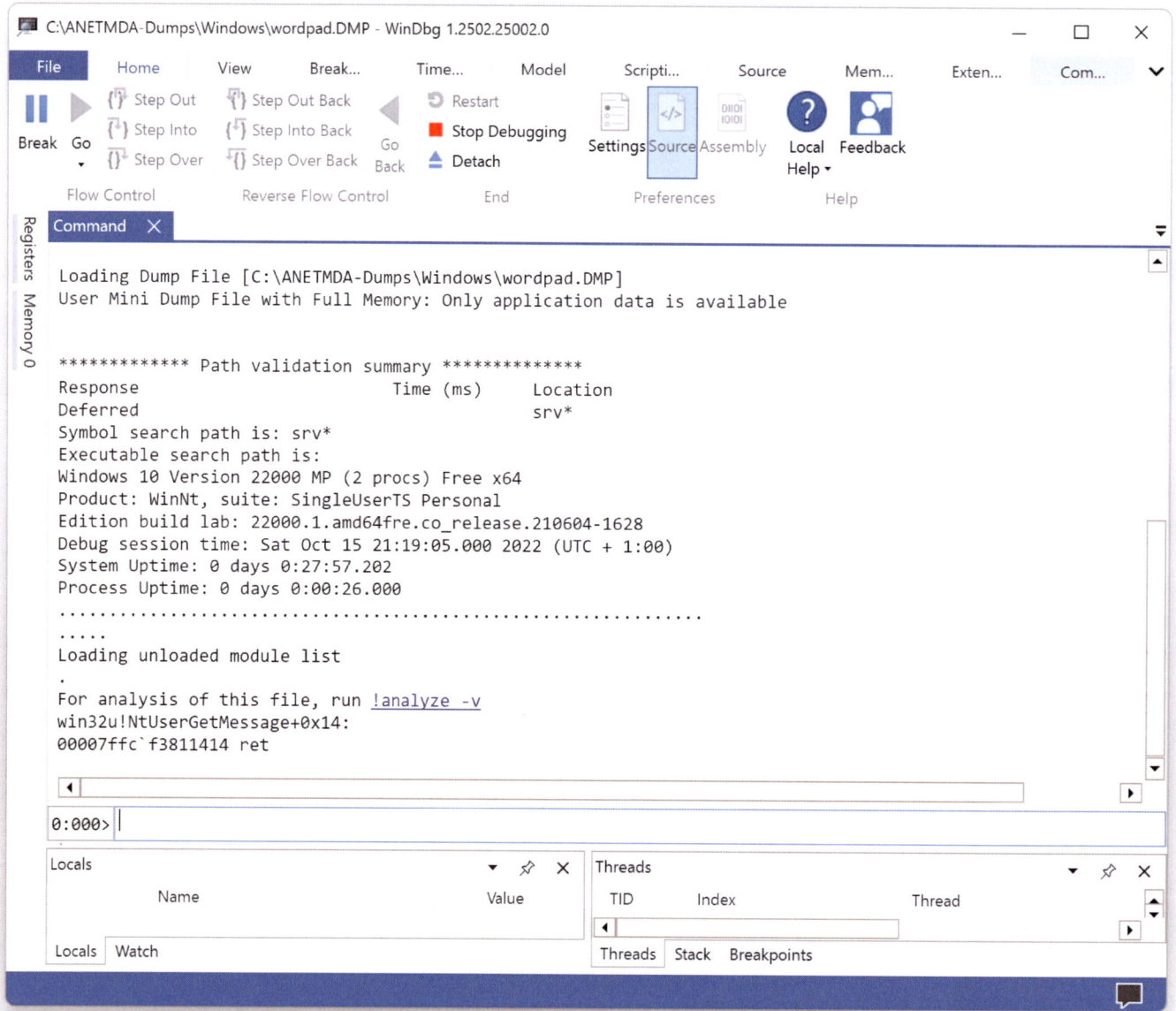

The screenshot shows the WinDbg window titled "C:\ANETMDA-Dumps\Windows\wordpad.DMP - WinDbg 1.2502.25002.0" with the Command window displaying:

```
Loading Dump File [C:\ANETMDA-Dumps\Windows\wordpad.DMP]
User Mini Dump File with Full Memory: Only application data is available

************* Path validation summary **************
Response                      Time (ms)      Location
Deferred                                     srv*
Symbol search path is: srv*
Executable search path is:
Windows 10 Version 22000 MP (2 procs) Free x64
Product: WinNt, suite: SingleUserTS Personal
Edition build lab: 22000.1.amd64fre.co_release.210604-1628
Debug session time: Sat Oct 15 21:19:05.000 2022 (UTC + 1:00)
System Uptime: 0 days 0:27:57.202
Process Uptime: 0 days 0:00:26.000
..........................................................
.....
Loading unloaded module list
.
For analysis of this file, run !analyze -v
win32u!NtUserGetMessage+0x14:
00007ffc`f3811414 ret
```

5. Type the **k** command to verify the correctness of the stack trace:

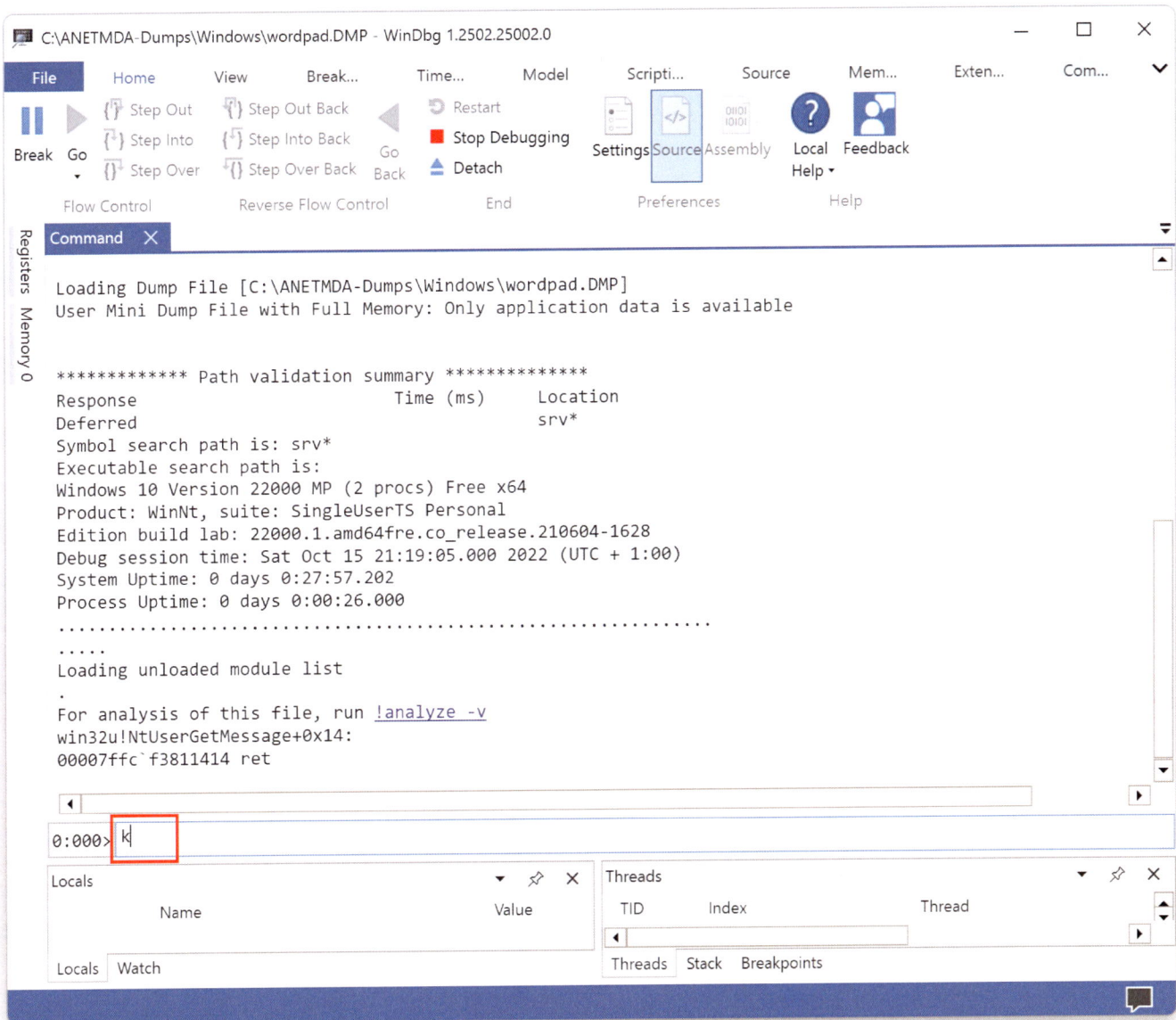

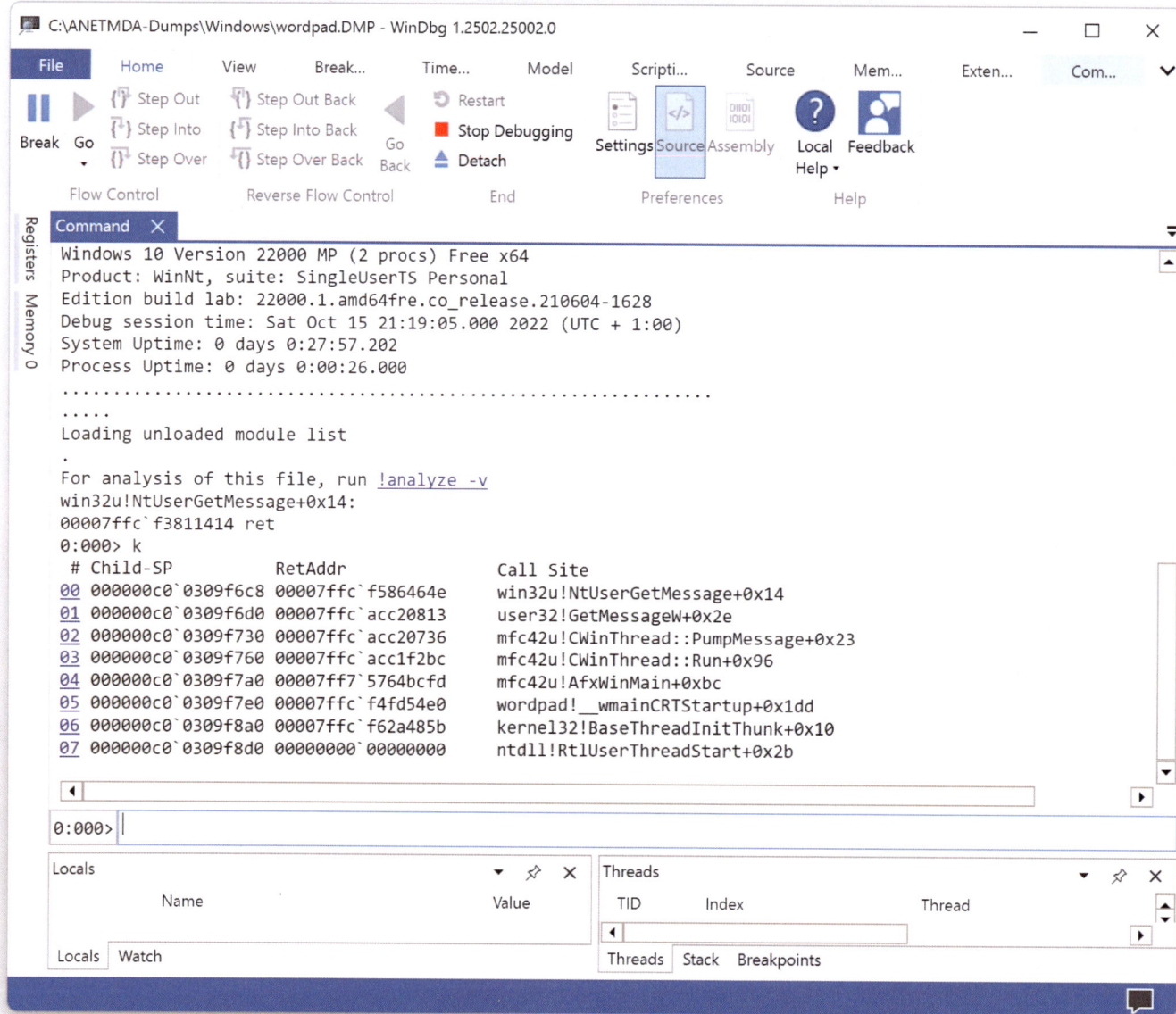

Windows 10 Version 22000 MP (2 procs) Free x64
Product: WinNt, suite: SingleUserTS Personal
Edition build lab: 22000.1.amd64fre.co_release.210604-1628
Debug session time: Sat Oct 15 21:19:05.000 2022 (UTC + 1:00)
System Uptime: 0 days 0:27:57.202
Process Uptime: 0 days 0:00:26.000
....
.....
Loading unloaded module list
.
For analysis of this file, run !analyze -v
win32u!NtUserGetMessage+0x14:
00007ffc`f3811414 ret
0:000> k
 # Child-SP   RetAddr   Call Site
00 000000c0`0309f6c8 00007ffc`f586464e   win32u!NtUserGetMessage+0x14
01 000000c0`0309f6d0 00007ffc`acc20813   user32!GetMessageW+0x2e
02 000000c0`0309f730 00007ffc`acc20736   mfc42u!CWinThread::PumpMessage+0x23
03 000000c0`0309f760 00007ffc`acc1f2bc   mfc42u!CWinThread::Run+0x96
04 000000c0`0309f7a0 00007ff7`5764bcfd   mfc42u!AfxWinMain+0xbc
05 000000c0`0309f7e0 00007ffc`f4fd54e0   wordpad!__wmainCRTStartup+0x1dd
06 000000c0`0309f8a0 00007ffc`f62a485b   kernel32!BaseThreadInitThunk+0x10
07 000000c0`0309f8d0 00000000`00000000   ntdll!RtlUserThreadStart+0x2b

6.   The output of the command should be this:

```
0:000> k
 # Child-SP          RetAddr               Call Site
00 000000c0`0309f6c8 00007ffc`f586464e   win32u!NtUserGetMessage+0x14
01 000000c0`0309f6d0 00007ffc`acc20813   user32!GetMessageW+0x2e
02 000000c0`0309f730 00007ffc`acc20736   mfc42u!CWinThread::PumpMessage+0x23
03 000000c0`0309f760 00007ffc`acc1f2bc   mfc42u!CWinThread::Run+0x96
04 000000c0`0309f7a0 00007ff7`5764bcfd   mfc42u!AfxWinMain+0xbc
05 000000c0`0309f7e0 00007ffc`f4fd54e0   wordpad!__wmainCRTStartup+0x1dd
06 000000c0`0309f8a0 00007ffc`f62a485b   kernel32!BaseThreadInitThunk+0x10
07 000000c0`0309f8d0 00000000`00000000   ntdll!RtlUserThreadStart+0x2b
```

If it has this form below with a large offset, then your symbol files were not set up correctly – **Incorrect Stack Trace** pattern:

```
0:000> k
 # Child-SP          RetAddr           Call Site
00 000000c0`0309f6c8 00007ffc`f586464e win32u!NtUserGetMessage+0x14
01 000000c0`0309f6d0 00007ffc`acc20813 user32!GetMessageW+0x2e
02 000000c0`0309f730 00007ffc`acc20736 mfc42u!Ordinal5730+0x23
03 000000c0`0309f760 00007ffc`acc1f2bc mfc42u!Ordinal6054+0x96
04 000000c0`0309f7a0 00007ff7`5764bcfd mfc42u!Ordinal1584+0xbc
05 000000c0`0309f7e0 00007ffc`f4fd54e0 wordpad+0xbcfd
06 000000c0`0309f8a0 00007ffc`f62a485b kernel32!BaseThreadInitThunk+0x10
07 000000c0`0309f8d0 00000000`00000000 ntdll!RtlUserThreadStart+0x2b
```

It is also possible that the stack trace becomes truncated if no symbols are available:

```
0:000> k
 # Child-SP          RetAddr           Call Site
00 000000c0`0309f6c8 00007ffc`f586464e win32u!NtUserGetMessage+0x14
01 000000c0`0309f6d0 00007ffc`acc20813 user32!GetMessageW+0x2e
02 000000c0`0309f730 00000000`00000000 00007ffc`acc20813
```

7. [Optional] Download and install the recommended version of Debugging Tools for Windows (See windbg.org for quick links, WinDbg Quick Links \ Download Debugging Tools for Windows). For this part, we use WinDbg 10.0.26100.3624 from Windows SDK 10.0.26100 for Windows 11, version 24H2.

8.   Launch WinDbg from Windows Kits \ WinDbg (X64).

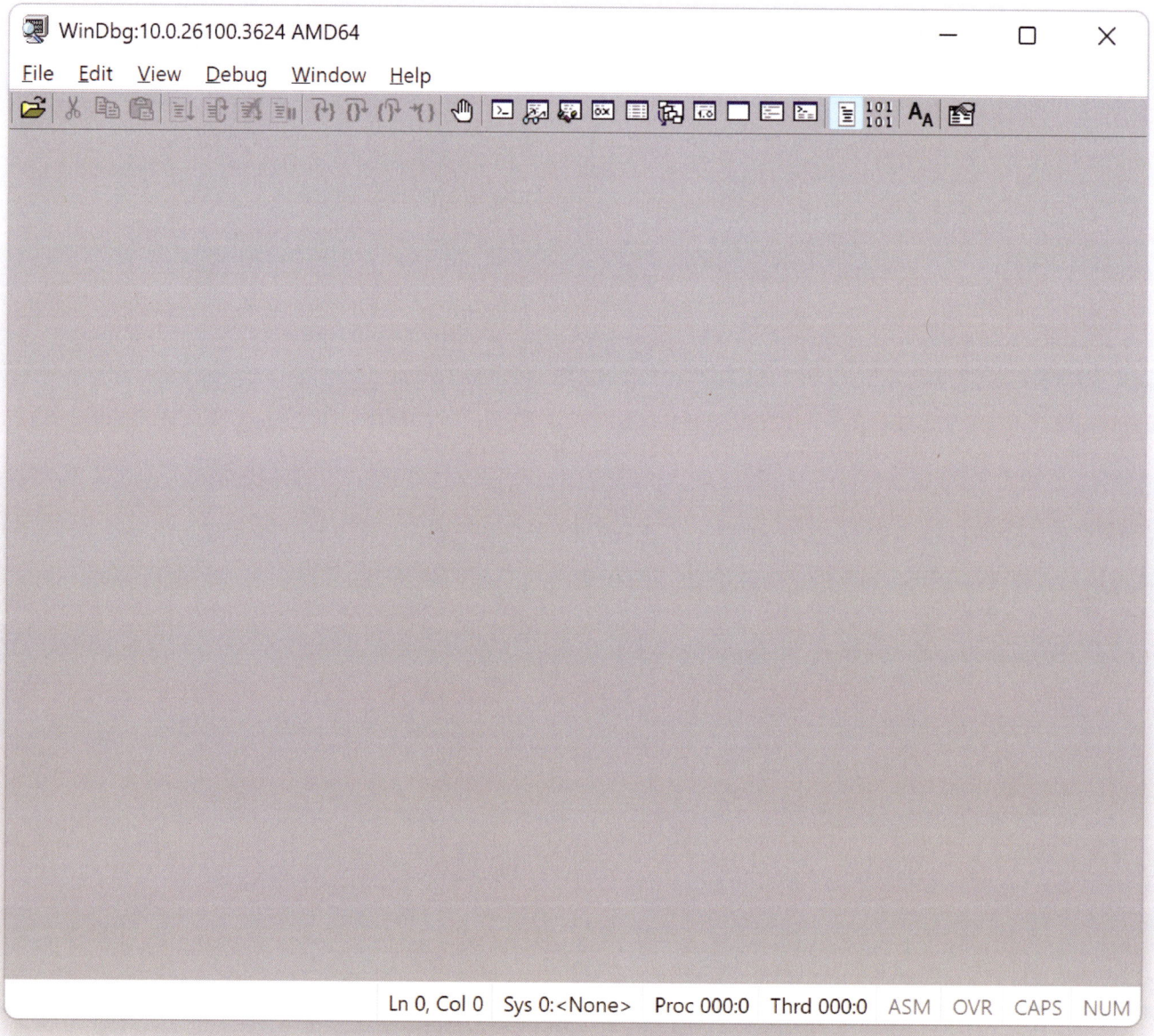

9. Open \ANETMDA-Dumps\Windows\wordpad.DMP:

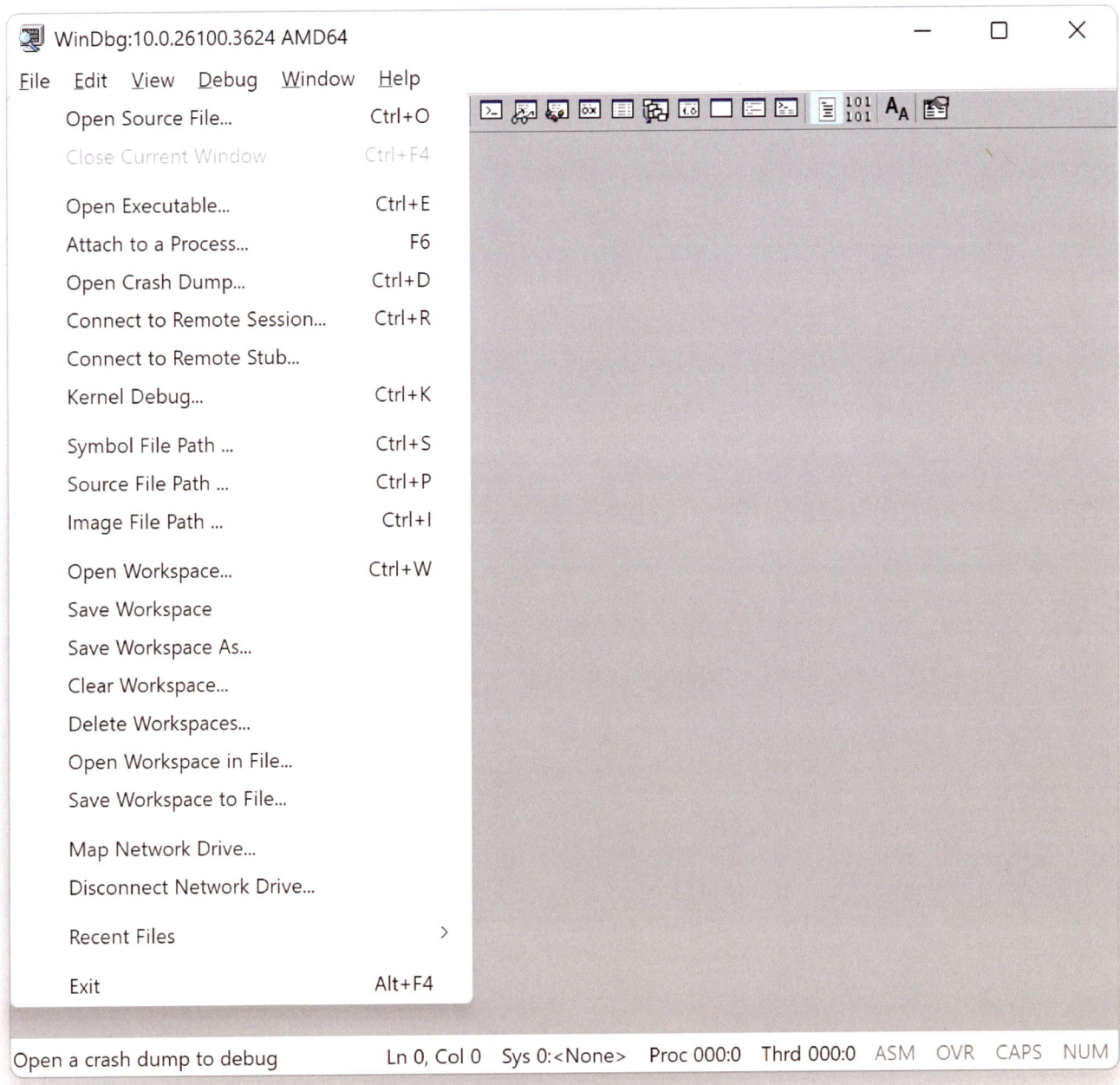

WinDbg:10.0.26100.3624 AMD64

File	Edit	View	Debug	Window	Help

Open Source File...	Ctrl+O
Close Current Window	Ctrl+F4
Open Executable...	Ctrl+E
Attach to a Process...	F6
Open Crash Dump...	Ctrl+D
Connect to Remote Session...	Ctrl+R
Connect to Remote Stub...	
Kernel Debug...	Ctrl+K
Symbol File Path ...	Ctrl+S
Source File Path ...	Ctrl+P
Image File Path ...	Ctrl+I
Open Workspace...	Ctrl+W
Save Workspace	
Save Workspace As...	
Clear Workspace...	
Delete Workspaces...	
Open Workspace in File...	
Save Workspace to File...	
Map Network Drive...	
Disconnect Network Drive...	
Recent Files	>
Exit	Alt+F4

Open a crash dump to debug   Ln 0, Col 0   Sys 0:<None>   Proc 000:0   Thrd 000:0   ASM   OVR   CAPS   NUM

10.   We get the dump file loaded:

```
Dump C:\ANETMDA-Dumps\Windows\wordpad.DMP - WinDbg:10.0.26100.3624 AMD64    —    □    ×

File  Edit  View  Debug  Window  Help

Command - Dump C:\ANETMDA-Dumps\Windows\wordpad.DMP - W...    —    □    ×

Microsoft (R) Windows Debugger Version 10.0.26100.3624 AMD64
Copyright (c) Microsoft Corporation. All rights reserved.


Loading Dump File [C:\ANETMDA-Dumps\Windows\wordpad.DMP]
User Mini Dump File with Full Memory: Only application data is available

Symbol search path is: srv*
Executable search path is:
Windows 10 Version 22000 MP (2 procs) Free x64
Product: WinNt, suite: SingleUserTS Personal
Edition build lab: 22000.1.amd64fre.co_release.210604-1628
Debug session time: Sat Oct 15 21:19:05.000 2022 (UTC + 1:00)
System Uptime: 0 days 0:27:57.202
Process Uptime: 0 days 0:00:26.000
.............................................................
.....
Loading unloaded module list
.
For analysis of this file, run !analyze -v
win32u!NtUserGetMessage+0x14:
00007ffc`f3811414 c3              ret


0:000>

Ln 0, Col 0   Sys 0:C:\ANET   Proc 000:12e8   Thrd 000:928   ASM  OVR  CAPS  NUM
```

11. Type **k** command to verify the correctness of stack trace:

```
Microsoft (R) Windows Debugger Version 10.0.26100.3624 AMD64
Copyright (c) Microsoft Corporation. All rights reserved.


Loading Dump File [C:\ANETMDA-Dumps\Windows\wordpad.DMP]
User Mini Dump File with Full Memory: Only application data is available

Symbol search path is: srv*
Executable search path is:
Windows 10 Version 22000 MP (2 procs) Free x64
Product: WinNt, suite: SingleUserTS Personal
Edition build lab: 22000.1.amd64fre.co_release.210604-1628
Debug session time: Sat Oct 15 21:19:05.000 2022 (UTC + 1:00)
System Uptime: 0 days 0:27:57.202
Process Uptime: 0 days 0:00:26.000
.................................................................
.....
Loading unloaded module list
.
For analysis of this file, run !analyze -v
win32u!NtUserGetMessage+0x14:
00007ffc`f3811414 c3              ret
```

0:000> k

```
Product: WinNt, suite: SingleUserTS Personal
Edition build lab: 22000.1.amd64fre.co_release.210604-1628
Debug session time: Sat Oct 15 21:19:05.000 2022 (UTC + 1:00)
System Uptime: 0 days 0:27:57.202
Process Uptime: 0 days 0:00:26.000
.................................................................
.....
Loading unloaded module list
.
For analysis of this file, run !analyze -v
win32u!NtUserGetMessage+0x14:
00007ffc`f3811414 c3              ret
0:000> k
 # Child-SP          RetAddr               Call Site
00 000000c0`0309f6c8 00007ffc`f586464e     win32u!NtUserGetMessage+0x14
01 000000c0`0309f6d0 00007ffc`acc20813     user32!GetMessageW+0x2e
02 000000c0`0309f730 00007ffc`acc20736     mfc42u!CWinThread::PumpMessage+0x23
03 000000c0`0309f760 00007ffc`acc1f2bc     mfc42u!CWinThread::Run+0x96
04 000000c0`0309f7a0 00007ff7`5764bcfd     mfc42u!AfxWinMain+0xbc
05 000000c0`0309f7e0 00007ffc`f4fd54e0     wordpad!__wmainCRTStartup+0x1dd
06 000000c0`0309f8a0 00007ffc`f62a485b     kernel32!BaseThreadInitThunk+0x10
07 000000c0`0309f8d0 00000000`00000000     ntdll!RtlUserThreadStart+0x2b
0:000>
```

Exercise PN0 (Linux)

- **Goal:** Download and verify the LLDB installation

- \ANETMDA-Dumps\Exercise-PN0-Linux.pdf

Exercise PN0 (LLDB)

Goal: Download and verify the LLDB installation.

1.   Download memory dump files if you haven't done that already and unpack the archive:

https://www.patterndiagnostics.com/Downloads/Training/ANETMDA/ANETMDA-Dumps-Linux.zip

2.   Download and install the version of LLDB available for your distribution. For x64 WSL2 Debian, we used the following command:

```
$ sudo apt install lldb
```

3.   Verify that LLDB is accessible and then exit it (**q** command):

```
$ lldb
(lldb) q
$
```

4.   Install the latest .NET SDK (.NET 9 at the time of this writing, https://dotnet.microsoft.com/en-us/download/dotnet/9.0):

```
$ wget https://builds.dotnet.microsoft.com/dotnet/Sdk/9.0.203/dotnet-sdk-9.0.203-linux-x64.tar.gz

$ sudo tar zxf dotnet-sdk-9.0.203-linux-x64.tar.gz -C /usr/share/dotnet

$ /usr/share/dotnet/dotnet --info
.NET SDK:
 Version:           9.0.203
 Commit:            dc7acfa194
 Workload version:  9.0.200-manifests.9df47798
 MSBuild version:   17.13.20+a4ef1e90f

Runtime Environment:
 OS Name:     debian
 OS Version:  10
 OS Platform: Linux
 RID:         linux-x64
 Base Path:   /usr/share/dotnet/sdk/9.0.203/

Host:
  Version:      9.0.4
  Architecture: x64
  Commit:       f57e6dc747

.NET SDKs installed:
  7.0.409 [/usr/share/dotnet/sdk]
  9.0.203 [/usr/share/dotnet/sdk]

.NET runtimes installed:
  Microsoft.AspNetCore.App 7.0.19 [/usr/share/dotnet/shared/Microsoft.AspNetCore.App]
  Microsoft.AspNetCore.App 9.0.4 [/usr/share/dotnet/shared/Microsoft.AspNetCore.App]
```

```
Microsoft.NETCore.App 7.0.19 [/usr/share/dotnet/shared/Microsoft.NETCore.App]
Microsoft.NETCore.App 9.0.4 [/usr/share/dotnet/shared/Microsoft.NETCore.App]
...
```

5.   Install the SOS extension plugin:

```
$ /usr/share/dotnet/dotnet tool install --global dotnet-sos
```

```
$ dotnet-sos install
Installing SOS to /home/coredump/.dotnet/sos
Creating installation directory...
Copying files from /home/coredump/.dotnet/tools/.store/dotnet-sos/9.0.621003/dotnet-
sos/9.0.621003/tools/net8.0/any/linux-x64
Copying files from /home/coredump/.dotnet/tools/.store/dotnet-sos/9.0.621003/dotnet-
sos/9.0.621003/tools/net8.0/any/lib
Creating new /home/coredump/.lldbinit file - LLDB will load SOS automatically at startup
SOS install succeeded
```

```
$ lldb
Current symbol store settings:
-> Cache: /home/coredump/.dotnet/symbolcache
-> Server: https://msdl.microsoft.com/download/symbols/ Timeout: 4 RetryCount: 0
(lldb) q
```

6.   Install the symbol tool:

```
$ dotnet tool install --global dotnet-symbol
```

Process Memory Dumps

Practice Exercises PN1 – PN8

All exercises were modeled on real-life examples using specially constructed applications. Windows process memory dumps were saved from an isolated Windows 11 x64 system configured with .NET 9 and LINQPad 8. Linux process core dumps were saved from WSL2 configured with .NET 9. In exercises, we learn how to recognize and use 22 .NET analysis patterns and 21 general unmanaged ones.

LINQPad 8 Setup

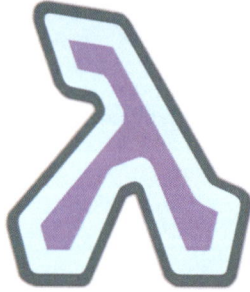

LINQPad 8

© 2007-2025 LINQPad Pty Ltd
Written by Joseph Albahari

Version 8.8.9 (X64)

Loading...

http://www.linqpad.net/

LINQPad

This machine has both .NET 9 and .NET 8 installed.
Which would you prefer as a default for executing queries?

(You can change your mind later in Edit | Preferences > Query)

.NET 9·   .NET 8

Modeling with LINQPad 8

```
void Main()
{
    new ClassMain().Main();
}

// Define other methods and classes here

public class ClassMain
{
    public bool time2stop = false;

    public void Main()
    {
        while (!time2stop)
        {
            DoWork();
        }
    }

    volatile int inSensor, outSensor;

    void DoWork()
    {
        outSensor ^= inSensor;
    }
}
```

I used C# for the applications' source code. Some Windows .NET exercises were modeled using the LINQPad 8 application (www.linqpad.net), where you can write code and instantly execute it. For example, when it hangs, I use Task Manager to save a process memory dump. All Linux exercises were modeled using console applications. The source code of Linux applications may be almost identical to the Windows ones except for some small changes.

Exercise PN1 (Windows)

- **Goal:** Learn how to use the SOS WinDbg extension to analyze managed space for the presence of exceptions

- **Patterns:** Manual Dump (Process); Stack Trace Collection (Unmanaged Space); CLR Thread; Technology-Specific Subtrace (JIT .NET Code); Software Exception; Exception Stack Trace; Managed Code Exception; Mixed Exception; Managed Stack Trace; Invalid Pointer; NULL Pointer (Data)

- **Commands:** .logopen, version, !peb, ~*k, ~*kL, .load, !pe, ~*e, lmv, .chain, .unload, !analyze -v, kL, u, .cxr, !CLRStack, .sympath+, .srcpath+, .frame, !help, .logclose

- \ANETMDA-Dumps\Exercise-PN1-Windows.pdf

Goal: Learn how to use the SOS WinDbg extension to analyze managed space for the presence of exceptions.

Patterns: Manual Dump (Process); Stack Trace Collection (Unmanaged Space); CLR Thread; Technology-Specific Subtrace (JIT .NET Code); Technology-Specific Subtrace (JIT .NET Code); Software Exception; Exception Stack Trace; Managed Code Exception; Managed Stack Trace; Stack Trace Collection (Managed Space); Mixed Exception; Invalid Pointer; NULL Pointer (Data).

Commands: .logopen, version, !peb, ~*k, ~*kL, .load, !pe, ~*e, lmv, .chain, .unload, !analyze -v, kL, u, .cxr, !CLRStack, .sympath+, .srcpath+, .frame, !help, .logclose

1.   Launch WinDbg.

2.   Open \ANETMDA-Dumps\Windows\x64\ApplicationA.DMP

3.   We get the dump file loaded:

```
Microsoft (R) Windows Debugger Version 10.0.27829.1001 AMD64
Copyright (c) Microsoft Corporation. All rights reserved.


Loading Dump File [C:\ANETMDA-Dumps\Windows\x64\ApplicationA.DMP]
User Mini Dump File with Full Memory: Only application data is available


************ Path validation summary **************
Response                    Time (ms)     Location
Deferred                                  srv*
Symbol search path is: srv*
Executable search path is:
Windows 10 Version 22000 MP (4 procs) Free x64
Product: WinNt, suite: SingleUserTS
Edition build lab: 22000.1.amd64fre.co_release.210604-1628
Debug session time: Sat Apr 26 13:45:10.000 2025 (UTC + 1:00)
System Uptime: 0 days 0:15:37.058
Process Uptime: 0 days 0:00:42.000
....................................................................
......................................
For analysis of this file, run !analyze -v
win32u!NtUserWaitMessage+0x14:
00007ffb`e61814d4 ret
```

Note: *ApplicationA* shows this window when launched:

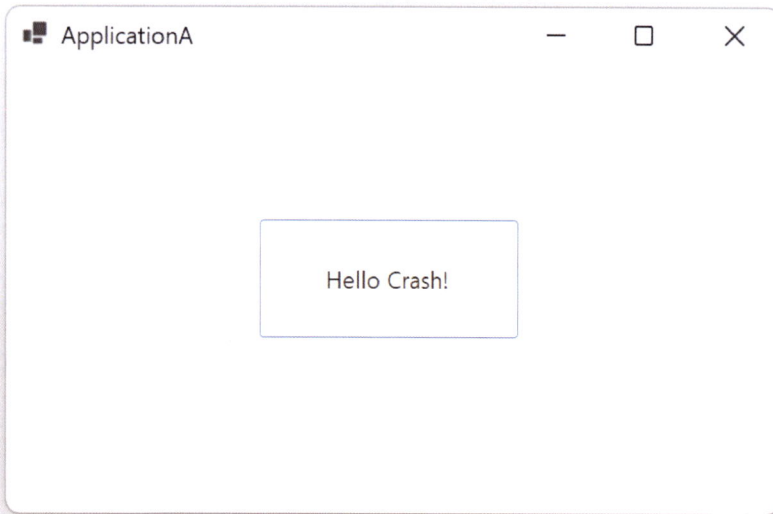

When we click on a button, it shows an exception dialog:

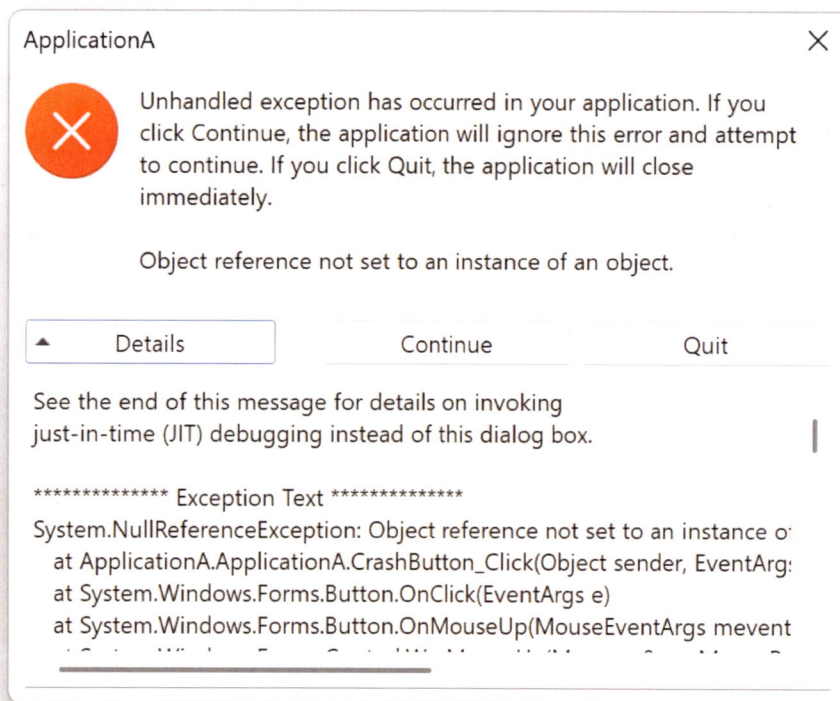

At this time, we use Task Manager to save a memory dump.

4.   Open a log file using the **.logopen** command:

```
0:000> .logopen C:\ANETMDA-Dumps\Windows\x64\ApplicationA.log
Opened log file 'C:\ANETMDA-Dumps\Windows\x64\ApplicationA.log'
```

Note: The WinDbg output may be slightly different on your system if you have a different WinDbg version, a different SOS extension version, you don't have .NET 9 installed, or you have a .NET version different from version 9.0.4 that was on a virtual machine where all the dumps were saved.

5.   WinDbg **version** command shows information about the operating system and when the dump was taken:

```
0:000> version
Windows 10 Version 19042 MP (2 procs) Free x64
Product: WinNt, suite: SingleUserTS Personal
Edition build lab: 19041.1.amd64fre.vb_release.191206-1406
Machine Name:
Debug session time: Thu Apr  1 23:15:28.000 2021 (UTC + 0:00)
System Uptime: 0 days 0:12:42.262
Process Uptime: 0 days 0:01:43.000
  Kernel time: 0 days 0:00:00.000
  User time: 0 days 0:00:01.000
Full memory user mini dump: C:\ANETCMDA-Dumps\Windows\x64\ApplicationA.exe.9152.dmp
[...]
```

6.   We can get the computer name from where the dump was taken using **!peb** command:

```
0:000> !peb
PEB at 000000d076d70000
    InheritedAddressSpace:    No
    ReadImageFileExecOptions: No
    BeingDebugged:            No
    ImageBaseAddress:         00007ff609cd0000
    NtGlobalFlag:             400
    NtGlobalFlag2:            0
    Ldr                       00007ffbe8e9a140
    Ldr.Initialized:          Yes
    Ldr.InInitializationOrderModuleList: 0000020ece432000 . 0000020ecff5c5c0
    Ldr.InLoadOrderModuleList:           0000020ece432180 . 0000020ecff5c5a0
    Ldr.InMemoryOrderModuleList:         0000020ece432190 . 0000020ecff5c5b0
[...]
    SubSystemData:      0000000000000000
    ProcessHeap:        0000020ece430000
    ProcessParameters:  0000020ece436500
    CurrentDirectory:   'C:\Work\'
    WindowTitle:  'C:\Work\ApplicationA.exe'
    ImageFile:    'C:\Work\ApplicationA.exe'
    CommandLine:  '"C:\Work\ApplicationA.exe" '
    DllPath:      '< Name not readable >'
    Environment:  0000020ece4311f0
        ALLUSERSPROFILE=C:\ProgramData
        APPDATA=C:\Users\User\AppData\Roaming
        CLIENTNAME=DESKTOP-IS6V2L0
        CommonProgramFiles=C:\Program Files\Common Files
        CommonProgramFiles(x86)=C:\Program Files (x86)\Common Files
        CommonProgramW6432=C:\Program Files\Common Files
        COMPUTERNAME=WINDEV2204EVAL
        ComSpec=C:\WINDOWS\system32\cmd.exe
        DriverData=C:\Windows\System32\Drivers\DriverData
        HOMEDRIVE=C:
        HOMEPATH=\Users\User
        LOCALAPPDATA=C:\Users\User\AppData\Local
        LOGONSERVER=\\WINDEV2204EVAL
        NUMBER_OF_PROCESSORS=4
```

```
        OneDrive=C:\Users\User\OneDrive
        OS=Windows_NT

Path=C:\Windows\system32;C:\Windows;C:\Windows\System32\Wbem;C:\Windows\System32\WindowsPowerSh
ell\v1.0\;C:\Windows\System32\OpenSSH\;C:\Program Files\Microsoft SQL
Server\150\Tools\Binn\;C:\Program Files\Microsoft SQL Server\Client
SDK\ODBC\170\Tools\Binn\;C:\Program
Files\dotnet\;C:\Users\User\AppData\Local\Microsoft\WindowsApps;C:\Users\User\.dotnet\tools
        PATHEXT=.COM;.EXE;.BAT;.CMD;.VBS;.VBE;.JS;.JSE;.WSF;.WSH;.MSC
        PROCESSOR_ARCHITECTURE=AMD64
        PROCESSOR_IDENTIFIER=Intel64 Family 6 Model 142 Stepping 10, GenuineIntel
        PROCESSOR_LEVEL=6
        PROCESSOR_REVISION=8e0a
        ProgramData=C:\ProgramData
        ProgramFiles=C:\Program Files
        ProgramFiles(x86)=C:\Program Files (x86)
        ProgramW6432=C:\Program Files
        PSModulePath=C:\Program
Files\WindowsPowerShell\Modules;C:\WINDOWS\system32\WindowsPowerShell\v1.0\Modules
        PUBLIC=C:\Users\Public
        SESSIONNAME=31C5CE94259D4006A9E4#0
        SystemDrive=C:
        SystemRoot=C:\WINDOWS
        TEMP=C:\Users\User\AppData\Local\Temp
        TMP=C:\Users\User\AppData\Local\Temp
        USERDOMAIN=WINDEV2204EVAL
        USERDOMAIN_ROAMINGPROFILE=WINDEV2204EVAL
        USERNAME=User
        USERPROFILE=C:\Users\User
        windir=C:\WINDOWS
```

7.   Type ~*kL command to verify the correctness of all stack traces (the command execution time may be longer for the first time because symbol files need to be downloaded from the Microsoft symbol server). The ~*k command output includes references to the .NET CLR source code, and we use the ~*kL command variant to reduce output clutter.

```
0:000> ~*kL

.  0  Id: 1bcc.19fc Suspend: 0 Teb: 000000d0`76d71000 Unfrozen
 # Child-SP          RetAddr           Call Site
00 000000d0`76b9b218 00007ffb`55d9c454 win32u!NtUserWaitMessage+0x14
01 000000d0`76b9b220 00007ffb`b5237d33 System_Windows_Forms_Primitives!Windows.Win32.PInvoke.WaitMessage+0x74
02 000000d0`76b9b2d0 00007ffb`b5237c1a System_Windows_Forms!System.Windows.Forms.Application.LightThreadContext.FPushMessageLoop+0x43
03 000000d0`76b9b360 00007ffb`b5239597 System_Windows_Forms!System.Windows.Forms.Application.LightThreadContext.RunMessageLoop+0xa
04 000000d0`76b9b390 00007ffb`b52392d2 System_Windows_Forms!System.Windows.Forms.Application.ThreadContext.RunMessageLoopInner+0x287
05 000000d0`76b9b410 00007ffb`b517feae System_Windows_Forms!System.Windows.Forms.Application.ThreadContext.RunMessageLoop+0x42
06 000000d0`76b9b490 00007ffb`b52390d9 System_Windows_Forms!System.Windows.Forms.Form.ShowDialog+0x27e
07 000000d0`76b9b520 00007ffb`55d83d0e System_Windows_Forms!System.Windows.Forms.Application.ThreadContext.OnThreadException+0x99
08 000000d0`76b9b590 00007ffb`b58cc4ef System_Windows_Forms!System.Windows.Forms.NativeWindow.Callback+0x26e
09 000000d0`76b9b5f0 00007ffb`b09e7a56 coreclr!CallCatchFunclet+0x17f
0a 000000d0`76b9b700 00007ffb`b09e717a System_Private_CoreLib!System.Runtime.EH.DispatchEx+0x536
0b 000000d0`76b9b860 00007ffb`b5942eb3 System_Private_CoreLib!System.Runtime.EH.RhThrowHwEx+0xaa
0c 000000d0`76b9b8a0 00007ffb`b58c1568 coreclr!CallDescrWorkerInternal+0x83
0d 000000d0`76b9b8e0 00007ffb`b59f5cde coreclr!DispatchCallSimple+0x60
0e 000000d0`76b9b970 00007ffb`b59cf58a coreclr!HandleManagedFaultNew+0x192
0f 000000d0`76b9d480 00007ffb`e8d9ca2a coreclr!CLRVectoredExceptionHandlerShim+0xa84ca
10 000000d0`76b9d4d0 00007ffb`e8d559f2 ntdll!RtlpCallVectoredHandlers+0x112
11 000000d0`76b9d570 00007ffb`e8dc805e ntdll!RtlDispatchException+0x62
12 000000d0`76b9d7c0 00007ffb`55d8cb36 ntdll!KiUserExceptionDispatch+0x2e
13 000000d0`76b9def0 00007ffb`b4f78dd5 ApplicationA!ApplicationA.ApplicationA.CrashButton_Click+0x26
14 000000d0`76b9df10 00007ffb`b4f78f69 System_Windows_Forms!System.Windows.Forms.Button.OnClick+0x195
15 000000d0`76b9dfc0 00007ffb`b4f63d6d System_Windows_Forms!System.Windows.Forms.Button.OnMouseUp+0xe9
16 000000d0`76b9e020 00007ffb`55d84d09 System_Windows_Forms!System.Windows.Forms.Control.WmMouseUp+0x2bd
17 000000d0`76b9e0b0 00007ffb`55d8b5d7 System_Windows_Forms!System.Windows.Forms.Control.WndProc+0x8d9
18 000000d0`76b9e140 00007ffb`55d83b69 System_Windows_Forms!System.Windows.Forms.ButtonBase.WndProc+0x97
19 000000d0`76b9e1a0 00007ffb`55d7347c System_Windows_Forms!System.Windows.Forms.NativeWindow.Callback+0xc9
1a 000000d0`76b9e220 00007ffb`e7701cac System_Windows_Forms_Primitives!ILStubClass.IL_STUB_ReversePInvoke(Windows.Win32.Foundation.HWND,
Windows.Win32.MessageId, Windows.Win32.Foundation.WPARAM, Windows.Win32.Foundation.LPARAM)+0x5c
```

```
1b 000000d0`76b9e2a0 00007ffb`e7700f06     user32!UserCallWinProcCheckWow+0x33c
1c 000000d0`76b9e410 00007ffb`b2d2291f     user32!DispatchMessageWorker+0x2a6
1d 000000d0`76b9e490 00007ffb`b5237e7e     System_Windows_Forms_Primitives!
1e 000000d0`76b9e560 00007ffb`b5237c1a     System_Windows_Forms!System.Windows.Forms.Application.LightThreadContext.FPushMessageLoop+0x18e
1f 000000d0`76b9e5f0 00007ffb`b5239597     System_Windows_Forms!System.Windows.Forms.Application.LightThreadContext.RunMessageLoop+0xa
20 000000d0`76b9e620 00007ffb`b52392d2     System_Windows_Forms!System.Windows.Forms.Application.ThreadContext.RunMessageLoopInner+0x287
21 000000d0`76b9e6a0 00007ffb`55d7189d     System_Windows_Forms!System.Windows.Forms.Application.ThreadContext.RunMessageLoop+0x42
22 000000d0`76b9e700 00007ffb`b5942eb3     ApplicationA!ApplicationA.Program.Main+0x3d
23 000000d0`76b9e740 00007ffb`b58c180c     coreclr!CallDescrWorkerInternal+0x83
24 000000d0`76b9e780 00007ffb`b58abab8     coreclr!MethodDescCallSite::CallTargetWorker+0x208
25 (Inline Function) --------`--------     coreclr!MethodDescCallSite::Call+0xb
26 000000d0`76b9e8c0 00007ffb`b58acc19     coreclr!RunMainInternal+0x11c
27 000000d0`76b9e9e0 00007ffb`b58acf2d     coreclr!RunMain+0xd1
28 000000d0`76b9ea70 00007ffb`b58ac1bb     coreclr!Assembly::ExecuteMainMethod+0x199
29 000000d0`76b9ed40 00007ffb`b58a704c     coreclr!CorHost2::ExecuteAssembly+0x1cb
2a 000000d0`76b9ee50 00007ffb`bec8e8ec     coreclr!coreclr_execute_assembly+0xcc
2b (Inline Function) --------`--------     hostpolicy!coreclr_t::execute_assembly+0x2d
2c 000000d0`76b9eef0 00007ffb`bec8ebbc     hostpolicy!run_app_for_context+0x58c
2d 000000d0`76b9f020 00007ffb`bec8f4ca     hostpolicy!run_app+0x3c
2e 000000d0`76b9f060 00007ffb`c83bd986     hostpolicy!corehost_main+0x15a
2f 000000d0`76b9f160 00007ffb`c83bff66     hostfxr!execute_app+0x2e6
30 000000d0`76b9f1f0 00007ffb`c83c204c     hostfxr!`anonymous namespace'::read_config_and_execute+0xa6
31 000000d0`76b9f2e0 00007ffb`c83c0533     hostfxr!fx_muxer_t::handle_exec_host_command+0x16c
32 000000d0`76b9f390 00007ffb`c83b8460     hostfxr!fx_muxer_t::execute+0x483
33 000000d0`76b9f4d0 00007ffb`09cdaae3     hostfxr!hostfxr_main_startupinfo+0xa0
34 000000d0`76b9f5d0 00007ff6`09cdaef6     ApplicationA_exe!exe_start+0x793
35 000000d0`76b9f780 00007ff6`09ce2818     ApplicationA_exe!wmain+0x146
36 (Inline Function) --------`--------     ApplicationA_exe!invoke_main+0x22
37 000000d0`76b9f7f0 00007ffb`e86253e0     ApplicationA_exe!__scrt_common_main_seh+0x10c
38 000000d0`76b9f830 00007ffb`e8d2485b     kernel32!BaseThreadInitThunk+0x10
39 000000d0`76b9f860 00000000`00000000     ntdll!RtlUserThreadStart+0x2b

   1  Id: 1bcc.e34 Suspend: 0 Teb: 000000d0`76d73000 Unfrozen
 # Child-SP          RetAddr               Call Site
00 000000d0`76f7f4d8 00007ffb`e8d36cdf     ntdll!NtWaitForWorkViaWorkerFactory+0x14
01 000000d0`76f7f4e0 00007ffb`e86253e0     ntdll!TppWorkerThread+0x2df
02 000000d0`76f7f7d0 00007ffb`e8d2485b     kernel32!BaseThreadInitThunk+0x10
03 000000d0`76f7f800 00000000`00000000     ntdll!RtlUserThreadStart+0x2b

   2  Id: 1bcc.1e10 Suspend: 0 Teb: 000000d0`76d75000 Unfrozen
 # Child-SP          RetAddr               Call Site
00 000000d0`770ff738 00007ffb`e8d36cdf     ntdll!NtWaitForWorkViaWorkerFactory+0x14
01 000000d0`770ff740 00007ffb`e86253e0     ntdll!TppWorkerThread+0x2df
02 000000d0`770ffa30 00007ffb`e8d2485b     kernel32!BaseThreadInitThunk+0x10
03 000000d0`770ffa60 00000000`00000000     ntdll!RtlUserThreadStart+0x2b

   3  Id: 1bcc.1d58 Suspend: 0 Teb: 000000d0`76d77000 Unfrozen
 # Child-SP          RetAddr               Call Site
00 000000d0`7727f788 00007ffb`e8d36cdf     ntdll!NtWaitForWorkViaWorkerFactory+0x14
01 000000d0`7727f790 00007ffb`e86253e0     ntdll!TppWorkerThread+0x2df
02 000000d0`7727fa80 00007ffb`e8d2485b     kernel32!BaseThreadInitThunk+0x10
03 000000d0`7727fab0 00000000`00000000     ntdll!RtlUserThreadStart+0x2b

   4  Id: 1bcc.1a9c Suspend: 0 Teb: 000000d0`76d79000 Unfrozen ".NET EventPipe"
 # Child-SP          RetAddr               Call Site
00 000000d0`773ff398 00007ffb`e644dcb0     ntdll!NtWaitForMultipleObjects+0x14
01 000000d0`773ff3a0 00007ffb`e644dbae     KERNELBASE!WaitForMultipleObjectsEx+0xf0
02 000000d0`773ff690 00007ffb`b591693f     KERNELBASE!WaitForMultipleObjects+0xe
03 000000d0`773ff6d0 00007ffb`b59168a0     coreclr!ds_ipc_poll+0x7f
04 000000d0`773ff950 00007ffb`b5916784     coreclr!ds_ipc_stream_factory_get_next_available_stream+0x108
05 000000d0`773ffa20 00007ffb`e86253e0     coreclr!server_thread+0x54
06 000000d0`773ffa90 00007ffb`e8d2485b     kernel32!BaseThreadInitThunk+0x10
07 000000d0`773ffac0 00000000`00000000     ntdll!RtlUserThreadStart+0x2b

   5  Id: 1bcc.17ec Suspend: 0 Teb: 000000d0`76d7b000 Unfrozen ".NET Debugger"
 # Child-SP          RetAddr               Call Site
00 000000d0`7757f888 00007ffb`e644dcb0     ntdll!NtWaitForMultipleObjects+0x14
01 000000d0`7757f890 00007ffb`b5907a9e     KERNELBASE!WaitForMultipleObjectsEx+0xf0
02 000000d0`7757fb80 00007ffb`b5907e26     coreclr!DebuggerRCThread::MainLoop+0xee
03 000000d0`7757fc40 00007ffb`b590785b     coreclr!DebuggerRCThread::ThreadProc+0x12e
04 000000d0`7757fca0 00007ffb`e86253e0     coreclr!DebuggerRCThread::ThreadProcStatic+0x5b
05 000000d0`7757fcd0 00007ffb`e8d2485b     kernel32!BaseThreadInitThunk+0x10
06 000000d0`7757fd00 00000000`00000000     ntdll!RtlUserThreadStart+0x2b

   6  Id: 1bcc.470 Suspend: 0 Teb: 000000d0`76d7d000 Unfrozen ".NET Finalizer"
 # Child-SP          RetAddr               Call Site
00 000000d0`776ff308 00007ffb`e644dcb0     ntdll!NtWaitForMultipleObjects+0x14
01 000000d0`776ff310 00007ffb`b5908a90     KERNELBASE!WaitForMultipleObjectsEx+0xf0
02 000000d0`776ff600 00007ffb`b590889f     coreclr!FinalizerThread::WaitForFinalizerEvent+0x78
03 000000d0`776ff640 00007ffb`b58aef05     coreclr!FinalizerThread::FinalizerThreadWorker+0x4f
04 (Inline Function) --------`--------     coreclr!ManagedThreadBase_DispatchInner+0xd
05 000000d0`776ff890 00007ffb`b58aee2d     coreclr!ManagedThreadBase_DispatchMiddle+0x79
06 000000d0`776ff940 00007ffb`b58fe921     coreclr!ManagedThreadBase_DispatchOuter+0x8d
07 (Inline Function) --------`--------     coreclr!ManagedThreadBase_NoADTransition+0x28
08 (Inline Function) --------`--------     coreclr!ManagedThreadBase::FinalizerBase+0x28
09 000000d0`776ff9b0 00007ffb`e86253e0     coreclr!FinalizerThread::FinalizerThreadStart+0x91
0a 000000d0`776ffac0 00007ffb`e8d2485b     kernel32!BaseThreadInitThunk+0x10
0b 000000d0`776ffaf0 00000000`00000000     ntdll!RtlUserThreadStart+0x2b

   7  Id: 1bcc.1a4 Suspend: 0 Teb: 000000d0`76d83000 Unfrozen
 # Child-SP          RetAddr               Call Site
```

```
00 000000d0`779ffc88 00007ffb`e770d2de    win32u!NtUserMsgWaitForMultipleObjectsEx+0x14
01 000000d0`779ffc90 00007ffb`e770d1d5    user32!RealMsgWaitForMultipleObjectsEx+0x1e
02 000000d0`779ffcd0 00007ffb`c2509970    user32!MsgWaitForMultipleObjects+0x55
03 000000d0`779ffd10 00007ffb`c25098c9    GdiPlus!BackgroundThreadProc+0x70
04 000000d0`779ffd80 00007ffb`e86253e0    GdiPlus!DllRefCountSafeThreadThunk+0x29
05 000000d0`779ffdb0 00007ffb`e8d2485b    kernel32!BaseThreadInitThunk+0x10
06 000000d0`779ffde0 00000000`00000000    ntdll!RtlUserThreadStart+0x2b

   8  Id: 1bcc.c6c Suspend: 0 Teb: 000000d0`76d85000 Unfrozen
 # Child-SP          RetAddr           Call Site
00 000000d0`77b7f208 00007ffb`e644dcb0    ntdll!NtWaitForMultipleObjects+0x14
01 000000d0`77b7f210 00007ffb`e7b2f598    KERNELBASE!WaitForMultipleObjectsEx+0xf0
02 000000d0`77b7f500 00007ffb`e7b2f40a    combase!WaitCoalesced+0xa4
03 000000d0`77b7f790 00007ffb`e7b2f20c    combase!CROIDTable::WorkerThreadLoop+0x5a
04 000000d0`77b7f7e0 00007ffb`e7b2f189    combase!CRpcThread::WorkerLoop+0x58
05 000000d0`77b7f850 00007ffb`e86253e0    combase!CRpcThreadCache::RpcWorkerThreadEntry+0x29
06 000000d0`77b7f880 00007ffb`e8d2485b    kernel32!BaseThreadInitThunk+0x10
07 000000d0`77b7f8b0 00000000`00000000    ntdll!RtlUserThreadStart+0x2b

   9  Id: 1bcc.1044 Suspend: 0 Teb: 000000d0`76d87000 Unfrozen
 # Child-SP          RetAddr           Call Site
00 000000d0`77cff6c8 00007ffb`e8d36cdf    ntdll!NtWaitForWorkViaWorkerFactory+0x14
01 000000d0`77cff6d0 00007ffb`e86253e0    ntdll!TppWorkerThread+0x2df
02 000000d0`77cff9c0 00007ffb`e8d2485b    kernel32!BaseThreadInitThunk+0x10
03 000000d0`77cff9f0 00000000`00000000    ntdll!RtlUserThreadStart+0x2b

  10  Id: 1bcc.1d40 Suspend: 0 Teb: 000000d0`76d89000 Unfrozen
 # Child-SP          RetAddr           Call Site
00 000000d0`77e7f448 00007ffb`e8d36cdf    ntdll!NtWaitForWorkViaWorkerFactory+0x14
01 000000d0`77e7f450 00007ffb`e86253e0    ntdll!TppWorkerThread+0x2df
02 000000d0`77e7f740 00007ffb`e8d2485b    kernel32!BaseThreadInitThunk+0x10
03 000000d0`77e7f770 00000000`00000000    ntdll!RtlUserThreadStart+0x2b

  11  Id: 1bcc.1cf8 Suspend: 0 Teb: 000000d0`76d8b000 Unfrozen ".NET System Events"
 # Child-SP          RetAddr           Call Site
00 000000d0`77fff338 00007ffb`e771472e    win32u!NtUserGetMessage+0x14
01 000000d0`77fff340 00007ffb`c0bb6979    user32!GetMessageW+0x2e
02 000000d0`77fff3a0 00007ffb`c0bb63f2    Microsoft_Win32_SystemEvents!
03 000000d0`77fff480 00007ffb`b5942eb3    Microsoft_Win32_SystemEvents!Microsoft.Win32.SystemEvents.WindowThreadProc+0x92
04 000000d0`77fff4f0 00007ffb`b58c1568    coreclr!CallDescrWorkerInternal+0x83
05 000000d0`77fff530 00007ffb`b59315a3    coreclr!DispatchCallSimple+0x60
06 000000d0`77fff5c0 00007ffb`b58aef05    coreclr!ThreadNative::KickOffThread_Worker+0x63
07 (Inline Function) --------`--------    coreclr!ManagedThreadBase_DispatchInner+0xd
08 000000d0`77fff620 00007ffb`b58aee2d    coreclr!ManagedThreadBase_DispatchMiddle+0x79
09 000000d0`77fff6d0 00007ffb`b58aefbb    coreclr!ManagedThreadBase_DispatchOuter+0x8d
0a (Inline Function) --------`--------    coreclr!ManagedThreadBase_FullTransition+0x28
0b (Inline Function) --------`--------    coreclr!ManagedThreadBase::KickOff+0x28
0c 000000d0`77fff740 00007ffb`e86253e0    coreclr!ThreadNative::KickOffThread+0x7b
0d 000000d0`77fff7a0 00007ffb`e8d2485b    kernel32!BaseThreadInitThunk+0x10
0e 000000d0`77fff7d0 00000000`00000000    ntdll!RtlUserThreadStart+0x2b
```

Note: We see that threads #0, #4 - #6, #11 have **coreclr** module on their stack traces (the previous versions of .NET Framework used the **clr** module and **mscorwks** module). We also see signs of software exception (in red) and exception stack trace #0, which has signs of managed code exception processing (in yellow). Finally, the stack trace fragment from our *ApplicationA* module is shown in green.

8.   We now check the version of .NET used when *ApplicationA* was running:

```
0:000> lmv m coreclr
Browse full module list
start             end               module name
00007ffb`b57f0000 00007ffb`b5c9a000   coreclr    (private pdb symbols)
C:\ProgramData\Dbg\sym\coreclr.pdb\80E26C0B98AE42B2AAB3114358114E551\coreclr.pdb
    Loaded symbol image file: coreclr.dll
    Image path: C:\Program Files\dotnet\shared\Microsoft.NETCore.App\9.0.4\coreclr.dll
    Image name: coreclr.dll
    Browse all global symbols  functions  data  Symbol Reload
    Timestamp:        Thu Mar 13 22:01:10 2025 (67D355A6)
    CheckSum:         0049FD9A
    ImageSize:        004AA000
    File version:     9.0.425.16305
    Product version:  9.0.425.16305
    File flags:       0 (Mask 3F)
    File OS:          4 Unknown Win32
    File type:        0.0 Unknown
```

```
File date:           00000000.00000000
Translations:        0409.04b0
Information from resource tables:
    CompanyName:      Microsoft Corporation
    ProductName:      Microsoft® .NET
    InternalName:     CoreCLR.dll
    OriginalFilename: CoreCLR.dll
    ProductVersion:   9,0,425,16305 @Commit: f57e6dc747158ab7ade4e62a75a6750d16b771e8
    FileVersion:      9,0,425,16305 @Commit: f57e6dc747158ab7ade4e62a75a6750d16b771e8
    FileDescription:  .NET Runtime
    LegalCopyright:   © Microsoft Corporation. All rights reserved.
    Comments:         Flavor=Retail
```

9.   WinDbg may load the SOS extension automatically and its version may not be exactly the same as the SOS extension from the process memory dump .NET version.

```
0:000> .chain
Extension DLL search Path:
[...]
Extension DLL chain:
    C:\Program Files\WindowsApps\Microsoft.WinDbg_1.2504.15001.0_x64__8wekyb3d8bbwe\amd64\winext\sos\sos: image 9,0,12,7501 @Commit:
a651406e39038aef1dbc7c8097b52953284dba27, API 2.0.0, built Sat Jan 25 08:30:17 2025
        [path: C:\Program Files\WindowsApps\Microsoft.WinDbg_1.2504.15001.0_x64__8wekyb3d8bbwe\amd64\winext\sos\sos.dll]
    DbgEngCoreDMExt: image 10.0.27829.1001, API 0.0.0,
        [path: C:\Program Files\WindowsApps\Microsoft.WinDbg_1.2504.15001.0_x64__8wekyb3d8bbwe\amd64\winext\DbgEngCoreDMExt.dll]
    CLRComposition: image 10.0.27829.1001, API 0.0.0,
        [path: C:\Program Files\WindowsApps\Microsoft.WinDbg_1.2504.15001.0_x64__8wekyb3d8bbwe\amd64\winext\CLRComposition.dll]
    MachOBinComposition: image 10.0.27829.1001, API 0.0.0,
        [path: C:\Program Files\WindowsApps\Microsoft.WinDbg_1.2504.15001.0_x64__8wekyb3d8bbwe\amd64\winext\MachOBinComposition.dll]
    ELFBinComposition: image 10.0.27829.1001, API 0.0.0,
        [path: C:\Program Files\WindowsApps\Microsoft.WinDbg_1.2504.15001.0_x64__8wekyb3d8bbwe\amd64\winext\ELFBinComposition.dll]
    dbghelp: image 10.0.27829.1001, API 10.0.6,
        [path: C:\Program Files\WindowsApps\Microsoft.WinDbg_1.2504.15001.0_x64__8wekyb3d8bbwe\amd64\dbghelp.dll]
    exts: image 10.0.27829.1001, API 1.0.0,
        [path: C:\Program Files\WindowsApps\Microsoft.WinDbg_1.2504.15001.0_x64__8wekyb3d8bbwe\amd64\WINXP\exts.dll]
    uext: image 10.0.27829.1001, API 1.0.0,
        [path: C:\Program Files\WindowsApps\Microsoft.WinDbg_1.2504.15001.0_x64__8wekyb3d8bbwe\amd64\winext\uext.dll]
    ntsdexts: image 10.0.27829.1001, API 1.0.0,
        [path: C:\Program Files\WindowsApps\Microsoft.WinDbg_1.2504.15001.0_x64__8wekyb3d8bbwe\amd64\WINXP\ntsdexts.dll]
```

Note: if this extension is not loaded, all commands related to .NET will not be available:

```
0:000> .unload C:\Program
Files\WindowsApps\Microsoft.WinDbg_1.2504.15001.0_x64__8wekyb3d8bbwe\amd64\winext\sos\sos
Unloading C:\Program
Files\WindowsApps\Microsoft.WinDbg_1.2504.15001.0_x64__8wekyb3d8bbwe\amd64\winext\sos\sos
extension DLL
```

```
0:000> .chain
Extension DLL search Path:
[...]
Extension DLL chain:
    DbgEngCoreDMExt: image 10.0.27829.1001, API 0.0.0,
        [path: C:\Program Files\WindowsApps\Microsoft.WinDbg_1.2504.15001.0_x64__8wekyb3d8bbwe\amd64\winext\DbgEngCoreDMExt.dll]
    CLRComposition: image 10.0.27829.1001, API 0.0.0,
        [path: C:\Program Files\WindowsApps\Microsoft.WinDbg_1.2504.15001.0_x64__8wekyb3d8bbwe\amd64\winext\CLRComposition.dll]
    MachOBinComposition: image 10.0.27829.1001, API 0.0.0,
        [path: C:\Program Files\WindowsApps\Microsoft.WinDbg_1.2504.15001.0_x64__8wekyb3d8bbwe\amd64\winext\MachOBinComposition.dll]
    ELFBinComposition: image 10.0.27829.1001, API 0.0.0,
        [path: C:\Program Files\WindowsApps\Microsoft.WinDbg_1.2504.15001.0_x64__8wekyb3d8bbwe\amd64\winext\ELFBinComposition.dll]
    dbghelp: image 10.0.27829.1001, API 10.0.6,
        [path: C:\Program Files\WindowsApps\Microsoft.WinDbg_1.2504.15001.0_x64__8wekyb3d8bbwe\amd64\dbghelp.dll]
    exts: image 10.0.27829.1001, API 1.0.0,
        [path: C:\Program Files\WindowsApps\Microsoft.WinDbg_1.2504.15001.0_x64__8wekyb3d8bbwe\amd64\WINXP\exts.dll]
    uext: image 10.0.27829.1001, API 1.0.0,
        [path: C:\Program Files\WindowsApps\Microsoft.WinDbg_1.2504.15001.0_x64__8wekyb3d8bbwe\amd64\winext\uext.dll]
    ntsdexts: image 10.0.27829.1001, API 1.0.0,
        [path: C:\Program Files\WindowsApps\Microsoft.WinDbg_1.2504.15001.0_x64__8wekyb3d8bbwe\amd64\WINXP\ntsdexts.dll]
```

```
0:000> !pe
```
pe is not extension gallery command
No export pe found

Note: The SOS version can also be checked by listing all loaded WinDbg extensions (**sos.dll** is used for .NET analysis):

10.   We load the SOS extension we previosly installed with the *dotnet-sos* tool. See the **SOS Setup (Specific .NET)** slide.


```
0:000> .load C:\Users\dmitr\.dotnet\sos\sos.dll
```


```
0:000> .chain
Extension DLL search Path:
[...]
Extension DLL chain:
    C:\Users\dmitr\.dotnet\sos\sos.dll: image 9,0,12,21003 @Commit: ebd1db46a2395bd7de706694ff54f1c9526951d7, API 2.0.0, built Fri Apr
11 05:48:49 2025
        [path: C:\Users\dmitr\.dotnet\sos\sos.dll]
    DbgEngCoreDMExt: image 10.0.27829.1001, API 0.0.0,
        [path: C:\Program Files\WindowsApps\Microsoft.WinDbg_1.2504.15001.0_x64__8wekyb3d8bbwe\amd64\winext\DbgEngCoreDMExt.dll]
    CLRComposition: image 10.0.27829.1001, API 0.0.0,
        [path: C:\Program Files\WindowsApps\Microsoft.WinDbg_1.2504.15001.0_x64__8wekyb3d8bbwe\amd64\winext\CLRComposition.dll]
    MachOBinComposition: image 10.0.27829.1001, API 0.0.0,
        [path: C:\Program Files\WindowsApps\Microsoft.WinDbg_1.2504.15001.0_x64__8wekyb3d8bbwe\amd64\winext\MachOBinComposition.dll]
    ELFBinComposition: image 10.0.27829.1001, API 0.0.0,
        [path: C:\Program Files\WindowsApps\Microsoft.WinDbg_1.2504.15001.0_x64__8wekyb3d8bbwe\amd64\winext\ELFBinComposition.dll]
    dbghelp: image 10.0.27829.1001, API 10.0.6,
        [path: C:\Program Files\WindowsApps\Microsoft.WinDbg_1.2504.15001.0_x64__8wekyb3d8bbwe\amd64\dbghelp.dll]
    exts: image 10.0.27829.1001, API 1.0.0,
        [path: C:\Program Files\WindowsApps\Microsoft.WinDbg_1.2504.15001.0_x64__8wekyb3d8bbwe\amd64\WINXP\exts.dll]
    uext: image 10.0.27829.1001, API 1.0.0,
        [path: C:\Program Files\WindowsApps\Microsoft.WinDbg_1.2504.15001.0_x64__8wekyb3d8bbwe\amd64\winext\uext.dll]
    ntsdexts: image 10.0.27829.1001, API 1.0.0,
        [path: C:\Program Files\WindowsApps\Microsoft.WinDbg_1.2504.15001.0_x64__8wekyb3d8bbwe\amd64\WINXP\ntsdexts.dll]
```


11.   Now, we check if there is a .NET exception on the current thread 0 (W):


```
0:000> !pe
Exception object: 0000020ed20130f8
Exception type:    System.NullReferenceException
Message:           Object reference not set to an instance of an object.
InnerException:    <none>
StackTrace (generated):
    SP               IP               Function
    000000D076B9DEF0 00007FFB55D8CB37 ApplicationA!ApplicationA.ApplicationA.CrashButton_Click(System.Object, System.EventArgs)+0x27
    000000D076B9DF10 00007FFBB4F78DD5 System_Windows_Forms!System.Windows.Forms.Button.OnClick(System.EventArgs)+0x195
    000000D076B9DFC0 00007FFBB4F78F69 System_Windows_Forms!System.Windows.Forms.Button.OnMouseUp(System.Windows.Forms.MouseEventArgs)+0xe9
    000000D076B9E020 00007FFBB4F63D6D System_Windows_Forms!System.Windows.Forms.Control.WmMouseUp(System.Windows.Forms.Message ByRef,
System.Windows.Forms.MouseButtons, Int32)+0x2bd
    000000D076B9E0B0 00007FFB55D84D09 System_Windows_Forms!System.Windows.Forms.Control.WndProc(System.Windows.Forms.Message ByRef)+0x8d9
    000000D076B9E140 00007FFB55D8B5D7 System_Windows_Forms!System.Windows.Forms.ButtonBase.WndProc(System.Windows.Forms.Message ByRef)+0x97
    000000D076B9E1A0 00007FFB55D83B69 System_Windows_Forms!System.Windows.Forms.NativeWindow.Callback(Windows.Win32.Foundation.HWND, Windows.Win32.MessageId,
Windows.Win32.Foundation.WPARAM, Windows.Win32.Foundation.LPARAM)+0xc9

StackTraceString: <none>
HResult: 80004003
```


Note: We also double-check that no other threads have exceptions by executing **!pe** command for each thread using **~*e** command:


```
0:000> ~*e !pe
Exception object: 0000020ed20130f8
Exception type:    System.NullReferenceException
Message:           Object reference not set to an instance of an object.
InnerException:    <none>
StackTrace (generated):
    SP               IP               Function
    000000D076B9DEF0 00007FFB55D8CB37 ApplicationA!ApplicationA.ApplicationA.CrashButton_Click(System.Object, System.EventArgs)+0x27
    000000D076B9DF10 00007FFBB4F78DD5 System_Windows_Forms!System.Windows.Forms.Button.OnClick(System.EventArgs)+0x195
    000000D076B9DFC0 00007FFBB4F78F69 System_Windows_Forms!System.Windows.Forms.Button.OnMouseUp(System.Windows.Forms.MouseEventArgs)+0xe9
    000000D076B9E020 00007FFBB4F63D6D System_Windows_Forms!System.Windows.Forms.Control.WmMouseUp(System.Windows.Forms.Message ByRef,
System.Windows.Forms.MouseButtons, Int32)+0x2bd
    000000D076B9E0B0 00007FFB55D84D09 System_Windows_Forms!System.Windows.Forms.Control.WndProc(System.Windows.Forms.Message ByRef)+0x8d9
    000000D076B9E140 00007FFB55D8B5D7 System_Windows_Forms!System.Windows.Forms.ButtonBase.WndProc(System.Windows.Forms.Message ByRef)+0x97
```

```
000000D076B9E1A0 00007FFB55D83B69 System_Windows_Forms!System.Windows.Forms.NativeWindow.Callback(Windows.Win32.Foundation.HWND, Windows.Win32.MessageId,
Windows.Win32.Foundation.WPARAM, Windows.Win32.Foundation.LPARAM)+0xc9

StackTraceString: <none>
HResult: 80004003
The current thread is unmanaged
The current thread is unmanaged
The current thread is unmanaged
The current thread is unmanaged
The current thread is unmanaged
There is no current managed exception on this thread
The current thread is unmanaged
The current thread is unmanaged
The current thread is unmanaged
The current thread is unmanaged
There is no current managed exception on this thread
```

12.   Let's see what **!analyze -v** command says:

0:000> **!analyze -v**

```
.............................................
.......................................
ClrmaManagedAnalysis::AssociateClient
AssociateClient trying managed CLRMA
AssociateClient trying DAC CLRMA
************************************************************************
*                                                                      *
*                    Exception Analysis                                *
*                                                                      *
************************************************************************

*** WARNING: Unable to verify checksum for ApplicationA.dll
*** WARNING: Unable to verify checksum for ApplicationA.exe
ClrmaManagedAnalysis::GetThread 19fc
ClrmaThread::Initialize 19fc
~ClrmaThread
ClrmaManagedAnalysis::GetThread 0e34
ClrmaThread::Initialize 0e34
ClrmaThread::Initialize FAILED managed thread not found
~ClrmaThread
ClrmaManagedAnalysis::GetThread 1e10
ClrmaThread::Initialize 1e10
ClrmaThread::Initialize FAILED managed thread not found
~ClrmaThread
ClrmaManagedAnalysis::GetThread 1d58
ClrmaThread::Initialize 1d58
ClrmaThread::Initialize FAILED managed thread not found
~ClrmaThread
ClrmaManagedAnalysis::GetThread 1a9c
ClrmaThread::Initialize 1a9c
ClrmaThread::Initialize FAILED managed thread not found
~ClrmaThread
ClrmaManagedAnalysis::GetThread 17ec
ClrmaThread::Initialize 17ec
ClrmaThread::Initialize FAILED managed thread not found
~ClrmaThread
ClrmaManagedAnalysis::GetThread 0470
ClrmaThread::Initialize 0470
~ClrmaThread
ClrmaManagedAnalysis::GetThread 01a4
ClrmaThread::Initialize 01a4
ClrmaThread::Initialize FAILED managed thread not found
~ClrmaThread
ClrmaManagedAnalysis::GetThread 0c6c
ClrmaThread::Initialize 0c6c
ClrmaThread::Initialize FAILED managed thread not found
~ClrmaThread
ClrmaManagedAnalysis::GetThread 1044
ClrmaThread::Initialize 1044
ClrmaThread::Initialize FAILED managed thread not found
~ClrmaThread
ClrmaManagedAnalysis::GetThread 1d40
ClrmaThread::Initialize 1d40
ClrmaThread::Initialize FAILED managed thread not found
~ClrmaThread
ClrmaManagedAnalysis::GetThread 1cf8
ClrmaThread::Initialize 1cf8
~ClrmaThread
ClrmaManagedAnalysis::get_ProviderName
ClrmaManagedAnalysis::GetThread ffffffff
ClrmaThread::Initialize 19fc
ClrmaThread::get_CurrentException
~ClrmaException
ClrmaThread::get_NestedExceptionCount
~ClrmaThread
Failed to request MethodData, not in JIT code range

KEY_VALUES_STRING: 1

    Key  : Analysis.CPU.mSec
    Value: 4531

    Key  : Analysis.Elapsed.mSec
    Value: 6221

    Key  : Analysis.IO.Other.Mb
    Value: 4

    Key  : Analysis.IO.Read.Mb
    Value: 4

    Key  : Analysis.IO.Write.Mb
    Value: 13

    Key  : Analysis.Init.CPU.mSec
    Value: 13140

    Key  : Analysis.Init.Elapsed.mSec
    Value: 3614105
```

```
Key   : Analysis.Memory.CommitPeak.Mb
Value: 407

Key   : Analysis.Version.DbgEng
Value: 10.0.27829.1001

Key   : Analysis.Version.Description
Value: 10.2503.24.01 amd64fre

Key   : Analysis.Version.Ext
Value: 1.2503.24.1

Key   : CLR.Engine
Value: CORECLR

Key   : CLR.Version
Value: 9.0.425.16305

Key   : Failure.Bucket
Value: BREAKPOINT_80000003_win32u.dll!NtUserWaitMessage

Key   : Failure.Exception.Code
Value: 0x80000003

Key   : Failure.Exception.Record
Value: 0x7ffbb57856e8

Key   : Failure.Hash
Value: {a106cd41-a8b1-c51d-6d94-a75661270841}

Key   : Failure.ProblemClass.Primary
Value: BREAKPOINT

Key   : Faulting.IP.Type
Value: Null

Key   : Timeline.OS.Boot.DeltaSec
Value: 937

Key   : Timeline.Process.Start.DeltaSec
Value: 42

Key   : WER.OS.Branch
Value: co_release

Key   : WER.OS.Version
Value: 10.0.22000.1

Key   : WER.Process.Version
Value: 1.0.0.0


FILE_IN_CAB:  ApplicationA.DMP

NTGLOBALFLAG:   400

APPLICATION_VERIFIER_FLAGS:   0

EXCEPTION_RECORD:  00007ffbb57856e8 -- (.exr 0x7ffbb57856e8)
ExceptionAddress: 00007ffbb52de4f8 (System_Windows_Forms+0x000000000080e4f8)
   ExceptionCode: 560bb828
  ExceptionFlags: 00007ffb
NumberParameters: -1255283464
   Parameter[0]: 00007ffb56039788
   Parameter[1]: 00007ffb560b07b0
   Parameter[2]: 00007ffb560b07f8
   Parameter[3]: 00007ffbb52de4f8
   Parameter[4]: 00007ffbb52de4f8
   Parameter[5]: 00007ffbb52de4f8
   Parameter[6]: 00007ffbb52de4f8
   Parameter[7]: 00007ffbb52de4f8
   Parameter[8]: 00007ffbb52de4f8
   Parameter[9]: 00007ffbb52de4f8
   Parameter[10]: 00007ffbb52de4f8
   Parameter[11]: 00007ffbb52de4f8
   Parameter[12]: 00007ffbb52de4f8
   Parameter[13]: 00007ffb560b8078
   Parameter[14]: 00007ffbb52de4f8


FAULTING_THREAD:  19fc

PROCESS_NAME:  ApplicationA.dll

ERROR_CODE: (NTSTATUS) 0x80000003 - {EXCEPTION}  Breakpoint  A breakpoint has been reached.

EXCEPTION_CODE_STR:  80000003

CONTEXT:  00007ffbe8d496fd -- (.cxr 0x7ffbe8d496fd)
rax=4080ce8040000001 rbx=c35b5d5e5f5c415d rcx=4810438d480f7388
rdx=415e415f4178c483 rsi=17b08fb60f000000 rdi=618d4448708b0000
rip=001786e8e5b4894a rsp=0030253c8b4865cc rbp=3025048b48650000
 r8=0000c824a48944ff  r9=39480e78e4854500 r10=840f001786e0cdb4
r11=ef0d1d8bfffffdbd r12=440007f644e80014 r13=a48944e32344e08b
r14=4c8d41000000c824 r15=000017b08f880124
iopl=0         nv dn di pl nz na po cy
cs=0f3f  ss=0030  ds=7485  es=0944  fs=8300  gs=247c         efl=02a1850f
001786e8`e5b4894a ???
Resetting default scope

IP_ON_HEAP:  001786e8e5b4894a
The fault address in not in any loaded module, please check your build's rebase
log at <releasedir>\bin\build_logs\timebuild\ntrebase.log for module which may
contain the address if it were loaded.

FRAME_ONE_INVALID: 1

STACK_TEXT:
000000d0`76b9b218 00007ffb`55d9c454     : 000000d0`00000000 00000000`00000000 000037c7`aacf9f22 00007ffb`b5bc1d60 : win32u!NtUserWaitMessage+0x14
000000d0`76b9b220 00007ffb`b5237d33     : 0000020e`d200d860 000000d0`76b9b2f8 000000d0`76b9b108 00000000`00000000 : System_Windows_Forms_Primitives!Windows.Win32.PInvoke.WaitMessage+0x74
000000d0`76b9b2d0 00007ffb`b5237c1a     : 0000020e`d2812da8 00000000`00000000 00000000`00000001 00000000`0000000d :
System_Windows_Forms!System.Windows.Forms.Application.LightThreadContext.FPushMessageLoop+0x43
000000d0`76b9b360 00007ffb`b5239597     : 0000020e`d2825fa8 00000000`00000001 00000000`0000051a 00000000`00000030 :
System_Windows_Forms!System.Windows.Forms.Application.LightThreadContext.RunMessageLoop+0xa
000000d0`76b9b390 00007ffb`b52392d2     : 0000020e`d200d860 000000d0`76b9b2d0 0000020e`d20201d8 00007ffb`5602f3b0 :
System_Windows_Forms!System.Windows.Forms.Application.ThreadContext.RunMessageLoopInner+0x287
000000d0`76b9b410 00007ffb`b517feae     : 0000020e`d2812da8 00000000`00000000 0000020e`d2846d88 00007ffb`5602f3b0 :
System_Windows_Forms!System.Windows.Forms.Application.ThreadContext.RunMessageLoop+0x42
000000d0`76b9b470 00007ffb`b52390d9     : 0000020e`d2013b18 00000000`00000000 00000000`00000200 000000d0`76b9b2d0 : System_Windows_Forms!System.Windows.Forms.Form.ShowDialog+0x27e
```

```
000000d0`76b9b520 00007ffb`55d83d0e     : 0000020e`d200d860 0000020e`d28249b0 0000020e`ce458c50 00007ffb`55f93ff0 :
System_Windows_Forms!System.Windows.Forms.Application.ThreadContext.OnThreadException+0x99
000000d0`76b9b590 00007ffb`b58cc4ef     : 000000d0`76b9b810 000000d0`76b9b850 000000d0`76b9c308 000000d0`76b9e1a0 : System_Windows_Forms!System.Windows.Forms.NativeWindow.Callback+0x26e
000000d0`76b9b5f0 00007ffb`b09e7a56     : 000000d0`76b9bf90 00007ffb`55d83cdb 000000d0`76b9bed0 000000d0`76b9bed0 : coreclr!CallCatchFunclet+0x17f
000000d0`76b9b700 00007ffb`b09e717a     : 000000d0`76b9bf90 000000d0`76b9bed0 00000000`00000001 0000020e`ce50d000 : System_Private_CoreLib!System.Runtime.EH.DispatchEx+0x536
000000d0`76b9b860 00007ffb`b5942eb3     : 00000000`00000000 000000d0`76b9dcb0 00000000`00000000 00007ffb`55d62874 : System_Private_CoreLib!System.Runtime.EH.RhThrowHwEx+0xaa
000000d0`76b9b8a0 00007ffb`b58c1568     : 000000d0`76d70000 0000020e`cfd50890 00007ffb`b5b95230 00007ffb`55d50af0 : coreclr!CallDescrWorkerInternal+0x83
000000d0`76b9b8e0 00007ffb`b59f5cde     : 00000000`00000000 000000d0`76b9dcb0 0000020e`ce458c50 0000020e`cfd50890 : coreclr!DispatchCallSimple+0x60
000000d0`76b9b970 00007ffb`b59cf58a     : 00000000`00000000 000000d0`76ba0000 000000d0`76ba0000 000000d0`76b9d510 : coreclr!HandleManagedFaultNew+0x192
000000d0`76b9d480 00007ffb`e8d9ca2a     : 00007ffb`b59270c0 00000000`00000000 0000020e`cfd50880 00000000`00000000 : coreclr!CLRVectoredExceptionHandlerShim+0xa84ca
000000d0`76b9d4d0 00007ffb`e8d559f2     : 000000d0`76b9dcb0 00000000`00000000 000000d0`76b9dfb0 00000000`00000000 : ntdll!RtlpCallVectoredHandlers+0x112
000000d0`76b9d570 00007ffb`e8dc805e     : 00007ffb`b57856e8 00007ffb`e8d496fd 0000020e`d28179c0 00007ffb`00000000 : ntdll!RtlDispatchException+0x62
000000d0`76b9d7c0 00007ffb`55d8cb36     : 00000000`000002af 00000000`00000000 000000d0`76b9dfb0 00007ffb`b4f78dd5 : ntdll!KiUserExceptionDispatch+0x2e
000000d0`76b9def0 00007ffb`b4f78dd5     : 0000020e`d2811050 0000020e`d28179c0 0000020e`d2824168 00000000`00000006 : ApplicationA!ApplicationA.ApplicationA.CrashButton_Click+0x26
000000d0`76b9df10 00007ffb`b4f78f69     : 0000020e`d28179c0 0000020e`d2824168 000000d0`76b9dee8 000000d0`76b9dfb0 : System_Windows_Forms!System.Windows.Forms.Button.OnClick+0x195
000000d0`76b9dfc0 00007ffb`b4f63d6d     : 0000020e`d28179c0 0000020e`d2824168 00000000`00000001 00000033`000000b5 : System_Windows_Forms!System.Windows.Forms.Button.OnMouseUp+0xe9
000000d0`76b9e020 00007ffb`55d84d09     : 0000020e`d28179c0 000000d0`76b9e1d0 00000000`00000000 00000000`00000001 : System_Windows_Forms!System.Windows.Forms.Control.WmMouseUp+0x2bd
000000d0`76b9e0b0 00007ffb`55d8b5d7     : 0000020e`ce517d90 000000d0`76b9e550 00000000`00000202 0000020e`ce517d90 : System_Windows_Forms!System.Windows.Forms.Control.WndProc+0x8d9
000000d0`76b9e140 00007ffb`55d83b69     : 0000020e`d28179c0 00000000`00000000 00000000`00000000 00007ffb`e8d5ff83 : System_Windows_Forms!System.Windows.Forms.ButtonBase.WndProc+0x97
000000d0`76b9e1a0 00007ffb`55d7347c     : 0000020e`d200eef0 000000d0`76b9e290 00000000`00000202 00000000`00000001 : System_Windows_Forms!System.Windows.Forms.NativeWindow.Callback+0xc9
000000d0`76b9e220 00007ffb`e7701cac     : 00000000`00000000 00000000`00000000 00000000`00000001 00000000`00000000 :
System_Windows_Forms_Primitives!ILStubClass.IL_STUB_ReversePInvoke(Windows.Win32.Foundation.HWND, Windows.Win32.Foundation.MessageId, Windows.Win32.Foundation.WPARAM,
Windows.Win32.Foundation.LPARAM)+0x5c
000000d0`76b9e2a0 00007ffb`e7700f06     : 00007ffb`e8dc4060 00007ffb`55c33124 00000000`002b0572 00000000`00000202 : user32!UserCallWinProcCheckWow+0x33c
000000d0`76b9e410 00007ffb`b2d2291f     : 00007ffb`55c33124 00000000`ffffffff 0000020e`d2812da8 00007ffb`55d8bd30 : user32!DispatchMessageWorker+0x2a6
000000d0`76b9e490 00007ffb`b5237e7e     : 0000020e`d2812da8 000000d0`76b9e588 00000000`00000001 00000000`0000000d : System_Windows_Forms_Primitives!
000000d0`76b9e560 00007ffb`b5237c1a     : 0000020e`d2812da8 00000000`ffffffff 00000000`00000000 00007ffb`55f92a10 :
System_Windows_Forms!System.Windows.Forms.Application.LightThreadContext.FPushMessageLoop+0x18e
000000d0`76b9e5f0 00007ffb`b5239597     : 0000020e`d2812da8 00000000`ffffffff 00000000`00000000 00007ffb`55f92a10 :
System_Windows_Forms!System.Windows.Forms.Application.LightThreadContext.RunMessageLoop+0xa
000000d0`76b9e620 00007ffb`b52392d2     : 0000020e`d200d860 00000000`ffffffff 0000020e`d200f3c8 0000020e`cff15fd0 :
System_Windows_Forms!System.Windows.Forms.Application.ThreadContext.RunMessageLoopInner+0x287
000000d0`76b9e6a0 00007ffb`55d7189d     : 0000020e`d2812da8 00000000`ffffffff 0000020e`d2818838 00007ffb`5602f3b0 :
System_Windows_Forms!System.Windows.Forms.Application.ThreadContext.RunMessageLoop+0x42
000000d0`76b9e700 00007ffb`b5942eb3     : 00007ffb`b58c168b 000000d0`76b9ed68 000000d0`76b9e979 : ApplicationA!ApplicationA.Program.Main+0x3d
000000d0`76b9e740 00007ffb`b58c180c     : 000000d0`76b9ea30 00000000`00000008 000000d0`76b9e7b0 00007ffb`00000001 : coreclr!CallDescrWorkerInternal+0x83
000000d0`76b9e780 00007ffb`b58abab8     : 000000d0`76b9ea30 00000000`00000001 00000000`00000000 00007ffb`b58db606 : coreclr!MethodDescCallSite::CallTargetWorker+0x208
(Inline Function) --------`--------     : --------`-------- --------`-------- --------`-------- --------`-------- : coreclr!MethodDescCallSite::Call+0xb
000000d0`76b9e8c0 00007ffb`b58acc19     : 00000000`00000000 00000000`00000000 00000000`00000001 000000d0`76b9ed68 : coreclr!RunMainInternal+0x11c
000000d0`76b9e9e0 00007ffb`b58acf2d     : 0000020e`ce50d000 00007ffb`00000001 00007ffb`55e25778 00000000`00000001 : coreclr!RunMain+0xd1
000000d0`76b9ea70 00007ffb`b58ac1bb     : 00000000`00000000 00000000`00000000 00000000`00000000 00000000`00000000 : coreclr!Assembly::ExecuteMainMethod+0x199
000000d0`76b9ed40 00007ffb`b58a704c     : 00000000`00000001 000000d0`76b9ee01 00000000`00000000 00007ffb`bec72350 : coreclr!CorHost2::ExecuteAssembly+0x1cb
000000d0`76b9ee50 00007ffb`bec8e8ec     : 0000020e`ce47a6d0 0000020e`ce47a6e0 0000020e`ce44b440 0000020e`ce447040 : coreclr!coreclr_execute_assembly+0xcc
(Inline Function) --------`--------     : --------`-------- --------`-------- --------`-------- --------`-------- : hostpolicy!corehost_t::execute_assembly+0x2d
000000d0`76b9eef0 00007ffb`bec8ebbc     : 0000020e`ce447048 000000d0`76b9f0f9 00007ffb`becc61e0 0000020e`ce447048 : hostpolicy!run_app_for_context+0x58c
000000d0`76b9f020 00007ffb`bec8f4ca     : 00000000`00000000 0000020e`ce447040 000000d0`76b9f0f9 0000020e`ce447040 : hostpolicy!run_app+0x3c
000000d0`76b9f060 00007ffb`c83bd986     : 0000020e`ce43da38 0000020e`ce43d920 00000000`00000000 000000d0`76b9f299 : hostpolicy!corehost_main+0x15a
000000d0`76b9f160 00007ffb`c83bff66     : 0000020e`ce44b040 000000d0`76b9f510 00000000`00000000 00000000`00000000 : hostfxr!execute_app+0x2e6
000000d0`76b9f1f0 00007ffb`c83c204c     : 00007ffb`c83f2898 0000020e`ce447630 000000d0`76b9f450 000000d0`76b9f400 : hostfxr!`anonymous namespace'::read_config_and_execute+0xa6
000000d0`76b9f2e0 00007ffb`c83c0533     : 000000d0`76b9f510 0000020e`ce447040 000000d0`76b9f481 000000d0`76b9f510 : hostfxr!fx_muxer_t::handle_exec_host_command+0x16c
000000d0`76b9f390 00007ffb`c83b8460     : 000000d0`76b9f530 0000020e`ce447d10 00000000`00000001 00007ff6`09d9b5e3 : hostfxr!fx_muxer_t::execute+0x483
000000d0`76b9f4d0 00007ff6`09cdaae3     : 00007ffb`e693f4f8 00007ffb`c83b99c0 000000d0`76b9f6d0 0000020e`ce447f90 : hostfxr!hostfxr_main_startupinfo+0xa0
000000d0`76b9f5d0 00007ff6`09cdaef6     : 00007ff6`09ced040 00000000`00000007 0000020e`ce447040 00000000`0000005d : ApplicationA_exe!exe_start+0x793
000000d0`76b9f780 00007ff6`09ce2818     : 00000000`00000000 00007ff6`09ce2899 0000020e`ce447040 00000000`00000000 : ApplicationA_exe!wmain+0x146
(Inline Function) --------`--------     : --------`-------- --------`-------- --------`-------- --------`-------- : ApplicationA_exe!invoke_main+0x22
000000d0`76b9f7f0 00007ff6`e86253e0     : 00000000`00000000 00000000`00000000 00000000`00000000 00000000`00000000 : ApplicationA_exe!__scrt_common_main_seh+0x10c
000000d0`76b9f830 00007ffb`e8d2485b     : 00000000`00000000 00000000`00000000 00000000`00000000 00000000`00000000 : kernel32!BaseThreadInitThunk+0x10
000000d0`76b9f860 00000000`00000000     : 00000000`00000000 00000000`00000000 00000000`00000000 00000000`00000000 : ntdll!RtlUserThreadStart+0x2b

STACK_COMMAND: ~0s; .ecxr ; kb

SYMBOL_NAME:  win32u!NtUserWaitMessage+14

MODULE_NAME: win32u

IMAGE_NAME:  win32u.dll

FAILURE_BUCKET_ID:  BREAKPOINT_80000003_win32u.dll!NtUserWaitMessage

OS_VERSION: 10.0.22000.1

BUILDLAB_STR:  co_release

OSPLATFORM_TYPE: x64

OSNAME:  Windows 10

IMAGE_VERSION: 10.0.22000.3260

FAILURE_ID_HASH:  {a106cd41-a8b1-c51d-6d94-a75661270841}

Followup:    MachineOwner
---------

CLRMAReleaseInstance
~ClrmaManagedAnalysis
```

Note: We see that this version of WinDbg was not able to provide the unmanaged NULL pointer exception diagnostics. Rather, it points to the manual dump creation.

13.   What we saw from the exception thread stack trace is that the unmanaged exception was enveloped into the managed exception. We now try to get the unmanaged exception context.

```
0:000> kL 16
 # Child-SP          RetAddr           Call Site
00 000000d0`76b9b218 00007ffb`55d9c454 win32u!NtUserWaitMessage+0x14
01 000000d0`76b9b220 00007ffb`b5237d33 System_Windows_Forms_Primitives!Windows.Win32.PInvoke.WaitMessage+0x74
02 000000d0`76b9b2d0 00007ffb`b5237c1a System_Windows_Forms!System.Windows.Forms.Application.LightThreadContext.FPushMessageLoop+0x43
03 000000d0`76b9b360 00007ffb`b5239597 System_Windows_Forms!System.Windows.Forms.Application.LightThreadContext.RunMessageLoop+0xa
04 000000d0`76b9b390 00007ffb`b52392d2 System_Windows_Forms!System.Windows.Forms.Application.ThreadContext.RunMessageLoopInner+0x287
05 000000d0`76b9b410 00007ffb`b517feae System_Windows_Forms!System.Windows.Forms.Application.ThreadContext.RunMessageLoop+0x42
06 000000d0`76b9b470 00007ffb`b52390d9 System_Windows_Forms!System.Windows.Forms.Form.ShowDialog+0x27e
07 000000d0`76b9b520 00007ffb`55d83d0e System_Windows_Forms!System.Windows.Forms.Application.ThreadContext.OnThreadException+0x99
```

```
08 000000d0`76b9b590 00007ffb`b58cc4ef   System_Windows_Forms!System.Windows.Forms.NativeWindow.Callback+0x26e
09 000000d0`76b9b5f0 00007ffb`b09e7a56   coreclr!CallCatchFunclet+0x17f
0a 000000d0`76b9b700 00007ffb`b09e717a   System_Private_CoreLib!System.Runtime.EH.DispatchEx+0x536
0b 000000d0`76b9b860 00007ffb`b5942eb3   System_Private_CoreLib!System.Runtime.EH.RhThrowHwEx+0xaa
0c 000000d0`76b9b8a0 00007ffb`b58c1568   coreclr!CallDescrWorkerInternal+0x83
0d 000000d0`76b9b8e0 00007ffb`b59f5cde   coreclr!DispatchCallSimple+0x60
0e 000000d0`76b9b970 00007ffb`b59cf58a   coreclr!HandleManagedFaultNew+0x192
0f 000000d0`76b9d480 00007ffb`e8d9ca2a   coreclr!CLRVectoredExceptionHandlerShim+0xa84ca
10 000000d0`76b9d4d0 00007ffb`e8d559f2   ntdll!RtlpCallVectoredHandlers+0x112
11 000000d0`76b9d570 00007ffb`e8dc805e   ntdll!RtlDispatchException+0x62
12 000000d0`76b9d7c0 00007ffb`55d8cb36   ntdll!KiUserExceptionDispatch+0x2e
13 000000d0`76b9def0 00007ffb`b4f78dd5   ApplicationA!ApplicationA.ApplicationA.CrashButton_Click+0x26
14 000000d0`76b9df10 00007ffb`b4f78f69   System_Windows_Forms!System.Windows.Forms.Button.OnClick+0x195
15 000000d0`76b9dfc0 00007ffb`b4f63d6d   System_Windows_Forms!System.Windows.Forms.Button.OnMouseUp+0xe9
```

```
0:000> u 00007ffb`55d8cb36
ApplicationA!ApplicationA.ApplicationA.CrashButton_Click+0x26:
00007ffb`55d8cb36 mov     dword ptr [rax],1
00007ffb`55d8cb3c add     rsp,10h
00007ffb`55d8cb40 pop     rbp
00007ffb`55d8cb41 ret
00007ffb`55d8cb42 add     byte ptr [rax],al
00007ffb`55d8cb44 sbb     dword ptr [00007ffb`67ddcb4c],eax
00007ffb`55d8cb4a add     dword ptr [rax],edx
00007ffb`55d8cb4d add     byte ptr [rax],al
```

```
0:000> .cxr 000000d0`76b9d7c0
rax=0000000000000000 rbx=0000020ed28179c0 rcx=0000020ed2811050
rdx=0000020ed28179c0 rsi=0000020ed2824168 rdi=0000000000000018
rip=00007ffb55d8cb36 rsp=000000d076b9def0 rbp=000000d076b9df00
 r8=0000020ed2824168  r9=0000000000000006 r10=0000020ece300000
r11=000000d076b9d8c0 r12=0000000000000000 r13=00000000000002af
r14=0000000000000048 r15=00000000000005fd
iopl=0         nv up ei pl zr na po nc
cs=0033  ss=002b  ds=002b  es=002b  fs=0053  gs=002b             efl=00010246
ApplicationA!ApplicationA.ApplicationA.CrashButton_Click+0x26:
00007ffb`55d8cb36 mov     dword ptr [rax],1      ds:00000000`00000000=????????
```

14. If we dump the stack trace, we see it starts from the exception frame. To reset it to the original stack trace, just use the .cxr command:

```
0:000> kL 5
# Child-SP          RetAddr          Call Site
00 000000d0`76b9def0 00007ffb`b4f78dd5 ApplicationA!ApplicationA.ApplicationA.CrashButton_Click+0x26
01 000000d0`76b9df10 00007ffb`b4f78f69 System_Windows_Forms!System.Windows.Forms.Button.OnClick+0x195
02 000000d0`76b9dfc0 00007ffb`b4f63d6d System_Windows_Forms!System.Windows.Forms.Button.OnMouseUp+0xe9
03 000000d0`76b9e020 00007ffb`55d84d09 System_Windows_Forms!System.Windows.Forms.Control.WmMouseUp+0x2bd
04 000000d0`76b9e0b0 00007ffb`55d8b5d7 System_Windows_Forms!System.Windows.Forms.Control.WndProc+0x8d9
```

```
0:000> .cxr
Resetting default scope
```

```
0:000> kL 5
# Child-SP          RetAddr          Call Site
00 000000d0`76b9b218 00007ffb`55d9c454 win32u!NtUserWaitMessage+0x14
01 000000d0`76b9b220 00007ffb`b5237d33 System_Windows_Forms_Primitives!Windows.Win32.PInvoke.WaitMessage+0x74
02 000000d0`76b9b2d0 00007ffb`b5237c1a System_Windows_Forms!System.Windows.Forms.Application.LightThreadContext.FPushMessageLoop+0x43
03 000000d0`76b9b360 00007ffb`b5239597 System_Windows_Forms!System.Windows.Forms.Application.LightThreadContext.RunMessageLoop+0xa
04 000000d0`76b9b390 00007ffb`b52392d2 System_Windows_Forms!System.Windows.Forms.Application.ThreadContext.RunMessageLoopInner+0x287
```

15. Finally, we get the managed stack trace of the current thread:

```
0:000> !CLRStack
OS Thread Id: 0x19fc (0)
        Child SP           IP Call Site
000000D076B9B250 00007ffbe61814d4 [InlinedCallFrame: 000000d076b9b250] Windows.Win32.PInvoke.g__LocalExternFunction|3644_0()
000000D076B9B250 00007ffb55d9c454 [InlinedCallFrame: 000000d076b9b250] Windows.Win32.PInvoke.g__LocalExternFunction|3644_0()
000000D076B9B220 00007ffb55d9c454 Windows.Win32.PInvoke.WaitMessage()
000000D076B9B2D0 00007ffbb5237d33 System.Windows.Forms.Application+LightThreadContext.FPushMessageLoop(Microsoft.Office.msoloop)
```

```
000000D076B9B360 00007ffbb5237c1a System.Windows.Forms.Application+LightThreadContext.RunMessageLoop(Microsoft.Office.msoloop, Boolean)
000000D076B9B390 00007ffbb5239597 System.Windows.Forms.Application+ThreadContext.RunMessageLoopInner(Microsoft.Office.msoloop,
System.Windows.Forms.ApplicationContext)
000000D076B9B410 00007ffbb52392d2 System.Windows.Forms.Application+ThreadContext.RunMessageLoop(Microsoft.Office.msoloop,
System.Windows.Forms.ApplicationContext)
000000D076B9B470 00007ffbb517feae System.Windows.Forms.Form.ShowDialog(System.Windows.Forms.IWin32Window)
000000D076B9B520 00007ffbb52390d9 System.Windows.Forms.Application+ThreadContext.OnThreadException(System.Exception)
000000D076B9B590 00007ffbb55d83d0e System.Windows.Forms.NativeWindow.Callback(Windows.Win32.Foundation.HWND, Windows.Win32.MessageId,
Windows.Win32.Foundation.WPARAM, Windows.Win32.Foundation.LPARAM)
000000D076B9B760 00007ffbb58cc4ef [InlinedCallFrame: 000000d076b9b760]
000000D076B9B760 00007ffbb09e7a31 [InlinedCallFrame: 000000d076b9b760]
000000D076B9B700 00007ffbb09e7a31 System.Runtime.EH.DispatchEx(System.Runtime.StackFrameIterator ByRef, ExInfo ByRef)
000000D076B9B860 00007ffbb09e717a System.Runtime.EH.RhThrowHwEx(UInt32, ExInfo ByRef)
000000D076B9B9D0 00007ffbb5942eb3 [FaultingExceptionFrame: 000000d076b9b9d0]
000000D076B9DEF0 00007ffbb55d8cb36 ApplicationA.ApplicationA.CrashButton_Click(System.Object, System.EventArgs)
000000D076B9DF10 00007ffbb4f78dd5 System.Windows.Forms.Button.OnClick(System.EventArgs)
000000D076B9DFC0 00007ffbb4f78f69 System.Windows.Forms.Button.OnMouseUp(System.Windows.Forms.MouseEventArgs)
000000D076B9E020 00007ffbb4f63d6d System.Windows.Forms.Control.WmMouseUp(System.Windows.Forms.Message ByRef, System.Windows.Forms.MouseButtons, Int32)
000000D076B9E0B0 00007ffbb55d84d09 System.Windows.Forms.Control.WndProc(System.Windows.Forms.Message ByRef)
000000D076B9E140 00007ffbb55d8b5d7 System.Windows.Forms.ButtonBase.WndProc(System.Windows.Forms.Message ByRef)
000000D076B9E1A0 00007ffbb55d83b69 System.Windows.Forms.NativeWindow.Callback(Windows.Win32.Foundation.HWND, Windows.Win32.MessageId,
Windows.Win32.Foundation.WPARAM, Windows.Win32.Foundation.LPARAM)
000000D076B9E220 00007ffbb55d7347c ILStubClass.IL_STUB_ReversePInvoke(Windows.Win32.Foundation.HWND, Windows.Win32.MessageId, Windows.Win32.Foundation.WPARAM,
Windows.Win32.Foundation.LPARAM)
000000D076B9E4C8 00007ffbe7701cac [InlinedCallFrame: 000000d076b9e4c8]
000000D076B9E4C8 00007ffbb2d2290f [InlinedCallFrame: 000000d076b9e4c8]
000000D076B9E490 00007ffbb2d2290f Windows.Win32.PInvoke.DispatchMessage(Windows.Win32.UI.WindowsAndMessaging.MSG*)
000000D076B9E560 00007ffbb5237e7e System.Windows.Forms.Application+LightThreadContext.FPushMessageLoop(Microsoft.Office.msoloop)
000000D076B9E5F0 00007ffbb5237c1a System.Windows.Forms.Application+LightThreadContext.RunMessageLoop(Microsoft.Office.msoloop, Boolean)
000000D076B9E620 00007ffbb5239597 System.Windows.Forms.Application+ThreadContext.RunMessageLoopInner(Microsoft.Office.msoloop,
System.Windows.Forms.ApplicationContext)
000000D076B9E6A0 00007ffbb52392d2 System.Windows.Forms.Application+ThreadContext.RunMessageLoop(Microsoft.Office.msoloop,
System.Windows.Forms.ApplicationContext)
000000D076B9E700 00007ffbb55d7189d ApplicationA.Program.Main()
```

16.   If we want to see *ApplicationA* source code lines in stack traces, we need to specify the symbol files. It is also possible to see the problem source code if we specify the path to the source code.

```
0:000> .sympath+ C:\ANETMDA-Dumps\Windows\x64\Symbols
Symbol search path is: srv*;C:\ANETMDA-Dumps\Windows\x64\Symbols
Expanded Symbol search path is:
cache*;SRV*https://msdl.microsoft.com/download/symbols;c:\anetmda-dumps\windows\x64\symbols

************ Path validation summary ************
Response                         Time (ms)        Location
Deferred                                          srv*
OK                                                C:\ANETMDA-Dumps\Windows\x64\Symbols
```

```
0:000> k 16
 # Child-SP          RetAddr           Call Site
00 000000d0`76b9b218 00007ffb`55d9c454 win32u!NtUserWaitMessage+0x14
01 000000d0`76b9b220 00007ffb`b5237d33 System_Windows_Forms_Primitives!Windows.Win32.PInvoke.WaitMessage+0x74
[/_/artifacts/obj/System.Windows.Forms.Primitives/Release/net9.0/Microsoft.Windows.CsWin32/Microsoft.Windows.CsWin32.SourceGenerator/Windows.Win32.PInvoke.USER32.dll.g.cs @ 4487]
02 000000d0`76b9b360 00007ffb`b5237c1a System_Windows_Forms!System.Windows.Forms.Application.LightThreadContext.FPushMessageLoop+0x43 [/_/src/System.Windows.Forms/src/System/Windows/Forms/Application.LightThreadContext.cs @ 83]
03 000000d0`76b9b360 00007ffb`b5239597 System_Windows_Forms!System.Windows.Forms.Application.LightThreadContext.RunMessageLoop+0xa [/_/src/System.Windows.Forms/src/System/Windows/Forms/Application.LightThreadContext.cs @ 26]
04 000000d0`76b9b390 00007ffb`b52392d2 System_Windows_Forms!System.Windows.Forms.Application.ThreadContext.RunMessageLoopInner+0x287 [/_/src/System.Windows.Forms/src/System/Windows/Forms/Application.ThreadContext.cs @ 809]
05 000000d0`76b9b410 00007ffb`b517feae System_Windows_Forms!System.Windows.Forms.Application.ThreadContext.RunMessageLoop+0x42 [/_/src/System.Windows.Forms/src/System/Windows/Forms/Application.ThreadContext.cs @ 696]
06 000000d0`76b9b470 00007ffb`b52390d9 System_Windows_Forms!System.Windows.Forms.Form.ShowDialog+0x27e [/_/src/System.Windows.Forms/src/System/Windows/Forms/Form.cs @ 5892]
07 000000d0`76b9b520 00007ffb`b55d83d0e System_Windows_Forms!System.Windows.Forms.Application.ThreadContext.OnThreadException+0x99 [/_/src/System.Windows.Forms/src/System/Windows/Forms/Application.ThreadContext.cs @ 624]
08 000000d0`76b9b590 00007ffb`b58cc4ef System_Windows_Forms!System.Windows.Forms.NativeWindow.Callback+0x26e [/_/src/System.Windows.Forms/src/System/Windows/Forms/NativeWindow.cs @ 363]
09 000000d0`76b9b5f0 00007ffb`b09e7a56 coreclr!CallCatchFunclet+0x17f [D:\a\_work\1\s\src\coreclr\vm\exceptionhandling.cpp @ 7751]
0a 000000d0`76b9b700 00007ffb`b09e717a System_Private_CoreLib!System.Runtime.EH.DispatchEx+0x536 [/_/src/coreclr/nativeaot/Runtime.Base/src/System/Runtime/ExceptionHandling.cs @ 928]
0b 000000d0`76b9b860 00007ffb`b5942eb3 System_Private_CoreLib!System.Runtime.EH.RhThrowHwEx+0xaa [/_/src/coreclr/nativeaot/Runtime.Base/src/System/Runtime/ExceptionHandling.cs @ 620]
0c 000000d0`76b9b8a0 00007ffb`b58c1568 coreclr!CallDescrWorkerInternal+0x83 [D:\a\_work\1\s\src\coreclr\vm\amd64\CallDescrWorkerAMD64.asm @ 74]
0d 000000d0`76b9b8e0 00007ffb`b59f5cde coreclr!DispatchCallSimple+0x60 [D:\a\_work\1\s\src\coreclr\vm\callhelpers.cpp @ 248]
0e 000000d0`76b9b970 00007ffb`b59cf58a coreclr!HandleManagedFaultNew+0x192 [D:\a\_work\1\s\src\coreclr\vm\excep.cpp @ 6304]
0f 000000d0`76b9d480 00007ffb`e8d9ca2a coreclr!CLRVectoredExceptionHandlerShim+0xa84ca [D:\a\_work\1\s\src\coreclr\vm\excep.cpp @ 7276]
10 000000d0`76b9d4d0 00007ffb`e8d559f2 ntdll!RtlpCallVectoredHandlers+0x112
11 000000d0`76b9d570 00007ffb`e8dc805e ntdll!RtlDispatchException+0x62
12 000000d0`76b9d7c0 00007ffb`55d8cb36 ntdll!KiUserExceptionDispatch+0x2e
13 000000d0`76b9def0 00007ffb`b4f78dd5 ApplicationA!ApplicationA.ApplicationA.CrashButton_Click+0x26 [C:\ANETMDA-Examples\ApplicationA\ApplicationA.cs @ 15]
14 000000d0`76b9df10 00007ffb`b4f78f69 System_Windows_Forms!System.Windows.Forms.Button.OnClick+0x195 [/_/src/System.Windows.Forms/src/System/Windows/Forms/Controls/Buttons/Button.cs @ 209]
15 000000d0`76b9dfc0 00007ffb`b4f63d6d System_Windows_Forms!System.Windows.Forms.Button.OnMouseUp+0xe9 [/_/src/System.Windows.Forms/src/System/Windows/Forms/Controls/Buttons/Button.cs @ 239]
```

```
0:000> .srcpath+ C:\ANETMDA-Dumps\Windows\Source\ApplicationA
Source search path is: SRV*;C:\ANETMDA-Dumps\Windows\Source\ApplicationA

************ Path validation summary ************
Response                         Time (ms)        Location
Deferred                                          SRV*
OK                                                C:\ANETMDA-Dumps\Windows\Source\ApplicationA
```

```
0:000> .frame 13
13 000000d0`76b9def0 00007ffb`b4f78dd5
ApplicationA!ApplicationA.ApplicationA.CrashButton_Click+0x26 [C:\ANETMDA-
Examples\ApplicationA\ApplicationA.cs @ 15]
```

ApplicationA.cs ✕   ⯯

```
 1 namespace ApplicationA
 2 {
 3     public partial class ApplicationA :
 4     {
 5         public ApplicationA()
 6         {
 7             InitializeComponent();
 8         }
 9
10         private void CrashButton_Click(
11         {
12             unsafe
13             {
14                 int* p = (int*)0;
15                 *p = 1;
16             }
17         }
18     }
19 }
20
```

17.   The help command shows all available SOS extension commands:

```
0:000> !sos.help
analyzeoom, AnalyzeOOM                          Displays the info of the last OOM that occurred on an
allocation request to the GC heap.
assemblies, clrmodules                          Lists the managed assemblies in the process.
clrstack <arguments>                            Provides a stack trace of managed code only.
clrthreads <arguments>                          Lists the managed threads running.
comstate <arguments>                            Lists the COM apartment model for each thread.
crashinfo                                       Displays the crash details that created the dump.
d, readmemory <address>                         Dumps memory contents.
da <address>                                    Dumps memory as zero-terminated byte strings.
db <address>                                    Dumps memory as bytes.
dbgout <arguments>                              Enables/disables (-off) internal SOS logging.
dc <address>                                    Dumps memory as chars.
dd <address>                                    Dumps memory as dwords (uint).
dp <address>                                    Dumps memory as pointers.
dq <address>                                    Dumps memory as qwords (ulong).
du <address>                                    Dumps memory as zero-terminated char strings.
dumpalc <arguments>                             Displays details about a collectible AssemblyLoadContext into
which the specified object is loaded.
dumparray <arguments>                           Displays details about a managed array.
dumpassembly <arguments>                        Displays details about an assembly.
```

dumpasync, DumpAsync   Displays information about async "stacks" on the garbage-
collected heap.
dumpccw <arguments>   Displays information about a COM Callable Wrapper.
dumpclass <arguments>   Displays information about a EE class structure at the
specified address.
dumpconcurrentdictionary, dcd <address>   Displays concurrent dictionary content.
dumpconcurrentqueue, dcq <address>   Displays concurrent queue content.
dumpdelegate <arguments>   Displays information about a delegate.
dumpdomain <arguments>   Displays the Microsoft intermediate language (MSIL) that's
associated with a managed method.
dumpexceptions   Displays a list of all managed exceptions.
dumpgcdata <arguments>   Displays information about the GC data.
dumpgen, dg <generation>   Displays heap content for the specified generation.
dumpheap, DumpHeap <memoryrange>   Displays a list of all managed objects.
dumphttp, DumpHttp   Displays information about HTTP requests.
dumpil <arguments>   Displays the Microsoft intermediate language (MSIL) that is
associated with a managed method.
dumplog <arguments>   Writes the contents of an in-memory stress log to the
specified file.
dumpmd <arguments>   Displays information about a MethodDesc structure at the
specified address.
dumpmodule <arguments>   Displays information about a EE module structure at the
specified address.
dumpmt <arguments>   Displays information about a method table at the specified
address.
dumpobj, do <arguments>   Displays info about an object at the specified address.
dumpobjgcrefs <object>   A helper command to implement !dumpobj -refs
dumppermissionset <arguments>   Displays a PermissionSet object (debug build only).
dumprcw <arguments>   Displays information about a Runtime Callable Wrapper.
dumprequests, DumpRequests   Displays all currently active incoming HTTP requests.
dumpruntimetypes, DumpRuntimeTypes   Finds all System.RuntimeType objects in the GC heap and
prints the type name and MethodTable they refer too.
dumpsig <arguments>   Dumps the signature of a method or field specified by
<sigaddr> <moduleaddr>.
dumpsigelem <arguments>   Dumps a single element of a signature object.
dumpstackobjects, dso, DumpStackObjects <stackbounds> Displays all managed objects found within the bounds of the
current stack.
dumpvc <arguments>   Displays info about the fields of a value class.
dw <address>   Dumps memory as words (ushort).
eeheap, EEHeap <memoryrange>   Displays information about native memory that CLR has
allocated.
eeversion <arguments>   Displays information about the runtime version.
ehinfo <arguments>   Displays the exception handling blocks in a JIT-ed method.
enummem <arguments>   ICLRDataEnumMemoryRegions.EnumMemoryRegions test command.
ephrefs   Finds older generation objects which reference objects in the
ephemeral segment.
ephtoloh   Finds ephemeral objects which reference the large object
heap.
finalizequeue, fq, FinalizeQueue   Displays all objects registered for finalization.
findappdomain <arguments>   Attempts to resolve the AppDomain of a GC object.
findpointersin <regions>   Finds pointers to the GC heap within the given memory
regions.
gchandleleaks <arguments>   Helps in tracking down GCHandle leaks.
gchandles <arguments>   Provides statistics about GCHandles in the process.
gcheapstat, GCHeapStat   Displays various GC heap stats.
gcinfo <arguments>   Displays JIT GC encoding for a method.
gcroot, GCRoot <target>   Displays info about references (or roots) to an object at the
specified address.
gctonative <memorytypes>   Finds GC objects which point to the given native memory
ranges.
gcwhere, GCWhere <address>   Displays the location in the GC heap of the specified
address.
help, soshelp <command>   Displays help for a command.
histclear <arguments>   Releases any resources used by the family of Hist commands.
histinit <arguments>   Initializes the SOS structures from the stress log saved in
the debuggee.
histobj <arguments>   Examines all stress log relocation records and displays the
chain of garbage collection relocations that may have led to the address passed in as an argument.
histobjfind <arguments>   Displays all the log entries that reference an object at the
specified address.
histroot <arguments>   Displays information related to both promotions and
relocations of the specified root.
histstats <arguments>   Displays stress log stats.

```
ip2md <arguments>                                Displays the MethodDesc structure at the specified address in
code that has been JIT-compiled.
listnearobj, lno, ListNearObj <address>          Displays the object preceding and succeeding the specified
address.
loadsymbols <url>                                Loads symbols for all modules.
logclose <path>                                  Disables console file logging.
logging <path>                                   Enables/disables internal diagnostic logging.
logopen <path>                                   Enables console file logging.
maddress                                         Displays a breakdown of the virtual address space.
modules, lm                                      Displays the native modules in the process.
name2ee <arguments>                              Displays the MethodTable structure and EEClass structure for
the specified type or method in the specified module.
notreachableinrange <start> <end>               A helper command for !finalizerqueue
objsize, ObjSize <objectaddress>                 Lists the sizes of the all the objects found on managed
threads.
parallelstacks, pstacks                          Displays the merged threads stack similarly to the Visual
Studio 'Parallel Stacks' panel.
pathto, PathTo <source> <target>                 Displays the GC path from <root> to <target>.
printexception, pe <arguments>                   Displays and formats fields of any object derived from the
Exception class at the specified address.
registers, r                                     Displays the thread's registers.
runtimes, setruntime <id>                        Lists the runtimes in the target or changes the default
runtime.
setclrpath <path>                                Sets the path to load coreclr DAC/DBI files.
setsymbolserver, SetSymbolServer <url>           Enables and sets symbol server support for symbols and module
download.
sizestats                                        Size statistics for the GC heap.
sosflush                                         Resets the internal cached state.
sosstatus                                        Displays internal status.
syncblk <arguments>                              Displays the SyncBlock holder info.
taskstate, tks <address>                         Displays a Task state in a human readable format.
threadpool, ThreadPool                           Displays info about the runtime thread pool.
threadpoolqueue, tpq                             Displays queued ThreadPool work items.
threads, setthread <thread>                      Lists the threads in the target or sets the current thread.
threadstate <arguments>                          Pretty prints the meaning of a threads state.
timerinfo, ti                                    Displays information about running timers.
traverseheap, TraverseHeap <filename>            Writes out heap information to a file in a format understood
by the CLR Profiler.
verifyheap, VerifyHeap <memoryrange>             Searches the managed heap for memory corruption..
verifyobj, VerifyObj <objectaddress>             Checks the given object for signs of corruption.
watsonbuckets <arguments>                        Displays the Watson buckets.
```

18.   Another way to see the list of the SOS extension commands is to filter all available extension commands:

```
0:000> .extmatch /e sos *
!sos.AnalyzeOOM
!sos.BPMD
!sos.CLRMACreateInstance
!sos.CLRMAReleaseInstance
!sos.CLRStack
!sos.COMState
!sos.ClrStack
!sos.DumpALC
!sos.DumpArray
!sos.DumpAssembly
!sos.DumpAsync
!sos.DumpCCW
!sos.DumpClass
!sos.DumpDelegate
!sos.DumpDomain
!sos.DumpGCConfigLog
!sos.DumpGCData
!sos.DumpHeap
!sos.DumpHttp
!sos.DumpIL
!sos.DumpLocks
```

```
!sos.DumpLog
!sos.DumpMD
!sos.DumpMT
!sos.DumpModule
!sos.DumpObj
!sos.DumpRCW
!sos.DumpRequests
!sos.DumpRuntimeTypes
!sos.DumpSig
!sos.DumpSigElem
!sos.DumpStack
!sos.DumpStackObjects
!sos.DumpVC
!sos.Dumpccw
!sos.Dumplog
!sos.Dumprcw
!sos.Dumpruntimetypes
!sos.EEHeap
!sos.EEStack
!sos.EEVersion
!sos.EHInfo
!sos.Ehinfo
!sos.ExposeDML
!sos.FinalizeQueue
!sos.FindAppDomain
!sos.FindRoots
!sos.Findappdomain
!sos.GCHandleLeaks
!sos.GCHandleleaks
!sos.GCHandles
!sos.GCHeapStat
!sos.GCInfo
!sos.GCRoot
!sos.GCWhere
!sos.GcHeapStat
!sos.GcWhere
!sos.Gchandleleaks
!sos.GetCodeTypeFlags
!sos.HeapStat
!sos.Help
!sos.HistClear
!sos.HistInit
!sos.HistObj
!sos.HistObjFind
!sos.HistRoot
!sos.HistStats
!sos.IP2MD
!sos.InitializeHostServices
!sos.ListNearObj
!sos.MinidumpMode
!sos.Minidumpmode
!sos.Name2EE
!sos.ObjSize
!sos.PathTo
!sos.PrintException
!sos.Printexception
!sos.ProcInfo
!sos.RCWCleanupList
!sos.Rcwcleanuplist
```

```
!sos.SOSFlush
!sos.SOSHandleCLRN
!sos.SOSInitializeByHost
!sos.SOSStatus
!sos.SOSUninitializeByHost
!sos.SaveAllModules
!sos.SaveModule
!sos.SaveState
!sos.SetClrPath
!sos.SetHostRuntime
!sos.SetSymbolServer
!sos.StopOnCatch
!sos.StopOnException
!sos.Stoponexception
!sos.SuppressJitOptimization
!sos.SyncBlk
!sos.ThreadPool
!sos.ThreadState
!sos.Threads
!sos.Token2EE
!sos.TraceToCode
!sos.TraverseHeap
!sos.Traverseheap
!sos.U
!sos.VMMap
!sos.VMStat
!sos.VerifyGMT
!sos.VerifyHeap
!sos.VerifyObj
!sos.VerifyStackTrace
!sos.Verifyheap
!sos.Watch
!sos.WatsonBuckets
!sos.analyzeoom
!sos.ao
!sos.assemblies
!sos.bpmd
!sos.clrmaconfig
!sos.clrmodules
!sos.clrstack
!sos.clrthreads
!sos.clru
!sos.comstate
!sos.crashinfo
!sos.da
!sos.dbgout
!sos.dclog
!sos.dg
!sos.dgc
!sos.do
!sos.dso
!sos.dumpalc
!sos.dumparray
!sos.dumpassembly
!sos.dumpasync
!sos.dumpccw
!sos.dumpclass
!sos.dumpdelegate
!sos.dumpdomain
```

```
!sos.dumpexceptions
!sos.dumpgcconfiglog
!sos.dumpgcdata
!sos.dumpgen
!sos.dumpheap
!sos.dumphttp
!sos.dumpil
!sos.dumplocks
!sos.dumplog
!sos.dumpmd
!sos.dumpmodule
!sos.dumpmt
!sos.dumpobj
!sos.dumprcw
!sos.dumprequests
!sos.dumpruntimetypes
!sos.dumpsig
!sos.dumpsigelem
!sos.dumpstack
!sos.dumpstackobjects
!sos.dumpvc
!sos.eeheap
!sos.eestack
!sos.eeversion
!sos.ehinfo
!sos.enummem
!sos.exposeDML
!sos.ext
!sos.finalizequeue
!sos.findappdomain
!sos.findroots
!sos.fq
!sos.gchandleleaks
!sos.gchandles
!sos.gcheapstat
!sos.gcinfo
!sos.gcroot
!sos.gcwhere
!sos.getCodeTypeFlags
!sos.heapstat
!sos.help
!sos.histclear
!sos.histinit
!sos.histobj
!sos.histobjfind
!sos.histroot
!sos.histstats
!sos.hof
!sos.ip2md
!sos.listnearobj
!sos.lno
!sos.logging
!sos.maddress
!sos.minidumpmode
!sos.name2ee
!sos.objsize
!sos.pathto
!sos.pe
!sos.printexception
```

```
!sos.processor
!sos.procinfo
!sos.rcwcleanuplist
!sos.runtimes
!sos.saveallmodules
!sos.savemodule
!sos.savestate
!sos.setclrpath
!sos.sethostruntime
!sos.setsymbolserver
!sos.sizestats
!sos.sjo
!sos.soe
!sos.sos
!sos.sosflush
!sos.soshelp
!sos.sosstatus
!sos.stoponcatch
!sos.stoponexception
!sos.suppressjitoptimization
!sos.syncblk
!sos.t
!sos.threadpool
!sos.threads
!sos.threadstate
!sos.token2ee
!sos.tp
!sos.tracetocode
!sos.traverseheap
!sos.u
!sos.verifyheap
!sos.verifyobj
!sos.vh
!sos.vmmap
!sos.vmstat
!sos.vo
!sos.watch
```

Note: Command help https://learn.microsoft.com/en-us/dotnet/core/diagnostics/sos-debugging-extension

19.   We close logging before exiting WinDbg:

```
0:000> .logclose
Closing open log file C:\ANETMDA-Dumps\Windows\x64\ApplicationA.log
```

Note: To avoid possible confusion and glitches, we recommend exiting WinDbg after each exercise.

Exercise PN1 (Linux)

- **Goal:** Learn how to analyze managed space for the presence of exceptions

- **Patterns:** Stack Trace Collection (Unmanaged Space); CLR Thread; JIT Code (.NET); Software Exception; Exception Stack Trace; Managed Code Exception; Mixed Exception; Managed Stack Trace; Invalid Pointer; NULL Pointer (Data)

- **Commands:** bt all, pe, ip2md, clru, clrthreads, thread select, clrstack, image list -p -f

- \ANETMDA-Dumps\Exercise-PN1-Linux.pdf

Exercise PN1 (Linux)

Goal: Learn how to analyze managed space for the presence of exceptions.

Patterns: Stack Trace Collection (Unmanaged Space); CLR Thread; JIT Code (.NET); Software Exception; Exception Stack Trace; Managed Code Exception; Managed Stack Trace; Stack Trace Collection (Managed Space); Mixed Exception; Invalid Pointer; NULL Pointer (Data).

Commands: bt all, pe, ip2md, clru, clrthreads, thread select, clrstack, image list -p -f

1.   Open \ANETMDA-Dumps\Linux\ApplicationG\core.ApplicationG.276.dmp in LLDB:

```
/mnt/c/ANETMDA-Dumps/Linux/ApplicationG$ lldb -c core.ApplicationG.276.dmp
bin/Release/net9.0/ApplicationG
Current symbol store settings:
-> Cache: /home/coredump/.dotnet/symbolcache
-> Server: https://msdl.microsoft.com/download/symbols/ Timeout: 4 RetryCount: 0
(lldb) target create "bin/Release/net9.0/ApplicationG" --core "core.ApplicationG.276.dmp"
warning: (x86_64) /usr/share/dotnet/host/fxr/9.0.4/libhostfxr.so unsupported DW_FORM values:
0x1b 0x21 0x22 0x23 0x25 0x26 0x64
warning: (x86_64) /usr/share/dotnet/shared/Microsoft.NETCore.App/9.0.4/libhostpolicy.so
unsupported DW_FORM values: 0x1b 0x21 0x22 0x23 0x25 0x26 0x64
warning: (x86_64) /usr/share/dotnet/shared/Microsoft.NETCore.App/9.0.4/libcoreclr.so
unsupported DW_FORM values: 0x1b 0x21 0x22 0x23 0x25 0x26 0x64
warning: (x86_64) /usr/share/dotnet/shared/Microsoft.NETCore.App/9.0.4/libSystem.Native.so
unsupported DW_FORM values: 0x1b 0x21 0x22 0x23 0x25 0x26
warning: (x86_64) /usr/share/dotnet/shared/Microsoft.NETCore.App/9.0.4/libclrjit.so unsupported
DW_FORM values: 0x1b 0x21 0x22 0x23 0x25 0x26 0x64
Warning: (x86_64) /mnt/c/ANETMDA-Dumps/Linux/ApplicationG/bin/Release/net9.0/ApplicationG
unsupported DW_FORM values: 0x1b 0x21 0x22 0x23 0x25 0x26 0x64
Core file '/mnt/c/ANETMDA-Dumps/Linux/ApplicationG/core.ApplicationG.276.dmp' (x86_64) was
loaded.
(lldb)
```

2.   List all unmanaged stack traces from all threads:

```
(lldb) bt all
* thread #1, name = 'ApplicationG', stop reason = signal SIGABRT
  * frame #0: 0x00007fdc25bad0ca libpthread.so.0`__waitpid(pid=284, stat_loc=0x00007ffc0b136634, options=0) at waitpid.c:30
    frame #1: 0x00007fdc25521d97 libcoreclr.so`PROCCreateCrashDump(std::vector<char const*, std::allocator<char const*> >&, char*, int, bool) + 647
    frame #2: 0x00007fdc2552324b libcoreclr.so`PROCCreateCrashDumpIfEnabled + 3227
    frame #3: 0x00007fdc2552097d libcoreclr.so`PROCAbort + 45
    frame #4: 0x00007fdc252508a9 libcoreclr.so`TerminateProcess + 137
    frame #5: 0x00007fdc252ac977 libcoreclr.so`SfiNext + 1703
    frame #6: 0x00007fdba61a6df9
    frame #7: 0x00007fdba61a6582
    frame #8: 0x00007fdc25371e04 libcoreclr.so`CallDescrWorkerInternal + 124
    frame #9: 0x00007fdc251afa05 libcoreclr.so`DispatchCallSimple(unsigned long*, unsigned int, unsigned long, unsigned int) + 245
    frame #10: 0x00007fdc252a1749 libcoreclr.so`HandleHardwareException(PAL_SEHException*) + 921
    frame #11: 0x00007fdc254f445c libcoreclr.so`SEHProcessException(PAL_SEHException*) + 316
    frame #12: 0x00007fdc254f6000 libcoreclr.so`common_signal_handler(int, siginfo_t*, void*, int, ...) + 656
    frame #13: 0x00007fdc254f5d06 libcoreclr.so`signal_handler_worker + 118
    frame #14: 0x00007fdc25526cb2 libcoreclr.so`CallSignalHandlerWrapper0 + 6
    frame #15: 0x00007fdba6eb188a
    frame #16: 0x00007fdc25371e04 libcoreclr.so`CallDescrWorkerInternal + 124
    frame #17: 0x00007fdc251b011c libcoreclr.so`MethodDescCallSite::CallTargetWorker(unsigned long const*, unsigned long*, int) + 1708
    frame #18: 0x00007fdc250970c4 libcoreclr.so`RunMain(MethodDesc*, short, int*, PtrArray**) + 836
    frame #19: 0x00007fdc2509753c libcoreclr.so`Assembly::ExecuteMainMethod(PtrArray**, int) + 460
    frame #20: 0x00007fdc250c0b34 libcoreclr.so`CorHost2::ExecuteAssembly(unsigned int, char16_t const*, int, char16_t const**, unsigned int*) + 740
    frame #21: 0x00007fdc25083340 libcoreclr.so`coreclr_execute_assembly + 144
    frame #22: 0x00007fdc2564b301 libhostpolicy.so`run_app_for_context(hostpolicy_context_t const&, int, char const**) + 1089
    frame #23: 0x00007fdc2564c3f9 libhostpolicy.so`corehost_main + 345
    frame #24: 0x00007fdc2568b685 libhostfxr.so`fx_muxer_t::handle_exec_host_command(std::__cxx11::basic_string<char, std::char_traits<char>,
std::allocator<char> > const&, host_startup_info_t const&, std::__cxx11::basic_string<char, std::char_traits<char>, std::allocator<char> > const&,
std::unordered_map<known_options, std::vector<std::__cxx11::basic_string<char, std::char_traits<char>, std::allocator<char> >,
std::allocator<std::__cxx11::basic_string<char, std::char_traits<char>, std::allocator<char> > > >, known_options_hash, std::equal_to<known_options>,
std::allocator<std::pair<known_options const, std::vector<std::__cxx11::basic_string<char, std::char_traits<char>, std::allocator<char> >,
```

```
std::allocator<std::__cxx11::basic_string<char, std::char_traits<char>, std::allocator<char> > > > > > > const&, int, char const**, int, host_mode_t, bool,
char*, int, int*) + 1477
    frame #25: 0x00007fdc2568a67d libhostfxr.so`fx_muxer_t::execute(std::__cxx11::basic_string<char, std::char_traits<char>, std::allocator<char> >, int, char
const**, host_startup_info_t const&, char*, int, int*) + 765
    frame #26: 0x00007fdc256845f2 libhostfxr.so`hostfxr_main_startupinfo + 242
    frame #27: 0x000055956b1ac21b ApplicationG`exe_start(int, char const**) + 1131
    frame #28: 0x000055956b1ac53f ApplicationG`main + 175
    frame #29: 0x00007fdc256de09b libc.so.6`__libc_start_main(main=(ApplicationG`main), argc=1, argv=0x00007ffc0b13c2c8, init=<unavailable>,
fini=<unavailable>, rtld_fini=<unavailable>, stack_end=0x00007ffc0b13c2b8) at libc-start.c:308
    frame #30: 0x000055956b1ab399 ApplicationG`_start + 41
  thread #2, stop reason = signal 0
    frame #0: 0x00007fdc257a86f9 libc.so.6`__GI___poll(fds=0x0000000000000000, nfds=0, timeout=-1) at poll.c:29
    frame #1: 0x00007fdc2551b18e libcoreclr.so`CorUnix::CPalSynchronizationManager::WorkerThread(void*) + 958
    frame #2: 0x00007fdc255249ae libcoreclr.so`CorUnix::CPalThread::ThreadEntry(void*) + 510
    frame #3: 0x00007fdc25ba2fa3 libpthread.so.0`start_thread(arg=<unavailable>) at pthread_create.c:486
    frame #4: 0x00007fdc257b306f libc.so.6`__GI___clone at clone.S:95
  thread #3, stop reason = signal 0
    frame #0: 0x00007fdc257a86f9 libc.so.6`__GI___poll(fds=0x00007fdb98000f20, nfds=1, timeout=-1) at poll.c:29
    frame #1: 0x00007fdc25422d5c libcoreclr.so`ds_ipc_poll(_DiagnosticsIpcPollHandle*, unsigned long, unsigned int, void (*)(char const*, unsigned int)) + 172
    frame #2: 0x00007fdc2539cf4b libcoreclr.so`ds_ipc_stream_factory_get_next_available_stream(void (*)(char const*, unsigned int)) + 731
    frame #3: 0x00007fdc253a1ca6 libcoreclr.so`server_thread(void*) + 198
    frame #4: 0x00007fdc255249ae libcoreclr.so`CorUnix::CPalThread::ThreadEntry(void*) + 510
    frame #5: 0x00007fdc25ba2fa3 libpthread.so.0`start_thread(arg=<unavailable>) at pthread_create.c:486
    frame #6: 0x00007fdc257b306f libc.so.6`__GI___clone at clone.S:95
  thread #4, stop reason = signal 0
    frame #0: 0x00007fdc25bacd0e libpthread.so.0`__libc_open64(file="/tmp/clr-debug-pipe-276-113357-in", oflag=0) at open64.c:48
    frame #1: 0x00007fdc2542277f libcoreclr.so`TwoWayPipe::WaitForConnection() + 31
    frame #2: 0x00007fdc2541d797 libcoreclr.so`DbgTransportSession::TransportWorker() + 183
    frame #3: 0x00007fdc2541c905 libcoreclr.so`DbgTransportSession::TransportWorkerStatic(void*) + 37
    frame #4: 0x00007fdc255249ae libcoreclr.so`CorUnix::CPalThread::ThreadEntry(void*) + 510
    frame #5: 0x00007fdc25ba2fa3 libpthread.so.0`start_thread(arg=<unavailable>) at pthread_create.c:486
    frame #6: 0x00007fdc257b306f libc.so.6`__GI___clone at clone.S:95
  thread #5, stop reason = signal 0
    frame #0: 0x00007fdc25ba900c libpthread.so.0`__pthread_cond_wait at futex-internal.h:88
    frame #1: 0x00007fdc25ba8ff1 libpthread.so.0`__pthread_cond_wait at pthread_cond_wait.c:502
    frame #2: 0x00007fdc25ba8f30 libpthread.so.0`__pthread_cond_wait(cond=0x0000559596323f38, mutex=0x0000559596323f10) at pthread_cond_wait.c:655
    frame #3: 0x00007fdc25519172 libcoreclr.so`CorUnix::CPalSynchronizationManager::ThreadNativeWait(CorUnix::_ThreadNativeWaitData*, unsigned int,
CorUnix::ThreadWakeupReason*, unsigned int*) + 354
    frame #4: 0x00007fdc25518d7a libcoreclr.so`CorUnix::CPalSynchronizationManager::BlockThread(CorUnix::CPalThread*, unsigned int, bool, bool,
CorUnix::ThreadWakeupReason*, unsigned int*) + 378
    frame #5: 0x00007fdc2551d952 libcoreclr.so`CorUnix::InternalWaitForMultipleObjectsEx(CorUnix::CPalThread*, unsigned int, void* const*, int, unsigned int,
int, int) + 1906
    frame #6: 0x00007fdc2551dc03 libcoreclr.so`WaitForMultipleObjectsEx + 83
    frame #7: 0x00007fdc2541b0ad libcoreclr.so`DebuggerRCThread::MainLoop() + 269
    frame #8: 0x00007fdc2541af28 libcoreclr.so`DebuggerRCThread::ThreadProc() + 312
    frame #9: 0x00007fdc2541ac25 libcoreclr.so`DebuggerRCThread::ThreadProcStatic(void*) + 53
    frame #10: 0x00007fdc255249ae libcoreclr.so`CorUnix::CPalThread::ThreadEntry(void*) + 510
    frame #11: 0x00007fdc25ba2fa3 libpthread.so.0`start_thread(arg=<unavailable>) at pthread_create.c:486
    frame #12: 0x00007fdc257b306f libc.so.6`__GI___clone at clone.S:95
  thread #6, stop reason = signal 0
    frame #0: 0x00007fdc25ba93f9 libpthread.so.0`__pthread_cond_timedwait at futex-internal.h:142
    frame #1: 0x00007fdc25ba93da libpthread.so.0`__pthread_cond_timedwait at pthread_cond_wait.c:533
    frame #2: 0x00007fdc25ba92c0 libpthread.so.0`__pthread_cond_timedwait(cond=0x000055959632f628, mutex=0x000055959632f600, abstime=0x00007fdc22d4d730) at
pthread_cond_wait.c:667
    frame #3: 0x00007fdc25519115 libcoreclr.so`CorUnix::CPalSynchronizationManager::ThreadNativeWait(CorUnix::_ThreadNativeWaitData*, unsigned int,
CorUnix::ThreadWakeupReason*, unsigned int*) + 261
    frame #4: 0x00007fdc25518d7a libcoreclr.so`CorUnix::CPalSynchronizationManager::BlockThread(CorUnix::CPalThread*, unsigned int, bool, bool,
CorUnix::ThreadWakeupReason*, unsigned int*) + 378
    frame #5: 0x00007fdc2551d952 libcoreclr.so`CorUnix::InternalWaitForMultipleObjectsEx(CorUnix::CPalThread*, unsigned int, void* const*, int, unsigned int,
int, int) + 1906
    frame #6: 0x00007fdc2551db29 libcoreclr.so`WaitForSingleObjectEx + 89
    frame #7: 0x00007fdc25279efe libcoreclr.so`CLREventBase::WaitEx(unsigned int, WaitMode, PendingSync*) + 238
    frame #8: 0x00007fdc251ec07f libcoreclr.so`FinalizerThread::WaitForFinalizerEvent(CLREvent*) + 31
    frame #9: 0x00007fdc251ec27f libcoreclr.so`FinalizerThread::FinalizerThreadWorker(void*) + 239
    frame #10: 0x00007fdc2517dc08 libcoreclr.so`ManagedThreadBase_DispatchOuter(ManagedThreadCallState*) + 344
    frame #11: 0x00007fdc2517e10d libcoreclr.so`ManagedThreadBase::FinalizerBase(void (*)(void*)) + 45
    frame #12: 0x00007fdc251ec4b8 libcoreclr.so`FinalizerThread::FinalizerThreadStart(void*) + 88
    frame #13: 0x00007fdc255249ae libcoreclr.so`CorUnix::CPalThread::ThreadEntry(void*) + 510
    frame #14: 0x00007fdc25ba2fa3 libpthread.so.0`start_thread(arg=<unavailable>) at pthread_create.c:486
    frame #15: 0x00007fdc257b306f libc.so.6`__GI___clone at clone.S:95
  thread #7, stop reason = signal 0
    frame #0: 0x00007fdc25ba93f9 libpthread.so.0`__pthread_cond_timedwait at futex-internal.h:142
    frame #1: 0x00007fdc25ba93da libpthread.so.0`__pthread_cond_timedwait at pthread_cond_wait.c:533
    frame #2: 0x00007fdc25ba92c0 libpthread.so.0`__pthread_cond_timedwait(cond=0x0000559596345388, mutex=0x0000559596345360, abstime=0x00007fdc21311b50) at
pthread_cond_wait.c:667
    frame #3: 0x00007fdc25519115 libcoreclr.so`CorUnix::CPalSynchronizationManager::ThreadNativeWait(CorUnix::_ThreadNativeWaitData*, unsigned int,
CorUnix::ThreadWakeupReason*, unsigned int*) + 261
    frame #4: 0x00007fdc25518d7a libcoreclr.so`CorUnix::CPalSynchronizationManager::BlockThread(CorUnix::CPalThread*, unsigned int, bool, bool,
CorUnix::ThreadWakeupReason*, unsigned int*) + 378
    frame #5: 0x00007fdc2551e089 libcoreclr.so`SleepEx + 153
    frame #6: 0x00007fdc251814aa libcoreclr.so`TieredCompilationManager::BackgroundWorkerStart() + 186
    frame #7: 0x00007fdc25181368 libcoreclr.so`TieredCompilationManager::BackgroundWorkerBootstrapper1(void*) + 104
    frame #8: 0x00007fdc2517dc08 libcoreclr.so`ManagedThreadBase_DispatchOuter(ManagedThreadCallState*) + 344
    frame #9: 0x00007fdc2517e0bd libcoreclr.so`ManagedThreadBase::KickOff(void (*)(void*), void*) + 45
    frame #10: 0x00007fdc25181290 libcoreclr.so`TieredCompilationManager::BackgroundWorkerBootstrapper0(void*) + 32
    frame #11: 0x00007fdc255249ae libcoreclr.so`CorUnix::CPalThread::ThreadEntry(void*) + 510
    frame #12: 0x00007fdc25ba2fa3 libpthread.so.0`start_thread(arg=<unavailable>) at pthread_create.c:486
    frame #13: 0x00007fdc257b306f libc.so.6`__GI___clone at clone.S:95
  thread #8, stop reason = signal 0
    frame #0: 0x00007fdc25bac544 libpthread.so.0`__libc_read at read.c:26
    frame #1: 0x00007fdc25bac530 libpthread.so.0`__libc_read(fd=29, buf=0x00007fdc1e7e9ebf, nbytes=1) at read.c:24
    frame #2: 0x00007fdc20b087ff libSystem.Native.so`SignalHandlerLoop + 95
    frame #3: 0x00007fdc25ba2fa3 libpthread.so.0`start_thread(arg=<unavailable>) at pthread_create.c:486
    frame #4: 0x00007fdc257b306f libc.so.6`__GI___clone at clone.S:95
```

Note: We see *libcoreclr.so* in almost all threads. We also see hardware exception processing (in red) and JIT code (in blue). The exception processing code called the *crashdump* tool to save a compatible memory dump.

3.   We check the current thread managed exception:

```
(lldb) pe
Exception object: 00007f9b9280fec8
Exception type:    System.NullReferenceException
Message:           Object reference not set to an instance of an object.
InnerException:    <none>
StackTrace (generated):
    SP                IP                Function
    00007FFC0B13B340 00007FDBA6EB188B ApplicationG.dll!Program.Main()+0x2b

StackTraceString: <none>
HResult: 80004003
```

4.   Let's verify the identified three JIT code frames:

```
(lldb) ip2md 0x00007fdba61a6df9
MethodDesc:    00007fdba6ea0520
Method Name:        System.Runtime.EH.DispatchEx(System.Runtime.StackFrameIterator ByRef, ExInfo ByRef)
Class:              00007fdba6ea0600
MethodTable:        00007fdba6ea0600
mdToken:            000000000600489E
Module:             00007fdba5f04000
IsJitted:           yes
Current CodeAddr:   00007fdba61a6940
Version History:
  ILCodeVersion:      0000000000000000
  ReJIT ID:           0
  IL Addr:            00007fdba6651250
     CodeAddr:           00007fdba61a6940  (ReadyToRun)
     NativeCodeVersion:  0000000000000000
Source file:  /_/src/coreclr/nativeaot/Runtime.Base/src/System/Runtime/ExceptionHandling.cs @ 865
```

```
(lldb) ip2md 0x00007fdba61a6582
MethodDesc:    00007fdba6ea04a0
Method Name:        System.Runtime.EH.RhThrowHwEx(UInt32, ExInfo ByRef)
Class:              00007fdba6ea0600
MethodTable:        00007fdba6ea0600
mdToken:            000000000600489A
Module:             00007fdba5f04000
IsJitted:           yes
Current CodeAddr:   00007fdba61a64d0
Version History:
  ILCodeVersion:      0000000000000000
  ReJIT ID:           0
  IL Addr:            00007fdba665106c
     CodeAddr:           00007fdba61a64d0  (ReadyToRun)
     NativeCodeVersion:  0000000000000000
Source file:  /_/src/coreclr/nativeaot/Runtime.Base/src/System/Runtime/ExceptionHandling.cs @ 620
```

```
(lldb) ip2md 0x00007fdba6eb188a
MethodDesc:    00007fdba6f59728
Method Name:        Program.Main()
Class:              00007fdba6f59760
MethodTable:        00007fdba6f59760
mdToken:            0000000006000001
Module:             00007fdba6f57038
IsJitted:           yes
```

116

```
Current CodeAddr:        00007fdba6eb1860
Version History:
  ILCodeVersion:         0000000000000000
  ReJIT ID:              0
  IL Addr:               00007fdc20af2250
     CodeAddr:               00007fdba6eb1860   (QuickJitted)
     NativeCodeVersion:  0000000000000000
Source file:  /mnt/c/ANETMDA-Examples/ApplicationG/Program.cs @ 12
```

5.   Since the *Program.Main()* method figures in both exception and stack trace, let's unassemble the JIT address:

```
(lldb) clru 0x00007fdba6eb188a
Normal JIT generated code
Program.Main()
ilAddr is 00007FDC20AF2250 pImport is 0000000037646840
Begin 00007FDBA6EB1860, size 36

/mnt/c/ANETMDA-Examples/ApplicationG/Program.cs @ 8:
00007fdba6eb1860 55                      push    rbp
00007fdba6eb1861 4883ec10                sub     rsp, 0x10
00007fdba6eb1865 488d6c2410              lea     rbp, [rsp + 0x10]
00007fdba6eb186a 33c0                    xor     eax, eax
00007fdba6eb186c 488945f8                mov     qword ptr [rbp - 0x8], rax
00007fdba6eb1870 48bf20373221dc7f0000 movabs  rdi, 0x7fdc21323720
00007fdba6eb187a ff15085af8ff            call    qword ptr [rip - 0x7a5f8]

/mnt/c/ANETMDA-Examples/ApplicationG/Program.cs @ 11:
00007fdba6eb1880 33c0                    xor     eax, eax
00007fdba6eb1882 488945f8                mov     qword ptr [rbp - 0x8], rax

/mnt/c/ANETMDA-Examples/ApplicationG/Program.cs @ 12:
00007fdba6eb1886 488b45f8                mov     rax, qword ptr [rbp - 0x8]
>>> 00007fdba6eb188a c70001000000            mov     dword ptr [rax], 0x1

/mnt/c/ANETMDA-Examples/ApplicationG/Program.cs @ 14:
00007fdba6eb1890 4883c410                add     rsp, 0x10
00007fdba6eb1894 5d                      pop     rbp
00007fdba6eb1895 c3                      ret
```

Note: We see an invalid data null pointer access.

6.   Let's now list all managed threads, their managed stack traces, and managed exceptions, if any:

```
(lldb) clrthreads
ThreadCount:       3
UnstartedThread: 0
BackgroundThread: 2
PendingThread:   0
DeadThread:      0
Hosted Runtime:  no
                                                                                        Lock
 DBG   ID    OSID ThreadOBJ         State GC Mode  GC Alloc Context                         Domain            Count Apt Exception
   1    1     114 0000559596326870   20020 Preemptive 00007F9B928163B8:00007F9B92817030 000055959630EAC0 -00001 Ukn System.NullReferenceException
00007f9b9280fec8
   6    2     119 000055959632DF70   21220 Preemptive 0000000000000000:0000000000000000 000055959630EAC0 -00001 Ukn (Finalizer)
   7    3     11a 0000559596344D00   21220 Preemptive 0000000000000000:0000000000000000 000055959630EAC0 -00001 Ukn

(lldb) clrstack
OS Thread Id: 0x114 (1)
        Child SP               IP Call Site
00007FFC0B1368E0 00007fdc25bad0ca [InlinedCallFrame: 00007ffc0b1368e0]
```

```
00007FFC0B1368E0 00007fdba61a6dd4 [InlinedCallFrame: 00007ffc0b1368e0]
00007FFC0B1368A0 00007FDBA61A6DD4
System.Runtime.EH.DispatchEx(System.Runtime.StackFrameIterator ByRef, ExInfo ByRef)
[/_/src/coreclr/nativeaot/Runtime.Base/src/System/Runtime/ExceptionHandling.cs @ 865]
00007FFC0B1369E0 00007FDBA61A6582 System.Runtime.EH.RhThrowHwEx(UInt32, ExInfo ByRef)
[/_/src/coreclr/nativeaot/Runtime.Base/src/System/Runtime/ExceptionHandling.cs @ 619]
00007FFC0B139680 00007fdc25371e04 [FaultingExceptionFrame: 00007ffc0b139680]
00007FFC0B13B340 00007FDBA6EB188A Program.Main() [/mnt/c/ANETMDA-
Examples/ApplicationG/Program.cs @ 12]
```

```
(lldb) thread select 6
* thread #6, stop reason = signal 0
    frame #0: 0x00007fdc25ba93f9 libpthread.so.0`__pthread_cond_timedwait at futex-
internal.h:142
```

```
(lldb) clrstack
OS Thread Id: 0x119 (6)
        Child SP               IP Call Site
00007FDC22D4DD10 00007fdc25ba93f9 [DebuggerU2MCatchHandlerFrame: 00007fdc22d4dd10]
```

```
(lldb) pe
There is no current managed exception on this thread
```

```
(lldb) thread select 7
* thread #7, stop reason = signal 0
    frame #0: 0x00007fdc25ba93f9 libpthread.so.0`__pthread_cond_timedwait at futex-
internal.h:142
```

```
(lldb) clrstack
OS Thread Id: 0x11a (7)
        Child SP               IP Call Site
00007FDC21311D10 00007fdc25ba93f9 [DebuggerU2MCatchHandlerFrame: 00007fdc21311d10]
```

```
(lldb) pe
There is no current managed exception on this thread
```

7.   Finally, we can list all loaded shared libraries:

```
(lldb) image list -p -f
[  0] 0x29cc440 /mnt/c/ANETMDA-Dumps/Linux/ApplicationG/bin/Release/net9.0/ApplicationG
[  1] 0x2add6f0 [vdso](0x00007ffc0b1e2000)
[  2] 0x2aff430 linux-vdso.so.1(0x00007ffc0b1e2000)
[  3] 0x2b07a90 /lib/x86_64-linux-gnu/libdl.so.2
[  4] 0x2b30120 /lib/x86_64-linux-gnu/libpthread.so.0
[  5] 0x7f050c014f80 /usr/lib/x86_64-linux-gnu/libstdc++.so.6
[  6] 0x7f053001dd60 /lib/x86_64-linux-gnu/libm.so.6
[  7] 0x7f05280e5380 /lib/x86_64-linux-gnu/libgcc_s.so.1
[  8] 0x7f05280b6ce0 /lib/x86_64-linux-gnu/libc.so.6
[  9] 0x7f05100a2df0 /lib64/ld-linux-x86-64.so.2
[ 10] 0x7f0528103790 /usr/share/dotnet/host/fxr/9.0.4/libhostfxr.so
[ 11] 0x7f0524119470 /usr/share/dotnet/shared/Microsoft.NETCore.App/9.0.4/libhostpolicy.so
[ 12] 0x397ad30 /usr/share/dotnet/shared/Microsoft.NETCore.App/9.0.4/libcoreclr.so
[ 13] 0x4088340 /lib/x86_64-linux-gnu/librt.so.1
[ 14] 0x7f051010ccb0 /usr/share/dotnet/shared/Microsoft.NETCore.App/9.0.4/libSystem.Native.so
[ 15] 0x7f05280f4b10 /usr/share/dotnet/shared/Microsoft.NETCore.App/9.0.4/libclrjit.so
[ 16] 0x40e6e50 /usr/lib/x86_64-linux-gnu/libicuuc.so.63
[ 17] 0x40ebee0 /usr/lib/x86_64-linux-gnu/libicudata.so.63
[ 18] 0x2cfa6d0 /usr/lib/x86_64-linux-gnu/libicui18n.so.63
```

Mechanisms (Invalid Pointer)

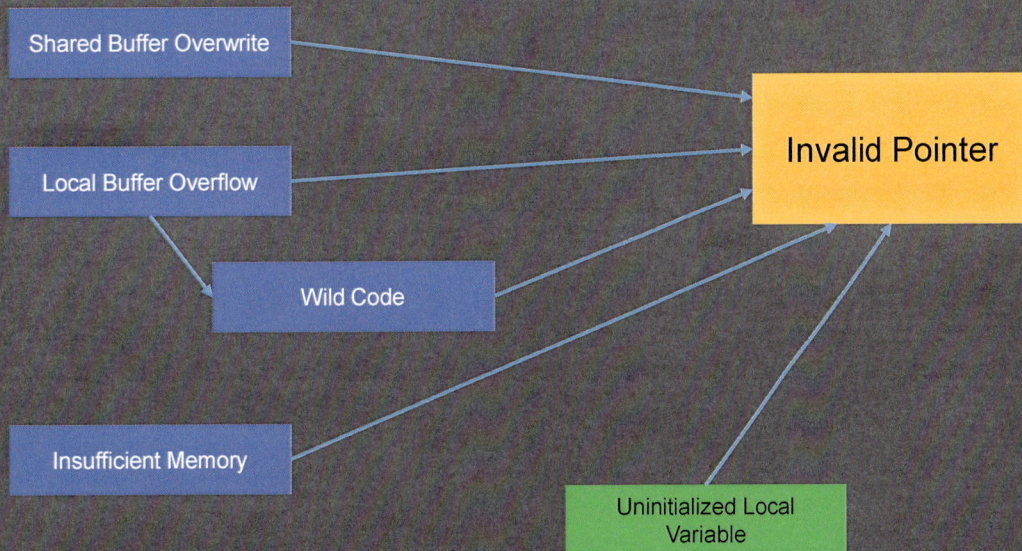

Patterns-Based Root Cause Analysis Methodology
https://www.dumpanalysis.org/pattern-oriented-root-cause-analysis

Exercise PN2 (Windows)

- **Goal:** Compare the 64-bit process memory dump from exercise PN1 with a 32-bit process memory dump

- **Patterns:** Platform-Specific Debugger; Hidden Exception (User Space); Execution Residue (Unmanaged Space, User)

- **Commands:** !teb, dps

- \ANETMDA-Dumps\Exercise-PN2-Windows.pdf

Exercise PN2 (Windows)

Goal: Compare the 64-bit process memory dump from exercise PN1 with a 32-bit process memory dump.

Patterns: Platform-Specific Debugger; Hidden Exception (User Space); Execution Residue (Unmanaged Space, User).

Commands: !teb, dps

1.   Launch WinDbg.

2.   Open \ANETMDA-Dumps\Windows\x86\ApplicationA.DMP

3.   We get the dump file loaded:

```
Microsoft (R) Windows Debugger Version 10.0.27829.1001 X86
Copyright (c) Microsoft Corporation. All rights reserved.


Loading Dump File [C:\ANETMDA-Dumps\Windows\x86\ApplicationA.DMP]
User Mini Dump File with Full Memory: Only application data is available


************* Path validation summary **************
Response                      Time (ms)      Location
Deferred                                     srv*
Symbol search path is: srv*
Executable search path is:
Windows 10 Version 22000 MP (4 procs) Free x86 compatible
Product: WinNt, suite: SingleUserTS
Edition build lab: 22000.1.amd64fre.co_release.210604-1628
Debug session time: Sat Apr 26 16:59:59.000 2025 (UTC + 1:00)
System Uptime: 0 days 0:04:34.312
Process Uptime: 0 days 0:03:01.000
.........................................................
.....................................
For analysis of this file, run !analyze -v
eax=00000000 ebx=00000001 ecx=00000000 edx=00000000 esi=03057998 edi=02d7dc54
eip=75fc112c esp=02d7dc4c ebp=02d7dc7c iopl=0         nv up ei pl nz na po nc
cs=0023  ss=002b  ds=002b  es=002b  fs=0053  gs=002b          efl=00000202
win32u!NtUserWaitMessage+0xc:
75fc112c ret
```

Note: This is a process memory dump of a 32-bit application. However, if you launch the 64-bit (AMD64) WinDbg from Debugging Tools for Windows, SOS extension commands do not work:

```
0:000> !pe
SOS does not support the current target architecture 'x86' (0x014c). A 32 bit target may
require a 32 bit debugger or vice versa. In general, try to use the same bitness for the
debugger and target process.
```

Note: We need a platform-specific X86 WinDbg version for 32-bit process memory dumps to analyze managed space. **If you use the WinDbg app, the appropriate process/extension is used automatically.**

4. Open a log file using .logopen:

```
0:000> .logopen C:\ANETMDA-Dumps\Windows\x86\ApplicationA.log
Opened log file 'C:\ANETMDA-Dumps\Windows\x86\ApplicationA.log'
```

Note: The WinDbg output may be slightly different on your system if you have a different WinDbg version, a different SOS extension version, you don't have .NET 9 installed, or you have a .NET version different from version 9.0.4 that was on a virtual machine where all the dumps were saved.

5. WinDbg **version** command shows information about the operating system and when the dump was taken:

```
0:000> version
Windows 10 Version 22000 MP (4 procs) Free x86 compatible
Product: WinNt, suite: SingleUserTS
Edition build lab: 22000.1.amd64fre.co_release.210604-1628
Debug session time: Sat Apr 26 16:59:59.000 2025 (UTC + 1:00)
System Uptime: 0 days 0:04:34.312
Process Uptime: 0 days 0:03:01.000
  Kernel time: 0 days 0:00:00.000
  User time: 0 days 0:00:01.000
Full memory user mini dump: C:\ANETMDA-Dumps\Windows\x86\ApplicationA.DMP [...]
```

6. We can get the computer name from where the dump was taken using the **!peb** command:

```
0:000> !peb
PEB at 02ade000
    InheritedAddressSpace:    No
    ReadImageFileExecOptions: No
    BeingDebugged:            No
    ImageBaseAddress:         003c0000
    NtGlobalFlag:             400
    NtGlobalFlag2:            0
    Ldr                       77a689c0
    Ldr.Initialized:          Yes
    Ldr.InInitializationOrderModuleList: 02fe18a0 . 104689a8
    Ldr.InLoadOrderModuleList:           02fe1988 . 10468998
    Ldr.InMemoryOrderModuleList:         02fe1990 . 104689a0
[...]
    SubSystemData:     00000000
    ProcessHeap:       02fe0000
    ProcessParameters: 02fe51e8
    CurrentDirectory:   'C:\Work\'
    WindowTitle:   'C:\Work\ApplicationA.exe'
    ImageFile:     'C:\Work\ApplicationA.exe'
    CommandLine:   '"C:\Work\ApplicationA.exe" '
    DllPath:       '< Name not readable >'
    Environment:   02fe6b38
        =::=::\
        ALLUSERSPROFILE=C:\ProgramData
        APPDATA=C:\Users\User\AppData\Roaming
        CommonProgramFiles=C:\Program Files (x86)\Common Files
        CommonProgramFiles(x86)=C:\Program Files (x86)\Common Files
        CommonProgramW6432=C:\Program Files\Common Files
        COMPUTERNAME=WINDEV2204EVAL
        ComSpec=C:\WINDOWS\system32\cmd.exe
        DriverData=C:\Windows\System32\Drivers\DriverData
        HOMEDRIVE=C:
```

```
        HOMEPATH=\Users\User
        LOCALAPPDATA=C:\Users\User\AppData\Local
        LOGONSERVER=\\WINDEV2204EVAL
        NUMBER_OF_PROCESSORS=4
        OneDrive=C:\Users\User\OneDrive
        OS=Windows_NT

Path=C:\Windows\system32;C:\Windows;C:\Windows\System32\Wbem;C:\Windows\System32\WindowsPowerSh
ell\v1.0\;C:\Windows\System32\OpenSSH\;C:\Program Files\Microsoft SQL
Server\150\Tools\Binn\;C:\Program Files\Microsoft SQL Server\Client
SDK\ODBC\170\Tools\Binn\;C:\Program
Files\dotnet\;C:\Users\User\AppData\Local\Microsoft\WindowsApps;C:\Users\User\.dotnet\tools
        PATHEXT=.COM;.EXE;.BAT;.CMD;.VBS;.VBE;.JS;.JSE;.WSF;.WSH;.MSC
        PROCESSOR_ARCHITECTURE=x86
        PROCESSOR_ARCHITEW6432=AMD64
        PROCESSOR_IDENTIFIER=Intel64 Family 6 Model 142 Stepping 10, GenuineIntel
        PROCESSOR_LEVEL=6
        PROCESSOR_REVISION=8e0a
        ProgramData=C:\ProgramData
        ProgramFiles=C:\Program Files (x86)
        ProgramFiles(x86)=C:\Program Files (x86)
        ProgramW6432=C:\Program Files
        PSModulePath=C:\Program
Files\WindowsPowerShell\Modules;C:\WINDOWS\system32\WindowsPowerShell\v1.0\Modules
        PUBLIC=C:\Users\Public
        SESSIONNAME=Console
        SystemDrive=C:
        SystemRoot=C:\WINDOWS
        TEMP=C:\Users\User\AppData\Local\Temp
        TMP=C:\Users\User\AppData\Local\Temp
        USERDOMAIN=WINDEV2204EVAL
        USERDOMAIN_ROAMINGPROFILE=WINDEV2204EVAL
        USERNAME=User
        USERPROFILE=C:\Users\User
        windir=C:\WINDOWS
```

7.   Type ~*kL command to verify the correctness of all stack traces (the command execution time may be longer for the first time because symbol files need to be downloaded from the Microsoft symbol server):

```
0:000> ~*kL

.  0  Id: 1c1c.1c20 Suspend: 0 Teb: 02ae1000 Unfrozen
 # ChildEBP RetAddr
00 02d7dc7c 0e27035a     win32u!NtUserWaitMessage+0xc
01 02d7dc7c 72ea3b24     System_Windows_Forms_Primitives!Windows.Win32.PInvoke.WaitMessage()+0x9bd5799a
02 02d7dcb4 72ea3a39     System_Windows_Forms!System.Windows.Forms.Application.LightThreadContext.FPushMessageLoop+0x34
03 02d7dcbc 72ea4f4c     System_Windows_Forms!System.Windows.Forms.Application.LightThreadContext.RunMessageLoop+0x9
04 02d7dd1c 72ea4cc8     System_Windows_Forms!System.Windows.Forms.Application.ThreadContext.RunMessageLoopInner+0x25c
05 02d7dd48 72c5565f     System_Windows_Forms!System.Windows.Forms.Application.ThreadContext.RunMessageLoop+0x38
06 02d7dd60 72e0d5cc     System_Windows_Forms!System.Windows.Forms.Application.RunDialog+0x3f
07 02d7ddb8 72ea4af9     System_Windows_Forms!System.Windows.Forms.Form.ShowDialog+0x22c
08 02d7ddf0 72e9b93c     System_Windows_Forms!System.Windows.Forms.Application.ThreadContext.OnThreadException+0x89
09 02d7ddfc 08b0e070     System_Windows_Forms!System.Windows.Forms.Control.ControlNativeWindow.OnThreadException+0x3c
0a 02d7ef4c 08b0261f     System_Windows_Forms!System.Windows.Forms.NativeWindow.Callback(Windows.Win32.Foundation.HWND,
Windows.Win32.MessageId, Windows.Win32.Foundation.WPARAM, Windows.Win32.Foundation.LPARAM)+0x95ce9390
0b 02d7ef90 76117c02     System_Windows_Forms_Primitives!ILStubClass.IL_STUB_ReversePInvoke(Windows.Win32.Foundation.HWND,
Windows.Win32.MessageId, Windows.Win32.Foundation.WPARAM, Windows.Win32.Foundation.LPARAM)+0x37
0c 02d7efbc 760f6fea     user32!_InternalCallWinProc+0x2a
0d 02d7f0ac 760f5908     user32!UserCallWinProcCheckWow+0x4aa
0e 02d7f128 760f5440     user32!DispatchMessageWorker+0x4b8
0f 02d7f134 7251513d     user32!DispatchMessageW+0x10
10 02d7f18c 72ea3c41     System_Windows_Forms_Primitives!put_Top+0x2c
11 02d7f1c4 72ea3a39     System_Windows_Forms!System.Windows.Forms.Application.LightThreadContext.FPushMessageLoop+0x151
12 02d7f1cc 72ea4f4c     System_Windows_Forms!System.Windows.Forms.Application.LightThreadContext.RunMessageLoop+0x9
13 02d7f22c 72ea4cc8     System_Windows_Forms!System.Windows.Forms.Application.ThreadContext.RunMessageLoopInner+0x25c
14 02d7f258 72c555df     System_Windows_Forms!System.Windows.Forms.Application.ThreadContext.RunMessageLoop+0x38
```

```
15 02d7f270 08b0184e    System_Windows_Forms!System.Windows.Forms.Application.Run+0x3f
16 02d7f27c 745b65c3    ApplicationA!ApplicationA.Program.Main()+0x2e
17 02d7f288 7452177a    coreclr!CallDescrWorkerInternal+0x34
18 (Inline) --------    coreclr!CallDescrWorkerWithHandler+0x5c
19 02d7f304 744fa5d2    coreclr!MethodDescCallSite::CallTargetWorker+0x12c
1a (Inline) --------    coreclr!MethodDescCallSite::Call+0x11
1b 02d7f418 744fac9a    coreclr!RunMainInternal+0xe4
1c 02d7f480 744fab37    coreclr!RunMain+0x9b
1d 02d7f6e0 744fb928    coreclr!Assembly::ExecuteMainMethod+0x16e
1e 02d7f774 744fb327    coreclr!CorHost2::ExecuteAssembly+0x168
1f 02d7f7c4 7488b2a2    coreclr!coreclr_execute_assembly+0xa7
20 (Inline) --------    hostpolicy!coreclr_t::execute_assembly+0x27
21 02d7f870 7488b4c2    hostpolicy!run_app_for_context+0x452
22 02d7f8b0 7488beaa    hostpolicy!run_app+0x52
23 02d7f954 748cb7d8    hostpolicy!corehost_main+0xda
24 02d7f9c8 748cd20d    hostfxr!execute_app+0x2d8
25 02d7fa50 748cede5    hostfxr!`anonymous namespace'::read_config_and_execute+0xbd
26 02d7fabc 748cd5c1    hostfxr!fx_muxer_t::handle_exec_host_command+0x115
27 02d7fbc0 748c700b    hostfxr!fx_muxer_t::execute+0x261
28 02d7fc60 003c9311    hostfxr!hostfxr_main_startupinfo+0x7b
29 02d7fd90 003c96f7    ApplicationA_exe!exe_start+0x6b1
2a 02d7fde0 003d002c    ApplicationA_exe!wmain+0x127
2b (Inline) --------    ApplicationA_exe!invoke_main+0x1c
2c 02d7fe28 77566839    ApplicationA_exe!__scrt_common_main_seh+0xfa
2d 02d7fe38 779a90ef    kernel32!BaseThreadInitThunk+0x19
2e 02d7fe90 779a90bd    ntdll!__RtlUserThreadStart+0x2b
2f 02d7fea0 00000000    ntdll!_RtlUserThreadStart+0x1b

   1  Id: 1c1c.1c78 Suspend: 0 Teb: 02af1000 Unfrozen ".NET EventPipe"
 # ChildEBP RetAddr
00 04faf9cc 770ba933    ntdll!NtWaitForMultipleObjects+0xc
01 04faf9cc 770ba7e8    KERNELBASE!WaitForMultipleObjectsEx+0x133
02 04faf9e8 7458710f    KERNELBASE!WaitForMultipleObjects+0x18
03 (Inline) --------    coreclr!ds_ipc_poll+0x6b
04 (Inline) --------    coreclr!ds_ipc_stream_factory_get_next_available_stream+0x147
05 04fafba4 77566839    coreclr!server_thread+0x19f
06 04fafbb4 779a90ef    kernel32!BaseThreadInitThunk+0x19
07 04fafc0c 779a90bd    ntdll!__RtlUserThreadStart+0x2b
08 04fafc1c 00000000    ntdll!_RtlUserThreadStart+0x1b

   2  Id: 1c1c.1c7c Suspend: 0 Teb: 02af5000 Unfrozen ".NET Debugger"
 # ChildEBP RetAddr
00 052ffb0c 770ba933    ntdll!NtWaitForMultipleObjects+0xc
01 052ffb0c 745a945c    KERNELBASE!WaitForMultipleObjectsEx+0x133
02 (Inline) --------    coreclr!DebuggerRCThread::MainLoop+0x8c
03 (Inline) --------    coreclr!DebuggerRCThread::ThreadProc+0x12a
04 052ffb8c 77566839    coreclr!DebuggerRCThread::ThreadProcStatic+0x17c
05 052ffb9c 779a90ef    kernel32!BaseThreadInitThunk+0x19
06 052ffbf4 779a90bd    ntdll!__RtlUserThreadStart+0x2b
07 052ffc04 00000000    ntdll!_RtlUserThreadStart+0x1b

   3  Id: 1c1c.1c80 Suspend: 0 Teb: 02af9000 Unfrozen ".NET Finalizer"
 # ChildEBP RetAddr
00 0847fa0c 770ba933    ntdll!NtWaitForMultipleObjects+0xc
01 0847fa0c 74582f08    KERNELBASE!WaitForMultipleObjectsEx+0x133
02 0847fa38 74582d5c    coreclr!FinalizerThread::WaitForFinalizerEvent+0x63
03 0847fc60 7457b273    coreclr!FinalizerThread::FinalizerThreadWorker+0x3c
04 (Inline) --------    coreclr!ManagedThreadBase_DispatchInner+0x12
05 0847fccc 7457b1ca    coreclr!ManagedThreadBase_DispatchMiddle+0x65
06 0847fd1c 74564fed    coreclr!ManagedThreadBase_DispatchOuter+0x62
07 (Inline) --------    coreclr!ManagedThreadBase_NoADTransition+0x1b
08 (Inline) --------    coreclr!ManagedThreadBase::FinalizerBase+0x1b
09 0847fd30 77566839    coreclr!FinalizerThread::FinalizerThreadStart+0x6d
0a 0847fd40 779a90ef    kernel32!BaseThreadInitThunk+0x19
0b 0847fd98 779a90bd    ntdll!__RtlUserThreadStart+0x2b
0c 0847fda8 00000000    ntdll!_RtlUserThreadStart+0x1b

   4  Id: 1c1c.1cf8 Suspend: 0 Teb: 02b05000 Unfrozen
 # ChildEBP RetAddr
00 09b9f9a0 760fed3f    win32u!NtUserMsgWaitForMultipleObjectsEx+0xc
01 09b9f9a0 760febde    user32!RealMsgWaitForMultipleObjectsEx+0x8f
02 09b9f9c4 72046a44    user32!MsgWaitForMultipleObjects+0x3e
03 09b9fa0c 720469ca    GdiPlus!BackgroundThreadProc+0x54
04 09b9fa24 77566839    GdiPlus!DllRefCountSafeThreadThunk+0x1a
05 09b9fa34 779a90ef    kernel32!BaseThreadInitThunk+0x19
06 09b9fa8c 779a90bd    ntdll!__RtlUserThreadStart+0x2b
07 09b9fa9c 00000000    ntdll!_RtlUserThreadStart+0x1b

   5  Id: 1c1c.1d34 Suspend: 0 Teb: 02b0d000 Unfrozen
 # ChildEBP RetAddr
00 0c09feb0 77971b58    ntdll!NtWaitForWorkViaWorkerFactory+0xc
01 0c09feb0 77566839    ntdll!TppWorkerThread+0x338
02 0c09fec0 779a90ef    kernel32!BaseThreadInitThunk+0x19
03 0c09ff18 779a90bd    ntdll!__RtlUserThreadStart+0x2b
```

```
04 0c09ff28 00000000    ntdll!_RtlUserThreadStart+0x1b


    6  Id: 1c1c.1d38 Suspend: 0 Teb: 02b11000 Unfrozen
 # ChildEBP RetAddr
00 0c25fb50 77971b58    ntdll!NtWaitForWorkViaWorkerFactory+0xc
01 0c25fb50 77566839    ntdll!TppWorkerThread+0x338
02 0c25fb60 779a90ef    kernel32!BaseThreadInitThunk+0x19
03 0c25fbb8 779a90bd    ntdll!__RtlUserThreadStart+0x2b
04 0c25fbc8 00000000    ntdll!_RtlUserThreadStart+0x1b


    7  Id: 1c1c.1d50 Suspend: 0 Teb: 02b15000 Unfrozen ".NET System Events"
 # ChildEBP RetAddr
00 0c48fca8 760fff80    win32u!NtUserGetMessage+0xc
01 0c48fca8 71544b80    user32!GetMessageW+0x30
02 0c48fd30 739d5d85    Microsoft_Win32_SystemEvents!Microsoft.Win32.SystemEvents.WindowThreadProc+0xc0
03 0c48fd40 745b65c3    System_Private_CoreLib!System.Threading.Thread.StartCallback+0x35
04 0c48fd4c 744e62fb    coreclr!CallDescrWorkerInternal+0x34
05 (Inline) --------    coreclr!CallDescrWorkerWithHandler+0x42
06 0c48fda8 7457b2eb    coreclr!DispatchCallSimple+0xa5
07 0c48fdc8 7457b273    coreclr!ThreadNative::KickOffThread_Worker+0x4b
08 (Inline) --------    coreclr!ManagedThreadBase_DispatchInner+0x12
09 0c48fe34 7457b1ca    coreclr!ManagedThreadBase_DispatchMiddle+0x65
0a 0c48fe84 7457b39d    coreclr!ManagedThreadBase_DispatchOuter+0x62
0b (Inline) --------    coreclr!ManagedThreadBase_FullTransition+0x1c
0c (Inline) --------    coreclr!ManagedThreadBase::KickOff+0x1c
0d 0c48fec8 77566839    coreclr!ThreadNative::KickOffThread+0x7d
0e 0c48fee0 779a90ef    kernel32!BaseThreadInitThunk+0x19
0f 0c48ff38 779a90bd    ntdll!__RtlUserThreadStart+0x2b
10 0c48ff48 00000000    ntdll!_RtlUserThreadStart+0x1b


    8  Id: 1c1c.16a8 Suspend: 0 Teb: 02b25000 Unfrozen
 # ChildEBP RetAddr
00 0325feac 77971b58    ntdll!NtWaitForWorkViaWorkerFactory+0xc
01 0325feac 77566839    ntdll!TppWorkerThread+0x338
02 0325febc 779a90ef    kernel32!BaseThreadInitThunk+0x19
03 0325ff14 779a90bd    ntdll!__RtlUserThreadStart+0x2b
04 0325ff24 00000000    ntdll!_RtlUserThreadStart+0x1b
```

Note: The thread #0 stack trace only shows signs of managed code exception processing (in yellow) compared to the x64 memory dump.

8.   However, we can get managed code exception information (using the SOS extension that comes from WinDbg):

```
0:000> !pe
Loading extension C:\Program
Files\WindowsApps\Microsoft.WinDbg_1.2504.15001.0_x64__8wekyb3d8bbwe\x86\winext\sos\extensions\Microsoft.Diagnostics.DataContractReader.dll
Loading extension C:\Program
Files\WindowsApps\Microsoft.WinDbg_1.2504.15001.0_x64__8wekyb3d8bbwe\x86\winext\sos\extensions\Microsoft.Diagnostics.DataContractReader.Extension.dll
Loading extension C:\Program
Files\WindowsApps\Microsoft.WinDbg_1.2504.15001.0_x64__8wekyb3d8bbwe\x86\winext\sos\extensions\Microsoft.Diagnostics.DebuggerCommands.dll
Exception object: 05311be0
Exception type:   System.NullReferenceException
Message:          Object reference not set to an instance of an object.
InnerException:   <none>
StackTrace (generated):
    SP       IP       Function
    02D7EDC0 08B0FCB1 ApplicationA!ApplicationA.ApplicationA.CrashButton_Click(System.Object, System.EventArgs)+0x19
    02D7EDD8 72C3E7DC System_Windows_Forms!System.Windows.Forms.Control.OnClick(System.EventArgs)+0x3c
    02D7EDEC 72C57810 System_Windows_Forms!System.Windows.Forms.Button.OnClick(System.EventArgs)+0x140
    02D7EE28 72C57955 System_Windows_Forms!System.Windows.Forms.Button.OnMouseUp(System.Windows.Forms.MouseEventArgs)+0xd5
    02D7EE4C 72C465C8 System_Windows_Forms!System.Windows.Forms.Control.WmMouseUp(System.Windows.Forms.Message ByRef, System.Windows.Forms.MouseButtons,
Int32)+0x218
    02D7EEA0 08B0EA53 System_Windows_Forms!System.Windows.Forms.Control.WndProc(System.Windows.Forms.Message ByRef)+0x79b
    02D7EEB4 08B0F0D4 System_Windows_Forms!System.Windows.Forms.ButtonBase.WndProc(System.Windows.Forms.Message ByRef)+0xfc63509c
    02D7EF14 08B0DFBF System_Windows_Forms!System.Windows.Forms.NativeWindow.Callback(Windows.Win32.Foundation.HWND, Windows.Win32.MessageId,
Windows.Win32.Foundation.WPARAM, Windows.Win32.Foundation.LPARAM)+0x157

StackTraceString: <none>
HResult: 80004003

0:000> u 08B0FCB1
ApplicationA!ApplicationA.ApplicationA.CrashButton_Click(System.Object, System.EventArgs)+0x19:
08b0fcb1 mov     dword ptr [eax],1
08b0fcb7 mov     esp,ebp
08b0fcb9 pop     ebp
08b0fcba ret     4
08b0fcbd add     byte ptr [eax],al
08b0fcbf add     byte ptr [eax],al
```

```
08b0fcc1 add        byte ptr [eax],al
08b0fcc3 add        byte ptr [eax-3Eh],ch
```

Note: We don't know the value of the EAX register to see if this was a null pointer.

9.   Let's see what the **!analyze -v** command says:

```
0:000> !analyze -v
.........................................................
.........................................................
ClrmaManagedAnalysis::AssociateClient
AssociateClient trying managed CLRMA
AssociateClient trying DAC CLRMA
*******************************************************************************
*                                                                             *
*                        Exception Analysis                                   *
*                                                                             *
*******************************************************************************

*** WARNING: Unable to verify checksum for ApplicationA.exe
ClrmaManagedAnalysis::GetThread 1c20
ClrmaThread::Initialize 1c20
~ClrmaThread
ClrmaManagedAnalysis::GetThread 1c78
ClrmaThread::Initialize 1c78
ClrmaThread::Initialize FAILED managed thread not found
~ClrmaThread
ClrmaManagedAnalysis::GetThread 1c7c
ClrmaThread::Initialize 1c7c
ClrmaThread::Initialize FAILED managed thread not found
~ClrmaThread
ClrmaManagedAnalysis::GetThread 1c80
ClrmaThread::Initialize 1c80
~ClrmaThread
ClrmaManagedAnalysis::GetThread 1cf8
ClrmaThread::Initialize 1cf8
ClrmaThread::Initialize FAILED managed thread not found
~ClrmaThread
ClrmaManagedAnalysis::GetThread 1d34
ClrmaThread::Initialize 1d34
ClrmaThread::Initialize FAILED managed thread not found
~ClrmaThread
ClrmaManagedAnalysis::GetThread 1d38
ClrmaThread::Initialize 1d38
ClrmaThread::Initialize FAILED managed thread not found
~ClrmaThread
ClrmaManagedAnalysis::GetThread 1d50
ClrmaThread::Initialize 1d50
~ClrmaThread
ClrmaManagedAnalysis::GetThread 16a8
ClrmaThread::Initialize 16a8
ClrmaThread::Initialize FAILED managed thread not found
~ClrmaThread
ClrmaManagedAnalysis::get_ProviderName
ClrmaManagedAnalysis::GetThread ffffffff
ClrmaThread::Initialize 1c20
ClrmaThread::get_CurrentException
~ClrmaException
ClrmaThread::get_NestedExceptionCount
~ClrmaThread

KEY_VALUES_STRING: 1

    Key  : Analysis.CPU.mSec
    Value: 3453

    Key  : Analysis.Elapsed.mSec
    Value: 7595

    Key  : Analysis.IO.Other.Mb
    Value: 4

    Key  : Analysis.IO.Read.Mb
    Value: 2

    Key  : Analysis.IO.Write.Mb
    Value: 17

    Key  : Analysis.Init.CPU.mSec
    Value: 6359

    Key  : Analysis.Init.Elapsed.mSec
    Value: 666385

    Key  : Analysis.Memory.CommitPeak.Mb
    Value: 327

    Key  : Analysis.Version.DbgEng
    Value: 10.0.27829.1001

    Key  : Analysis.Version.Description
    Value: 10.2503.24.01 x86fre

    Key  : Analysis.Version.Ext
    Value: 1.2503.24.1

    Key  : CLR.Engine
    Value: CORECLR

    Key  : CLR.Version
    Value: 9.0.425.16305

    Key  : Failure.Bucket
    Value: BREAKPOINT_80000003_win32u.dll!NtUserWaitMessage

    Key  : Failure.Exception.Code
    Value: 0x80000003
```

126

```
       Key  : Failure.Hash
       Value: {a106cd41-a8b1-c51d-6d94-a75661270841}

       Key  : Failure.ProblemClass.Primary
       Value: BREAKPOINT

       Key  : Faulting.IP.Type
       Value: Null

       Key  : Timeline.OS.Boot.DeltaSec
       Value: 274

       Key  : Timeline.Process.Start.DeltaSec
       Value: 181

       Key  : WER.OS.Branch
       Value: co_release

       Key  : WER.OS.Version
       Value: 10.0.22000.1

       Key  : WER.Process.Version
       Value: 1.0.0.0


FILE_IN_CAB:  ApplicationA.DMP

NTGLOBALFLAG:  400

APPLICATION_VERIFIER_FLAGS:  0

EXCEPTION_RECORD:  (.exr -1)
ExceptionAddress: 00000000
   ExceptionCode: 80000003 (Break instruction exception)
  ExceptionFlags: 00000000
NumberParameters: 0

FAULTING_THREAD:  1c20

PROCESS_NAME:  ApplicationA.dll

ERROR_CODE: (NTSTATUS) 0x80000003 - {EXCEPTION}  Breakpoint  A breakpoint has been reached.

EXCEPTION_CODE_STR:  80000003

IP_ON_HEAP:  0e27035a
The fault address in not in any loaded module, please check your build's rebase
log at <releasedir>\bin\build_logs\timebuild\ntrebase.log for module which may
contain the address if it were loaded.

FRAME_ONE_INVALID: 1

STACK_TEXT:
02d7dc7c 0e27035a  fd1aa344 747d1220 02d7f144 win32u!NtUserWaitMessage+0xc
02d7dc7c 72ea3b24  00000000 00000000 00000000 System_Windows_Forms_Primitives!Windows.Win32.PInvoke.WaitMessage()+0x9bd5799a
02d7dcb4 72ea3a39  00000000 00000000 00000000 System_Windows_Forms!System.Windows.Forms.Application.LightThreadContext.FPushMessageLoop+0x34
02d7dcbc 72ea4f4c  00000000 00000000 00000000 System_Windows_Forms!System.Windows.Forms.Application.LightThreadContext.RunMessageLoop+0x9
02d7dd1c 72ea4cc8  00000000 00000000 00000000 System_Windows_Forms!System.Windows.Forms.Application.ThreadContext.RunMessageLoopInner+0x25c
02d7dd48 72c5565f  00000000 00000000 00000000 System_Windows_Forms!System.Windows.Forms.Application.ThreadContext.RunMessageLoop+0x38
02d7dd60 72e0d5cc  00000000 00000000 00000000 System_Windows_Forms!System.Windows.Forms.Application.RunDialog+0x3f
02d7ddb8 72ea4af9  00000000 00000000 00000000 System_Windows_Forms!System.Windows.Forms.Form.ShowDialog+0x22c
02d7ddf0 72e9b93c  00000000 00000000 00000000 System_Windows_Forms!System.Windows.Forms.Application.ThreadContext.OnThreadException+0x89
02d7ddfc 08b0e070  00000000 00000000 00000000 System_Windows_Forms!System.Windows.Forms.Control.ControlNativeWindow.OnThreadException+0x3c
02d7ef4c 08b0261f  00000000 00000000 00000000 System_Windows_Forms!System.Windows.Forms.NativeWindow.Callback(Windows.Win32.Foundation.HWND, Windows.Win32.MessageId,
Windows.Win32.Foundation.WPARAM, Windows.Win32.Foundation.LPARAM)+0x95ce9390
02d7ef90 76117c02  00000000 00000000 00000000 System_Windows_Forms_Primitives!ILStubClass.IL_STUB_ReversePInvoke(Windows.Win32.Foundation.HWND, Windows.Win32.MessageId,
Windows.Win32.Foundation.WPARAM, Windows.Win32.Foundation.LPARAM)+0x37
02d7efbc 760f6fea  04e1332e 0001044c 00000202 user32!_InternalCallWinProc+0x2a
02d7f0ac 760f5908  04e1332e 00000000 00000202 user32!UserCallWinProcCheckWow+0x4aa
02d7f128 760f5440  02d7f144 02d7f18c 7251513d user32!DispatchMessageWorker+0x4b8
02d7f134 7251513d  02d7f19c fd1aa344 747d1220 user32!DispatchMessageW+0x10
02d7f18c 72ea3c41  00000000 00000000 00000000 System_Windows_Forms_Primitives!put_Top+0x2c
02d7f1c4 72ea3a39  00000000 00000000 00000000 System_Windows_Forms!System.Windows.Forms.Application.LightThreadContext.FPushMessageLoop+0x151
02d7f1cc 72ea4f4c  00000000 00000000 00000000 System_Windows_Forms!System.Windows.Forms.Application.LightThreadContext.RunMessageLoop+0x9
02d7f22c 72ea4cc8  00000000 00000000 00000000 System_Windows_Forms!System.Windows.Forms.Application.ThreadContext.RunMessageLoopInner+0x25c
02d7f258 72c555df  00000000 00000000 00000000 System_Windows_Forms!System.Windows.Forms.Application.ThreadContext.RunMessageLoop+0x38
02d7f270 08b0184e  00000000 00000000 00000000 System_Windows_Forms!System.Windows.Forms.Application.Run+0x3f
02d7f27c 745b65c3  02d7f2a0 02d7f304 7452177a ApplicationA!ApplicationA.Program.Main()+0x2e
02d7f288 7452177a  02d7f2e0 02d7f40c 74577e90 coreclr!CallDescrWorkerInternal+0x34
(Inline) --------  -------- -------- -------- coreclr!CallDescrWorkerWithHandler+0x5c
02d7f304 744fa5d2  02d7f400 00000000 00000000 coreclr!MethodDescCallSite::CallTargetWorker+0x12c
(Inline) --------  -------- -------- -------- coreclr!MethodDescCallSite::Call+0x11
02d7f418 744fac9a  ffcc0d79 03057998 08b44f4c coreclr!RunMainInternal+0xe4
02d7f480 744fab37  02d7f75c ffcc0f19 coreclr!RunMain+0x9b
02d7f6e0 744fb928  02d7f75c 74589760 ffcc0e8d coreclr!Assembly::ExecuteMainMethod+0x16e
02d7f774 744fb327  02ff4208 00000001 030b22c0 coreclr!CorHost2::ExecuteAssembly+0x168
02d7f7c4 7488b2a2  02ff4208 00000001 00000000 coreclr!coreclr_execute_assembly+0xa7
(Inline) --------  -------- -------- -------- hostpolicy!coreclr_t::execute_assembly+0x27
02d7f870 7488b4c2  02fef494 c993cdbd 02fef490 hostpolicy!run_app_for_context+0x452
02d7f8b0 7488beaa  00000000 02fef494 7488bdd0 hostpolicy!run_app+0x52
02d7f954 748cb7d8  00000001 02fef490 ce9da6bb hostpolicy!corehost_main+0xda
02d7f9c8 748cd20d  00000001 02fef490 ce9da523 hostfxr!execute_app+0x2d8
02d7fa50 748cede5  02d7fb94 02d7faf8 00000001 hostfxr!`anonymous namespace'::read_config_and_execute+0xbd
02d7fabc 748cd5c1  02d7fb94 02d7faf8 00000001 hostfxr!fx_muxer_t::handle_exec_host_command+0x115
02d7fbc0 748c700b  02d7fc10 00000000 00000000 hostfxr!fx_muxer_t::execute+0x261
02d7fc60 003c9311  00000001 02fef490 02fef5b0 hostfxr!hostfxr_main_startupinfo+0x7b
02d7f990 003c96f7  02fe8ff0 02fef490 02fef490 ApplicationA_exe!exe_start+0x6b1
02d7fde0 003d002c  00000001 02fef490 02fe8ff0 ApplicationA_exe!wmain+0x127
(Inline) --------  -------- -------- -------- ApplicationA_exe!invoke_main+0x1c
02d7fe28 77566839  02ade000 77566820 02d7fe90 ApplicationA_exe!__scrt_common_main_seh+0xfa
02d7fe38 779a90ef  02ade000 87efe4cc 00000000 kernel32!BaseThreadInitThunk+0x19
02d7fe90 779a90bd  ffffffff 779d8f24 00000000 ntdll!__RtlUserThreadStart+0x2b
02d7fea0 00000000  00000000 00000000 00000000 ntdll!_RtlUserThreadStart+0x1b


STACK_COMMAND:  ~0s; .ecxr ; kb

SYMBOL_NAME:  win32u!NtUserWaitMessage+c

MODULE_NAME: win32u

IMAGE_NAME:  win32u.dll

FAILURE_BUCKET_ID:  BREAKPOINT_80000003_win32u.dll!NtUserWaitMessage

OS_VERSION:  10.0.22000.1

BUILDLAB_STR:  co_release
```

OSPLATFORM_TYPE: x86

OSNAME: Windows 10

IMAGE_VERSION: 10.0.22000.3147

FAILURE_ID_HASH: {a106cd41-a8b1-c51d-6d94-a75661270841}

Followup: MachineOwner

CLRMAReleaseInstance
~ClrmaManagedAnalysis

Note: the output of the command is similar to its x64 variant. We get such a managed stack trace using **!CLRStack** command but it doesn't show the exception, only signs of managed exception processing:

```
0:000> !CLRStack
OS Thread Id: 0x1c20 (0)
Child SP       IP Call Site
02D7DC54 75fc112c [InlinedCallFrame: 02d7dc54] Windows.Win32.PInvoke.g__LocalExternFunction|3644_0()
02D7DC50 0e27035a Windows.Win32.PInvoke.WaitMessage()
[/_/artifacts/obj/System.Windows.Forms.Primitives/Release/net9.0/Microsoft.Windows.CsWin32/Microsoft.Windows.CsWin32.SourceGenerator/Windows.Win32.PInvoke.USE
R32.dll.g.cs @ 4487]
02D7DC84 72ea3b24 System.Windows.Forms.Application+LightThreadContext.FPushMessageLoop(Microsoft.Office.msoloop)
[/_/src/System.Windows.Forms/src/System/Windows/Forms/Application.LightThreadContext.cs @ 136]
02D7DCBC 72ea3a39 System.Windows.Forms.Application+LightThreadContext.RunMessageLoop(Microsoft.Office.msoloop, Boolean)
[/_/src/System.Windows.Forms/src/System/Windows/Forms/Application.LightThreadContext.cs @ 26]
02D7DCC8 72ea4f4c System.Windows.Forms.Application+ThreadContext.RunMessageLoopInner(Microsoft.Office.msoloop, System.Windows.Forms.ApplicationContext)
[/_/src/System.Windows.Forms/src/System/Windows/Forms/Application.ThreadContext.cs @ 809]
02D7DD28 72ea4cc8 System.Windows.Forms.Application+ThreadContext.RunMessageLoop(Microsoft.Office.msoloop, System.Windows.Forms.ApplicationContext)
[/_/src/System.Windows.Forms/src/System/Windows/Forms/Application.ThreadContext.cs @ 696]
02D7DD54 72c5565f System.Windows.Forms.Application.RunDialog(System.Windows.Forms.Form) [/_/src/System.Windows.Forms/src/System/Windows/Forms/Application.cs @
1339]
02D7DD68 72e0d5cc System.Windows.Forms.Form.ShowDialog(System.Windows.Forms.IWin32Window) [/_/src/System.Windows.Forms/src/System/Windows/Forms/Form.cs @
5892]
02D7DDC0 72ea4af9 System.Windows.Forms.Application+ThreadContext.OnThreadException(System.Exception)
[/_/src/System.Windows.Forms/src/System/Windows/Forms/Application.ThreadContext.cs @ 624]
02D7DDF8 72e9b93c System.Windows.Forms.Control+ControlNativeWindow.OnThreadException(System.Exception)
[/_/src/System.Windows.Forms/src/System/Windows/Forms/Control.ControlNativeWindow.cs @ 59]
02D7DE04 08b0e070 System.Windows.Forms.NativeWindow.Callback(Windows.Win32.Foundation.HWND, Windows.Win32.MessageId, Windows.Win32.Foundation.WPARAM,
Windows.Win32.Foundation.LPARAM) [/_/src/System.Windows.Forms/src/System/Windows/Forms/NativeWindow.cs @ 364]
02D7EF60 08b0261f ILStubClass.IL_STUB_ReversePInvoke(Windows.Win32.Foundation.HWND, Windows.Win32.MessageId, Windows.Win32.Foundation.WPARAM,
Windows.Win32.Foundation.LPARAM)
02D7F144 76117c02 [InlinedCallFrame: 02d7f144]
02D7F140 72515136 Windows.Win32.PInvoke.DispatchMessage(Windows.Win32.UI.WindowsAndMessaging.MSG*)
02D7F194 72ea3c41 System.Windows.Forms.Application+LightThreadContext.FPushMessageLoop(Microsoft.Office.msoloop)
[/_/src/System.Windows.Forms/src/System/Windows/Forms/Application.LightThreadContext.cs @ 109]
02D7F1CC 72ea3a39 System.Windows.Forms.Application+LightThreadContext.RunMessageLoop(Microsoft.Office.msoloop, Boolean)
[/_/src/System.Windows.Forms/src/System/Windows/Forms/Application.LightThreadContext.cs @ 26]
02D7F1D8 72ea4f4c System.Windows.Forms.Application+ThreadContext.RunMessageLoopInner(Microsoft.Office.msoloop, System.Windows.Forms.ApplicationContext)
[/_/src/System.Windows.Forms/src/System/Windows/Forms/Application.ThreadContext.cs @ 809]
02D7F238 72ea4cc8 System.Windows.Forms.Application+ThreadContext.RunMessageLoop(Microsoft.Office.msoloop, System.Windows.Forms.ApplicationContext)
[/_/src/System.Windows.Forms/src/System/Windows/Forms/Application.ThreadContext.cs @ 696]
02D7F264 72c555df System.Windows.Forms.Application.Run(System.Windows.Forms.Form) [/_/src/System.Windows.Forms/src/System/Windows/Forms/Application.cs @ 1324]
02D7F278 08b0184e ApplicationA.Program.Main()
```

10.   To see the hidden exception and set the corresponding exception context, we need to dump execution residue from the raw stack region.

```
0:000> !teb
TEB at 02ae1000
    ExceptionList:        02d7df24
    StackBase:            02d80000
    StackLimit:           02d76000
    SubSystemTib:         00000000
    FiberData:            00001e00
    ArbitraryUserPointer: 00000000
    Self:                 02ae1000
    EnvironmentPointer:   00000000
    ClientId:             00001c1c . 00001c20
    RpcHandle:            00000000
    Tls Storage:          03087080
    PEB Address:          02ade000
    LastErrorValue:       0
    LastStatusValue:      c000007c
    Count Owned Locks:    0
    HardErrorMode:        0
```

128

```
0:000> dps 02d76000 02d80000
02d76000  00000000
02d76004  00000000
02d76008  00000000
...
...
...
02d7e8d4  00000000
02d7e8d8  00000000
02d7e8dc  00000000
02d7e8e0  00000000
02d7e8e4  00000000
02d7e8e8  00000000
02d7e8ec  87eff228
02d7e8f0  02d7edcc
02d7e8f4  779b72b6 ntdll!KiUserExceptionDispatcher+0x26
02d7e8f8  02d7e908
02d7e8fc  02d7e958
02d7e900  02d7e908
02d7e904  02d7e958
02d7e908  c0000005
02d7e90c  00000000
02d7e910  00000000
02d7e914  08b0fcb1 ApplicationA!ApplicationA.ApplicationA.CrashButton_Click(System.Object,
System.EventArgs)+0x19
02d7e918  00000002
02d7e91c  00000001
02d7e920  00000000
02d7e924  00000000
02d7e928  00000000
02d7e92c  00000000
02d7e930  00000000
02d7e934  00000000
02d7e938  00000000
02d7e93c  00000000
02d7e940  00000000
02d7e944  00000000
02d7e948  00000000
02d7e94c  00000000
02d7e950  00000000
02d7e954  00000000
02d7e958  0001007f
02d7e95c  00000000
02d7e960  00000000
02d7e964  00000000
02d7e968  00000000
02d7e96c  00000000
02d7e970  00000000
02d7e974  0000027f
02d7e978  00000100
02d7e97c  0000ffff
02d7e980  70fc1e0a
UIAutomationCore!std::_Hash<std::_Umap_traits<_GUID,ContainerManagerApi::ClientContainerActivit
yData,std::_Uhash_compare<_GUID,std::hash<_GUID>,std::equal_to<_GUID>
>,std::allocator<std::pair<_GUID const ,ContainerManagerApi::ClientContainerActivityData> >,0>
>::_Hash<std::_Umap_traits<_GUID,ContainerManagerApi::ClientContainerActivityData,std::_Uhash_c
ompare<_GUID,std::hash<_GUID>,std::equal_to<_GUID> >,std::allocator<std::pair<_GUID const
,ContainerManagerApi::ClientContainerActivityData> >,0> >+0x44
```

```
02d7e984  00000000
02d7e988  00000000
02d7e98c  00000000
02d7e990  00000000
02d7e994  00000000
02d7e998  00000000
02d7e99c  00000000
02d7e9a0  40078700
02d7e9a4  00000000
02d7e9a8  87000000
02d7e9ac  00004007
02d7e9b0  00000000
02d7e9b4  4005f000
02d7e9b8  00000000
02d7e9bc  80000000
02d7e9c0  00003fff
02d7e9c4  00000000
02d7e9c8  40028000
02d7e9cc  00000000
02d7e9d0  c0000000
02d7e9d4  00003ffe
02d7e9d8  00000000
02d7e9dc  3fff8000
02d7e9e0  00000000
02d7e9e4  0000002b
02d7e9e8  00000053
02d7e9ec  0000002b
02d7e9f0  0000002b
02d7e9f4  0531e758
02d7e9f8  053150a8
02d7e9fc  05315258
02d7ea00  053150a8
02d7ea04  053100a0
02d7ea08  00000000
02d7ea0c  02d7edcc
02d7ea10  08b0fcb1 ApplicationA!ApplicationA.ApplicationA.CrashButton_Click(System.Object,
System.EventArgs)+0x19
02d7ea14  00000023
02d7ea18  00210246
02d7ea1c  02d7edc0
02d7ea20  0000002b
...
...
...

0:000> .cxr 02d7e958
eax=00000000 ebx=05315258 ecx=053100a0 edx=053150a8 esi=053150a8 edi=0531e758
eip=08b0fcb1 esp=02d7edc0 ebp=02d7edcc iopl=0         nv up ei pl zr na pe nc
cs=0023  ss=002b  ds=002b  es=002b  fs=0053  gs=002b              efl=00210246
ApplicationA!ApplicationA.ApplicationA.CrashButton_Click(System.Object, System.EventArgs)+0x19:
08b0fcb1 mov      dword ptr [eax],1                    ds:002b:00000000=????????
```

```
0:000> kL
 *** Stack trace for last set context - .thread/.cxr resets it
 # ChildEBP RetAddr
00 02d7edcc 72c3e7dc      ApplicationA!ApplicationA.ApplicationA.CrashButton_Click(System.Object, System.EventArgs)+0x19
01 02d7ede4 72c57810      System_Windows_Forms!System.Windows.Forms.Control.OnClick+0x3c
02 02d7ee20 72c57955      System_Windows_Forms!System.Windows.Forms.Button.OnClick+0x140
03 02d7ee44 72c465c8      System_Windows_Forms!System.Windows.Forms.Button.OnMouseUp+0xd5
04 02d7ee90 08b0ea53      System_Windows_Forms!System.Windows.Forms.Control.WmMouseUp+0x218
05 02d7eeac 08b0f0d4      System_Windows_Forms!System.Windows.Forms.Control.WndProc(System.Windows.Forms.Message ByRef)+0x95ec7403
06 02d7ef0c 08b0dfbf      System_Windows_Forms!System.Windows.Forms.ButtonBase.WndProc(System.Windows.Forms.Message ByRef)+0x95eb54f4
07 02d7ef4c 08b0261f      System_Windows_Forms!System.Windows.Forms.NativeWindow.Callback(Windows.Win32.Foundation.HWND,
Windows.Win32.MessageId, Windows.Win32.Foundation.WPARAM, Windows.Win32.Foundation.LPARAM)+0x95ce92df
08 02d7ef90 76117c02      System_Windows_Forms_Primitives!ILStubClass.IL_STUB_ReversePInvoke(Windows.Win32.Foundation.HWND,
Windows.Win32.MessageId, Windows.Win32.Foundation.WPARAM, Windows.Win32.Foundation.LPARAM)+0x37
09 02d7efbc 760f6fea      user32!_InternalCallWinProc+0x2a
0a 02d7f0ac 760f5908      user32!UserCallWinProcCheckWow+0x4aa
0b 02d7f128 760f5440      user32!DispatchMessageWorker+0x4b8
0c 02d7f134 7251513d      user32!DispatchMessageW+0x10
0d 02d7f18c 72ea3c41      System_Windows_Forms_Primitives!put_Top+0x2c
0e 02d7f1c4 72ea3a39      System_Windows_Forms!System.Windows.Forms.Application.LightThreadContext.FPushMessageLoop+0x151
0f 02d7f1cc 72ea4f4c      System_Windows_Forms!System.Windows.Forms.Application.LightThreadContext.RunMessageLoop+0x9
10 02d7f22c 72ea4cc8      System_Windows_Forms!System.Windows.Forms.Application.ThreadContext.RunMessageLoopInner+0x25c
11 02d7f258 72c555df      System_Windows_Forms!System.Windows.Forms.Application.ThreadContext.RunMessageLoop+0x38
12 02d7f270 08b0184e      System_Windows_Forms!System.Windows.Forms.Application.Run+0x3f
13 02d7f27c 745b65c3      ApplicationA!ApplicationA.Program.Main()+0x2e
14 02d7f288 7452177a      coreclr!CallDescrWorkerInternal+0x34
15 (Inline) --------      coreclr!CallDescrWorkerWithHandler+0x5c
16 02d7f304 744fa5d2      coreclr!MethodDescCallSite::CallTargetWorker+0x12c
17 (Inline) --------      coreclr!MethodDescCallSite::Call+0x11
18 02d7f418 744fac9a      coreclr!RunMainInternal+0xe4
19 02d7f480 744fab37      coreclr!RunMain+0x9b
1a 02d7f6e0 744fb928      coreclr!Assembly::ExecuteMainMethod+0x16e
1b 02d7f774 744fb327      coreclr!CorHost2::ExecuteAssembly+0x168
1c 02d7f7c4 7488b2a2      coreclr!coreclr_execute_assembly+0xa7
1d (Inline) --------      hostpolicy!coreclr_t::execute_assembly+0x27
1e 02d7f870 7488b4c2      hostpolicy!run_app_for_context+0x452
1f 02d7f8b0 7488beaa      hostpolicy!run_app+0x52
20 02d7f954 748cb7d8      hostpolicy!corehost_main+0xda
21 02d7f9c8 748cd20d      hostfxr!execute_app+0x2d8
22 02d7fa50 748cede5      hostfxr!`anonymous namespace'::read_config_and_execute+0xbd
23 02d7fabc 748cd5c1      hostfxr!fx_muxer_t::handle_exec_host_command+0x115
24 02d7fbc0 748c700b      hostfxr!fx_muxer_t::execute+0x261
25 02d7fc60 003c9311      hostfxr!hostfxr_main_startupinfo+0x7b
26 02d7fd90 003c96f7      ApplicationA_exe!exe_start+0x6b1
27 02d7fde0 003d002c      ApplicationA_exe!wmain+0x127
28 (Inline) --------      ApplicationA_exe!invoke_main+0x1c
29 02d7fe28 77566839      ApplicationA_exe!__scrt_common_main_seh+0xfa
2a 02d7fe38 779a90ef      kernel32!BaseThreadInitThunk+0x19
2b 02d7fe90 779a90bd      ntdll!__RtlUserThreadStart+0x2b
2c 02d7fea0 00000000      ntdll!_RtlUserThreadStart+0x1b
```

11.   We close logging before exiting WinDbg:

```
0:000> .logclose
Closing open log file C:\ANETMDA-Dumps\Windows\x86\ApplicationA.log
```

Note: If the memory dump of a 32-bit process is saved using the 64-bit Task Manager instead of the 32-bit Task Manager from the *SysWOW64* folder, then we won't be able to load the corresponding 32-bit SOS extension even if we specify the x86 target in WinDbg or run the WinDbg (X86) from Debugging Tools for Windows.

Exercise PN3 (Windows)

- **Goal:** Learn how to find problem assemblies, modules, classes, and methods, disassemble code, and analyze CPU spikes

- **Patterns:** Active Thread; Spiking Thread; JIT Code (.NET); Annotated Disassembly (JIT .NET Code); Distributed Spike

- **Commands:** !analyze -v -hang, !IP2MD, !runaway, ~<>k, !U, !DumpMD, !DumpClass, !DumpMT, !DumpModule, !DumpAssembly, !DumpDomain, !DumpIL, .logappend

- \ANETMDA-Dumps\Exercise-PN3-Windows.pdf

Exercise PN3 (Windows)

Goal: Learn how to find problem assemblies, modules, classes, and methods, disassemble code, and analyze CPU spikes.

Patterns: Active Thread; Spiking Thread; JIT Code (.NET); Annotated Disassembly (JIT .NET Code); Distributed Spike.

Commands: !analyze -v -hang, !IP2MD, !runaway, ~<>k, !U, !DumpMD, !DumpClass, !DumpMT, !DumpModule, !DumpAssembly, !DumpDomain, !DumpIL, .logappend

1.　　Launch WinDbg.

2.　　Open \ANETMDA-Dumps\Windows\x64\LINQPad8.DMP

3.　　We get the dump file loaded:

```
Microsoft (R) Windows Debugger Version 10.0.27829.1001 AMD64
Copyright (c) Microsoft Corporation. All rights reserved.


Loading Dump File [C:\ANETMDA-Dumps\Windows\x64\LINQPad8.DMP]
User Mini Dump File with Full Memory: Only application data is available


************* Path validation summary **************
Response                      Time (ms)     Location
Deferred                                    srv*
Symbol search path is: srv*
Executable search path is:
Windows 10 Version 22000 MP (4 procs) Free x64
Product: WinNt, suite: SingleUserTS
Edition build lab: 22000.1.amd64fre.co_release.210604-1628
Debug session time: Sun Apr 27 10:03:00.000 2025 (UTC + 1:00)
System Uptime: 0 days 0:36:06.753
Process Uptime: 0 days 0:07:01.000
.......................................................
.......................................................

For analysis of this file, run !analyze -v
*** WARNING: Unable to verify checksum for LINQPadQuery.dll
LINQPadQuery!UserQuery.ClassMain.DoWork+0x16:
00007ffe`fbbf8446 je      LINQPadQuery!UserQuery.ClassMain.DoWork+0x1d (00007ffe`fbbf844d)
[br=1]
```

4.　　Open a log file using **.logopen** command:

```
0:000> .logopen C:\ANETMDA-Dumps\Windows\x64\LINQPadB.log
Opened log file 'C:\ANETMDA-Dumps\Windows\x64\LINQPadB.log'
```

Note: The WinDbg output may be slightly different on your system if you have a different WinDbg version, a different SOS extension version, you don't have .NET 9 installed, or you have a .NET version different from version 9.0.4 that were on a virtual machine where all the dumps were saved.

5. Type **~*kL** command to verify the correctness of all stack traces (the command execution time may be longer for the first time because symbol files need to be downloaded from the Microsoft symbol server):

```
0:000> ~*kL

.  0  Id: e5c.8d0 Suspend: 0 Teb: 00000047`46cb2000 Unfrozen
 # Child-SP          RetAddr               Call Site
00 00000047`46b2d250 00007ffe`fbbf83f0     LINQPadQuery!UserQuery.ClassMain.DoWork+0x16
01 00000047`46b2d290 00007ffe`fbbf834b     LINQPadQuery!UserQuery.ClassMain.Main+0x30
02 00000047`46b2d2d0 00007ffe`fbbf370c     LINQPadQuery!UserQuery.Main+0x4b
03 00000047`46b2d310 00007ffe`fbbf023f     LINQPad_Runtime!LINQPad.ExecutionModel.ClrQueryRunner.Run+0x1dec
04 00000047`46b2dc60 00007ffe`fb37311a     LINQPad_Runtime!LINQPad.ExecutionModel.Server.RunQuery+0x21f
05 00000047`46b2df40 00007ffe`fb372c42     LINQPad_Runtime!LINQPad.ExecutionModel.Server.PrepareAndRunQuery+0x3ea
06 00000047`46b2e080 00007ffe`fb372b6c     LINQPad_Runtime!LINQPad.ExecutionModel.Server.<ExecuteClrQuery>b__147_0+0x52
07 00000047`46b2e0c0 00007ffe`fb31dc60     LINQPad_Runtime!LINQPad.ExecutionModel.SyncPCQ.<>c__DisplayClass14_0.<Enqueue>b__0+0x4c
08 00000047`46b2e110 00007ffe`fb31d9ae     LINQPad_Runtime!LINQPad.ExecutionModel.SyncPCQ.Consume+0x100
09 00000047`46b2e190 00007ffe`fb31659f     LINQPad_Runtime!LINQPad.ExecutionModel.SyncPCQ.Start+0x2ee
0a 00000047`46b2e290 00007ffe`fb31604b     LINQPad_Runtime!LINQPad.ExecutionModel.ProcessServer.TryRun+0x4cf
0b 00000047`46b2e450 00007ffe`fb315fd4     LINQPad_Runtime!LINQPad.ExecutionModel.ProcessServer.Run+0x3b
0c 00000047`46b2e4a0 00007ffe`fb3156f3     LINQPad_Runtime!LINQPad.RuntimeLoader.Run+0x84
0d 00000047`46b2e4f0 00007ffe`fb31566c     LINQPad_Runtime!LINQPad.RuntimeLoader.Start+0x43
0e 00000047`46b2e570 00007fff`5aee2eb3     LINQPad_Runtime!LINQPad.EntryPoint.Main+0x4c
0f 00000047`46b2e5c0 00007fff`5adc5559     coreclr!CallDescrWorkerInternal+0x83
10 00000047`46b2e600 00007fff`5a32e325     coreclr!RuntimeMethodHandle::InvokeMethod+0x3a9
11 00000047`46b2e930 00007fff`5a32dc2b     System_Private_CoreLib!System.Reflection.MethodBaseInvoker.InvokeDirectByRefWithFewArgs+0xb5
12 00000047`46b2e9b0 00007fff`5a33f910     System_Private_CoreLib!System.Reflection.MethodBaseInvoker.InvokeWithOneArg+0x1bb
13 00000047`46b2ea90 00007fff`5a32d203     System_Private_CoreLib!System.Reflection.RuntimeMethodInfo.Invoke+0x1b0
14 00000047`46b2eb00 00007ffe`fb3119ff     System_Private_CoreLib!System.Reflection.MethodBase.Invoke+0x23
15 00000047`46b2eb40 00007fff`5aee2eb3     LINQPad_Query!LINQPad.ProcessServer.ProcessServerProgram.Main+0x19f
16 00000047`46b2ec10 00007fff`5ae6180c     coreclr!CallDescrWorkerInternal+0x83
17 00000047`46b2ec50 00007fff`5ae4ba54     coreclr!MethodDescCallSite::CallTargetWorker+0x208
18 (Inline Function) --------`--------     coreclr!MethodDescCallSite::Call_RetArgSlot+0xd
19 00000047`46b2ed90 00007fff`5ae4cc19     coreclr!RunMainInternal+0xb8
1a 00000047`46b2eeb0 00007fff`5ae4cf2d     coreclr!RunMain+0xd1
1b 00000047`46b2ef40 00007fff`5ae4c1bb     coreclr!Assembly::ExecuteMainMethod+0x199
1c 00000047`46b2f210 00007fff`5ae4704c     coreclr!CorHost2::ExecuteAssembly+0x1cb
1d 00000047`46b2f320 00007fff`61bee8ec     coreclr!coreclr_execute_assembly+0xcc
1e (Inline Function) --------`--------     hostpolicy!coreclr_t::execute_assembly+0x2d
1f 00000047`46b2f3c0 00007fff`61beebbc     hostpolicy!run_app_for_context+0x58c
20 00000047`46b2f4f0 00007fff`64c61be9     hostpolicy!run_app+0x3c
21 00000047`46b2f530 00007ff6`1e4f7377     hostfxr!fx_muxer_t::run_app+0x109
22 00000047`46b2f5a0 00007ff6`1e505a72     LINQPad8+0x17377
23 00000047`46b2fef0 00007fff`a72853e0     LINQPad8+0x25a72
24 00000047`46b2ff30 00007fff`a82c485b     kernel32!BaseThreadInitThunk+0x10
25 00000047`46b2ff60 00000000`00000000     ntdll!RtlUserThreadStart+0x2b

   1  Id: e5c.484 Suspend: 0 Teb: 00000047`46cb8000 Unfrozen ".NET EventPipe"
 # Child-SP          RetAddr               Call Site
00 00000047`470ff558 00007fff`a5bddcb0     ntdll!NtWaitForMultipleObjects+0x14
01 00000047`470ff560 00007fff`a5bddbae     KERNELBASE!WaitForMultipleObjectsEx+0xf0
02 00000047`470ff850 00007fff`5aeb693f     KERNELBASE!WaitForMultipleObjects+0xe
03 00000047`470ff890 00007fff`5aeb68a0     coreclr!ds_ipc_poll+0x7f
04 00000047`470ffb10 00007fff`5aeb6784     coreclr!ds_ipc_stream_factory_get_next_available_stream+0x108
05 00000047`470ffbe0 00007fff`a72853e0     coreclr!server_thread+0x54
06 00000047`470ffc50 00007fff`a82c485b     kernel32!BaseThreadInitThunk+0x10
07 00000047`470ffc80 00000000`00000000     ntdll!RtlUserThreadStart+0x2b

   2  Id: e5c.df0 Suspend: 0 Teb: 00000047`46cba000 Unfrozen ".NET Debugger"
 # Child-SP          RetAddr               Call Site
00 00000047`471ff408 00007fff`a5bddcb0     ntdll!NtWaitForMultipleObjects+0x14
01 00000047`471ff410 00007fff`5aea7a9e     KERNELBASE!WaitForMultipleObjectsEx+0xf0
02 00000047`471ff700 00007fff`5aea7e26     coreclr!DebuggerRCThread::MainLoop+0xee
03 00000047`471ff7c0 00007fff`5aea785b     coreclr!DebuggerRCThread::ThreadProc+0x12e
04 00000047`471ff820 00007fff`a72853e0     coreclr!DebuggerRCThread::ThreadProcStatic+0x5b
05 00000047`471ff850 00007fff`a82c485b     kernel32!BaseThreadInitThunk+0x10
06 00000047`471ff880 00000000`00000000     ntdll!RtlUserThreadStart+0x2b

   3  Id: e5c.890 Suspend: 0 Teb: 00000047`46cbc000 Unfrozen ".NET Finalizer"
 # Child-SP          RetAddr               Call Site
00 00000047`472ff3b8 00007fff`a5bddcb0     ntdll!NtWaitForMultipleObjects+0x14
01 00000047`472ff3c0 00007fff`5aea8a90     KERNELBASE!WaitForMultipleObjectsEx+0xf0
02 00000047`472ff6b0 00007fff`5aea889f     coreclr!FinalizerThread::WaitForFinalizerEvent+0x78
03 00000047`472ff6f0 00007fff`5ae4ef05     coreclr!FinalizerThread::FinalizerThreadWorker+0x4f
04 (Inline Function) --------`--------     coreclr!ManagedThreadBase_DispatchInner+0xd
05 00000047`472ff940 00007fff`5ae4ee2d     coreclr!ManagedThreadBase_DispatchMiddle+0x79
06 00000047`472ff9f0 00007fff`5ae9e921     coreclr!ManagedThreadBase_DispatchOuter+0x8d
07 (Inline Function) --------`--------     coreclr!ManagedThreadBase_NoADTransition+0x28
08 (Inline Function) --------`--------     coreclr!ManagedThreadBase::FinalizerBase+0x28
09 00000047`472ffa60 00007fff`a72853e0     coreclr!FinalizerThread::FinalizerThreadStart+0x91
0a 00000047`472ffb70 00007fff`a82c485b     kernel32!BaseThreadInitThunk+0x10
0b 00000047`472ffba0 00000000`00000000     ntdll!RtlUserThreadStart+0x2b
```

```
   4  Id: e5c.b80 Suspend: 0 Teb: 00000047`46cc2000 Unfrozen ".NET TP Wait"
 #  Child-SP          RetAddr            Call Site
00 00000047`46b6f2e8 00007fff`a5bddcb0  ntdll!NtWaitForMultipleObjects+0x14
01 00000047`46b6f2f0 00007fff`5ad9e800  KERNELBASE!WaitForMultipleObjectsEx+0xf0
02 00000047`46b6f5e0 00007fff`5ad9e523  coreclr!Thread::DoAppropriateAptStateWait+0x5c
03 00000047`46b6f620 00007fff`5ad9e35a  coreclr!Thread::DoAppropriateWaitWorker+0x17b
04 00000047`46b6f6f0 00007fff`5ad9cd19  coreclr!Thread::DoAppropriateWait+0xa6
05 00000047`46b6f790 00007ffe`fbc66250  coreclr!WaitHandleNative::CorWaitMultipleNative+0xf9
06 00000047`46b6f930 00007fff`5a2c2dcc  System_Private_CoreLib!System.Threading.WaitHandle.WaitAnyMultiple+0xf0
07 00000047`46b6f9b0 00007fff`5aee2eb3  System_Private_CoreLib!System.Threading.PortableThreadPool.WaitThread.WaitThreadStart+0x8c
08 00000047`46b6fa10 00007fff`5ae61568  coreclr!CallDescrWorkerInternal+0x83
09 00000047`46b6fa50 00007fff`5aed15a3  coreclr!DispatchCallSimple+0x60
0a 00000047`46b6fae0 00007fff`5ae4ef05  coreclr!ThreadNative::KickOffThread_Worker+0x63
0b (Inline Function) --------`--------  coreclr!ManagedThreadBase_DispatchInner+0xd
0c 00000047`46b6fb40 00007fff`5ae4ee2d  coreclr!ManagedThreadBase_DispatchMiddle+0x79
0d 00000047`46b6fbf0 00007fff`5ae4efbb  coreclr!ManagedThreadBase_DispatchOuter+0x8d
0e (Inline Function) --------`--------  coreclr!ManagedThreadBase_FullTransition+0x28
0f (Inline Function) --------`--------  coreclr!ManagedThreadBase::KickOff+0x28
10 00000047`46b6fc60 00007fff`a72853e0  coreclr!ThreadNative::KickOffThread+0x7b
11 00000047`46b6fcc0 00007fff`a82c485b  kernel32!BaseThreadInitThunk+0x10
12 00000047`46b6fcf0 00000000`00000000  ntdll!RtlUserThreadStart+0x2b

   5  Id: e5c.878 Suspend: 0 Teb: 00000047`46cc6000 Unfrozen ".NET TP Gate"
 #  Child-SP          RetAddr            Call Site
00 00000047`46baf2d8 00007fff`a5bddcb0  ntdll!NtWaitForMultipleObjects+0x14
01 00000047`46baf2e0 00007fff`5ad9e800  KERNELBASE!WaitForMultipleObjectsEx+0xf0
02 00000047`46baf5d0 00007fff`5ad9e523  coreclr!Thread::DoAppropriateAptStateWait+0x5c
03 00000047`46baf610 00007fff`5ad9e35a  coreclr!Thread::DoAppropriateWaitWorker+0x17b
04 00000047`46baf6e0 00007fff`5ad9e24a  coreclr!Thread::DoAppropriateWait+0xa6
05 00000047`46baf780 00007ffe`fbe43f63  coreclr!WaitHandleNative::CorWaitOneNative+0xdb
06 00000047`46baf8f0 00007fff`5a2c08ed  System_Private_CoreLib!System.Threading.WaitHandle.WaitOneNoCheck+0xc3
07 00000047`46baf970 00007fff`5aee2eb3  System_Private_CoreLib!System.Threading.PortableThreadPool.GateThread.GateThreadStart+0x18d
08 00000047`46bafae0 00007fff`5ae61568  coreclr!CallDescrWorkerInternal+0x83
09 00000047`46bafb20 00007fff`5aed15a3  coreclr!DispatchCallSimple+0x60
0a 00000047`46bafbb0 00007fff`5ae4ef05  coreclr!ThreadNative::KickOffThread_Worker+0x63
0b (Inline Function) --------`--------  coreclr!ManagedThreadBase_DispatchInner+0xd
0c 00000047`46bafc10 00007fff`5ae4ee2d  coreclr!ManagedThreadBase_DispatchMiddle+0x79
0d 00000047`46bafcc0 00007fff`5ae4efbb  coreclr!ManagedThreadBase_DispatchOuter+0x8d
0e (Inline Function) --------`--------  coreclr!ManagedThreadBase_FullTransition+0x28
0f (Inline Function) --------`--------  coreclr!ManagedThreadBase::KickOff+0x28
10 00000047`46bafd30 00007fff`a72853e0  coreclr!ThreadNative::KickOffThread+0x7b
11 00000047`46bafd90 00007fff`a82c485b  kernel32!BaseThreadInitThunk+0x10
12 00000047`46bafdc0 00000000`00000000  ntdll!RtlUserThreadStart+0x2b

   6  Id: e5c.1b24 Suspend: 0 Teb: 00000047`46cce000 Unfrozen ".NET Timer"
 #  Child-SP          RetAddr            Call Site
00 00000047`478ff0f8 00007fff`a5bddcb0  ntdll!NtWaitForMultipleObjects+0x14
01 00000047`478ff100 00007fff`5ad9e800  KERNELBASE!WaitForMultipleObjectsEx+0xf0
02 00000047`478ff3f0 00007fff`5ad9e523  coreclr!Thread::DoAppropriateAptStateWait+0x5c
03 00000047`478ff430 00007fff`5ad9e35a  coreclr!Thread::DoAppropriateWaitWorker+0x17b
04 00000047`478ff500 00007fff`5ad9e24a  coreclr!Thread::DoAppropriateWait+0xa6
05 00000047`478ff5a0 00007fff`5a2a6653  coreclr!WaitHandleNative::CorWaitOneNative+0xdb
06 00000047`478ff710 00007fff`5a2b945f  System_Private_CoreLib!System.Threading.WaitHandle.WaitOneNoCheck+0x83
07 00000047`478ff780 00007fff`5aee2eb3  System_Private_CoreLib!System.Threading.TimerQueue.TimerThread+0x7f
08 00000047`478ff810 00007fff`5ae61568  coreclr!CallDescrWorkerInternal+0x83
09 00000047`478ff850 00007fff`5aed15a3  coreclr!DispatchCallSimple+0x60
0a 00000047`478ff8e0 00007fff`5ae4ef05  coreclr!ThreadNative::KickOffThread_Worker+0x63
0b (Inline Function) --------`--------  coreclr!ManagedThreadBase_DispatchInner+0xd
0c 00000047`478ff940 00007fff`5ae4ee2d  coreclr!ManagedThreadBase_DispatchMiddle+0x79
0d 00000047`478ff9f0 00007fff`5ae4efbb  coreclr!ManagedThreadBase_DispatchOuter+0x8d
0e (Inline Function) --------`--------  coreclr!ManagedThreadBase_FullTransition+0x28
0f (Inline Function) --------`--------  coreclr!ManagedThreadBase::KickOff+0x28
10 00000047`478ffa60 00007fff`a72853e0  coreclr!ThreadNative::KickOffThread+0x7b
11 00000047`478ffac0 00007fff`a82c485b  kernel32!BaseThreadInitThunk+0x10
12 00000047`478ffaf0 00000000`00000000  ntdll!RtlUserThreadStart+0x2b

   7  Id: e5c.1c98 Suspend: 0 Teb: 00000047`46cd2000 Unfrozen
 #  Child-SP          RetAddr            Call Site
00 00000047`47affb48 00007fff`a82d6cdf  ntdll!NtWaitForWorkViaWorkerFactory+0x14
01 00000047`47affb50 00007fff`a72853e0  ntdll!TppWorkerThread+0x2df
02 00000047`47affe40 00007fff`a82c485b  kernel32!BaseThreadInitThunk+0x10
03 00000047`47affe70 00000000`00000000  ntdll!RtlUserThreadStart+0x2b

   8  Id: e5c.1898 Suspend: 0 Teb: 00000047`46cdc000 Unfrozen ".NET TP Worker"
 #  Child-SP          RetAddr            Call Site
00 00000047`474ff348 00007fff`a5bdebd3  ntdll!NtRemoveIoCompletion+0x14
01 00000047`474ff350 00007ffe`fbc63387  KERNELBASE!GetQueuedCompletionStatus+0x53
02 00000047`474ff3b0 00007ffe`fbc5510b  System_Private_CoreLib!System.Threading.LowLevelLifoSemaphore.WaitForSignal+0x107
03 00000047`474ff480 00007fff`5a2c35be  System_Private_CoreLib!System.Threading.LowLevelLifoSemaphore.Wait+0x2ab
04 00000047`474ff530 00007fff`5aee2eb3
System_Private_CoreLib!System.Threading.PortableThreadPool.WorkerThread.WorkerThreadStart+0x12e
05 00000047`474ff640 00007fff`5ae61568  coreclr!CallDescrWorkerInternal+0x83
06 00000047`474ff680 00007fff`5aed15a3  coreclr!DispatchCallSimple+0x60
```

```
07 00000047`474ff710 00007fff`5ae4ef05     coreclr!ThreadNative::KickOffThread_Worker+0x63
08 (Inline Function) --------`--------      coreclr!ManagedThreadBase_DispatchInner+0xd
09 00000047`474ff770 00007fff`5ae4ee2d     coreclr!ManagedThreadBase_DispatchMiddle+0x79
0a 00000047`474ff820 00007fff`5ae4efbb     coreclr!ManagedThreadBase_DispatchOuter+0x8d
0b (Inline Function) --------`--------      coreclr!ManagedThreadBase_FullTransition+0x28
0c (Inline Function) --------`--------      coreclr!ManagedThreadBase::KickOff+0x28
0d 00000047`474ff890 00007fff`a72853e0     coreclr!ThreadNative::KickOffThread+0x7b
0e 00000047`474ff8f0 00007fff`a82c485b     kernel32!BaseThreadInitThunk+0x10
0f 00000047`474ff920 00000000`00000000     ntdll!RtlUserThreadStart+0x2b

    9  Id: e5c.1e7c Suspend: 0 Teb: 00000047`46cde000 Unfrozen ".NET TP Worker"
 # Child-SP          RetAddr               Call Site
00 00000047`47bff6c8 00007fff`a831b903     ntdll!NtDelayExecution+0x14
01 00000047`47bff6d0 00007fff`a5bad031     ntdll!RtlDelayExecution+0x43
02 00000047`47bff700 00007ffe`fbc54f89     KERNELBASE!SleepEx+0x71
03 00000047`47bff780 00007fff`5a2c35be     System_Private_CoreLib!System.Threading.LowLevelLifoSemaphore.Wait+0x129
04 00000047`47bff830 00007fff`5aee2eb3     System_Private_CoreLib!System.Threading.PortableThreadPool.WorkerThread.WorkerThreadStart+0x12e
05 00000047`47bff940 00007fff`5ae61568     coreclr!CallDescrWorkerInternal+0x83
06 00000047`47bff980 00007fff`5aed15a3     coreclr!DispatchCallSimple+0x60
07 00000047`47bffa10 00007fff`5ae4ef05     coreclr!ThreadNative::KickOffThread_Worker+0x63
08 (Inline Function) --------`--------      coreclr!ManagedThreadBase_DispatchInner+0xd
09 00000047`47bffa70 00007fff`5ae4ee2d     coreclr!ManagedThreadBase_DispatchMiddle+0x79
0a 00000047`47bffb20 00007fff`5ae4efbb     coreclr!ManagedThreadBase_DispatchOuter+0x8d
0b (Inline Function) --------`--------      coreclr!ManagedThreadBase_FullTransition+0x28
0c (Inline Function) --------`--------      coreclr!ManagedThreadBase::KickOff+0x28
0d 00000047`47bffb90 00007fff`a72853e0     coreclr!ThreadNative::KickOffThread+0x7b
0e 00000047`47bffbf0 00007fff`a82c485b     kernel32!BaseThreadInitThunk+0x10
0f 00000047`47bffc20 00000000`00000000     ntdll!RtlUserThreadStart+0x2b

   10  Id: e5c.f40 Suspend: 0 Teb: 00000047`46ce0000 Unfrozen ".NET TP Worker"
 # Child-SP          RetAddr               Call Site
00 00000047`479ff788 00007fff`a5bdebd3     ntdll!NtRemoveIoCompletion+0x14
01 00000047`479ff790 00007ffe`fbc63387     KERNELBASE!GetQueuedCompletionStatus+0x53
02 00000047`479ff7f0 00007ffe`fbc5510b     System_Private_CoreLib!System.Threading.LowLevelLifoSemaphore.WaitForSignal+0x107
03 00000047`479ff8c0 00007fff`5a2c35be     System_Private_CoreLib!System.Threading.LowLevelLifoSemaphore.Wait+0x2ab
04 00000047`479ff970 00007fff`5aee2eb3     System_Private_CoreLib!System.Threading.PortableThreadPool.WorkerThread.WorkerThreadStart+0x12e
05 00000047`479ffa80 00007fff`5ae61568     coreclr!CallDescrWorkerInternal+0x83
06 00000047`479ffac0 00007fff`5aed15a3     coreclr!DispatchCallSimple+0x60
07 00000047`479ffb50 00007fff`5ae4ef05     coreclr!ThreadNative::KickOffThread_Worker+0x63
08 (Inline Function) --------`--------      coreclr!ManagedThreadBase_DispatchInner+0xd
09 00000047`479ffbb0 00007fff`5ae4ee2d     coreclr!ManagedThreadBase_DispatchMiddle+0x79
0a 00000047`479ffc60 00007fff`5ae4efbb     coreclr!ManagedThreadBase_DispatchOuter+0x8d
0b (Inline Function) --------`--------      coreclr!ManagedThreadBase_FullTransition+0x28
0c (Inline Function) --------`--------      coreclr!ManagedThreadBase::KickOff+0x28
0d 00000047`479ffcd0 00007fff`a72853e0     coreclr!ThreadNative::KickOffThread+0x7b
0e 00000047`479ffd30 00007fff`a82c485b     kernel32!BaseThreadInitThunk+0x10
0f 00000047`479ffd60 00000000`00000000     ntdll!RtlUserThreadStart+0x2b

   11  Id: e5c.1940 Suspend: 0 Teb: 00000047`46cf6000 Unfrozen
 # Child-SP          RetAddr               Call Site
00 00000047`46effa88 00007fff`a82d6cdf     ntdll!NtWaitForWorkViaWorkerFactory+0x14
01 00000047`46effa90 00007fff`a72853e0     ntdll!TppWorkerThread+0x2df
02 00000047`46effd80 00007fff`a82c485b     kernel32!BaseThreadInitThunk+0x10
03 00000047`46effdb0 00000000`00000000     ntdll!RtlUserThreadStart+0x2b

   12  Id: e5c.1ee4 Suspend: 0 Teb: 00000047`46d00000 Unfrozen ".NET TP Worker"
 # Child-SP          RetAddr               Call Site
00 00000047`46fff378 00007fff`a5bdebd3     ntdll!NtRemoveIoCompletion+0x14
01 00000047`46fff380 00007ffe`fbc63387     KERNELBASE!GetQueuedCompletionStatus+0x53
02 00000047`46fff3e0 00007ffe`fbc5510b     System_Private_CoreLib!System.Threading.LowLevelLifoSemaphore.WaitForSignal+0x107
03 00000047`46fff4b0 00007fff`5a2c35be     System_Private_CoreLib!System.Threading.LowLevelLifoSemaphore.Wait+0x2ab
04 00000047`46fff560 00007fff`5aee2eb3     System_Private_CoreLib!System.Threading.PortableThreadPool.WorkerThread.WorkerThreadStart+0x12e
05 00000047`46fff670 00007fff`5ae61568     coreclr!CallDescrWorkerInternal+0x83
06 00000047`46fff6b0 00007fff`5aed15a3     coreclr!DispatchCallSimple+0x60
07 00000047`46fff740 00007fff`5ae4ef05     coreclr!ThreadNative::KickOffThread_Worker+0x63
08 (Inline Function) --------`--------      coreclr!ManagedThreadBase_DispatchInner+0xd
09 00000047`46fff7a0 00007fff`5ae4ee2d     coreclr!ManagedThreadBase_DispatchMiddle+0x79
0a 00000047`46fff850 00007fff`5ae4efbb     coreclr!ManagedThreadBase_DispatchOuter+0x8d
0b (Inline Function) --------`--------      coreclr!ManagedThreadBase_FullTransition+0x28
0c (Inline Function) --------`--------      coreclr!ManagedThreadBase::KickOff+0x28
0d 00000047`46fff8c0 00007fff`a72853e0     coreclr!ThreadNative::KickOffThread+0x7b
0e 00000047`46fff920 00007fff`a82c485b     kernel32!BaseThreadInitThunk+0x10
0f 00000047`46fff950 00000000`00000000     ntdll!RtlUserThreadStart+0x2b

   13  Id: e5c.1454 Suspend: 0 Teb: 00000047`46d02000 Unfrozen
 # Child-SP          RetAddr               Call Site
00 00000047`475ff648 00007fff`a82d6cdf     ntdll!NtWaitForWorkViaWorkerFactory+0x14
01 00000047`475ff650 00007fff`a72853e0     ntdll!TppWorkerThread+0x2df
02 00000047`475ff940 00007fff`a82c485b     kernel32!BaseThreadInitThunk+0x10
03 00000047`475ff970 00000000`00000000     ntdll!RtlUserThreadStart+0x2b
```

```
 14  Id: e5c.980 Suspend: 0 Teb: 00000047`46d06000 Unfrozen ".NET Tiered Compilation Worker"
 # Child-SP          RetAddr               Call Site
00 00000047`473ff6d8 00007fff`a5bd10ce   ntdll!NtWaitForSingleObject+0x14
01 00000047`473ff6e0 00007fff`5aea93a3   KERNELBASE!WaitForSingleObjectEx+0x8e
02 (Inline Function) --------`--------    coreclr!CLREventWaitHelper2+0x6
03 00000047`473ff780 00007fff`5aea87a0   coreclr!CLREventWaitHelper+0xf
04 (Inline Function) --------`--------    coreclr!CLREventBase::WaitEx+0x12
05 (Inline Function) --------`--------    coreclr!CLREventBase::Wait+0x12
06 00000047`473ff7d0 00007fff`5aea8645   coreclr!TieredCompilationManager::BackgroundWorkerStart+0x11c
07 00000047`473ff820 00007fff`5ae4ef05   coreclr!TieredCompilationManager::BackgroundWorkerBootstrapper1+0x55
08 (Inline Function) --------`--------    coreclr!ManagedThreadBase_DispatchInner+0xd
09 00000047`473ff860 00007fff`5ae4ee2d   coreclr!ManagedThreadBase_DispatchMiddle+0x79
0a 00000047`473ff910 00007fff`5aedc8da   coreclr!ManagedThreadBase_DispatchOuter+0x8d
0b (Inline Function) --------`--------    coreclr!ManagedThreadBase_FullTransition+0x24
0c (Inline Function) --------`--------    coreclr!ManagedThreadBase::KickOff+0x24
0d 00000047`473ff980 00007fff`a72853e0   coreclr!TieredCompilationManager::BackgroundWorkerBootstrapper0+0x3a
0e 00000047`473ff9d0 00007fff`a82c485b   kernel32!BaseThreadInitThunk+0x10
0f 00000047`473ffa00 00000000`00000000   ntdll!RtlUserThreadStart+0x2b
```

Note: We see that most threads have the **coreclr** module on their stack traces. We also see active thread #0 since its top frame is not inside any waiting function.

6.   We load the corresponding SOS extension (and unload the previous, if any).

```
0:000> .unload sos
No extension named 'sos' in chain

0:000> .load C:\Users\dmitr\.dotnet\sos\sos.dll
```

7.   We check if there are .NET exceptions on each thread:

```
0:000> ~*e !pe
There is no current managed exception on this thread
The current thread is unmanaged
The current thread is unmanaged
There is no current managed exception on this thread
There is no current managed exception on this thread
There is no current managed exception on this thread
There is no current managed exception on this thread
The current thread is unmanaged
There is no current managed exception on this thread
There is no current managed exception on this thread
There is no current managed exception on this thread
The current thread is unmanaged
There is no current managed exception on this thread
The current thread is unmanaged
There is no current managed exception on this thread
```

8.   "The customer" reported that one of the application windows was unresponsive. We now try the default WinDbg analysis command with **-hang** switch:

```
0:000> !analyze -v -hang
..............................................
..............................................
..............................
*** WARNING: Unable to verify checksum for LINQPadQuery.dll

************** Symbol Loading Error Summary **************
Module name         Error
LINQPadQuery        The system cannot find the file specified

You can troubleshoot most symbol related issues by turning on symbol loading diagnostics (!sym noisy) and repeating the command that caused symbols to be loaded.
You should also verify that your symbol search path (.sympath) is correct.
ClrmaManagedAnalysis::AssociateClient
AssociateClient trying managed CLRMA
AssociateClient trying DAC CLRMA
*************************************************************
*                                                         *
*                    Exception Analysis                   *
*                                                         *
*************************************************************
```

```
ClrmaManagedAnalysis::GetThread 08d0
ClrmaThread::Initialize 08d0
~ClrmaThread
ClrmaManagedAnalysis::GetThread 0484
ClrmaThread::Initialize 0484
ClrmaThread::Initialize FAILED managed thread not found
~ClrmaThread
ClrmaManagedAnalysis::GetThread 0df0
ClrmaThread::Initialize 0df0
ClrmaThread::Initialize FAILED managed thread not found
~ClrmaThread
ClrmaManagedAnalysis::GetThread 0890
ClrmaThread::Initialize 0890
~ClrmaThread
ClrmaManagedAnalysis::GetThread 0b80
ClrmaThread::Initialize 0b80
~ClrmaThread
ClrmaManagedAnalysis::GetThread 0878
ClrmaThread::Initialize 0878
~ClrmaThread
ClrmaManagedAnalysis::GetThread 1b24
ClrmaThread::Initialize 1b24
~ClrmaThread
ClrmaManagedAnalysis::GetThread 1c98
ClrmaThread::Initialize 1c98
ClrmaThread::Initialize FAILED managed thread not found
~ClrmaThread
ClrmaManagedAnalysis::GetThread 1898
ClrmaThread::Initialize 1898
~ClrmaThread
ClrmaManagedAnalysis::GetThread 1e7c
ClrmaThread::Initialize 1e7c
~ClrmaThread
ClrmaManagedAnalysis::GetThread 0f40
ClrmaThread::Initialize 0f40
~ClrmaThread
ClrmaManagedAnalysis::GetThread 1940
ClrmaThread::Initialize 1940
ClrmaThread::Initialize FAILED managed thread not found
~ClrmaThread
ClrmaManagedAnalysis::GetThread 1ee4
ClrmaThread::Initialize 1ee4
~ClrmaThread
ClrmaManagedAnalysis::GetThread 1454
ClrmaThread::Initialize 1454
ClrmaThread::Initialize FAILED managed thread not found
~ClrmaThread
ClrmaManagedAnalysis::GetThread 0980
ClrmaThread::Initialize 0980
~ClrmaThread
ClrmaManagedAnalysis::get_ProviderName
ClrmaManagedAnalysis::GetThread ffffffff
ClrmaThread::Initialize 08d0
ClrmaThread:get_CurrentException
ClrmaThread:get_NestedExceptionCount
~ClrmaThread


KEY_VALUES_STRING: 1

    Key  : Analysis.CPU.mSec
    Value: 2718

    Key  : Analysis.Elapsed.mSec
    Value: 5047

    Key  : Analysis.IO.Other.Mb
    Value: 0

    Key  : Analysis.IO.Read.Mb
    Value: 2

    Key  : Analysis.IO.Write.Mb
    Value: 0

    Key  : Analysis.Init.CPU.mSec
    Value: 8031

    Key  : Analysis.Init.Elapsed.mSec
    Value: 1310616

    Key  : Analysis.Memory.CommitPeak.Mb
    Value: 314

    Key  : Analysis.Version.DbgEng
    Value: 10.0.27829.1001

    Key  : Analysis.Version.Description
    Value: 10.2503.24.01 amd64fre

    Key  : Analysis.Version.Ext
    Value: 1.2503.24.1

    Key  : CLR.Engine
    Value: CORECLR

    Key  : CLR.Version
    Value: 9.0.425.16305

    Key  : Failure.Bucket
    Value: APPLICATION_HANG_BusyHang_cfffffff_LINQPadQuery.dll!UserQuery.ClassMain.DoWork

    Key  : Failure.Exception.Code
    Value: 0xcfffffff

    Key  : Failure.Hash
    Value: {a511eba0-c4ce-8c81-b092-0b342efebb2b}

    Key  : Failure.ProblemClass.Primary
    Value: BusyHang

    Key  : Faulting.IP.Type
    Value: Null

    Key  : Timeline.OS.Boot.DeltaSec
    Value: 2166

    Key  : Timeline.Process.Start.DeltaSec
    Value: 421
```

```
        Key  : WER.OS.Branch
        Value: co_release

        Key  : WER.OS.Version
        Value: 10.0.22000.1

        Key  : WER.Process.Version
        Value: 1.0.8.0


    FILE_IN_CAB:  LINQPad8.DMP

    NTGLOBALFLAG:  400

    APPLICATION_VERIFIER_FLAGS:  0

    CONTEXT:  (.cxr;r)
    rax=0000000000000001 rbx=0000004746b2e7c0 rcx=00000155d5cbbd98
    rdx=0000004746b2d290 rsi=0000004746b2e668 rdi=00007ffefb5dc640
    rip=00007ffefbbf8446 rsp=0000004746b2d250 rbp=0000004746b2d280
     r8=0000004746b2d008  r9=0000004746b2d150 r10=0000000000000000
    r11=0000004746b2d150 r12=00000155cf238b40 r13=0000000000000000
    r14=00007ffefb297408 r15=0000000000000000
    iopl=0         nv up ei pl zr na po nc
    cs=0033  ss=002b  ds=002b  es=002b  fs=0053  gs=002b             efl=00000246
    LINQPadQuery!UserQuery.ClassMain.DoWork+0x16:
    00007ffe`fbbf8446 je      LINQPadQuery!UserQuery.ClassMain.DoWork+0x1d (00007ffe`fbbf844d) [br=1]

    EXCEPTION_RECORD:  (.exr -1)
    ExceptionAddress: 0000000000000000
       ExceptionCode: 80000003 (Break instruction exception)
      ExceptionFlags: 00000000
    NumberParameters: 0

    FAULTING_THREAD:  8d0

    PROCESS_NAME:  LINQPad8.exe

    WATSON_BKT_EVENT:  AppHang

    BLOCKING_THREAD:  8d0

    ERROR_CODE: (NTSTATUS) 0xcfffffff - <Unable to get error code text>

    EXCEPTION_CODE_STR:  cfffffff

    DERIVED_WAIT_CHAIN:

    Dl Eid Cid      WaitType
    -- --- ------- -------------------------
     0   e5c.8d0 Unknown

    WAIT_CHAIN_COMMAND:  ~0s;k;;

    STACK_TEXT:
    00000047`46b2d250 00007ffe`fbbf83f0     : 00000155`d5cbbd98 00000000`000008d0 00000155`cf231428 00007ffe`fbc70958 : LINQPadQuery!UserQuery.ClassMain.DoWork+0x16
    00000047`46b2d290 00007ffe`fbbf834b     : 00000155`d5cbbd98 000000000`000008d0 00000155`cf231428 00007ffe`fbc70958 : LINQPadQuery!UserQuery.ClassMain.Main+0x30
    00000047`46b2d2d0 00007ffe`fbbf370c     : 00000155`d5cbb408 00000155`d3090010 00000155`d3090010 00007ffe`fbb7a3d0 : LINQPadQuery!UserQuery.Main+0x4b
    00000047`46b2d310 00007ffe`fbbf023f     : 00000155`d5cb3420 00000000`00000000 00000000`00000155 d5c21a88 00000155`cf238b40 : LINQPad_Runtime!LINQPad.ExecutionModel.ClrQueryRunner.Run+0x1dec
    00000047`46b2dc60 00007ffe`fb37311a     : 00000155`d5c4bfc0 00000155`d5cb3420 00000155`d3804500 00000155`cf238b40 : LINQPad_Runtime!LINQPad.ExecutionModel.Server.RunQuery+0x21f
    00000047`46b2df40 00007ffe`fb372c42     : 00000155`d5c4bfc0 00000155`d5cb3420 00000195`d3290100 00000195`d8f5f840 : LINQPad_Runtime!LINQPad.ExecutionModel.Server.PrepareAndRunQuery+0x3ea
    00000047`46b2e080 00007ffe`fb372b6c     : 00000155`d5c4bfc0 00000000`00000000 00000155`d5c27570 00000155`cf238b40 : LINQPad_Runtime!LINQPad.ExecutionModel.Server.<ExecuteClrQuery>b__147_0+0x52
    00000047`46b2e0c0 00007ffe`fb31dc60     : 00000155`d5cb3328 00000000`00000000 00000000`00000000 00000155`d5c27570 00000155`cf238b40 : LINQPad_Runtime!LINQPad.ExecutionModel.SyncPCQ.<>c__DisplayClass14_0.<Enqueue>b__0+0x4c
    00000047`46b2e110 00007ffe`fb31d9ae     : 00000155`d5c26c48 00000000`00000000 00000000`00000000 00000155`d39644b0 00000155`cf238b40 : LINQPad_Runtime!LINQPad.ExecutionModel.SyncPCQ.Consume+0x100
    00000047`46b2e190 00007ffe`fb31659f     : 00000155`d5c26c48 00000000`00000000 00000000`00000000 00000000`00000000 : LINQPad_Runtime!LINQPad.ExecutionModel.SyncPCQ.Start+0x2ee
    00000047`46b2e290 00007ffe`fb31604b     : 00000155`d5c0b738 00000196`65c143f4 00000000`00000000 00000155`d3400000 : LINQPad_Runtime!LINQPad.ExecutionModel.ProcessServer.TryRun+0x4cf
    00000047`46b2e450 00007ffe`fb315fd4     : 00000155`d5c0b738 00000196`65c143f4 00000000`00000000 00000155`d3400000 : LINQPad_Runtime!LINQPad.ExecutionModel.ProcessServer.Run+0x3b
    00000047`46b2e4a0 00007ffe`fb3156f3     : 00000155`d5c0b738 00000000`00000000 00000000`00000000 00000155`d3400000 : LINQPad_Runtime!LINQPad.RuntimeLoader.Run+0x84
    00000047`46b2e4f0 00007ffe`fb31566c     : 00000155`d5c0b738 00007ffe`fb50f398 00007fff`5adc51b0 00000047`46b2e719 : LINQPad_Runtime!LINQPad.RuntimeLoader.Start+0x43
    00000047`46b2e570 00007fff`5aee2eb3     : 00000155`d5c0b738 00007ffe`fb50f398 00007fff`5adc51b0 00000047`46b2e719 : LINQPad_Runtime!LINQPad.EntryPoint.Main+0x4c
    00000047`46b2e5c0 00007fff`5adc5559     : 00007ffe`fb3c5328 00007ffe`fb3c5328 00000000`00000000 00007ffe`fb5dc640 : coreclr!CallDescrWorkerInternal+0x83
    00000047`46b2e600 00007fff`5a32e325     : 00000000`00000000 00000047`46b2e960 00000155`d383c028 00000000`00000000 : coreclr!RuntimeMethodHandle::InvokeMethod+0x3a9
    00000047`46b2e930 00007fff`5a32dc2b     : 00000155`d383bfd8 00000000`00000000 00000000`00000000 00000000`00000000 : System_Private_CoreLib!System.Reflection.MethodBaseInvoker.InvokeDirectByRefWithFewArgs+0xb5
    00000047`46b2e9b0 00007fff`5a33f910     : 00000155`d383bfd8 00000000`00000000 00000000`00000000 00000000`00000000 : System_Private_CoreLib!System.Reflection.MethodBaseInvoker.InvokeWithOneArg+0x1bb
    00000047`46b2ea08 00007fff`5a32d203     : 00000155`d383bf50 00000000`00000000 00000000`00000000 00000000`00000000 : System_Private_CoreLib!System.Reflection.RuntimeMethodInfo.Invoke+0x1b0
    00000047`46b2eb00 00007fff`fb3119ff     : 00000155`d383bf50 00000000`00000000 00000155`d383bfb8 00007ffe`fb292170 : System_Private_CoreLib!System.Reflection.MethodBase.Invoke+0x23
    00000047`46b2eb40 00007fff`5aee2eb3     : 00000155`d5c0b738 00000047`46b2f238 00000047`46b2f238 00000047`46b2ee49 : LINQPad_Query!LINQPad.ProcessServer.ProcessServerProgram.Main+0x19f
    00000047`46b2ec10 00007fff`5ae6180c     : 00000047`46b2f238 00000000`00000000 00000000`00000000 00000047`46b2ee58 00007fff`00000001 : coreclr!CallDescrWorkerInternal+0x83
    00000047`46b2ec50 00007fff`5ae4ba54     : 00000047`46b2ef00 00000000`00000000 00000000`00000000 00007fff`5ae7b606 : coreclr!MethodDescCallSite::CallTargetWorker+0x208
    (Inline Function) --------`--------     : --------`-------- --------`-------- --------`-------- --------`-------- : coreclr!MethodDescCallSite::Call_RetArgSlot+0xd
    00000047`46b2ed90 00007fff`5ae4cc19     : 00000155`d5c0b738 00000155`d380f070 00000000`00000000 00000047`46b2f238 : coreclr!RunMainInternal+0xb8
    00000047`46b2eeb0 00007fff`5ae4cf2d     : 00000155`cf238b40 00007ffe`00000000 00007ffe`fb3c5848 00000000`00000000 : coreclr!RunMain+0xd1
    00000047`46b2ef40 00007fff`5ae4c1bb     : 00000000`00000000 00000047`46b2f210 00000000`00000000 00000155`cf2ce670 : coreclr!Assembly::ExecuteMainMethod+0x199
    00000047`46b2f210 00007fff`5ae4704c     : 00000000`00000001 00000047`46b2f210 00000000`0000000e 00007fff`61bd2350 : coreclr!CorHost2::ExecuteAssembly+0x1cb
    00000047`46b2f320 00007fff`61bee8ec     : 00000155`cf27aca0 00000155`cf27acb0 00000155`cf229840 00000155`cf28b8f0 : coreclr!coreclr_execute_assembly+0xcc
    (Inline Function) --------`--------     : --------`-------- --------`-------- --------`-------- --------`-------- : hostpolicy!coreclr_t::execute_assembly+0x2d
    00000047`46b2f3c0 00007fff`61beebbc     : 00000155`cf2cccf0 00000000`00000000 00007fff`61c261e0 00000155`cf2cccf0 : hostpolicy!run_app_for_context+0x58c
    00000047`46b2f4f0 00007fff`64c61be9     : 00000155`cf2cccf0 00000155`cf229390 00000155`cf229390 00000000`00000000 : hostpolicy!run_app+0x3c
    00000047`46b2f530 00007ff6`1e4f7377     : 00000155`cf23b210 00000155`cf229390 00000000`00000000 00007ff6`1e55dc50 : hostfxr!fx_muxer_t::run_app+0x109
    00000047`46b2f5a0 00007ff6`1e505a72     : 00000000`0000000a 00000000`00000000 00000000`00000000 00000000`00000000 : LINQPad8!0x17377
    00000047`46b2fef0 00007fff`a72853e0     : 00000000`00000000 00000000`00000000 00000000`00000000 00000000`00000000 : LINQPad8!0x25a72
    00000047`46b2ff30 00007fff`a82c485b     : 00000000`00000000 00000000`00000000 00000000`00000000 00000000`00000000 : kernel32!BaseThreadInitThunk+0x10
    00000047`46b2ff60 00000000`00000000     : 00000000`00000000 00000000`00000000 00000000`00000000 00000000`00000000 : ntdll!RtlUserThreadStart+0x2b


    STACK_COMMAND:  ~0s; .ecxr ; kb

    SYMBOL_NAME:  LINQPadQuery!UserQuery.ClassMain.DoWork+16

    MODULE_NAME:  LINQPadQuery

    IMAGE_NAME:  LINQPadQuery.dll

    FAILURE_BUCKET_ID:  APPLICATION_HANG_BusyHang_cfffffff_LINQPadQuery.dll!UserQuery.ClassMain.DoWork

    OS_VERSION:  10.0.22000.1

    BUILDLAB_STR:  co_release

    OSPLATFORM_TYPE:  x64

    OSNAME:  Windows 10
```

139

FAILURE_ID_HASH: {a511eba0-c4ce-8c81-b092-0b342efebb2b}

Followup: MachineOwner

CLRMAReleaseInstance
~ClrmaManagedAnalysis

Note: We see the command didn't find anything useful except the hint at the **DoWork** method call, but at the same time, it shows only the unmanaged stack trace from the main (#0) thread. If we execute **!analyze -v** command instead, it only suggests that the dump was manually generated via a breakpoint:

ERROR_CODE: (NTSTATUS) 0x80000003 - {EXCEPTION} Breakpoint A breakpoint has been reached.

...

FAILURE_BUCKET_ID: BREAKPOINT_80000003_LINQPadQuery.dll!UserQuery.ClassMain.DoWork

9.   Let's now check the managed stack trace for thread #0 (**!CLRStack** command):

```
0:000> !CLRStack
OS Thread Id: 0x8d0 (0)
        Child SP           IP Call Site
0000004746B2D250 00007ffefbbf8446 UserQuery+ClassMain.DoWork()
0000004746B2D290 00007ffefbbf83f0 UserQuery+ClassMain.Main()
0000004746B2D2D0 00007ffefbbf834b UserQuery.Main()
0000004746B2D310 00007ffefbbf370c LINQPad.ExecutionModel.ClrQueryRunner.Run()
0000004746B2DC60 00007ffefbbf023f LINQPad.ExecutionModel.Server.RunQuery(LINQPad.ExecutionModel.QueryRunner)
0000004746B2DF40 00007ffefb37311a LINQPad.ExecutionModel.Server.PrepareAndRunQuery(LINQPad.ExecutionModel.QueryRunner)
0000004746B2E080 00007ffefb372c42 LINQPad.ExecutionModel.Server.b__147_0()
0000004746B2E0C0 00007ffefb372b6c LINQPad.ExecutionModel.SyncPCQ+c__DisplayClass14_0.b__0()
0000004746B2E110 00007ffefb31dc60 LINQPad.ExecutionModel.SyncPCQ.Consume()
0000004746B2E190 00007ffefb31d9ae LINQPad.ExecutionModel.SyncPCQ.Start(Boolean, System.String, Boolean)
0000004746B2E290 00007ffefb31659f LINQPad.ExecutionModel.ProcessServer.TryRun(System.String[])
0000004746B2E450 00007ffefb31604b LINQPad.ExecutionModel.ProcessServer.Run(System.String[])
0000004746B2E4A0 00007ffefb315fd4 LINQPad.RuntimeLoader.Run(System.String[])
0000004746B2E4F0 00007ffefb3156f3 LINQPad.RuntimeLoader.Start(System.String[])
0000004746B2E570 00007ffefb31566c LINQPad.EntryPoint.Main(System.String[])
0000004746B2E7F8 00007fff5aee2eb3 [HelperMethodFrame_PROTECTOBJ: 0000004746b2e7f8]
System.RuntimeMethodHandle.InvokeMethod(System.Object, Void**, System.Signature, Boolean)
0000004746B2E930 00007fff5a32e325 System.Reflection.MethodBaseInvoker.InvokeDirectByRefWithFewArgs(System.Object,
System.Span`1<System.Object>, System.Reflection.BindingFlags)
0000004746B2E9B0 00007fff5a32dc2b System.Reflection.MethodBaseInvoker.InvokeWithOneArg(System.Object,
System.Reflection.BindingFlags, System.Reflection.Binder, System.Object[], System.Globalization.CultureInfo)
0000004746B2EA90 00007fff5a33f910 System.Reflection.RuntimeMethodInfo.Invoke(System.Object,
System.Reflection.BindingFlags, System.Reflection.Binder, System.Object[], System.Globalization.CultureInfo)
0000004746B2EB00 00007fff5a32d203 System.Reflection.MethodBase.Invoke(System.Object, System.Object[])
0000004746B2EB40 00007ffefb3119ff LINQPad.ProcessServer.ProcessServerProgram.Main(System.String[])
```

Note: If we compare **!CLRStack** with **k**, we see that return addresses are on different lines:

```
0:000> k 5
 # Child-SP          RetAddr               Call Site
00 00000047`46b2d250 00007ffe`fbbf83f0     LINQPadQuery!UserQuery.ClassMain.DoWork+0x16
01 00000047`46b2d290 00007ffe`fbbf834b     LINQPadQuery!UserQuery.ClassMain.Main+0x30
02 00000047`46b2d2d0 00007ffe`fbbf370c     LINQPadQuery!UserQuery.Main+0x4b
03 00000047`46b2d310 00007ffe`fbbf023f     LINQPad_Runtime!LINQPad.ExecutionModel.ClrQueryRunner.Run+0x1dec
04 00000047`46b2dc60 00007ffe`fb37311a     LINQPad_Runtime!LINQPad.ExecutionModel.Server.RunQuery+0x21f
```

```
0:000> !CLRStack
OS Thread Id: 0x8d0 (0)
        Child SP           IP Call Site
0000004746B2D250 00007ffefbbf8446 UserQuery+ClassMain.DoWork()
0000004746B2D290 00007ffefbbf83f0 UserQuery+ClassMain.Main()
0000004746B2D2D0 00007ffefbbf834b UserQuery.Main()
0000004746B2D310 00007ffefbbf370c LINQPad.ExecutionModel.ClrQueryRunner.Run()
0000004746B2DC60 00007ffefbbf023f LINQPad.ExecutionModel.Server.RunQuery(LINQPad.ExecutionModel.QueryRunner)
[...]
```

10.   In the previous versions of .NET versions of the unmanaged stack trace, we also see technology-specific subtraces with possible JIT calls and double-check them using the **!IP2MD** command, for example, from the previous edition that used .NET 5 and .NET 6:

```
0:000> kL
 # Child-SP          RetAddr           Call Site
00 00000049`e1d7cf60 00007ffc`c79405ef 0x00007ffc`c794063a
01 00000049`e1d7cf90 00007ffc`c7940548 0x00007ffc`c79405ef
02 00000049`e1d7cfd0 00007ffc`c7755a05 0x00007ffc`c7940548
03 00000049`e1d7d010 00007ffc`c77523ee 0x00007ffc`c7755a05
04 00000049`e1d7d890 00007ffc`c774d330 0x00007ffc`c77523ee
05 00000049`e1d7db60 00007ffc`c774babf 0x00007ffc`c774d330
06 00000049`e1d7dca0 00007ffc`c774b5dc 0x00007ffc`c774babf
07 00000049`e1d7dce0 00007ffc`c7717f15 0x00007ffc`c774b5dc
08 00000049`e1d7dd30 00007ffc`c7717c6b 0x00007ffc`c7717f15
09 00000049`e1d7ddc0 00007ffc`c715a761 0x00007ffc`c7717c6b
0a 00000049`e1d7deb0 00007ffc`c7157cca 0x00007ffc`c715a761
0b 00000049`e1d7e010 00007ffc`c7157c55 0x00007ffc`c7157cca
0c 00000049`e1d7e060 00007ffc`c7156689 0x00007ffc`c7157c55
0d 00000049`e1d7e0b0 00007ffc`c7155cd5 0x00007ffc`c7156689
0e 00000049`e1d7e130 00007ffd`26c99373 0x00007ffc`c7155cd5
0f 00000049`e1d7e170 00007ffd`26bc8efa coreclr!CallDescrWorkerInternal+0x83
10 00000049`e1d7e1b0 00007ffd`26bc8741 coreclr!CallDescrWorkerReflectionWrapper+0x1a
11 00000049`e1d7e200 00007ffd`26806f76 coreclr!RuntimeMethodHandle::InvokeMethod+0x3d1
12 00000049`e1d7e740 00007ffd`268017ee
System_Private_CoreLib!System.Reflection.RuntimeMethodInfo.Invoke(System.Object, System.Reflection.BindingFlags,
System.Reflection.Binder, System.Object[], System.Globalization.CultureInfo)$##6004B40+0xa6
13 00000049`e1d7e7b0 00007ffc`c71466e1 System_Private_CoreLib!System.Reflection.MethodBase.Invoke(System.Object,
System.Object[])$##6004A46+0x1e
14 00000049`e1d7e7f0 00007ffd`26c99373 0x00007ffc`c71466e1
15 00000049`e1d7e870 00007ffd`26b7d0fa coreclr!CallDescrWorkerInternal+0x83
16 00000049`e1d7e8b0 00007ffd`26c0077b coreclr!MethodDescCallSite::CallTargetWorker+0x3d2
17 (Inline Function) --------`-------- coreclr!MethodDescCallSite::Call_RetArgSlot+0xd
18 00000049`e1d7ea40 00007ffd`26c005aa coreclr!RunMainInternal+0xbb
19 00000049`e1d7eb70 00007ffd`26c00309 coreclr!RunMain+0xd2
1a 00000049`e1d7ec20 00007ffd`26c000c8 coreclr!Assembly::ExecuteMainMethod+0x1cd
1b 00000049`e1d7efb0 00007ffd`26bc2962 coreclr!CorHost2::ExecuteAssembly+0x1c8
1c 00000049`e1d7f120 00007ffd`4b522b26 coreclr!coreclr_execute_assembly+0xe2
1d (Inline Function) --------`-------- hostpolicy!coreclr_t::execute_assembly+0x2b
1e 00000049`e1d7f1c0 00007ffd`4b522d67 hostpolicy!run_app_for_context+0x3be
1f 00000049`e1d7f350 00007ffd`4b5239eb hostpolicy!run_app+0x37
20 00000049`e1d7f390 00007ffd`4b67399e hostpolicy!corehost_main+0xfb
21 00000049`e1d7f550 00007ffd`4b677210 hostfxr!execute_app+0x1de
22 (Inline Function) --------`-------- hostfxr!?A0xeb1db345::read_config_and_execute+0x10a
23 00000049`e1d7f640 00007ffd`4b675a7b hostfxr!fx_muxer_t::handle_exec_host_command+0x214
24 00000049`e1d7f730 00007ffd`4b672029 hostfxr!fx_muxer_t::execute+0x39b
25 00000049`e1d7f870 00007ff7`60eefa1f hostfxr!hostfxr_main_startupinfo+0x89
26 00000049`e1d7f970 00007ff7`60eefdf7 LINQPad6_Query_exe!exe_start+0x63f
27 00000049`e1d7fb80 00007ff7`60ef1fa8 LINQPad6_Query_exe!wmain+0xc7
28 (Inline Function) --------`-------- LINQPad6_Query_exe!invoke_main+0x22
29 00000049`e1d7fca0 00007ffd`557f7034 LINQPad6_Query_exe!__scrt_common_main_seh+0x10c
2a 00000049`e1d7fce0 00007ffd`575e2651 kernel32!BaseThreadInitThunk+0x14
2b 00000049`e1d7fd10 00000000`00000000 ntdll!RtlUserThreadStart+0x21


0:000> !IP2MD 0x00007ffc`c794063a
MethodDesc:    00007ffcc794d388
Method Name:        UserQuery+ClassMain.DoWork()
Class:              00007ffcc794d2a8
MethodTable:        00007ffcc794d3c8
mdToken:            0000000006000005
Module:             00007ffcc794c080
IsJitted:           yes
Current CodeAddr:   00007ffcc7940630
Version History:
  ILCodeVersion:    0000000000000000
  ReJIT ID:         0
  IL Addr:          0000017c79ee20a6
```

```
              CodeAddr:            00007ffcc7940630  (MinOptJitted)
              NativeCodeVersion:   0000000000000000
```

```
0:000> !IP2MD 0x00007ffc`c79405ef
MethodDesc:      00007ffcc794d370
Method Name:            UserQuery+ClassMain.Main()
Class:                  00007ffcc794d2a8
MethodTable:            00007ffcc794d3c8
mdToken:                0000000006000004
Module:                 00007ffcc794c080
IsJitted:               yes
Current CodeAddr:       00007ffcc79405c0
Version History:
  ILCodeVersion:        0000000000000000
  ReJIT ID:             0
  IL Addr:              0000017c79ee2080
      CodeAddr:            00007ffcc79405c0  (MinOptJitted)
      NativeCodeVersion:   0000000000000000
```

```
0:000> !IP2MD 0x00007ffc`c7940548
MethodDesc:      00007ffcc794cdd0
Method Name:            UserQuery.Main()
Class:                  00007ffcc794cd00
MethodTable:            00007ffcc794ce10
mdToken:                0000000006000002
Module:                 00007ffcc794c080
IsJitted:               yes
Current CodeAddr:       00007ffcc7940500
Version History:
  ILCodeVersion:        0000000000000000
  ReJIT ID:             0
  IL Addr:              0000017c79ee205d
      CodeAddr:            00007ffcc7940500  (MinOptJitted)
      NativeCodeVersion:   0000000000000000
```

```
0:000> !IP2MD 0x00007ffc`c71466e1
MethodDesc:      00007ffcc71e4908
Method Name:            ProcessServer.ProcessServerProgram.Main(System.String[])
Class:                  00007ffcc71fa900
MethodTable:            00007ffcc71e4948
mdToken:                0000000006000001
Module:                 00007ffcc71e27d8
IsJitted:               yes
Current CodeAddr:       00007ffcc7146570
Version History:
  ILCodeVersion:        0000000000000000
  ReJIT ID:             0
  IL Addr:              0000017c78452050
      CodeAddr:            00007ffcc7146570  (QuickJitted)
      NativeCodeVersion:   0000000000000000
```

11.   We can see more information for .NET calls on our stack trace, too:

```
0:000> kL 3
 # Child-SP          RetAddr            Call Site
00 00000047`46b2d250 00007ffe`fbbf83f0   LINQPadQuery!UserQuery.ClassMain.DoWork+0x16
01 00000047`46b2d290 00007ffe`fbbf834b   LINQPadQuery!UserQuery.ClassMain.Main+0x30
02 00000047`46b2d2d0 00007ffe`fbbf370c   LINQPadQuery!UserQuery.Main+0x4b
```

```
0:000> !IP2MD 00007ffe`fbbf83f0
MethodDesc:     00007ffefbc70900
Method Name:            UserQuery+ClassMain.Main()
Class:                  00007ffefbc70958
MethodTable:            00007ffefbc70958
mdToken:                0000000006000006
Module:                 00007ffefbbc8f30
IsJitted:               yes
Current CodeAddr:       00007ffefbbf83c0
Version History:
  ILCodeVersion:        0000000000000000
  ReJIT ID:             0
  IL Addr:              000001966a3b20f8
     CodeAddr:             00007ffefbbf83c0  (MinOptJitted)
     NativeCodeVersion:  0000000000000000
```

12.   We now check thread CPU consumption (**!runaway** command):

```
0:000> !runaway f
User Mode Time
  Thread       Time
   0:8d0       0 days 0:04:53.421
   9:1e7c      0 days 0:00:00.500
   8:1898      0 days 0:00:00.437
  10:f40       0 days 0:00:00.250
   3:890       0 days 0:00:00.109
  12:1ee4      0 days 0:00:00.078
  14:980       0 days 0:00:00.000
  13:1454      0 days 0:00:00.000
  11:1940      0 days 0:00:00.000
   7:1c98      0 days 0:00:00.000
   6:1b24      0 days 0:00:00.000
   5:878       0 days 0:00:00.000
   4:b80       0 days 0:00:00.000
   2:df0       0 days 0:00:00.000
   1:484       0 days 0:00:00.000
Kernel Mode Time
  Thread       Time
   0:8d0       0 days 0:00:01.000
  10:f40       0 days 0:00:00.234
   9:1e7c      0 days 0:00:00.218
   8:1898      0 days 0:00:00.125
   6:1b24      0 days 0:00:00.109
   3:890       0 days 0:00:00.093
  12:1ee4      0 days 0:00:00.062
   4:b80       0 days 0:00:00.062
   5:878       0 days 0:00:00.046
  14:980       0 days 0:00:00.000
  13:1454      0 days 0:00:00.000
  11:1940      0 days 0:00:00.000
   7:1c98      0 days 0:00:00.000
   2:df0       0 days 0:00:00.000
   1:484       0 days 0:00:00.000
Elapsed Time
  Thread       Time
   0:8d0       0 days 0:07:00.585
   1:484       0 days 0:07:00.524
```

```
 2:df0     0 days 0:07:00.523
 3:890     0 days 0:07:00.521
 4:b80     0 days 0:07:00.258
 5:878     0 days 0:07:00.255
 6:1b24    0 days 0:07:00.189
 7:1c98    0 days 0:06:59.645
 8:1898    0 days 0:05:17.316
10:f40     0 days 0:05:17.031
 9:1e7c    0 days 0:05:17.031
11:1940    0 days 0:02:00.571
12:1ee4    0 days 0:01:04.307
13:1454    0 days 0:00:59.194
14:980     0 days 0:00:02.534
```

Note: We see that thread #0 spent most of the time (04:53) spiking CPU in user mode since its creation 07:00 minutes ago.

13.   We now check what is the currently executing instruction of the current thread:

```
0:000> r
rax=0000000000000001 rbx=0000004746b2e7c0 rcx=00000155d5cbbd98
rdx=0000004746b2d290 rsi=0000004746b2e668 rdi=00007ffefb5dc640
rip=00007ffefbbf8446 rsp=0000004746b2d250 rbp=0000004746b2d280
 r8=0000004746b2d008  r9=0000004746b2d150 r10=0000000000000000
r11=0000004746b2d150 r12=00000155cf238b40 r13=0000000000000000
r14=00007ffefb297408 r15=0000000000000000
iopl=0         nv up ei pl zr na po nc
cs=0033  ss=002b  ds=002b  es=002b  fs=0053  gs=002b            efl=00000246
LINQPadQuery!UserQuery.ClassMain.DoWork+0x16:
00007ffe`fbbf8446 je        LINQPadQuery!UserQuery.ClassMain.DoWork+0x1d (00007ffe`fbbf844d)
[br=1]
```

```
0:000> kL 3
 # Child-SP          RetAddr           Call Site
00 00000047`46b2d250 00007ffe`fbbf83f0 LINQPadQuery!UserQuery.ClassMain.DoWork+0x16
01 00000047`46b2d290 00007ffe`fbbf834b LINQPadQuery!UserQuery.ClassMain.Main+0x30
02 00000047`46b2d2d0 00007ffe`fbbf370c LINQPadQuery!UserQuery.Main+0x4b
```

Note: We see that it is executing some code instead of waiting like other threads, for example:

```
0:000> ~2kL
 # Child-SP          RetAddr           Call Site
00 00000047`471ff408 00007fff`a5bddcb0 ntdll!NtWaitForMultipleObjects+0x14
01 00000047`471ff410 00007fff`5aea7a9e KERNELBASE!WaitForMultipleObjectsEx+0xf0
02 00000047`471ff700 00007fff`5aea7e26 coreclr!DebuggerRCThread::MainLoop+0xee
03 00000047`471ff7c0 00007fff`5aea785b coreclr!DebuggerRCThread::ThreadProc+0x12e
04 00000047`471ff820 00007fff`a72853e0 coreclr!DebuggerRCThread::ThreadProcStatic+0x5b
05 00000047`471ff850 00007fff`a82c485b kernel32!BaseThreadInitThunk+0x10
06 00000047`471ff880 00000000`00000000 ntdll!RtlUserThreadStart+0x2b
```

14.   We check if the instruction pointer address belongs to the JIT-compiled code:

```
0:000> !IP2MD 00007ffe`fbbf8446
MethodDesc:     00007ffefbc70920
Method Name:            UserQuery+ClassMain.DoWork()
Class:                  00007ffefbc70958
```

```
MethodTable:           00007ffefbc70958
mdToken:               0000000006000007
Module:                00007ffefbbc8f30
IsJitted:              yes
Current CodeAddr:      00007ffefbbf8430
Version History:
  ILCodeVersion:       0000000000000000
  ReJIT ID:            0
  IL Addr:             000001966a3b211e
     CodeAddr:            00007ffefbbf8430   (MinOptJitted)
     NativeCodeVersion:  0000000000000000
```

15.   We double check our findings with **!CLRStack** command:

```
0:000> !CLRStack
OS Thread Id: 0x8d0 (0)
        Child SP             IP Call Site
0000004746B2D250 00007ffefbbf8446 UserQuery+ClassMain.DoWork()
0000004746B2D290 00007ffefbbf83f0 UserQuery+ClassMain.Main()
0000004746B2D2D0 00007ffefbbf834b UserQuery.Main()
0000004746B2D310 00007ffefbbf370c LINQPad.ExecutionModel.ClrQueryRunner.Run()
0000004746B2DC60 00007ffefbbf023f LINQPad.ExecutionModel.Server.RunQuery(LINQPad.ExecutionModel.QueryRunner)
0000004746B2DF40 00007ffefb37311a LINQPad.ExecutionModel.Server.PrepareAndRunQuery(LINQPad.ExecutionModel.QueryRunner)
0000004746B2E080 00007ffefb372c42 LINQPad.ExecutionModel.Server.b__147_0()
0000004746B2E0C0 00007ffefb372b6c LINQPad.ExecutionModel.SyncPCQ+c__DisplayClass14_0.b__0()
0000004746B2E110 00007ffefb31dc60 LINQPad.ExecutionModel.SyncPCQ.Consume()
0000004746B2E190 00007ffefb31d9ae LINQPad.ExecutionModel.SyncPCQ.Start(Boolean, System.String, Boolean)
0000004746B2E290 00007ffefb31659f LINQPad.ExecutionModel.ProcessServer.TryRun(System.String[])
0000004746B2E450 00007ffefb31604b LINQPad.ExecutionModel.ProcessServer.Run(System.String[])
0000004746B2E4A0 00007ffefb315fd4 LINQPad.RuntimeLoader.Run(System.String[])
0000004746B2E4F0 00007ffefb3156f3 LINQPad.RuntimeLoader.Start(System.String[])
0000004746B2E570 00007ffefb31566c LINQPad.EntryPoint.Main(System.String[])
0000004746B2E7F8 00007fff5aee2eb3 [HelperMethodFrame_PROTECTOBJ: 0000004746b2e7f8]
System.RuntimeMethodHandle.InvokeMethod(System.Object, Void**, System.Signature, Boolean)
0000004746B2E930 00007fff5a32e325 System.Reflection.MethodBaseInvoker.InvokeDirectByRefWithFewArgs(System.Object,
System.Span`1<System.Object>, System.Reflection.BindingFlags)
0000004746B2E9B0 00007fff5a32dc2b System.Reflection.MethodBaseInvoker.InvokeWithOneArg(System.Object,
System.Reflection.BindingFlags, System.Reflection.Binder, System.Object[], System.Globalization.CultureInfo)
0000004746B2EA90 00007fff5a33f910 System.Reflection.RuntimeMethodInfo.Invoke(System.Object,
System.Reflection.BindingFlags, System.Reflection.Binder, System.Object[], System.Globalization.CultureInfo)
0000004746B2EB00 00007fff5a32d203 System.Reflection.MethodBase.Invoke(System.Object, System.Object[])
0000004746B2EB40 00007ffefb3119ff LINQPad.ProcessServer.ProcessServerProgram.Main(System.String[])
```

16.   We now dump the method descriptor, class, method table (with or without method descriptors), module, and assembly information using **!DumpMD**, **!DumpClass**, **!DumpMT**, **!DumpModule**, **!DumpAssembly** and **!DumpDomain** SOS extension commands, respectively:

```
0:000> !IP2MD 00007ffe`fbbf8446
MethodDesc:    00007ffefbc70920
Method Name:        UserQuery+ClassMain.DoWork()
Class:             00007ffefbc70958
MethodTable:       00007ffefbc70958
mdToken:           0000000006000007
Module:            00007ffefbbc8f30
IsJitted:          yes
Current CodeAddr:  00007ffefbbf8430
Version History:
  ILCodeVersion:       0000000000000000
  ReJIT ID:            0
  IL Addr:             000001966a3b211e
     CodeAddr:            00007ffefbbf8430   (MinOptJitted)
     NativeCodeVersion:  0000000000000000
```

```
0:000> !DumpMD 00007ffefbc70920
Method Name:           UserQuery+ClassMain.DoWork()
Class:                 00007ffefbc70958
MethodTable:           00007ffefbc70958
mdToken:               0000000006000007
Module:                00007ffefbbc8f30
IsJitted:              yes
Current CodeAddr:      00007ffefbbf8430
Version History:
  ILCodeVersion:       0000000000000000
  ReJIT ID:            0
  IL Addr:             000001966a3b211e
     CodeAddr:            00007ffefbbf8430  (MinOptJitted)
     NativeCodeVersion:  0000000000000000


0:000> !DumpClass 00007ffefbc70958
Class Name:        UserQuery+ClassMain
mdToken:           0000000002000004
File:              C:\Users\User\AppData\Local\Temp\LINQPad8\_ibiqaikn\lfpjux\LINQPadQuery.dll
Parent MethodTable: 00007ffefb1d4730
Module:            00007ffefbbc8f30
Method Table:      00007ffefbc70958
Canonical MethodTable: 00007ffefbc70958
Class Attributes:     100002
NumInstanceFields:    3
NumStaticFields:      0
              MT    Field   Offset                 Type VT     Attr            Value Name
00007ffefb292f78   4000003       10        System.Boolean  1 instance               time2stop
00007ffefb297408   4000004        8         System.Int32   1 instance               inSensor
00007ffefb297408   4000005        c         System.Int32   1 instance               outSensor


0:000> !DumpMT 00007ffefbc70958
Canonical MethodTabl 00007ffefbc70958
Module:                00007ffefbbc8f30
Name:                  UserQuery+ClassMain
mdToken:               0000000002000004
File:
C:\Users\User\AppData\Local\Temp\LINQPad8\_ibiqaikn\lfpjux\LINQPadQuery.dll
AssemblyLoadContext: 00000155d5cba5f0
BaseSize:              0x20
ComponentSize:         0x0
DynamicStatics:        false
ContainsPointers:      false
Number of Methods:     7
Number of IFaces in IFaceMap: 0


0:000> !DumpMT -md 00007ffefbc70958
Canonical MethodTabl 00007ffefbc70958
Module:                00007ffefbbc8f30
Name:                  UserQuery+ClassMain
mdToken:               0000000002000004
File:
C:\Users\User\AppData\Local\Temp\LINQPad8\_ibiqaikn\lfpjux\LINQPadQuery.dll
AssemblyLoadContext: 00000155d5cba5f0
BaseSize:              0x20
ComponentSize:         0x0
DynamicStatics:        false
ContainsPointers:      false
```

146

```
Number of Methods:   7
Number of IFaces in IFaceMap: 0
--------------------------------------
MethodDesc Table
           Entry        MethodDesc     JIT Slot          Name
00007FFEFB280000 00007ffefb1d4690   NONE 0000000000000000 System.Object.Finalize()
00007FFEFB2800A8 00007ffefb1d46a8   NONE 0000000000000001 System.Object.ToString()
00007FFEFBB71230 00007ffefb1d46c0   JIT 0000000000000002 System.Object.Equals(System.Object)
00007FFEFBE40390 00007ffefb1d4718   JIT 0000000000000003 System.Object.GetHashCode()
00007FFEFBB7A3E8 00007ffefbc70940   JIT 0000000000000004 UserQuery+ClassMain..ctor()
00007FFEFBB7A400 00007ffefbc70900   JIT 0000000000000005 UserQuery+ClassMain.Main()
00007FFEFBB7A418 00007ffefbc70920   JIT 0000000000000006 UserQuery+ClassMain.DoWork()


0:000> !DumpModule 00007ffefbbc8f30
Name: C:\Users\User\AppData\Local\Temp\LINQPad8\_ibiqaikn\lfpjux\LINQPadQuery.dll
Attributes:            PEFile
TransientFlags:        00009011
Assembly:              00000155d0d3b1c0
BaseAddress:           000001966A3B0000
LoaderHeap:            00007FFF5B1FE9E8
TypeDefToMethodTableMap: 00007FFEFBB9FA08
TypeRefToMethodTableMap: 00007FFEFBB9FA30
MethodDefToDescMap:    00007FFEFBB9FB50
FieldDefToDescMap:     00007FFEFBB9FBA0
MemberRefToDescMap:    00007FFEFBB9FAD8
FileReferencesMap:     0000000000000000
AssemblyReferencesMap: 00007FFEFBB9FBD8
MetaData start address: 000001966A3B214C (2200 bytes)


0:000> !DumpAssembly 00000155d0d3b1c0
Parent Domain:         00000155d0c6c830
Name:                  C:\Users\User\AppData\Local\Temp\LINQPad8\_ibiqaikn\lfpjux\LINQPadQuery.dll
  Module
  00007ffefbbc8f30
C:\Users\User\AppData\Local\Temp\LINQPad8\_ibiqaikn\lfpjux\LINQPadQuery.dll


0:000> !DumpDomain 00000155d0c6c830
--------------------------------------
Domain 1:              00000155d0c6c830
LowFrequencyHeap:      00007FFF5B1FE9F8
HighFrequencyHeap:     00007FFF5B1FEA88
StubHeap:              00007FFF5B1FEB18
Stage:                 OPEN
Name:                  clrhost
Assembly:              00000155cf2cb080 [C:\Program Files\dotnet\shared\Microsoft.NETCore.App\9.0.4\System.Private.CoreLib.dll]
  Module
  00007ffefb1d4000   C:\Program Files\dotnet\shared\Microsoft.NETCore.App\9.0.4\System.Private.CoreLib.dll

Assembly:              00000155cf2cc5e0 [C:\Users\User\AppData\Local\LINQPad\8.8.9\ProcessServer\9.0.4\LINQPad.Query.dll]
  Module
  00007ffefb3c3368   C:\Users\User\AppData\Local\LINQPad\8.8.9\ProcessServer\9.0.4\LINQPad.Query.dll

Assembly:              00000155cf2cc6a0 [C:\Program Files\dotnet\shared\Microsoft.NETCore.App\9.0.4\System.Runtime.dll]
  Module
  00007ffefb3c5478   C:\Program Files\dotnet\shared\Microsoft.NETCore.App\9.0.4\System.Runtime.dll

Assembly:              00000155cf2cc400 [C:\Program Files\dotnet\shared\Microsoft.WindowsDesktop.App\9.0.4\System.Windows.Forms.dll]
  Module
  00007ffefb3c7130   C:\Program Files\dotnet\shared\Microsoft.WindowsDesktop.App\9.0.4\System.Windows.Forms.dll

Assembly:              00000155cf2cc3a0 [C:\Program Files\dotnet\shared\Microsoft.NETCore.App\9.0.4\System.Runtime.Loader.dll]
  Module
  00007ffefb3c89f0   C:\Program Files\dotnet\shared\Microsoft.NETCore.App\9.0.4\System.Runtime.Loader.dll

Assembly:              00000155cf2cc460 [C:\Program Files\dotnet\shared\Microsoft.NETCore.App\9.0.4\System.Console.dll]
  Module
  00007ffefb3c9ae0   C:\Program Files\dotnet\shared\Microsoft.NETCore.App\9.0.4\System.Console.dll

Assembly:              00000155cf2cc7c0 [C:\Program Files\dotnet\shared\Microsoft.NETCore.App\9.0.4\System.Runtime.Extensions.dll]
  Module
  00007ffefb3cb058   C:\Program Files\dotnet\shared\Microsoft.NETCore.App\9.0.4\System.Runtime.Extensions.dll

Assembly:              00000155cf221b10 [C:\Program Files\dotnet\shared\Microsoft.WindowsDesktop.App\9.0.4\System.Private.Windows.Core.dll]
  Module
```

```
        00007ffefb3cbfe0    C:\Program Files\dotnet\shared\Microsoft.WindowsDesktop.App\9.0.4\System.Private.Windows.Core.dll

Assembly:               00000155cf221b70 [C:\Program Files\dotnet\shared\Microsoft.WindowsDesktop.App\9.0.4\System.Windows.Forms.Primitives.dll]
  Module
        00007ffefb485550    C:\Program Files\dotnet\shared\Microsoft.WindowsDesktop.App\9.0.4\System.Windows.Forms.Primitives.dll

Assembly:               00000155cf221690 [C:\Program Files\dotnet\shared\Microsoft.NETCore.App\9.0.4\System.Runtime.InteropServices.dll]
  Module
        00007ffefb4d03a8    C:\Program Files\dotnet\shared\Microsoft.NETCore.App\9.0.4\System.Runtime.InteropServices.dll

Assembly:               00000155cf221570 [C:\Program Files\dotnet\shared\Microsoft.NETCore.App\9.0.4\System.Threading.dll]
  Module
        00007ffefb4d38c0    C:\Program Files\dotnet\shared\Microsoft.NETCore.App\9.0.4\System.Threading.dll

Assembly:               00000155cf221630 [C:\Program Files\dotnet\shared\Microsoft.NETCore.App\9.0.4\System.Collections.dll]
  Module
        00007ffefb4d66a0    C:\Program Files\dotnet\shared\Microsoft.NETCore.App\9.0.4\System.Collections.dll

Assembly:               00000155cf221330 [C:\Program Files\dotnet\shared\Microsoft.NETCore.App\9.0.4\System.ComponentModel.Primitives.dll]
  Module
        00007ffefb4dbba0    C:\Program Files\dotnet\shared\Microsoft.NETCore.App\9.0.4\System.ComponentModel.Primitives.dll

Assembly:               00000155cf222050 [C:\Program Files\dotnet\shared\Microsoft.NETCore.App\9.0.4\System.Drawing.Primitives.dll]
  Module
        00007ffefb4f6f88    C:\Program Files\dotnet\shared\Microsoft.NETCore.App\9.0.4\System.Drawing.Primitives.dll

Assembly:               00000155cf2215d0 [C:\Program Files\dotnet\shared\Microsoft.NETCore.App\9.0.4\System.IO.FileSystem.dll]
  Module
        00007ffefb4f7d20    C:\Program Files\dotnet\shared\Microsoft.NETCore.App\9.0.4\System.IO.FileSystem.dll

Assembly:               00000155cf2fe660 [C:\Program Files\LINQPad8\LINQPad.Runtime.dll]
  Module
        00007ffefb531440    C:\Program Files\LINQPad8\LINQPad.Runtime.dll

Assembly:               00000155cf2fdd00 [C:\Program Files\dotnet\shared\Microsoft.NETCore.App\9.0.4\System.Linq.dll]
  Module
        00007ffefb539650    C:\Program Files\dotnet\shared\Microsoft.NETCore.App\9.0.4\System.Linq.dll

Assembly:               00000155cf2fddc0 [C:\Program Files\dotnet\shared\Microsoft.NETCore.App\9.0.4\System.IO.Compression.dll]
  Module
        00007ffefb5d8e80    C:\Program Files\dotnet\shared\Microsoft.NETCore.App\9.0.4\System.IO.Compression.dll

Assembly:               00000155cf2fde20 [C:\Program Files\dotnet\shared\Microsoft.NETCore.App\9.0.4\System.Diagnostics.Process.dll]
  Module
        00007ffefb5e8508    C:\Program Files\dotnet\shared\Microsoft.NETCore.App\9.0.4\System.Diagnostics.Process.dll

Assembly:               00000155cf2fe6c0 [C:\Program Files\dotnet\shared\Microsoft.NETCore.App\9.0.4\System.Transactions.Local.dll]
  Module
        00007ffefb5efc08    C:\Program Files\dotnet\shared\Microsoft.NETCore.App\9.0.4\System.Transactions.Local.dll

Assembly:               00000155cf2fe000 [C:\Program Files\dotnet\shared\Microsoft.NETCore.App\9.0.4\System.Threading.Tasks.dll]
  Module
        00007ffefb624e68    C:\Program Files\dotnet\shared\Microsoft.NETCore.App\9.0.4\System.Threading.Tasks.dll

Assembly:               00000155cf2fdc40 [C:\Program Files\dotnet\shared\Microsoft.NETCore.App\9.0.4\System.IO.MemoryMappedFiles.dll]
  Module
        00007ffefb629dc8    C:\Program Files\dotnet\shared\Microsoft.NETCore.App\9.0.4\System.IO.MemoryMappedFiles.dll

Assembly:               00000155cf2fe5a0 [C:\Program Files\dotnet\shared\Microsoft.NETCore.App\9.0.4\System.Threading.ThreadPool.dll]
  Module
        00007ffefb634e18    C:\Program Files\dotnet\shared\Microsoft.NETCore.App\9.0.4\System.Threading.ThreadPool.dll

Assembly:               00000155cf2fe9c0 [C:\Program Files\dotnet\shared\Microsoft.NETCore.App\9.0.4\System.Threading.Thread.dll]
  Module
        00007ffefb653ae0    C:\Program Files\dotnet\shared\Microsoft.NETCore.App\9.0.4\System.Threading.Thread.dll

Assembly:               00000155cf2cb920 [C:\Program Files\dotnet\shared\Microsoft.NETCore.App\9.0.4\System.Diagnostics.Debug.dll]
  Module
        00007ffefb656470    C:\Program Files\dotnet\shared\Microsoft.NETCore.App\9.0.4\System.Diagnostics.Debug.dll

Assembly:               00000155d0d3bc40 [C:\Program Files\dotnet\shared\Microsoft.NETCore.App\9.0.4\System.Runtime.InteropServices.RuntimeInformation.dll]
  Module
        00007ffefb67b528    C:\Program Files\dotnet\shared\Microsoft.NETCore.App\9.0.4\System.Runtime.InteropServices.RuntimeInformation.dll

Assembly:               00000155d0d3b700 [C:\Program Files\dotnet\shared\Microsoft.NETCore.App\9.0.4\System.Memory.dll]
  Module
        00007ffefb69e1a0    C:\Program Files\dotnet\shared\Microsoft.NETCore.App\9.0.4\System.Memory.dll

Assembly:               00000155d0d3b040 [C:\Program Files\dotnet\shared\Microsoft.NETCore.App\9.0.4\Microsoft.Win32.Primitives.dll]
  Module
        00007ffefb69eb18    C:\Program Files\dotnet\shared\Microsoft.NETCore.App\9.0.4\Microsoft.Win32.Primitives.dll

Assembly:               00000155d0d3ba00 [C:\Program Files\dotnet\shared\Microsoft.NETCore.App\9.0.4\System.IO.Pipes.dll]
  Module
        00007ffefb69f5c0    C:\Program Files\dotnet\shared\Microsoft.NETCore.App\9.0.4\System.IO.Pipes.dll

Assembly:               00000155d0d3bac0 [C:\Program Files\dotnet\shared\Microsoft.NETCore.App\9.0.4\System.Private.Uri.dll]
  Module
        00007ffefb6b4b30    C:\Program Files\dotnet\shared\Microsoft.NETCore.App\9.0.4\System.Private.Uri.dll

Assembly:               00000155d0d3bb20 [C:\Program Files\dotnet\shared\Microsoft.NETCore.App\9.0.4\System.Text.RegularExpressions.dll]
  Module
        00007ffefb6bcc68    C:\Program Files\dotnet\shared\Microsoft.NETCore.App\9.0.4\System.Text.RegularExpressions.dll

Assembly:               00000155d0d3bd00 [C:\Program Files\dotnet\shared\Microsoft.NETCore.App\9.0.4\System.Reflection.Emit.Lightweight.dll]
  Module
        00007ffefb6f8588    C:\Program Files\dotnet\shared\Microsoft.NETCore.App\9.0.4\System.Reflection.Emit.Lightweight.dll
```

```
Assembly:          00000155d0d3b460 [C:\Program Files\dotnet\shared\Microsoft.NETCore.App\9.0.4\System.Reflection.Emit.ILGeneration.dll]
  Module
  00007ffefb6faef8    C:\Program Files\dotnet\shared\Microsoft.NETCore.App\9.0.4\System.Reflection.Emit.ILGeneration.dll

Assembly:          00000155d0d3bdc0 [C:\Program Files\dotnet\shared\Microsoft.NETCore.App\9.0.4\System.Reflection.Primitives.dll]
  Module
  00007ffefb72fbb0    C:\Program Files\dotnet\shared\Microsoft.NETCore.App\9.0.4\System.Reflection.Primitives.dll

Assembly:          00000155d0d3be20 [C:\Program Files\dotnet\shared\Microsoft.NETCore.App\9.0.4\System.Xml.XDocument.dll]
  Module
  00007ffefb7817b8    C:\Program Files\dotnet\shared\Microsoft.NETCore.App\9.0.4\System.Xml.XDocument.dll

Assembly:          00000155d0d5e920 [C:\Program Files\dotnet\shared\Microsoft.NETCore.App\9.0.4\System.Private.Xml.Linq.dll]
  Module
  00007ffefb781b40    C:\Program Files\dotnet\shared\Microsoft.NETCore.App\9.0.4\System.Private.Xml.Linq.dll

Assembly:          00000155d0d5e8c0 [C:\Program Files\dotnet\shared\Microsoft.NETCore.App\9.0.4\System.Private.Xml.dll]
  Module
  00007ffefb7820c8    C:\Program Files\dotnet\shared\Microsoft.NETCore.App\9.0.4\System.Private.Xml.dll

Assembly:          00000155d0d5dc00 [C:\Program Files\dotnet\shared\Microsoft.NETCore.App\9.0.4\System.Collections.Concurrent.dll]
  Module
  00007ffefb78d3f0    C:\Program Files\dotnet\shared\Microsoft.NETCore.App\9.0.4\System.Collections.Concurrent.dll

Assembly:          00000155d0d5dfc0 [C:\Program Files\dotnet\shared\Microsoft.NETCore.App\9.0.4\System.Data.Common.dll]
  Module
  00007ffefb82b8f0    C:\Program Files\dotnet\shared\Microsoft.NETCore.App\9.0.4\System.Data.Common.dll

Assembly:          00000155d0d5e440 [C:\Program Files\dotnet\shared\Microsoft.NETCore.App\9.0.4\System.ComponentModel.TypeConverter.dll]
  Module
  00007ffefb82be88    C:\Program Files\dotnet\shared\Microsoft.NETCore.App\9.0.4\System.ComponentModel.TypeConverter.dll

Assembly:          00000155d0d5eb00 [C:\Program Files\dotnet\shared\Microsoft.NETCore.App\9.0.4\System.ComponentModel.dll]
  Module
  00007ffefb82c410    C:\Program Files\dotnet\shared\Microsoft.NETCore.App\9.0.4\System.ComponentModel.dll

Assembly:          00000155d0d5e5c0 [C:\Program Files\dotnet\shared\Microsoft.NETCore.App\9.0.4\System.Xml.ReaderWriter.dll]
  Module
  00007ffefb82cfb0    C:\Program Files\dotnet\shared\Microsoft.NETCore.App\9.0.4\System.Xml.ReaderWriter.dll

Assembly:          00000155d0d5e4a0 [C:\Program Files\dotnet\shared\Microsoft.NETCore.App\9.0.4\System.Linq.Expressions.dll]
  Module
  00007ffefb86e708    C:\Program Files\dotnet\shared\Microsoft.NETCore.App\9.0.4\System.Linq.Expressions.dll

Assembly:          00000155d0d5e380 [C:\Program Files\dotnet\shared\Microsoft.NETCore.App\9.0.4\System.Diagnostics.FileVersionInfo.dll]
  Module
  00007ffefb8a1bf8    C:\Program Files\dotnet\shared\Microsoft.NETCore.App\9.0.4\System.Diagnostics.FileVersionInfo.dll

Assembly:          00000155d0d5e980 [C:\Program Files\dotnet\shared\Microsoft.NETCore.App\9.0.4\System.Reflection.Metadata.dll]
  Module
  00007ffefb8a3b38    C:\Program Files\dotnet\shared\Microsoft.NETCore.App\9.0.4\System.Reflection.Metadata.dll

Assembly:          00000155d0d5dde0 [C:\Program Files\dotnet\shared\Microsoft.NETCore.App\9.0.4\System.Collections.Immutable.dll]
  Module
  00007ffefb8aeb90    C:\Program Files\dotnet\shared\Microsoft.NETCore.App\9.0.4\System.Collections.Immutable.dll

Assembly:          00000155d0d5de40 [C:\Program Files\dotnet\shared\Microsoft.NETCore.App\9.0.4\System.Text.Encoding.Extensions.dll]
  Module
  00007ffefb8f0000    C:\Program Files\dotnet\shared\Microsoft.NETCore.App\9.0.4\System.Text.Encoding.Extensions.dll

Assembly:          00000155d0d5e9e0 [C:\Program Files\dotnet\shared\Microsoft.NETCore.App\9.0.4\System.Text.Json.dll]
  Module
  00007ffefb905298    C:\Program Files\dotnet\shared\Microsoft.NETCore.App\9.0.4\System.Text.Json.dll

Assembly:          00000155d0d5dea0 [C:\Program Files\dotnet\shared\Microsoft.NETCore.App\9.0.4\System.ObjectModel.dll]
  Module
  00007ffefb909340    C:\Program Files\dotnet\shared\Microsoft.NETCore.App\9.0.4\System.ObjectModel.dll

Assembly:          00000155d0d5e560 [C:\Program Files\dotnet\shared\Microsoft.NETCore.App\9.0.4\Microsoft.CSharp.dll]
  Module
  00007ffefb90ded0    C:\Program Files\dotnet\shared\Microsoft.NETCore.App\9.0.4\Microsoft.CSharp.dll

Assembly:          000001966a2468b0 []
  Module
  00007ffefb93e8d0    Hyperlinq.dll

Assembly:          000001966a218920 [C:\Program Files\dotnet\shared\Microsoft.NETCore.App\9.0.4\netstandard.dll]
  Module
  00007ffefb93ee18    C:\Program Files\dotnet\shared\Microsoft.NETCore.App\9.0.4\netstandard.dll

Assembly:          000001966a2183e0 [C:\Program Files\dotnet\shared\Microsoft.NETCore.App\9.0.4\System.Runtime.Serialization.Formatters.dll]
  Module
  00007ffefb9e2e78    C:\Program Files\dotnet\shared\Microsoft.NETCore.App\9.0.4\System.Runtime.Serialization.Formatters.dll

Assembly:          000001966a218440 []
  Module
  00007ffefb9f9cc8    NuGet.Versioning.dll

Assembly:          000001966a218b60 []
  Module
  00007ffefba26018    LINQPad.Runtime.UI.dll

Assembly:          000001966a218680 (Dynamic) []
  Module
  00007ffefbb37130    Dynamic Module

Assembly:          000001966a218800 [C:\Program Files\dotnet\shared\Microsoft.NETCore.App\9.0.4\System.Diagnostics.StackTrace.dll]
  Module
```

```
00007ffefbb5a648    C:\Program Files\dotnet\shared\Microsoft.NETCore.App\9.0.4\System.Diagnostics.StackTrace.dll

Assembly:           000001966a2182c0 []
  Module
00007ffefbb5ceb8    NuGet.Packaging.dll

Assembly:           000001966a218b00 [C:\Program Files\dotnet\shared\Microsoft.NETCore.App\9.0.4\System.Diagnostics.TraceSource.dll]
  Module
00007ffefbbb0e00    C:\Program Files\dotnet\shared\Microsoft.NETCore.App\9.0.4\System.Diagnostics.TraceSource.dll

Assembly:           000001966a218320 [C:\Program Files\dotnet\shared\Microsoft.NETCore.App\9.0.4\System.Diagnostics.TextWriterTraceListener.dll]
  Module
00007ffefbbb20c8    C:\Program Files\dotnet\shared\Microsoft.NETCore.App\9.0.4\System.Diagnostics.TextWriterTraceListener.dll

Assembly:           00000155d0d3b1c0 [C:\Users\User\AppData\Local\Temp\LINQPad8\_ibiqaikn\lfpjux\LINQPadQuery.dll]
  Module
00007ffefbbc8f30    C:\Users\User\AppData\Local\Temp\LINQPad8\_ibiqaikn\lfpjux\LINQPadQuery.dll
```

17.   At the end of this exercise, we revisit our stack trace again and disassemble the previous methods:

```
0:000> k 3
 # Child-SP          RetAddr           Call Site
00 00000047`46b2d250 00007ffe`fbbf83f0 LINQPadQuery!UserQuery.ClassMain.DoWork+0x16
01 00000047`46b2d290 00007ffe`fbbf834b LINQPadQuery!UserQuery.ClassMain.Main+0x30
02 00000047`46b2d2d0 00007ffe`fbbf370c LINQPadQuery!UserQuery.Main+0x4b

0:000> !U 00007ffe`fbbf83f0
Normal JIT generated code
UserQuery+ClassMain.Main()
ilAddr is 000001966A3B20F8 pImport is 0000027BD6AFE5F0
Begin 00007FFEFBBF83C0, size 52
00007ffe`fbbf83c0 push    rbp
00007ffe`fbbf83c1 sub     rsp,30h
00007ffe`fbbf83c5 lea     rbp,[rsp+30h]
00007ffe`fbbf83ca xor     eax,eax
00007ffe`fbbf83cc mov     dword ptr [rbp-4],eax
00007ffe`fbbf83cf mov     qword ptr [rbp+10h],rcx
00007ffe`fbbf83d3 cmp     dword ptr [00007ffe`fbbc9178],0
00007ffe`fbbf83da je      LINQPadQuery!UserQuery.ClassMain.Main+0x21 (00007ffe`fbbf83e1)
00007ffe`fbbf83dc call    coreclr!JIT_DbgIsJustMyCode (00007fff`5aff33c0)
00007ffe`fbbf83e1 nop
00007ffe`fbbf83e2 nop
00007ffe`fbbf83e3 jmp     LINQPadQuery!UserQuery.ClassMain.Main+0x32 (00007ffe`fbbf83f2)
00007ffe`fbbf83e5 nop
00007ffe`fbbf83e6 mov     rcx,qword ptr [rbp+10h]
00007ffe`fbbf83ea call    qword ptr [CLRStub[MethodDescPrestub]@00007FFEFBB7E418 (00007ffe`fbb7e418)]
>>> 00007ffe`fbbf83f0 nop
00007ffe`fbbf83f1 nop
00007ffe`fbbf83f2 mov     rax,qword ptr [rbp+10h]
00007ffe`fbbf83f6 movzx   eax,byte ptr [rax+10h]
00007ffe`fbbf83fa test    eax,eax
00007ffe`fbbf83fc sete    al
00007ffe`fbbf83ff movzx   eax,al
00007ffe`fbbf8402 mov     dword ptr [rbp-4],eax
00007ffe`fbbf8405 cmp     dword ptr [rbp-4],0
00007ffe`fbbf8409 jne     LINQPadQuery!UserQuery.ClassMain.Main+0x25 (00007ffe`fbbf83e5)
00007ffe`fbbf840b nop
00007ffe`fbbf840c add     rsp,30h
00007ffe`fbbf8410 pop     rbp
00007ffe`fbbf8411 ret

0:000> dps 00007ffe`fbb7e418 L1
00007ffe`fbb7e418  00007ffe`fbbf8430 LINQPadQuery!UserQuery.ClassMain.DoWork

0:000> !U 00007ffe`fbbf834b
Normal JIT generated code
UserQuery.Main()
ilAddr is 000001966A3B20D3 pImport is 0000027BD6FFE290
Begin 00007FFEFBBF8300, size 54
```

```
00007ffe`fbbf8300 push    rbp
00007ffe`fbbf8301 push    rdi
00007ffe`fbbf8302 sub     rsp,28h
00007ffe`fbbf8306 lea     rbp,[rsp+30h]
00007ffe`fbbf830b xor     eax,eax
00007ffe`fbbf830d mov     qword ptr [rbp-10h],rax
00007ffe`fbbf8311 mov     qword ptr [rbp+10h],rcx
00007ffe`fbbf8315 cmp     dword ptr [00007ffe`fbbc9178],0
00007ffe`fbbf831c je      LINQPadQuery!UserQuery.Main+0x23 (00007ffe`fbbf8323)
00007ffe`fbbf831e call    coreclr!JIT_DbgIsJustMyCode (00007fff`5aff33c0)
00007ffe`fbbf8323 nop
00007ffe`fbbf8324 mov     rcx,7FFEFBC70958h
00007ffe`fbbf832e call    coreclr!JIT_NewS_MP_FastPortable (00007fff`5adce710)
00007ffe`fbbf8333 mov     qword ptr [rbp-10h],rax
00007ffe`fbbf8337 mov     rcx,qword ptr [rbp-10h]
00007ffe`fbbf833b call    qword ptr [CLRStub[MethodDescPrestub]@00007FFEFBB7E3E8 (00007ffe`fbb7e3e8)]
00007ffe`fbbf8341 mov     rcx,qword ptr [rbp-10h]
00007ffe`fbbf8345 call    qword ptr [CLRStub[MethodDescPrestub]@00007FFEFBB7E400 (00007ffe`fbb7e400)]
>>> 00007ffe`fbbf834b nop
00007ffe`fbbf834c nop
00007ffe`fbbf834d add     rsp,28h
00007ffe`fbbf8351 pop     rdi
00007ffe`fbbf8352 pop     rbp
00007ffe`fbbf8353 ret
```

```
0:000> dps 00007ffe`fbb7e400 L1
00007ffe`fbb7e400  00007ffe`fbbf83c0 LINQPadQuery!UserQuery.ClassMain.Main
```

Note: We see that JIT code is annotated with method names, and this can be helpful with reverse engineering of an unknown method.

18.   If you know the method descriptor, you can also dump IL code:

```
MethodDesc:     00007ffefbc70920
Method Name:            UserQuery+ClassMain.DoWork()
Class:                  00007ffefbc70958
MethodTable:            00007ffefbc70958
mdToken:                0000000006000007
Module:                 00007ffefbbc8f30
IsJitted:               yes
Current CodeAddr:       00007ffefbbf8430
Version History:
  ILCodeVersion:        0000000000000000
  ReJIT ID:             0
  IL Addr:              000001966a3b211e
    CodeAddr:             00007ffefbbf8430  (MinOptJitted)
    NativeCodeVersion:  0000000000000000
```

```
0:000> !DumpIL 00007ffefbc70920
ilAddr is 000001966A3B211E pImport is 0000027BD6FFFA30
ilAddr = 000001966A3B211E
IL_0000: nop
IL_0001: ldarg.0
IL_0002: ldarg.0
IL_0003: volatile.
IL_0005: ldfld ClassMain::outSensor
IL_000a: ldarg.0
IL_000b: volatile.
IL_000d: ldfld ClassMain::inSensor
IL_0012: xor
```

```
IL_0013: volatile.
IL_0015: stfld ClassMain::outSensor
IL_001a: ret
```

```
0:000> !U 00007ffefbbf8430
Normal JIT generated code
UserQuery+ClassMain.DoWork()
ilAddr is 000001966A3B211E pImport is 0000027BD6FFF130
Begin 00007FFEFBBF8430, size 34
>>> 00007ffe`fbbf8430 push     rbp
00007ffe`fbbf8431 push     rdi
00007ffe`fbbf8432 sub      rsp,28h
00007ffe`fbbf8436 lea      rbp,[rsp+30h]
00007ffe`fbbf843b mov      qword ptr [rbp+10h],rcx
00007ffe`fbbf843f cmp      dword ptr [00007ffe`fbbc9178],0
00007ffe`fbbf8446 je       LINQPadQuery!UserQuery.ClassMain.DoWork+0x1d (00007ffe`fbbf844d)
00007ffe`fbbf8448 call     coreclr!JIT_DbgIsJustMyCode (00007fff`5aff33c0)
00007ffe`fbbf844d nop
00007ffe`fbbf844e mov      rax,qword ptr [rbp+10h]
00007ffe`fbbf8452 mov      eax,dword ptr [rax+8]
00007ffe`fbbf8455 mov      rcx,qword ptr [rbp+10h]
00007ffe`fbbf8459 xor      dword ptr [rcx+0Ch],eax
00007ffe`fbbf845c nop
00007ffe`fbbf845d add      rsp,28h
00007ffe`fbbf8461 pop      rdi
00007ffe`fbbf8462 pop      rbp
00007ffe`fbbf8463 ret
```

19.   We close logging before exiting WinDbg:

```
0:000> .logclose
Closing open log file C:\ANETMDA-Dumps\Windows\x64\LINQPadB.log
```

20.   There was another spiking process at the problem time, and its process memory dump was saved, too. We launch WinDbg and open \ANETMDA-Dumps\Windows\x64\LINQPad8-2.DMP

21.   We get the dump file loaded:

```
Microsoft (R) Windows Debugger Version 10.0.27829.1001 AMD64
Copyright (c) Microsoft Corporation. All rights reserved.


Loading Dump File [C:\ANETMDA-Dumps\Windows\x64\LINQPad8-2.DMP]
User Mini Dump File with Full Memory: Only application data is available


************* Path validation summary **************
Response                      Time (ms)     Location
Deferred                                    srv*
Symbol search path is: srv*
Executable search path is:
Windows 10 Version 22000 MP (4 procs) Free x64
Product: WinNt, suite: SingleUserTS
Edition build lab: 22000.1.amd64fre.co_release.210604-1628
Debug session time: Sun Apr 27 10:04:57.000 2025 (UTC + 1:00)
System Uptime: 0 days 0:38:04.297
```

```
Process Uptime: 0 days 0:09:04.000
.......................................................
.......................................................
.......................................................
.......................................................
.......................................................
Loading unloaded module list
..............
For analysis of this file, run !analyze -v
win32u!NtUserWaitMessage+0x14:
00007fff`a5f414d4 ret
```

22.   Open a log file using the **.logappend** command and load the SOS extension:

```
0:000> .logappend C:\ANETMDA-Dumps\Windows\x64\LINQPadB.log
Opened log file 'C:\ANETMDA-Dumps\Windows\x64\LINQPadB.log'

0:000> .load C:\Users\dmitr\.dotnet\sos\sos.dll
```

23.   We check the current thread stack trace, where we see some JIT code:

```
0:000> kL
 # Child-SP          RetAddr           Call Site
00 0000001c`59f1dd38 00007fff`907b632e win32u!NtUserWaitMessage+0x14
01 0000001c`59f1dd40 00007fff`5e24d77f System_Windows_Forms_Primitives!
02 0000001c`59f1de00 00007fff`5e24fc0d
System_Windows_Forms!System.Windows.Forms.Application.ComponentManager.Interop.Mso.IMsoComponentManager.FPushMessageLoop+0x43f
03 0000001c`59f1def0 00007fff`5e24f8f8 System_Windows_Forms!System.Windows.Forms.Application.ThreadContext.RunMessageLoopInner+0x2cd
04 0000001c`59f1df90 00007fff`5df44996 System_Windows_Forms!System.Windows.Forms.Application.ThreadContext.RunMessageLoop+0x48
05 0000001c`59f1dff0 00007ffe`fffe527f System_Windows_Forms!System.Windows.Forms.Application.Run+0x56
06 0000001c`59f1e030 00007ffe`ffb91d86 LINQPad_GUI!
07 0000001c`59f1e320 00007ffe`ff7b2121 LINQPad_GUI!
08 0000001c`59f1e650 00007ffe`ff7afdf1 LINQPad_GUI!
09 0000001c`59f1e6b0 00007ffe`ff7adeec LINQPad_GUI!
0a 0000001c`59f1e7d0 00007fff`5f33a6d3 LINQPad_GUI!
0b 0000001c`59f1e820 00007fff`5f2602d0 coreclr!CallDescrWorkerInternal+0x83
0c (Inline Function) --------`-------- coreclr!CallDescrWorkerWithHandler+0x30
0d 0000001c`59f1e860 00007fff`5f26202c coreclr!CallDescrWorkerReflectionWrapper+0x48
0e 0000001c`59f1e8b0 00007fff`5eafe297 coreclr!RuntimeMethodHandle::InvokeMethod+0x91c
0f 0000001c`59f1ef30 00007fff`5eaf0e36 System_Private_CoreLib!System.Reflection.RuntimeMethodInfo.Invoke+0xe7
10 0000001c`59f1f000 00007ffe`ff79b654 System_Private_CoreLib!System.Reflection.MethodBase.Invoke+0x26
11 0000001c`59f1f040 00007ffe`ff798373 LINQPad_GUI!LINQPad.UI.TestHarness.Go+0x164
12 0000001c`59f1f0f0 00007ffe`ff797d9f LINQPad_GUI!LINQPad.UI.TestHarness.Test+0x173
13 0000001c`59f1f1c0 00007ff6`1e4f513b System_Private_CoreLib!ILStubClass.IL_STUB_ReversePInvoke(Int64, Int32)+0x4f
14 0000001c`59f1f220 00007ff6`1e4f7df3 LINQPad8+0x1513b
15 0000001c`59f1f3b0 00007ff6`1e505a72 LINQPad8+0x17df3
16 0000001c`59f1fd00 00007fff`a72853e0 LINQPad8+0x25a72
17 0000001c`59f1fd40 00007fff`a82c485b kernel32!BaseThreadInitThunk+0x10
18 0000001c`59f1fd70 00000000`00000000 ntdll!RtlUserThreadStart+0x2b
```

```
0:000> !IP2MD 00007ffe`fffe527f
MethodDesc:    00007ffeffa5fdc0
Method Name:        LINQPad.UIProgram.Run()
Class:              00007ffeffa626a0
MethodTable:        00007ffeffa716c0
mdToken:            0000000006000216
Module:             00007ffeff949a98
IsJitted:           yes
Current CodeAddr:   00007ffefffe4700
Version History:
  ILCodeVersion:      0000000000000000
  ReJIT ID:           0
  IL Addr:            000001b778c5c418
     CodeAddr:           00007ffefffe4700  (MinOptJitted)
     NativeCodeVersion:  0000000000000000
```

```
0:000> !IP2MD 00007ffe`ffb91d86
MethodDesc:    00007ffeffa5fc70
Method Name:        LINQPad.UIProgram.Go(System.String[])
```

```
Class:                    00007ffeffa626a0
MethodTable:              00007ffeffa716c0
mdToken:                  000000000600020A
Module:                   00007ffeff949a98
IsJitted:                 yes
Current CodeAddr:         00007ffeffb913a0
Version History:
   ILCodeVersion:         0000000000000000
   ReJIT ID:              0
   IL Addr:               000001b778c5b474
      CodeAddr:               00007ffeffb913a0  (MinOptJitted)
      NativeCodeVersion:  0000000000000000
```

24.   Then we check the spiking thread stack traces:

```
0:000> !runaway
User Mode Time
   Thread       Time
      0:1cec    0 days 0:00:16.328
     13:198c    0 days 0:00:11.578
     20:19b0    0 days 0:00:07.234
     19:978     0 days 0:00:06.453
     21:1f88    0 days 0:00:05.828
     24:1608    0 days 0:00:03.390
     26:1d0c    0 days 0:00:00.265
     10:1d38    0 days 0:00:00.250
      3:bcc     0 days 0:00:00.218
     12:12b0    0 days 0:00:00.046
     15:144c    0 days 0:00:00.031
     14:1790    0 days 0:00:00.031
     11:1370    0 days 0:00:00.031
     16:11e8    0 days 0:00:00.015
      8:bac     0 days 0:00:00.015
      7:1a9c    0 days 0:00:00.015
      6:1c88    0 days 0:00:00.015
     27:1070    0 days 0:00:00.000
     25:11e4    0 days 0:00:00.000
     23:103c    0 days 0:00:00.000
     22:458     0 days 0:00:00.000
     18:1c04    0 days 0:00:00.000
     17:c48     0 days 0:00:00.000
      9:1074    0 days 0:00:00.000
      5:c3c     0 days 0:00:00.000
      4:1d2c    0 days 0:00:00.000
      2:cdc     0 days 0:00:00.000
      1:18f4    0 days 0:00:00.000
```

```
0:000> ~13kL
 #  Child-SP         RetAddr          Call Site
00 0000001c`5bdff318 00007fff`a5bdebd3 ntdll!NtRemoveIoCompletion+0x14
01 0000001c`5bdff320 00007fff`5e9583a1 KERNELBASE!GetQueuedCompletionStatus+0x53
02 0000001c`5bdff380 00007fff`042a3ed2 System_Private_CoreLib!
03 0000001c`5bdff480 00007fff`0429e416 System_Private_CoreLib!System.Threading.LowLevelLifoSemaphore.WaitForSignal+0x32
04 0000001c`5bdff4e0 00007fff`5ea8de28 System_Private_CoreLib!System.Threading.LowLevelLifoSemaphore.Wait+0x176
05 0000001c`5bdff5a0 00007fff`5ea7278f System_Private_CoreLib!System.Threading.PortableThreadPool.WorkerThread.WorkerThreadStart+0x1e8
06 0000001c`5bdff6b0 00007fff`5f33a6d3 System_Private_CoreLib!System.Threading.Thread.StartCallback+0x3f
07 0000001c`5bdff6f0 00007fff`5f22d3bc coreclr!CallDescrWorkerInternal+0x83
08 0000001c`5bdff730 00007fff`5f31bf03 coreclr!DispatchCallSimple+0x80
09 0000001c`5bdff7c0 00007fff`5f288615 coreclr!ThreadNative::KickOffThread_Worker+0x63
0a (Inline Function) --------`-------- coreclr!ManagedThreadBase_DispatchInner+0xd
0b 0000001c`5bdff820 00007fff`5f28851a coreclr!ManagedThreadBase_DispatchMiddle+0x85
0c 0000001c`5bdff900 00007fff`5f288339 coreclr!ManagedThreadBase_DispatchOuter+0xae
0d (Inline Function) --------`-------- coreclr!ManagedThreadBase_FullTransition+0x2d
0e (Inline Function) --------`-------- coreclr!ManagedThreadBase::KickOff+0x2d
0f 0000001c`5bdff9a0 00007fff`a72853e0 coreclr!ThreadNative::KickOffThread+0x79
10 0000001c`5bdffa00 00007fff`a82c485b kernel32!BaseThreadInitThunk+0x10
```

```
11 0000001c`5bdffa30 00000000`00000000     ntdll!RtlUserThreadStart+0x2b
```

```
0:000> ~20kL
 # Child-SP          RetAddr           Call Site
00 0000001c`5c0ff728 00007fff`a5bdebd3   ntdll!NtRemoveIoCompletion+0x14
01 0000001c`5c0ff730 00007fff`5e9583a1   KERNELBASE!GetQueuedCompletionStatus+0x53
02 0000001c`5c0ff790 00007fff`042a3ed2   System_Private_CoreLib!
03 0000001c`5c0ff890 00007fff`0429e416   System_Private_CoreLib!System.Threading.LowLevelLifoSemaphore.WaitForSignal+0x32
04 0000001c`5c0ff8f0 00007fff`5ea8de28   System_Private_CoreLib!System.Threading.LowLevelLifoSemaphore.Wait+0x176
05 0000001c`5c0ff9b0 00007fff`5ea7278f   System_Private_CoreLib!System.Threading.PortableThreadPool.WorkerThread.WorkerThreadStart+0x1e8
06 0000001c`5c0ffac0 00007fff`5f33a6d3   System_Private_CoreLib!System.Threading.Thread.StartCallback+0x3f
07 0000001c`5c0ffb00 00007fff`5f22d3bc   coreclr!CallDescrWorkerInternal+0x83
08 0000001c`5c0ffb40 00007fff`5f31bf03   coreclr!DispatchCallSimple+0x80
09 0000001c`5c0ffbd0 00007fff`5f288615   coreclr!ThreadNative::KickOffThread_Worker+0x63
0a (Inline Function) --------`--------   coreclr!ManagedThreadBase_DispatchInner+0xd
0b 0000001c`5c0ffc30 00007fff`5f28851a   coreclr!ManagedThreadBase_DispatchMiddle+0x85
0c 0000001c`5c0ffd10 00007fff`5f288339   coreclr!ManagedThreadBase_DispatchOuter+0xae
0d (Inline Function) --------`--------   coreclr!ManagedThreadBase_FullTransition+0x2d
0e (Inline Function) --------`--------   coreclr!ManagedThreadBase::KickOff+0x2d
0f 0000001c`5c0ffdb0 00007fff`a72853e0   coreclr!ThreadNative::KickOffThread+0x79
10 0000001c`5c0ffe10 00007fff`a82c485b   kernel32!BaseThreadInitThunk+0x10
11 0000001c`5c0ffe40 00000000`00000000   ntdll!RtlUserThreadStart+0x2b
```

```
0:000> ~19kL
 # Child-SP          RetAddr           Call Site
00 0000001c`5cdff168 00007fff`a5bdebd3   ntdll!NtRemoveIoCompletion+0x14
01 0000001c`5cdff170 00007fff`5e9583a1   KERNELBASE!GetQueuedCompletionStatus+0x53
02 0000001c`5cdff1d0 00007fff`042a3ed2   System_Private_CoreLib!
03 0000001c`5cdff2d0 00007fff`0429e416   System_Private_CoreLib!System.Threading.LowLevelLifoSemaphore.WaitForSignal+0x32
04 0000001c`5cdff330 00007fff`5ea8de28   System_Private_CoreLib!System.Threading.LowLevelLifoSemaphore.Wait+0x176
05 0000001c`5cdff3f0 00007fff`5ea7278f   System_Private_CoreLib!System.Threading.PortableThreadPool.WorkerThread.WorkerThreadStart+0x1e8
06 0000001c`5cdff500 00007fff`5f33a6d3   System_Private_CoreLib!System.Threading.Thread.StartCallback+0x3f
07 0000001c`5cdff540 00007fff`5f22d3bc   coreclr!CallDescrWorkerInternal+0x83
08 0000001c`5cdff580 00007fff`5f31bf03   coreclr!DispatchCallSimple+0x80
09 0000001c`5cdff610 00007fff`5f288615   coreclr!ThreadNative::KickOffThread_Worker+0x63
0a (Inline Function) --------`--------   coreclr!ManagedThreadBase_DispatchInner+0xd
0b 0000001c`5cdff670 00007fff`5f28851a   coreclr!ManagedThreadBase_DispatchMiddle+0x85
0c 0000001c`5cdff750 00007fff`5f288339   coreclr!ManagedThreadBase_DispatchOuter+0xae
0d (Inline Function) --------`--------   coreclr!ManagedThreadBase_FullTransition+0x2d
0e (Inline Function) --------`--------   coreclr!ManagedThreadBase::KickOff+0x2d
0f 0000001c`5cdff7f0 00007fff`a72853e0   coreclr!ThreadNative::KickOffThread+0x79
10 0000001c`5cdff850 00007fff`a82c485b   kernel32!BaseThreadInitThunk+0x10
11 0000001c`5cdff880 00000000`00000000   ntdll!RtlUserThreadStart+0x2b
```

```
0:000> ~21kL
 # Child-SP          RetAddr           Call Site
00 0000001c`5c9ff408 00007fff`a5bdebd3   ntdll!NtRemoveIoCompletion+0x14
01 0000001c`5c9ff410 00007fff`5e9583a1   KERNELBASE!GetQueuedCompletionStatus+0x53
02 0000001c`5c9ff470 00007fff`042a3ed2   System_Private_CoreLib!
03 0000001c`5c9ff570 00007fff`0429e416   System_Private_CoreLib!System.Threading.LowLevelLifoSemaphore.WaitForSignal+0x32
04 0000001c`5c9ff5d0 00007fff`5ea8de28   System_Private_CoreLib!System.Threading.LowLevelLifoSemaphore.Wait+0x176
05 0000001c`5c9ff690 00007fff`5ea7278f   System_Private_CoreLib!System.Threading.PortableThreadPool.WorkerThread.WorkerThreadStart+0x1e8
06 0000001c`5c9ff7a0 00007fff`5f33a6d3   System_Private_CoreLib!System.Threading.Thread.StartCallback+0x3f
07 0000001c`5c9ff7e0 00007fff`5f22d3bc   coreclr!CallDescrWorkerInternal+0x83
08 0000001c`5c9ff820 00007fff`5f31bf03   coreclr!DispatchCallSimple+0x80
09 0000001c`5c9ff8b0 00007fff`5f288615   coreclr!ThreadNative::KickOffThread_Worker+0x63
0a (Inline Function) --------`--------   coreclr!ManagedThreadBase_DispatchInner+0xd
0b 0000001c`5c9ff910 00007fff`5f28851a   coreclr!ManagedThreadBase_DispatchMiddle+0x85
0c 0000001c`5c9ff9f0 00007fff`5f288339   coreclr!ManagedThreadBase_DispatchOuter+0xae
0d (Inline Function) --------`--------   coreclr!ManagedThreadBase_FullTransition+0x2d
0e (Inline Function) --------`--------   coreclr!ManagedThreadBase::KickOff+0x2d
0f 0000001c`5c9ffa90 00007fff`a72853e0   coreclr!ThreadNative::KickOffThread+0x79
10 0000001c`5c9ffaf0 00007fff`a82c485b   kernel32!BaseThreadInitThunk+0x10
11 0000001c`5c9ffb20 00000000`00000000   ntdll!RtlUserThreadStart+0x2b
```

```
0:000> ~24kL
 # Child-SP          RetAddr           Call Site
00 0000001c`5abff678 00007fff`a5bdebd3   ntdll!NtRemoveIoCompletion+0x14
01 0000001c`5abff680 00007fff`5e9583a1   KERNELBASE!GetQueuedCompletionStatus+0x53
02 0000001c`5abff6e0 00007fff`042a3ed2   System_Private_CoreLib!
03 0000001c`5abff7e0 00007fff`0429e416   System_Private_CoreLib!System.Threading.LowLevelLifoSemaphore.WaitForSignal+0x32
04 0000001c`5abff840 00007fff`5ea8de28   System_Private_CoreLib!System.Threading.LowLevelLifoSemaphore.Wait+0x176
05 0000001c`5abff900 00007fff`5ea7278f   System_Private_CoreLib!System.Threading.PortableThreadPool.WorkerThread.WorkerThreadStart+0x1e8
06 0000001c`5abffa10 00007fff`5f33a6d3   System_Private_CoreLib!System.Threading.Thread.StartCallback+0x3f
07 0000001c`5abffa50 00007fff`5f22d3bc   coreclr!CallDescrWorkerInternal+0x83
08 0000001c`5abffa90 00007fff`5f31bf03   coreclr!DispatchCallSimple+0x80
09 0000001c`5abffb20 00007fff`5f288615   coreclr!ThreadNative::KickOffThread_Worker+0x63
0a (Inline Function) --------`--------   coreclr!ManagedThreadBase_DispatchInner+0xd
0b 0000001c`5abffb80 00007fff`5f28851a   coreclr!ManagedThreadBase_DispatchMiddle+0x85
0c 0000001c`5abffc60 00007fff`5f288339   coreclr!ManagedThreadBase_DispatchOuter+0xae
0d (Inline Function) --------`--------   coreclr!ManagedThreadBase_FullTransition+0x2d
0e (Inline Function) --------`--------   coreclr!ManagedThreadBase::KickOff+0x2d
0f 0000001c`5abffd00 00007fff`a72853e0   coreclr!ThreadNative::KickOffThread+0x79
10 0000001c`5abffd60 00007fff`a82c485b   kernel32!BaseThreadInitThunk+0x10
11 0000001c`5abffd90 00000000`00000000   ntdll!RtlUserThreadStart+0x2b
```

25.   We close logging before exiting WinDbg:

```
0:000> .logclose
Closing open log file C:\ANETMDA-Dumps\Windows\x64\LINQPadB.log
```

Exercise PN3 (Linux)

- **Goal:** Learn how to find problem assemblies, modules, classes, and methods, disassemble code, and analyze CPU spikes

- **Patterns:** Paratext; Manual Dump (Process); Active Thread; Spiking Thread

- **Commands:** x/i, dumpmd, dumpclass, dumpmt, dumpmodule, dumpassembly, dumpdomain, dumpil

- \ANETMDA-Dumps\Exercise-PN3-Linux.pdf

Exercise PN3 (Linux)

Goal: Learn how to find problem assemblies, modules, classes, and methods, disassemble code, and analyze CPU spikes.

Patterns: Paratext; Manual Dump (Process); Active Thread; Spiking Thread.

Commands: x/i, dumpmd, dumpclass, dumpmt, dumpmodule, dumpassembly, dumpdomain, dumpil

1. The *ApplicationH* process was consuming 100% CPU, and its dump was saved manually.

```
top - 20:50:04 up 18:07,  0 users,  load average: 0.72, 0.22, 0.08
Tasks:   7 total,   2 running,   5 sleeping,   0 stopped,   0 zombie
%Cpu(s): 12.5 us,  0.0 sy,  0.0 ni, 87.4 id,  0.0 wa,  0.0 hi,  0.0 si,  0.0 st
MiB Mem :   7904.0 total,   7382.1 free,    395.9 used,    126.0 buff/cache
MiB Swap:   2048.0 total,   2048.0 free,      0.0 used.   7314.7 avail Mem

  PID USER      PR  NI    VIRT    RES    SHR S  %CPU  %MEM     TIME+ COMMAND
  408 coredump  20   0  260.6g  22160  18380 R 100.0   0.3   1:18.86 ApplicationH
    1 root      20   0    2776   1948   1828 S   0.0   0.0   0:00.77 init(Debian)
    5 root      20   0    2776      4      0 S   0.0   0.0   0:00.00 init
    8 root      20   0    2784    204     80 S   0.0   0.0   0:00.00 SessionLeader
    9 root      20   0    2784    212     80 S   0.0   0.0   0:00.50 Relay(10)
   10 coredump  20   0    7640   4436   3208 S   0.0   0.1   0:00.68 bash
  416 coredump  20   0   10984   3328   2864 R   0.0   0.0   0:00.02 top
```

2. Open \ANETMDA-Dumps\Linux\ApplicationH\core.ApplicationH.408.dmp in LLDB:

```
/mnt/c/ANETMDA-Dumps/Linux/ApplicationH$ lldb -c core.ApplicationH.408.dmp
bin/Release/net9.0/ApplicationH
Current symbol store settings:
-> Cache: /home/coredump/.dotnet/symbolcache
-> Server: https://msdl.microsoft.com/download/symbols/ Timeout: 4 RetryCount: 0
(lldb) target create "bin/Release/net9.0/ApplicationH" --core "core.ApplicationH.408.dmp"
Warning: (x86_64) /usr/share/dotnet/host/fxr/9.0.4/libhostfxr.so unsupported DW_FORM values:
0x1b 0x21 0x22 0x23 0x25 0x26 0x64
Warning: (x86_64) /usr/share/dotnet/shared/Microsoft.NETCore.App/9.0.4/libhostpolicy.so
unsupported DW_FORM values: 0x1b 0x21 0x22 0x23 0x25 0x26 0x64
Warning: (x86_64) /usr/share/dotnet/shared/Microsoft.NETCore.App/9.0.4/libcoreclr.so
unsupported DW_FORM values: 0x1b 0x21 0x22 0x23 0x25 0x26 0x64
Warning: (x86_64) /usr/share/dotnet/shared/Microsoft.NETCore.App/9.0.4/libSystem.Native.so
unsupported DW_FORM values: 0x1b 0x21 0x22 0x23 0x25 0x26
Warning: (x86_64) /usr/share/dotnet/shared/Microsoft.NETCore.App/9.0.4/libclrjit.so unsupported
DW_FORM values: 0x1b 0x21 0x22 0x23 0x25 0x26 0x64
Warning: (x86_64) /mnt/c/ANETMDA-Dumps/Linux/ApplicationH/bin/Release/net9.0/ApplicationH
unsupported DW_FORM values: 0x1b 0x21 0x22 0x23 0x25 0x26 0x64

Core file '/mnt/c/ANETMDA-Dumps/Linux/ApplicationH/core.ApplicationH.408.dmp' (x86_64) was
loaded.
```

3. Verify all stack traces:

```
(lldb) bt all
* thread #1, name = 'ApplicationH', stop reason = signal SIGSTOP
  * frame #0: 0x00007f3318e319f8
    frame #1: 0x00007f3318e3194c
    frame #2: 0x00007f33972f8e04 libcoreclr.so`CallDescrWorkerInternal + 124
    frame #3: 0x00007f339713711c libcoreclr.so`MethodDescCallSite::CallTargetWorker(unsigned long const*, unsigned long*, int) + 1708
```

157

```
    frame #4: 0x00007f339701e0c4 libcoreclr.so`RunMain(MethodDesc*, short, int*, PtrArray**) + 836
    frame #5: 0x00007f339701e53c libcoreclr.so`Assembly::ExecuteMainMethod(PtrArray**, int) + 460
    frame #6: 0x00007f3397047b34 libcoreclr.so`CorHost2::ExecuteAssembly(unsigned int, char16_t const*, int, char16_t const**, unsigned int*) + 740
    frame #7: 0x00007f339700a340 libcoreclr.so`coreclr_execute_assembly + 144
    frame #8: 0x00007f33975d2301 libhostpolicy.so`run_app_for_context(hostpolicy_context_t const&, int, char const**) + 1089
    frame #9: 0x00007f33975d33f9 libhostpolicy.so`corehost_main + 345
    frame #10: 0x00007f3397612685 libhostfxr.so`fx_muxer_t::handle_exec_host_command(std::__cxx11::basic_string<char, std::char_traits<char>,
std::allocator<char> > const&, host_startup_info_t const&, std::__cxx11::basic_string<char, std::char_traits<char>, std::allocator<char> > const&,
std::unordered_map<known_options, std::vector<std::__cxx11::basic_string<char, std::char_traits<char>, std::allocator<char> >,
std::allocator<std::__cxx11::basic_string<char, std::char_traits<char>, std::allocator<char> > > >, known_options_hash, std::equal_to<known_options>,
std::allocator<std::pair<known_options const, std::vector<std::__cxx11::basic_string<char, std::char_traits<char>, std::allocator<char> >,
std::allocator<std::__cxx11::basic_string<char, std::char_traits<char>, std::allocator<char> > > > > > const&, int, char const**, int, host_mode_t, bool,
char*, int, int*) + 1477
    frame #11: 0x00007f339761167d libhostfxr.so`fx_muxer_t::execute(std::__cxx11::basic_string<char, std::char_traits<char>, std::allocator<char> >, int, char
const**, host_startup_info_t const&, char*, int, int*) + 765
    frame #12: 0x00007f339760b5f2 libhostfxr.so`hostfxr_main_startupinfo + 242
    frame #13: 0x000055d67db9a21b ApplicationH`exe_start(int, char const**) + 1131
    frame #14: 0x000055d67db9a53f ApplicationH`main + 175
    frame #15: 0x00007f339766509b libc.so.6`__libc_start_main(main=(ApplicationH`main), argc=1, argv=0x00007ffc0722fa28, init=<unavailable>,
fini=<unavailable>, rtld_fini=<unavailable>, stack_end=0x00007ffc0722fa18) at libc-start.c:308
    frame #16: 0x000055d67db99399 ApplicationH`_start + 41
  thread #2, stop reason = signal 0
    frame #0: 0x00007f339772f6f9 libc.so.6`__GI___poll(fds=0x00007f3396e2ad98, nfds=1, timeout=-1) at poll.c:29
    frame #1: 0x00007f33974a2800 libcoreclr.so`CorUnix::CPalSynchronizationManager::ReadBytesFromProcessPipe(int, unsigned char*, int) + 288
    frame #2: 0x00007f33974a1e63 libcoreclr.so`CorUnix::CPalSynchronizationManager::WorkerThread(void*) + 147
    frame #3: 0x00007f33974ab9ae libcoreclr.so`CorUnix::CPalThread::ThreadEntry(void*) + 510
    frame #4: 0x00007f3397b29fa3 libpthread.so.0`start_thread(arg=<unavailable>) at pthread_create.c:486
    frame #5: 0x00007f339773a06f libc.so.6`__GI___clone at clone.S:95
  thread #3, stop reason = signal 0
    frame #0: 0x00007f339772f6f9 libc.so.6`__GI___poll(fds=0x00007f3308000f20, nfds=1, timeout=-1) at poll.c:29
    frame #1: 0x00007f33973a9d5c libcoreclr.so`ds_ipc_poll(_DiagnosticsIpcPollHandle*, unsigned long, unsigned int, void (*)(char const*, unsigned int)) + 172
    frame #2: 0x00007f3397323f4b libcoreclr.so`ds_ipc_stream_factory_get_next_available_stream(void (*)(char const*, unsigned int)) + 731
    frame #3: 0x00007f3397328ca6 libcoreclr.so`server_thread(void*) + 198
    frame #4: 0x00007f33974ab9ae libcoreclr.so`CorUnix::CPalThread::ThreadEntry(void*) + 510
    frame #5: 0x00007f3397b29fa3 libpthread.so.0`start_thread(arg=<unavailable>) at pthread_create.c:486
    frame #6: 0x00007f339773a06f libc.so.6`__GI___clone at clone.S:95
  thread #4, stop reason = signal 0
    frame #0: 0x00007f3397b33d0e libpthread.so.0`__libc_open64(file="/tmp/clr-debug-pipe-408-6516106-in", oflag=0) at open64.c:48
    frame #1: 0x00007f33973a977f libcoreclr.so`TwoWayPipe::WaitForConnection() + 31
    frame #2: 0x00007f33973a4797 libcoreclr.so`DbgTransportSession::TransportWorker() + 183
    frame #3: 0x00007f33973a3905 libcoreclr.so`DbgTransportSession::TransportWorkerStatic(void*) + 37
    frame #4: 0x00007f33974ab9ae libcoreclr.so`CorUnix::CPalThread::ThreadEntry(void*) + 510
    frame #5: 0x00007f3397b29fa3 libpthread.so.0`start_thread(arg=<unavailable>) at pthread_create.c:486
    frame #6: 0x00007f339773a06f libc.so.6`__GI___clone at clone.S:95
  thread #5, stop reason = signal 0
    frame #0: 0x00007f3397b3000c libpthread.so.0`__pthread_cond_wait at futex-internal.h:88
    frame #1: 0x00007f3397b2fff1 libpthread.so.0`__pthread_cond_wait at pthread_cond_wait.c:502
    frame #2: 0x00007f3397b2ff30 libpthread.so.0`__pthread_cond_wait(cond=0x000055d6802afc08, mutex=0x000055d6802afbe0) at pthread_cond_wait.c:655
    frame #3: 0x00007f33974a0172 libcoreclr.so`CorUnix::CPalSynchronizationManager::ThreadNativeWait(CorUnix::_ThreadNativeWaitData*, unsigned int,
CorUnix::ThreadWakeupReason*, unsigned int*) + 354
    frame #4: 0x00007f3397497f d7a libcoreclr.so`CorUnix::CPalSynchronizationManager::BlockThread(CorUnix::CPalThread*, unsigned int, bool, bool,
CorUnix::ThreadWakeupReason*, unsigned int*) + 378
    frame #5: 0x00007f33974a4952 libcoreclr.so`CorUnix::InternalWaitForMultipleObjectsEx(CorUnix::CPalThread*, unsigned int, void* const*, int, unsigned int,
int, int) + 1906
    frame #6: 0x00007f33974a4c03 libcoreclr.so`WaitForMultipleObjectsEx + 83
    frame #7: 0x00007f33973a20ad libcoreclr.so`DebuggerRCThread::MainLoop() + 269
    frame #8: 0x00007f33973a1f28 libcoreclr.so`DebuggerRCThread::ThreadProc() + 312
    frame #9: 0x00007f33973a1c25 libcoreclr.so`DebuggerRCThread::ThreadProcStatic(void*) + 53
    frame #10: 0x00007f33974ab9ae libcoreclr.so`CorUnix::CPalThread::ThreadEntry(void*) + 510
    frame #11: 0x00007f3397b29fa3 libpthread.so.0`start_thread(arg=<unavailable>) at pthread_create.c:486
    frame #12: 0x00007f339773a06f libc.so.6`__GI___clone at clone.S:95
  thread #6, stop reason = signal 0
    frame #0: 0x00007f3397b303f9 libpthread.so.0`__pthread_cond_timedwait at futex-internal.h:142
    frame #1: 0x00007f3397b303da libpthread.so.0`__pthread_cond_timedwait at pthread_cond_wait.c:533
    frame #2: 0x00007f3397b302c0 libpthread.so.0`__pthread_cond_timedwait(cond=0x000055d6802bb2f8, mutex=0x000055d6802bb2d0, abstime=0x00007f3394cd57d0) at
pthread_cond_wait.c:667
    frame #3: 0x00007f33974a0115 libcoreclr.so`CorUnix::CPalSynchronizationManager::ThreadNativeWait(CorUnix::_ThreadNativeWaitData*, unsigned int,
CorUnix::ThreadWakeupReason*, unsigned int*) + 261
    frame #4: 0x00007f3397497f d7a libcoreclr.so`CorUnix::CPalSynchronizationManager::BlockThread(CorUnix::CPalThread*, unsigned int, bool, bool,
CorUnix::ThreadWakeupReason*, unsigned int*) + 378
    frame #5: 0x00007f33974a4952 libcoreclr.so`CorUnix::InternalWaitForMultipleObjectsEx(CorUnix::CPalThread*, unsigned int, void* const*, int, unsigned int,
int, int) + 1906
    frame #6: 0x00007f33974a4c03 libcoreclr.so`WaitForMultipleObjectsEx + 83
    frame #7: 0x00007f3397173111 libcoreclr.so`FinalizerThread::WaitForFinalizerEvent(CLREvent*) + 177
    frame #8: 0x00007f339717327f libcoreclr.so`FinalizerThread::FinalizerThreadWorker(void*) + 239
    frame #9: 0x00007f3397104c08 libcoreclr.so`ManagedThreadBase_DispatchOuter(ManagedThreadCallState*) + 344
    frame #10: 0x00007f339710510d libcoreclr.so`ManagedThreadBase::FinalizerBase(void (*)(void*)) + 45
    frame #11: 0x00007f33971734b8 libcoreclr.so`FinalizerThread::FinalizerThreadStart(void*) + 88
    frame #12: 0x00007f33974ab9ae libcoreclr.so`CorUnix::CPalThread::ThreadEntry(void*) + 510
    frame #13: 0x00007f3397b29fa3 libpthread.so.0`start_thread(arg=<unavailable>) at pthread_create.c:486
    frame #14: 0x00007f339773a06f libc.so.6`__GI___clone at clone.S:95
```

Note: We see active thread #1 since its top frame #0 is not inside any waiting function.

4.   We check if there are .NET exceptions on each managed thread:

```
(lldb) pe
There is no current managed exception on this thread
```

```
(lldb) clrthreads
ThreadCount:       2
UnstartedThread:   0
BackgroundThread:  1
PendingThread:     0
DeadThread:        0
Hosted Runtime:    no

Lock
 DBG   ID    OSID ThreadOBJ            State GC Mode      GC Alloc Context
Domain             Count Apt Exception
   1    1     198 000055D6802B2540    20020 Cooperative 00007EF302809380:00007EF302809E60
000055D68029A790 -00001 Ukn
   6    2     19d 000055D6802B9C40    21220 Preemptive  0000000000000000:0000000000000000
000055D68029A790 -00001 Ukn (Finalizer)

(lldb) thread select 6
* thread #6, stop reason = signal 0
    frame #0: 0x00007f3397b303f9 libpthread.so.0`__pthread_cond_timedwait at futex-
internal.h:142

(lldb) pe
There is no current managed exception on this thread

(lldb) thread select 1
* thread #1, name = 'ApplicationH', stop reason = signal SIGSTOP
    frame #0: 0x00007f3318e319f8
->  0x7f3318e319f8: cmpb    $0x0, 0x10(%rdi)
    0x7f3318e319fc: je      0x7f3318e319f2
    0x7f3318e319fe: addq    $0x50, %rsp
    0x7f3318e31a02: popq    %rbp
```

5.   Let's now check the managed stack trace for thread #1:

```
(lldb) clrstack
OS Thread Id: 0x198 (1)
        Child SP               IP Call Site
00007FFC0722EA40 00007F3318E319F8 ClassMain.Main() [/mnt/c/ANETMDA-Examples/ApplicationH/Program.cs @ 9]
00007FFC0722EAA0 00007F3318E3189B Program.<Main>$(System.String[]) [/mnt/c/ANETMDA-Examples/ApplicationH/Program.cs @
1]
```

6.   We also see that the top IP address in the unmanaged stack trace corresponds to the top IP address in the managed stack trace and the current CPU instruction:

```
(lldb) bt 3
* thread #1, name = 'ApplicationH', stop reason = signal SIGSTOP
  * frame #0: 0x00007f3318e319f8
    frame #1: 0x00007f3318e3194c
    frame #2: 0x00007f33972f8e04 libcoreclr.so`CallDescrWorkerInternal + 124

(lldb) ip2md 0x00007f3318e319f8
MethodDesc:     00007f3318eda058
Method Name:            ClassMain.Main()
Class:                  00007f3318eda0b0
MethodTable:            00007f3318eda0b0
mdToken:                0000000006000003
Module:                 00007f3318ed7038
IsJitted:               yes
```

```
Current CodeAddr:        00007f3318e319e0
Version History:
  ILCodeVersion:         0000000000000000
  ReJIT ID:              0
  IL Addr:               00007f3392a7a264
     CodeAddr:              00007f3318e319e0  (OptimizedTier1OSR)
     NativeCodeVersion:  000055D6802C8C10
     CodeAddr:              00007f3318e31900  (QuickJitted)
     NativeCodeVersion:  0000000000000000
Source file:  /mnt/c/ANETMDA-Examples/ApplicationH/Program.cs @ 9
```

7.   We now check what is the currently executing instruction of the current thread:

```
(lldb) x/i $pc
-> 0x7f3318e319f8: 80 7f 10 00  cmpb    $0x0, 0x10(%rdi)
```

```
(lldb) bt 2
* thread #1, name = 'ApplicationH', stop reason = signal SIGSTOP
  * frame #0: 0x00007f3318e319f8
    frame #1: 0x00007f3318e3194c
```

Note: We see that it is executing some code instead of waiting like other threads, for example:

```
(lldb) thread select 2
* thread #2, stop reason = signal 0
    frame #0: 0x00007f339772f6f9 libc.so.6`__GI___poll(fds=0x00007f3396e2ad98, nfds=1,
timeout=-1) at poll.c:29
```

```
(lldb) bt 2
* thread #2, stop reason = signal 0
  * frame #0: 0x00007f339772f6f9 libc.so.6`__GI___poll(fds=0x00007f3396e2ad98, nfds=1, timeout=-1) at poll.c:29
    frame #1: 0x00007f33974a2800 libcoreclr.so`CorUnix::CPalSynchronizationManager::ReadBytesFromProcessPipe(int,
unsigned char*, int) + 288
```

8.   We now dump the method descriptor, class, method table (with or without method descriptors), module, and assembly information using **dumpmd**, **dumpclass**, **dumpmt**, **dumpmodule**, **dumpassembly**, and **dumpdomain** commands, respectively:

```
(lldb) ip2md 0x00007f3318e319f8
MethodDesc:     00007f3318eda058
Method Name:         ClassMain.Main()
Class:               00007f3318eda0b0
MethodTable:         00007f3318eda0b0
mdToken:             0000000006000003
Module:              00007f3318ed7038
IsJitted:            yes
Current CodeAddr:    00007f3318e319e0
Version History:
  ILCodeVersion:       0000000000000000
  ReJIT ID:            0
  IL Addr:             00007f3392a7a264
     CodeAddr:              00007f3318e319e0  (OptimizedTier1OSR)
     NativeCodeVersion:  000055D6802C8C10
     CodeAddr:              00007f3318e31900  (QuickJitted)
     NativeCodeVersion:  0000000000000000
Source file:  /mnt/c/ANETMDA-Examples/ApplicationH/Program.cs @ 9
```

```
(lldb) dumpmd 00007f3318eda058
Method Name:        ClassMain.Main()
Class:              00007f3318eda0b0
MethodTable:        00007f3318eda0b0
mdToken:            0000000006000003
Module:             00007f3318ed7038
IsJitted:           yes
Current CodeAddr:   00007f3318e31900
Version History:
  ILCodeVersion:    0000000000000000
  ReJIT ID:         0
  IL Addr:          00007f3392a7a264
     CodeAddr:          00007f3318e319e0  (OptimizedTier1OSR)
     NativeCodeVersion: 000055D6802C8C10
     CodeAddr:          00007f3318e31900  (QuickJitted)
     NativeCodeVersion: 0000000000000000

(lldb) dumpclass 00007f3318eda0b0
Class Name:         ClassMain
mdToken:            0000000002000003
File:               /mnt/c/ANETMDA-Examples/ApplicationH/bin/Release/net9.0/ApplicationH.dll
Parent MethodTable: 00007f3317e84910
Module:             00007f3318ed7038
Method Table:       00007f3318eda0b0
Canonical MethodTable: 00007f3318eda0b0
Class Attributes:   100001
NumInstanceFields:  3
NumStaticFields:    0
              MT    Field   Offset                 Type VT     Attr            Value Name
00007f3318dc3080  4000001      10       System.Boolean  1 instance                  time2stop
00007f3318dc74f0  4000002       8         System.Int32  1 instance                  inSensor
00007f3318dc74f0  4000003       c         System.Int32  1 instance                  outSensor

(lldb) dumpmt 00007f3318eda0b0
Canonical MethodTabl 00007F3318EDA0B0
Module:             00007F3318ED7038
Name:               ClassMain
mdToken:            0000000002000003
File:               /mnt/c/ANETMDA-Examples/ApplicationH/bin/Release/net9.0/ApplicationH.dll
AssemblyLoadContext: Default ALC - The managed instance of this context doesn't exist yet.
BaseSize:           0x20
ComponentSize:      0x0
DynamicStatics:     false
ContainsPointers:   false
Number of Methods:  7
Number of IFaces in IFaceMap: 0

(lldb) dumpmt -md 00007f3318eda0b0
Canonical MethodTabl 00007F3318EDA0B0
Module:             00007F3318ED7038
Name:               ClassMain
mdToken:            0000000002000003
File:               /mnt/c/ANETMDA-Examples/ApplicationH/bin/Release/net9.0/ApplicationH.dll
AssemblyLoadContext: Default ALC - The managed instance of this context doesn't exist yet.
BaseSize:           0x20
ComponentSize:      0x0
DynamicStatics:     false
ContainsPointers:   false
Number of Methods:  7
```

```
Number of IFaces in IFaceMap: 0
----------------------------------------
MethodDesc Table
           Entry         MethodDesc    JIT Slot                Name
00007F3318DB0000 00007F3317E84870  NONE 0000000000000000 System.Object.Finalize()
00007F3318DB00A8 00007F3317E84888  NONE 0000000000000001 System.Object.ToString()
00007F3318DB0E70 00007F3317E848A0  NONE 0000000000000002 System.Object.Equals(System.Object)
00007F3318DB0E88 00007F3317E848F8  NONE 0000000000000003 System.Object.GetHashCode()
00007F3318DB3288 00007F3318EDA098   JIT 0000000000000004 ClassMain..ctor()
00007F3318DB32A0 00007F3318EDA058   JIT 0000000000000005 ClassMain.Main()
00007F3318DB32D0 00007F3318EDA078   JIT 0000000000000006 ClassMain.DoWork()
```

```
(lldb) dumpmodule 00007F3318ED7038
Name: /mnt/c/ANETMDA-Examples/ApplicationH/bin/Release/net9.0/ApplicationH.dll
Attributes:             PEFile IsFileLayout
TransientFlags:         00008811
Assembly:               000055d6802c6010
BaseAddress:            00007F3392A7A000
LoaderHeap:             00007F33975461B0
TypeDefToMethodTableMap: 00007F3318EB78D0
TypeRefToMethodTableMap: 00007F3318EB78F0
MethodDefToDescMap:     00007F3318EB79E0
FieldDefToDescMap:      00007F3318EB7A18
MemberRefToDescMap:     00007F3318EB7970
FileReferencesMap:      0000000000000000
AssemblyReferencesMap:  00007F3318EB7A40
MetaData start address: 00007F3392A7A29C (1440 bytes)
```

```
(lldb) dumpassembly 000055d6802c6010
Parent Domain:          000055d68029a790
Name:                   /mnt/c/ANETMDA-Examples/ApplicationH/bin/Release/net9.0/ApplicationH.dll
  Module
  00007f3318ed7038        /mnt/c/ANETMDA-Examples/ApplicationH/bin/Release/net9.0/ApplicationH.dll
```

```
(lldb) dumpdomain 000055d68029a790
--------------------------------------
Domain 1:          000055d68029a790
LowFrequencyHeap:  00007F33975461C0
HighFrequencyHeap: 00007F3397546250
StubHeap:          00007F33975462E0
Stage:             OPEN
Name:              clrhost
Assembly:          000055d6802bca10 [/usr/share/dotnet/shared/Microsoft.NETCore.App/9.0.4/System.Private.CoreLib.dll]
  Module
  00007f3317e84000   /usr/share/dotnet/shared/Microsoft.NETCore.App/9.0.4/System.Private.CoreLib.dll

Assembly:          000055d6802c6010 [/mnt/c/ANETMDA-Examples/ApplicationH/bin/Release/net9.0/ApplicationH.dll]
  Module
  00007f3318ed7038   /mnt/c/ANETMDA-Examples/ApplicationH/bin/Release/net9.0/ApplicationH.dll

Assembly:          000055d6802c95d0 [/usr/share/dotnet/shared/Microsoft.NETCore.App/9.0.4/System.Runtime.dll]
  Module
  00007f3318ed9208   /usr/share/dotnet/shared/Microsoft.NETCore.App/9.0.4/System.Runtime.dll
```

9.   At the end of this exercise, we revisit our CLR stack trace again and disassemble the current function:

```
(lldb) thread select 1
* thread #1, name = 'ApplicationH', stop reason = signal SIGSTOP
    frame #0: 0x00007f3318e319f8
-> 0x7f3318e319f8: cmpb   $0x0, 0x10(%rdi)
   0x7f3318e319fc: je     0x7f3318e319f2
   0x7f3318e319fe: addq   $0x50, %rsp
   0x7f3318e31a02: popq   %rbp
```

```
(lldb) clru 0x7f3318e319f8
Normal JIT generated code
ClassMain.Main()
ilAddr is 00007F3392A7A264 pImport is 000000001FF489F0
Begin 00007F3318E319E0, size 24
00007f3318e319e0 488b4500           mov      rax, qword ptr [rbp]
00007f3318e319e4 50                 push     rax
00007f3318e319e5 488bec             mov      rbp, rsp
00007f3318e319e8 488b7d20           mov      rdi, qword ptr [rbp + 0x20]

/mnt/c/ANETMDA-Examples/ApplicationH/Program.cs @ 9:
00007f3318e319ec 807f1000           cmp      byte ptr [rdi + 0x10], 0x0
00007f3318e319f0 750c               jne      0x7f3318e319fe

/mnt/c/ANETMDA-Examples/ApplicationH/Program.cs @ 11:
00007f3318e319f2 8b4708             mov      eax, dword ptr [rdi + 0x8]
00007f3318e319f5 31470c             xor      dword ptr [rdi + 0xc], eax

/mnt/c/ANETMDA-Examples/ApplicationH/Program.cs @ 9:
>>> 00007f3318e319f8 807f1000       cmp      byte ptr [rdi + 0x10], 0x0
00007f3318e319fc 74f4               je       0x7f3318e319f2

/mnt/c/ANETMDA-Examples/ApplicationH/Program.cs @ 13:
00007f3318e319fe 4883c450           add      rsp, 0x50
00007f3318e31a02 5d                 pop      rbp
00007f3318e31a03 c3                 ret
```

Note: We see that JIT code is annotated with method names, and this can be helpful with reverse engineering of an unknown method. We also see the infinite loop in the code.

10.   If you know the method descriptor, you can also dump IL code:

```
MethodDesc:     00007f3318eda058
Method Name:            ClassMain.Main()
Class:                  00007f3318eda0b0
MethodTable:            00007f3318eda0b0
mdToken:                0000000006000003
Module:                 00007f3318ed7038
IsJitted:               yes
Current CodeAddr:       00007f3318e319e0
Version History:
  ILCodeVersion:        0000000000000000
  ReJIT ID:             0
  IL Addr:              00007f3392a7a264
     CodeAddr:             00007f3318e319e0  (OptimizedTier1OSR)
     NativeCodeVersion:    000055D6802C8C10
     CodeAddr:             00007f3318e31900  (QuickJitted)
     NativeCodeVersion:    0000000000000000

(lldb) dumpil 00007f3318eda058
ilAddr is 00007F3392A7A264 pImport is 000000001FF489F0
ilAddr = 00007F3392A7A264
IL_0000: br.s IL_0008
IL_0002: ldarg.0
IL_0003: call void ClassMain::DoWork()
IL_0008: ldarg.0
IL_0009: ldfld ClassMain::time2stop
IL_000e: brfalse.s IL_0102
IL_0010: ret
```

163

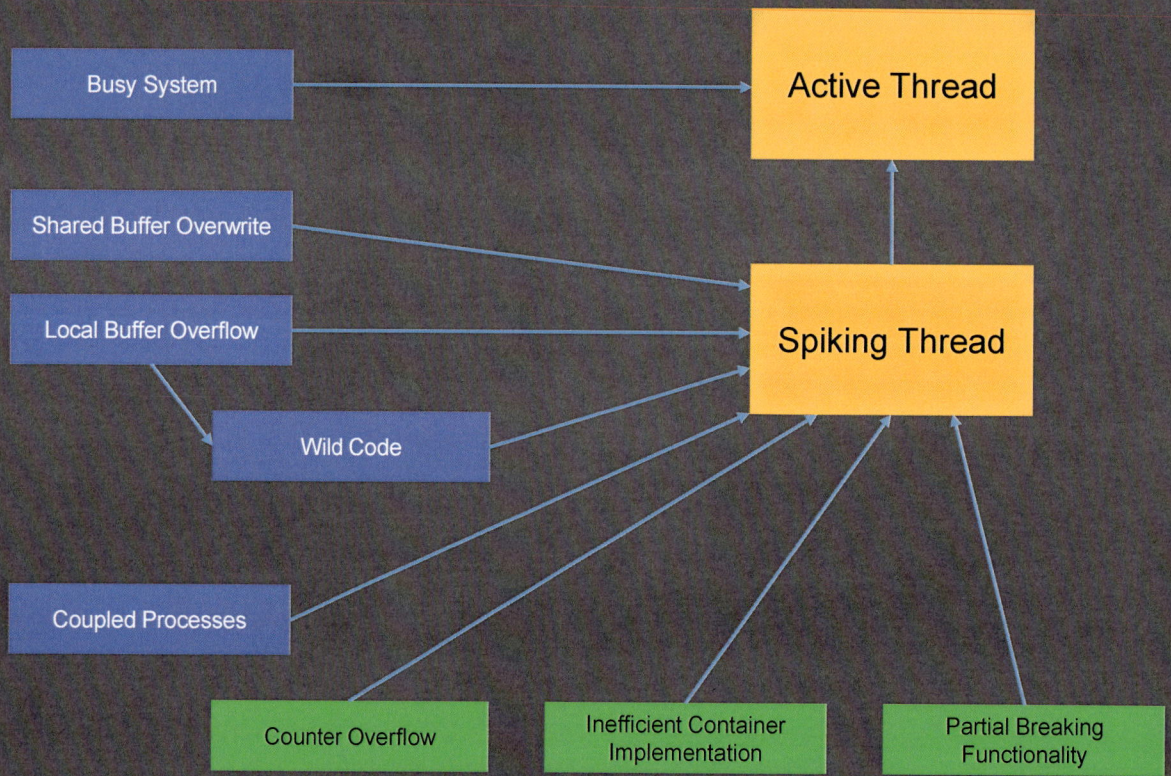

Defect Mechanism Patterns (DMP), Part 1

https://dumpanalysis.org/defect-mechanism-patterns-part1

Exercise PN4 (Windows)

- **Goal:** Learn how to recognize and analyze deadlocks using SOS, execution residue, handled exceptions, and dump object references

- **Patterns:** Special Thread (.NET CLR); Wait Chain (CLR Monitors); Deadlock (Managed Space); Execution Residue (Managed Space); Value References; Hidden Exception (Managed Space); Handled Exception (.NET CLR); Coincidental Symbolic Information; Rough Stack Trace (Unmanaged Space); Caller-n-Callee

- **Commands:** ~<>s, !Threads, !syncblk, !DumpObj, ub, !DumpStack, dpS, !DumpStackObjects

- \ANETMDA-Dumps\Exercise-PN4-Windows.pdf

Goal: Learn how to recognize and analyze deadlocks using SOS, execution residue, handled exceptions, and dump object references.

Patterns: Special Thread (.NET CLR); Wait Chain (CLR Monitors); Deadlock (Managed Space); Execution Residue (Managed Space); Value References; Hidden Exception (Managed Space); Handled Exception (.NET CLR); Coincidental Symbolic Information; Rough Stack Trace (Unmanaged Space); Caller-n-Callee.

Commands: ~<>s, !Threads, !syncblk, !DumpObj, ub,!DumpStack, dpS, !DumpStackObjects

1.   Launch WinDbg.

2.   Open \ANETMDA-Dumps\Windows\x64\LINQPad8-PN4.DMP

3.   We get the dump file loaded:


```
Microsoft (R) Windows Debugger Version 10.0.27829.1001 AMD64
Copyright (c) Microsoft Corporation. All rights reserved.



Loading Dump File [C:\ANETMDA-Dumps\Windows\x64\LINQPad8-PN4.DMP]
User Mini Dump File with Full Memory: Only application data is available



************* Path validation summary **************
Response                        Time (ms)      Location
Deferred                                       srv*
Symbol search path is: srv*
Executable search path is:
Windows 10 Version 22000 MP (4 procs) Free x64
Product: WinNt, suite: SingleUserTS
Edition build lab: 22000.1.amd64fre.co_release.210604-1628
Debug session time: Sun Apr 27 15:34:11.000 2025 (UTC + 1:00)
System Uptime: 0 days 0:19:52.082
Process Uptime: 0 days 0:17:15.000
................................................................
................................................................

For analysis of this file, run !analyze -v
win32u!NtUserMsgWaitForMultipleObjectsEx+0x14:
00007ffa`c012abf4 ret
```

4.   Open a log file using **.logopen** command:

```
0:000> .logopen C:\ANETMDA-Dumps\Windows\x64\LINQPadC.log
Opened log file 'C:\ANETMDA-Dumps\Windows\x64\LINQPadC.log'
```

Note: The WinDbg output may be slightly different on your system if you have a different WinDbg version, a different SOS extension version, you don't have .NET 9 installed, or you have a .NET version different from version 9.0.4 that was on a virtual machine where all the dumps were saved.

5. Type ~*kL command to verify the correctness of all stack traces (the command execution time may be longer for the first time because symbol files need to be downloaded from the Microsoft symbol server):

```
0:000> ~*kL

.  0  Id: 1ef4.1cc0 Suspend: 0 Teb: 0000003f`525f4000 Unfrozen
 # Child-SP          RetAddr               Call Site
00 0000003f`523ac918 00007ffa`c1bcd2de     win32u!NtUserMsgWaitForMultipleObjectsEx+0x14
01 0000003f`523ac920 00007ffa`c1198ea6     user32!RealMsgWaitForMultipleObjectsEx+0x1e
02 0000003f`523ac960 00007ffa`c1195c55     combase!CCliModalLoop::BlockFn+0x196
03 0000003f`523aca10 00007ffa`c11e79c0     combase!ClassicSTAThreadWaitForHandles+0xa5
04 0000003f`523acb30 00007ffa`73f3d7ec     combase!CoWaitForMultipleHandles+0x80
05 0000003f`523acb70 00007ffa`73e95948     coreclr!MsgWaitHelper+0x44
06 0000003f`523acbb0 00007ffa`73d1e523     coreclr!Thread::DoAppropriateAptStateWait+0x1771a4
07 0000003f`523acbf0 00007ffa`73d1e35a     coreclr!Thread::DoAppropriateWaitWorker+0x17b
08 0000003f`523accc0 00007ffa`73e571bf     coreclr!Thread::DoAppropriateWait+0xa6
09 0000003f`523acd60 00007ffa`73e570f5     coreclr!Thread::JoinEx+0x6b
0a 0000003f`523acdb0 00007ffa`73e56fab     coreclr!ThreadNative::DoJoin+0xd9
0b 0000003f`523ace00 00007ffa`732244af     coreclr!ThreadNative::Join+0xcb
0c 0000003f`523acf80 00007ffa`14b68550     System_Private_CoreLib!System.Threading.Thread.Join+0xf
0d 0000003f`523acfb0 00007ffa`14b6834b     LINQPadQuery!UserQuery.ClassMain.Main+0x190
0e 0000003f`523ad030 00007ffa`14b63c4c     LINQPadQuery!UserQuery.Main+0x4b
0f 0000003f`523ad070 00007ffa`14b6023f     LINQPad_Runtime!LINQPad.ExecutionModel.ClrQueryRunner.Run+0x1dec
10 0000003f`523ad9c0 00007ffa`142f314a     LINQPad_Runtime!LINQPad.ExecutionModel.Server.RunQuery+0x21f
11 0000003f`523adca0 00007ffa`142f2c72     LINQPad_Runtime!LINQPad.ExecutionModel.Server.PrepareAndRunQuery+0x3ea
12 0000003f`523adde0 00007ffa`142f2b9c     LINQPad_Runtime!LINQPad.ExecutionModel.Server.<ExecuteClrQuery>b__147_0+0x52
13 0000003f`523ade20 00007ffa`1429dc70     LINQPad_Runtime!LINQPad.ExecutionModel.SyncPCQ.<>c__DisplayClass14_0.<Enqueue>b__0+0x4c
14 0000003f`523ade70 00007ffa`1429d9be     LINQPad_Runtime!LINQPad.ExecutionModel.SyncPCQ.Consume+0x100
15 0000003f`523adef0 00007ffa`1429659f     LINQPad_Runtime!LINQPad.ExecutionModel.SyncPCQ.Start+0x2ee
16 0000003f`523adff0 00007ffa`1429604b     LINQPad_Runtime!LINQPad.ExecutionModel.ProcessServer.TryRun+0x4cf
17 0000003f`523ae1b0 00007ffa`14295fd4     LINQPad_Runtime!LINQPad.ExecutionModel.ProcessServer.Run+0x3b
18 0000003f`523ae200 00007ffa`142956f3     LINQPad_Runtime!LINQPad.RuntimeLoader.Run+0x84
19 0000003f`523ae250 00007ffa`1429566c     LINQPad_Runtime!LINQPad.RuntimeLoader.Start+0x43
1a 0000003f`523ae2d0 00007ffa`73e62eb3     LINQPad_Runtime!LINQPad.EntryPoint.Main+0x4c
1b 0000003f`523ae320 00007ffa`73d45559     coreclr!CallDescrWorkerInternal+0x83
1c 0000003f`523ae360 00007ffa`732ae325     coreclr!RuntimeMethodHandle::InvokeMethod+0x3a9
1d 0000003f`523ae690 00007ffa`732adc2b     System_Private_CoreLib!System.Reflection.MethodBaseInvoker.InvokeDirectByRefWithFewArgs+0xb5
1e 0000003f`523ae710 00007ffa`732bf910     System_Private_CoreLib!System.Reflection.MethodBaseInvoker.InvokeWithOneArg+0x1bb
1f 0000003f`523ae7f0 00007ffa`732ad203     System_Private_CoreLib!System.Reflection.RuntimeMethodInfo.Invoke+0x1b0
20 0000003f`523ae860 00007ffa`142919ff     System_Private_CoreLib!System.Reflection.MethodBase.Invoke+0x23
21 0000003f`523ae8a0 00007ffa`73e62eb3     LINQPad_Query!LINQPad.ProcessServer.ProcessServerProgram.Main+0x19f
22 0000003f`523ae970 00007ffa`73de180c     coreclr!CallDescrWorkerInternal+0x83
23 0000003f`523ae9b0 00007ffa`73dcba54     coreclr!MethodDescCallSite::CallTargetWorker+0x208
24 (Inline Function) --------`--------     coreclr!MethodDescCallSite::Call_RetArgSlot+0xd
25 0000003f`523aeaf0 00007ffa`73dccc19     coreclr!RunMainInternal+0xb8
26 0000003f`523aec10 00007ffa`73dccf2d     coreclr!RunMain+0xd1
27 0000003f`523aeca0 00007ffa`73dcc1bb     coreclr!Assembly::ExecuteMainMethod+0x199
28 0000003f`523aef70 00007ffa`73dc704c     coreclr!CorHost2::ExecuteAssembly+0x1cb
29 0000003f`523af080 00007ffa`741de8ec     coreclr!coreclr_execute_assembly+0xcc
2a (Inline Function) --------`--------     hostpolicy!coreclr_t::execute_assembly+0x2d
2b 0000003f`523af120 00007ffa`741debbc     hostpolicy!run_app_for_context+0x58c
2c 0000003f`523af250 00007ffa`74231be9     hostpolicy!run_app+0x3c
2d 0000003f`523af290 00007ff6`958c7377     hostfxr!fx_muxer_t::run_app+0x109
2e 0000003f`523af300 00007ff6`958d5a72     LINQPad8+0x17377
2f 0000003f`523afc50 00007ffa`c1d753e0     LINQPad8+0x25a72
30 0000003f`523afc90 00007ffa`c2cc485b     kernel32!BaseThreadInitThunk+0x10
31 0000003f`523afcc0 00000000`00000000     ntdll!RtlUserThreadStart+0x2b

   1  Id: 1ef4.131c Suspend: 0 Teb: 0000003f`525fa000 Unfrozen ".NET EventPipe"
 # Child-SP          RetAddr               Call Site
00 0000003f`528ff4e8 00007ffa`c04bdcb0     ntdll!NtWaitForMultipleObjects+0x14
01 0000003f`528ff4f0 00007ffa`c04bdbae     KERNELBASE!WaitForMultipleObjectsEx+0xf0
02 0000003f`528ff7e0 00007ffa`73e3693f     KERNELBASE!WaitForMultipleObjects+0xe
03 0000003f`528ff820 00007ffa`73e368a0     coreclr!ds_ipc_poll+0x7f
04 0000003f`528ffaa0 00007ffa`73e36784     coreclr!ds_ipc_stream_factory_get_next_available_stream+0x108
05 0000003f`528ffb70 00007ffa`c1d753e0     coreclr!server_thread+0x54
06 0000003f`528ffbe0 00007ffa`c2cc485b     kernel32!BaseThreadInitThunk+0x10
07 0000003f`528ffc10 00000000`00000000     ntdll!RtlUserThreadStart+0x2b

   2  Id: 1ef4.1b30 Suspend: 0 Teb: 0000003f`525fc000 Unfrozen ".NET Debugger"
 # Child-SP          RetAddr               Call Site
00 0000003f`529ff9e8 00007ffa`c04bdcb0     ntdll!NtWaitForMultipleObjects+0x14
01 0000003f`529ff9f0 00007ffa`73e27a9e     KERNELBASE!WaitForMultipleObjectsEx+0xf0
02 0000003f`529ffce0 00007ffa`73e27e26     coreclr!DebuggerRCThread::MainLoop+0xee
03 0000003f`529ffda0 00007ffa`73e2785b     coreclr!DebuggerRCThread::ThreadProc+0x12e
04 0000003f`529ffe00 00007ffa`c1d753e0     coreclr!DebuggerRCThread::ThreadProcStatic+0x5b
05 0000003f`529ffe30 00007ffa`c2cc485b     kernel32!BaseThreadInitThunk+0x10
06 0000003f`529ffe60 00000000`00000000     ntdll!RtlUserThreadStart+0x2b

   3  Id: 1ef4.1b18 Suspend: 0 Teb: 0000003f`525fe000 Unfrozen ".NET Finalizer"
 # Child-SP          RetAddr               Call Site
00 0000003f`52aff1c8 00007ffa`c04b10ce     ntdll!NtWaitForSingleObject+0x14
01 0000003f`52aff1d0 00007ffa`73e293a3     KERNELBASE!WaitForSingleObjectEx+0x8e
02 (Inline Function) --------`--------     coreclr!CLREventWaitHelper2+0x6
03 0000003f`52aff270 00007ffa`73e28a39     coreclr!CLREventWaitHelper+0xf
04 (Inline Function) --------`--------     coreclr!CLREventBase::WaitEx+0x10
05 (Inline Function) --------`--------     coreclr!CLREventBase::Wait+0x10
06 0000003f`52aff2c0 00007ffa`73e2889f     coreclr!FinalizerThread::WaitForFinalizerEvent+0x21
07 0000003f`52aff300 00007ffa`73dcef05     coreclr!FinalizerThread::FinalizerThreadWorker+0x4f
08 (Inline Function) --------`--------     coreclr!ManagedThreadBase_DispatchInner+0xd
09 0000003f`52aff550 00007ffa`73dcee2d     coreclr!ManagedThreadBase_DispatchMiddle+0x79
0a 0000003f`52aff600 00007ffa`73e1e921     coreclr!ManagedThreadBase_DispatchOuter+0x8d
0b (Inline Function) --------`--------     coreclr!ManagedThreadBase_NoADTransition+0x28
0c (Inline Function) --------`--------     coreclr!ManagedThreadBase::FinalizerBase+0x28
```

```
0d 0000003f`52aff670 00007ffa`c1d753e0     coreclr!FinalizerThread::FinalizerThreadStart+0x91
0e 0000003f`52aff780 00007ffa`c2cc485b     kernel32!BaseThreadInitThunk+0x10
0f 0000003f`52aff7b0 00000000`00000000     ntdll!RtlUserThreadStart+0x2b

   4  Id: 1ef4.11e0 Suspend: 0 Teb: 0000003f`52404000 Unfrozen ".NET TP Wait"
 # Child-SP          RetAddr               Call Site
00 0000003f`523ef018 00007ffa`c04bdcb0     ntdll!NtWaitForMultipleObjects+0x14
01 0000003f`523ef020 00007ffa`73d1e800     KERNELBASE!WaitForMultipleObjectsEx+0xf0
02 0000003f`523ef310 00007ffa`73d1e523     coreclr!Thread::DoAppropriateAptStateWait+0x5c
03 0000003f`523ef350 00007ffa`73d1e35a     coreclr!Thread::DoAppropriateWaitWorker+0x17b
04 0000003f`523ef420 00007ffa`73d1cd19     coreclr!Thread::DoAppropriateWait+0xa6
05 0000003f`523ef4c0 00007ffa`14db3e30     coreclr!WaitHandleNative::CorWaitMultipleNative+0xf9
06 0000003f`523ef660 00007ffa`73242dcc     System_Private_CoreLib!System.Threading.WaitHandle.WaitAnyMultiple+0xf0
07 0000003f`523ef6e0 00007ffa`73e62eb3     System_Private_CoreLib!System.Threading.PortableThreadPool.WaitThread.WaitThreadStart+0x8c
08 0000003f`523ef740 00007ffa`73de1568     coreclr!CallDescrWorkerInternal+0x83
09 0000003f`523ef780 00007ffa`73e515a3     coreclr!DispatchCallSimple+0x60
0a 0000003f`523ef810 00007ffa`73dcef05     coreclr!ThreadNative::KickOffThread_Worker+0x63
0b (Inline Function) --------`--------     coreclr!ManagedThreadBase_DispatchInner+0xd
0c 0000003f`523ef870 00007ffa`73dcee2d     coreclr!ManagedThreadBase_DispatchMiddle+0x79
0d 0000003f`523ef920 00007ffa`73dcefbb     coreclr!ManagedThreadBase_DispatchOuter+0x8d
0e (Inline Function) --------`--------     coreclr!ManagedThreadBase_FullTransition+0x28
0f (Inline Function) --------`--------     coreclr!ManagedThreadBase::KickOff+0x28
10 0000003f`523ef990 00007ffa`c1d753e0     coreclr!ThreadNative::KickOffThread+0x7b
11 0000003f`523ef9f0 00007ffa`c2cc485b     kernel32!BaseThreadInitThunk+0x10
12 0000003f`523efa20 00000000`00000000     ntdll!RtlUserThreadStart+0x2b

   5  Id: 1ef4.1964 Suspend: 0 Teb: 0000003f`52408000 Unfrozen ".NET TP Gate"
 # Child-SP          RetAddr               Call Site
00 0000003f`52d3f348 00007ffa`c04bdcb0     ntdll!NtWaitForMultipleObjects+0x14
01 0000003f`52d3f350 00007ffa`73d1e800     KERNELBASE!WaitForMultipleObjectsEx+0xf0
02 0000003f`52d3f640 00007ffa`73d1e523     coreclr!Thread::DoAppropriateAptStateWait+0x5c
03 0000003f`52d3f680 00007ffa`73d1e35a     coreclr!Thread::DoAppropriateWaitWorker+0x17b
04 0000003f`52d3f750 00007ffa`73d1e24b     coreclr!Thread::DoAppropriateWait+0xa6
05 0000003f`52d3f7f0 00007ffa`14dbc9a3     coreclr!WaitHandleNative::CorWaitOneNative+0xdb
06 0000003f`52d3f960 00007ffa`732408ed     System_Private_CoreLib!System.Threading.WaitHandle.WaitOneNoCheck+0xc3
07 0000003f`52d3f9e0 00007ffa`73e62eb3     System_Private_CoreLib!System.Threading.PortableThreadPool.GateThread.GateThreadStart+0x18d
08 0000003f`52d3fb50 00007ffa`73de1568     coreclr!CallDescrWorkerInternal+0x83
09 0000003f`52d3fb90 00007ffa`73e515a3     coreclr!DispatchCallSimple+0x60
0a 0000003f`52d3fc20 00007ffa`73dcef05     coreclr!ThreadNative::KickOffThread_Worker+0x63
0b (Inline Function) --------`--------     coreclr!ManagedThreadBase_DispatchInner+0xd
0c 0000003f`52d3fc80 00007ffa`73dcee2d     coreclr!ManagedThreadBase_DispatchMiddle+0x79
0d 0000003f`52d3fd30 00007ffa`73dcefbb     coreclr!ManagedThreadBase_DispatchOuter+0x8d
0e (Inline Function) --------`--------     coreclr!ManagedThreadBase_FullTransition+0x28
0f (Inline Function) --------`--------     coreclr!ManagedThreadBase::KickOff+0x28
10 0000003f`52d3fda0 00007ffa`c1d753e0     coreclr!ThreadNative::KickOffThread+0x7b
11 0000003f`52d3fe00 00007ffa`c2cc485b     kernel32!BaseThreadInitThunk+0x10
12 0000003f`52d3fe30 00000000`00000000     ntdll!RtlUserThreadStart+0x2b

   6  Id: 1ef4.12a8 Suspend: 0 Teb: 0000003f`52410000 Unfrozen ".NET Timer"
 # Child-SP          RetAddr               Call Site
00 0000003f`5313ee38 00007ffa`c04bdcb0     ntdll!NtWaitForMultipleObjects+0x14
01 0000003f`5313ee40 00007ffa`73d1e800     KERNELBASE!WaitForMultipleObjectsEx+0xf0
02 0000003f`5313f130 00007ffa`73d1e523     coreclr!Thread::DoAppropriateAptStateWait+0x5c
03 0000003f`5313f170 00007ffa`73d1e35a     coreclr!Thread::DoAppropriateWaitWorker+0x17b
04 0000003f`5313f240 00007ffa`73d1e24b     coreclr!Thread::DoAppropriateWait+0xa6
05 0000003f`5313f2e0 00007ffa`732266513    coreclr!WaitHandleNative::CorWaitOneNative+0xdb
06 0000003f`5313f450 00007ffa`7323945f     System_Private_CoreLib!System.Threading.WaitHandle.WaitOneNoCheck+0x83
07 0000003f`5313f4c0 00007ffa`73e62eb3     System_Private_CoreLib!System.Threading.TimerQueue.TimerThread+0x7f
08 0000003f`5313f550 00007ffa`73de1568     coreclr!CallDescrWorkerInternal+0x83
09 0000003f`5313f590 00007ffa`73e515a3     coreclr!DispatchCallSimple+0x60
0a 0000003f`5313f620 00007ffa`73dcef05     coreclr!ThreadNative::KickOffThread_Worker+0x63
0b (Inline Function) --------`--------     coreclr!ManagedThreadBase_DispatchInner+0xd
0c 0000003f`5313f680 00007ffa`73dcee2d     coreclr!ManagedThreadBase_DispatchMiddle+0x79
0d 0000003f`5313f730 00007ffa`73dcefbb     coreclr!ManagedThreadBase_DispatchOuter+0x8d
0e (Inline Function) --------`--------     coreclr!ManagedThreadBase_FullTransition+0x28
0f (Inline Function) --------`--------     coreclr!ManagedThreadBase::KickOff+0x28
10 0000003f`5313f7a0 00007ffa`c1d753e0     coreclr!ThreadNative::KickOffThread+0x7b
11 0000003f`5313f800 00007ffa`c2cc485b     kernel32!BaseThreadInitThunk+0x10
12 0000003f`5313f830 00000000`00000000     ntdll!RtlUserThreadStart+0x2b

   7  Id: 1ef4.12c4 Suspend: 0 Teb: 0000003f`52414000 Unfrozen
 # Child-SP          RetAddr               Call Site
00 0000003f`5333f628 00007ffa`c2cd6cdf     ntdll!NtWaitForWorkViaWorkerFactory+0x14
01 0000003f`5333f630 00007ffa`c1d753e0     ntdll!TppWorkerThread+0x2df
02 0000003f`5333f920 00007ffa`c2cc485b     kernel32!BaseThreadInitThunk+0x10
03 0000003f`5333f950 00000000`00000000     ntdll!RtlUserThreadStart+0x2b

   8  Id: 1ef4.640 Suspend: 0 Teb: 0000003f`52424000 Unfrozen
 # Child-SP          RetAddr               Call Site
00 0000003f`5353f068 00007ffa`c04bdcb0     ntdll!NtWaitForMultipleObjects+0x14
01 0000003f`5353f070 00007ffa`73d1e800     KERNELBASE!WaitForMultipleObjectsEx+0xf0
02 0000003f`5353f360 00007ffa`73d1e523     coreclr!Thread::DoAppropriateAptStateWait+0x5c
03 0000003f`5353f3a0 00007ffa`73d1e35a     coreclr!Thread::DoAppropriateWaitWorker+0x17b
04 0000003f`5353f470 00007ffa`73e28fc1     coreclr!Thread::DoAppropriateWait+0xa6
05 (Inline Function) --------`--------     coreclr!CLREventBase::WaitEx+0x53
06 0000003f`5353f510 00007ffa`73e28d0f     coreclr!CLREventBase::Wait+0x59
07 0000003f`5353f560 00007ffa`73e28bb2     coreclr!AwareLock::EnterEpilogHelper+0x12f
08 0000003f`5353f640 00007ffa`73e28b51     coreclr!AwareLock::EnterEpilog+0x42
09 0000003f`5353f6c0 00007ffa`73dfbbcb     coreclr!AwareLock::Enter+0xad
```

```
0a (Inline Function) --------`--------     coreclr!SyncBlock::EnterMonitor+0x8
0b (Inline Function) --------`--------     coreclr!ObjHeader::EnterObjMonitor+0xd
0c (Inline Function) --------`--------     coreclr!Object::EnterObjMonitor+0x16
0d 0000003f`5353f6f0 00007ffa`73d49bf7     coreclr!JIT_MonEnter_Helper+0x12f
0e 0000003f`5353f870 00007ffa`14b6863d     coreclr!JIT_MonEnter_Portable+0x147
```

```
0f 0000003f`5353f8b0 00007ffa`7322bf14     LINQPadQuery!UserQuery.ClassMain.thread_proc_1+0xbd
```

```
10 0000003f`5353f900 00007ffa`73e62eb3     System_Private_CoreLib!System.Threading.ExecutionContext.RunInternal+0x94
11 0000003f`5353f970 00007ffa`73de1568     coreclr!CallDescrWorkerInternal+0x83
12 0000003f`5353f9b0 00007ffa`73e515a3     coreclr!DispatchCallSimple+0x60
```

```
13 0000003f`5353fa40 00007ffa`73dcef05     coreclr!ThreadNative::KickOffThread_Worker+0x63
14 (Inline Function) --------`--------     coreclr!ManagedThreadBase_DispatchInner+0xd
15 0000003f`5353faa0 00007ffa`73dcee2d     coreclr!ManagedThreadBase_DispatchMiddle+0x79
16 0000003f`5353fb50 00007ffa`73dcefbb     coreclr!ManagedThreadBase_DispatchOuter+0x8d
17 (Inline Function) --------`--------     coreclr!ManagedThreadBase_FullTransition+0x28
18 (Inline Function) --------`--------     coreclr!ManagedThreadBase::KickOff+0x28
19 0000003f`5353fbc0 00007ffa`c1d753e0     coreclr!ThreadNative::KickOffThread+0x7b
1a 0000003f`5353fc20 00007ffa`c2cc485b     kernel32!BaseThreadInitThunk+0x10
1b 0000003f`5353fc50 00000000`00000000     ntdll!RtlUserThreadStart+0x2b

   9  Id: 1ef4.1b0c Suspend: 0 Teb: 0000003f`52426000 Unfrozen
 # Child-SP          RetAddr               Call Site
00 0000003f`5363f098 00007ffa`c04bdcb0     ntdll!NtWaitForMultipleObjects+0x14
01 0000003f`5363f0a0 00007ffa`73d1e800     KERNELBASE!WaitForMultipleObjectsEx+0xf0
02 0000003f`5363f390 00007ffa`73d1e523     coreclr!Thread::DoAppropriateAptStateWait+0x5c
03 0000003f`5363f3d0 00007ffa`73d1e35a     coreclr!Thread::DoAppropriateWaitWorker+0x17b
04 0000003f`5363f4a0 00007ffa`73e28fc1     coreclr!Thread::DoAppropriateWait+0xa6
05 (Inline Function) --------`--------     coreclr!CLREventBase::WaitEx+0x53
06 0000003f`5363f540 00007ffa`73e28d0f     coreclr!CLREventBase::Wait+0x59
07 0000003f`5363f590 00007ffa`73e28bb2     coreclr!AwareLock::EnterEpilogHelper+0x12f
08 0000003f`5363f670 00007ffa`73e28b51     coreclr!AwareLock::EnterEpilog+0x42
09 0000003f`5363f6f0 00007ffa`73dfbbcb     coreclr!AwareLock::Enter+0xad
0a (Inline Function) --------`--------     coreclr!SyncBlock::EnterMonitor+0x8
0b (Inline Function) --------`--------     coreclr!ObjHeader::EnterObjMonitor+0xd
0c (Inline Function) --------`--------     coreclr!Object::EnterObjMonitor+0x16
0d 0000003f`5363f720 00007ffa`73d49bf7     coreclr!JIT_MonEnter_Helper+0x12f
0e 0000003f`5363f8a0 00007ffa`14b86a86     coreclr!JIT_MonEnter_Portable+0x147
0f 0000003f`5363f8e0 00007ffa`7322bf14     LINQPadQuery!UserQuery.ClassMain.thread_proc_2+0x46
10 0000003f`5363f910 00007ffa`73e62eb3     System_Private_CoreLib!System.Threading.ExecutionContext.RunInternal+0x94
11 0000003f`5363f980 00007ffa`73de1568     coreclr!CallDescrWorkerInternal+0x83
12 0000003f`5363f9c0 00007ffa`73e515a3     coreclr!DispatchCallSimple+0x60
13 0000003f`5363fa50 00007ffa`73dcef05     coreclr!ThreadNative::KickOffThread_Worker+0x63
14 (Inline Function) --------`--------     coreclr!ManagedThreadBase_DispatchInner+0xd
15 0000003f`5363fab0 00007ffa`73dcee2d     coreclr!ManagedThreadBase_DispatchMiddle+0x79
16 0000003f`5363fb60 00007ffa`73dcefbb     coreclr!ManagedThreadBase_DispatchOuter+0x8d
17 (Inline Function) --------`--------     coreclr!ManagedThreadBase_FullTransition+0x28
18 (Inline Function) --------`--------     coreclr!ManagedThreadBase::KickOff+0x28
19 0000003f`5363fbd0 00007ffa`c1d753e0     coreclr!ThreadNative::KickOffThread+0x7b
1a 0000003f`5363fc30 00007ffa`c2cc485b     kernel32!BaseThreadInitThunk+0x10
1b 0000003f`5363fc60 00000000`00000000     ntdll!RtlUserThreadStart+0x2b

  10  Id: 1ef4.13c8 Suspend: 0 Teb: 0000003f`52484000 Unfrozen ".NET TP Worker"
 # Child-SP          RetAddr               Call Site
00 0000003f`526ff5b8 00007ffa`c04bebd3     ntdll!NtRemoveIoCompletion+0x14
01 0000003f`526ff5c0 00007ffa`14bd2c67     KERNELBASE!GetQueuedCompletionStatus+0x53
02 0000003f`526ff620 00007ffa`14bcf102     System_Private_CoreLib!System.Threading.LowLevelLifoSemaphore.WaitForSignal+0x107
03 0000003f`526ff6f0 00007ffa`732435be     System_Private_CoreLib!System.Threading.LowLevelLifoSemaphore.Wait+0x282
04 0000003f`526ff7a0 00007ffa`73e62eb3     System_Private_CoreLib!System.Threading.PortableThreadPool.WorkerThread.WorkerThreadStart+0x12e
05 0000003f`526ff8b0 00007ffa`73de1568     coreclr!CallDescrWorkerInternal+0x83
06 0000003f`526ff8f0 00007ffa`73e515a3     coreclr!DispatchCallSimple+0x60
07 0000003f`526ff980 00007ffa`73dcef05     coreclr!ThreadNative::KickOffThread_Worker+0x63
08 (Inline Function) --------`--------     coreclr!ManagedThreadBase_DispatchInner+0xd
09 0000003f`526ff9e0 00007ffa`73dcee2d     coreclr!ManagedThreadBase_DispatchMiddle+0x79
0a 0000003f`526ffa90 00007ffa`73dcefbb     coreclr!ManagedThreadBase_DispatchOuter+0x8d
0b (Inline Function) --------`--------     coreclr!ManagedThreadBase_FullTransition+0x28
0c (Inline Function) --------`--------     coreclr!ManagedThreadBase::KickOff+0x28
0d 0000003f`526ffb00 00007ffa`c1d753e0     coreclr!ThreadNative::KickOffThread+0x7b
0e 0000003f`526ffb60 00007ffa`c2cc485b     kernel32!BaseThreadInitThunk+0x10
0f 0000003f`526ffb90 00000000`00000000     ntdll!RtlUserThreadStart+0x2b

  11  Id: 1ef4.13cc Suspend: 0 Teb: 0000003f`52486000 Unfrozen ".NET TP Worker"
 # Child-SP          RetAddr               Call Site
00 0000003f`527ff8b8 00007ffa`c04bebd3     ntdll!NtRemoveIoCompletion+0x14
01 0000003f`527ff8c0 00007ffa`14bd2c67     KERNELBASE!GetQueuedCompletionStatus+0x53
02 0000003f`527ff920 00007ffa`14bcf102     System_Private_CoreLib!System.Threading.LowLevelLifoSemaphore.WaitForSignal+0x107
03 0000003f`527ff9f0 00007ffa`732435be     System_Private_CoreLib!System.Threading.LowLevelLifoSemaphore.Wait+0x282
04 0000003f`527ffaa0 00007ffa`73e62eb3     System_Private_CoreLib!System.Threading.PortableThreadPool.WorkerThread.WorkerThreadStart+0x12e
05 0000003f`527ffbb0 00007ffa`73de1568     coreclr!CallDescrWorkerInternal+0x83
06 0000003f`527ffbf0 00007ffa`73e515a3     coreclr!DispatchCallSimple+0x60
07 0000003f`527ffc80 00007ffa`73dcef05     coreclr!ThreadNative::KickOffThread_Worker+0x63
08 (Inline Function) --------`--------     coreclr!ManagedThreadBase_DispatchInner+0xd
09 0000003f`527ffce0 00007ffa`73dcee2d     coreclr!ManagedThreadBase_DispatchMiddle+0x79
0a 0000003f`527ffd90 00007ffa`73dcefbb     coreclr!ManagedThreadBase_DispatchOuter+0x8d
0b (Inline Function) --------`--------     coreclr!ManagedThreadBase_FullTransition+0x28
0c (Inline Function) --------`--------     coreclr!ManagedThreadBase::KickOff+0x28
0d 0000003f`527ffe00 00007ffa`c1d753e0     coreclr!ThreadNative::KickOffThread+0x7b
0e 0000003f`527ffe60 00007ffa`c2cc485b     kernel32!BaseThreadInitThunk+0x10
0f 0000003f`527ffe90 00000000`00000000     ntdll!RtlUserThreadStart+0x2b

  12  Id: 1ef4.13c4 Suspend: 0 Teb: 0000003f`52488000 Unfrozen ".NET TP Worker"
 # Child-SP          RetAddr               Call Site
00 0000003f`52bff4d8 00007ffa`c04bebd3     ntdll!NtRemoveIoCompletion+0x14
01 0000003f`52bff4e0 00007ffa`14bd2c67     KERNELBASE!GetQueuedCompletionStatus+0x53
02 0000003f`52bff540 00007ffa`14bcf102     System_Private_CoreLib!System.Threading.LowLevelLifoSemaphore.WaitForSignal+0x107
03 0000003f`52bff610 00007ffa`732435be     System_Private_CoreLib!System.Threading.LowLevelLifoSemaphore.Wait+0x282
04 0000003f`52bff6c0 00007ffa`73e62eb3     System_Private_CoreLib!System.Threading.PortableThreadPool.WorkerThread.WorkerThreadStart+0x12e
05 0000003f`52bff7d0 00007ffa`73de1568     coreclr!CallDescrWorkerInternal+0x83
06 0000003f`52bff810 00007ffa`73e515a3     coreclr!DispatchCallSimple+0x60
07 0000003f`52bff8a0 00007ffa`73dcef05     coreclr!ThreadNative::KickOffThread_Worker+0x63
08 (Inline Function) --------`--------     coreclr!ManagedThreadBase_DispatchInner+0xd
09 0000003f`52bff900 00007ffa`73dcee2d     coreclr!ManagedThreadBase_DispatchMiddle+0x79
0a 0000003f`52bff9b0 00007ffa`73dcefbb     coreclr!ManagedThreadBase_DispatchOuter+0x8d
0b (Inline Function) --------`--------     coreclr!ManagedThreadBase_FullTransition+0x28
0c (Inline Function) --------`--------     coreclr!ManagedThreadBase::KickOff+0x28
0d 0000003f`52bffa20 00007ffa`c1d753e0     coreclr!ThreadNative::KickOffThread+0x7b
0e 0000003f`52bffa80 00007ffa`c2cc485b     kernel32!BaseThreadInitThunk+0x10
0f 0000003f`52bffab0 00000000`00000000     ntdll!RtlUserThreadStart+0x2b
```

```
 13  Id: 1ef4.13b8 Suspend: 0 Teb: 0000003f`5248c000 Unfrozen ".NET TP Worker"
 # Child-SP          RetAddr           Call Site
00 0000003f`52e3f1c8 00007ffa`c04bebd3 ntdll!NtRemoveIoCompletion+0x14
01 0000003f`52e3f1d0 00007ffa`14bd2c67 KERNELBASE!GetQueuedCompletionStatus+0x53
02 0000003f`52e3f230 00007ffa`14bcf102 System_Private_CoreLib!System.Threading.LowLevelLifoSemaphore.WaitForSignal+0x107
03 0000003f`52e3f300 00007ffa`732435be System_Private_CoreLib!System.Threading.LowLevelLifoSemaphore.Wait+0x282
04 0000003f`52e3f3b0 00007ffa`73e62eb3 System_Private_CoreLib!System.Threading.PortableThreadPool.WorkerThread.WorkerThreadStart+0x12e
05 0000003f`52e3f4c0 00007ffa`73de1568 coreclr!CallDescrWorkerInternal+0x83
06 0000003f`52e3f500 00007ffa`73e515a3 coreclr!DispatchCallSimple+0x60
07 0000003f`52e3f590 00007ffa`73dcef05 coreclr!ThreadNative::KickOffThread_Worker+0x63
08 (Inline Function) --------`-------- coreclr!ManagedThreadBase_DispatchInner+0xd
09 0000003f`52e3f5f0 00007ffa`73dcee2d coreclr!ManagedThreadBase_DispatchMiddle+0x79
0a 0000003f`52e3f6a0 00007ffa`73dcefbb coreclr!ManagedThreadBase_DispatchOuter+0x8d
0b (Inline Function) --------`-------- coreclr!ManagedThreadBase_FullTransition+0x28
0c (Inline Function) --------`-------- coreclr!ManagedThreadBase::KickOff+0x28
0d 0000003f`52e3f710 00007ffa`c1d753e0 coreclr!ThreadNative::KickOffThread+0x7b
0e 0000003f`52e3f770 00007ffa`c2cc485b kernel32!BaseThreadInitThunk+0x10
0f 0000003f`52e3f7a0 00000000`00000000 ntdll!RtlUserThreadStart+0x2b

 14  Id: 1ef4.13b0 Suspend: 0 Teb: 0000003f`5248e000 Unfrozen ".NET Tiered Compilation Worker"
 # Child-SP          RetAddr           Call Site
00 0000003f`52cff7b8 00007ffa`c04b10ce ntdll!NtWaitForSingleObject+0x14
01 0000003f`52cff7c0 00007ffa`73e293a3 KERNELBASE!WaitForSingleObjectEx+0x8e
02 (Inline Function) --------`-------- coreclr!CLREventWaitHelper2+0x6
03 0000003f`52cff860 00007ffa`73e287a0 coreclr!CLREventWaitHelper+0xf
04 (Inline Function) --------`-------- coreclr!CLREventBase::WaitEx+0x12
05 (Inline Function) --------`-------- coreclr!CLREventBase::Wait+0x12
06 0000003f`52cff8b0 00007ffa`73e28645 coreclr!TieredCompilationManager::BackgroundWorkerStart+0x11c
07 0000003f`52cff900 00007ffa`73dcef05 coreclr!TieredCompilationManager::BackgroundWorkerBootstrapper1+0x55
08 (Inline Function) --------`-------- coreclr!ManagedThreadBase_DispatchInner+0xd
09 0000003f`52cff940 00007ffa`73dcee2d coreclr!ManagedThreadBase_DispatchMiddle+0x79
0a 0000003f`52cff9f0 00007ffa`73e5c8da coreclr!ManagedThreadBase_DispatchOuter+0x8d
0b (Inline Function) --------`-------- coreclr!ManagedThreadBase_FullTransition+0x24
0c (Inline Function) --------`-------- coreclr!ManagedThreadBase::KickOff+0x24
0d 0000003f`52cffa60 00007ffa`c1d753e0 coreclr!TieredCompilationManager::BackgroundWorkerBootstrapper0+0x3a
0e 0000003f`52cffab0 00007ffa`c2cc485b kernel32!BaseThreadInitThunk+0x10
0f 0000003f`52cffae0 00000000`00000000 ntdll!RtlUserThreadStart+0x2b
```

Note: We see two threads, #8 and #9, entered synchronization monitor functions (*MonEnter*, *EnterMonitor*). So we have a possible wait chain there. If we try the **!analyze -v -hang** command, it will only point to the manual dump.

6.   We load the corresponding SOS extension (and unload the previous, if any).

```
0:000> .unload sos
No extension named 'sos' in chain
```

```
0:000> .load C:\Users\dmitr\.dotnet\sos\sos.dll
```

7.   Now we check managed threads and list special CLR threads (**!Threads** -**special** command, the output is shown in smaller font for visual clarity):

```
0:000> !Threads -special
ThreadCount:      18
UnstartedThread:  0
BackgroundThread: 9
PendingThread:    0
DeadThread:       6
Hosted Runtime:   no

                                                                                              Lock
 DBG   ID   OSID ThreadOBJ          State GC Mode     GC Alloc Context                  Domain         Count Apt Exception
   0    1   1cc0 000001DF4421A450 2024020 Preemptive  0000000000000000:0000000000000000 000001df44255c90 -00001 STA
   3    2   1b18 000001DF45BD0BB0    2b220 Preemptive  000001DF4B402310:000001DF4B4042E8 000001df44255c90 -00001 MTA (Finalizer)
   4    4   11e0 000001DF442892E0  302b220 Preemptive  000001DF4B404380:000001DF4B406308 000001df44255c90 -00001 MTA (Threadpool Worker)
   5    6   1964 000001DF45C5D640  302b220 Preemptive  0000000000000000:0000000000000000 000001df44255c90 -00001 MTA (Threadpool Worker)
   6    7   12a8 000001DF45C7E590  202b220 Preemptive  0000000000000000:0000000000000000 000001df44255c90 -00001 MTA
XXXX   13      0 000001DF45C6F180 1039820 Preemptive  0000000000000000:0000000000000000 000001df44255c90 -00001 Ukn (Threadpool Worker)
   8   14    640 000001DF45C5AE00  202b020 Preemptive  0000000000000000:0000000000000000 000001df44255c90 -00001 MTA
   9   15   1b0c 0000021FDF123250  202b020 Preemptive  0000000000000000:0000000000000000 000001df44255c90 -00001 MTA
XXXX    9      0 000001DF44264550 1039820 Preemptive  0000000000000000:0000000000000000 000001df44255c90 -00001 Ukn (Threadpool Worker)
XXXX    3      0 000001DF45C82AA0 1039820 Preemptive  0000000000000000:0000000000000000 000001df44255c90 -00001 Ukn (Threadpool Worker)
XXXX   11      0 0000021FDEEB58D0 1039820 Preemptive  0000000000000000:0000000000000000 000001df44255c90 -00001 Ukn (Threadpool Worker)
XXXX   10      0 0000021FDEEB4590 1039820 Preemptive  0000000000000000:0000000000000000 000001df44255c90 -00001 Ukn (Threadpool Worker)
XXXX    8      0 0000021FDEEB5400 1039820 Preemptive  0000000000000000:0000000000000000 000001df44255c90 -00001 Ukn (Threadpool Worker)
  10   12   13c8 0000021FDEEB5DA0  102b220 Preemptive  0000000000000000:0000000000000000 000001df44255c90 -00001 MTA (Threadpool Worker)
  11   16   13cc 0000021FDEEB4A60  102b220 Preemptive  000001DF4B434DB0:000001DF4B436608 000001df44255c90 -00001 MTA (Threadpool Worker)
  12    5   13c4 0000021FDEEB40C0  102b220 Preemptive  000001DF4B4090F0:000001DF4B40A348 000001df44255c90 -00001 MTA (Threadpool Worker)
  13   17   13b8 0000021FDEEB3BF0  102b220 Preemptive  000001DF4B447E30:000001DF4B448728 000001df44255c90 -00001 MTA (Threadpool Worker)
  14   18   13b0 0000021FDEEB4F30    2b220 Preemptive  0000000000000000:0000000000000000 000001df44255c90 -00001 MTA

       OSID Special thread type
```

```
  2 1b30 DbgHelper
  3 1b18 Finalizer
```

Note: The application was reported hanging, but we don't see anything suspicious.

8.   However, when we check the output of the **!syncblk** command, we suspect a deadlock between threads **#8** and **#9**:

```
0:000> !syncblk
Index       SyncBlock MonitorHeld Recursion Owning Thread Info      SyncBlock Owner
    3 000001DF45C81B78          3         1 000001DF45C5AE00 640   8 0000021fda9d7058 System.String
    6 000001DF45C81C80          3         1 0000021FDF123250 1b0c  9 0000021fda9d7098 System.String
-----------------------------
Total            14
CCW               0
RCW               0
ComClassFactory   0
Free              3
```

Note: What we see here is that thread **#9** holds a lock on **000001DF45C81C80** synchronization block that is owned by **0000021fda9d7098** String object with "**critical section 2**" value:

```
0:000> !DumpObj 0000021fda9d7098
Name:        System.String
MethodTable: 00007ffa1426bf40
Canonical MethodTable: 00007ffa1426bf40
Tracked Type: false
Size:        58(0x3a) bytes
File:        C:\Program Files\dotnet\shared\Microsoft.NETCore.App\9.0.4\System.Private.CoreLib.dll
String:      critical section 2
Fields:
              MT    Field   Offset                 Type VT     Attr            Value Name
00007ffa14217408  4000355        8         System.Int32  1 instance              18 _stringLength
00007ffa14232f60  4000356        c          System.Char  1 instance              63 _firstChar
00007ffa1426bf40  4000354        8        System.String  0   static 0000021fda9b0008 Empty
```

and that thread **#8** holds a lock on **000001DF45C81B78** block that is owned by **0000021fda9d7058** String object with "**critical section 1**" value:

```
0:000> !DumpObj 0000021fda9d7058
Name:        System.String
MethodTable: 00007ffa1426bf40
Canonical MethodTable: 00007ffa1426bf40
Tracked Type: false
Size:        58(0x3a) bytes
File:        C:\Program Files\dotnet\shared\Microsoft.NETCore.App\9.0.4\System.Private.CoreLib.dll
String:      critical section 1
Fields:
              MT    Field   Offset                 Type VT     Attr            Value Name
00007ffa14217408  4000355        8         System.Int32  1 instance              18 _stringLength
00007ffa14232f60  4000356        c          System.Char  1 instance              63 _firstChar
00007ffa1426bf40  4000354        8        System.String  0   static 0000021fda9b0008 Empty
```

9.   However, to verify whether thread **#8** is waiting for the sync block owner from thread **#9** and vice versa, we need to inspect execution residue on their thread stack regions to see if there are any value references there:

```
0:000> ~8kL 10
 # Child-SP          RetAddr               Call Site
00 0000003f`5353f068 00007ffa`c04bdcb0     ntdll!NtWaitForMultipleObjects+0x14
```

```
01 0000003f`5353f070 00007ffa`73d1e800    KERNELBASE!WaitForMultipleObjectsEx+0xf0
02 0000003f`5353f360 00007ffa`73d1e523    coreclr!Thread::DoAppropriateAptStateWait+0x5c
03 0000003f`5353f3a0 00007ffa`73d1e35a    coreclr!Thread::DoAppropriateWaitWorker+0x17b
04 0000003f`5353f470 00007ffa`73e28fc1    coreclr!Thread::DoAppropriateWait+0xa6
05 (Inline Function) --------`--------    coreclr!CLREventBase::WaitEx+0x53
06 0000003f`5353f510 00007ffa`73e28d0f    coreclr!CLREventBase::Wait+0x59
07 0000003f`5353f560 00007ffa`73e28bb2    coreclr!AwareLock::EnterEpilogHelper+0x12f
08 0000003f`5353f640 00007ffa`73e28b51    coreclr!AwareLock::EnterEpilog+0x42
09 0000003f`5353f6c0 00007ffa`73dfbbcb    coreclr!AwareLock::Enter+0xad
0a (Inline Function) --------`--------    coreclr!SyncBlock::EnterMonitor+0x8
0b (Inline Function) --------`--------    coreclr!ObjHeader::EnterObjMonitor+0xd
0c (Inline Function) --------`--------    coreclr!Object::EnterObjMonitor+0x16
0d 0000003f`5353f6f0 00007ffa`73d49bf7    coreclr!JIT_MonEnter_Helper+0x12f
0e 0000003f`5353f870 00007ffa`14b6863d    coreclr!JIT_MonEnter_Portable+0x147
0f 0000003f`5353f8b0 00007ffa`7322bf14    LINQPadQuery!UserQuery.ClassMain.thread_proc_1+0xbd
```

```
0:000> !IP2MD 00007ffa`14b6863d
MethodDesc:      00007ffa14b48458
Method Name:         UserQuery+ClassMain.thread_proc_1()
Class:               00007ffa14b484e8
MethodTable:         00007ffa14b484e8
mdToken:             0000000006000007
Module:              00007ffa14b40be8
IsJitted:            yes
Current CodeAddr:    00007ffa14b68580
Version History:
  ILCodeVersion:     0000000000000000
  ReJIT ID:          0
  IL Addr:           0000021fdf3b2110
     CodeAddr:           00007ffa14b68580  (MinOptJitted)
     NativeCodeVersion:  0000000000000000
```

```
0:000> dps 0000003f`5353f6c0 0000003f`5353f8b0
0000003f`5353f6c0  00000000`00000000
0000003f`5353f6c8  00000000`00000000
0000003f`5353f6d0  000001df`4808b200
0000003f`5353f6d8  000001df`4808c8f8
0000003f`5353f6e0  000001df`4808b200
0000003f`5353f6e8  00007ffa`73dfbbcb coreclr!JIT_MonEnter_Helper+0x12f
[D:\a\_work\1\s\src\coreclr\vm\jithelpers.cpp @ 2634]
0000003f`5353f6f0  00000000`00000000
0000003f`5353f6f8  00007ffa`741700c0 coreclr!g_SyncBlockCacheInstance+0x10
0000003f`5353f700  000001df`45c81c80
0000003f`5353f708  00000000`00000000
0000003f`5353f710  ffffffff`ffffffff
0000003f`5353f718  0000021f`da9d7098
0000003f`5353f720  00007ffa`c048d09f KERNELBASE!SleepEx+0xdf
0000003f`5353f728  00000000`00000000
0000003f`5353f730  00000000`00000000
0000003f`5353f738  000001df`45c5ae00
0000003f`5353f740  0000003f`5353f728
0000003f`5353f748  00000001`00000001
0000003f`5353f750  ffffffff`feced300
0000003f`5353f758  00000000`00000000
0000003f`5353f760  000017d2`4e91ba65
0000003f`5353f768  00007ffa`740e05f8 coreclr!HelperMethodFrame_1OBJ::`vftable'
0000003f`5353f770  0000003f`5353fb98
0000003f`5353f778  00007ffa`14271048
0000003f`5353f780  00000000`00000030
```

```
0000003f`5353f788   000001df`45c5ae00
0000003f`5353f790   00007ffa`73d49ab0 coreclr!JIT_MonEnter_Portable
[D:\a\_work\1\s\src\coreclr\vm\jithelpers.cpp @ 2659]
0000003f`5353f798   00007ffa`14b6863d LINQPadQuery!UserQuery.ClassMain.thread_proc_1+0xbd
0000003f`5353f7a0   0000003f`5353f8b0
0000003f`5353f7a8   000001df`4808b208
0000003f`5353f7b0   000001df`4acbc368
0000003f`5353f7b8   0000021f`da9d7098
0000003f`5353f7c0   0000003f`5353f8f0
0000003f`5353f7c8   00000000`00000000
0000003f`5353f7d0   00000000`00000000
0000003f`5353f7d8   00000000`00000000
0000003f`5353f7e0   00000000`00000000
0000003f`5353f7e8   0000003f`5353f860
0000003f`5353f7f0   0000003f`5353f7b0
0000003f`5353f7f8   0000003f`5353f8a0
0000003f`5353f800   0000003f`5353f7c0
0000003f`5353f808   0000003f`5353f7c8
0000003f`5353f810   0000003f`5353f7d0
0000003f`5353f818   0000003f`5353f7d8
0000003f`5353f820   0000003f`5353f7e0
0000003f`5353f828   0000003f`5353f798
0000003f`5353f830   00007ffa`73dfbb14 coreclr!JIT_MonEnter_Helper+0x78
[D:\a\_work\1\s\src\coreclr\vm\jithelpers.cpp @ 2621]
0000003f`5353f838   0000003f`5353f6e8
0000003f`5353f840   0000003f`5353f718
0000003f`5353f848   00000000`00000000
0000003f`5353f850   000017ed`1dc02819
0000003f`5353f858   000001df`4808b208
0000003f`5353f860   000001df`4acbc260
0000003f`5353f868   00007ffa`73d49bf7 coreclr!JIT_MonEnter_Portable+0x147
[D:\a\_work\1\s\src\coreclr\vm\jithelpers.cpp @ 2668]
0000003f`5353f870   0000021f`da9d7098
0000003f`5353f878   0000003f`5353f8f0
0000003f`5353f880   00007ffa`73d49ab0 coreclr!JIT_MonEnter_Portable
[D:\a\_work\1\s\src\coreclr\vm\jithelpers.cpp @ 2659]
0000003f`5353f888   0000021f`da9d7098
0000003f`5353f890   00000000`00000000
0000003f`5353f898   00000000`00000000
0000003f`5353f8a0   000001df`48013360
0000003f`5353f8a8   00007ffa`14b6863d LINQPadQuery!UserQuery.ClassMain.thread_proc_1+0xbd
0000003f`5353f8b0   00000000`00000000
```

Note: We see thread #8 is waiting for the sync block owner (String) from thread #9.

10.   We repeat the same exercise for the thread #9:

```
0:000> ~9kL 10
 # Child-SP          RetAddr           Call Site
00 0000003f`5363f098 00007ffa`c04bdcb0 ntdll!NtWaitForMultipleObjects+0x14
01 0000003f`5363f0a0 00007ffa`73d1e800 KERNELBASE!WaitForMultipleObjectsEx+0xf0
02 0000003f`5363f390 00007ffa`73d1e523 coreclr!Thread::DoAppropriateAptStateWait+0x5c
03 0000003f`5363f3d0 00007ffa`73d1e35a coreclr!Thread::DoAppropriateWaitWorker+0x17b
04 0000003f`5363f4a0 00007ffa`73e28fc1 coreclr!Thread::DoAppropriateWait+0xa6
05 (Inline Function) --------`-------- coreclr!CLREventBase::WaitEx+0x53
06 0000003f`5363f540 00007ffa`73e28d0f coreclr!CLREventBase::Wait+0x59
07 0000003f`5363f590 00007ffa`73e28bb2 coreclr!AwareLock::EnterEpilogHelper+0x12f
08 0000003f`5363f670 00007ffa`73e28b51 coreclr!AwareLock::EnterEpilog+0x42
```

173

```
09 0000003f`5363f6f0 00007ffa`73dfbbcb    coreclr!AwareLock::Enter+0xad
0a (Inline Function) --------`--------     coreclr!SyncBlock::EnterMonitor+0x8
0b (Inline Function) --------`--------     coreclr!ObjHeader::EnterObjMonitor+0xd
0c (Inline Function) --------`--------     coreclr!Object::EnterObjMonitor+0x16
0d 0000003f`5363f720 00007ffa`73d49bf7    coreclr!JIT_MonEnter_Helper+0x12f
0e 0000003f`5363f8a0 00007ffa`14b86a86    coreclr!JIT_MonEnter_Portable+0x147
0f 0000003f`5363f8e0 00007ffa`7322bf14    LINQPadQuery!UserQuery.ClassMain.thread_proc_2+0x46
```

```
0:000> !IP2MD 00007ffa`14b86a86
MethodDesc:          00007ffa14b48478
Method Name:         UserQuery+ClassMain.thread_proc_2()
Class:               00007ffa14b484e8
MethodTable:         00007ffa14b484e8
mdToken:             0000000006000008
Module:              00007ffa14b40be8
IsJitted:            yes
Current CodeAddr:    00007ffa14b86a40
Version History:
  ILCodeVersion:     0000000000000000
  ReJIT ID:          0
  IL Addr:           0000021fdf3b219c
     CodeAddr:          00007ffa14b86a40  (MinOptJitted)
     NativeCodeVersion: 0000000000000000
```

```
0:000> dps 0000003f`5363f6f0 0000003f`5363f8e0
0000003f`5363f6f0  00000000`00000000
0000003f`5363f6f8  00000000`00000000
0000003f`5363f700  000001df`4808b200
0000003f`5363f708  000001df`4808c8f8
0000003f`5363f710  000001df`4808b200
0000003f`5363f718  00007ffa`73dfbbcb coreclr!JIT_MonEnter_Helper+0x12f
[D:\a\_work\1\s\src\coreclr\vm\jithelpers.cpp @ 2634]
0000003f`5363f720  00000000`00000000
0000003f`5363f728  00007ffa`741700c0 coreclr!g_SyncBlockCacheInstance+0x10
0000003f`5363f730  000001df`45c81b78
0000003f`5363f738  00000000`00000000
0000003f`5363f740  000072a3`42a8fb7c
0000003f`5363f748  0000021f`da9d7058
0000003f`5363f750  0000003f`5363f970
0000003f`5363f758  00000000`00000000
0000003f`5363f760  00000000`00000000
0000003f`5363f768  0000021f`df123250
0000003f`5363f770  0000003f`5363f758
0000003f`5363f778  00000001`00000001
0000003f`5363f780  00090f04`0001005f
0000003f`5363f788  00000000`80000000
0000003f`5363f790  000017d2`4e91ba65
0000003f`5363f798  00007ffa`740e05f8 coreclr!HelperMethodFrame_1OBJ::`vftable'
0000003f`5363f7a0  0000003f`5363fba8
0000003f`5363f7a8  00007ffa`14271048
0000003f`5363f7b0  00000000`00000030
0000003f`5363f7b8  0000021f`df123250
0000003f`5363f7c0  00007ffa`73d49ab0 coreclr!JIT_MonEnter_Portable
[D:\a\_work\1\s\src\coreclr\vm\jithelpers.cpp @ 2659]
0000003f`5363f7c8  00007ffa`14b86a86 LINQPadQuery!UserQuery.ClassMain.thread_proc_2+0x46
0000003f`5363f7d0  0000003f`5363f8e0
0000003f`5363f7d8  000001df`4808b2d0
0000003f`5363f7e0  000001df`4acbc368
0000003f`5363f7e8  0000021f`da9d7058
```

```
0000003f`5363f7f0    0000003f`5363f900
0000003f`5363f7f8    00000000`00000000
0000003f`5363f800    00000000`00000000
0000003f`5363f808    00000000`00000000
0000003f`5363f810    00000000`00000000
0000003f`5363f818    0000003f`5363f890
0000003f`5363f820    0000003f`5363f7e0
0000003f`5363f828    0000003f`5363f8d0
0000003f`5363f830    0000003f`5363f7f0
0000003f`5363f838    0000003f`5363f7f8
0000003f`5363f840    0000003f`5363f800
0000003f`5363f848    0000003f`5363f808
0000003f`5363f850    0000003f`5363f810
0000003f`5363f858    0000003f`5363f7c8
0000003f`5363f860    00007ffa`73dfbb14 coreclr!JIT_MonEnter_Helper+0x78
[D:\a\_work\1\s\src\coreclr\vm\jithelpers.cpp @ 2621]
0000003f`5363f868    0000003f`5363f718
0000003f`5363f870    0000003f`5363f748
0000003f`5363f878    00000000`00000000
0000003f`5363f880    000017ed`1df029c9
0000003f`5363f888    000001df`4808b2d0
0000003f`5363f890    000001df`4acbc328
0000003f`5363f898    00007ffa`73d49bf7 coreclr!JIT_MonEnter_Portable+0x147
[D:\a\_work\1\s\src\coreclr\vm\jithelpers.cpp @ 2668]
0000003f`5363f8a0    0000021f`da9d7058
0000003f`5363f8a8    0000003f`5363f900
0000003f`5363f8b0    00007ffa`73d49ab0 coreclr!JIT_MonEnter_Portable
[D:\a\_work\1\s\src\coreclr\vm\jithelpers.cpp @ 2659]
0000003f`5363f8b8    0000021f`da9d7058
0000003f`5363f8c0    000001df`4808b2d0
0000003f`5363f8c8    000001df`4808b2d0
0000003f`5363f8d0    000001df`48013360
0000003f`5363f8d8    00007ffa`14b86a86 LINQPadQuery!UserQuery.ClassMain.thread_proc_2+0x46
0000003f`5363f8e0    0000003f`5363f970
```

Note: We see thread #9 is waiting for the sync block owner (String) from thread #8. Since both threads are mutually waiting for each other, we consider them deadlocked.

11.   How did this deadlock happen? We can look at both threads' execution residue, and we would see that in the case of thread #8, there were valid (not coincidental) symbolic references of exception processing (**!teb** and **dpS** command):

```
0:000> ~8s
ntdll!NtWaitForMultipleObjects+0x14:
00007ffa`c2d64bd4 ret

0:008> !teb
TEB at 0000003f52424000
    ExceptionList:        0000000000000000
    StackBase:            0000003f53540000
    StackLimit:           0000003f53536000
    SubSystemTib:         0000000000000000
    FiberData:            0000000000001e00
    ArbitraryUserPointer: 0000000000000000
    Self:                 0000003f52424000
    EnvironmentPointer:   0000000000000000
    ClientId:             0000000000001ef4 . 0000000000000640
```

```
       RpcHandle:                 0000000000000000
       Tls Storage:               0000021fdf0e8040
       PEB Address:               0000003f525f3000
       LastErrorValue:            0
       LastStatusValue:           c0000034
       Count Owned Locks:         0
       HardErrorMode:             0


0:008> dpS 0000003f53536000 0000003f53540000
 00007ffa`c2ce96fd ntdll!RtlpLowFragHeapAllocFromContext+0x1cd
 [...]
 00007ffa`73dec601 coreclr!CallCatchFunclet+0x291 [D:\a\_work\1\s\src\coreclr\vm\exceptionhandling.cpp @ 7908]
 00007ffa`14b68681 LINQPadQuery!UserQuery.ClassMain.thread_proc_1+0x101
 00007ffa`14b68681 LINQPadQuery!UserQuery.ClassMain.thread_proc_1+0x101
 00007ffa`73277a56 System_Private_CoreLib!System.Runtime.EH.DispatchEx+0x536
[/_/src/coreclr/nativeaot/Runtime.Base/src/System/Runtime/ExceptionHandling.cs @ 928]
 00007ffa`14b68681 LINQPadQuery!UserQuery.ClassMain.thread_proc_1+0x101
 00007ffa`740e1d60 coreclr!InlinedCallFrame::`vftable'
 00007ffa`73277a31 System_Private_CoreLib!System.Runtime.EH.DispatchEx+0x511
[/_/src/coreclr/nativeaot/Runtime.Base/src/System/Runtime/ExceptionHandling.cs @ 928]
 00007ffa`73e64005 coreclr!ThePreStub+0x55 [D:\a\_work\1\s\src\coreclr\vm\amd64\ThePreStubAMD64.asm @ 21]
 00007ffa`14b68681 LINQPadQuery!UserQuery.ClassMain.thread_proc_1+0x101
 00007ffa`7327717a System_Private_CoreLib!System.Runtime.EH.RhThrowHwEx+0xaa
[/_/src/coreclr/nativeaot/Runtime.Base/src/System/Runtime/ExceptionHandling.cs @ 620]
 00007ffa`14af8090 System.Runtime.EH.RhThrowHwEx(UInt32, ExInfo ByRef)
 [...]
 00007ffa`c2d3ca2a ntdll!RtlpCallVectoredHandlers+0x112
 00007ffa`73e470c0 coreclr!CLRVectoredExceptionHandlerShim [D:\a\_work\1\s\src\coreclr\vm\excep.cpp @ 7125]
 00007ffa`c2cf59f2 ntdll!RtlDispatchException+0x62
 00007ffa`740a9d50 coreclr!CEEInfo::`vftable'
 00007ffa`c2cfff83 ntdll!RtlActivateActivationContextUnsafeFast+0x93
 00007ffa`14b68748 LINQPadQuery!UserQuery+ClassMain..cctor()+0x68
 00007ffa`14b68780 LINQPadQuery!UserQuery+ClassMain.DoWork()+0x30
 00007ffa`c04bdcb0 KERNELBASE!WaitForMultipleObjectsEx+0xf0
 00007ffa`c04bdd9c KERNELBASE!WaitForMultipleObjectsEx+0x1dc
 00007ffa`73d5f32c coreclr!MethodDesc::JitCompileCodeLocked+0x1a4 [D:\a\_work\1\s\src\coreclr\vm\prestub.cpp @ 1053]
 00007ffa`c2d6805e ntdll!KiUserExceptionDispatch+0x2e
 00007ffa`14b685e4 LINQPadQuery!UserQuery.ClassMain.thread_proc_1+0x64
 00007ffa`73d1e82e coreclr!Thread::GetFinalApartment+0x12 [D:\a\_work\1\s\src\coreclr\vm\threads.cpp @ 4772]
 00007ffa`73d1e800 coreclr!Thread::DoAppropriateAptStateWait+0x5c [D:\a\_work\1\s\src\coreclr\vm\threads.cpp @ 3184]
 00007ffa`73d1e523 coreclr!Thread::DoAppropriateWaitWorker+0x17b [D:\a\_work\1\s\src\coreclr\vm\threads.cpp @ 3363]
 00007ffa`73d1e35a coreclr!Thread::DoAppropriateWait+0xa6 [D:\a\_work\1\s\src\coreclr\vm\threads.cpp @ 3032]
 00007ffa`14b68580 LINQPadQuery!UserQuery.ClassMain.thread_proc_1
 00007ffa`73e28fc1 coreclr!CLREventBase::Wait+0x59 [D:\a\_work\1\s\src\coreclr\vm\synch.cpp @ 413]
 00007ffa`73e28d0f coreclr!AwareLock::EnterEpilogHelper+0x12f [D:\a\_work\1\s\src\coreclr\vm\syncblk.cpp @ 2617]
 00007ffa`c2cff207 ntdll!RtlDeactivateActivationContextUnsafeFast+0xc7
 00007ffa`73e28bb2 coreclr!AwareLock::EnterEpilog+0x42 [D:\a\_work\1\s\src\coreclr\vm\syncblk.cpp @ 2488]
 00007ffa`74170000 coreclr!ReJitManager::s_csGlobalRequest+0x28
 [...]
 00007ffa`740ab770 coreclr!vtable_DebuggerU2MCatchHandlerFrame
 00007ffa`73dcefbb coreclr!ThreadNative::KickOffThread+0x7b [D:\a\_work\1\s\src\coreclr\vm\comsynchronizable.cpp @ 230]
 00007ffa`73e51540 coreclr!ThreadNative::KickOffThread_Worker [D:\a\_work\1\s\src\coreclr\vm\comsynchronizable.cpp @ 141]
 00007ffa`c1d753e0 kernel32!BaseThreadInitThunk+0x10
 00007ffa`c2cc485b ntdll!RtlUserThreadStart+0x2b
 ????????`????????


0:008> ub 00007ffa`c2cf59f2 L1
ntdll!RtlDispatchException+0x5d:
00007ffa`c2cf59ed  call    ntdll!RtlpCallVectoredHandlers (00007ffa`c2d3c918)


0:008> ub 00007ffa`c2d6805e L1
ntdll!KiUserExceptionDispatch+0x29:
00007ffa`c2d68059  call    ntdll!RtlDispatchException (00007ffa`c2cf5990)
```

Note: !DumpStack may show the caller and callee relationship for some of the found symbolic references:

```
0:008> !DumpStack 0000003f53536000 0000003f53540000
OS Thread Id: 0x640 (8)
Current frame: ntdll!NtWaitForMultipleObjects + 0x14
Child-SP          RetAddr           Caller, Callee
```

```
[...]
0000003F5353CFA0 00007ffa73dec601 coreclr!CallCatchFunclet + 0x291
[D:\a\_work\1\s\src\coreclr\vm\exceptionhandling.cpp:7908], calling coreclr!ClrRestoreNonvolatileContext
[D:\a\_work\1\s\src\coreclr\vm\threads.cpp:7998]
0000003F5353D0B0 00007ffa73277a56 (MethodDesc 00007ffa14270a10 + 0x536
System.Runtime.EH.DispatchEx(System.Runtime.StackFrameIterator ByRef, ExInfo ByRef))
0000003F5353D138 00007ffa73277a31 (MethodDesc 00007ffa14270a10 + 0x511
System.Runtime.EH.DispatchEx(System.Runtime.StackFrameIterator ByRef, ExInfo ByRef)), calling coreclr!JIT_PInvokeBegin
[D:\a\_work\1\s\src\coreclr\vm\amd64\PInvokeStubs.asm:142]
[...]
0000003F5353EF20 00007ffac2cf59f2 ntdll!RtlDispatchException + 0x62, calling ntdll!RtlpCallVectoredHandlers
0000003F5353EF80 00007ffac2cfff83 ntdll!RtlActivateActivationContextUnsafeFast + 0x93, calling
ntdll!_security_check_cookie
0000003F5353F060 00007ffac04bdcb0 KERNELBASE!WaitForMultipleObjectsEx + 0xf0, calling ntdll!NtWaitForMultipleObjects
0000003F5353F100 00007ffac04bdd9c KERNELBASE!WaitForMultipleObjectsEx + 0x1dc, calling
ntdll!RtlActivateActivationContextUnsafeFast
0000003F5353F130 00007ffa73d5f32c coreclr!MethodDesc::JitCompileCodeLocked + 0x1a4
[D:\a\_work\1\s\src\coreclr\vm\prestub.cpp:1053], calling coreclr!__security_check_cookie
[D:\a\_work\1\s\src\vctools\crt\vcstartup\src\gs\amd64\amdsecgs.asm:45]
0000003F5353F170 00007ffac2d6805e ntdll!KiUserExceptionDispatch + 0x2e, calling ntdll!RtlDispatchException
0000003F5353F8B0 00007ffa14b685e4 (MethodDesc 00007ffa14b48458 + 0x64 UserQuery+ClassMain.thread_proc_1()) ====>
Exception Code 0 cxr@0000003F5353F180 exr@0000003F5353F670
0000003F5353F320 00007ffa73d1e82e
[...]
```

12.   In the output above, we also see the exception context address:

```
0:008> .cxr 0000003F5353F180
rax=0000000000000000 rbx=000001df48013360 rcx=0000000000000000
rdx=000000000000000e rsi=000001df4808c8f8 rdi=000001df4808b208
rip=00007ffa14b685e4 rsp=0000003f5353f8b0 rbp=0000003f5353f8f0
 r8=000001df45c5ae00  r9=0000000000000001 r10=000001df44020000
r11=0000003f5353f260 r12=0000000000000000 r13=0000000000000000
r14=0000000000000000 r15=0000000000000000
iopl=0         nv up ei pl zr na po nc
cs=0033  ss=002b  ds=002b  es=002b  fs=0053  gs=002b             efl=00010246
LINQPadQuery!UserQuery.ClassMain.thread_proc_1+0x64:
00007ffa`14b685e4 mov     dword ptr [rax],1           ds:00000000`00000000=????????
```

13.   We can also see a hidden exception object (**!DumpStackObjects** or **!dso** command):

```
0:008> !DumpStackObjects 0000003f53536000 0000003f53540000
OS Thread Id: 0x640 (8)
         SP/REG          Object Name
    003f5353f5b0     021fda9d7098 System.String
    003f5353f718     021fda9d7098 System.String
    003f5353f7b0     01df4acbc368 System.Threading.ContextCallback
    003f5353f7b8     021fda9d7098 System.String
    003f5353f860     01df4acbc260 System.Threading.Thread+StartHelper
    003f5353f870     021fda9d7098 System.String
    003f5353f888     021fda9d7098 System.String
    003f5353f8d8     01df4acbc430 System.NullReferenceException
    003f5353f8e0     01df4acbc430 System.NullReferenceException
    003f5353f940     01df4acbc218 System.Threading.Thread


0:008> !DumpObj 01df4acbc430
Name:           System.NullReferenceException
MethodTable: 00007ffa14b49b90
Canonical MethodTable: 00007ffa14b49b90
Tracked Type: false
Size:           120(0x78) bytes
File:           C:\Program Files\dotnet\shared\Microsoft.NETCore.App\9.0.4\System.Private.CoreLib.dll
Fields:
```
177

```
          MT       Field    Offset              Type VT     Attr        Value Name
00007ffa14349af0  4000271       8 ...ection.MethodBase  0 instance 0000000000000000 _exceptionMethod
00007ffa1426bf40  4000272      10       System.String  0 instance 000001df4acbc910 _message
00007ffa14274b60  4000273      18 ...tions.IDictionary  0 instance 0000000000000000 _data
00007ffa1426e260  4000274      20     System.Exception  0 instance 0000000000000000 _innerException
00007ffa1426bf40  4000275      28       System.String  0 instance 0000000000000000 _helpURL
00007ffa14154730  4000276      30       System.Object  0 instance 000001df4acbca30 _stackTrace
00007ffa1433e698  4000277      38       System.Byte[]  0 instance 0000000000000000 _watsonBuckets
00007ffa1426bf40  4000278      40       System.String  0 instance 0000000000000000 _stackTraceString
00007ffa1426bf40  4000279      48       System.String  0 instance 0000000000000000
_remoteStackTraceString
00007ffa1426bf40  400027a      50       System.String  0 instance 0000000000000000 _source
00007ffa142672e8  400027b      58      System.UIntPtr  1 instance 00007FFA14B685E4 _ipForWatsonBuckets
00007ffa14265270  400027c      60       System.IntPtr  1 instance 0000000000000000 _xptrs
00007ffa14217408  400027d      68       System.Int32  1 instance      -532462766 _xcode
00007ffa14217408  400027e      6c       System.Int32  1 instance     -2147467261 _HResult
```

```
0:008> !DumpObj 000001df4acbc910
Name:        System.String
MethodTable: 00007ffa1426bf40
Canonical MethodTable: 00007ffa1426bf40
Tracked Type: false
Size:        128(0x80) bytes
File:        C:\Program
Files\dotnet\shared\Microsoft.NETCore.App\9.0.4\System.Private.CoreLib.dll
String:      Object reference not set to an instance of an object.
Fields:
          MT       Field    Offset              Type VT     Attr        Value Name
00007ffa14217408  4000355       8       System.Int32  1 instance           53
_stringLength
00007ffa14232f60  4000356       c       System.Char  1 instance           4f _firstChar
00007ffa1426bf40  4000354       8     System.String  0   static 0000021fda9b0008 Empty
```

Note: We also double-check our hypothesis by looking at the thread unmanaged raw stack (**!DumpStackObjects** command doesn't show anything suspicious in managed residue):

```
0:008> ~9s
ntdll!NtWaitForMultipleObjects+0x14:
00007ffa`c2d64bd4 ret
```

```
0:009> !teb
TEB at 0000003f52426000
    ExceptionList:        0000000000000000
    StackBase:            0000003f53640000
    StackLimit:           0000003f5363d000
    SubSystemTib:         0000000000000000
    FiberData:            0000000000001e00
    ArbitraryUserPointer: 0000000000000000
    Self:                 0000003f52426000
    EnvironmentPointer:   0000000000000000
    ClientId:             0000000000001ef4 . 0000000000001b0c
    RpcHandle:            0000000000000000
    Tls Storage:          0000021fdf0e8580
    PEB Address:          0000003f525f3000
    LastErrorValue:       0
    LastStatusValue:      c000000d
    Count Owned Locks:    0
    HardErrorMode:        0
```

```
0:009> !DumpStackObjects 0000003f5363d000 0000003f53640000
OS Thread Id: 0x1b0c (9)
         SP/REG          Object Name
    003f5363f5e0    021fda9d7058 System.String
    003f5363f748    021fda9d7058 System.String
    003f5363f7e0    01df4acbc368 System.Threading.ContextCallback
    003f5363f7e8    021fda9d7058 System.String
    003f5363f890    01df4acbc328 System.Threading.Thread+StartHelper
    003f5363f8a0    021fda9d7058 System.String
    003f5363f8b8    021fda9d7058 System.String
    003f5363f950    01df4acbc2e0 System.Threading.Thread

0:009> dpS 0000003f5363d000 0000003f53640000
[... No symbolic references of exception processing ...]
```

Note: Here is the source code fragment explaining why the lock was never released and why we got exception processing residue:

```
            try
            {
                    Monitor.Enter(cs1);
                    {
                            DoWork();
                            unsafe
                            {
                                    int* p = (int *)0;
                                    *p = 1;
                            }
                    }
                    Monitor.Exit(cs1);
            }
            catch (Exception e)
            {
                    Console.WriteLine("We caught an exception.");
            }
```

14.   We close logging before exiting WinDbg:

```
0:009> .logclose
Closing open log file C:\ANETMDA-Dumps\Windows\x64\LINQPadC.log
```

Deadlock (Windows)

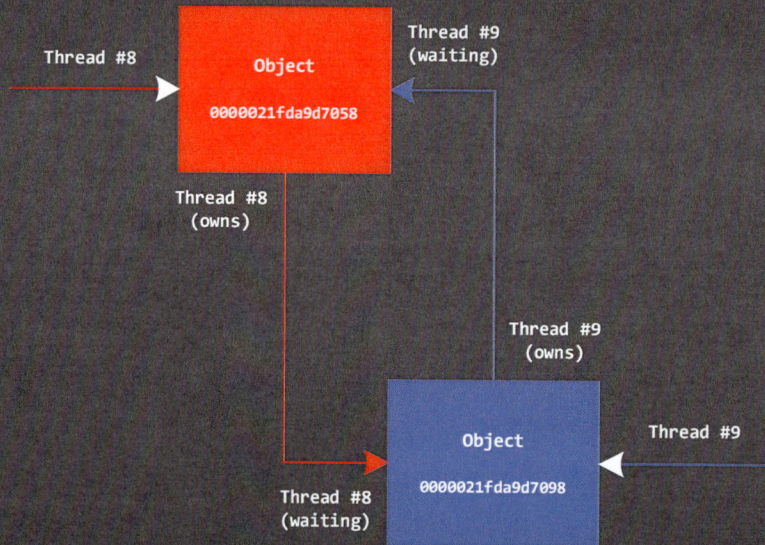

Exercise PN4 (Linux)

- **Goal:** Learn how to recognize and analyze deadlocks, execution residue, and dump object references

- **Patterns:** Wait Chain (CLR Monitors); Deadlock (Managed Space); Execution Residue (Managed Space); Value References; Hidden Exception (Managed Space)

- **Commands:** syncblk, dumpobj, frame select, register read, print, x/<n>gx, dumpstackobjects, x/<n>a

- \ANETMDA-Dumps\Exercise-PN4-Linux.pdf

Exercise PN4 (Linux)

Goal: Learn how to recognize and analyze deadlocks, execution residue, and dump object references.

Patterns: Wait Chain (CLR Monitors); Deadlock (Managed Space); Execution Residue (Managed Space); Value References; Hidden Exception (Managed Space).

Commands: syncblk, dumpobj, frame select, register read, print, x/<n>gx, dumpstackobjects, x/<n>a

1.   Open \ANETMDA-Dumps\Linux\ApplicationI\core.ApplicationI.804.dmp in LLDB:

```
/mnt/c/ANETMDA-Dumps/Linux/ApplicationI$ lldb -c core.ApplicationI.804.dmp
bin/Release/net9.0/ApplicationI
Current symbol store settings:
-> Cache: /home/coredump/.dotnet/symbolcache
-> Server: https://msdl.microsoft.com/download/symbols/ Timeout: 4 RetryCount: 0
(lldb) target create "bin/Release/net9.0/ApplicationI" --core "core.ApplicationI.804.dmp"
warning: (x86_64) /usr/share/dotnet/host/fxr/9.0.4/libhostfxr.so unsupported DW_FORM values:
0x1b 0x21 0x22 0x23 0x25 0x26 0x64
warning: (x86_64) /usr/share/dotnet/shared/Microsoft.NETCore.App/9.0.4/libhostpolicy.so
unsupported DW_FORM values: 0x1b 0x21 0x22 0x23 0x25 0x26 0x64
warning: (x86_64) /usr/share/dotnet/shared/Microsoft.NETCore.App/9.0.4/libcoreclr.so
unsupported DW_FORM values: 0x1b 0x21 0x22 0x23 0x25 0x26 0x64
warning: (x86_64) /usr/share/dotnet/shared/Microsoft.NETCore.App/9.0.4/libSystem.Native.so
unsupported DW_FORM values: 0x1b 0x21 0x22 0x23 0x25 0x26
warning: (x86_64) /usr/share/dotnet/shared/Microsoft.NETCore.App/9.0.4/libclrjit.so unsupported
DW_FORM values: 0x1b 0x21 0x22 0x23 0x25 0x26 0x64
warning: (x86_64) /mnt/c/ANETMDA-Dumps/Linux/ApplicationI/bin/Release/net9.0/ApplicationI
unsupported DW_FORM values: 0x1b 0x21 0x22 0x23 0x25 0x26 0x64
Core file '/mnt/c/ANETMDA-Dumps/Linux/ApplicationI/core.ApplicationI.804.dmp' (x86_64) was
loaded.
```

2.   Verify the correctness of all stack traces:

```
(lldb) bt all

* thread #1, name = 'ApplicationI', stop reason = signal SIGSTOP
  * frame #0: 0x00007f21e97c300c libpthread.so.0`__pthread_cond_wait at futex-internal.h:88
    frame #1: 0x00007f21e97c2ff1 libpthread.so.0`__pthread_cond_wait at pthread_cond_wait.c:502
    frame #2: 0x00007f21e97c2f30 libpthread.so.0`__pthread_cond_wait(cond=0x00005652bd824348, mutex=0x00005652bd824320) at pthread_cond_wait.c:655
    frame #3: 0x00007f21e9133172 libcoreclr.so`CorUnix::CPalSynchronizationManager::ThreadNativeWait(CorUnix::_ThreadNativeWaitData*, unsigned int,
CorUnix::ThreadWakeupReason*, unsigned int*) + 354
    frame #4: 0x00007f21e9132d7a libcoreclr.so`CorUnix::CPalSynchronizationManager::BlockThread(CorUnix::CPalThread*, unsigned int, bool, bool,
CorUnix::ThreadWakeupReason*, unsigned int*) + 378
    frame #5: 0x00007f21e9137952 libcoreclr.so`CorUnix::InternalWaitForMultipleObjectsEx(CorUnix::CPalThread*, unsigned int, void* const*, int, unsigned int,
int, int) + 1906
    frame #6: 0x00007f21e9137c03 libcoreclr.so`WaitForMultipleObjectsEx + 83
    frame #7: 0x00007f21e8d94255 libcoreclr.so`Thread::DoAppropriateWaitWorker(int, void**, int, unsigned int, WaitMode, void*) + 1429
    frame #8: 0x00007f21e8d8f424 libcoreclr.so`Thread::DoAppropriateWait(int, void**, int, unsigned int, WaitMode, PendingSync*) + 228
    frame #9: 0x00007f21e8d8f2ec libcoreclr.so`Thread::JoinEx(unsigned int, WaitMode) + 108
    frame #10: 0x00007f21e8de0c6c libcoreclr.so`ThreadNative::DoJoin(ThreadBaseObject*, int) + 220
    frame #11: 0x00007f21e8de089c libcoreclr.so`ThreadNative::Join(ThreadBaseObject*, int) + 268
    frame #12: 0x00007f2169d5854c
    frame #13: 0x00007f216aab189b
    frame #14: 0x00007f21e8f8be04 libcoreclr.so`CallDescrWorkerInternal + 124
    frame #15: 0x00007f21e8dca11c libcoreclr.so`MethodDescCallSite::CallTargetWorker(unsigned long const*, unsigned long*, int) + 1708
    frame #16: 0x00007f21e8cb10c4 libcoreclr.so`RunMain(MethodDesc*, short, int*, PtrArray**) + 836
    frame #17: 0x00007f21e8cb153c libcoreclr.so`Assembly::ExecuteMainMethod(PtrArray**) + 460
    frame #18: 0x00007f21e8cdab34 libcoreclr.so`CorHost2::ExecuteAssembly(unsigned int, char16_t const*, int, char16_t const**, unsigned int*) + 740
    frame #19: 0x00007f21e8c9d340 libcoreclr.so`coreclr_execute_assembly + 144
    frame #20: 0x00007f21e9265301 libhostpolicy.so`run_app_for_context(hostpolicy_context_t const&, int, char const**) + 1089
    frame #21: 0x00007f21e92663f9 libhostpolicy.so`corehost_main + 345
    frame #22: 0x00007f21e92a5685 libhostfxr.so`fx_muxer_t::handle_exec_host_command(std::__cxx11::basic_string<char, std::char_traits<char>,
std::allocator<char> > const&, host_startup_info_t const&, std::__cxx11::basic_string<char, std::char_traits<char>, std::allocator<char> > const&,
std::unordered_map<known_options, std::vector<std::__cxx11::basic_string<char, std::char_traits<char>, std::allocator<char> >,
std::allocator<std::__cxx11::basic_string<char, std::char_traits<char>, std::allocator<char> > > >, known_options_hash, std::equal_to<known_options>,
std::allocator<std::pair<known_options const, std::vector<std::__cxx11::basic_string<char, std::char_traits<char>, std::allocator<char> >,
std::allocator<std::__cxx11::basic_string<char, std::char_traits<char>, std::allocator<char> > > > > > const&, int, char const**, int, host_mode_t, bool,
char*, int, int*) + 1477
```

```
    frame #23: 0x00007f21e92a467d libhostfxr.so`fx_muxer_t::execute(std::__cxx11::basic_string<char, std::char_traits<char>, std::allocator<char> >, int, char
const**, host_startup_info_t const&, char*, int, int*) + 765
    frame #24: 0x00007f21e929e5f2 libhostfxr.so`hostfxr_main_startupinfo + 242
    frame #25: 0x00005652a7bb221b ApplicationI`exe_start(int, char const**) + 1131
    frame #26: 0x00005652a7bb253f ApplicationI`main + 175
    frame #27: 0x00007f21e92f809b libc.so.6`__libc_start_main(main=(ApplicationI`main), argc=1, argv=0x00007ffc4480e798, init=<unavailable>,
fini=<unavailable>, rtld_fini=<unavailable>, stack_end=0x00007ffc4480e788) at libc-start.c:308
    frame #28: 0x00005652a7bb1399 ApplicationI`_start + 41
  thread #2, stop reason = signal 0
    frame #0: 0x00007f21e93c26f9 libc.so.6`__GI___poll(fds=0x00007f21e8abdd98, nfds=1, timeout=-1) at poll.c:29
    frame #1: 0x00007f21e9135800 libcoreclr.so`CorUnix::CPalSynchronizationManager::ReadBytesFromProcessPipe(int, unsigned char*, int) + 288
    frame #2: 0x00007f21e9134e63 libcoreclr.so`CorUnix::CPalSynchronizationManager::WorkerThread(void*) + 147
    frame #3: 0x00007f21e913e9ae libcoreclr.so`CorUnix::CPalThread::ThreadEntry(void*) + 510
    frame #4: 0x00007f21e97bcfa3 libpthread.so.0`start_thread(arg=<unavailable>) at pthread_create.c:486
    frame #5: 0x00007f21e93cd06f libc.so.6`__GI___clone at clone.S:95
  thread #3, stop reason = signal 0
    frame #0: 0x00007f21e93c26f9 libc.so.6`__GI___poll(fds=0x00007f215c000f20, nfds=1, timeout=-1) at poll.c:29
    frame #1: 0x00007f21e903cd5c libcoreclr.so`ds_ipc_poll(_DiagnosticsIpcPollHandle*, unsigned long, unsigned int, void (*)(char const*, unsigned int)) + 172
    frame #2: 0x00007f21e8fb6f4b libcoreclr.so`ds_ipc_stream_factory_get_next_available_stream(void (*)(char const*, unsigned int)) + 731
    frame #3: 0x00007f21e8fbbca6 libcoreclr.so`server_thread(void*) + 198
    frame #4: 0x00007f21e913e9ae libcoreclr.so`CorUnix::CPalThread::ThreadEntry(void*) + 510
    frame #5: 0x00007f21e97bcfa3 libpthread.so.0`start_thread(arg=<unavailable>) at pthread_create.c:486
    frame #6: 0x00007f21e93cd06f libc.so.6`__GI___clone at clone.S:95
  thread #4, stop reason = signal 0
    frame #0: 0x00007f21e97c6d0e libpthread.so.0`__libc_open64(file="/tmp/clr-debug-pipe-804-11702264-in", oflag=0) at open64.c:48
    frame #1: 0x00007f21e903c77f libcoreclr.so`TwoWayPipe::WaitForConnection() + 31
    frame #2: 0x00007f21e9037797 libcoreclr.so`DbgTransportSession::TransportWorker() + 183
    frame #3: 0x00007f21e9036905 libcoreclr.so`DbgTransportSession::TransportWorkerStatic(void*) + 37
    frame #4: 0x00007f21e913e9ae libcoreclr.so`CorUnix::CPalThread::ThreadEntry(void*) + 510
    frame #5: 0x00007f21e97bcfa3 libpthread.so.0`start_thread(arg=<unavailable>) at pthread_create.c:486
    frame #6: 0x00007f21e93cd06f libc.so.6`__GI___clone at clone.S:95
  thread #5, stop reason = signal 0
    frame #0: 0x00007f21e97c300c libpthread.so.0`__pthread_cond_wait at futex-internal.h:88
    frame #1: 0x00007f21e97c2ff1 libpthread.so.0`__pthread_cond_wait at pthread_cond_wait.c:502
    frame #2: 0x00007f21e97c2f30 libpthread.so.0`__pthread_cond_wait(cond=0x00005652bd853c48, mutex=0x00005652bd853c20) at pthread_cond_wait.c:655
    frame #3: 0x00007f21e9133172 libcoreclr.so`CorUnix::CPalSynchronizationManager::ThreadNativeWait(CorUnix::_ThreadNativeWaitData*, unsigned int,
CorUnix::ThreadWakeupReason*, unsigned int*) + 354
    frame #4: 0x00007f21e9132d7a libcoreclr.so`CorUnix::CPalSynchronizationManager::BlockThread(CorUnix::CPalThread*, unsigned int, bool, bool,
CorUnix::ThreadWakeupReason*, unsigned int*) + 378
    frame #5: 0x00007f21e9137952 libcoreclr.so`CorUnix::InternalWaitForMultipleObjectsEx(CorUnix::CPalThread*, unsigned int, void* const*, int, unsigned int,
int, int) + 1906
    frame #6: 0x00007f21e9137c03 libcoreclr.so`WaitForMultipleObjectsEx + 83
    frame #7: 0x00007f21e90350ad libcoreclr.so`DebuggerRCThread::MainLoop() + 269
    frame #8: 0x00007f21e9034f28 libcoreclr.so`DebuggerRCThread::ThreadProc() + 312
    frame #9: 0x00007f21e9034c25 libcoreclr.so`DebuggerRCThread::ThreadProcStatic(void*) + 53
    frame #10: 0x00007f21e913e9ae libcoreclr.so`CorUnix::CPalThread::ThreadEntry(void*) + 510
    frame #11: 0x00007f21e97bcfa3 libpthread.so.0`start_thread(arg=<unavailable>) at pthread_create.c:486
    frame #12: 0x00007f21e93cd06f libc.so.6`__GI___clone at clone.S:95
  thread #6, stop reason = signal 0
    frame #0: 0x00007f21e97c33f9 libpthread.so.0`__pthread_cond_timedwait at futex-internal.h:142
    frame #1: 0x00007f21e97c33da libpthread.so.0`__pthread_cond_timedwait at pthread_cond_wait.c:533
    frame #2: 0x00007f21e97c32c0 libpthread.so.0`__pthread_cond_timedwait(cond=0x00005652bd85f338, mutex=0x00005652bd85f310, abstime=0x00007f21e69697d0) at
pthread_cond_wait.c:667
    frame #3: 0x00007f21e9133115 libcoreclr.so`CorUnix::CPalSynchronizationManager::ThreadNativeWait(CorUnix::_ThreadNativeWaitData*, unsigned int,
CorUnix::ThreadWakeupReason*, unsigned int*) + 261
    frame #4: 0x00007f21e9132d7a libcoreclr.so`CorUnix::CPalSynchronizationManager::BlockThread(CorUnix::CPalThread*, unsigned int, bool, bool,
CorUnix::ThreadWakeupReason*, unsigned int*) + 378
    frame #5: 0x00007f21e9137952 libcoreclr.so`CorUnix::InternalWaitForMultipleObjectsEx(CorUnix::CPalThread*, unsigned int, void* const*, int, unsigned int,
int, int) + 1906
    frame #6: 0x00007f21e9137c03 libcoreclr.so`WaitForMultipleObjectsEx + 83
    frame #7: 0x00007f21e8e06111 libcoreclr.so`FinalizerThread::WaitForFinalizerEvent(CLREvent*) + 177
    frame #8: 0x00007f21e8e0627f libcoreclr.so`FinalizerThread::FinalizerThreadWorker(void*) + 239
    frame #9: 0x00007f21e8d97c08 libcoreclr.so`ManagedThreadBase_DispatchOuter(ManagedThreadCallState*) + 344
    frame #10: 0x00007f21e8d9810d libcoreclr.so`ManagedThreadBase::FinalizerBase(void (*)(void*)) + 45
    frame #11: 0x00007f21e8e064b8 libcoreclr.so`FinalizerThread::FinalizerThreadStart(void*) + 88
    frame #12: 0x00007f21e913e9ae libcoreclr.so`CorUnix::CPalThread::ThreadEntry(void*) + 510
    frame #13: 0x00007f21e97bcfa3 libpthread.so.0`start_thread(arg=<unavailable>) at pthread_create.c:486
    frame #14: 0x00007f21e93cd06f libc.so.6`__GI___clone at clone.S:95
  thread #7, stop reason = signal 0
    frame #0: 0x00007f21e97c300c libpthread.so.0`__pthread_cond_wait at futex-internal.h:88
    frame #1: 0x00007f21e97c2ff1 libpthread.so.0`__pthread_cond_wait at pthread_cond_wait.c:502
    frame #2: 0x00007f21e97c2f30 libpthread.so.0`__pthread_cond_wait(cond=0x00005652bd8910d8, mutex=0x00005652bd8910b0) at pthread_cond_wait.c:655
    frame #3: 0x00007f21e9133172 libcoreclr.so`CorUnix::CPalSynchronizationManager::ThreadNativeWait(CorUnix::_ThreadNativeWaitData*, unsigned int,
CorUnix::ThreadWakeupReason*, unsigned int*) + 354
    frame #4: 0x00007f21e9132d7a libcoreclr.so`CorUnix::CPalSynchronizationManager::BlockThread(CorUnix::CPalThread*, unsigned int, bool, bool,
CorUnix::ThreadWakeupReason*, unsigned int*) + 378
    frame #5: 0x00007f21e9137952 libcoreclr.so`CorUnix::InternalWaitForMultipleObjectsEx(CorUnix::CPalThread*, unsigned int, void* const*, int, unsigned int,
int, int) + 1906
    frame #6: 0x00007f21e9137c03 libcoreclr.so`WaitForMultipleObjectsEx + 83
    frame #7: 0x00007f21e8d94255 libcoreclr.so`Thread::DoAppropriateWaitWorker(int, void**, int, unsigned int, WaitMode, void*) + 1429
    frame #8: 0x00007f21e8d8f424 libcoreclr.so`Thread::DoAppropriateWait(int, void**, int, unsigned int, WaitMode, PendingSync*) + 228
    frame #9: 0x00007f21e8e93e83 libcoreclr.so`CLREventBase::WaitEx(unsigned int, WaitMode, PendingSync*) + 115
    frame #10: 0x00007f21e8d8e83b libcoreclr.so`AwareLock::EnterEpilogHelper(Thread*, int) + 587
    frame #11: 0x00007f21e8d8e33c libcoreclr.so`AwareLock::Enter() + 252
    frame #12: 0x00007f21e8e27048 libcoreclr.so`JIT_MonEnter_Helper(Object*, unsigned char*, void*) + 376
    frame #13: 0x00007f21e8e272d2 libcoreclr.so`JIT_MonEnter_Portable + 82
    frame #14: 0x00007f216aab1b3d
    frame #15: 0x00007f21e8f8be04 libcoreclr.so`CallDescrWorkerInternal + 124
    frame #16: 0x00007f21e8dc9a05 libcoreclr.so`DispatchCallSimple(unsigned long*, unsigned int, unsigned long, unsigned int) + 245
    frame #17: 0x00007f21e8ddf6c2 libcoreclr.so`ThreadNative::KickOffThread_Worker(void*) + 146
    frame #18: 0x00007f21e8d97c08 libcoreclr.so`ManagedThreadBase_DispatchOuter(ManagedThreadCallState*) + 344
    frame #19: 0x00007f21e8d980bd libcoreclr.so`ManagedThreadBase::KickOff(void (*)(void*), void*) + 45
    frame #20: 0x00007f21e8ddf7dc libcoreclr.so`ThreadNative::KickOffThread(void*) + 252
    frame #21: 0x00007f21e913e9ae libcoreclr.so`CorUnix::CPalThread::ThreadEntry(void*) + 510
    frame #22: 0x00007f21e97bcfa3 libpthread.so.0`start_thread(arg=<unavailable>) at pthread_create.c:486
    frame #23: 0x00007f21e93cd06f libc.so.6`__GI___clone at clone.S:95
  thread #8, stop reason = signal 0
    frame #0: 0x00007f21e97c6544 libpthread.so.0`__libc_read at read.c:26
```

183

```
      frame #1: 0x00007f21e97c6530 libpthread.so.0`__libc_read(fd=31, buf=0x00007f21e1bfdebf, nbytes=1) at read.c:24
      frame #2: 0x00007f21e47247ff libSystem.Native.so`SignalHandlerLoop + 95
      frame #3: 0x00007f21e97bcfa3 libpthread.so.0`start_thread(arg=<unavailable>) at pthread_create.c:486
      frame #4: 0x00007f21e93cd06f libc.so.6`__GI___clone at clone.S:95
    thread #9, stop reason = signal 0
      frame #0: 0x00007f21e97c300c libpthread.so.0`__pthread_cond_wait at futex-internal.h:88
      frame #1: 0x00007f21e97c2ff1 libpthread.so.0`__pthread_cond_wait at pthread_cond_wait.c:502
      frame #2: 0x00007f21e97c2f30 libpthread.so.0`__pthread_cond_wait(cond=0x00005652bd892418, mutex=0x00005652bd8923f0) at pthread_cond_wait.c:655
      frame #3: 0x00007f21e9133172 libcoreclr.so`CorUnix::CPalSynchronizationManager::ThreadNativeWait(CorUnix::_ThreadNativeWaitData*, unsigned int,
CorUnix::ThreadWakeupReason*, unsigned int*) + 354
      frame #4: 0x00007f21e9132d7a libcoreclr.so`CorUnix::CPalSynchronizationManager::BlockThread(CorUnix::CPalThread*, unsigned int, bool, bool,
CorUnix::ThreadWakeupReason*, unsigned int*) + 378
      frame #5: 0x00007f21e9137952 libcoreclr.so`CorUnix::InternalWaitForMultipleObjectsEx(CorUnix::CPalThread*, unsigned int, void* const*, int, unsigned int,
int, int) + 1906
      frame #6: 0x00007f21e9137c03 libcoreclr.so`WaitForMultipleObjectsEx + 83
      frame #7: 0x00007f21e8d94255 libcoreclr.so`Thread::DoAppropriateWaitWorker(int, void**, int, unsigned int, WaitMode, void*) + 1429
      frame #8: 0x00007f21e8d8f424 libcoreclr.so`Thread::DoAppropriateWait(int, void**, int, unsigned int, WaitMode, PendingSync*) + 228
      frame #9: 0x00007f21e8e93e83 libcoreclr.so`CLREventBase::WaitEx(unsigned int, WaitMode, PendingSync*) + 115
      frame #10: 0x00007f21e8d8e83b libcoreclr.so`AwareLock::EnterEpilogHelper(Thread*, int) + 587
      frame #11: 0x00007f21e8d8e33c libcoreclr.so`AwareLock::Enter() + 252
      frame #12: 0x00007f21e8e27048 libcoreclr.so`JIT_MonEnter_Helper(Object*, unsigned char*, void*) + 376
      frame #13: 0x00007f21e8e272d2 libcoreclr.so`JIT_MonEnter_Portable + 82
      frame #14: 0x00007f216aab431e
      frame #15: 0x00007f21e8f8be04 libcoreclr.so`CallDescrWorkerInternal + 124
      frame #16: 0x00007f21e8dc9a05 libcoreclr.so`DispatchCallSimple(unsigned long*, unsigned int, unsigned long, unsigned int) + 245
      frame #17: 0x00007f21e8ddf6c2 libcoreclr.so`ThreadNative::KickOffThread_Worker(void*) + 146
      frame #18: 0x00007f21e8d97c08 libcoreclr.so`ManagedThreadBase_DispatchOuter(ManagedThreadCallState*) + 344
      frame #19: 0x00007f21e8d980bd libcoreclr.so`ManagedThreadBase::KickOff(void (*)(void*), void*) + 45
      frame #20: 0x00007f21e8ddf7dc libcoreclr.so`ThreadNative::KickOffThread(void*) + 252
      frame #21: 0x00007f21e913e9ae libcoreclr.so`CorUnix::CPalThread::ThreadEntry(void*) + 510
      frame #22: 0x00007f21e97bcfa3 libpthread.so.0`start_thread(arg=<unavailable>) at pthread_create.c:486
      frame #23: 0x00007f21e93cd06f libc.so.6`__GI___clone at clone.S:95
```

Note: We see two threads, #7 and #9, entered synchronization monitor functions (*MonEnter*). So we have a possible wait chain there.

3.   Now we check managed threads and list special CLR threads:

```
(lldb) clrthreads
ThreadCount:      4
UnstartedThread:  0
BackgroundThread: 1
PendingThread:    0
DeadThread:       0
Hosted Runtime:   no
                                                                                                    Lock
 DBG   ID   OSID ThreadOBJ        State GC Mode   GC Alloc Context                    Domain           Count Apt Exception
   1    1    324 00005652BD856580 2020020 Preemptive 00007EE156809600:00007EE156809E60 00005652BD83E7D0 -00001 Ukn
   6    2    329 00005652BD85DC80 21220 Preemptive 00007EE156813D8:00007EE156815010 00005652BD83E7D0 -00001 Ukn (Finalizer)
   7    4    32b 00005652BD86F040 2021020 Preemptive 00007EE156812308:00007EE156812FF0 00005652BD83E7D0 -00001 Ukn
   9    5    32d 00005652BD80DB90 2021020 Preemptive 0000000000000000:0000000000000000 00005652BD83E7D0 -00001 Ukn
```

Note: The application was reported hanging, but we don't see anything suspicious.

4.   However, when we check the output of the **syncblk** command, we suspect a deadlock between threads #7 and #9:

```
(lldb) syncblk
Index         SyncBlock MonitorHeld Recursion Owning Thread Info           SyncBlock Owner
    1 00007EE0A8001118           3         1 00005652BD86F040 32b    7 00007f21e4f3f810 System.String
    2 00007EE0A8001170           3         1 00005652BD80DB90 32d    9 00007f21e4f3f850 System.String
-----------------------------
Total         2
Free          0
```

Note: What we see here is that thread #9 holds a lock on 00007EE0A8001170 synchronization block that is owned by 00007f21e4f3f850 String object with "critical section 2" value:

```
(lldb) dumpobj 00007f21e4f3f850
Name:        System.String
MethodTable: 00007f216aa9be30
Canonical MethodTable: 00007f216aa9be30
Tracked Type: false
```

```
Size:          58(0x3a) bytes
File:          /usr/share/dotnet/shared/Microsoft.NETCore.App/9.0.4/System.Private.CoreLib.dll
String:        critical section 2
Fields:
              MT    Field   Offset                   Type VT     Attr            Value Name
00007f216aa474f0  40002ef       8         System.Int32  1 instance                18 _stringLength
00007f216aa53010  40002f0       c          System.Char  1 instance                63 _firstChar
00007f216aa9be30  40002ee       8        System.String  0    static 00007f21e4f3f008 Empty
```

and that thread **#7** holds a lock on **00007EE0A8001118** block that is owned by **00007f21e4f3f810** String object with "**critical section 1**" value:

```
(lldb) dumpobj 00007f21e4f3f810
Name:          System.String
MethodTable: 00007f216aa9be30
Canonical MethodTable: 00007f216aa9be30
Tracked Type: false
Size:          58(0x3a) bytes
File:          /usr/share/dotnet/shared/Microsoft.NETCore.App/9.0.4/System.Private.CoreLib.dll
String:        critical section 1
Fields:
              MT    Field   Offset                   Type VT     Attr            Value Name
00007f216aa474f0  40002ef       8         System.Int32  1 instance                18 _stringLength
00007f216aa53010  40002f0       c          System.Char  1 instance                63 _firstChar
00007f216aa9be30  40002ee       8        System.String  0    static 00007f21e4f3f008 Empty
```

5.   However, to verify whether thread **#7** is waiting for the sync block owner from thread **#9** and vice versa, we need to inspect execution residue on their thread stack regions to see if there are any value references there:

```
(lldb) thread select 7
* thread #7, stop reason = signal 0
    frame #0: 0x00007f21e97c300c libpthread.so.0`__pthread_cond_wait at futex-internal.h:88

(lldb) bt
* thread #7, stop reason = signal 0
  * frame #0: 0x00007f21e97c300c libpthread.so.0`__pthread_cond_wait at futex-internal.h:88
    frame #1: 0x00007f21e97c2ff1 libpthread.so.0`__pthread_cond_wait at pthread_cond_wait.c:502
    frame #2: 0x00007f21e97c2f30 libpthread.so.0`__pthread_cond_wait(cond=0x00005652bd8910d8, mutex=0x00005652bd8910b0) at pthread_cond_wait.c:655
    frame #3: 0x00007f21e9133172 libcoreclr.so`CorUnix::CPalSynchronizationManager::ThreadNativeWait(CorUnix::_ThreadNativeWaitData*, unsigned int,
CorUnix::ThreadWakeupReason*, unsigned int*) + 354
    frame #4: 0x00007f21e9132d7a libcoreclr.so`CorUnix::CPalSynchronizationManager::BlockThread(CorUnix::CPalThread*, unsigned int, bool, bool,
CorUnix::ThreadWakeupReason*, unsigned int*) + 378
    frame #5: 0x00007f21e9137952 libcoreclr.so`CorUnix::InternalWaitForMultipleObjectsEx(CorUnix::CPalThread*, unsigned int, void* const*, int, unsigned int,
int, int) + 1906
    frame #6: 0x00007f21e9137c03 libcoreclr.so`WaitForMultipleObjectsEx + 83
    frame #7: 0x00007f21e8d94255 libcoreclr.so`Thread::DoAppropriateWaitWorker(int, void**, int, unsigned int, WaitMode, void*) + 1429
    frame #8: 0x00007f21e8d8f424 libcoreclr.so`Thread::DoAppropriateWait(int, void**, int, unsigned int, WaitMode, PendingSync*) + 228
    frame #9: 0x00007f21e8e93e83 libcoreclr.so`CLREventBase::WaitEx(unsigned int, WaitMode, PendingSync*) + 115
    frame #10: 0x00007f21e8d8e83b libcoreclr.so`AwareLock::EnterEpilogHelper(Thread*, int) + 587
    frame #11: 0x00007f21e8d8e33c libcoreclr.so`AwareLock::Enter() + 252
    frame #12: 0x00007f21e8e27048 libcoreclr.so`JIT_MonEnter_Helper(Object*, unsigned char*, void*) + 376
    frame #13: 0x00007f21e8e272d2 libcoreclr.so`JIT_MonEnter_Portable + 82
    frame #14: 0x00007f216aab1b3d
    frame #15: 0x00007f21e8f8be04 libcoreclr.so`CallDescrWorkerInternal + 124
    frame #16: 0x00007f21e8dc9a05 libcoreclr.so`DispatchCallSimple(unsigned long*, unsigned int, unsigned long, unsigned int) + 245
    frame #17: 0x00007f21e8ddf6c2 libcoreclr.so`ThreadNative::KickOffThread_Worker(void*) + 146
    frame #18: 0x00007f21e8d97c08 libcoreclr.so`ManagedThreadBase_DispatchOuter(ManagedThreadCallState*) + 344
    frame #19: 0x00007f21e8d980bd libcoreclr.so`ManagedThreadBase::KickOff(void (*)(void*), void*) + 45
    frame #20: 0x00007f21e8ddf7dc libcoreclr.so`ThreadNative::KickOffThread(void*) + 252
    frame #21: 0x00007f21e913e9ae libcoreclr.so`CorUnix::CPalThread::ThreadEntry(void*) + 510
    frame #22: 0x00007f21e97bcfa3 libpthread.so.0`start_thread(arg=<unavailable>) at pthread_create.c:486
    frame #23: 0x00007f21e93cd06f libc.so.6`__GI___clone at clone.S:95

(lldb) ip2md 0x00007f216aab1b3d
MethodDesc:    00007f216ab5a088
Method Name:          ClassMain.thread_proc_1()
Class:                00007f216ab5a118
MethodTable:          00007f216ab5a118
mdToken:              0000000006000004
Module:               00007f216ab57038
IsJitted:             yes
```

```
Current CodeAddr:        00007f216aab1aa0
Version History:
  ILCodeVersion:         0000000000000000
  ReJIT ID:              0
  IL Addr:               00007f21e470d27c
     CodeAddr:              00007f216aab1aa0  (QuickJitted)
     NativeCodeVersion:  0000000000000000
Source file:  /mnt/c/ANETMDA-Examples/ApplicationI/Program.cs @ 39
```

(lldb) **frame select 11**
```
frame #11: 0x00007f21e8d8e33c libcoreclr.so`AwareLock::Enter() + 252
libcoreclr.so`AwareLock::Enter:
    0x7f21e8d8e33c <+252>: leaq   -0x60(%rbp), %rdi
    0x7f21e8d8e340 <+256>: callq  0x7f21e8e95ad0            ;
DebugBlockingItemHolder::~DebugBlockingItemHolder()
    0x7f21e8d8e345 <+261>: movq   %fs:0x28, %rax
    0x7f21e8d8e34e <+270>: cmpq   -0x18(%rbp), %rax
```

(lldb) **register read** sp
```
     rsp = 0x00007f21e42fd920
```

(lldb) **frame select 14**
```
frame #14: 0x00007f216aab1b3d
    0x7f216aab1b3d: callq  *-0x7a67b(%rip)
    0x7f216aab1b43: movabsq $0x7f216ab5a118, %rdi    ; imm = 0x7F216AB5A118
    0x7f216aab1b4d: callq  0x7f21e8e202d0           ; JIT_GetNonGCStaticBase_Portable
    0x7f216aab1b52: movabsq $0x7ee154000188, %rax    ; imm = 0x7EE154000188
```

(lldb) **register read** sp
```
     rsp = 0x00007f21e42fdb70
```

(lldb) p (0x00007f21e42fdb70 - 0x00007f21e42fd920)/8
```
(long) $5 = 74
```

(lldb) **x/74**gx 0x00007f21e42fd920
```
0x7f21e42fd920: 0x00005652bd86f040 0x00007ee0b0000c08
0x7f21e42fd930: 0x00007ee0a8001170 0xffffffff00000000
0x7f21e42fd940: 0x0000000000000000 0x00007ee0a8001170
0x7f21e42fd950: 0x00005652bd83e7d0 0xffffffff00000000
0x7f21e42fd960: 0x0000000000000000 0xd133c813b91b5700
0x7f21e42fd970: 0x00007f21e42fda20 0x00005652bd86f040
0x7f21e42fd980: 0x00007f21e42fdb40 0x00007f21e8e27048
0x7f21e42fd990: 0x00007f21e8e27280 0x00007ee0b0000bb8
0x7f21e42fd9a0: 0x0000000000000000 0x00005652bd86f040
0x7f21e42fd9b0: 0x00007f21e42fda10 0x0000000100000001
0x7f21e42fd9c0: 0x0000000000000000 0x0000000000000000
0x7f21e42fd9d0: 0xffffffffffffffff 0x0000000000000000
0x7f21e42fd9e0: 0x00000000000007d0 0x0000000000000000
0x7f21e42fd9f0: 0x0000000000000000 0x0000000000000000
0x7f21e42fda00: 0x00007f21e3afdac0 0x00007f21e4f3f850
0x7f21e42fda10: 0x0000000000000000 0x0000000006f99ff5
0x7f21e42fda20: 0x00007f21e918b1c0 0x00007f21e42fdcc0
0x7f21e42fda30: 0x0000000000000000 0x00007f2100000030
0x7f21e42fda40: 0x00005652bd86f040 0x00007f21e8e27280
0x7f21e42fda50: 0x00007f21e42fdac0 0x00007f21e8de23eb
0x7f21e42fda60: 0x00007f21e918aef0 0x00007f21e42fd9a0
0x7f21e42fda70: 0x00007f216aa33498 0x00007f21e91dbbc0
0x7f21e42fda80: 0x00007f21e42fda20 0x00007f21e42fdb40
0x7f21e42fda90: 0x0000000000000000 0x0000000000000008
```

```
0x7f21e42fdaa0: 0x00007f21e42fdad0 0x00007f21e9123a93
0x7f21e42fdab0: 0x00007f216aa33498 0x000000000001c920
0x7f21e42fdac0: 0x0000000000000000 0xd133c813b91b5700
0x7f21e42fdad0: 0x00007f21e42fdae0 0x00007f21e8e9bef9
0x7f21e42fdae0: 0x00007f21e42fdb40 0x00007f21e8d8d017
0x7f21e42fdaf0: 0x00007f21e42fdcc0 0x00007f21e8e26f88
0x7f21e42fdb00: 0x00007f21e42fd988 0x00007f21e42fda08
0x7f21e42fdb10: 0xd133c813b91b5700 0x00007f21e4f3f850
0x7f21e42fdb20: 0x0000000000000000 0x00007f21e42fdcc0
0x7f21e42fdb30: 0x00007f216aa33498 0x00007f21e42fdc50
0x7f21e42fdb40: 0x00007f21e42fdb60 0x00007f21e8e272d2
0x7f21e42fdb50: 0x00007ee154000188 0x00007f21e42fdbd8
0x7f21e42fdb60: 0x00007f21e42fdb90 0x00007f216aab1b3d
```

Note: We see thread **#7** is waiting for the sync block owner (String) from thread **#9**.

6.   We repeat the same exercise for the thread **#9**:

```
(lldb) thread select 9
* thread #9, stop reason = signal 0
    frame #0: 0x00007f21e97c300c libpthread.so.0`__pthread_cond_wait at futex-internal.h:88
```

```
(lldb) bt
* thread #9, stop reason = signal 0
  * frame #0: 0x00007f21e97c300c libpthread.so.0`__pthread_cond_wait at futex-internal.h:88
    frame #1: 0x00007f21e97c2ff1 libpthread.so.0`__pthread_cond_wait at pthread_cond_wait.c:502
    frame #2: 0x00007f21e97c2f30 libpthread.so.0`__pthread_cond_wait(cond=0x00005652bd892418, mutex=0x00005652bd8923f0) at pthread_cond_wait.c:655
    frame #3: 0x00007f21e9133172 libcoreclr.so`CorUnix::CPalSynchronizationManager::ThreadNativeWait(CorUnix::_ThreadNativeWaitData*, unsigned int,
CorUnix::ThreadWakeupReason*, unsigned int*) + 354
    frame #4: 0x00007f21e9132d7a libcoreclr.so`CorUnix::CPalSynchronizationManager::BlockThread(CorUnix::CPalThread*, unsigned int, bool, bool,
CorUnix::ThreadWakeupReason*, unsigned int*) + 378
    frame #5: 0x00007f21e9137952 libcoreclr.so`CorUnix::InternalWaitForMultipleObjectsEx(CorUnix::CPalThread*, unsigned int, void* const*, int, unsigned int,
int, int) + 1906
    frame #6: 0x00007f21e9137c03 libcoreclr.so`WaitForMultipleObjectsEx + 83
    frame #7: 0x00007f21e8d94255 libcoreclr.so`Thread::DoAppropriateWaitWorker(int, void**, int, unsigned int, WaitMode, void*) + 1429
    frame #8: 0x00007f21e8d8f424 libcoreclr.so`Thread::DoAppropriateWait(int, void**, int, unsigned int, WaitMode, PendingSync*) + 228
    frame #9: 0x00007f21e8e93e83 libcoreclr.so`CLREventBase::WaitEx(unsigned int, WaitMode, PendingSync*) + 115
    frame #10: 0x00007f21e8d8e83b libcoreclr.so`AwareLock::EnterEpilogHelper(Thread*, int) + 587
    frame #11: 0x00007f21e8d8e33c libcoreclr.so`AwareLock::Enter() + 252
    frame #12: 0x00007f21e8e27048 libcoreclr.so`JIT_MonEnter_Helper(Object*, unsigned char*, void*) + 376
    frame #13: 0x00007f21e8e272d2 libcoreclr.so`JIT_MonEnter_Portable + 82
    frame #14: 0x00007f216aab431e
    frame #15: 0x00007f21e8f8be04 libcoreclr.so`CallDescrWorkerInternal + 124
    frame #16: 0x00007f21e8dc9a05 libcoreclr.so`DispatchCallSimple(unsigned long*, unsigned int, unsigned long, unsigned int) + 245
    frame #17: 0x00007f21e8ddf6c2 libcoreclr.so`ThreadNative::KickOffThread_Worker(void*) + 146
    frame #18: 0x00007f21e8d97c08 libcoreclr.so`ManagedThreadBase_DispatchOuter(ManagedThreadCallState*) + 344
    frame #19: 0x00007f21e8d980bd libcoreclr.so`ManagedThreadBase::KickOff(void (*)(void*), void*) + 45
    frame #20: 0x00007f21e8ddf7dc libcoreclr.so`ThreadNative::KickOffThread(void*) + 252
    frame #21: 0x00007f21e913e9ae libcoreclr.so`CorUnix::CPalThread::ThreadEntry(void*) + 510
    frame #22: 0x00007f21e97bcfa3 libpthread.so.0`start_thread(arg=<unavailable>) at pthread_create.c:486
    frame #23: 0x00007f21e93cd06f libc.so.6`__GI___clone at clone.S:95
```

```
(lldb) ip2md 0x00007f216aab431e
MethodDesc:    00007f216ab5a0a8
Method Name:          ClassMain.thread_proc_2()
Class:                00007f216ab5a118
MethodTable:          00007f216ab5a118
mdToken:              0000000006000005
Module:               00007f216ab57038
IsJitted:             yes
Current CodeAddr:     00007f216aab42f0
Version History:
  ILCodeVersion:      0000000000000000
  ReJIT ID:           0
  IL Addr:            00007f21e470d2f4
     CodeAddr:           00007f216aab42f0  (QuickJitted)
     NativeCodeVersion:  0000000000000000
Source file:  /mnt/c/ANETMDA-Examples/ApplicationI/Program.cs @ 53
```

```
(lldb) frame select 11
frame #11: 0x00007f21e8d8e33c libcoreclr.so`AwareLock::Enter() + 252
libcoreclr.so`AwareLock::Enter:
    0x7f21e8d8e33c <+252>: leaq    -0x60(%rbp), %rdi
    0x7f21e8d8e340 <+256>: callq   0x7f21e8e95ad0              ;
DebugBlockingItemHolder::~DebugBlockingItemHolder()
    0x7f21e8d8e345 <+261>: movq    %fs:0x28, %rax
    0x7f21e8d8e34e <+270>: cmpq    -0x18(%rbp), %rax


(lldb) register read sp
    rsp = 0x00007f21e138b940


(lldb) frame select 14
frame #14: 0x00007f216aab431e
    0x7f216aab431e: callq   *-0x7ce5c(%rip)
    0x7f216aab4324: movl    $0xbb8, %edi               ; imm = 0xBB8
    0x7f216aab4329: callq   *-0x7cfff(%rip)
    0x7f216aab432f: callq   *-0x7ce6d(%rip)


(lldb) register read sp
    rsp = 0x00007f21e138bb90


(lldb) p (0x00007f21e138bb90 - 0x00007f21e138b940)/8
(long) $6 = 74


(lldb) x/74gx 0x00007f21e138b940
0x7f21e138b940: 0x00005652bd80db90 0x00007ee0a8000c08
0x7f21e138b950: 0x00007ee0a8001118 0xffffffff00000000
0x7f21e138b960: 0x0000000000000000 0x00007ee0a8001118
0x7f21e138b970: 0x00005652bd83e7d0 0xffffffff00000000
0x7f21e138b980: 0x0000000000000000 0xd133c813b91b5700
0x7f21e138b990: 0x00007f21e138ba40 0x00005652bd80db90
0x7f21e138b9a0: 0x00007f21e138bb60 0x00007f21e8e27048
0x7f21e138b9b0: 0x00007f21e8e27280 0x00007ee0a8000bb8
0x7f21e138b9c0: 0x0000000000000000 0x00005652bd80db90
0x7f21e138b9d0: 0x00007f21e138ba30 0x0000000100000001
0x7f21e138b9e0: 0x0000000000000000 0x0000000000000000
0x7f21e138b9f0: 0xffffffffffffffff 0x0000000000000000
0x7f21e138ba00: 0x0000000000000000 0x0000000000000000
0x7f21e138ba10: 0x0000000000000000 0x0000000000000000
0x7f21e138ba20: 0x00005652bd81fc30 0x00007f21e4f3f810
0x7f21e138ba30: 0x0000000000000000 0x0000000006f99ff5
0x7f21e138ba40: 0x00007f21e918b1c0 0x00007f21e138bcc0
0x7f21e138ba50: 0x00005652bd892250 0x0000000000000030
0x7f21e138ba60: 0x00005652bd80db90 0x00007f21e8e27280
0x7f21e138ba70: 0x00007f21e9124900 0x0000000000000002
0x7f21e138ba80: 0x00007f21e918aef0 0x00007f21e138b9c0
0x7f21e138ba90: 0x00007f216aa33498 0x00007f21e91dbbc0
0x7f21e138baa0: 0x00007f21e138ba40 0x00007f21e138bb60
0x7f21e138bab0: 0x0000000000000000 0x00007f21e138bc50
0x7f21e138bac0: 0x00007f21e138bb00 0x00007f21e912e5fa
0x7f21e138bad0: 0x6c5c6c5c00000000 0x00005652bd8412a0
0x7f21e138bae0: 0x0000000000000000 0xd133c813b91b5700
0x7f21e138baf0: 0x0000000000000001 0x0000000000000001
0x7f21e138bb00: 0x00007f21e138bb60 0x00007f21e8d8d017
0x7f21e138bb10: 0xffffffffffffffff 0x00007f21e8e26f88
0x7f21e138bb20: 0x00007f21e138b9a8 0x00007f21e138ba28
0x7f21e138bb30: 0xd133c813b91b5700 0x00007f21e4f3f810
0x7f21e138bb40: 0x0000000000000000 0x00007f21e138bcc0
```

```
0x7f21e138bb50: 0x00007f216aa33498 0x00007f21e138bc50
0x7f21e138bb60: 0x00007f21e138bb80 0x00007f21e8e272d2
0x7f21e138bb70: 0x00007ee154000180 0x00007f21e138bbd8
0x7f21e138bb80: 0x00007f21e138bb90 0x00007f216aab431e
```

Note: We see thread **#9** is waiting for the sync block owner (String) from thread **#7**. Since both threads are mutually waiting for each other, we consider them deadlocked.

7.   How did this deadlock happen? We can look at both threads' execution residue, and we would see that in the case of thread **#7,** there were hidden symbolic references of exception objects (**dumpstackobjects** or **dso** command):

```
(lldb) dumpstackobjects
OS Thread Id: 0x32d (9)
        SP/REG            Object Name
    7f21e138b8f8      7f21e4f3f810 System.String
    7f21e138ba28      7f21e4f3f810 System.String
    7f21e138bb38      7f21e4f3f810 System.String
    7f21e138bc50      7ee156809578 System.Threading.Thread


(lldb) thread select 7
* thread #7, stop reason = signal 0
    frame #0: 0x00007f21e97c300c libpthread.so.0`__pthread_cond_wait at futex-internal.h:88

(lldb) dso
OS Thread Id: 0x32b (7)
        SP/REG            Object Name
    7f21e42fd8d8      7f21e4f3f850 System.String
    7f21e42fda08      7f21e4f3f850 System.String
    7f21e42fdb18      7f21e4f3f850 System.String
    7f21e42fdb80      7ee156809e78 System.NullReferenceException
    7f21e42fdc50      7ee1568093b8 System.Threading.Thread

(lldb) x/20a 7f21e42fdb18
0x7f21e42fdb18: 0x00007f21e4f3f850
0x7f21e42fdb20: 0x0000000000000000
0x7f21e42fdb28: 0x00007f21e42fdcc0 -> 0x00007f21e918b480 libcoreclr.so`vtable for
DebuggerU2MCatchHandlerFrame + 16
0x7f21e42fdb30: 0x00007f216aa33498
0x7f21e42fdb38: 0x00007f21e42fdc50
0x7f21e42fdb40: 0x00007f21e42fdb60
0x7f21e42fdb48: 0x00007f21e8e272d2 libcoreclr.so`JIT_MonEnter_Portable + 82
0x7f21e42fdb50: 0x00007ee154000188
0x7f21e42fdb58: 0x00007f21e42fdbd8
0x7f21e42fdb60: 0x00007f21e42fdb90
0x7f21e42fdb68: 0x00007f216aab1b3d
0x7f21e42fdb70: 0x00007f21e42fdb70
0x7f21e42fdb78: 0x00007f216aa33498
0x7f21e42fdb80: 0x00007ee156809e78
0x7f21e42fdb88: 0x0000000000000000
0x7f21e42fdb90: 0x00007f21e42fdbb0
0x7f21e42fdb98: 0x00007f21e8f8be04 libcoreclr.so`CallDescrWorkerInternal + 124
0x7f21e42fdba0: 0x0000006e0000007c
0x7f21e42fdba8: 0x0000000000000000
0x7f21e42fdbb0: 0x00007f21e42fdc40
```

```
(lldb) dumpobj 7ee156809e78
Name:           System.NullReferenceException
MethodTable: 00007f216ac50970
Canonical MethodTable: 00007f216ac50970
Tracked Type: false
Size:           120(0x78) bytes
File:           /usr/share/dotnet/shared/Microsoft.NETCore.App/9.0.4/System.Private.CoreLib.dll
Fields:
              MT     Field   Offset                 Type VT     Attr            Value Name
00007f216aca0cb8   4000213        8 ...ection.MethodBase  0 instance 0000000000000000 _exceptionMethod
00007f216aa9be30   4000214       10          System.String  0 instance 00007ee15680bda8 _message
00007f216aaa4670   4000215       18 ...tions.IDictionary  0 instance 0000000000000000 _data
00007f216aa9e150   4000216       20        System.Exception  0 instance 0000000000000000 _innerException
00007f216aa9be30   4000217       28          System.String  0 instance 0000000000000000 _helpURL
00007f2169b04910   4000218       30          System.Object  0 instance 00007ee15680bee0 _stackTrace
00007f216ad61328   4000219       38          System.Byte[]  0 instance 0000000000000000 _watsonBuckets
00007f216aa9be30   400021a       40          System.String  0 instance 0000000000000000 _stackTraceString
00007f216aa9be30   400021b       48          System.String  0 instance 0000000000000000
_remoteStackTraceString
00007f216aa9be30   400021c       50          System.String  0 instance 0000000000000000 _source
00007f216aa971e8   400021d       58        System.UIntPtr  1 instance 0000000000000000 _ipForWatsonBuckets
00007f216aa95170   400021e       60         System.IntPtr  1 instance 0000000000000000 _xptrs
00007f216aa474f0   400021f       68          System.Int32  1 instance       -532462766 _xcode
00007f216aa474f0   4000220       6c          System.Int32  1 instance      -2147467261 _HResult1t

(lldb) dumpobj 00007ee15680bda8
Name:           System.String
MethodTable: 00007f216aa9be30
Canonical MethodTable: 00007f216aa9be30
Tracked Type: false
Size:           128(0x80) bytes
File:           /usr/share/dotnet/shared/Microsoft.NETCore.App/9.0.4/System.Private.CoreLib.dll
String:         Object reference not set to an instance of an object.
Fields:
              MT     Field   Offset                 Type VT     Attr            Value Name
00007f216aa474f0   40002ef        8          System.Int32  1 instance               53 _stringLength
00007f216aa53010   40002f0        c          System.Char  1 instance               4f _firstChar
00007f216aa9be30   40002ee        8          System.String  0   static 00007f21e4f3f008 Empty
```

Note: Here is the source code fragment explaining why the lock was never released and why we got exception processing residue:

```
try
{
        Monitor.Enter(cs1);
        {
                DoWork();
                unsafe
                {
                        int* p = (int *)0;
                        *p = 1;
                }
        }
        Monitor.Exit(cs1);
}
catch (Exception e)
{
        Console.WriteLine("We caught an exception.");
}
```

Deadlock (Linux)

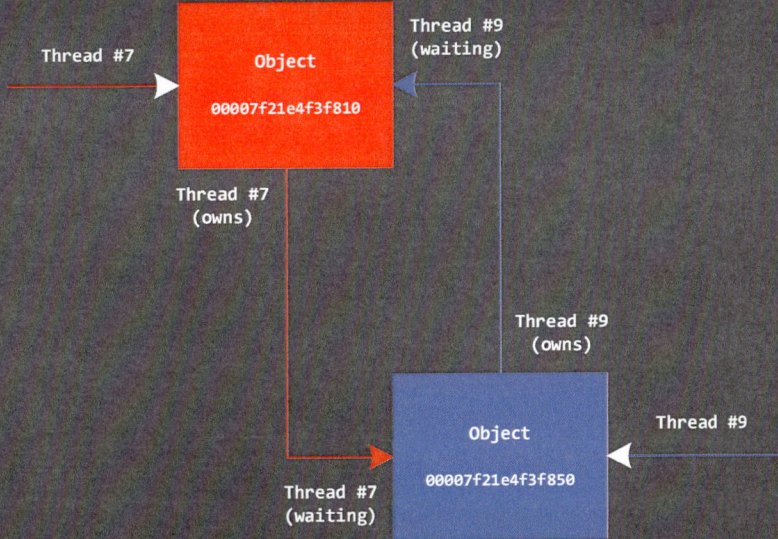

Mechanisms (Deadlock)

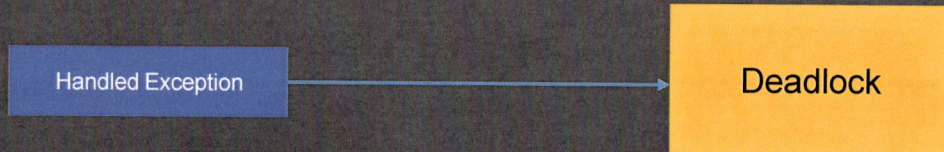

Handled Exception → Deadlock

Exercise PN5 (Windows)

- **Goal:** Learn how to analyze multiple managed exceptions

- **Patterns:** Stack Trace Collection (Managed Space); Multiple Exceptions (Managed Space); Nested Exceptions (Managed Code)

- **Commands:** !pe -nested, !CLRStack -all

- \ANETMDA-Dumps\Exercise-PN5-Windows.pdf

Exercise PN5 (Windows)

Goal: Learn how to analyze multiple managed exceptions.

Patterns: Stack Trace Collection (Managed Space); Multiple Exceptions (Managed Space); Nested Exceptions (Managed Code).

Commands: !pe -nested, !CLRStack -all

1.   Launch WinDbg.

2.   Open \ANETMDA-Dumps\Windows\x64\ApplicationD.exe.18196.dmp

3.   We get the dump file loaded:

```
Microsoft (R) Windows Debugger Version 10.0.27829.1001 AMD64
Copyright (c) Microsoft Corporation. All rights reserved.


Loading Dump File [C:\ANETMDA-Dumps\Windows\x64\ApplicationD.exe.18196.dmp]
User Mini Dump File with Full Memory: Only application data is available


************* Path validation summary **************
Response                        Time (ms)     Location
Deferred                                      srv*
OK                                            C:\ANETMDA-Dumps\Windows\x64\Symbols
Symbol search path is: srv*;C:\ANETMDA-Dumps\Windows\x64\Symbols
Executable search path is:
Windows 10 Version 22000 MP (4 procs) Free x64
Product: WinNt, suite: SingleUserTS
Edition build lab: 22000.1.amd64fre.co_release.210604-1628
Debug session time: Mon Apr 28 08:47:39.000 2025 (UTC + 1:00)
System Uptime: 0 days 0:02:37.539
Process Uptime: 0 days 0:00:04.000
.......................................................
This dump file has an exception of interest stored in it.
The stored exception information can be accessed via .ecxr
```
(4714.4764): CLR exception - code e0434352 (first/second chance not available)
```
For analysis of this file, run !analyze -v
ntdll!NtWaitForMultipleObjects+0x14:
00007ff8`f1624bd4 ret
```

4.   Open a log file using **.logopen** command:

```
0:008> .logopen C:\ANETMDA-Dumps\Windows\x64\ApplicationD.log
Opened log file 'C:\ANETMDA-Dumps\Windows\x64\ApplicationD.log'
```

Note: The WinDbg output may be slightly different on your system if you have a different WinDbg version, a different SOS extension version, you don't have .NET 9 installed, or you have a .NET version different from version 9.0.4 that was on a virtual machine where all the dumps were saved.

5.   It was reported that the program was terminating with the following exception stack trace screenshot below. After closing the message dialog, the crash dump was saved.

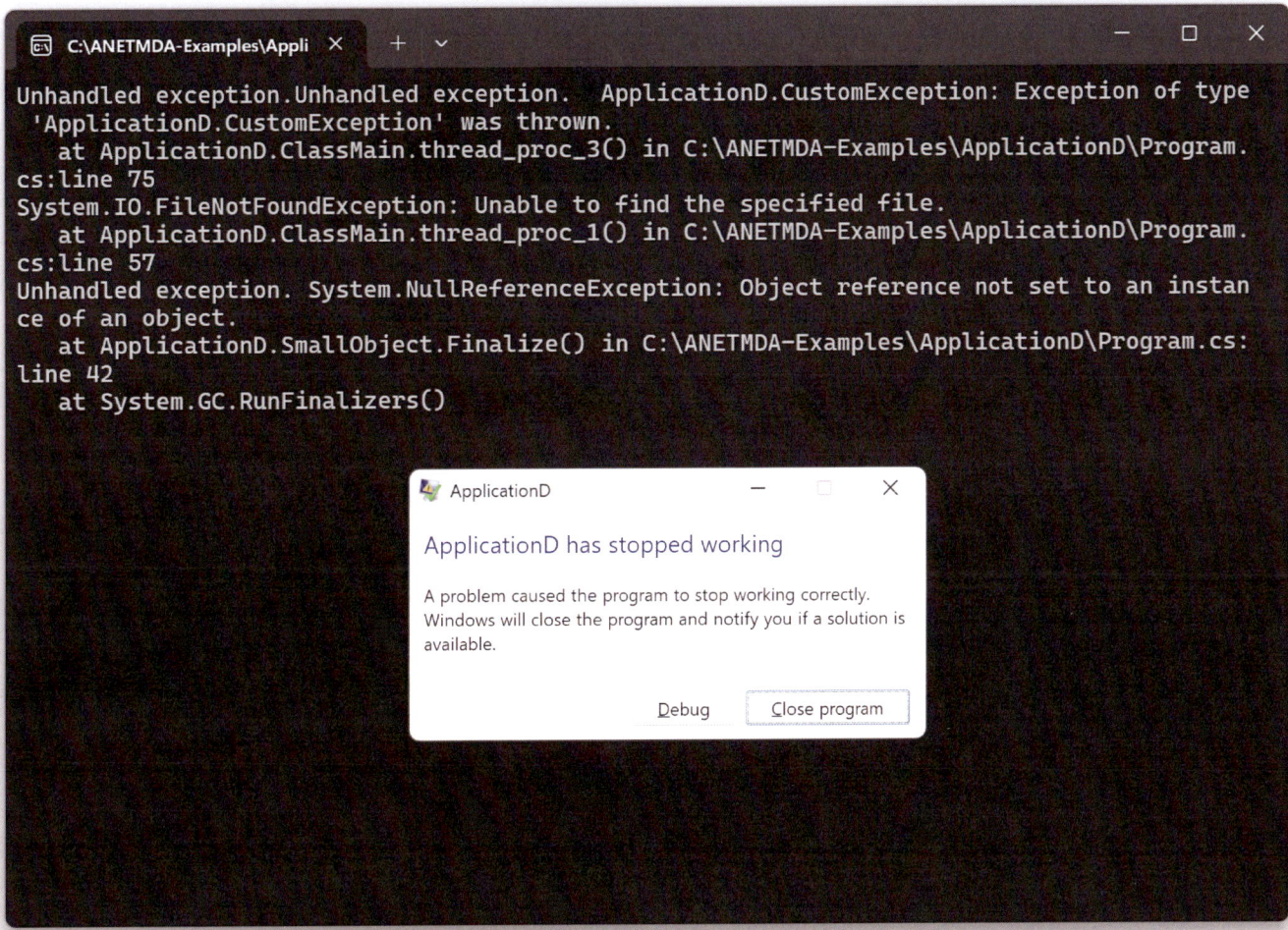

```
C:\ANETMDA-Examples\Appli   X    +  v                                          —   □   X

Unhandled exception.Unhandled exception.  ApplicationD.CustomException: Exception of type
 'ApplicationD.CustomException' was thrown.
   at ApplicationD.ClassMain.thread_proc_3() in C:\ANETMDA-Examples\ApplicationD\Program.
cs:line 75
System.IO.FileNotFoundException: Unable to find the specified file.
   at ApplicationD.ClassMain.thread_proc_1() in C:\ANETMDA-Examples\ApplicationD\Program.
cs:line 57
Unhandled exception. System.NullReferenceException: Object reference not set to an instan
ce of an object.
   at ApplicationD.SmallObject.Finalize() in C:\ANETMDA-Examples\ApplicationD\Program.cs:
line 42
   at System.GC.RunFinalizers()
```

ApplicationD   —   □   X

ApplicationD has stopped working

A problem caused the program to stop working correctly.
Windows will close the program and notify you if a solution is
available.

                              Debug   Close program

6.   Type ~*kL command to verify the correctness of all stack traces:

```
0:008> ~*kL

   0  Id: 4714.4718 Suspend: 0 Teb: 000000e9`3a185000 Unfrozen
 # Child-SP          RetAddr               Call Site
00 000000e9`39fddf68 00007ff8`eefcdcb0     ntdll!NtWaitForMultipleObjects+0x14
01 000000e9`39fddf70 00007ff8`c391e800     KERNELBASE!WaitForMultipleObjectsEx+0xf0
02 000000e9`39fde260 00007ff8`c391e523     coreclr!Thread::DoAppropriateAptStateWait+0x5c
03 000000e9`39fde2a0 00007ff8`c391e35a     coreclr!Thread::DoAppropriateWaitWorker+0x17b
04 000000e9`39fde370 00007ff8`c3a571bf     coreclr!Thread::DoAppropriateWait+0xa6
05 000000e9`39fde410 00007ff8`c3a570f5     coreclr!Thread::JoinEx+0x6b
06 000000e9`39fde460 00007ff8`c3a56fab     coreclr!ThreadNative::DoJoin+0xd9
07 000000e9`39fde4b0 00007ff8`a5be44af     coreclr!ThreadNative::Join+0xcb
08 000000e9`39fde630 00007ff8`63eb1a46     System_Private_CoreLib!System.Threading.Thread.Join+0xf
09 000000e9`39fde660 00007ff8`63eb189b     ApplicationD!ApplicationD.ClassMain.Main+0x146
0a 000000e9`39fde6d0 00007ff8`c3a62eb3     ApplicationD!ApplicationD.ClassMain.Main+0x3b
0b 000000e9`39fde710 00007ff8`c39e180c     coreclr!CallDescrWorkerInternal+0x83
0c 000000e9`39fde750 00007ff8`c39cbab8     coreclr!MethodDescCallSite::CallTargetWorker+0x208
0d (Inline Function) --------`--------     coreclr!MethodDescCallSite::Call+0xb
0e 000000e9`39fde890 00007ff8`c39ccc19     coreclr!RunMainInternal+0x11c
0f 000000e9`39fde9b0 00007ff8`c39ccf2d     coreclr!RunMain+0xd1
10 000000e9`39fdea40 00007ff8`c39cc1bb     coreclr!Assembly::ExecuteMainMethod+0x199
11 000000e9`39fded10 00007ff8`c39c704c     coreclr!CorHost2::ExecuteAssembly+0x1cb
12 000000e9`39fdee20 00007ff8`c732e8ec     coreclr!coreclr_execute_assembly+0xcc
13 (Inline Function) --------`--------     hostpolicy!coreclr_t::execute_assembly+0x2d
14 000000e9`39fdeec0 00007ff8`c732ebbc     hostpolicy!run_app_for_context+0x58c
```

```
15 000000e9`39fdeff0 00007ff8`c732f4ca     hostpolicy!run_app+0x3c
16 000000e9`39fdf030 00007ff8`c7eed986     hostpolicy!corehost_main+0x15a
17 000000e9`39fdf130 00007ff8`c7eeff66     hostfxr!execute_app+0x2e6
18 000000e9`39fdf1c0 00007ff8`c7ef204c     hostfxr!`anonymous namespace'::read_config_and_execute+0xa6
19 000000e9`39fdf2b0 00007ff8`c7ef0533     hostfxr!fx_muxer_t::handle_exec_host_command+0x16c
1a 000000e9`39fdf360 00007ff8`c7ee8460     hostfxr!fx_muxer_t::execute+0x483
1b 000000e9`39fdf4a0 00007ff7`ad98aae3     hostfxr!hostfxr_main_startupinfo+0xa0
1c 000000e9`39fdf5a0 00007ff7`ad98aef6     ApplicationD_exe!exe_start+0x793
1d 000000e9`39fdf750 00007ff7`ad992818     ApplicationD_exe!wmain+0x146
1e (Inline Function) --------`--------     ApplicationD_exe!invoke_main+0x22
1f 000000e9`39fdf7c0 00007ff8`ef6653e0     ApplicationD_exe!__scrt_common_main_seh+0x10c
20 000000e9`39fdf800 00007ff8`f158485b     kernel32!BaseThreadInitThunk+0x10
21 000000e9`39fdf830 00000000`00000000     ntdll!RtlUserThreadStart+0x2b

   1  Id: 4714.4744 Suspend: 0 Teb: 000000e9`3a187000 Unfrozen
 # Child-SP          RetAddr               Call Site
00 000000e9`3a37f598 00007ff8`f1596cdf     ntdll!NtWaitForWorkViaWorkerFactory+0x14
01 000000e9`3a37f5a0 00007ff8`ef6653e0     ntdll!TppWorkerThread+0x2df
02 000000e9`3a37f890 00007ff8`f158485b     kernel32!BaseThreadInitThunk+0x10
03 000000e9`3a37f8c0 00000000`00000000     ntdll!RtlUserThreadStart+0x2b

   2  Id: 4714.4748 Suspend: 0 Teb: 000000e9`3a189000 Unfrozen
 # Child-SP          RetAddr               Call Site
00 000000e9`3a4ffb38 00007ff8`f1596cdf     ntdll!NtWaitForWorkViaWorkerFactory+0x14
01 000000e9`3a4ffb40 00007ff8`ef6653e0     ntdll!TppWorkerThread+0x2df
02 000000e9`3a4ffe30 00007ff8`f158485b     kernel32!BaseThreadInitThunk+0x10
03 000000e9`3a4ffe60 00000000`00000000     ntdll!RtlUserThreadStart+0x2b

   3  Id: 4714.474c Suspend: 0 Teb: 000000e9`3a18b000 Unfrozen
 # Child-SP          RetAddr               Call Site
00 000000e9`3a67f768 00007ff8`f1596cdf     ntdll!NtWaitForWorkViaWorkerFactory+0x14
01 000000e9`3a67f770 00007ff8`ef6653e0     ntdll!TppWorkerThread+0x2df
02 000000e9`3a67fa60 00007ff8`f158485b     kernel32!BaseThreadInitThunk+0x10
03 000000e9`3a67fa90 00000000`00000000     ntdll!RtlUserThreadStart+0x2b

   4  Id: 4714.4750 Suspend: 0 Teb: 000000e9`3a18d000 Unfrozen ".NET EventPipe"
 # Child-SP          RetAddr               Call Site
00 000000e9`3a7ff5f8 00007ff8`eefcdcb0     ntdll!NtWaitForMultipleObjects+0x14
01 000000e9`3a7ff600 00007ff8`eefcdbae     KERNELBASE!WaitForMultipleObjectsEx+0xf0
02 000000e9`3a7ff8f0 00007ff8`c3a3693f     KERNELBASE!WaitForMultipleObjects+0xe
03 000000e9`3a7ff930 00007ff8`c3a368a0     coreclr!ds_ipc_poll+0x7f
04 000000e9`3a7ffbb0 00007ff8`c3a36784     coreclr!ds_ipc_stream_factory_get_next_available_stream+0x108
05 000000e9`3a7ffc80 00007ff8`ef6653e0     coreclr!server_thread+0x54
06 000000e9`3a7ffcf0 00007ff8`f158485b     kernel32!BaseThreadInitThunk+0x10
07 000000e9`3a7ffd20 00000000`00000000     ntdll!RtlUserThreadStart+0x2b

   5  Id: 4714.4754 Suspend: 0 Teb: 000000e9`3a18f000 Unfrozen ".NET Debugger"
 # Child-SP          RetAddr               Call Site
00 000000e9`3a97f3e8 00007ff8`eefcdcb0     ntdll!NtWaitForMultipleObjects+0x14
01 000000e9`3a97f3f0 00007ff8`c3a27a9e     KERNELBASE!WaitForMultipleObjectsEx+0xf0
02 000000e9`3a97f6e0 00007ff8`c3a27e26     coreclr!DebuggerRCThread::MainLoop+0xee
03 000000e9`3a97f7a0 00007ff8`c3a2785b     coreclr!DebuggerRCThread::ThreadProc+0x12e
04 000000e9`3a97f800 00007ff8`ef6653e0     coreclr!DebuggerRCThread::ThreadProcStatic+0x5b
05 000000e9`3a97f830 00007ff8`f158485b     kernel32!BaseThreadInitThunk+0x10
06 000000e9`3a97f860 00000000`00000000     ntdll!RtlUserThreadStart+0x2b

   6  Id: 4714.4758 Suspend: 0 Teb: 000000e9`3a191000 Unfrozen ".NET Finalizer"
 # Child-SP          RetAddr               Call Site
00 000000e9`3aafb6d8 00007ff8`f15db903     ntdll!NtDelayExecution+0x14
01 000000e9`3aafb6e0 00007ff8`eef9d031     ntdll!RtlDelayExecution+0x43
02 000000e9`3aafb710 00007ff8`ef6beaac     KERNELBASE!SleepEx+0x71
03 000000e9`3aafb790 00007ff8`ef0be2f3     kernel32!WerpReportFault+0xa4
04 000000e9`3aafb7d0 00007ff8`f162b0ec     KERNELBASE!UnhandledExceptionFilter+0x3e3
05 000000e9`3aafb8f0 00007ff8`f16140f6     ntdll!RtlUserThreadStart$filt$0+0xac
06 000000e9`3aafb930 00007ff8`f162906f     ntdll!_C_specific_handler+0x96
07 000000e9`3aafb9a0 00007ff8`f15b5bea     ntdll!RtlpExecuteHandlerForException+0xf
08 000000e9`3aafb9d0 00007ff8`f15b2ef1     ntdll!RtlDispatchException+0x25a
09 000000e9`3aafc120 00007ff8`eefc2e0c     ntdll!RtlRaiseException+0x1f1
0a 000000e9`3aafc900 00007ff8`c3ad873e     KERNELBASE!RaiseException+0x6c
0b 000000e9`3aafc9e0 00007ff8`a5c3796d     coreclr!SfiNext+0xe962e
0c 000000e9`3aafcb00 00007ff8`a5c3717a     System_Private_CoreLib!System.Runtime.EH.DispatchEx+0x44d
0d 000000e9`3aafcc60 00007ff8`c3a62eb3     System_Private_CoreLib!System.Runtime.EH.RhThrowHwEx+0xaa
0e 000000e9`3aafcca0 00007ff8`c39e1568     coreclr!CallDescrWorkerInternal+0x83
0f 000000e9`3aafcce0 00007ff8`c3b15cde     coreclr!DispatchCallSimple+0x60
```

```
10 000000e9`3aafcd70 00007ff8`c3aef58a     coreclr!HandleManagedFaultNew+0x192
11 000000e9`3aafe880 00007ff8`f15fca2a     coreclr!CLRVectoredExceptionHandlerShim+0xa84ca
12 000000e9`3aafe8d0 00007ff8`f15b59f2     ntdll!RtlpCallVectoredHandlers+0x112
13 000000e9`3aafe970 00007ff8`f162805e     ntdll!RtlDispatchException+0x62
14 000000e9`3aafebc0 00007ff8`63eb5132     ntdll!KiUserExceptionDispatch+0x2e
15 000000e9`3aaff2c0 00007ff8`a5adbe9f     ApplicationD!ApplicationD.SmallObject.Finalize+0x22
16 000000e9`3aaff300 00007ff8`c3a62eb3     System_Private_CoreLib!System.GC.RunFinalizers+0x8f
17 000000e9`3aaff3e0 00007ff8`c39e1568     coreclr!CallDescrWorkerInternal+0x83
18 000000e9`3aaff420 00007ff8`c3a2945f     coreclr!DispatchCallSimple+0x60
19 000000e9`3aaff4b0 00007ff8`c3a28950     coreclr!FinalizerThread::FinalizeAllObjects+0x7b
1a 000000e9`3aaff590 00007ff8`c39cef05     coreclr!FinalizerThread::FinalizerThreadWorker+0x100
1b (Inline Function) --------`--------     coreclr!ManagedThreadBase_DispatchInner+0xd
1c 000000e9`3aaff7e0 00007ff8`c39cee2d     coreclr!ManagedThreadBase_DispatchMiddle+0x79
1d 000000e9`3aaff890 00007ff8`c3a1e921     coreclr!ManagedThreadBase_DispatchOuter+0x8d
1e (Inline Function) --------`--------     coreclr!ManagedThreadBase_NoADTransition+0x28
1f (Inline Function) --------`--------     coreclr!ManagedThreadBase::FinalizerBase+0x28
20 000000e9`3aaff900 00007ff8`ef6653e0     coreclr!FinalizerThread::FinalizerThreadStart+0x91
21 000000e9`3aaffa10 00007ff8`f158485b     kernel32!BaseThreadInitThunk+0x10
22 000000e9`3aaffa40 00000000`00000000     ntdll!RtlUserThreadStart+0x2b

   7  Id: 4714.475c Suspend: 0 Teb: 000000e9`3a193000 Unfrozen ".NET Tiered Compilation Worker"
 # Child-SP          RetAddr               Call Site
00 000000e9`3ac7f668 00007ff8`eefc10ce     ntdll!NtWaitForSingleObject+0x14
01 000000e9`3ac7f670 00007ff8`c3a293a3     KERNELBASE!WaitForSingleObjectEx+0x8e
02 (Inline Function) --------`--------     coreclr!CLREventWaitHelper2+0x6
03 000000e9`3ac7f710 00007ff8`c3a287a0     coreclr!CLREventWaitHelper+0xf
04 (Inline Function) --------`--------     coreclr!CLREventBase::WaitEx+0x12
05 (Inline Function) --------`--------     coreclr!CLREventBase::Wait+0x12
06 000000e9`3ac7f760 00007ff8`c3a28645     coreclr!TieredCompilationManager::BackgroundWorkerStart+0x11c
07 000000e9`3ac7f7b0 00007ff8`c39cef05     coreclr!TieredCompilationManager::BackgroundWorkerBootstrapper1+0x55
08 (Inline Function) --------`--------     coreclr!ManagedThreadBase_DispatchInner+0xd
09 000000e9`3ac7f7f0 00007ff8`c39cee2d     coreclr!ManagedThreadBase_DispatchMiddle+0x79
0a 000000e9`3ac7f8a0 00007ff8`c3a5c8da     coreclr!ManagedThreadBase_DispatchOuter+0x8d
0b (Inline Function) --------`--------     coreclr!ManagedThreadBase_FullTransition+0x24
0c (Inline Function) --------`--------     coreclr!ManagedThreadBase::KickOff+0x24
0d 000000e9`3ac7f910 00007ff8`ef6653e0     coreclr!TieredCompilationManager::BackgroundWorkerBootstrapper0+0x3a
0e 000000e9`3ac7f960 00007ff8`f158485b     kernel32!BaseThreadInitThunk+0x10
0f 000000e9`3ac7f990 00000000`00000000     ntdll!RtlUserThreadStart+0x2b

#  8  Id: 4714.4764 Suspend: 0 Teb: 000000e9`3a197000 Unfrozen
 # Child-SP          RetAddr               Call Site
00 000000e9`3adfc3e8 00007ff8`eefcdcb0     ntdll!NtWaitForMultipleObjects+0x14
01 000000e9`3adfc3f0 00007ff8`eefcdbae     KERNELBASE!WaitForMultipleObjectsEx+0xf0
02 000000e9`3adfc6e0 00007ff8`ef6bf087     KERNELBASE!WaitForMultipleObjects+0xe
03 000000e9`3adfc720 00007ff8`ef6beac6     kernel32!WerpReportFaultInternal+0x587
04 000000e9`3adfc840 00007ff8`ef0be2f3     kernel32!WerpReportFault+0xbe
05 000000e9`3adfc880 00007ff8`f162b0ec     KERNELBASE!UnhandledExceptionFilter+0x3e3
06 000000e9`3adfc9a0 00007ff8`f16140f6     ntdll!RtlUserThreadStart$filt$0+0xac
07 000000e9`3adfc9e0 00007ff8`f162906f     ntdll!_C_specific_handler+0x96
08 000000e9`3adfca50 00007ff8`f15b5bea     ntdll!RtlpExecuteHandlerForException+0xf
09 000000e9`3adfca80 00007ff8`f15b2ef1     ntdll!RtlDispatchException+0x25a
0a 000000e9`3adfd1d0 00007ff8`eefc2e0c     ntdll!RtlRaiseException+0x1f1
0b 000000e9`3adfd9b0 00007ff8`c3ad873e     KERNELBASE!RaiseException+0x6c
0c 000000e9`3adfda90 00007ff8`a5c3796d     coreclr!SfiNext+0xe962e
0d 000000e9`3adfdbb0 00007ff8`a5c371cd     System_Private_CoreLib!System.Runtime.EH.DispatchEx+0x44d
0e 000000e9`3adfdd10 00007ff8`c3a62eb3     System_Private_CoreLib!System.Runtime.EH.RhThrowEx+0x2d
0f 000000e9`3adfdd40 00007ff8`c39e1568     coreclr!CallDescrWorkerInternal+0x83
10 000000e9`3adfdd80 00007ff8`c39d19b1     coreclr!DispatchCallSimple+0x60
11 000000e9`3adfde10 00007ff8`c39d1844     coreclr!DispatchManagedException+0x169
12 000000e9`3adff4d0 00007ff8`c39d1813     coreclr!DispatchManagedException+0x24
13 000000e9`3adff9d0 00007ff8`c39d179e     coreclr!ThrowNew+0x67
14 000000e9`3adffa20 00007ff8`63eb1aba     coreclr!IL_Throw+0x8e
15 000000e9`3adffb70 00007ff8`c3a62eb3     ApplicationD!ApplicationD.ClassMain.thread_proc_1+0x3a
16 000000e9`3adffbb0 00007ff8`c39e1568     coreclr!CallDescrWorkerInternal+0x83
17 000000e9`3adffbf0 00007ff8`c3a515a3     coreclr!DispatchCallSimple+0x60
18 000000e9`3adffc80 00007ff8`c39cef05     coreclr!ThreadNative::KickOffThread_Worker+0x63
19 (Inline Function) --------`--------     coreclr!ManagedThreadBase_DispatchInner+0xd
1a 000000e9`3adffce0 00007ff8`c39cee2d     coreclr!ManagedThreadBase_DispatchMiddle+0x79
1b 000000e9`3adffd90 00007ff8`c39cefbb     coreclr!ManagedThreadBase_DispatchOuter+0x8d
1c (Inline Function) --------`--------     coreclr!ManagedThreadBase_FullTransition+0x28
1d (Inline Function) --------`--------     coreclr!ManagedThreadBase::KickOff+0x28
1e 000000e9`3adffe00 00007ff8`ef6653e0     coreclr!ThreadNative::KickOffThread+0x7b
1f 000000e9`3adffe60 00007ff8`f158485b     kernel32!BaseThreadInitThunk+0x10
20 000000e9`3adffe90 00000000`00000000     ntdll!RtlUserThreadStart+0x2b
```

```
 9  Id: 4714.4768 Suspend: 0 Teb: 000000e9`3a199000 Unfrozen
# Child-SP          RetAddr            Call Site
00 000000e9`3af7f898 00007ff8`c39cfe71 KERNELBASE!OpenThreadToken
01 000000e9`3af7f8a0 00007ff8`c39cfdac coreclr!RevertIfImpersonated+0x2d
02 000000e9`3af7f8d0 00007ff8`c39cfb01 coreclr!Thread::CreateNewThread+0x5c
03 000000e9`3af7f940 00007ff8`c39ced90 coreclr!ThreadNative::Start+0xa1
04 000000e9`3af7f9d0 00007ff8`63eb5e5b coreclr!ThreadNative_Start+0x30
05 000000e9`3af7fa20 00007ff8`63eb5bb8 System_Private_CoreLib!System.Threading.Thread.StartCore+0xbb
06 000000e9`3af7fae0 00007ff8`63eb1b28 ApplicationD!ApplicationD.SmallObject..ctor+0xa8
07 000000e9`3af7fb30 00007ff8`c3a62eb3 ApplicationD!ApplicationD.ClassMain.thread_proc_2+0x58
08 000000e9`3af7fbb0 00007ff8`c39e1568 coreclr!CallDescrWorkerInternal+0x83
09 000000e9`3af7fbf0 00007ff8`c3a515a3 coreclr!DispatchCallSimple+0x60
0a 000000e9`3af7fc80 00007ff8`c39cef05 coreclr!ThreadNative::KickOffThread_Worker+0x63
0b (Inline Function) --------`-------- coreclr!ManagedThreadBase_DispatchInner+0xd
0c 000000e9`3af7fce0 00007ff8`c39cee2d coreclr!ManagedThreadBase_DispatchMiddle+0x79
0d 000000e9`3af7fd90 00007ff8`c39cefbb coreclr!ManagedThreadBase_DispatchOuter+0x8d
0e (Inline Function) --------`-------- coreclr!ManagedThreadBase_FullTransition+0x28
0f (Inline Function) --------`-------- coreclr!ManagedThreadBase::KickOff+0x28
10 000000e9`3af7fe00 00007ff8`ef6653e0 coreclr!ThreadNative::KickOffThread+0x7b
11 000000e9`3af7fe60 00007ff8`f158485b kernel32!BaseThreadInitThunk+0x10
12 000000e9`3af7fe90 00000000`00000000 ntdll!RtlUserThreadStart+0x2b

 10  Id: 4714.476c Suspend: 0 Teb: 000000e9`3a19b000 Unfrozen
# Child-SP          RetAddr            Call Site
00 000000e9`3b0fa4b8 00007ff8`f15db903 ntdll!NtDelayExecution+0x14
01 000000e9`3b0fa4c0 00007ff8`eef9d031 ntdll!RtlDelayExecution+0x43
02 000000e9`3b0fa4f0 00007ff8`ef6beaac KERNELBASE!SleepEx+0x71
03 000000e9`3b0fa570 00007ff8`ef0be2f3 kernel32!WerpReportFault+0xa4
04 000000e9`3b0fa5b0 00007ff8`f162b0ec KERNELBASE!UnhandledExceptionFilter+0x3e3
05 000000e9`3b0fa6d0 00007ff8`f16140f6 ntdll!RtlUserThreadStart$filt$0+0xac
06 000000e9`3b0fa710 00007ff8`f162906f ntdll!_C_specific_handler+0x96
07 000000e9`3b0fa780 00007ff8`f15b5bea ntdll!RtlpExecuteHandlerForException+0xf
08 000000e9`3b0fa7b0 00007ff8`f15b2ef1 ntdll!RtlDispatchException+0x25a
09 000000e9`3b0faf00 00007ff8`eefc2e0c ntdll!RtlRaiseException+0x1f1
0a 000000e9`3b0fb6e0 00007ff8`c3ad873e KERNELBASE!RaiseException+0x6c
0b 000000e9`3b0fb7c0 00007ff8`a5c3796d coreclr!SfiNext+0xe962e
0c 000000e9`3b0fb8e0 00007ff8`a5c371cd System_Private_CoreLib!System.Runtime.EH.DispatchEx+0x44d
0d 000000e9`3b0fba40 00007ff8`c3a62eb3 System_Private_CoreLib!System.Runtime.EH.RhThrowEx+0x2d
0e 000000e9`3b0fba70 00007ff8`c39e1568 coreclr!CallDescrWorkerInternal+0x83
0f 000000e9`3b0fbab0 00007ff8`c39d19b1 coreclr!DispatchCallSimple+0x60
10 000000e9`3b0fbb40 00007ff8`c39d1844 coreclr!DispatchManagedException+0x169
11 000000e9`3b0fd200 00007ff8`c39d1813 coreclr!DispatchManagedException+0x24
12 000000e9`3b0fd700 00007ff8`c39d179e coreclr!ThrowNew+0x67
13 000000e9`3b0fd750 00007ff8`63eb1d40 coreclr!IL_Throw+0x8e
14 000000e9`3b0fd8a0 00007ff8`c39ec4ef ApplicationD!ApplicationD.ClassMain.thread_proc_3+0xa0
15 000000e9`3b0fd8e0 00007ff8`a5c37a56 coreclr!CallCatchFunclet+0x17f
16 000000e9`3b0fd9f0 00007ff8`a5c371cd System_Private_CoreLib!System.Runtime.EH.DispatchEx+0x536
17 000000e9`3b0fdb50 00007ff8`c3a62eb3 System_Private_CoreLib!System.Runtime.EH.RhThrowEx+0x2d
18 000000e9`3b0fdb80 00007ff8`c39e1568 coreclr!CallDescrWorkerInternal+0x83
19 000000e9`3b0fdbc0 00007ff8`c39d19b1 coreclr!DispatchCallSimple+0x60
1a 000000e9`3b0fdc50 00007ff8`c39d1844 coreclr!DispatchManagedException+0x169
1b 000000e9`3b0ff310 00007ff8`c39d1813 coreclr!DispatchManagedException+0x24
1c 000000e9`3b0ff810 00007ff8`c39d179e coreclr!ThrowNew+0x67
1d 000000e9`3b0ff860 00007ff8`63eb1ce1 coreclr!IL_Throw+0x8e
1e 000000e9`3b0ff9b0 00007ff8`c3a62eb3 ApplicationD!ApplicationD.ClassMain.thread_proc_3+0x41
1f 000000e9`3b0ffa10 00007ff8`c39e1568 coreclr!CallDescrWorkerInternal+0x83
20 000000e9`3b0ffa50 00007ff8`c3a515a3 coreclr!DispatchCallSimple+0x60
21 000000e9`3b0ffae0 00007ff8`c39cef05 coreclr!ThreadNative::KickOffThread_Worker+0x63
22 (Inline Function) --------`-------- coreclr!ManagedThreadBase_DispatchInner+0xd
23 000000e9`3b0ffb40 00007ff8`c39cee2d coreclr!ManagedThreadBase_DispatchMiddle+0x79
24 000000e9`3b0ffbf0 00007ff8`c39cefbb coreclr!ManagedThreadBase_DispatchOuter+0x8d
25 (Inline Function) --------`-------- coreclr!ManagedThreadBase_FullTransition+0x28
26 (Inline Function) --------`-------- coreclr!ManagedThreadBase::KickOff+0x28
27 000000e9`3b0ffc60 00007ff8`ef6653e0 coreclr!ThreadNative::KickOffThread+0x7b
28 000000e9`3b0ffcc0 00007ff8`f158485b kernel32!BaseThreadInitThunk+0x10
29 000000e9`3b0ffcf0 00000000`00000000 ntdll!RtlUserThreadStart+0x2b
```

Note: We notice an exception on the finalizer thread #6, and there are two threads, #8 and #10, that have a thrown exception, and in thread #10, we have a rethrown exception.

7.	We check if the SOS extension is already loaded by using the **.chain** command. If it is loaded, we may either continue or unload it and load our own version:

```
0:008> .unload sos
Unloading sos extension DLL

0:008> .load C:\Users\dmitr\.dotnet\sos\sos.dll
```

8.	We now list managed stack traces:

```
0:008> ~*e !CLRStack
OS Thread Id: 0x4718 (0)
        Child SP               IP Call Site
000000E939FDE518 00007ff8f1624bd4 [HelperMethodFrame_1OBJ: 000000e939fde518] System.Threading.Thread.Join(Int32)
000000E939FDE630 00007ff8a5be44af System.Threading.Thread.Join()
[/_/src/libraries/System.Private.CoreLib/src/System/Threading/Thread.cs @ 539]
000000E939FDE660 00007ff863eb1a46 ApplicationD.ClassMain.Main()
000000E939FDE6D0 00007ff863eb189b ApplicationD.ClassMain.Main(System.String[])
OS Thread Id: 0x4744 (1)
Unable to walk the managed stack. The current thread is likely not a
managed thread. You can run !clrthreads to get a list of managed threads in
the process
Failed to start stack walk: 80070057
OS Thread Id: 0x4748 (2)
Unable to walk the managed stack. The current thread is likely not a
managed thread. You can run !clrthreads to get a list of managed threads in
the process
Failed to start stack walk: 80070057
OS Thread Id: 0x474c (3)
Unable to walk the managed stack. The current thread is likely not a
managed thread. You can run !clrthreads to get a list of managed threads in
the process
Failed to start stack walk: 80070057
OS Thread Id: 0x4750 (4)
Unable to walk the managed stack. The current thread is likely not a
managed thread. You can run !clrthreads to get a list of managed threads in
the process
Failed to start stack walk: 80070057
OS Thread Id: 0x4754 (5)
Unable to walk the managed stack. The current thread is likely not a
managed thread. You can run !clrthreads to get a list of managed threads in
the process
Failed to start stack walk: 80070057
OS Thread Id: 0x4758 (6)
        Child SP               IP Call Site
000000E93AAFCB60 00007ff8f1624704 [InlinedCallFrame: 000000e93aafcb60]
000000E93AAFCB60 00007ff8a5c37948 [InlinedCallFrame: 000000e93aafcb60]
000000E93AAFCB00 00007ff8a5c37948 System.Runtime.EH.DispatchEx(System.Runtime.StackFrameIterator ByRef, ExInfo ByRef)
[/_/src/coreclr/nativeaot/Runtime.Base/src/System/Runtime/ExceptionHandling.cs @ 865]
000000E93AAFCC60 00007ff8a5c3717a System.Runtime.EH.RhThrowHwEx(UInt32, ExInfo ByRef)
[/_/src/coreclr/nativeaot/Runtime.Base/src/System/Runtime/ExceptionHandling.cs @ 619]
000000E93AAFCDD0 00007ff8c3a62eb3 [FaultingExceptionFrame: 000000e93aafcdd0]
000000E93AAFF2C0 00007ff863eb5132 ApplicationD.SmallObject.Finalize()
000000E93AAFF300 00007ff8a5adbe9f System.GC.RunFinalizers()
[/_/src/coreclr/System.Private.CoreLib/src/System/GC.CoreCLR.cs @ 317]
000000E93AAFF8D8 00007ff8c3a62eb3 [DebuggerU2MCatchHandlerFrame: 000000e93aaff8d8]
OS Thread Id: 0x475c (7)
        Child SP               IP Call Site
000000E93AC7F8E8 00007ff8f1624104 [DebuggerU2MCatchHandlerFrame: 000000e93ac7f8e8]
OS Thread Id: 0x4764 (8)
        Child SP               IP Call Site
000000E93ADFDC10 00007ff8f1624bd4 [InlinedCallFrame: 000000e93adfdc10]
000000E93ADFDC10 00007ff8a5c37948 [InlinedCallFrame: 000000e93adfdc10]
000000E93ADFDBB0 00007ff8a5c37948 System.Runtime.EH.DispatchEx(System.Runtime.StackFrameIterator ByRef, ExInfo ByRef)
[/_/src/coreclr/nativeaot/Runtime.Base/src/System/Runtime/ExceptionHandling.cs @ 865]
000000E93ADFDD10 00007ff8a5c371cd System.Runtime.EH.RhThrowEx(System.Object, ExInfo ByRef)
[/_/src/coreclr/nativeaot/Runtime.Base/src/System/Runtime/ExceptionHandling.cs @ 645]
000000E93ADFFA78 00007ff8c3a62eb3 [HelperMethodFrame: 000000e93adffa78]
000000E93ADFFB70 00007ff863eb1aba ApplicationD.ClassMain.thread_proc_1()
000000E93ADFFDD8 00007ff8c3a62eb3 [DebuggerU2MCatchHandlerFrame: 000000e93adffdd8]
```

```
OS Thread Id: 0x4768 (9)
        Child SP               IP Call Site
000000E93AF7FA50 00007ff8eefb3b90 [InlinedCallFrame: 000000e93af7fa50]
System.Threading.Thread.StartInternal(System.Threading.ThreadHandle, Int32, Int32, Char*)
000000E93AF7FA50 00007ff863eb5e5b [InlinedCallFrame: 000000e93af7fa50]
System.Threading.Thread.StartInternal(System.Threading.ThreadHandle, Int32, Int32, Char*)
000000E93AF7FA20 00007ff863eb5e5b System.Threading.Thread.StartCore()
[/_/src/coreclr/System.Private.CoreLib/src/System/Threading/Thread.CoreCLR.cs @ 89]
000000E93AF7FAE0 00007ff863eb5bb8 ApplicationD.SmallObject..ctor()
000000E93AF7FB30 00007ff863eb1b28 ApplicationD.ClassMain.thread_proc_2()
000000E93AF7FDD8 00007ff8c3a62eb3 [DebuggerU2MCatchHandlerFrame: 000000e93af7fdd8]
OS Thread Id: 0x476c (10)
        Child SP               IP Call Site
000000E93B0FB940 00007ff8f1624704 [InlinedCallFrame: 000000e93b0fb940]
000000E93B0FB940 00007ff8a5c37948 [InlinedCallFrame: 000000e93b0fb940]
000000E93B0FB8E0 00007ff8a5c37948 System.Runtime.EH.DispatchEx(System.Runtime.StackFrameIterator ByRef, ExInfo ByRef)
[/_/src/coreclr/nativeaot/Runtime.Base/src/System/Runtime/ExceptionHandling.cs @ 865]
000000E93B0FBA40 00007ff8a5c371cd System.Runtime.EH.RhThrowEx(System.Object, ExInfo ByRef)
[/_/src/coreclr/nativeaot/Runtime.Base/src/System/Runtime/ExceptionHandling.cs @ 645]
000000E93B0FD7A8 00007ff8c3a62eb3 [HelperMethodFrame: 000000e93b0fd7a8]
000000E93B0FD8A0 00007ff863eb1d40 ApplicationD.ClassMain.thread_proc_3()
000000E93B0FDA50 00007ff8c39ec4ef [InlinedCallFrame: 000000e93b0fda50]
000000E93B0FDA50 00007ff8a5c37a31 [InlinedCallFrame: 000000e93b0fda50]
000000E93B0FD9F0 00007ff8a5c37a31 System.Runtime.EH.DispatchEx(System.Runtime.StackFrameIterator ByRef, ExInfo ByRef)
[/_/src/coreclr/nativeaot/Runtime.Base/src/System/Runtime/ExceptionHandling.cs @ 928]
000000E93B0FDB50 00007ff8a5c371cd System.Runtime.EH.RhThrowEx(System.Object, ExInfo ByRef)
[/_/src/coreclr/nativeaot/Runtime.Base/src/System/Runtime/ExceptionHandling.cs @ 645]
000000E93B0FF8B8 00007ff8c3a62eb3 [HelperMethodFrame: 000000e93b0ff8b8]
000000E93B0FF9B0 00007ff863eb1ce1 ApplicationD.ClassMain.thread_proc_3()
000000E93B0FFC38 00007ff8c3a62eb3 [DebuggerU2MCatchHandlerFrame: 000000e93b0ffc38]
```

Note: Another way is to use **-all** option for **!CLRStack** command (the output will exclude non-CLR threads):

```
0:008> !CLRStack -all
OS Thread Id: 0x4718
        Child SP               IP Call Site
000000E939FDE518 00007ff8f1624bd4 [HelperMethodFrame_1OBJ: 000000e939fde518] System.Threading.Thread.Join(Int32)
000000E939FDE630 00007ff8a5be44af System.Threading.Thread.Join()
[/_/src/libraries/System.Private.CoreLib/src/System/Threading/Thread.cs @ 539]
000000E939FDE660 00007ff863eb1a46 ApplicationD.ClassMain.Main()
000000E939FDE6D0 00007ff863eb189b ApplicationD.ClassMain.Main(System.String[])
OS Thread Id: 0x4758
        Child SP               IP Call Site
000000E93AAFCB60 00007ff8f1624704 [InlinedCallFrame: 000000e93aafcb60]
000000E93AAFCB60 00007ff8a5c37948 [InlinedCallFrame: 000000e93aafcb60]
000000E93AAFCB00 00007ff8a5c37948 System.Runtime.EH.DispatchEx(System.Runtime.StackFrameIterator ByRef, ExInfo ByRef)
[/_/src/coreclr/nativeaot/Runtime.Base/src/System/Runtime/ExceptionHandling.cs @ 865]
000000E93AAFCC60 00007ff8a5c3717a System.Runtime.EH.RhThrowHwEx(UInt32, ExInfo ByRef)
[/_/src/coreclr/nativeaot/Runtime.Base/src/System/Runtime/ExceptionHandling.cs @ 619]
000000E93AAFCDD0 00007ff8c3a62eb3 [FaultingExceptionFrame: 000000e93aafcdd0]
000000E93AAFF2C0 00007ff863eb5132 ApplicationD.SmallObject.Finalize()
000000E93AAFF300 00007ff8a5adbe9f System.GC.RunFinalizers()
[/_/src/coreclr/System.Private.CoreLib/src/System/GC.CoreCLR.cs @ 317]
000000E93AAFF8D8 00007ff8c3a62eb3 [DebuggerU2MCatchHandlerFrame: 000000e93aaff8d8]
OS Thread Id: 0x475c
        Child SP               IP Call Site
000000E93AC7F8E8 00007ff8f1624104 [DebuggerU2MCatchHandlerFrame: 000000e93ac7f8e8]
OS Thread Id: 0x4764
        Child SP               IP Call Site
000000E93ADFDC10 00007ff8f1624bd4 [InlinedCallFrame: 000000e93adfdc10]
000000E93ADFDC10 00007ff8a5c37948 [InlinedCallFrame: 000000e93adfdc10]
000000E93ADFDBB0 00007ff8a5c37948 System.Runtime.EH.DispatchEx(System.Runtime.StackFrameIterator ByRef, ExInfo ByRef)
[/_/src/coreclr/nativeaot/Runtime.Base/src/System/Runtime/ExceptionHandling.cs @ 865]
000000E93ADFDD10 00007ff8a5c371cd System.Runtime.EH.RhThrowEx(System.Object, ExInfo ByRef)
[/_/src/coreclr/nativeaot/Runtime.Base/src/System/Runtime/ExceptionHandling.cs @ 645]
000000E93ADFFA78 00007ff8c3a62eb3 [HelperMethodFrame: 000000e93adffa78]
000000E93ADFFB70 00007ff863eb1aba ApplicationD.ClassMain.thread_proc_1()
000000E93ADFFDD8 00007ff8c3a62eb3 [DebuggerU2MCatchHandlerFrame: 000000e93adffdd8]
OS Thread Id: 0x4768
        Child SP               IP Call Site
000000E93AF7FA50 00007ff8eefb3b90 [InlinedCallFrame: 000000e93af7fa50]
System.Threading.Thread.StartInternal(System.Threading.ThreadHandle, Int32, Int32, Char*)
```

```
000000E93AF7FA50 00007ff863eb5e5b [InlinedCallFrame: 000000e93af7fa50]
System.Threading.Thread.StartInternal(System.Threading.ThreadHandle, Int32, Int32, Char*)
000000E93AF7FA20 00007ff863eb5e5b System.Threading.Thread.StartCore()
[/_/src/coreclr/System.Private.CoreLib/src/System/Threading/Thread.CoreCLR.cs @ 89]
000000E93AF7FAE0 00007ff863eb5bb8 ApplicationD.SmallObject..ctor()
000000E93AF7FB30 00007ff863eb1b28 ApplicationD.ClassMain.thread_proc_2()
000000E93AF7FDD8 00007ff8c3a62eb3 [DebuggerU2MCatchHandlerFrame: 000000e93af7fdd8]
OS Thread Id: 0x476c
        Child SP               IP Call Site
000000E93B0FB940 00007ff8f1624704 [InlinedCallFrame: 000000e93b0fb940]
000000E93B0FB940 00007ff8a5c37948 [InlinedCallFrame: 000000e93b0fb940]
000000E93B0FB8E0 00007ff8a5c37948 System.Runtime.EH.DispatchEx(System.Runtime.StackFrameIterator ByRef, ExInfo ByRef)
[/_/src/coreclr/nativeaot/Runtime.Base/src/System/Runtime/ExceptionHandling.cs @ 865]
000000E93B0FBA40 00007ff8a5c371cd System.Runtime.EH.RhThrowEx(System.Object, ExInfo ByRef)
[/_/src/coreclr/nativeaot/Runtime.Base/src/System/Runtime/ExceptionHandling.cs @ 645]
000000E93B0FD7A8 00007ff8c3a62eb3 [HelperMethodFrame: 000000e93b0fd7a8]
000000E93B0FD8A0 00007ff863eb1d40 ApplicationD.ClassMain.thread_proc_3()
000000E93B0FDA50 00007ff8c39ec4ef [InlinedCallFrame: 000000e93b0fda50]
000000E93B0FDA50 00007ff8a5c37a31 [InlinedCallFrame: 000000e93b0fda50]
000000E93B0FD9F0 00007ff8a5c37a31 System.Runtime.EH.DispatchEx(System.Runtime.StackFrameIterator ByRef, ExInfo ByRef)
[/_/src/coreclr/nativeaot/Runtime.Base/src/System/Runtime/ExceptionHandling.cs @ 928]
000000E93B0FDB50 00007ff8a5c371cd System.Runtime.EH.RhThrowEx(System.Object, ExInfo ByRef)
[/_/src/coreclr/nativeaot/Runtime.Base/src/System/Runtime/ExceptionHandling.cs @ 645]
000000E93B0FF8B8 00007ff8c3a62eb3 [HelperMethodFrame: 000000e93b0ff8b8]
000000E93B0FF9B0 00007ff863eb1ce1 ApplicationD.ClassMain.thread_proc_3()
000000E93B0FFC38 00007ff8c3a62eb3 [DebuggerU2MCatchHandlerFrame: 000000e93b0ffc38]
```

9.   Then we list managed threads:

```
0:008> !Threads
ThreadCount:      1133
UnstartedThread:  1
BackgroundThread: 2
PendingThread:    0
DeadThread:       1126
Hosted Runtime:   no
                                                                                           Lock
 DBG   ID   OSID ThreadOBJ          State GC Mode   GC Alloc Context                Domain             Count Apt Exception
   0    1   4718 0000023E0B9D6B40  202a020 Preemptive 0000000000000000:0000000000000000 0000023e0b9fdcb0 -00001 MTA
   6    2   4758 0000023E0B9DB760   2b220 Preemptive 0000000000000000:0000000000000000 0000023e0b9fdcb0 -00001 MTA (Finalizer)
System.NullReferenceException 0000023e100083a0
   7    3   475c 0000023E0B9E38B0   2b220 Preemptive 0000000000000000:0000000000000000 0000023e0b9fdcb0 -00001 MTA
   8    4   4764 0000023E0BA79AD0   2b020 Preemptive 0000000000000000:0000000000000000 0000023e0b9fdcb0 -00001 MTA System.IO.FileNotFoundException
0000023e1240a6a0
   9    5   4768 0000023E0D450AD0   2b020 Preemptive 0000023E131EE808:0000023E131F0710 0000023e0b9fdcb0 -00001 MTA
  10    6   476c 0000023E0B9B53E0   2b020 Preemptive 0000000000000000:0000000000000000 0000023e0b9fdcb0 -00001 MTA ApplicationD.CustomException
0000023e124c56a0 (nested exceptions)
[...]
```

Note: We see that threads #6, #8, and #10 have exceptions. Thread #10 has a nested exception.

10.   We double-check managed exceptions by running **!PrintException** (**!pe**) for every thread:

```
0:008> ~*e !pe
There is no current managed exception on this thread
The current thread is unmanaged
The current thread is unmanaged
The current thread is unmanaged
The current thread is unmanaged
The current thread is unmanaged
Exception object: 0000023e100083a0
Exception type:   System.NullReferenceException
Message:          Object reference not set to an instance of an object.
InnerException:   <none>
StackTrace (generated):
    SP               IP               Function
    000000E93AAFF2C0 00007FF863EB5133 ApplicationD!ApplicationD.SmallObject.Finalize()+0x23
    000000E93AAFF300 00007FF8A5ADBE9F System_Private_CoreLib!System.GC.RunFinalizers()+0x8f

StackTraceString: <none>
```

HResult: 80004003
There is no current managed exception on this thread
Exception object: 0000023e1240a6a0
Exception type: System.IO.FileNotFoundException
Message: Unable to find the specified file.
InnerException: <none>
StackTrace (generated):
    SP   IP   Function
    000000E93ADFFB70 00007FF863EB1AB9 ApplicationD!ApplicationD.ClassMain.thread_proc_1()+0x39

StackTraceString: <none>
HResult: 80070002
There is no current managed exception on this thread
Exception object: 0000023e124c56a0
Exception type: ApplicationD.CustomException
Message: <none>
InnerException: <none>
StackTrace (generated):
    SP   IP   Function
    000000E93B0FD8A0 00007FF863EB1D3F ApplicationD!ApplicationD.ClassMain.thread_proc_3()+0x9f

StackTraceString: <none>
HResult: 80131500
There are nested exceptions on this thread. Run with -nested for details

11.   We now check ApplicationD.CustomException object:

```
0:008> !DumpObj 0000023e124c56a0
Name:        ApplicationD.CustomException
MethodTable: 00007ff863f6ae58
Canonical MethodTable: 00007ff863f6ae58
Tracked Type: false
Size:        136(0x88) bytes
File:        C:\Work\ApplicationD.dll
Fields:
              MT    Field   Offset                 Type VT     Attr            Value Name
00007ff863fb51a8  4000271        8 ...ection.MethodBase  0 instance 0000000000000000 _exceptionMethod
00007ff863e8bf40  4000272       10        System.String  0 instance 0000000000000000 _message
00007ff863e94b60  4000273       18 ...tions.IDictionary  0 instance 0000000000000000 _data
00007ff863e8e260  4000274       20     System.Exception  0 instance 0000000000000000 _innerException
00007ff863e8bf40  4000275       28        System.String  0 instance 0000000000000000 _helpURL
00007ff863d74730  4000276       30        System.Object  0 instance 0000023e124c5728 _stackTrace
00007ff863f5dea0  4000277       38        System.Byte[]  0 instance 0000023e124c5770 _watsonBuckets
00007ff863e8bf40  4000278       40        System.String  0 instance 0000000000000000 _stackTraceString
00007ff863e8bf40  4000279       48        System.String  0 instance 0000000000000000 _remoteStackTraceString
00007ff863e8bf40  400027a       50        System.String  0 instance 0000000000000000 _source
00007ff863e872e8  400027b       58      System.UIntPtr  1 instance 0000000000000000 _ipForWatsonBuckets
00007ff863e85270  400027c       60       System.IntPtr  1 instance 0000000000000000 _xptrs
00007ff863e37408  400027d       68        System.Int32  1 instance      -532462766 _xcode
00007ff863e37408  400027e       6c        System.Int32  1 instance     -2146233088 _HResult
00007ff863e8bf40  4000001       70        System.String  0 instance 0000027ea20b22a8 description
00007ff863e37408  4000002       78        System.Int32  1 instance               5 code
```

```
0:008> !DumpObj 0000027ea20b22a8
Name:        System.String
MethodTable: 00007ff863e8bf40
Canonical MethodTable: 00007ff863e8bf40
Tracked Type: false
Size:        50(0x32) bytes
File:        C:\Program Files\dotnet\shared\Microsoft.NETCore.App\9.0.4\System.Private.CoreLib.dll
String:      File Not Found
Fields:
              MT    Field   Offset                 Type VT     Attr            Value Name
00007ff863e37408  4000355        8        System.Int32  1 instance              14 _stringLength
00007ff863e52f60  4000356        c        System.Char   1 instance              46 _firstChar
00007ff863e8bf40  4000354        8        System.String  0   static 0000027ea20b0008 Empty
```

```
0:008> ~10s
ntdll!NtDelayExecution+0x14:
00007ff8`f1624704 ret

0:010> !pe -nested
Exception object: 0000023e124c56a0
Exception type:   ApplicationD.CustomException
Message:          <none>
InnerException:   <none>
StackTrace (generated):
    SP                IP                Function
    000000E93B0FD8A0  00007FF863EB1D3F  ApplicationD!ApplicationD.ClassMain.thread_proc_3()+0x9f

StackTraceString: <none>
HResult: 80131500


Nested exception -------------------------------------------------------------
Exception object: 0000023e12409068
Exception type:   System.IO.FileNotFoundException
Message:          Unable to find the specified file.
InnerException:   <none>
StackTrace (generated):
    SP                IP                Function
    000000E93B0FF9B0  00007FF863EB1CE0  ApplicationD!ApplicationD.ClassMain.thread_proc_3()+0x40

StackTraceString: <none>
HResult: 80070002
```

12. We also recall that the finalizer thread had exception processing code on its unmanaged thread stack trace:

```
0:010> ~6s
ntdll!NtDelayExecution+0x14:
00007ff8`f1624704 ret

0:006> kL
 # Child-SP          RetAddr           Call Site
00 000000e9`3aafb6d8 00007ff8`f15db903 ntdll!NtDelayExecution+0x14
01 000000e9`3aafb6e0 00007ff8`eef9d031 ntdll!RtlDelayExecution+0x43
02 000000e9`3aafb710 00007ff8`ef6beaac KERNELBASE!SleepEx+0x71
03 000000e9`3aafb790 00007ff8`ef0be2f3 kernel32!WerpReportFault+0xa4
04 000000e9`3aafb7d0 00007ff8`f162b0ec KERNELBASE!UnhandledExceptionFilter+0x3e3
05 000000e9`3aafb8f0 00007ff8`f16140f6 ntdll!RtlUserThreadStart$filt$0+0xac
06 000000e9`3aafb930 00007ff8`f162906f ntdll!_C_specific_handler+0x96
07 000000e9`3aafb9a0 00007ff8`f15b5bea ntdll!RtlpExecuteHandlerForException+0xf
08 000000e9`3aafb9d0 00007ff8`f15b2ef1 ntdll!RtlDispatchException+0x25a
09 000000e9`3aafc120 00007ff8`eefc2e0c ntdll!RtlRaiseException+0x1f1
0a 000000e9`3aafc900 00007ff8`c3ad873e KERNELBASE!RaiseException+0x6c
0b 000000e9`3aafc9e0 00007ff8`a5c3796d coreclr!SfiNext+0xe962e
0c 000000e9`3aafcb00 00007ff8`a5c3717a System_Private_CoreLib!System.Runtime.EH.DispatchEx+0x44d
0d 000000e9`3aafcc60 00007ff8`c3a62eb3 System_Private_CoreLib!System.Runtime.EH.RhThrowHwEx+0xaa
0e 000000e9`3aafcca0 00007ff8`c39e1568 coreclr!CallDescrWorkerInternal+0x83
0f 000000e9`3aafcce0 00007ff8`c3b15cde coreclr!DispatchCallSimple+0x60
10 000000e9`3aafcd70 00007ff8`c3aef58a coreclr!HandleManagedFaultNew+0x192
11 000000e9`3aafe880 00007ff8`f15fca2a coreclr!CLRVectoredExceptionHandlerShim+0xa84ca
12 000000e9`3aafe8d0 00007ff8`f15b59f2 ntdll!RtlpCallVectoredHandlers+0x112
13 000000e9`3aafe970 00007ff8`f162805e ntdll!RtlDispatchException+0x62
14 000000e9`3aafebc0 00007ff8`63eb5132 ntdll!KiUserExceptionDispatch+0x2e
15 000000e9`3aaff2c0 00007ff8`a5adbe9f ApplicationD!ApplicationD.SmallObject.Finalize+0x22
16 000000e9`3aaff300 00007ff8`c3a62eb3 System_Private_CoreLib!System.GC.RunFinalizers+0x8f
17 000000e9`3aaff3e0 00007ff8`c39e1568 coreclr!CallDescrWorkerInternal+0x83
18 000000e9`3aaff420 00007ff8`c3a2945f coreclr!DispatchCallSimple+0x60
19 000000e9`3aaff4b0 00007ff8`c3a28950 coreclr!FinalizerThread::FinalizeAllObjects+0x7b
1a 000000e9`3aaff590 00007ff8`c39cef05 coreclr!FinalizerThread::FinalizerThreadWorker+0x100
```

```
1b (Inline Function) --------`--------    coreclr!ManagedThreadBase_DispatchInner+0xd
1c 000000e9`3aaff7e0 00007ff8`c39cee2d    coreclr!ManagedThreadBase_DispatchMiddle+0x79
1d 000000e9`3aaff890 00007ff8`c3a1e921    coreclr!ManagedThreadBase_DispatchOuter+0x8d
1e (Inline Function) --------`--------    coreclr!ManagedThreadBase_NoADTransition+0x28
1f (Inline Function) --------`--------    coreclr!ManagedThreadBase::FinalizerBase+0x28
20 000000e9`3aaff900 00007ff8`ef6653e0    coreclr!FinalizerThread::FinalizerThreadStart+0x91
21 000000e9`3aaffa10 00007ff8`f158485b    kernel32!BaseThreadInitThunk+0x10
22 000000e9`3aaffa40 00000000`00000000    ntdll!RtlUserThreadStart+0x2b
```

13.   Since we see a JIT code address on the stack trace before exception processing, it suggests that we have a non-CLR exception. From the disassembly, we see it was a NULL pointer exception in the *SmallObject Finalize* method (RAX is zeroed, and its value propagated up to pointer dereference):

```
0:006> !IP2MD 00007ff8`63eb5132
MethodDesc:        00007ff863f672f8
Method Name:              ApplicationD.SmallObject.Finalize()
Class:                    00007ff863f67350
MethodTable:              00007ff863f67350
mdToken:                  0000000006000004
Module:                   00007ff863f63368
IsJitted:                 yes
Current CodeAddr:         00007ff863eb5110
Version History:
  ILCodeVersion:          0000000000000000
  ReJIT ID:               0
  IL Addr:                0000023e0d4c20bc
     CodeAddr:               00007ff863eb5110  (QuickJitted)
     NativeCodeVersion:   0000000000000000
```

```
0:006> !U 00007ff8`63eb5132
Normal JIT generated code
ApplicationD.SmallObject.Finalize()
ilAddr is 0000023E0D4C20BC pImport is 0000020CD38F9250
Begin 00007FF863EB5110, size 5a
00007ff8`63eb5110 push     rbp
00007ff8`63eb5111 sub      rsp,30h
00007ff8`63eb5115 lea      rbp,[rsp+30h]
00007ff8`63eb511a xor      eax,eax
00007ff8`63eb511c mov      qword ptr [rbp-8],rax
00007ff8`63eb5120 mov      qword ptr [rbp-10h],rsp
00007ff8`63eb5124 mov      qword ptr [rbp+10h],rcx
00007ff8`63eb5128 xor      eax,eax
00007ff8`63eb512a mov      qword ptr [rbp-8],rax
00007ff8`63eb512e mov      rax,qword ptr [rbp-8]
>>> 00007ff8`63eb5132 mov      dword ptr [rax],1
00007ff8`63eb5138 mov      rcx,rsp
00007ff8`63eb513b call     ApplicationD!ApplicationD.SmallObject.Finalize+0x37
(00007ff8`63eb5147)
00007ff8`63eb5140 nop
00007ff8`63eb5141 add      rsp,30h
00007ff8`63eb5145 pop      rbp
00007ff8`63eb5146 ret
00007ff8`63eb5147 push     rbp
00007ff8`63eb5148 sub      rsp,30h
00007ff8`63eb514c mov      rbp,qword ptr [rcx+20h]
00007ff8`63eb5150 mov      qword ptr [rsp+20h],rbp
00007ff8`63eb5155 lea      rbp,[rbp+30h]
00007ff8`63eb5159 mov      rcx,qword ptr [rbp+10h]
00007ff8`63eb515d call     qword ptr [00007ff8`63d74778]
```

```
00007ff8`63eb5163 nop
00007ff8`63eb5164 add       rsp,30h
00007ff8`63eb5168 pop       rbp
00007ff8`63eb5169 ret
```

14.   If we specify *ApplicationD* symbol file path via the **.sympath** command, we can see source code line references:

```
0:006> .sympath+ C:\ANETMDA-Dumps\Windows\x64\Symbols
Symbol search path is: srv*;C:\ANETMDA-Dumps\Windows\x64\Symbols
Expanded Symbol search path is:
cache*;SRV*https://msdl.microsoft.com/download/symbols;c:\anetmda-dumps\windows\x64\symbols

************* Path validation summary **************
Response                      Time (ms)    Location
Deferred                                   srv*
OK                                         C:\ANETMDA-Dumps\Windows\x64\Symbols

0:006> !IP2MD 00007ff8`63eb5132
MethodDesc:    00007ff863f672f8
Method Name:          ApplicationD.SmallObject.Finalize()
Class:                00007ff863f67350
MethodTable:          00007ff863f67350
mdToken:              0000000006000004
Module:               00007ff863f63368
IsJitted:             yes
Current CodeAddr:     00007ff863eb5110
Version History:
  ILCodeVersion:      0000000000000000
  ReJIT ID:           0
  IL Addr:            0000023e0d4c20bc
     CodeAddr:           00007ff863eb5110  (QuickJitted)
     NativeCodeVersion:  0000000000000000
Source file:  C:\ANETMDA-Examples\ApplicationD\Program.cs @ 42

0:006> !U 00007ff8`63eb5132
Normal JIT generated code
ApplicationD.SmallObject.Finalize()
ilAddr is 0000023E0D4C20BC pImport is 0000020CD38F9250
Begin 00007FF863EB5110, size 5a

C:\ANETMDA-Examples\ApplicationD\Program.cs @ 41:
00007ff8`63eb5110 push      rbp
00007ff8`63eb5111 sub       rsp,30h
00007ff8`63eb5115 lea       rbp,[rsp+30h]
00007ff8`63eb511a xor       eax,eax
00007ff8`63eb511c mov       qword ptr [rbp-8],rax
00007ff8`63eb5120 mov       qword ptr [rbp-10h],rsp
00007ff8`63eb5124 mov       qword ptr [rbp+10h],rcx
00007ff8`63eb5128 xor       eax,eax
00007ff8`63eb512a mov       qword ptr [rbp-8],rax

C:\ANETMDA-Examples\ApplicationD\Program.cs @ 42:
00007ff8`63eb512e mov       rax,qword ptr [rbp-8]
>>> 00007ff8`63eb5132 mov       dword ptr [rax],1
00007ff8`63eb5138 mov       rcx,rsp
00007ff8`63eb513b call      ApplicationD!ApplicationD.SmallObject.Finalize+0x37
(00007ff8`63eb5147)
```

```
00007ff8`63eb5140 nop

C:\ANETMDA-Examples\ApplicationD\Program.cs @ 45:
00007ff8`63eb5141 add       rsp,30h
00007ff8`63eb5145 pop       rbp
00007ff8`63eb5146 ret

C:\ANETMDA-Examples\ApplicationD\Program.cs @ 41:
00007ff8`63eb5147 push      rbp
00007ff8`63eb5148 sub       rsp,30h
00007ff8`63eb514c mov       rbp,qword ptr [rcx+20h]
00007ff8`63eb5150 mov       qword ptr [rsp+20h],rbp
00007ff8`63eb5155 lea       rbp,[rbp+30h]

C:\ANETMDA-Examples\ApplicationD\Program.cs @ 45:
00007ff8`63eb5159 mov       rcx,qword ptr [rbp+10h]
00007ff8`63eb515d call      qword ptr [00007ff8`63d74778]
00007ff8`63eb5163 nop
00007ff8`63eb5164 add       rsp,30h
00007ff8`63eb5168 pop       rbp
00007ff8`63eb5169 ret
```

15.   We close logging before exiting WinDbg:

```
0:006> .logclose
Closing open log file C:\ANETMDA-Dumps\Windows\x64\ApplicationD.log
```

Exercise PN5 (Linux)

- **Goal:** Learn how to analyze multiple managed exceptions

- **Patterns:** Stack Trace Collection (Managed Space); Multiple Exceptions (Managed Space); Nested Exceptions (Managed Code)

- **Commands:** pe -nested

- \ANETMDA-Dumps\Exercise-PN5-Linux.pdf

Goal: Learn how to analyze multiple managed exceptions.

Patterns: Stack Trace Collection (Managed Space); Multiple Exceptions (Managed Space); Nested Exceptions (Managed Code).

Commands: pe -nested

1.   Open \ANETMDA-Dumps\Linux\ApplicationJ\core.ApplicationJ.1620.dmp in LLDB:

```
/mnt/c/ANETMDA-Dumps/Linux/ApplicationJ$ lldb -c core.ApplicationJ.1620.dmp
bin/Release/net9.0/ApplicationJ
Current symbol store settings:
-> Cache: /home/coredump/.dotnet/symbolcache
-> Server: https://msdl.microsoft.com/download/symbols/ Timeout: 4 RetryCount: 0
(lldb) target create "bin/Release/net9.0/ApplicationJ" --core "core.ApplicationJ.1620.dmp"
warning: (x86_64) /usr/share/dotnet/host/fxr/9.0.4/libhostfxr.so unsupported DW_FORM values:
0x1b 0x21 0x22 0x23 0x25 0x26 0x64
warning: (x86_64) /usr/share/dotnet/shared/Microsoft.NETCore.App/9.0.4/libhostpolicy.so
unsupported DW_FORM values: 0x1b 0x21 0x22 0x23 0x25 0x26 0x64
warning: (x86_64) /usr/share/dotnet/shared/Microsoft.NETCore.App/9.0.4/libcoreclr.so
unsupported DW_FORM values: 0x1b 0x21 0x22 0x23 0x25 0x26 0x64
warning: (x86_64) /usr/share/dotnet/shared/Microsoft.NETCore.App/9.0.4/libSystem.Native.so
unsupported DW_FORM values: 0x1b 0x21 0x22 0x23 0x25 0x26
warning: (x86_64) /usr/share/dotnet/shared/Microsoft.NETCore.App/9.0.4/libclrjit.so unsupported
DW_FORM values: 0x1b 0x21 0x22 0x23 0x25 0x26 0x64
warning: (x86_64) /mnt/c/ANETMDA-Dumps/Linux/ApplicationJ/bin/Release/net9.0/ApplicationJ
unsupported DW_FORM values: 0x1b 0x21 0x22 0x23 0x25 0x26 0x64
Core file '/mnt/c/ANETMDA-Dumps/Linux/ApplicationJ/core.ApplicationJ.1620.dmp' (x86_64) was
loaded.
```

2.   It was reported that the program was terminating with the following exception stack trace below, and the core dump was saved after exporting the appropriate variables.

```
/mnt/c/ANETMDA-Examples/ApplicationJ$ dotnet run -c Release
Unhandled exception. Unhandled exception. ApplicationD.CustomException: Exception of type
'ApplicationD.CustomException' was thrown.
   at ApplicationD.ClassMain.thread_proc_3() in /mnt/c/ANETMDA-
Examples/ApplicationJ/Program.cs:line 67
System.IO.FileNotFoundException: Unable to find the specified file.
   at ApplicationD.ClassMain.thread_proc_1() in /mnt/c/ANETMDA-
Examples/ApplicationJ/Program.cs:line 49
[createdump] Gathering state for process 1620 ApplicationJ
[createdump] Crashing thread 065d signal 6 (0006)
[createdump] Problem suspending thread: ptrace(ATTACH, 1806) FAILED No such process (3)
[createdump] Writing full dump to file ./core.ApplicationJ.1620.dmp
[createdump] Written 188600320 bytes (46045 pages) to core file
[createdump] Target process is alive
[createdump] Dump successfully written in 4998ms
```

3.   Check all stack traces:

```
(lldb) bt all
* thread #1, name = 'ApplicationJ', stop reason = signal 0
  * frame #0: 0x00007f689689b00c libpthread.so.0`__pthread_cond_wait at futex-internal.h:88
    frame #1: 0x00007f689689aff1 libpthread.so.0`__pthread_cond_wait at pthread_cond_wait.c:502
    frame #2: 0x00007f689689af30 libpthread.so.0`__pthread_cond_wait(cond=0x000055b14ca81978, mutex=0x000055b14ca81950) at pthread_cond_wait.c:655
    frame #3: 0x00007f689620b172 libcoreclr.so`CorUnix::CPalSynchronizationManager::ThreadNativeWait(CorUnix::_ThreadNativeWaitData*, unsigned int,
CorUnix::ThreadWakeupReason*, unsigned int*) + 354
    frame #4: 0x00007f689620ad7a libcoreclr.so`CorUnix::CPalSynchronizationManager::BlockThread(CorUnix::CPalThread*, unsigned int, bool, bool,
CorUnix::ThreadWakeupReason*, unsigned int*) + 378
    frame #5: 0x00007f689620f952 libcoreclr.so`CorUnix::InternalWaitForMultipleObjectsEx(CorUnix::CPalThread*, unsigned int, void* const*, int, unsigned int,
int, int) + 1906
    frame #6: 0x00007f689620fc03 libcoreclr.so`WaitForMultipleObjectsEx + 83
    frame #7: 0x00007f6895e6c255 libcoreclr.so`Thread::DoAppropriateWaitWorker(int, void**, int, unsigned int, WaitMode, void*) + 1429
    frame #8: 0x00007f6895e67424 libcoreclr.so`Thread::DoAppropriateWait(int, void**, int, unsigned int, WaitMode, PendingSync*) + 228
    frame #9: 0x00007f6895e672ec libcoreclr.so`Thread::JoinEx(unsigned int, WaitMode) + 108
    frame #10: 0x00007f6895eb8c6c libcoreclr.so`ThreadNative::DoJoin(ThreadBaseObject*, int) + 220
    frame #11: 0x00007f6895eb889c libcoreclr.so`ThreadNative::Join(ThreadBaseObject*, int) + 268
    frame #12: 0x00007f6816e2854c
    frame #13: 0x00007f6817b8189b
    frame #14: 0x00007f6896063e04 libcoreclr.so`CallDescrWorkerInternal + 124
    frame #15: 0x00007f6895ea211c libcoreclr.so`MethodDescCallSite::CallTargetWorker(unsigned long const*, unsigned long*, int) + 1708
    frame #16: 0x00007f6895d890c4 libcoreclr.so`RunMain(MethodDesc*, short, int*, PtrArray**) + 836
    frame #17: 0x00007f6895d8953c libcoreclr.so`Assembly::ExecuteMainMethod(PtrArray**, int) + 460
    frame #18: 0x00007f6895db2b34 libcoreclr.so`CorHost2::ExecuteAssembly(unsigned int, char16_t const*, int, char16_t const**, unsigned int*) + 740
    frame #19: 0x00007f6895d75340 libcoreclr.so`coreclr_execute_assembly + 144
    frame #20: 0x00007f689633d301 libhostpolicy.so`run_app_for_context(hostpolicy_context_t const&, int, char const**) + 1089
    frame #21: 0x00007f689633e3f9 libhostpolicy.so`corehost_main + 345
    frame #22: 0x00007f689637d685 libhostfxr.so`fx_muxer_t::handle_exec_host_command(std::__cxx11::basic_string<char, std::char_traits<char>,
std::allocator<char> > const&, host_startup_info_t const&, std::__cxx11::basic_string<char, std::char_traits<char>, std::allocator<char> > const&,
std::unordered_map<known_options, std::vector<std::__cxx11::basic_string<char, std::char_traits<char>, std::allocator<char> > >,
std::allocator<std::__cxx11::basic_string<char, std::char_traits<char>, std::allocator<char> > > >, known_options_hash, std::equal_to<known_options>,
std::allocator<std::pair<known_options const, std::vector<std::__cxx11::basic_string<char, std::char_traits<char>, std::allocator<char> >
std::allocator<std::__cxx11::basic_string<char, std::char_traits<char>, std::allocator<char> > > > > > const&, int, char const**, int, host_mode_t, bool,
char*, int, int*) + 1477
    frame #23: 0x00007f689637c67d libhostfxr.so`fx_muxer_t::execute(std::__cxx11::basic_string<char, std::char_traits<char>, std::allocator<char> >, int, char
const**, host_startup_info_t const&, char*, int, int*) + 765
    frame #24: 0x00007f68963765f2 libhostfxr.so`hostfxr_main_startupinfo + 242
    frame #25: 0x000055b10cab421b ApplicationJ`exe_start(int, char const**) + 1131
    frame #26: 0x000055b10cab453f ApplicationJ`main + 175
    frame #27: 0x00007f68963d009b libc.so.6`__libc_start_main(main=(ApplicationJ`main), argc=1, argv=0x00007ffca0d2e798, init=<unavailable>,
fini=<unavailable>, rtld_fini=<unavailable>, stack_end=0x00007ffca0d2e788) at libc-start.c:308
    frame #28: 0x000055b10cab3399 ApplicationJ`_start + 41
  thread #2, stop reason = signal 0
    frame #0: 0x00007f689649a6f9 libc.so.6`__GI___poll(fds=0x0000000000000000, nfds=0, timeout=-1) at poll.c:29
    frame #1: 0x00007f689620d18e libcoreclr.so`CorUnix::CPalSynchronizationManager::WorkerThread(void*) + 958
    frame #2: 0x00007f68962169ae libcoreclr.so`CorUnix::CPalThread::ThreadEntry(void*) + 510
    frame #3: 0x00007f6896894fa3 libpthread.so.0`start_thread(arg=<unavailable>) at pthread_create.c:486
    frame #4: 0x00007f68964a506f libc.so.6`__GI___clone at clone.S:95
  thread #3, stop reason = signal 0
    frame #0: 0x00007f689649a6f9 libc.so.6`__GI___poll(fds=0x00007f6808000f20, nfds=1, timeout=-1) at poll.c:29
    frame #1: 0x00007f68961114d5c libcoreclr.so`ds_ipc_poll(_DiagnosticsIpcPollHandle*, unsigned long, unsigned int, void (*)(char const*, unsigned int)) + 172
    frame #2: 0x00007f689608ef4b libcoreclr.so`ds_ipc_stream_factory_get_next_available_stream(void (*)(char const*, unsigned int)) + 731
    frame #3: 0x00007f6896093ca6 libcoreclr.so`server_thread(void*) + 198
    frame #4: 0x00007f68962169ae libcoreclr.so`CorUnix::CPalThread::ThreadEntry(void*) + 510
    frame #5: 0x00007f6896894fa3 libpthread.so.0`start_thread(arg=<unavailable>) at pthread_create.c:486
    frame #6: 0x00007f68964a506f libc.so.6`__GI___clone at clone.S:95
  thread #4, stop reason = signal 0
    frame #0: 0x00007f689689ed0e libpthread.so.0`__libc_open64(file="/tmp/clr-debug-pipe-1620-15950716-in", oflag=0) at open64.c:48
    frame #1: 0x00007f689611477f libcoreclr.so`TwoWayPipe::WaitForConnection() + 31
    frame #2: 0x00007f689610f797 libcoreclr.so`DbgTransportSession::TransportWorker() + 183
    frame #3: 0x00007f689610e905 libcoreclr.so`DbgTransportSession::TransportWorkerStatic(void*) + 37
    frame #4: 0x00007f68962169ae libcoreclr.so`CorUnix::CPalThread::ThreadEntry(void*) + 510
    frame #5: 0x00007f6896894fa3 libpthread.so.0`start_thread(arg=<unavailable>) at pthread_create.c:486
    frame #6: 0x00007f68964a506f libc.so.6`__GI___clone at clone.S:95
  thread #5, stop reason = signal 0
    frame #0: 0x00007f689689b00c libpthread.so.0`__pthread_cond_wait at futex-internal.h:88
    frame #1: 0x00007f689689aff1 libpthread.so.0`__pthread_cond_wait at pthread_cond_wait.c:502
    frame #2: 0x00007f689689af30 libpthread.so.0`__pthread_cond_wait(cond=0x000055b14cab2f18, mutex=0x000055b14cab2ef0) at pthread_cond_wait.c:655
    frame #3: 0x00007f689620b172 libcoreclr.so`CorUnix::CPalSynchronizationManager::ThreadNativeWait(CorUnix::_ThreadNativeWaitData*, unsigned int,
CorUnix::ThreadWakeupReason*, unsigned int*) + 354
    frame #4: 0x00007f689620ad7a libcoreclr.so`CorUnix::CPalSynchronizationManager::BlockThread(CorUnix::CPalThread*, unsigned int, bool, bool,
CorUnix::ThreadWakeupReason*, unsigned int*) + 378
    frame #5: 0x00007f689620f952 libcoreclr.so`CorUnix::InternalWaitForMultipleObjectsEx(CorUnix::CPalThread*, unsigned int, void* const*, int, unsigned int,
int, int) + 1906
    frame #6: 0x00007f689620fc03 libcoreclr.so`WaitForMultipleObjectsEx + 83
    frame #7: 0x00007f689610d0ad libcoreclr.so`DebuggerRCThread::MainLoop() + 269
    frame #8: 0x00007f689610cf28 libcoreclr.so`DebuggerRCThread::ThreadProc() + 312
    frame #9: 0x00007f689610cc25 libcoreclr.so`DebuggerRCThread::ThreadProcStatic(void*) + 53
    frame #10: 0x00007f68962169ae libcoreclr.so`CorUnix::CPalThread::ThreadEntry(void*) + 510
    frame #11: 0x00007f6896894fa3 libpthread.so.0`start_thread(arg=<unavailable>) at pthread_create.c:486
    frame #12: 0x00007f68964a506f libc.so.6`__GI___clone at clone.S:95
  thread #6, stop reason = signal 0
    frame #0: 0x00007f689689b3f9 libpthread.so.0`__pthread_cond_timedwait at futex-internal.h:142
    frame #1: 0x00007f689689b3da libpthread.so.0`__pthread_cond_timedwait at pthread_cond_wait.c:533
    frame #2: 0x00007f689689b2c0 libpthread.so.0`__pthread_cond_timedwait(cond=0x000055b14cabe608, mutex=0x000055b14cabe5e0, abstime=0x00007f6893a3d730) at
pthread_cond_wait.c:667
    frame #3: 0x00007f689620b115 libcoreclr.so`CorUnix::CPalSynchronizationManager::ThreadNativeWait(CorUnix::_ThreadNativeWaitData*, unsigned int,
CorUnix::ThreadWakeupReason*, unsigned int*) + 261
    frame #4: 0x00007f689620ad7a libcoreclr.so`CorUnix::CPalSynchronizationManager::BlockThread(CorUnix::CPalThread*, unsigned int, bool, bool,
CorUnix::ThreadWakeupReason*, unsigned int*) + 378
    frame #5: 0x00007f689620f952 libcoreclr.so`CorUnix::InternalWaitForMultipleObjectsEx(CorUnix::CPalThread*, unsigned int, void* const*, int, unsigned int,
int, int) + 1906
    frame #6: 0x00007f689620fb29 libcoreclr.so`WaitForSingleObjectEx + 89
    frame #7: 0x00007f6895f6befe libcoreclr.so`CLREventBase::WaitEx(unsigned int, WaitMode, PendingSync*) + 238
```

209

```
        frame #8: 0x00007f6895ede07f libcoreclr.so`FinalizerThread::WaitForFinalizerEvent(CLREvent*) + 31
        frame #9: 0x00007f6895ede27f libcoreclr.so`FinalizerThread::FinalizerThreadWorker(void*) + 239
        frame #10: 0x00007f6895e6fc08 libcoreclr.so`ManagedThreadBase_DispatchOuter(ManagedThreadCallState*) + 344
        frame #11: 0x00007f6895e7010d libcoreclr.so`ManagedThreadBase::FinalizerBase(void (*)(void*)) + 45
        frame #12: 0x00007f6895ede4b8 libcoreclr.so`FinalizerThread::FinalizerThreadStart(void*) + 88
        frame #13: 0x00007f68962169ae libcoreclr.so`CorUnix::CPalThread::ThreadEntry(void*) + 510
        frame #14: 0x00007f6896894fa3 libpthread.so.0`start_thread(arg=<unavailable>) at pthread_create.c:486
        frame #15: 0x00007f68964a506f libc.so.6`__GI___clone at clone.S:95
  thread #7, stop reason = signal 0
        frame #0: 0x00007f689689b3f9 libpthread.so.0`__pthread_cond_timedwait at futex-internal.h:142
        frame #1: 0x00007f689689b3da libpthread.so.0`__pthread_cond_timedwait at pthread_cond_wait.c:533
        frame #2: 0x00007f689689b2c0 libpthread.so.0`__pthread_cond_timedwait(cond=0x000055b14cac4968, mutex=0x000055b14cac4940, abstime=0x00007f6892005b50) at
pthread_cond_wait.c:667
        frame #3: 0x00007f689620b115 libcoreclr.so`CorUnix::CPalSynchronizationManager::ThreadNativeWait(CorUnix::_ThreadNativeWaitData*, unsigned int,
CorUnix::ThreadWakeupReason*, unsigned int*) + 261
        frame #4: 0x00007f689620ad7a libcoreclr.so`CorUnix::CPalSynchronizationManager::BlockThread(CorUnix::CPalThread*, unsigned int, bool, bool,
CorUnix::ThreadWakeupReason*, unsigned int*) + 378
        frame #5: 0x00007f6896210089 libcoreclr.so`SleepEx + 153
        frame #6: 0x00007f6895e734aa libcoreclr.so`TieredCompilationManager::BackgroundWorkerStart() + 186
        frame #7: 0x00007f6895e73368 libcoreclr.so`TieredCompilationManager::BackgroundWorkerBootstrapper1(void*) + 104
        frame #8: 0x00007f6895e6fc08 libcoreclr.so`ManagedThreadBase_DispatchOuter(ManagedThreadCallState*) + 344
        frame #9: 0x00007f6895e700bd libcoreclr.so`ManagedThreadBase::KickOff(void (*)(void*), void*) + 45
        frame #10: 0x00007f6895e73290 libcoreclr.so`TieredCompilationManager::BackgroundWorkerBootstrapper0(void*) + 32
        frame #11: 0x00007f68962169ae libcoreclr.so`CorUnix::CPalThread::ThreadEntry(void*) + 510
        frame #12: 0x00007f6896894fa3 libpthread.so.0`start_thread(arg=<unavailable>) at pthread_create.c:486
        frame #13: 0x00007f68964a506f libc.so.6`__GI___clone at clone.S:95
  thread #8, stop reason = signal 0
        frame #0: 0x00007f689649a6f9 libc.so.6`__GI___poll(fds=0x0000000000000000, nfds=0, timeout=-1) at poll.c:29
        frame #1: 0x00007f689621293e libcoreclr.so`CorUnix::TerminateCurrentProcessNoExit(int) + 110
        frame #2: 0x00007f6896212891 libcoreclr.so`TerminateProcess + 113
        frame #3: 0x00007f6895f9e977 libcoreclr.so`SfiNext + 1703
        frame #4: 0x00007f6816e76df9
        frame #5: 0x00007f6816e765d0
        frame #6: 0x00007f6896063e04 libcoreclr.so`CallDescrWorkerInternal + 124
        frame #7: 0x00007f6895ea1a05 libcoreclr.so`DispatchCallSimple(unsigned long*, unsigned int, unsigned long, unsigned int) + 245
        frame #8: 0x00007f6895f9a00c libcoreclr.so`DispatchManagedException(Object*, _CONTEXT*) + 364
        frame #9: 0x00007f6895f9a4b6 libcoreclr.so`DispatchManagedException(Object*) + 70
        frame #10: 0x00007f6895f01250 libcoreclr.so`ThrowNew(Object*) + 224
        frame #11: 0x00007f6895f013c6 libcoreclr.so`IL_Throw(Object*) + 278
        frame #12: 0x00007f6817b81aca
        frame #13: 0x00007f6896063e04 libcoreclr.so`CallDescrWorkerInternal + 124
        frame #14: 0x00007f6895ea1a05 libcoreclr.so`DispatchCallSimple(unsigned long*, unsigned int, unsigned long, unsigned int) + 245
        frame #15: 0x00007f6895eb76c2 libcoreclr.so`ThreadNative::KickOffThread_Worker(void*) + 146
        frame #16: 0x00007f6895e6fc08 libcoreclr.so`ManagedThreadBase_DispatchOuter(ManagedThreadCallState*) + 344
        frame #17: 0x00007f6895e700bd libcoreclr.so`ManagedThreadBase::KickOff(void (*)(void*), void*) + 45
        frame #18: 0x00007f6895eb77dc libcoreclr.so`ThreadNative::KickOffThread(void*) + 252
        frame #19: 0x00007f68962169ae libcoreclr.so`CorUnix::CPalThread::ThreadEntry(void*) + 510
        frame #20: 0x00007f6896894fa3 libpthread.so.0`start_thread(arg=<unavailable>) at pthread_create.c:486
        frame #21: 0x00007f68964a506f libc.so.6`__GI___clone at clone.S:95
  thread #9, stop reason = signal 0
        frame #0: 0x00007f68965088bd libc.so.6`__memset_avx2_erms at memset-vec-unaligned-erms.S:151
        frame #1: 0x00007f6896026ed8 libcoreclr.so`WKS::gc_heap::adjust_limit_clr(unsigned char*, unsigned long, unsigned long, alloc_context*, unsigned int,
WKS::heap_segment*, int, int) + 792
        frame #2: 0x00007f6896029741 libcoreclr.so`WKS::gc_heap::a_fit_segment_end_p(int, WKS::heap_segment*, unsigned long, alloc_context*, unsigned int, int,
int*) + 673
        frame #3: 0x00007f689602a5da libcoreclr.so`WKS::gc_heap::soh_try_fit(int, unsigned long, alloc_context*, unsigned int, int, int*, int*) + 1482
        frame #4: 0x00007f689602a86c libcoreclr.so`WKS::gc_heap::allocate_soh(int, unsigned long, alloc_context*, unsigned int, int) + 252
        frame #5: 0x00007f689602c0fa libcoreclr.so`WKS::gc_heap::try_allocate_more_space(alloc_context*, unsigned long, unsigned int, int) + 714
        frame #6: 0x00007f689605b850 libcoreclr.so`WKS::GCHeap::Alloc(gc_alloc_context*, unsigned long, unsigned int) + 240
        frame #7: 0x00007f6895ee3640 libcoreclr.so`Alloc(unsigned long, GC_ALLOC_FLAGS) + 192
        frame #8: 0x00007f6895ee339f libcoreclr.so`AllocateSzArray(MethodTable*, int, GC_ALLOC_FLAGS) + 175
        frame #9: 0x00007f6895efb026 libcoreclr.so`JIT_NewArr1(CORINFO_CLASS_STRUCT_*, long) + 262
        frame #10: 0x00007f6817b81c84
        frame #11: 0x00007f6817b81b39
        frame #12: 0x00007f6896063e04 libcoreclr.so`CallDescrWorkerInternal + 124
        frame #13: 0x00007f6895ea1a05 libcoreclr.so`DispatchCallSimple(unsigned long*, unsigned int, unsigned long, unsigned int) + 245
        frame #14: 0x00007f6895eb76c2 libcoreclr.so`ThreadNative::KickOffThread_Worker(void*) + 146
        frame #15: 0x00007f6895e6fc08 libcoreclr.so`ManagedThreadBase_DispatchOuter(ManagedThreadCallState*) + 344
        frame #16: 0x00007f6895e700bd libcoreclr.so`ManagedThreadBase::KickOff(void (*)(void*), void*) + 45
        frame #17: 0x00007f6895eb77dc libcoreclr.so`ThreadNative::KickOffThread(void*) + 252
        frame #18: 0x00007f68962169ae libcoreclr.so`CorUnix::CPalThread::ThreadEntry(void*) + 510
        frame #19: 0x00007f6896894fa3 libpthread.so.0`start_thread(arg=<unavailable>) at pthread_create.c:486
        frame #20: 0x00007f68964a506f libc.so.6`__GI___clone at clone.S:95
  thread #10, stop reason = signal SIGABRT
        frame #0: 0x00007f689689f0ca libpthread.so.0`__waitpid(pid=1794, stat_loc=0x00007f68903c3df4, options=0) at waitpid.c:30
        frame #1: 0x00007f6896213d97 libcoreclr.so`PROCCreateCrashDump(std::vector<char const*, std::allocator<char const*> >&, char*, int, bool) + 647
        frame #2: 0x00007f6896215124b libcoreclr.so`PROCCreateCrashDumpIfEnabled + 3227
        frame #3: 0x00007f689621297d libcoreclr.so`PROCAbort + 45
        frame #4: 0x00007f68962128a9 libcoreclr.so`TerminateProcess + 137
        frame #5: 0x00007f6895f9e977 libcoreclr.so`SfiNext + 1703
        frame #6: 0x00007f6816e76df9
        frame #7: 0x00007f6816e765d0
        frame #8: 0x00007f6896063e04 libcoreclr.so`CallDescrWorkerInternal + 124
        frame #9: 0x00007f6895ea1a05 libcoreclr.so`DispatchCallSimple(unsigned long*, unsigned int, unsigned long, unsigned int) + 245
        frame #10: 0x00007f6895f9a00c libcoreclr.so`DispatchManagedException(Object*, _CONTEXT*) + 364
        frame #11: 0x00007f6895f9a4b6 libcoreclr.so`DispatchManagedException(Object*) + 70
        frame #12: 0x00007f6895f01250 libcoreclr.so`ThrowNew(Object*) + 224
        frame #13: 0x00007f6895f013c6 libcoreclr.so`IL_Throw(Object*) + 278
        frame #14: 0x00007f6817b81d58
        frame #15: 0x00007f6896063e04 libcoreclr.so`CallDescrWorkerInternal + 124
        frame #16: 0x00007f6895ea1a05 libcoreclr.so`DispatchCallSimple(unsigned long*, unsigned int, unsigned long, unsigned int) + 245
        frame #17: 0x00007f6895eb76c2 libcoreclr.so`ThreadNative::KickOffThread_Worker(void*) + 146
        frame #18: 0x00007f6895e6fc08 libcoreclr.so`ManagedThreadBase_DispatchOuter(ManagedThreadCallState*) + 344
        frame #19: 0x00007f6895e700bd libcoreclr.so`ManagedThreadBase::KickOff(void (*)(void*), void*) + 45
        frame #20: 0x00007f6895eb77dc libcoreclr.so`ThreadNative::KickOffThread(void*) + 252
        frame #21: 0x00007f68962169ae libcoreclr.so`CorUnix::CPalThread::ThreadEntry(void*) + 510
        frame #22: 0x00007f6896894fa3 libpthread.so.0`start_thread(arg=<unavailable>) at pthread_create.c:486
        frame #23: 0x00007f68964a506f libc.so.6`__GI___clone at clone.S:95
```

Note: We notice an active thread #9, and there are two threads, #8 and #10, that have a thrown exception.

4.   We first list managed threads:

```
(lldb) clrthreads
ThreadCount:      184
UnstartedThread:  0
BackgroundThread: 2
PendingThread:    0
DeadThread:       178
Hosted Runtime:   no
                                                                                                Lock
   DBG   ID   OSID ThreadOBJ          State GC Mode  GC Alloc Context                          Domain          Count Apt Exception
     1    1    654 000055B14CAB5850  2020020 Preemptive 0000000000000000:0000000000000000    000055B14CA9DAA0 -00001 Ukn
     6    2    659 000055B14CABCF50   21220 Preemptive 00007F28020101D8:00007F2802010FD0    000055B14CA9DAA0 -00001 Ukn (Finalizer)
     7    3    65a 000055B14CAD3CE0   21220 Preemptive 0000000000000000:0000000000000000    000055B14CA9DAA0 -00001 Ukn
     8    4    65b 000055B14CAEEBF0   21020 Preemptive 00007F280227A690:00007F280227B110    000055B14CA9DAA0 -00001 Ukn System.IO.FileNotFoundException
00007f2802809e78
     9    5    65c 000055B14CAF06E0   21020 Cooperative 00007F28022E7EA8:00007F28022ED2A0   000055B14CA9DAA0 -00001 Ukn
    10    6    65d 000055B14CA6D390   21020 Preemptive 00007F28022A98A0:00007F28022AB1D0    000055B14CA9DAA0 -00001 Ukn ApplicationD.CustomException
00007f2802008200 (nested exceptions)
  XXXX    7      0 00007F2760001360   31820 Preemptive 0000000000000000:0000000000000000    000055B14CA9DAA0 -00001 Ukn
  XXXX    8      0 00007F2760003180   31820 Preemptive 0000000000000000:0000000000000000    000055B14CA9DAA0 -00001 Ukn
  XXXX    9      0 00007F2760004FA0   31820 Preemptive 0000000000000000:0000000000000000    000055B14CA9DAA0 -00001 Ukn
  XXXX   10      0 00007F2760006C40   31820 Preemptive 0000000000000000:0000000000000000    000055B14CA9DAA0 -00001 Ukn
  XXXX   11      0 00007F2760008710   31820 Preemptive 0000000000000000:0000000000000000    000055B14CA9DAA0 -00001 Ukn
  XXXX   12      0 00007F276000A1E0   31820 Preemptive 0000000000000000:0000000000000000    000055B14CA9DAA0 -00001 Ukn
  XXXX   13      0 00007F276000BCB0   31820 Preemptive 0000000000000000:0000000000000000    000055B14CA9DAA0 -00001 Ukn
  XXXX   14      0 00007F276000D780   31820 Preemptive 0000000000000000:0000000000000000    000055B14CA9DAA0 -00001 Ukn
  XXXX   15      0 00007F276000F250   31820 Preemptive 0000000000000000:0000000000000000    000055B14CA9DAA0 -00001 Ukn
[...]

  XXXX  180      0 00007F2760125B10   31820 Preemptive 0000000000000000:0000000000000000    000055B14CA9DAA0 -00001 Ukn
  XXXX  181      0 00007F27601275E0   31820 Preemptive 0000000000000000:0000000000000000    000055B14CA9DAA0 -00001 Ukn
  XXXX  182      0 00007F27601290B0   31820 Preemptive 0000000000000000:0000000000000000    000055B14CA9DAA0 -00001 Ukn
  XXXX  183      0 00007F276012AB80   31820 Preemptive 0000000000000000:0000000000000000    000055B14CA9DAA0 -00001 Ukn
  XXXX  184      0 00007F276012C650   31820 Preemptive 0000000000000000:0000000000000000    000055B14CA9DAA0 -00001 Ukn
```

5.   We then analyze the managed threads one by one and their exceptions:

```
(lldb) thread select 8
* thread #8, stop reason = signal 0
    frame #0: 0x00007f689649a6f9 libc.so.6`__GI___poll(fds=0x0000000000000000, nfds=0,
timeout=-1) at poll.c:29
```

```
(lldb) pe
Exception object: 00007f2802809e78
Exception type:   System.IO.FileNotFoundException
Message:          Unable to find the specified file.
InnerException:   <none>
StackTrace (generated):
    SP               IP                Function
    00007F68913D5B80 00007F6817B81AC9
ApplicationJ.dll!ApplicationD.ClassMain.thread_proc_1()+0x39

StackTraceString: <none>
HResult: 80070002
```

```
(lldb) clrstack
OS Thread Id: 0x65b (8)
        Child SP         IP Call Site
00007F68913D1ED0 00007f689649a6f9 [InlinedCallFrame: 00007f68913d1ed0]
00007F68913D1ED0 00007f6816e76dd4 [InlinedCallFrame: 00007f68913d1ed0]
00007F68913D1E90 00007f6816E76DD4 System.Runtime.EH.DispatchEx(System.Runtime.StackFrameIterator ByRef, ExInfo ByRef)
[/_/src/coreclr/nativeaot/Runtime.Base/src/System/Runtime/ExceptionHandling.cs @ 865]
00007F68913D1FD0 00007f6816E765D0 System.Runtime.EH.RhThrowEx(System.Object, ExInfo ByRef)
[/_/src/coreclr/nativeaot/Runtime.Base/src/System/Runtime/ExceptionHandling.cs @ 645]
00007F68913D5A60 00007f6896063e04 [HelperMethodFrame: 00007f68913d5a60]
00007F68913D5B80 00007f6817B81ACA ApplicationD.ClassMain.thread_proc_1() [/mnt/c/ANETMDA-Examples/ApplicationJ/Program.cs @ 49]
00007F68913D5CC0 00007f6896063e04 [DebuggerU2MCatchHandlerFrame: 00007f68913d5cc0]
```

```
(lldb) thread select 10
* thread #10, stop reason = signal SIGABRT
```

```
    frame #0: 0x00007f689689f0ca libpthread.so.0`__waitpid(pid=1794,
stat_loc=0x00007f68903c3df4, options=0) at waitpid.c:30
```

(lldb) **pe**
Exception object: 00007f2802008200
Exception type: ApplicationD.CustomException
Message: <none>
InnerException: <none>
StackTrace (generated):
    SP   IP   Function
    00007F68903C7D50 00007F6817B81D57
ApplicationJ.dll!ApplicationD.ClassMain.thread_proc_3()+0xa7

StackTraceString: <none>
HResult: 80131500
There are nested exceptions on this thread. Run with -nested for details

(lldb) **pe -nested**
Exception object: 00007f2802008200
Exception type: ApplicationD.CustomException
Message: <none>
InnerException: <none>
StackTrace (generated):
    SP   IP   Function
    00007F68903C7D50 00007F6817B81D57
ApplicationJ.dll!ApplicationD.ClassMain.thread_proc_3()+0xa7

StackTraceString: <none>
HResult: 80131500

Nested exception ---
Exception object: 00007f2802008098
Exception type: System.IO.FileNotFoundException
Message: Unable to find the specified file.
InnerException: <none>
StackTrace (generated):
    SP   IP   Function
    00007F68903CBB60 00007F6817B81CFB
ApplicationJ.dll!ApplicationD.ClassMain.thread_proc_3()+0x4b

StackTraceString: <none>
HResult: 80070002

(lldb) **clrstack**
OS Thread Id: 0x65d (10)
        Child SP   IP Call Site
00007F68903C40A0 00007f689689f0ca [InlinedCallFrame: 00007f68903c40a0]
00007F68903C40A0 00007f6816e76dd4 [InlinedCallFrame: 00007f68903c40a0]
00007F68903C4060 00007F6816E76DD4 System.Runtime.EH.DispatchEx(System.Runtime.StackFrameIterator ByRef, ExInfo ByRef)
[/_/src/coreclr/nativeaot/Runtime.Base/src/System/Runtime/ExceptionHandling.cs @ 865]
00007F68903C41A0 00007F6816E765D0 System.Runtime.EH.RhThrowEx(System.Object, ExInfo ByRef)
[/_/src/coreclr/nativeaot/Runtime.Base/src/System/Runtime/ExceptionHandling.cs @ 645]
00007F68903C7C30 00007f6896063e04 [HelperMethodFrame: 00007f68903c7c30]
00007F68903C7D50 00007F6817B81D58 ApplicationD.ClassMain.thread_proc_3() [/mnt/c/ANETMDA-Examples/ApplicationJ/Program.cs @ 67]
00007F68903C7EB0 00007f6895f9bde3 [InlinedCallFrame: 00007f68903c7eb0]
00007F68903C7EB0 00007f6816e76ed7 [InlinedCallFrame: 00007f68903c7eb0]
00007F68903C7E70 00007F6816E76ED7 System.Runtime.EH.DispatchEx(System.Runtime.StackFrameIterator ByRef, ExInfo ByRef)
[/_/src/coreclr/nativeaot/Runtime.Base/src/System/Runtime/ExceptionHandling.cs @ 928]
00007F68903C7FB0 00007F6816E765D0 System.Runtime.EH.RhThrowEx(System.Object, ExInfo ByRef)
[/_/src/coreclr/nativeaot/Runtime.Base/src/System/Runtime/ExceptionHandling.cs @ 645]
00007F68903CBA40 00007f6896063e04 [HelperMethodFrame: 00007f68903cba40]
00007F68903CBB60 00007F6817B81CFC ApplicationD.ClassMain.thread_proc_3() [/mnt/c/ANETMDA-Examples/ApplicationJ/Program.cs @ 63]
00007F68903CBCC0 00007f6896063e04 [DebuggerU2MCatchHandlerFrame: 00007f68903cbcc0]

```
(lldb) thread select 9
* thread #9, stop reason = signal 0
    frame #0: 0x00007f68965088bd libc.so.6`__memset_avx2_erms at memset-vec-unaligned-
erms.S:151

(lldb) x/i $pc
-> 0x7f68965088bd: f3 aa  rep    stosb %al, %es:(%rdi)

(lldb) register read $rdi
    rdi = 0x00007f28022ea000

(lldb) x 0x00007f28022ea000
0x7f28022ea000: 00 00 00 00 00 00 00 00 00 00 00 00 00 00 00 00  ................
0x7f28022ea010: 00 00 00 00 00 00 00 00 00 00 00 00 00 00 00 00  ................

(lldb) clrstack
OS Thread Id: 0x65c (9)
        Child SP               IP Call Site
00007F6890BD09D8 00007f68965088bd [HelperMethodFrame: 00007f6890bd09d8]
00007F6890BD0B00 00007F6817B81C84 ApplicationD.SmallObject..ctor() [/mnt/c/ANETMDA-Examples/ApplicationJ/Program.cs @ 31]
00007F6890BD0B40 00007F6817B81B39 ApplicationD.ClassMain.thread_proc_2() [/mnt/c/ANETMDA-Examples/ApplicationJ/Program.cs @ 56]
00007F6890BD0CC0 00007f6896063e04 [DebuggerU2MCatchHandlerFrame: 00007f6890bd0cc0]
```

6.   We now check **ApplicationD.CustomException** object:

```
(lldb) dumpobj 00007f2802008200
Name:           ApplicationD.CustomException
MethodTable:    00007f6817c48390
Canonical MethodTable: 00007f6817c48390
Tracked Type: false
Size:           136(0x88) bytes
File:           /mnt/c/ANETMDA-Examples/ApplicationJ/bin/Release/net9.0/ApplicationJ.dll
Fields:
              MT    Field   Offset                 Type VT     Attr            Value Name
00007f6817c7ed38  4000213        8 ...ection.MethodBase  0 instance 0000000000000000 _exceptionMethod
00007f6817b6be30  4000214       10        System.String  0 instance 0000000000000000 _message
00007f6817b74670  4000215       18 ...tions.IDictionary  0 instance 0000000000000000 _data
00007f6817b6e150  4000216       20     System.Exception  0 instance 0000000000000000 _innerException
00007f6817b6be30  4000217       28        System.String  0 instance 0000000000000000 _helpURL
00007f6816bd4910  4000218       30        System.Object  0 instance 00007f2802008288 _stackTrace
00007f6817d2d528  4000219       38        System.Byte[]  0 instance 0000000000000000 _watsonBuckets
00007f6817b6be30  400021a       40        System.String  0 instance 0000000000000000 _stackTraceString
00007f6817b6be30  400021b       48        System.String  0 instance 0000000000000000 _remoteStackTraceString
00007f6817b6be30  400021c       50        System.String  0 instance 0000000000000000 _source
00007f6817b671e8  400021d       58      System.UIntPtr  1 instance 0000000000000000 _ipForWatsonBuckets
00007f6817b65170  400021e       60       System.IntPtr  1 instance 0000000000000000 _xptrs
00007f6817b174f0  400021f       68        System.Int32  1 instance      -532462766 _xcode
00007f6817b174f0  4000220       6c        System.Int32  1 instance     -2146233088 _HResult
00007f6817b6be30  4000001       70        System.String  0 instance 00007f6892019280 description
00007f6817b174f0  4000002       78        System.Int32  1 instance               5 code
```

```
(lldb) dumpobj 00007f6892019280
Name:           System.String
MethodTable:    00007f6817b6be30
Canonical MethodTable: 00007f6817b6be30
Tracked Type: false
Size:           50(0x32) bytes
File:           /usr/share/dotnet/shared/Microsoft.NETCore.App/9.0.4/System.Private.CoreLib.dll
String:         File Not Found
Fields:
              MT    Field   Offset                 Type VT     Attr            Value Name
00007f6817b174f0  40002ef        8        System.Int32  1 instance              14 _stringLength
00007f6817b23010  40002f0        c         System.Char  1 instance              46 _firstChar
00007f6817b6be30  40002ee        8        System.String  0   static 00007f6892017008 Empty
```

Exercise PN6 (Windows)

- **Goal:** Learn how to diagnose heap and handle leaks

- **Patterns:** Handle Leak; Object Distribution Anomaly (.NET Heap); Memory Leak (.NET Heap)

- **Commands:** !heap, !address -summary, !DumpHeap, ?, !eeheap, !GCHandles, !FinalizeQueue, !handle

- \ANETMDA-Dumps\Exercise-PN6-Windows.pdf

Goal: Learn how to diagnose heap and handle leaks.

Patterns: Handle Leak; Object Distribution Anomaly (.NET Heap); Memory Leak (.NET Heap).

Commands: !heap, !address -summary, !DumpHeap, ?, !eeheap, !GCHandles, !FinalizeQueue, !handle

1.   Launch WinDbg.

2.   Open \ANETMDA-Dumps\Windows\x64\LINQPad8-PN6.DMP

3.   We get the dump file loaded:

```
Microsoft (R) Windows Debugger Version 10.0.27829.1001 AMD64
Copyright (c) Microsoft Corporation. All rights reserved.



Loading Dump File [C:\ANETMDA-Dumps\Windows\x64\LINQPad8-PN6.DMP]
User Mini Dump File with Full Memory: Only application data is available



************* Path validation summary **************
Response                      Time (ms)      Location
Deferred                                     srv*
Symbol search path is: srv*
Executable search path is:
Windows 10 Version 22000 MP (4 procs) Free x64
Product: WinNt, suite: SingleUserTS
Edition build lab: 22000.1.amd64fre.co_release.210604-1628
Debug session time: Mon Apr 28 18:05:18.000 2025 (UTC + 1:00)
System Uptime: 0 days 0:07:06.468
Process Uptime: 0 days 0:04:55.000
...............................................................
...............................................................
....
For analysis of this file, run !analyze -v
win32u!NtUserMsgWaitForMultipleObjectsEx+0x14:
00007ffa`7c60abf4 ret
```

4.   Open a log file using the **.logopen** command (you will need to inspect the log file from time to time as the WinDbg output is voluminous in this exercise), and load the SOS extension if necessary:

```
0:000> .logopen C:\ANETMDA-Dumps\Windows\x64\LINQPadD.log
Opened log file 'C:\ANETMDA-Dumps\Windows\x64\LINQPadD.log'

0:000> .unload sos
Unloading sos extension DLL

0:000> .load C:\Users\dmitr\.dotnet\sos\sos.dll
```

215

Note: The WinDbg output may be slightly different on your system if you have a different WinDbg version, a different SOS extension version, you don't have .NET 9 installed, or you have a .NET version different from version 9.0.4 that was on a virtual machine where all the dumps were saved.

5.   The C# modeling code used in this exercise is the same as in *ApplicationD* in exercise PN5, so we skip unmanaged stack trace analysis of exceptions. The main difference here is that a process memory dump size is over 1GB, suggesting a memory leak. We check the process unmanaged heap:

```
0:000> !heap -s
```

```
****************************************************************************
                          NT HEAP STATS BELOW
****************************************************************************
LFH Key                : 0xa29fb143f033d861
Termination on corruption : ENABLED
          Heap     Flags   Reserv  Commit  Virt   Free  List   UCR  Virt  Lock  Fast
                            (k)     (k)     (k)    (k) length       blocks cont. heap
-------------------------------------------------------------------------------------
0000027fcfc20000 00000002 145896 139556 145868   2817   212    13    1     c   LFH
0000027fcfa20000 00008000     64      4     64      2     1     1    0     0
0000027fcfda0000 00001002     88     64     60     20     5     1    0     0   LFH
0000027fcfd50000 00001002     60      8     60      5     1     1    0     0
0000027fd1610000 00001002     60     20     60      4     2     1    0     0
0000027fd16e0000 00041002     60      8     60      5     1     1    0     0
-------------------------------------------------------------------------------------
```

Note: We see that the unmanaged process heap is less than 20% of the memory dump file size, so we double-check the address region usage statistics:

```
0:000> !address -summary
```

```
Mapping file section regions...
Mapping module regions...
Mapping PEB regions...
Mapping TEB and stack regions...
Mapping heap regions...
Mapping page heap regions...
Mapping other regions...
Mapping stack trace database regions...
Mapping activation context regions...
```

--- Usage Summary ---------------	RgnCount	----------- Total Size --------	%ofBusy	%ofTotal
Free	146	7fbe`514c1000 (127.743 TB)		99.80%
<unknown>	380	41`9b6a4800 (262.428 GB)	99.89%	0.20%
Image	645	0`0950a800 (149.041 MB)	0.06%	0.00%
Heap	957	0`0902d000 (144.176 MB)	0.05%	0.00%
Stack	45	0`00d80000 (13.500 MB)	0.01%	0.00%
Other	11	0`001b4000 (1.703 MB)	0.00%	0.00%
TEB	15	0`0001e000 (120.000 kB)	0.00%	0.00%
PEB	1	0`00001000 (4.000 kB)	0.00%	0.00%

--- Type Summary (for busy) ------	RgnCount	----------- Total Size --------	%ofBusy	%ofTotal
MEM_PRIVATE	1097	41`a0f6c000 (262.515 GB)	99.92%	0.20%
MEM_IMAGE	641	0`093ab000 (147.668 MB)	0.05%	0.00%
MEM_MAPPED	316	0`04818000 (72.094 MB)	0.03%	0.00%

```
--- State Summary --------------- RgnCount ----------- Total Size -------- %ofBusy %ofTotal
MEM_FREE                              146    7fbe`514c1000 ( 127.743 TB)             99.80%
MEM_RESERVE                           193      41`67715000 ( 261.616 GB)   99.58%     0.20%
MEM_COMMIT                           1861       0`4741a000 (   1.113 GB)    0.42%     0.00%

--- Protect Summary (for commit) - RgnCount ----------- Total Size -------- %ofBusy %ofTotal
PAGE_READWRITE                        865       0`3bc9d000 ( 956.613 MB)    0.36%     0.00%
PAGE_EXECUTE_READ                     125       0`05d1d000 (  93.113 MB)    0.03%     0.00%
PAGE_READONLY                         316       0`05623000 (  86.137 MB)    0.03%     0.00%
PAGE_WRITECOPY                         79       0`00240000 (   2.250 MB)    0.00%     0.00%
PAGE_NOACCESS                         460       0`001cc000 (   1.797 MB)    0.00%     0.00%
PAGE_READWRITE | PAGE_GUARD            15       0`0002f000 ( 188.000 kB)    0.00%     0.00%
PAGE_EXECUTE_READWRITE                  1       0`00002000 (   8.000 kB)    0.00%     0.00%

--- Largest Region by Usage ----------- Base Address -------- Region Size ----------
Free                                  2c0`73730000    7d34`59130000 ( 125.204 TB)
<unknown>                             280`07801000      3f`c9eef000 ( 255.155 GB)
Image                                 2c0`66be2000       0`02135000 (  33.207 MB)
Heap                                  2c0`731fc000       0`00513000 (   5.074 MB)
Stack                                  9a`5e100000       0`000fc000 (1008.000 kB)
Other                                 27f`cffb0000       0`00181000 (   1.504 MB)
TEB                                    9a`5de19000       0`00002000 (   8.000 kB)
PEB                                    9a`5de18000       0`00001000 (   4.000 kB)
```

Note: This prompts us to suspect a managed heap leak.

6.   We check managed heap statistics:

```
0:000> !DumpHeap -stat
Statistics:
          MT   Count    TotalSize Class Name
[...]
7ff9d3895328     246       18,456 System.String[]
7ff9d3aaee60     129       21,872 System.Reflection.RuntimeMethodInfo[]
7ff9d3aaf898     308       24,640 System.Signature
7ff9d3f7ded0     386       33,968 Microsoft.CSharp.RuntimeBinder.Semantics.AggregateType
7ff9d36aa038   1,079       43,160 System.RuntimeType
7ff9d3762170     348       47,400 System.Object[]
7ff9d3bd7518     551       48,488 System.Reflection.RuntimeParameterInfo
7ff9d388dea0     444       82,520 System.Byte[]
7ff9d3aadbc8   2,003      208,312 System.Reflection.RuntimeMethodInfo
027fcfce3ab0   2,724      340,848 Free
7ff9d37bbf40   3,974      352,852 System.String
7ff9d3b331d0  42,042    1,009,008 LINQPad.Disposable
7ff9d4126c68  50,000    1,600,000 UserQuery+SmallObject
7ff9d3ab1f58  42,331    2,709,184 System.Action
7ff9d37bfda0  50,018    3,601,296 System.Threading.Thread
7ff9d37b8e48  50,269  820,446,200 System.Int32[]
Total 257,956 objects, 831,243,473 bytes
```

Note: We see 50,000 *UserQuery+SmallObject* objects and almost the same amount of *Int32* arrays and *System.Threading.Thread* objects. We check the object class:

```
0:000> !DumpMT 7ff9d4126c68
Canonical MethodTabl 00007ff9d4126c68
Module:              00007ff9d407f2b0
```

217

```
Name:                   UserQuery+SmallObject
mdToken:                0000000002000005
File:
C:\Users\User\AppData\Local\Temp\LINQPad8\_cpfjtgxi\otjvmd\LINQPadQuery.dll
AssemblyLoadContext: 0000027fd64bda68
BaseSize:               0x20
ComponentSize:          0x0
DynamicStatics:         false
ContainsPointers:       true
Number of Methods:      6
Number of IFaces in IFaceMap: 0
```

```
0:000> !DumpClass 7ff9d4126c68
Class Name:             UserQuery+SmallObject
mdToken:                0000000002000005
File:                   C:\Users\User\AppData\Local\Temp\LINQPad8\_cpfjtgxi\otjvmd\LINQPadQuery.dll
Parent MethodTable: 00007ff9d36a4730
Module:                 00007ff9d407f2b0
Method Table:           00007ff9d4126c68
Canonical MethodTable: 00007ff9d4126c68
Class Attributes:       100002
NumInstanceFields:      2
NumStaticFields:        0
              MT    Field   Offset                 Type VT     Attr            Value Name
00007ff9d37b8e48 4000005        8         System.Int32[]  0 instance          buffer
00007ff9d37bfda0 4000006       10 ....Threading.Thread  0 instance          thread
```

7.   We can calculate the average array size and dump all heap objects that satisfy the minimum size:

```
0:000> ? 0n820446200/0n50269
Evaluate expression: 16321 = 00000000`00003fc1
```

```
0:000> !DumpHeap -min 16000
       Address               MT       Size
    027fd1802020      7ff9d3762170       16,344
    027fd3800090      7ff9d37b8e48       16,408
    027fd3804110      7ff9d37b8e48       16,408
    027fd3808190      7ff9d37b8e48       16,408
    027fd380c210      7ff9d37b8e48       16,408
    027fd3810290      7ff9d37b8e48       16,408
    027fd3814310      7ff9d37b8e48       16,408
    027fd3818390      7ff9d37b8e48       16,408
    027fd381c410      7ff9d37b8e48       16,408
    027fd3820490      7ff9d37b8e48       16,408
[...]
    028006eb1540      7ff9d37b8e48       16,408
    028006eb55c0      7ff9d37b8e48       16,408
    028006eb9640      7ff9d37b8e48       16,408
    028006ebd6c0      7ff9d37b8e48       16,408
    028006ec1740      7ff9d37b8e48       16,408
    028006ec57c0      7ff9d37b8e48       16,408
    028006ec9840      7ff9d37b8e48       16,408
    028006ecd8c0      7ff9d37b8e48       16,408
    028006ed1940      7ff9d37b8e48       16,408
    028006ed59c0      7ff9d37b8e48       16,408
    028006ed9a40      7ff9d37b8e48       16,408
    028006eddac0      7ff9d37b8e48       16,408
    028006ee1b40      7ff9d37b8e48       16,408
```

```
028006ee5bc0        7ff9d37b8e48                16,408
028007000048        7ff9d37b8e48                16,408
0280070040e0        7ff9d37b8e48                16,408
028007008178        7ff9d37b8e48                16,408
02800700c210        7ff9d37b8e48                16,408
0280070102a8        7ff9d37b8e48                16,408
028007014340        7ff9d37b8e48                16,408
0280070183d8        7ff9d37b8e48                16,408
02800701c470        7ff9d37b8e48                16,408
028007020508        7ff9d37b8e48                16,408
0280070245a0        7ff9d37b8e48                16,408
028007028638        7ff9d37b8e48                16,408
02800702c6d0        7ff9d37b8e48                16,408

Statistics:
          MT  Count   TotalSize Class Name
7ff9d3762170      1      16,344 System.Object[]
7ff9d3f87ef8      1      17,264
System.Collections.Generic.Dictionary<Microsoft.CSharp.RuntimeBinder.Semantics.TypeTable+KeyPai
r<Microsoft.CSharp.RuntimeBinder.Semantics.AggregateSymbol,
Microsoft.CSharp.RuntimeBinder.Semantics.TypeTable+KeyPair<Microsoft.CSharp.RuntimeBinder.Seman
tics.AggregateType, Microsoft.CSharp.RuntimeBinder.Semantics.TypeArray>>,
Microsoft.CSharp.RuntimeBinder.Semantics.AggregateType>+Entry[]
7ff9d37bbf40      1      40,814 System.String
027fcfce3ab0     12     243,872 Free
7ff9d37b8e48 50,001 820,424,624 System.Int32[]
Total 50,016 objects, 820,742,918 bytes

0:000> !DumpObj 028007020508
Name:        System.Int32[]
MethodTable: 00007ff9d37b8e48
Canonical MethodTable: 00007ff9d37b8e48
Tracked Type: false
Size:        16408(0x4018) bytes
Array:       Rank 1, Number of elements 4096, Type Int32 (Print Array)
Fields:
None
```

8. We can also dump all *UserQuery+SmallObject* objects from the managed heap:

```
0:000> !DumpHeap -type UserQuery+SmallObject
       Address              MT    Size
   027fd3800028    7ff9d4126c68      32
   027fd38040a8    7ff9d4126c68      32
   027fd3808128    7ff9d4126c68      32
   027fd380c1a8    7ff9d4126c68      32
   027fd3810228    7ff9d4126c68      32
   027fd38142a8    7ff9d4126c68      32
   027fd3818328    7ff9d4126c68      32
   027fd381c3a8    7ff9d4126c68      32
   027fd3820428    7ff9d4126c68      32
   027fd38244a8    7ff9d4126c68      32
   027fd3828528    7ff9d4126c68      32
   027fd382c5a8    7ff9d4126c68      32
   027fd3830628    7ff9d4126c68      32
   027fd38346a8    7ff9d4126c68      32
   027fd3838728    7ff9d4126c68      32
   027fd383c7a8    7ff9d4126c68      32
```

```
        027fd3840828        7ff9d4126c68                32
[...]
        028006eb14d8        7ff9d4126c68                32
        028006eb5558        7ff9d4126c68                32
        028006eb95d8        7ff9d4126c68                32
        028006ebd658        7ff9d4126c68                32
        028006ec16d8        7ff9d4126c68                32
        028006ec5758        7ff9d4126c68                32
        028006ec97d8        7ff9d4126c68                32
        028006ecd858        7ff9d4126c68                32
        028006ed18d8        7ff9d4126c68                32
        028006ed5958        7ff9d4126c68                32
        028006ed99d8        7ff9d4126c68                32
        028006edda58        7ff9d4126c68                32
        028006ee1ad8        7ff9d4126c68                32
        028006ee5b58        7ff9d4126c68                32
        028007004078        7ff9d4126c68                32
        0280070080f8        7ff9d4126c68                32
        02800700c1a8        7ff9d4126c68                32
        028007010240        7ff9d4126c68                32
        0280070142d8        7ff9d4126c68                32
        028007018370        7ff9d4126c68                32
        02800701c408        7ff9d4126c68                32
        0280070204a0        7ff9d4126c68                32
        028007024538        7ff9d4126c68                32
        0280070285b8        7ff9d4126c68                32
        02800702c668        7ff9d4126c68                32

Statistics:
          MT  Count TotalSize Class Name
7ff9d4126c68 50,000 1,600,000 UserQuery+SmallObject
Total 50,000 objects, 1,600,000 bytes


0:000> !DumpObj 02800702c668
Name:       UserQuery+SmallObject
MethodTable: 00007ff9d4126c68
Canonical MethodTable: 00007ff9d4126c68
Tracked Type: false
Size:       32(0x20) bytes
File:       C:\Users\User\AppData\Local\Temp\LINQPad8\_cpfjtgxi\otjvmd\LINQPadQuery.dll
Fields:
              MT   Field  Offset                 Type VT    Attr          Value Name
00007ff9d37b8e48 4000005     8         System.Int32[]  0 instance 000002800702c6d0 buffer
00007ff9d37bfda0 4000006    10 ....Threading.Thread  0 instance 000002800702c688 thread

0:000> !DumpObj 000002800702c6d0
Name:       System.Int32[]
MethodTable: 00007ff9d37b8e48
Canonical MethodTable: 00007ff9d37b8e48
Tracked Type: false
Size:       16408(0x4018) bytes
Array:      Rank 1, Number of elements 4096, Type Int32 (Print Array)
Fields:
None

0:000> !DumpObj 000002800702c688
Name:       System.Threading.Thread
MethodTable: 00007ff9d37bfda0
Canonical MethodTable: 00007ff9d37bfda0
Tracked Type: false
```

```
Size:          72(0x48) bytes
File:          C:\Program Files\dotnet\shared\Microsoft.NETCore.App\9.0.4\System.Private.CoreLib.dll
Fields:
              MT    Field   Offset                 Type VT     Attr            Value Name
00007ff9d3b0a860  4000c80        8 ....ExecutionContext  0 instance 0000000000000000 _executionContext
00007ff9d3b49390  4000c81       10 ...ronizationContext  0 instance 0000000000000000 _synchronizationContext
00007ff9d37bbf40  4000c82       18         System.String  0 instance 0000000000000000 _name
00007ff9d3b0b6d8  4000c83       20 ...hread+StartHelper  0 instance 0000000000000000 _startHelper
00007ff9d37b5270  4000c84       28         System.IntPtr  1 instance 000002C0731B3D30 _DONT_USE_InternalThread
00007ff9d3767408  4000c85       30         System.Int32  1 instance                2 _priority
00007ff9d3767408  4000c86       34         System.Int32  1 instance            50015 _managedThreadId
00007ff9d3762f78  4000c87       38       System.Boolean  1 instance                0 _mayNeedResetForThreadPool
00007ff9d3767408  4000c89        8         System.Int32  1   static                0
<OptimalMaxSpinWaitsPerSpinIteration>k__BackingField
0000000000000000  4000c8a        8                        0   static 0000000000000000 s_asyncLocalPrincipal
00007ff9d3762f78  4000c8c        c       System.Boolean  1   static                0 s_isProcessorNumberReallyFast
00007ff9d37bfda0  4000c8b       10 ....Threading.Thread  0 TLstatic  t_currentThread
    Thread static values (Thread:Value)
        1c84:0000027fd6423018
        1c9c:0000027fd64005c0
        1c68:0000027fd6423aa8
        1324:0000027fd6424170
        207c:0000027fd6426b40
        a88:0000027fd6448640
        99c:0000027fd6448318
        1d04:0000027fd644ce00
        2244:0000027fd64bf4f8
        2290:0000027fd64bf648
        32ce0:0000028007315148
```

Note: We see that every object has a thread object reference, and we have almost the same amount of *Thread* objects on the managed heap, so this could have also contributed to the thread handle leak we see if we run the **!handle** command (the output can take some time):

```
0:000> !handle
[...]
Handle 00000000000aa8f0
  Type              Thread
Handle 00000000000aa8f4
  Type              Event
Handle 00000000000aa8f8
  Type              Event
Handle 00000000000aa8fc
  Type              Thread
Handle 00000000000aa900
  Type              Event
Handle 00000000000aa904
  Type              Event
Handle 00000000000aa908
  Type              Event
Handle 00000000000aa90c
  Type              Thread
Handle 00000000000aa910
  Type              Event
Handle 00000000000aa914
  Type              Event
Handle 00000000000aa918
  Type              Thread
Handle 00000000000aa91c
  Type              Event
Handle 00000000000aa920
  Type              Event
Handle 00000000000aa924
```

```
    Type            Thread
Handle 00000000000aa928
    Type            Event
Handle 00000000000aa92c
    Type            Event
Handle 00000000000aa930
    Type            Thread
Handle 00000000000aa934
    Type            Event
Handle 00000000000aa938
    Type            Event
Handle 00000000000aa93c
    Type            Event
Handle 00000000000aa940
    Type            Thread
Handle 00000000000aa944
    Type            Event
Handle 00000000000aa948
    Type            Event
Handle 00000000000aa94c
    Type            Thread
Handle 00000000000aa950
    Type            Event
Handle 00000000000aa954
    Type            Event
Handle 00000000000aa958
    Type            Thread
Handle 00000000000aa95c
    Type            Thread
Handle 00000000000aa960
    Type            Event
Handle 00000000000aa964
    Type            Thread
Handle 00000000000aa968
    Type            Event
Handle 00000000000aa96c
    Type            Event
Handle 00000000000aa970
    Type            Event
Handle 00000000000aa974
    Type            Thread
Handle 00000000000aa978
    Type            Event
Handle 00000000000aa97c
    Type            Event
Handle 00000000000aa980
    Type            Thread
Handle 00000000000aa984
    Type            Event
Handle 00000000000aa988
    Type            Event
Handle 00000000000aa98c
    Type            Thread
174006 Handles
Type                    Count
None                    101
Event                   123735
Section                 11
File                    64
```

```
Directory            2
Mutant               8
WindowStation        2
Semaphore            9
Key                  18
Process              3
Thread               50024
Desktop              1
IoCompletion         6
TpWorkerFactory      3
ALPC Port            6
WaitCompletionPacket 13
```

9.   Then we list managed threads:

```
0:000> !Threads
ThreadCount:      50019
UnstartedThread:  0
BackgroundThread: 11
PendingThread:    0
DeadThread:       50007
Hosted Runtime:   no
                                                                              Lock
 DBG    ID   OSID ThreadOBJ          State GC Mode  GC Alloc Context               Domain              Count Apt Exception
   0     1   1c84 0000027FCFC5A280 2024020 Preemptive 0000000000000000:0000000000000000 0000027fcfc55eb0 -00001 STA
   3     2   1c9c 000002BFD1730BB0 202b220 Preemptive 0000000000000000:0000000000000000 0000027fcfc55eb0 -00001 MTA (Finalizer)
System.NullReferenceException 0000027fd40042d8
   4     4   1c68 000002BFD174FDB0 302b220 Preemptive 0000028007035110:00000280070365B8 0000027fcfc55eb0 -00001 MTA (Threadpool Worker)
   5     6   1324 000002BFD17C3760 302b220 Preemptive 0000000000000000:0000000000000000 0000027fcfc55eb0 -00001 MTA (Threadpool Worker)
   6     7   207c 000002BFD17E13A0 202b220 Preemptive 0000000000000000:0000000000000000 0000027fcfc55eb0 -00001 MTA
XXXX     5      0 000002BFD174E640 1039820 Preemptive 0000000000000000:0000000000000000 0000027fcfc55eb0 -00001 Ukn (Threadpool Worker)
XXXX     8      0 000002BFD17E3650 1039820 Preemptive 0000000000000000:0000000000000000 0000027fcfc55eb0 -00001 Ukn (Threadpool Worker)
   8     9    a88 000002BFD17EA720 102b220 Preemptive 00000280073741F0:0000028007375978 0000027fcfc55eb0 -00001 MTA (Threadpool Worker)
  10    10    99c 000002C06ABC2BC0 102b220 Preemptive 00000280073FDA30:00000280073FE1F8 0000027fcfc55eb0 -00001 MTA (Threadpool Worker)
   9    11   1d04 000002C06ABC1D40 102b220 Preemptive 0000028007413560:0000028007415010 0000027fcfc55eb0 -00001 MTA (Threadpool Worker)
  11    12   2244 000002C06ABA4850 202b220 Preemptive 0000000000000000:0000000000000000 0000027fcfc55eb0 -00001 MTA System.IO.FileNotFoundException
0000027fd64bf6f0
XXXX    13      0 000002C06A9E1440   39820 Preemptive 0000000000000000:0000000000000000 0000027fcfc55eb0 -00001 Ukn
  12    14   2290 000002C06A9E1DD0 202b220 Preemptive 0000000000000000:0000000000000000 0000027fcfc55eb0 -00001 MTA UserQuery+CustomException
0000027fd64bff00
XXXX    15      0 000002C06AA30690   39820 Preemptive 0000000000000000:0000000000000000 0000027fcfc55eb0 -00001 Ukn
XXXX    16      0 000002C06AA52F80   39820 Preemptive 0000000000000000:0000000000000000 0000027fcfc55eb0 -00001 Ukn
XXXX    17      0 000002C06ABC26D0   39820 Preemptive 0000000000000000:0000000000000000 0000027fcfc55eb0 -00001 Ukn
XXXX    18      0 000002C06AA539A0   39820 Preemptive 0000000000000000:0000000000000000 0000027fcfc55eb0 -00001 Ukn
XXXX    19      0 000002C06AA54840   39820 Preemptive 0000000000000000:0000000000000000 0000027fcfc55eb0 -00001 Ukn
XXXX    20      0 000002C06AA53EA0   39820 Preemptive 0000000000000000:0000000000000000 0000027fcfc55eb0 -00001 Ukn
XXXX    21      0 000002C06AA56050   39820 Preemptive 0000000000000000:0000000000000000 0000027fcfc55eb0 -00001 Ukn
XXXX    22      0 000002C06AA551E0   39820 Preemptive 0000000000000000:0000000000000000 0000027fcfc55eb0 -00001 Ukn
XXXX    23      0 000002C06AA556B0   39820 Preemptive 0000000000000000:0000000000000000 0000027fcfc55eb0 -00001 Ukn
XXXX    24      0 000002C06AA54370   39820 Preemptive 0000000000000000:0000000000000000 0000027fcfc55eb0 -00001 Ukn
XXXX    25      0 000002C06AA55B80   39820 Preemptive 0000000000000000:0000000000000000 0000027fcfc55eb0 -00001 Ukn
XXXX    26      0 000002C06AA57390   39820 Preemptive 0000000000000000:0000000000000000 0000027fcfc55eb0 -00001 Ukn
[...]
XXXX 50003      0 000002C0731B16B0   39820 Preemptive 0000000000000000:0000000000000000 0000027fcfc55eb0 -00001 Ukn
XXXX 50004      0 000002C0731B0370   39820 Preemptive 0000000000000000:0000000000000000 0000027fcfc55eb0 -00001 Ukn
XXXX 50005      0 000002C0731B2050   39820 Preemptive 0000000000000000:0000000000000000 0000027fcfc55eb0 -00001 Ukn
XXXX 50006      0 000002C0731AD820   39820 Preemptive 0000000000000000:0000000000000000 0000027fcfc55eb0 -00001 Ukn
XXXX 50007      0 000002C0731AE690   39820 Preemptive 0000000000000000:0000000000000000 0000027fcfc55eb0 -00001 Ukn
XXXX 50008      0 000002C0731B0840   39820 Preemptive 0000000000000000:0000000000000000 0000027fcfc55eb0 -00001 Ukn
XXXX 50009      0 000002C0731B46D0   39820 Preemptive 0000000000000000:0000000000000000 0000027fcfc55eb0 -00001 Ukn
XXXX 50010      0 000002C0731B3860   39820 Preemptive 0000000000000000:0000000000000000 0000027fcfc55eb0 -00001 Ukn
XXXX 50011      0 000002C0731B0D10   39820 Preemptive 0000000000000000:0000000000000000 0000027fcfc55eb0 -00001 Ukn
XXXX 50012      0 000002C0731B3390   39820 Preemptive 0000000000000000:0000000000000000 0000027fcfc55eb0 -00001 Ukn
XXXX 50013      0 000002C0731ADCF0   39820 Preemptive 0000000000000000:0000000000000000 0000027fcfc55eb0 -00001 Ukn
XXXX 50014      0 000002C0731B11E0   39820 Preemptive 0000000000000000:0000000000000000 0000027fcfc55eb0 -00001 Ukn
XXXX 50015      0 000002C0731B3D30   39820 Preemptive 0000000000000000:0000000000000000 0000027fcfc55eb0 -00001 Ukn
XXXX  1150      0 000002C0731AF500 1039820 Preemptive 0000000000000000:0000000000000000 0000027fcfc55eb0 -00001 Ukn (Threadpool Worker)
XXXX     3      0 000002C0731B2520 1039820 Preemptive 0000000000000000:0000000000000000 0000027fcfc55eb0 -00001 Ukn (Threadpool Worker)
XXXX 50016      0 000002C0731AD350 1039820 Preemptive 0000000000000000:0000000000000000 0000027fcfc55eb0 -00001 Ukn (Threadpool Worker)
XXXX 50017      0 000002C0731B4200 1039820 Preemptive 0000000000000000:0000000000000000 0000027fcfc55eb0 -00001 Ukn (Threadpool Worker)
  13 50018   32ce0 000002C0731B29F0 102b220 Preemptive 0000028007359B60:000002800735B7D8 0000027fcfc55eb0 -00001 MTA (Threadpool Worker)
  14 50019   32ef0 000002C0731B1B80   2b220 Preemptive 0000000000000000:0000000000000000 0000027fcfc55eb0 -00001 MTA
```

Note: We see an endless list of threads. The thread count is more than 50,000, and all of them are dead but not released.

10. We also check the GC heap, GC handles, and the finalizer queue:

```
0:000> !eeheap -gc
DATAS =
========================================
Number of GC Heaps: 1
----------------------------------------
Small object heap
       segment          begin         allocated        committed allocated size      committed size
    02bfe58278b0    028007000028     0280073fffc0      028007400000 0x3fff98 (4194200)  0x400000 (4194304)
    02bfe5827958    028007400028     028007415028      028007421000 0x15000 (86016)     0x21000 (135168)
generation 1:
    02bfe5827760    028006800028     028006a19048      028006c00000 0x219020 (2199584)  0x400000 (4194304)
generation 2:
    02bfe581f180    027fd3800028     027fd3bfd328      027fd3c00000 0x3fd300 (4182784)  0x400000 (4194304)
    02bfe581f228    027fd3c00028     027fd3fffe58      027fd4000000 0x3ffe30 (4193840)  0x400000 (4194304)
    02bfe581f2d0    027fd4000028     027fd43ff188      027fd4400000 0x3ff160 (4190560)  0x400000 (4194304)
    02bfe581f8b8    027fd6400028     027fd67ffff8      027fd6800000 0x3fffd0 (4194256)  0x400000 (4194304)
    02bfe581f960    027fd6800028     027fd6bfff90      027fd6c00000 0x3fff68 (4194152)  0x400000 (4194304)
    02bfe581fa08    027fd6c00028     027fd6fffe70      027fd7000000 0x3ffe48 (4193864)  0x400000 (4194304)
    02bfe581fab0    027fd7000028     027fd73ffdf0      027fd7400000 0x3ffdc8 (4193736)  0x400000 (4194304)
[...]
    02bfe5827568    028005c00028     028005fffdf0      028006000000 0x3ffdc8 (4193736)  0x400000 (4194304)
    02bfe5827610    028006000028     0280063ffe58      028006400000 0x3ffe30 (4193840)  0x400000 (4194304)
    02bfe58276b8    028006400028     0280067fff28      028006800000 0x3fff00 (4194048)  0x400000 (4194304)
    02bfe5827808    028006c00028     028006ee9bd8      028007000000 0x2e9bb0 (3054512)  0x400000 (4194304)
NonGC heap
       segment          begin         allocated        committed allocated size      committed size
    027fcfc5d200    02c0664a0008     02c0664cca98      02c0664d0000 0x2ca90 (182928)    0x30000 (196608)
Large object heap
       segment          begin         allocated        committed allocated size      committed size
    02bfe581f378    027fd4400028     027fd4400028      027fd4421000                     0x21000 (135168)
Pinned object heap
       segment          begin         allocated        committed allocated size      committed size
    02bfe581ec40    027fd1800028     027fd1806410      027fd1811000 0x63e8 (25576)      0x11000 (69632)
------------------------------
GC Allocated Heap Size:    Size: 0x318c6b80 (831286144) bytes.
GC Committed Heap Size:    Size: 0x31c7f000 (835186688) bytes.
```

```
0:000> !GCHandles
        Handle Type              Object          Size        Data Type
0000027FCFD71098 WeakShort    0000027fd64bf648    72              System.Threading.Thread
0000027FCFD710A0 WeakShort    0000027fd64bf580    72              System.Threading.Thread
0000027FCFD710A8 WeakShort    0000027fd64bf4f8    72              System.Threading.Thread
0000027FCFD710B0 WeakShort    0000027fd644ce00    72              System.Threading.Thread
0000027FCFD710B8 WeakShort    0000027fd6448318    72              System.Threading.Thread
0000027FCFD710C0 WeakShort    0000027fd6448640    72              System.Threading.Thread
0000027FCFD710C8 WeakShort    0000027fd64482d0    72              System.Threading.Thread
[...]
000002C0737139C0 WeakShort    0000028007315148    72              System.Threading.Thread
000002C0737139C8 WeakShort    00000280071e1850    72              System.Threading.Thread
000002C0737139D0 WeakShort    000000280071e1850   72              System.Threading.Thread
0000027FCFD71770 WeakLong     0000027fd642c808    160             System.RuntimeType+RuntimeTypeCache
0000027FCFD71778 WeakLong     0000027fd6428de0    160             System.RuntimeType+RuntimeTypeCache
0000027FCFD71780 WeakLong     0000027fd6428bb8    160             System.RuntimeType+RuntimeTypeCache
0000027FCFD71788 WeakLong     0000027fd6427bb8    160             System.RuntimeType+RuntimeTypeCache
[…]
0000027FCFD713A0 Strong       0000027fd640b2f0    64              System.Diagnostics.Tracing.EventPipeEventProvider
0000027FCFD713A8 Strong       0000027fd640b240    88              System.Diagnostics.Tracing.EtwEventProvider
0000027FCFD713B0 Strong       0000027fd640af20    64              System.Diagnostics.Tracing.EventPipeEventProvider
0000027FCFD713B8 Strong       0000027fd640ae70    88              System.Diagnostics.Tracing.EtwEventProvider
0000027FCFD713C8 Strong       0000027fd6400178    120             System.ExecutionEngineException
0000027FCFD713D0 Strong       0000027fd6400100    120             System.StackOverflowException
0000027FCFD713D8 Strong       0000027fd6400088    120             System.OutOfMemoryException
0000027FCFD713E0 Strong       0000027fd6400028    96              System.Int32[]
0000027FCFD713E8 Strong       0000027fd1800028    8184            System.Object[]
0000027FCFD713F0 Strong       0000027fd64005c0    72              System.Threading.Thread
0000027FCFD713F8 Strong       0000027fd6423018    72              System.Threading.Thread
0000027FCFD73788 Strong       0000027fd40042d8    120             System.NullReferenceException
0000027FCFD73790 Strong       0000027fd40042d8    120             System.NullReferenceException
0000027FCFD73B60 Strong       0000027fd64bf6f0    136             System.IO.FileNotFoundException
000002C073713738 Strong       0000028007315148    72              System.Threading.Thread
0000027FCFD715F8 Pinned       0000027fd40001f0    24              System.Object
0000027FCFD71B40 Dependent    0000027fd80804e8    456 0000000000000000 System.Buffers.SharedArrayPoolThreadLocalArray[]
0000027FCFD71B48 Dependent    0000027fd427e880    456 0000000000000000 System.Buffers.SharedArrayPoolThreadLocalArray[]
0000027FCFD71B50 Dependent    0000027fd427d868    456 0000000000000000 System.Buffers.SharedArrayPoolThreadLocalArray[]
```

```
0000027FCFD71B58 Dependent    0000027fd4260870       456 0000000000000000 System.Buffers.SharedArrayPoolThreadLocalArray[]
[...]
0000027FCFD71BF8 Dependent    0000027fd6418f48       456 0000000000000000 System.Buffers.SharedArrayPoolThreadLocalArray[]

Statistics:
          MT     Count    TotalSize Class Name
00007ff9d36a4730     1           24 System.Object
00007ff9d41ffa38     1           40 System.Buffers.SharedArrayPool`1[[System.ValueTuple`2[[System.String,
System.Private.CoreLib],[System.Reflection.FieldInfo, System.Private.CoreLib]], System.Private.CoreLib]]
00007ff9d41f2af8     1           40 System.Buffers.SharedArrayPool`1[[Hyperlinq.HNode, Hyperlinq]]
00007ff9d3dd2d48     1           40 System.Buffers.SharedArrayPool`1[[System.Reflection.AssemblyName, System.Private.CoreLib]]
00007ff9d3d710b0     1           40 System.Buffers.SharedArrayPool`1[[System.Byte, System.Private.CoreLib]]
00007ff9d3cc1d90     1           40 System.Buffers.SharedArrayPool`1[[System.Boolean, System.Private.CoreLib]]
00007ff9d3cbd400     1           40 System.Buffers.SharedArrayPool`1[[System.ReadOnlyMemory`1[[System.Char,
System.Private.CoreLib]], System.Private.CoreLib]]
00007ff9d3bc9b88     1           40 System.Buffers.SharedArrayPool`1[[System.Char, System.Private.CoreLib]]
00007ff9d3a7fc78     1           40 System.Buffers.SharedArrayPool`1[[System.Int32, System.Private.CoreLib]]
00007ff9d389f8b0     2           96 System.Reflection.RuntimeAssembly
00007ff9d37b8e48     1           96 System.Int32[]
00007ff9d37be7a0     1          120 System.ExecutionEngineException
00007ff9d37be678     1          120 System.StackOverflowException
00007ff9d37be550     1          120 System.OutOfMemoryException
00007ff9d407f1c8     2          160 LINQPad.ExecutionModel.QueryLoadContext
00007ff9d3a7c758     2          160 System.Runtime.Loader.DefaultAssemblyLoadContext
00007ff9d3898d78     2          176 LINQPad.ProcessServer.LINQPadRuntimeLoadContext
00007ff9d3b09090     1          184 System.Diagnostics.Tracing.FrameworkEventSource
00007ff9d3aa21d8     1          184 System.Buffers.ArrayPoolEventSource
00007ff9d3869da0     1          184 System.Diagnostics.Tracing.NativeRuntimeEventSource
00007ff9d3b0e830     1          192 System.Threading.Tasks.TplEventSource
00007ff9d4163a10     2          240 System.NullReferenceException
00007ff9d3ecbd70     2          256 LINQPad.ExecutionModel.UserLoadContext
00007ff9d4126b28     2          272 UserQuery+CustomException
00007ff9d3d729e8     2          272 System.IO.FileNotFoundException
00007ff9d3873c78     6          384 System.Diagnostics.Tracing.EventPipeEventProvider
00007ff9d3876d30     1          400 System.Diagnostics.Tracing.RuntimeEventSource
00007ff9d386ae68     6          528 System.Diagnostics.Tracing.EtwEventProvider
00007ff9d386b508    12          768 System.Diagnostics.Tracing.EventSource+OverrideEventProvider
00007ff9d3e778e8    30         2160 System.Reflection.Emit.DynamicResolver
00007ff9d37bfda0    56         4032 System.Threading.Thread
00007ff9d3aa0288    16         7296 System.Buffers.SharedArrayPoolThreadLocalArray[]
00007ff9d39d2a80    73        11680 System.RuntimeType+RuntimeTypeCache
00007ff9d3762170     3        25576 System.Object[]
Total 236 objects

Handles:
    Strong Handles:       40
    Pinned Handles:        1
    Weak Long Handles:   107
    Weak Short Handles:   70
    Dependent Handles:    18


0:000> !FinalizeQueue
SyncBlocks to be cleaned up: 0
Free-Threaded Interfaces to be released: 0
MTA Interfaces to be released: 0
STA Interfaces to be released: 0
---------------------------------

Heap 0
generation 0 has 2 objects (2c071c305c8->2c071c305d8)
generation 1 has 181 objects (2c071c30020->2c071c305c8)
generation 2 has 0 objects (2c071c30020->2c071c30020)
Ready for finalization 99,987 objects (2c071c30638->2c071cf3ad0)
---------------------------------
Statistics for all finalizable objects (including all objects ready for finalization):
      Address          MT        Size
   027fd64005c0  7ff9d37bfda0       72
   027fd640abc0  7ff9d3869da0      184
   027fd640ae30  7ff9d386b508       64
   027fd640aec8  7ff9d3874018       24
   027fd640aee0  7ff9d386b508       64
   027fd640af60  7ff9d3874018       24
   027fd640af98  7ff9d3875ae8       24
   027fd640afb0  7ff9d3876d30      400
   027fd640b200  7ff9d386b508       64
   027fd640b298  7ff9d3874018       24
[...]

   028006854cb8  7ff9d4126c68       32
   028006858d50  7ff9d4126c68       32
   02800685cde8  7ff9d4126c68       32
   028006860e80  7ff9d4126c68       32
   028006864f18  7ff9d4126c68       32
   028006868fb0  7ff9d4126c68       32
   02800686d048  7ff9d4126c68       32
   028007004078  7ff9d4126c68       32
   0280070080f8  7ff9d4126c68       32
   02800700c1a8  7ff9d4126c68       32
   028007010240  7ff9d4126c68       32
```

```
0280070142d8    7ff9d4126c68            32
028007018370    7ff9d4126c68            32
02800701c408    7ff9d4126c68            32
0280070204a0    7ff9d4126c68            32
028007024538    7ff9d4126c68            32

Statistics:
          MT  Count  TotalSize  Class Name
7ff9d3c58cf8      1         24  System.LocalDataStoreSlot
7ff9d3da3fe0      1         24  System.Reflection.Internal.NativeHeapMemoryBlock+DisposableData
7ff9d3b6e010      1         32  Microsoft.Win32.SafeHandles.SafeProcessHandle
7ff9d3aac0e0      1         32  System.IO.FileStream
7ff9d3c598e0      1         40  System.Threading.ThreadLocal<System.Object>
7ff9d3ef7560      1         72  LINQPad.ExecutionModel.Proxy<LINQPad.ExecutionModel.IPluginWindowClient>
7ff9d3ebc278      1         72  LINQPad.ExecutionModel.Proxy<LINQPad.ExecutionModel.ProcessServer>
7ff9d3ec6a18      1         72  LINQPad.ExecutionModel.Proxy<LINQPad.ExecutionModel.IServer>
7ff9d3ec7880      1         72  LINQPad.ExecutionModel.Proxy<LINQPad.ExecutionModel.AppHost>
7ff9d3ef71f0      1         72  LINQPad.ExecutionModel.Proxy<LINQPad.ExecutionModel.IClient>
7ff9d3b032f0      1         72  Microsoft.Win32.SafeHandles.SafeFileHandle
7ff9d3a7c758      1         80  System.Runtime.Loader.DefaultAssemblyLoadContext
7ff9d3ef5a88      1         80  LINQPad.ExecutionModel.Proxy<LINQPad.AppHost>+CastProxy<LINQPad.GuiAppHost>
7ff9d407f1c8      1         80  LINQPad.ExecutionModel.QueryLoadContext
7ff9d3898d78      1         88  LINQPad.ProcessServer.LINQPadRuntimeLoadContext
7ff9d39ff200      4         96  System.WeakReference<System.Runtime.Loader.AssemblyLoadContext>
7ff9d4027840      1         96  LINQPad.ExecutionModel.SharedMemoryValueWrapper<LINQPad.ExecutionModel.LockFreeExecutionInfo>
7ff9d3b03b80      1        112  LINQPad.ExecutionModel.InPipe
7ff9d4137140      2        112  System.Runtime.CompilerServices.ConditionalWeakTable<System.Reflection.Assembly,
System.Reflection.Metadata.MetadataReaderProvider>+Container
7ff9d3875ae8      5        120  System.WeakReference<System.Diagnostics.Tracing.EventSource>
7ff9d3abdda8      1        120  LINQPad.ExecutionModel.FastChannel
7ff9d3afea68      4        128  Microsoft.Win32.SafeHandles.SafeMemoryMappedFileHandle
7ff9d3ecbd70      1        128  LINQPad.ExecutionModel.UserLoadContext
7ff9d3b01168      4        160  Microsoft.Win32.SafeHandles.SafeMemoryMappedViewHandle
7ff9d3b0f450      1        176  System.Threading.LowLevelLifoSemaphore
7ff9d3869da0      1        184  System.Diagnostics.Tracing.NativeRuntimeEventSource
7ff9d3aa21d8      1        184  System.Buffers.ArrayPoolEventSource
7ff9d3b09090      1        184  System.Diagnostics.Tracing.FrameworkEventSource
7ff9d3b0e830      1        192  System.Threading.Tasks.TplEventSource
7ff9d3cb5d48      8        192  System.WeakReference<System.Text.RegularExpressions.RegexReplacement>
7ff9d3b06f60      5        200  System.Threading.LowLevelLock
7ff9d3af9538      3        240  LINQPad.ExecutionModel.MMFileWrapper
7ff9d3b06010      2        240  System.Threading.RegisteredWaitHandle
7ff9d3b21638     10        240  System.Threading.ThreadInt64PersistentCounter+ThreadLocalNodeFinalizationHelper
7ff9d3af9218      2        256  LINQPad.ExecutionModel.OutPipe
7ff9d3874018     12        288  System.WeakReference<System.Diagnostics.Tracing.EventProvider>
7ff9d3b03718      9        288  Microsoft.Win32.SafeHandles.SafeWaitHandle
7ff9d3aba588      1        288  System.Diagnostics.Process
7ff9d3aa2510      9        360  System.Gen2GcCallback
7ff9d3876d30      1        400  System.Diagnostics.Tracing.RuntimeEventSource
7ff9d3aa1428      8        448  System.Runtime.CompilerServices.ConditionalWeakTable<System.Buffers.SharedArrayPoolThreadLocalArray[], System.Object>+Container
7ff9d3b0eaa8     10        720  System.Threading.ThreadPoolWorkQueueThreadLocals
7ff9d386b508     12        768  System.Diagnostics.Tracing.EventSource+OverrideEventProvider
7ff9d3e778e8     30      2,160  System.Reflection.Emit.DynamicResolver
7ff9d4126c68 49,999  1,599,968  UserQuery+SmallObject
7ff9d37bfda0 50,018  3,601,296  System.Threading.Thread
Total 100,182 objects, 5,211,256 bytes
```

Note: This is because the finalizer thread is hanging due to an exception in the *SmallObject Finalize* method (see also exercise **PN5**). We can see it by examining JIT code disassembly:

```
0:000> ~3kL
 #  Child-SP          RetAddr           Call Site
00  0000009a`5e6fc358  00007ffa`7e95b903  ntdll!NtDelayExecution+0x14
01  0000009a`5e6fc360  00007ffa`7c29d031  ntdll!RtlDelayExecution+0x43
02  0000009a`5e6fc390  00007ffa`3325ce9c  KERNELBASE!SleepEx+0x71
03  0000009a`5e6fc410  00007ffa`3325cdc9  coreclr!Thread::UserSleep+0xc0
04  0000009a`5e6fc470  00007ffa`32763f82  coreclr!ThreadNative_Sleep+0x39
05  0000009a`5e6fc4b0  00007ff9`d40a8bbf  System_Private_CoreLib!System.Threading.Thread.Sleep+0x42
06  0000009a`5e6fc580  00007ffa`333a2eb3  LINQPad_Runtime!LINQPad.ExecutionModel.Server.CurrentDomain_UnhandledException+0x21f
07  0000009a`5e6fc660  00007ffa`33321568  coreclr!CallDescrWorkerInternal+0x83
08  0000009a`5e6fc6a0  00007ffa`33453ef6  coreclr!DispatchCallSimple+0x60
09  0000009a`5e6fc730  00007ffa`3348af68  coreclr!ExceptionNotifications::DeliverExceptionNotification+0x46
0a  0000009a`5e6fc790  00007ffa`3348acff  coreclr!InvokeUnhandledSwallowing+0x74
0b  0000009a`5e6fc820  00007ffa`3343d189  coreclr!DistributeUnhandledExceptionReliably+0x15f
0c  0000009a`5e6fc8e0  00007ffa`3343cafa  coreclr!AppDomain::RaiseUnhandledExceptionEvent+0xa9
0d  0000009a`5e6fc940  00007ffa`33456baf  coreclr!AppDomain::OnUnhandledException+0x8a
0e  0000009a`5e6fc9e0  00007ffa`334560a3  coreclr!NotifyAppDomainsOfUnhandledException+0x133
0f  0000009a`5e6fcaa0  00007ffa`33418703  coreclr!InternalUnhandledExceptionFilter_Worker+0x20b
10  0000009a`5e6fcb60  00007ffa`327b77c9  coreclr!SfiNext+0xe95f3
11  0000009a`5e6fcc80  00007ffa`327b717a  System_Private_CoreLib!System.Runtime.EH.DispatchEx+0x2a9
12  0000009a`5e6fcde0  00007ffa`333a2eb3  System_Private_CoreLib!System.Runtime.EH.RhThrowHwEx+0xaa
13  0000009a`5e6fce20  00007ffa`33321568  coreclr!CallDescrWorkerInternal+0x83
14  0000009a`5e6fce60  00007ffa`33455cde  coreclr!DispatchCallSimple+0x60
15  0000009a`5e6fcef0  00007ffa`3342f58a  coreclr!HandleManagedFaultNew+0x192
16  0000009a`5e6fea00  00007ffa`7e97ca2a  coreclr!CLRVectoredExceptionHandlerShim+0xa84ca
17  0000009a`5e6fea50  00007ffa`7e9359f2  ntdll!RtlpCallVectoredHandlers+0x112
18  0000009a`5e6feaf0  00007ffa`7e9a805e  ntdll!RtlDispatchException+0x62
19  0000009a`5e6fed40  00007ff9`d40b5205  ntdll!KiUserExceptionDispatch+0x2e
```

226

```
1a 0000009a`5e6ff440 00007ffa`3265be9f   LINQPadQuery!UserQuery.SmallObject.Finalize+0x35
1b 0000009a`5e6ff480 00007ffa`333a2eb3   System_Private_CoreLib!System.GC.RunFinalizers+0x8f
1c 0000009a`5e6ff560 00007ffa`33321568   coreclr!CallDescrWorkerInternal+0x83
1d 0000009a`5e6ff5a0 00007ffa`3336945f   coreclr!DispatchCallSimple+0x60
1e 0000009a`5e6ff630 00007ffa`33368950   coreclr!FinalizerThread::FinalizeAllObjects+0x7b
1f 0000009a`5e6ff710 00007ffa`3330ef05   coreclr!FinalizerThread::FinalizerThreadWorker+0x100
20 (Inline Function) --------`--------   coreclr!ManagedThreadBase_DispatchInner+0xd
21 0000009a`5e6ff960 00007ffa`3330ee2d   coreclr!ManagedThreadBase_DispatchMiddle+0x79
22 0000009a`5e6ffa10 00007ffa`3335e921   coreclr!ManagedThreadBase_DispatchOuter+0x8d
23 (Inline Function) --------`--------   coreclr!ManagedThreadBase_NoADTransition+0x28
24 (Inline Function) --------`--------   coreclr!ManagedThreadBase::FinalizerBase+0x28
25 0000009a`5e6ffa80 00007ffa`7dd853e0   coreclr!FinalizerThread::FinalizerThreadStart+0x91
26 0000009a`5e6ffb90 00007ffa`7e90485b   kernel32!BaseThreadInitThunk+0x10
27 0000009a`5e6ffbc0 00000000`00000000   ntdll!RtlUserThreadStart+0x2b


0:000> !U 00007ff9`d40b5205
Normal JIT generated code
UserQuery+SmallObject.Finalize()
ilAddr is 000002C06AE72168 pImport is 000001681C8F6C70
Begin 00007FF9D40B51D0, size 72
00007ff9`d40b51d0 push    rbp
00007ff9`d40b51d1 sub     rsp,30h
00007ff9`d40b51d5 lea     rbp,[rsp+30h]
00007ff9`d40b51da xor     eax,eax
00007ff9`d40b51dc mov     qword ptr [rbp-8],rax
00007ff9`d40b51e0 mov     qword ptr [rbp-10h],rsp
00007ff9`d40b51e4 mov     qword ptr [rbp+10h],rcx
00007ff9`d40b51e8 cmp     dword ptr [00007ff9`d407f4f8],0
00007ff9`d40b51ef je      LINQPadQuery!UserQuery.SmallObject.Finalize+0x26 (00007ff9`d40b51f6)
00007ff9`d40b51f1 call    coreclr!JIT_DbgIsJustMyCode (00007ffa`334b33c0)
00007ff9`d40b51f6 nop
00007ff9`d40b51f7 nop
00007ff9`d40b51f8 nop
00007ff9`d40b51f9 xor     eax,eax
00007ff9`d40b51fb mov     eax,eax
00007ff9`d40b51fd mov     qword ptr [rbp-8],rax
00007ff9`d40b5201 mov     rax,qword ptr [rbp-8]
>>> 00007ff9`d40b5205 mov     dword ptr [rax],1
00007ff9`d40b520b nop
00007ff9`d40b520c nop
00007ff9`d40b520d nop
00007ff9`d40b520e mov     rcx,rsp
00007ff9`d40b5211 call    LINQPadQuery!UserQuery.SmallObject.Finalize+0x4e (00007ff9`d40b521e)
00007ff9`d40b5216 nop
00007ff9`d40b5217 nop
00007ff9`d40b5218 add     rsp,30h
00007ff9`d40b521c pop     rbp
00007ff9`d40b521d ret
00007ff9`d40b521e push    rbp
00007ff9`d40b521f sub     rsp,30h
00007ff9`d40b5223 mov     rbp,qword ptr [rcx+20h]
00007ff9`d40b5227 mov     qword ptr [rsp+20h],rbp
00007ff9`d40b522c lea     rbp,[rbp+30h]
00007ff9`d40b5230 mov     rcx,qword ptr [rbp+10h]
00007ff9`d40b5234 call    qword ptr [00007ff9`d36a4778]
00007ff9`d40b523a nop
00007ff9`d40b523b nop
00007ff9`d40b523c add     rsp,30h
00007ff9`d40b5240 pop     rbp
00007ff9`d40b5241 ret
```

11.   We close logging before exiting WinDbg:

```
0:000> .logclose
Closing open log file C:\ANETMDA-Dumps\Windows\x64\LINQPadD.log
```

Exercise PN6 (Linux)

- **Goal:** Learn how to diagnose heap leaks

- **Patterns:** Special Thread (.NET CLR); Object Distribution Anomaly (.NET Heap); Memory Leak (.NET Heap)

- **Commands:** dumpheap, eeheap, gchandles, finalizequeue

- \ANETMDA-Dumps\Exercise-PN6-Linux.pdf

Exercise PN6 (Linux)

Goal: Learn how to diagnose heap handle leaks.

Patterns: Special Thread (.NET CLR); Object Distribution Anomaly (.NET Heap); Memory Leak (.NET Heap).

Commands: dumpheap, eeheap, gchandles, finalizequeu

1.   Open \ANETMDA-Dumps\Linux\ApplicationK\core.ApplicationK.12997.dmp in LLDB:

```
/mnt/c/ANETMDA-Dumps/Linux/ApplicationK$ lldb -c core.ApplicationK.12997.dmp
bin/Release/net9.0/ApplicationK
Current symbol store settings:
-> Cache: /home/coredump/.dotnet/symbolcache
-> Server: https://msdl.microsoft.com/download/symbols/ Timeout: 4 RetryCount: 0
(lldb) target create "bin/Release/net9.0/ApplicationK" --core "core.ApplicationK.12997.dmp"
```

Core file '/mnt/c/ANETMDA-Dumps/Linux/ApplicationK/core.ApplicationK.12997.dmp' (x86_64) was
loaded.

2.   The process memory dump size is unexpectedly over 1GB, suggesting a managed heap leak. We check

managed heap statistics:

```
(lldb) dumpheap -stat
Statistics:
          MT  Count    TotalSize Class Name
7fc3577acbf0      1           24 System.Collections.Generic.StringEqualityComparer
7fc357840838      1           24 System.OrdinalCaseSensitiveComparer
7fc3577afe30      1           24
System.Collections.Generic.NonRandomizedStringEqualityComparer+OrdinalIgnoreCaseComparer
7fc357840c38      1           24 System.OrdinalIgnoreCaseComparer
7fc35785a0c0      1           24 ApplicationD.ClassMain
7fc35788dfb0      1           24 System.Text.EncoderReplacementFallback
7fc35788dc60      1           24 System.Text.DecoderReplacementFallback
7fc3578a79e0      1           24 System.Reflection.Missing
7fc3578a7b60      1           24 System.Type+<>c
7fc3578a84f0      1           24 System.Resources.ResourceManager+ResourceManagerMediator
7fc3578a8180      1           24 System.Resources.ManifestBasedResourceGroveler
7fc3578c6900      1           24 System.Resources.FastResourceComparer
7fc3578bc390      1           26 System.Globalization.CalendarId[]
7fc357845238      1           32 System.Collections.Generic.List<System.Char>
7fc35784bd18      1           32 System.Diagnostics.Tracing.ActivityTracker
7fc357852488      1           32 System.Collections.Generic.List<System.Func<System.Diagnostics.Tracing.EventSource>>
7fc357853d68      1           32
System.Collections.Generic.List<System.WeakReference<System.Diagnostics.Tracing.EventSource>>
7fc357859a88      1           32 System.Collections.Generic.List<System.String>
7fc3578a8288      1           32 System.Resources.ResourceManager+CultureNameResourceSetPair
7fc3578542f8      1           40 System.WeakReference<System.Diagnostics.Tracing.EventSource>[]
7fc35785ba98      1           40 System.Threading.ExecutionContext
7fc35787f7f0      1           40 System.Reflection.RuntimeModule
```

```
7fc3577afbd8      2        48 System.Collections.Generic.NonRandomizedStringEqualityComparer+OrdinalComparer
7fc357849f38      2        48 System.Diagnostics.Tracing.TraceLoggingEventHandleTable
7fc357853c78      2        48 System.WeakReference<System.Diagnostics.Tracing.EventSource>
7fc35787db08      1        48 System.Reflection.RuntimeAssembly
7fc35788d7d0      1        48 System.Text.UTF8Encoding+UTF8EncodingSealed
7fc3578a78b8      2        48 System.Type[]
7fc35787ae68      1        56 System.IO.BinaryReader
7fc357847d30      2        64 System.Char[]
7fc35787a810      1        64 System.Resources.RuntimeResourceSet
7fc357842bb0      2        64 System.Guid
7fc356804910      3        72 System.Object
7fc35784bad0      3        72 System.WeakReference<System.Diagnostics.Tracing.EventProvider>
7fc3577a6388      1        80 System.Collections.Generic.Dictionary<System.String, System.Object>
7fc357846de8      1        80 System.Collections.Generic.Dictionary<System.Char, System.String>
7fc357852f70      2        80 System.Func<System.Diagnostics.Tracing.EventSource>[]
7fc35784d488      1        80 System.Collections.Generic.Dictionary<System.Guid,
System.Diagnostics.Tracing.EventSource+OverrideEventProvider>
7fc35784bf88      1        80 System.Collections.Generic.Dictionary<System.String,
System.Diagnostics.Tracing.EventSource+OverrideEventProvider>
7fc3578a8568      1        80 System.Collections.Generic.Dictionary<System.String, System.Resources.ResourceSet>
7fc3578ba4b0      1        80 System.Collections.Generic.Dictionary<System.String, System.Globalization.CultureInfo>
7fc3578bcb70      1        80 System.Collections.Generic.Dictionary<System.String, System.Globalization.CultureData>
7fc3578c58a0      1        80 System.Collections.Generic.Dictionary<System.String, System.Resources.ResourceLocator>
7fc357856e78      1        96 System.Collections.Generic.Dictionary<System.String,
System.Diagnostics.Tracing.EventSource+OverrideEventProvider>+Entry[]
7fc3578799e8      1        96 System.Resources.ResourceManager
7fc3578bd880      1        96 System.Collections.Generic.Dictionary<System.String,
System.Globalization.CultureData>+Entry[]
7fc3578bdb40      1        96 System.Collections.Generic.Dictionary<System.String,
System.Globalization.CultureInfo>+Entry[]
7fc3578bfd48      1        96 System.Reflection.RuntimeAssembly+ManifestResourceStream
7fc3578c6cd0      1        96 System.Collections.Generic.Dictionary<System.String,
System.Resources.ResourceSet>+Entry[]
7fc3578c8c28      1       120 System.NullReferenceException
7fc35779e440      1       120 System.OutOfMemoryException
7fc35779e568      1       120 System.StackOverflowException
7fc35779e690      1       120 System.ExecutionEngineException
7fc35784a470      3       120 System.Diagnostics.Tracing.EventProviderImpl
7fc357856ba8      1       120 System.Collections.Generic.Dictionary<System.Guid,
System.Diagnostics.Tracing.EventSource+OverrideEventProvider>+Entry[]
7fc3578c7778      1       120 System.Collections.Generic.Dictionary<System.String,
System.Resources.ResourceLocator>+Entry[]
7fc35787a1d0      1       128 System.Resources.ResourceReader
7fc3578781a8      1       136 ApplicationD.CustomException
7fc3578bc9d0      1       160 System.Globalization.CalendarData
7fc357849d58      1       184 System.Diagnostics.Tracing.NativeRuntimeEventSource
7fc3578481d0      1       192 System.Collections.Generic.Dictionary<System.Char, System.String>+Entry[]
7fc3578433f8      3       192 System.Func<System.Diagnostics.Tracing.EventSource>
7fc35784abd8      3       192 System.Diagnostics.Tracing.EventPipeEventProvider
7fc3578a7550      3       192 System.Reflection.MemberFilter
7fc357849ff0      2       208 System.IntPtr[]
7fc3578bca70      1       208 System.Globalization.CalendarData[]
7fc35785a720      4       256 System.Threading.ThreadStart
7fc35785e768      2       272 System.IO.FileNotFoundException
7fc3578c7d60      4       288 System.SByte[]
7fc3577ab7d0      1       288 System.Collections.Generic.Dictionary<System.String, System.Object>+Entry[]
7fc3578b48a0      3       336 System.Globalization.CultureInfo
7fc35784b2e8      6       384 System.Diagnostics.Tracing.EventSource+OverrideEventProvider
7fc357854ec0      1       400 System.Diagnostics.Tracing.RuntimeEventSource
7fc3578590b8     17       920 System.String[]
7fc35680a160     29     1,160 System.RuntimeType
7fc3578bc1d0      3     1,344 System.Globalization.CultureData
7fc35785b620    134     8,576 System.Threading.Thread+StartHelper
7fc357742278     12     8,936 System.Object[]
7fc35779be30    199    38,794 System.String
7fc35785e968 50,000 1,600,000 ApplicationD.SmallObject
55b74dd3dc20 28,376 1,625,800 Free
7fc35779fc10 50,005 3,600,360 System.Threading.Thread
7fc357798d38 50,013 820,403,632 System.Int32[]
Total 178,895 objects, 827,296,980 bytes
```

Note: We see 50,000 *ApplicationD.SmallObject* objects and almost the same amount of *Int32* arrays and *System.Threading.Thread* objects. We check the object class:

```
(lldb) dumpmt 7fc35785e968
Canonical MethodTabl 00007FC35785E968
Module:              00007FC357857038
Name:                ApplicationD.SmallObject
mdToken:             0000000002000004
File:                /mnt/c/ANETMDA-Examples/ApplicationK/bin/Release/net9.0/ApplicationK.dll
AssemblyLoadContext: Default ALC - The managed instance of this context doesn't exist yet.
BaseSize:            0x20
ComponentSize:       0x0
DynamicStatics:      false
ContainsPointers:    true
Number of Methods:   6
Number of IFaces in IFaceMap: 0

(lldb) dumpclass 7fc35785e968
Class Name:          ApplicationD.SmallObject
mdToken:             0000000002000004
File:                /mnt/c/ANETMDA-Examples/ApplicationK/bin/Release/net9.0/ApplicationK.dll
Parent MethodTable:  00007fc356804910
Module:              00007fc357857038
Method Table:        00007fc35785e968
Canonical MethodTable: 00007fc35785e968
Class Attributes:    100001
NumInstanceFields:   2
NumStaticFields:     0
          MT    Field    Offset                 Type VT    Attr     Value Name
00007fc357798d38  4000003     8         System.Int32[]  0 instance       buffer
00007fc35779fc10  4000004    10    ....Threading.Thread  0 instance       thread
```

3.   We can calculate the average array size and dump all heap objects that satisfy the minimum size:

```
(lldb) p 820403632/50013
(int) $0 = 16403

(lldb) dumpheap -min 16000
      Address            MT         Size
[...]
    7f8375b93ff8    7fc357798d38      16,408
    7f8375b980d0    7fc357798d38      16,408
    7f8375b9c1a8    7fc357798d38      16,408
    7f8375ba0280    7fc357798d38      16,408
    7f8375ba4358    7fc357798d38      16,408
    7f8375ba8430    7fc357798d38      16,408
    7f8375bac508    7fc357798d38      16,408
    7f8375bb05e0    7fc357798d38      16,408
    7f8375bb46b8    7fc357798d38      16,408
    7f8375bb8790    7fc357798d38      16,408
    7f8375bbc868    7fc357798d38      16,408
    7f8375bc0940    7fc357798d38      16,408
    7f8375bc4a18    7fc357798d38      16,408
    7f8375bc8af0    7fc357798d38      16,408
    7f8375bccbc8    7fc357798d38      16,408
    7f8375bd0ca0    7fc357798d38      16,408
    7f8375bd4d78    7fc357798d38      16,408
```

```
7f8375bd8e50        7fc357798d38              16,408
7f8375bdcf40        7fc357798d38              16,408
7f8375be1018        7fc357798d38              16,408
7f8375be50f0        7fc357798d38              16,408
7f8375be91c8        7fc357798d38              16,408
7f8375bed2a0        7fc357798d38              16,408
7f8375bf1378        7fc357798d38              16,408
7f8375bf5450        7fc357798d38              16,408
7f8375bf9528        7fc357798d38              16,408

Statistics:
          MT   Count    TotalSize Class Name
7fc35779be30       1       28,242 System.String
7fc357798d38 50,000 820,400,000 System.Int32[]
Total 50,001 objects, 820,428,242 bytes

(lldb) dumpobj 7f8375bf9528
Name:        System.Int32[]
MethodTable: 00007fc357798d38
Canonical MethodTable: 00007fc357798d38
Tracked Type: false
Size:        16408(0x4018) bytes
Array:       Rank 1, Number of elements 4096, Type Int32
Fields:
None
```

4.   We can also dump all *ApplicationD.SmallObject* objects from the managed heap:

```
(lldb) dumpheap -type ApplicationD.SmallObject
         Address            MT    Size
[...]
    7f8375ba01c0    7fc35785e968              32
    7f8375ba4298    7fc35785e968              32
    7f8375ba8370    7fc35785e968              32
    7f8375bac448    7fc35785e968              32
    7f8375bb0520    7fc35785e968              32
    7f8375bb45f8    7fc35785e968              32
    7f8375bb86d0    7fc35785e968              32
    7f8375bbc7a8    7fc35785e968              32
    7f8375bc0880    7fc35785e968              32
    7f8375bc4958    7fc35785e968              32
    7f8375bc8a30    7fc35785e968              32
    7f8375bccb08    7fc35785e968              32
    7f8375bd0be0    7fc35785e968              32
    7f8375bd4cb8    7fc35785e968              32
    7f8375bd8d90    7fc35785e968              32
    7f8375bdce80    7fc35785e968              32
    7f8375be0f58    7fc35785e968              32
    7f8375be5030    7fc35785e968              32
    7f8375be9108    7fc35785e968              32
    7f8375bed1e0    7fc35785e968              32
    7f8375bf12b8    7fc35785e968              32
    7f8375bf5390    7fc35785e968              32
    7f8375bf9468    7fc35785e968              32
    7f8375bfd540    7fc35785e968              32

Statistics:
          MT  Count TotalSize Class Name
```

```
7fc35785e968    50,000 1,600,000 ApplicationD.SmallObject
Total 50,000 objects, 1,600,000 bytes
```

```
(lldb) dumpobj 7f8375bfd540
Name:           ApplicationD.SmallObject
MethodTable: 00007fc35785e968
Canonical MethodTable: 00007fc35785e968
Tracked Type: false
Size:           32(0x20) bytes
File:           /mnt/c/ANETMDA-Examples/ApplicationK/bin/Release/net9.0/ApplicationK.dll
Fields:
              MT    Field   Offset                 Type VT     Attr            Value Name
00007fc357798d38  4000003        8        System.Int32[]  0 instance 00007f8375400028 buffer
00007fc35779fc10  4000004       10   ....Threading.Thread  0 instance 00007f8375bfd560 thread
```

```
(lldb) dumpobj 00007f8375400028
Name:           System.Int32[]
MethodTable: 00007fc357798d38
Canonical MethodTable: 00007fc357798d38
Tracked Type: false
Size:           16408(0x4018) bytes
Array:          Rank 1, Number of elements 4096, Type Int32
Fields:
None
```

```
(lldb) dumpobj 00007f8375bfd560
Name:           System.Threading.Thread
MethodTable: 00007fc35779fc10
Canonical MethodTable: 00007fc35779fc10
Tracked Type: false
Size:           72(0x48) bytes
File:           /usr/share/dotnet/shared/Microsoft.NETCore.App/9.0.4/System.Private.CoreLib.dll
Fields:
              MT    Field   Offset                 Type VT     Attr            Value Name
00007fc35785ba98  4000c07        8   ....ExecutionContext  0 instance 0000000000000000 _executionContext
0000000000000000  4000c08       10   ...ronizationContext  0 instance 0000000000000000 _synchronizationContext
00007fc35779be30  4000c09       18         System.String  0 instance 0000000000000000 _name
00007fc35785b620  4000c0a       20   ...hread+StartHelper  0 instance 0000000000000000 _startHelper
00007fc357795170  4000c0b       28        System.IntPtr  1 instance 00007F82747B6DE0 _DONT_USE_InternalThread
00007fc3577474f0  4000c0c       30         System.Int32  1 instance                2 _priority
00007fc3577474f0  4000c0d       34         System.Int32  1 instance            49872 _managedThreadId
00007fc357743080  4000c0e       38       System.Boolean  1 instance                0 _mayNeedResetForThreadPool
00007fc3577474f0  4000c10        8         System.Int32  1   static                0
<OptimalMaxSpinWaitsPerSpinIteration>k__BackingField
0000000000000000  4000c11        8                       0   static 0000000000000000 s_asyncLocalPrincipal
00007fc357743080  4000c13        c       System.Boolean  1   static                0 s_isProcessorNumberReallyFast
00007fc35779fc10  4000c12       10   ....Threading.Thread  0 TLstatic  t_currentThread
    Thread static values (Thread:Value)
        32c5:00007f8344c09348
        32ca:00007f8344c170d8
```

Note: We see that every object has a thread object reference, and we have almost the same amount of *Thread* objects:

```
(lldb) clrthreads
[...]
XXXX 49987       0 00007F8274877950   31820 Preemptive 0000000000000000:0000000000000000 000055B74DD499A0 -00001 Ukn
XXXX 49988       0 00007F8274879420   31820 Preemptive 0000000000000000:0000000000000000 000055B74DD499A0 -00001 Ukn
XXXX 49989       0 00007F827487AEF0   31820 Preemptive 0000000000000000:0000000000000000 000055B74DD499A0 -00001 Ukn
XXXX 49990       0 00007F827487C9C0   31820 Preemptive 0000000000000000:0000000000000000 000055B74DD499A0 -00001 Ukn
XXXX 49991       0 00007F827487E490   31820 Preemptive 0000000000000000:0000000000000000 000055B74DD499A0 -00001 Ukn
XXXX 49992       0 00007F827487FF60   31820 Preemptive 0000000000000000:0000000000000000 000055B74DD499A0 -00001 Ukn
XXXX 49993       0 00007F8274881A30   31820 Preemptive 0000000000000000:0000000000000000 000055B74DD499A0 -00001 Ukn
XXXX 49994       0 00007F8274883500   31820 Preemptive 0000000000000000:0000000000000000 000055B74DD499A0 -00001 Ukn
XXXX 49995       0 00007F8274884FD0   31820 Preemptive 0000000000000000:0000000000000000 000055B74DD499A0 -00001 Ukn
```

```
XXXX 49996      0 00007F8274886AA0   31820 Preemptive  0000000000000000:0000000000000000 000055B74DD499A0 -00001 Ukn
XXXX 49997      0 00007F8274888570   31820 Preemptive  0000000000000000:0000000000000000 000055B74DD499A0 -00001 Ukn
XXXX 49998      0 00007F827488A040   31820 Preemptive  0000000000000000:0000000000000000 000055B74DD499A0 -00001 Ukn
XXXX 49999      0 00007F827488BB10   31820 Preemptive  0000000000000000:0000000000000000 000055B74DD499A0 -00001 Ukn
XXXX 50000      0 00007F827488D5E0   31820 Preemptive  0000000000000000:0000000000000000 000055B74DD499A0 -00001 Ukn
XXXX 50001      0 00007F827488F0B0   31820 Preemptive  0000000000000000:0000000000000000 000055B74DD499A0 -00001 Ukn
XXXX 50002      0 00007F8274890B80   31820 Preemptive  0000000000000000:0000000000000000 000055B74DD499A0 -00001 Ukn
XXXX 50003      0 00007F8274892650   31820 Preemptive  0000000000000000:0000000000000000 000055B74DD499A0 -00001 Ukn
XXXX 50004      0 00007F8274894120   31820 Preemptive  0000000000000000:0000000000000000 000055B74DD499A0 -00001 Ukn
XXXX 50005      0 00007F8274895BF0   31820 Preemptive  0000000000000000:0000000000000000 000055B74DD499A0 -00001 Ukn
XXXX 50006      0 00007F82748976C0   31820 Preemptive  0000000000000000:0000000000000000 000055B74DD499A0 -00001 Ukn
```

Note: We see an endless list of threads. The thread count is more than 50,000.

5.   We also check the GC heap, GC handles, and the finalizer queue:


```
(lldb) eeheap -gc
DATAS =
========================================
Number of GC Heaps: 1
----------------------------------------
Small object heap
         segment            begin          allocated           committed allocated size      committed size
generation 0:
    7f82bf587b60     7f8375000028       7f837521f9a8      7f8375400000 0x21f980 (2226560) 0x400000 (4194304)
generation 1:
    7f82bf587ab8     7f8374c00028       7f8374ffd660      7f8375000000 0x3fd638 (4183608) 0x400000 (4194304)
    7f82bf587c08     7f8375400028       7f8375404040      7f8375800000 0x4018 (16408)     0x400000 (4194304)
    7f82bf587cb0     7f8375800028       7f8375bfd5a8      7f8375c00000 0x3fd580 (4183424) 0x400000 (4194304)
generation 2:
    7f82bf57f580     7f8342000028       7f83423ffec0      7f8342400000 0x3ffe98 (4193944) 0x400000 (4194304)
    7f82bf57f628     7f8342400028       7f83427fd5a8      7f8342800000 0x3fd580 (4183424) 0x400000 (4194304)
    7f82bf57f6d0     7f8342800028       7f8342bfd978      7f8342c00000 0x3fd950 (4184400) 0x400000 (4194304)
[...]
    7f82bf587818     7f8373c00028       7f8373ffd640      7f8374000000 0x3fd618 (4183576) 0x400000 (4194304)
    7f82bf5878c0     7f8374000028       7f83743fd5a8      7f8374400000 0x3fd580 (4183424) 0x400000 (4194304)
    7f82bf587968     7f8374400028       7f83747fd5e0      7f8374800000 0x3fd5b8 (4183480) 0x400000 (4194304)
    7f82bf587a10     7f8374800028       7f8374bfbdf0      7f8374c00000 0x3fbdc8 (4177352) 0x400000 (4194304)
NonGC heap
         segment            begin          allocated           committed allocated size      committed size
    55b74dd6ba70     7fc3d1c23008       7fc3d1c25668      7fc3d1c33000 0x2660 (9824)       0x10000 (65536)
Large object heap
         segment            begin          allocated           committed allocated size      committed size
    7f82bf57f778     7f8342c00028       7f8342c00028      7f8342c01000                     0x1000 (4096)
Pinned object heap
         segment            begin          allocated           committed allocated size      committed size
    7f82bf57f040     7f8340000028       7f8340002020      7f8340011000 0x1ff8 (8184)       0x11000 (69632)
------------------------------
GC Allocated Heap Size:    Size: 0x314f8f80 (827297664) bytes.
GC Committed Heap Size:    Size: 0x31c22000 (834805760) bytes.
```


```
(lldb) gchandles
        Handle Type                Object    Size        Data Type
00007FC3CD841200 WeakShort   00007F83750AA3B8      72        System.Threading.Thread
00007FC3CD841208 WeakShort   00007F83750A62E0      72        System.Threading.Thread
[...]
00007FC3D47811B0 WeakShort   00007F8344C093F8      72        System.Threading.Thread
00007FC3D47811B8 WeakShort   00007F8344C09278      72        System.Threading.Thread
00007FC3D47811C0 WeakShort   00007F8344C09020      64        System.Diagnostics.Tracing.EventSource+OverrideEventProvider
00007FC3D47811C8 WeakShort   00007F8344C08B38     400        System.Diagnostics.Tracing.RuntimeEventSource
00007FC3D47811D0 WeakShort   00007F8344C08DF0      64        System.Diagnostics.Tracing.EventSource+OverrideEventProvider
00007FC3D47811D8 WeakShort   00007F8344C08768     184        System.Diagnostics.Tracing.NativeRuntimeEventSource
00007FC3D47811E0 WeakShort   00007F8344C08A40      64        System.Diagnostics.Tracing.EventSource+OverrideEventProvider
00007FC3D47811F0 WeakShort   00007F8344C170D8      72        System.Threading.Thread
00007FC3D47811F8 WeakShort   00007F8344C09348      72        System.Threading.Thread
00007FC3D4789270 WeakShort   00007F8346800048      72        System.Threading.Thread
00007FC3D4781208 Strong      00007F8344C0D868     136        ApplicationD.CustomException
00007FC3D4781220 Strong      00007F8344C0D868     136        ApplicationD.CustomException
00007FC3D4781228 Strong      00007F8344C0D700     136        System.IO.FileNotFoundException
00007FC3D4781230 Strong      00007F8344C094C8     136        System.IO.FileNotFoundException
00007FC3D4781238 Strong      00007F8344C094C8     136        System.IO.FileNotFoundException
```

```
00007FC3D4781390 Strong    00007F8344C09480      72                System.Threading.Thread
00007FC3D47813A0 Strong    00007F8344C09278      72                System.Threading.Thread
00007FC3D47813A8 Strong    00007F8344C09060      64                System.Diagnostics.Tracing.EventPipeEventProvider
00007FC3D47813B0 Strong    00007F8344C08E30      64                System.Diagnostics.Tracing.EventPipeEventProvider
00007FC3D47813B8 Strong    00007F8344C08A80      64                System.Diagnostics.Tracing.EventPipeEventProvider
00007FC3D47813C8 Strong    00007F8344C00178     120                System.ExecutionEngineException
00007FC3D47813D0 Strong    00007F8344C00100     120                System.StackOverflowException
00007FC3D47813D8 Strong    00007F8344C00088     120                System.OutOfMemoryException
00007FC3D47813E0 Strong    00007F8344C00028      96                System.Int32[]
00007FC3D47813E8 Strong    00007F8340000028    8184                System.Object[]
00007FC3D47813F0 Strong    00007F8344C170D8      72                System.Threading.Thread
00007FC3D47813F8 Strong    00007F8344C09348      72                System.Threading.Thread
00007FC3D4782568 Strong    00007F83428083A0     120                System.NullReferenceException
00007FC3D4782570 Strong    00007F83428083A0     120                System.NullReferenceException
00007FC3D47815F8 Pinned    00007F83428001F0      24                System.Object

Statistics:
              MT    Count    TotalSize Class Name
00007fc356804910        1           24 System.Object
00007fc357798d38        1           96 System.Int32[]
00007fc35779e690        1          120 System.ExecutionEngineException
00007fc35779e568        1          120 System.StackOverflowException
00007fc35779e440        1          120 System.OutOfMemoryException
00007fc357849d58        1          184 System.Diagnostics.Tracing.NativeRuntimeEventSource
00007fc35784b2e8        3          192 System.Diagnostics.Tracing.EventSource+OverrideEventProvider
00007fc35784abd8        3          192 System.Diagnostics.Tracing.EventPipeEventProvider
00007fc3578c8c28        2          240 System.NullReferenceException
00007fc3578781a8        2          272 ApplicationD.CustomException
00007fc357854ec0        1          400 System.Diagnostics.Tracing.RuntimeEventSource
00007fc35785e768        3          408 System.IO.FileNotFoundException
00007fc357742278        1         8184 System.Object[]
00007fc35779fc10      151        10872 System.Threading.Thread
Total 172 objects

Handles:
    Strong Handles:       19
    Pinned Handles:        1
    Weak Short Handles:   152
```

```
(lldb) finalizequeue
[...]
    7f83504409a8      7fc35785e968                32
    7f8350444a40      7fc35785e968                32
    7f8350448ad8      7fc35785e968                32
    7f835044cb70      7fc35785e968                32
    7f8350450c08      7fc35785e968                32
    7f8350454ca0      7fc35785e968                32

Statistics:
          MT  Count TotalSize Class Name
7fc357853c78      2        48 System.WeakReference<System.Diagnostics.Tracing.EventSource>
7fc35784bad0      3        72 System.WeakReference<System.Diagnostics.Tracing.EventProvider>
7fc357849d58      1       184 System.Diagnostics.Tracing.NativeRuntimeEventSource
7fc35784b2e8      6       384 System.Diagnostics.Tracing.EventSource+OverrideEventProvider
7fc357854ec0      1       400 System.Diagnostics.Tracing.RuntimeEventSource
7fc35785e968 49,999 1,599,968 ApplicationD.SmallObject
7fc35779fc10 50,005 3,600,360 System.Threading.Thread
Total 100,017 objects, 5,201,416 bytes
```

Note: We have the large number of objects in the finalizer queue because the finalizer thread is hanging due to an exception in the *SmallObject Finalize* method. We can see it by examining the finalizer thread stack trace and its execution residue:

```
(lldb) bt all
* thread #1, name = 'ApplicationK', stop reason = signal SIGSTOP
  * frame #0: 0x00007fc3d64aa00c libpthread.so.0`__pthread_cond_wait at futex-internal.h:88
    frame #1: 0x00007fc3d64a9ff1 libpthread.so.0`__pthread_cond_wait at pthread_cond_wait.c:502
    frame #2: 0x00007fc3d64a9f30 libpthread.so.0`__pthread_cond_wait(cond=0x000055b74dd2f348, mutex=0x000055b74dd2f320) at pthread_cond_wait.c:655
    frame #3: 0x00007fc3d5e1a172 libcoreclr.so`CorUnix::CPalSynchronizationManager::ThreadNativeWait(CorUnix::_ThreadNativeWaitData*, unsigned int,
CorUnix::ThreadWakeupReason*, unsigned int*) + 354
    frame #4: 0x00007fc3d5e19d7a libcoreclr.so`CorUnix::CPalSynchronizationManager::BlockThread(CorUnix::CPalThread*, unsigned int, bool, bool,
CorUnix::ThreadWakeupReason*, unsigned int*) + 378
```

```
    frame #5: 0x00007fc3d5e1e952 libcoreclr.so`CorUnix::InternalWaitForMultipleObjectsEx(CorUnix::CPalThread*, unsigned int, void* const*, int, unsigned int,
int, int) + 1906
    frame #6: 0x00007fc3d5e1ec03 libcoreclr.so`WaitForMultipleObjectsEx + 83
    frame #7: 0x00007fc3d5a7b255 libcoreclr.so`Thread::DoAppropriateWaitWorker(int, void**, int, unsigned int, WaitMode, void*) + 1429
    frame #8: 0x00007fc3d5a76424 libcoreclr.so`Thread::DoAppropriateWait(int, void**, int, unsigned int, WaitMode, PendingSync*) + 228
    frame #9: 0x00007fc3d5a762ec libcoreclr.so`Thread::JoinEx(unsigned int, WaitMode) + 108
    frame #10: 0x00007fc3d5ac7c6c libcoreclr.so`ThreadNative::DoJoin(ThreadBaseObject*, int) + 220
    frame #11: 0x00007fc3d5ac679c libcoreclr.so`ThreadNative::Join(ThreadBaseObject*, int) + 268
    frame #12: 0x00007fc356a5854c
    frame #13: 0x00007fc3577b189b
    frame #14: 0x00007fc3d5c72e04 libcoreclr.so`CallDescrWorkerInternal + 124
    frame #15: 0x00007fc3d5ab111c libcoreclr.so`MethodDescCallSite::CallTargetWorker(unsigned long const*, unsigned long*, int) + 1708
    frame #16: 0x00007fc3d59980c4 libcoreclr.so`RunMain(MethodDesc*, short, int*, PtrArray**) + 836
    frame #17: 0x00007fc3d599853c libcoreclr.so`Assembly::ExecuteMainMethod(PtrArray**, int) + 460
    frame #18: 0x00007fc3d59c1b34 libcoreclr.so`CorHost2::ExecuteAssembly(unsigned int, char16_t const*, int, char16_t const**, unsigned int*) + 740
    frame #19: 0x00007fc3d5984340 libcoreclr.so`coreclr_execute_assembly + 144
    frame #20: 0x00007fc3d5f4c301 libhostpolicy.so`run_app_for_context(hostpolicy_context_t const&, int, char const**) + 1089
    frame #21: 0x00007fc3d5f4d3f9 libhostpolicy.so`corehost_main + 345
    frame #22: 0x00007fc3d5f8c685 libhostfxr.so`fx_muxer_t::handle_exec_host_command(std::__cxx11::basic_string<char, std::char_traits<char>,
std::allocator<char> > const&, host_startup_info_t const&, std::__cxx11::basic_string<char, std::char_traits<char>, std::allocator<char> > const&,
std::unordered_map<known_options, std::vector<std::__cxx11::basic_string<char, std::char_traits<char>, std::allocator<char> >,
std::allocator<std::__cxx11::basic_string<char, std::char_traits<char>, std::allocator<char> > > >, known_options_hash, std::equal_to<known_options>,
std::allocator<std::pair<known_options const, std::vector<std::__cxx11::basic_string<char, std::char_traits<char>, std::allocator<char> >,
std::allocator<std::__cxx11::basic_string<char, std::char_traits<char>, std::allocator<char> > > > > > const&, int, char const**, int, host_mode_t, bool,
char*, int, int*) + 1477
    frame #23: 0x00007fc3d5f8b67d libhostfxr.so`fx_muxer_t::execute(std::__cxx11::basic_string<char, std::char_traits<char>, std::allocator<char> >, int, char
const**, host_startup_info_t const&, char*, int, int*) + 765
    frame #24: 0x00007fc3d5f855f2 libhostfxr.so`hostfxr_main_startupinfo + 242
    frame #25: 0x000055b74906a21b ApplicationK`exe_start(int, char const**) + 1131
    frame #26: 0x000055b74906a53f ApplicationK`main + 175
    frame #27: 0x00007fc3d5fdf09b libc.so.6`__libc_start_main(main=(ApplicationK`main), argc=1, argv=0x00007ffc03c4fb28, init=<unavailable>,
fini=<unavailable>, rtld_fini=<unavailable>, stack_end=0x00007ffc03c4fb18) at libc-start.c:308
    frame #28: 0x000055b749069399 ApplicationK`_start + 41
  thread #2, stop reason = signal 0
    frame #0: 0x00007fc3d60a96f9 libc.so.6`__GI___poll(fds=0x00007fc3d57a4d98, nfds=1, timeout=-1) at poll.c:29
    frame #1: 0x00007fc3d5e1c800 libcoreclr.so`CorUnix::CPalSynchronizationManager::ReadBytesFromProcessPipe(int, unsigned char*, int) + 288
    frame #2: 0x00007fc3d5e1be63 libcoreclr.so`CorUnix::CPalSynchronizationManager::WorkerThread(void*) + 147
    frame #3: 0x00007fc3d5e259ae libcoreclr.so`CorUnix::CPalThread::ThreadEntry(void*) + 510
    frame #4: 0x00007fc3d64a3fa3 libpthread.so.0`start_thread(arg=<unavailable>) at pthread_create.c:486
    frame #5: 0x00007fc3d60b406f libc.so.6`__GI___clone at clone.S:95
  thread #3, stop reason = signal 0
    frame #0: 0x00007fc3d60a96f9 libc.so.6`__GI___poll(fds=0x00007fc348000f20, nfds=1, timeout=-1) at poll.c:29
    frame #1: 0x00007fc3d5d23d5c libcoreclr.so`ds_ipc_poll(_DiagnosticsIpcPollHandle*, unsigned long, unsigned int, void (*)(char const*, unsigned int)) + 172
    frame #2: 0x00007fc3d5c9df4b libcoreclr.so`ds_ipc_stream_factory_get_next_available_stream(void (*)(char const*, unsigned int)) + 731
    frame #3: 0x00007fc3d5ca2ca6 libcoreclr.so`server_thread(void*) + 198
    frame #4: 0x00007fc3d5e259ae libcoreclr.so`CorUnix::CPalThread::ThreadEntry(void*) + 510
    frame #5: 0x00007fc3d64a3fa3 libpthread.so.0`start_thread(arg=<unavailable>) at pthread_create.c:486
    frame #6: 0x00007fc3d60b406f libc.so.6`__GI___clone at clone.S:95
  thread #4, stop reason = signal 0
    frame #0: 0x00007fc3d64add0e libpthread.so.0`__libc_open64(file="/tmp/clr-debug-pipe-12997-20364698-in", oflag=0) at open64.c:48
    frame #1: 0x00007fc3d5d2377f libcoreclr.so`TwoWayPipe::WaitForConnection() + 31
    frame #2: 0x00007fc3d5d1e797 libcoreclr.so`DbgTransportSession::TransportWorker() + 183
    frame #3: 0x00007fc3d5d1d905 libcoreclr.so`DbgTransportSession::TransportWorkerStatic(void*) + 37
    frame #4: 0x00007fc3d5e259ae libcoreclr.so`CorUnix::CPalThread::ThreadEntry(void*) + 510
    frame #5: 0x00007fc3d64a3fa3 libpthread.so.0`start_thread(arg=<unavailable>) at pthread_create.c:486
    frame #6: 0x00007fc3d60b406f libc.so.6`__GI___clone at clone.S:95
  thread #5, stop reason = signal 0
    frame #0: 0x00007fc3d64aa00c libpthread.so.0`__pthread_cond_wait at futex-internal.h:88
    frame #1: 0x00007fc3d64a9ff1 libpthread.so.0`__pthread_cond_wait at pthread_cond_wait.c:502
    frame #2: 0x00007fc3d64a9f30 libpthread.so.0`__pthread_cond_wait(cond=0x000055b74dd5ee18, mutex=0x000055b74dd5edf0) at pthread_cond_wait.c:655
    frame #3: 0x00007fc3d5e1a172 libcoreclr.so`CorUnix::CPalSynchronizationManager::ThreadNativeWait(CorUnix::_ThreadNativeWaitData*, unsigned int,
CorUnix::ThreadWakeupReason*, unsigned int*) + 354
    frame #4: 0x00007fc3d5e19d7a libcoreclr.so`CorUnix::CPalSynchronizationManager::BlockThread(CorUnix::CPalThread*, unsigned int, bool, bool,
CorUnix::ThreadWakeupReason*, unsigned int*) + 378
    frame #5: 0x00007fc3d5e1e952 libcoreclr.so`CorUnix::InternalWaitForMultipleObjectsEx(CorUnix::CPalThread*, unsigned int, void* const*, int, unsigned int,
int, int) + 1906
    frame #6: 0x00007fc3d5e1ec03 libcoreclr.so`WaitForMultipleObjectsEx + 83
    frame #7: 0x00007fc3d5d1c0ad libcoreclr.so`DebuggerRCThread::MainLoop() + 269
    frame #8: 0x00007fc3d5d1bf28 libcoreclr.so`DebuggerRCThread::ThreadProc() + 312
    frame #9: 0x00007fc3d5d1bc25 libcoreclr.so`DebuggerRCThread::ThreadProcStatic(void*) + 53
    frame #10: 0x00007fc3d5e259ae libcoreclr.so`CorUnix::CPalThread::ThreadEntry(void*) + 510
    frame #11: 0x00007fc3d64a3fa3 libpthread.so.0`start_thread(arg=<unavailable>) at pthread_create.c:486
    frame #12: 0x00007fc3d60b406f libc.so.6`__GI___clone at clone.S:95
  thread #6, stop reason = signal 0
    frame #0: 0x00007fc3d64aa00c libpthread.so.0`__pthread_cond_wait at futex-internal.h:88
    frame #1: 0x00007fc3d64a9ff1 libpthread.so.0`__pthread_cond_wait at pthread_cond_wait.c:502
    frame #2: 0x00007fc3d64a9f30 libpthread.so.0`__pthread_cond_wait(cond=0x000055b74dd6a508, mutex=0x000055b74dd6a4e0) at pthread_cond_wait.c:655
    frame #3: 0x00007fc3d5e1a172 libcoreclr.so`CorUnix::CPalSynchronizationManager::ThreadNativeWait(CorUnix::_ThreadNativeWaitData*, unsigned int,
CorUnix::ThreadWakeupReason*, unsigned int*) + 354
    frame #4: 0x00007fc3d5e19d7a libcoreclr.so`CorUnix::CPalSynchronizationManager::BlockThread(CorUnix::CPalThread*, unsigned int, bool, bool,
CorUnix::ThreadWakeupReason*, unsigned int*) + 378
    frame #5: 0x00007fc3d5e1f089 libcoreclr.so`SleepEx + 153
    frame #6: 0x00007fc3d5a7c988 libcoreclr.so`Thread::UserSleep(int) + 200
    frame #7: 0x00007fc3d5ac93eb libcoreclr.so`ThreadNative_Sleep + 91
    frame #8: 0x00007fc356a5804a
    frame #9: 0x00007fc3577b2706
    frame #10: 0x00007fc35695cc7c
    frame #11: 0x00007fc3d5c72e04 libcoreclr.so`CallDescrWorkerInternal + 124
    frame #12: 0x00007fc3d5ab0a05 libcoreclr.so`DispatchCallSimple(unsigned long*, unsigned int, unsigned long, unsigned int) + 245
    frame #13: 0x00007fc3d5aed011 libcoreclr.so`FinalizerThread::FinalizeAllObjects() + 145
    frame #14: 0x00007fc3d5aed249 libcoreclr.so`FinalizerThread::FinalizerThreadWorker(void*) + 185
    frame #15: 0x00007fc3d5a7ec08 libcoreclr.so`ManagedThreadBase_DispatchOuter(ManagedThreadCallState*) + 344
    frame #16: 0x00007fc3d5a7f10d libcoreclr.so`ManagedThreadBase::FinalizerBase(void (*)(void*)) + 45
    frame #17: 0x00007fc3d5aed4b8 libcoreclr.so`FinalizerThread::FinalizerThreadStart(void*) + 88
    frame #18: 0x00007fc3d5e259ae libcoreclr.so`CorUnix::CPalThread::ThreadEntry(void*) + 510
    frame #19: 0x00007fc3d64a3fa3 libpthread.so.0`start_thread(arg=<unavailable>) at pthread_create.c:486
    frame #20: 0x00007fc3d60b406f libc.so.6`__GI___clone at clone.S:95
  thread #7, stop reason = signal 0
```

```
      frame #0: 0x00007fc3d64aa00c libpthread.so.0`__pthread_cond_wait at futex-internal.h:88
      frame #1: 0x00007fc3d64a9ff1 libpthread.so.0`__pthread_cond_wait at pthread_cond_wait.c:502
      frame #2: 0x00007fc3d64a9f30 libpthread.so.0`__pthread_cond_wait(cond=0x000055b74dd9bfc8, mutex=0x000055b74dd9bfa0) at pthread_cond_wait.c:655
      frame #3: 0x00007fc3d5e1a172 libcoreclr.so`CorUnix::CPalSynchronizationManager::ThreadNativeWait(CorUnix::_ThreadNativeWaitData*, unsigned int,
CorUnix::ThreadWakeupReason*, unsigned int*) + 354
      frame #4: 0x00007fc3d5e19d7a libcoreclr.so`CorUnix::CPalSynchronizationManager::BlockThread(CorUnix::CPalThread*, unsigned int, bool, bool,
CorUnix::ThreadWakeupReason*, unsigned int*) + 378
      frame #5: 0x00007fc3d5e1f089 libcoreclr.so`SleepEx + 153
      frame #6: 0x00007fc3d5a7c988 libcoreclr.so`Thread::UserSleep(int) + 200
      frame #7: 0x00007fc3d5ac93eb libcoreclr.so`ThreadNative_Sleep + 91
      frame #8: 0x00007fc356a5804a
      frame #9: 0x00007fc3577b1af8
      frame #10: 0x00007fc3d5c72e04 libcoreclr.so`CallDescrWorkerInternal + 124
      frame #11: 0x00007fc3d5ab0a05 libcoreclr.so`DispatchCallSimple(unsigned long*, unsigned int, unsigned long, unsigned int) + 245
      frame #12: 0x00007fc3d5ac66c2 libcoreclr.so`ThreadNative::KickOffThread_Worker(void*) + 146
      frame #13: 0x00007fc3d5a7ec08 libcoreclr.so`ManagedThreadBase_DispatchOuter(ManagedThreadCallState*) + 344
      frame #14: 0x00007fc3d5a7f0bd libcoreclr.so`ManagedThreadBase::KickOff(void (*)(void*), void*) + 45
      frame #15: 0x00007fc3d5ac67dc libcoreclr.so`ThreadNative::KickOffThread(void*) + 252
      frame #16: 0x00007fc3d5e259ae libcoreclr.so`CorUnix::CPalThread::ThreadEntry(void*) + 510
      frame #17: 0x00007fc3d64a3fa3 libpthread.so.0`start_thread(arg=<unavailable>) at pthread_create.c:486
      frame #18: 0x00007fc3d60b406f libc.so.6`__GI___clone at clone.S:95
   thread #8, stop reason = signal 0
      frame #0: 0x00007fc3d64aa00c libpthread.so.0`__pthread_cond_wait at futex-internal.h:88
      frame #1: 0x00007fc3d64a9ff1 libpthread.so.0`__pthread_cond_wait at pthread_cond_wait.c:502
      frame #2: 0x00007fc3d64a9f30 libpthread.so.0`__pthread_cond_wait(cond=0x000055b74dd9f668, mutex=0x000055b74dd9f640) at pthread_cond_wait.c:655
      frame #3: 0x00007fc3d5e1a172 libcoreclr.so`CorUnix::CPalSynchronizationManager::ThreadNativeWait(CorUnix::_ThreadNativeWaitData*, unsigned int,
CorUnix::ThreadWakeupReason*, unsigned int*) + 354
      frame #4: 0x00007fc3d5e19d7a libcoreclr.so`CorUnix::CPalSynchronizationManager::BlockThread(CorUnix::CPalThread*, unsigned int, bool, bool,
CorUnix::ThreadWakeupReason*, unsigned int*) + 378
      frame #5: 0x00007fc3d5e1f089 libcoreclr.so`SleepEx + 153
      frame #6: 0x00007fc3d5a7c988 libcoreclr.so`Thread::UserSleep(int) + 200
      frame #7: 0x00007fc3d5ac93eb libcoreclr.so`ThreadNative_Sleep + 91
      frame #8: 0x00007fc356a5804a
      frame #9: 0x00007fc3577b1dea
      frame #10: 0x00007fc3d5c72e04 libcoreclr.so`CallDescrWorkerInternal + 124
      frame #11: 0x00007fc3d5ab0a05 libcoreclr.so`DispatchCallSimple(unsigned long*, unsigned int, unsigned long, unsigned int) + 245
      frame #12: 0x00007fc3d5ac66c2 libcoreclr.so`ThreadNative::KickOffThread_Worker(void*) + 146
      frame #13: 0x00007fc3d5a7ec08 libcoreclr.so`ManagedThreadBase_DispatchOuter(ManagedThreadCallState*) + 344
      frame #14: 0x00007fc3d5a7f0bd libcoreclr.so`ManagedThreadBase::KickOff(void (*)(void*), void*) + 45
      frame #15: 0x00007fc3d5ac67dc libcoreclr.so`ThreadNative::KickOffThread(void*) + 252
      frame #16: 0x00007fc3d5e259ae libcoreclr.so`CorUnix::CPalThread::ThreadEntry(void*) + 510
      frame #17: 0x00007fc3d64a3fa3 libpthread.so.0`start_thread(arg=<unavailable>) at pthread_create.c:486
      frame #18: 0x00007fc3d60b406f libc.so.6`__GI___clone at clone.S:95
(lldb) thread select 6
* thread #6, stop reason = signal 0
     frame #0: 0x00007fc3d64aa00c libpthread.so.0`__pthread_cond_wait at futex-internal.h:88

(lldb) dso
OS Thread Id: 0x32ca (6)
         SP/REG          Object Name
     7fc3d3648eb8     7f83428083a0 System.NullReferenceException
     7fc3d3648f10     7f83428083a0 System.NullReferenceException
     7fc3d3649130     7f83428083a0 System.NullReferenceException
     7fc3d364d8b8     7f83428083a0 System.NullReferenceException
     7fc3d364d8c8     7f8344c12f68 ApplicationD.SmallObject
     7fc3d364d8f0     7f8344c170d8 System.Threading.Thread
     7fc3d364d950     7f8344c12f68 ApplicationD.SmallObject
     7fc3d364f010     7f8375bccb08 ApplicationD.SmallObject
     7fc3d364f018     7f8375bd4cb8 ApplicationD.SmallObject
     7fc3d364f020     7f8375bdce80 ApplicationD.SmallObject
     7fc3d364f028     7f8375be5030 ApplicationD.SmallObject
     7fc3d364f030     7f8375bed1e0 ApplicationD.SmallObject
     7fc3d364f038     7f8375bf5390 ApplicationD.SmallObject
     7fc3d364f040     7f8375bfd540 ApplicationD.SmallObject
     7fc3d364f048     7f8375bc0880 ApplicationD.SmallObject
     7fc3d364f050     7f8344c08d88 System.Diagnostics.Tracing.EventSource+OverrideEventProvider
     7fc3d364f058     7f8344c08df0 System.Diagnostics.Tracing.EventSource+OverrideEventProvider
     7fc3d364f060     7f8344c08cc8 System.Diagnostics.Tracing.TraceLoggingEventHandleTable
     7fc3d364f068     7f8344c08af8 System.WeakReference<System.Diagnostics.Tracing.EventSource>[]
     7fc3d364f070     7f8344c08fa8 System.Collections.Generic.Dictionary<System.Guid,
System.Diagnostics.Tracing.EventSource+OverrideEventProvider>+Entry[]
     7fc3d364f090     7f8342800028 Free

(lldb) ip2md 0x00007fc356a5804a
MethodDesc:      00007fc35779f338
Method Name:         System.Threading.Thread.Sleep(Int32)
Class:               00007fc35779fc10
MethodTable:         00007fc35779fc10
```

237

```
mdToken:                0000000006003AE5
Module:                 00007fc356804000
IsJitted:               yes
Current CodeAddr:       00007fc356a58010
Version History:
  ILCodeVersion:        0000000000000000
  ReJIT ID:             0
  IL Addr:              00007fc356f1ef18
     CodeAddr:             00007fc356a58010  (ReadyToRun)
     NativeCodeVersion:    0000000000000000
Source file:  /_/src/libraries/System.Private.CoreLib/src/System/Threading/Thread.cs @ 368

(lldb) ip2md 0x00007fc3577b2706
MethodDesc:    00007fc35785e910
Method Name:            ApplicationD.SmallObject.Finalize()
Class:                  00007fc35785e968
MethodTable:            00007fc35785e968
mdToken:                0000000006000006
Module:                 00007fc357857038
IsJitted:               yes
Current CodeAddr:       00007fc3577b26a0
Version History:
  ILCodeVersion:        0000000000000000
  ReJIT ID:             0
  IL Addr:              00007fc3d47902d0
     CodeAddr:             00007fc3577b26a0  (QuickJitted)
     NativeCodeVersion:    0000000000000000
Source file:  /mnt/c/ANETMDA-Examples/ApplicationK/Program.cs @ 46

(lldb) ip2md 0x00007fc35695cc7c
MethodDesc:    00007fc35785ac30
Method Name:            System.GC.RunFinalizers()
Class:                  00007fc35785b3e8
MethodTable:            00007fc35785b3e8
mdToken:                00000000060004E0
Module:                 00007fc356804000
IsJitted:               yes
Current CodeAddr:       00007fc35695cbf0
Version History:
  ILCodeVersion:        0000000000000000
  ReJIT ID:             0
  IL Addr:              00007fc356e67e3c
     CodeAddr:             00007fc35695cbf0  (ReadyToRun)
     NativeCodeVersion:    0000000000000000
Source file:  /_/src/coreclr/System.Private.CoreLib/src/System/GC.CoreCLR.cs @ 318

(lldb) clrstack
OS Thread Id: 0x32ca (6)
        Child SP          IP Call Site
00007FC3D3648C68 00007fc3d64aa00c [InlinedCallFrame: 00007fc3d3648c68]
00007FC3D3648C68 00007fc356a5803b [InlinedCallFrame: 00007fc3d3648c68]
00007FC3D3648C50 00007FC356A5803B System.Threading.Thread.Sleep(Int32) [/_/src/libraries/System.Private.CoreLib/src/System/Threading/Thread.cs @ 368]
00007FC3D3648CF0 00007FC3577B2706 ApplicationD.SmallObject.Finalize() [/mnt/c/ANETMDA-Examples/ApplicationK/Program.cs @ 46]
00007FC3D3648E50 00007fc3d5baade3 [InlinedCallFrame: 00007fc3d3648e50]
00007FC3D3648E50 00007fc356aa6ed7 [InlinedCallFrame: 00007fc3d3648e50]
00007FC3D3648E10 00007FC356AA6ED7 System.Runtime.EH.DispatchEx(System.Runtime.StackFrameIterator ByRef, ExInfo ByRef)
[/_/src/coreclr/nativeaot/Runtime.Base/src/System/Runtime/ExceptionHandling.cs @ 928]
00007FC3D3648F50 00007FC356AA6582 System.Runtime.EH.RhThrowHwEx(UInt32, ExInfo ByRef)
[/_/src/coreclr/nativeaot/Runtime.Base/src/System/Runtime/ExceptionHandling.cs @ 619]
00007FC3D364BBF0 00007fc3d5c72e04 [FaultingExceptionFrame: 00007fc3d364bbf0]
00007FC3D364D8B0 00007FC3577B26C6 ApplicationD.SmallObject.Finalize() [/mnt/c/ANETMDA-Examples/ApplicationK/Program.cs @ 41]
00007FC3D364D8E0 00007FC35695CC7C System.GC.RunFinalizers() [/_/src/coreclr/System.Private.CoreLib/src/System/GC.CoreCLR.cs @ 317]
00007FC3D364DD10 00007fc3d5c72e04 [DebuggerU2MCatchHandlerFrame: 00007fc3d364dd10]
```

Mechanisms (Memory Leak)

Unbounded Container → Memory Leak

239

Exercise PN7 (Windows)

- **Goal:** Learn how to recognize and analyze heap corruption

- **Patterns:** Regular Data; Dynamic Memory Corruption (Managed Heap)

- **Commands:** .formats, !VerifyHeap, !ListNearObj

- \ANETMDA-Dumps\Exercise-PN7-Windows.pdf

Exercise PN7 (Windows)

Goal: Learn how to recognize and analyze heap corruption.

Patterns: Regular Data; Dynamic Memory Corruption (Managed Heap).

Commands: .formats, !VerifyHeap, !ListNearObj

1.   Launch WinDbg.

2.   Open \ANETMDA-Dumps\Windows\x64\LINQPad8.exe.4976.dmp

3.   We get the dump file loaded:

```
Microsoft (R) Windows Debugger Version 10.0.27829.1001 AMD64
Copyright (c) Microsoft Corporation. All rights reserved.


Loading Dump File [C:\ANETMDA-Dumps\Windows\x64\LINQPad8.exe.4976.dmp]
User Mini Dump File with Full Memory: Only application data is available


************* Path validation summary **************
Response                        Time (ms)     Location
Deferred                                      srv*
Symbol search path is: srv*
Executable search path is:
Windows 10 Version 22000 MP (4 procs) Free x64
Product: WinNt, suite: SingleUserTS
Edition build lab: 22000.1.amd64fre.co_release.210604-1628
Debug session time: Tue Apr 29 08:20:11.000 2025 (UTC + 1:00)
System Uptime: 0 days 0:27:07.884
Process Uptime: 0 days 0:01:41.000
........................................................
........................................................

This dump file has an exception of interest stored in it.
The stored exception information can be accessed via .ecxr
```
```
(1370.420): Access violation - code c0000005 (first/second chance not available)
```
```
For analysis of this file, run !analyze -v
coreclr!MethodTable::GetFlag [inlined in coreclr!WKS::gc_heap::plan_phase+0x578]:
00007ffe`e135bd28 mov        eax,dword ptr [rcx]      ds:00620075`00670070=????????
```

Open a log file using **.logopen** command and load the SOS extension if necessary:

```
0:000> .logopen C:\ANETMDA-Dumps\Windows\x64\LINQPadE.log
Opened log file 'C:\ANETMDA-Dumps\Windows\x64\LINQPadE.log'

0:000> .unload sos
Unloading sos extension DLL

0:000> .load C:\Users\dmitr\.dotnet\sos\sos.dll
```

Note: The WinDbg output may be slightly different on your system if you have a different WinDbg version, a different SOS extension version, you don't have .NET 9 installed, or you have a .NET version different from version 9.0.4 that was on a virtual machine where all the dumps were saved.

4. Verify the correctness of all stack traces:

```
0:000> ~*kL
```

```
.  0  Id: 1370.420 Suspend: 0 Teb: 0000002a`8b0f1000 Unfrozen
 # Child-SP          RetAddr               Call Site
00 (Inline Function) --------`--------     coreclr!MethodTable::GetFlag
01 (Inline Function) --------`--------     coreclr!MethodTable::HasComponentSize
02 (Inline Function) --------`--------     coreclr!WKS::my_get_size+0x8
03 0000002a`8b2fc9a0 00007ffe`e1357ede     coreclr!WKS::gc_heap::plan_phase+0x578
04 0000002a`8b2fcda0 00007ffe`e1354ea4     coreclr!WKS::gc_heap::gc1+0x6a
05 (Inline Function) --------`--------     coreclr!GCToOSInterface::GetLowPrecisionTimeStamp+0x5
06 0000002a`8b2fcdf0 00007ffe`e1357d16     coreclr!WKS::gc_heap::garbage_collect+0x1a0
07 0000002a`8b2fce40 00007ffe`e15e2660     coreclr!WKS::GCHeap::GarbageCollectGeneration+0x13e
08 0000002a`8b2fcea0 00007ffe`e152fc0e     coreclr!WKS::GCHeap::GarbageCollect+0x110
09 0000002a`8b2fcee0 00007ffe`e06fbae3     coreclr!GCInterface_Collect+0x5e
0a 0000002a`8b2fcf40 00007ffe`821884d9     System_Private_CoreLib!System.GC.Collect+0x53
0b 0000002a`8b2fd010 00007ffe`8218834b     LINQPadQuery!UserQuery.ClassMain.Main+0x119
0c 0000002a`8b2fd070 00007ffe`82183b0c     LINQPadQuery!UserQuery.Main+0x4b
0d 0000002a`8b2fd0b0 00007ffe`8218023f     LINQPad_Runtime!LINQPad.ExecutionModel.ClrQueryRunner.Run+0x1dec
0e 0000002a`8b2fda00 00007ffe`8190369a     LINQPad_Runtime!LINQPad.ExecutionModel.Server.RunQuery+0x21f
0f 0000002a`8b2fdce0 00007ffe`819031c2     LINQPad_Runtime!LINQPad.ExecutionModel.Server.PrepareAndRunQuery+0x3ea
10 0000002a`8b2fde20 00007ffe`819030ec     LINQPad_Runtime!LINQPad.ExecutionModel.Server.<ExecuteClrQuery>b__147_0+0x52
11 0000002a`8b2fde60 00007ffe`818adc70     LINQPad_Runtime!LINQPad.ExecutionModel.SyncPCQ.<>c__DisplayClass14_0.<Enqueue>b__0+0x4c
12 0000002a`8b2fdeb0 00007ffe`818ad9be     LINQPad_Runtime!LINQPad.ExecutionModel.SyncPCQ.Consume+0x100
13 0000002a`8b2fdf30 00007ffe`818a659f     LINQPad_Runtime!LINQPad.ExecutionModel.SyncPCQ.Start+0x2ee
14 0000002a`8b2fe030 00007ffe`818a604b     LINQPad_Runtime!LINQPad.ExecutionModel.ProcessServer.TryRun+0x4cf
15 0000002a`8b2fe1f0 00007ffe`818a5fd4     LINQPad_Runtime!LINQPad.ExecutionModel.ProcessServer.Run+0x3b
16 0000002a`8b2fe240 00007ffe`818a56f3     LINQPad_Runtime!LINQPad.RuntimeLoader.Run+0x84
17 0000002a`8b2fe290 00007ffe`818a566c     LINQPad_Runtime!LINQPad.RuntimeLoader.Start+0x43
18 0000002a`8b2fe310 00007ffe`e1442eb3     LINQPad_Runtime!LINQPad.EntryPoint.Main+0x4c
19 0000002a`8b2fe360 00007ffe`e1325559     coreclr!CallDescrWorkerInternal+0x83
1a 0000002a`8b2fe3a0 00007ffe`e088e325     coreclr!RuntimeMethodHandle::InvokeMethod+0x3a9
1b 0000002a`8b2fe6d0 00007ffe`e088dc2b     System_Private_CoreLib!System.Reflection.MethodBaseInvoker.InvokeDirectByRefWithFewArgs+0xb5
1c 0000002a`8b2fe750 00007ffe`e089f910     System_Private_CoreLib!System.Reflection.MethodBaseInvoker.InvokeWithOneArg+0x1bb
1d 0000002a`8b2fe830 00007ffe`e088d203     System_Private_CoreLib!System.Reflection.RuntimeMethodInfo.Invoke+0x1b0
1e 0000002a`8b2fe8a0 00007ffe`818a19ff     System_Private_CoreLib!System.Reflection.MethodBase.Invoke+0x23
1f 0000002a`8b2fe8e0 00007ffe`e1442eb3     LINQPad_Query!LINQPad.ProcessServer.ProcessServerProgram.Main+0x19f
20 0000002a`8b2fe9b0 00007ffe`e13c180c     coreclr!CallDescrWorkerInternal+0x83
21 0000002a`8b2fe9f0 00007ffe`e13aba54     coreclr!MethodDescCallSite::CallTargetWorker+0x208
22 (Inline Function) --------`--------     coreclr!MethodDescCallSite::Call_RetArgSlot+0xd
23 0000002a`8b2feb30 00007ffe`e13acc19     coreclr!RunMainInternal+0xb8
24 0000002a`8b2fec50 00007ffe`e13acf2d     coreclr!RunMain+0xd1
25 0000002a`8b2fece0 00007ffe`e13ac1bb     coreclr!Assembly::ExecuteMainMethod+0x199
26 0000002a`8b2fefb0 00007ffe`e13a704c     coreclr!CorHost2::ExecuteAssembly+0x1cb
27 0000002a`8b2ff0c0 00007ffe`e17be8ec     coreclr!coreclr_execute_assembly+0xcc
28 (Inline Function) --------`--------     hostpolicy!coreclr_t::execute_assembly+0x2d
29 0000002a`8b2ff160 00007ffe`e17bebbc     hostpolicy!run_app_for_context+0x58c
2a 0000002a`8b2ff290 00007ffe`e1811be9     hostpolicy!run_app+0x3c
2b 0000002a`8b2ff2d0 00007ff7`4a677377     hostfxr!fx_muxer_t::run_app+0x109
2c 0000002a`8b2ff340 00007ff7`4a685a72     LINQPad8+0x17377
2d 0000002a`8b2ffc90 00007fff`400f53e0     LINQPad8+0x25a72
2e 0000002a`8b2ffcd0 00007fff`4160485b     kernel32!BaseThreadInitThunk+0x10
2f 0000002a`8b2ffd00 00000000`00000000     ntdll!RtlUserThreadStart+0x2b
```

```
   1  Id: 1370.1b90 Suspend: 0 Teb: 0000002a`8b0f9000 Unfrozen ".NET EventPipe"
 # Child-SP          RetAddr               Call Site
00 0000002a`8b6ff1a8 00007fff`3f07dcb0     ntdll!NtWaitForMultipleObjects+0x14
01 0000002a`8b6ff1b0 00007fff`3f07dbae     KERNELBASE!WaitForMultipleObjectsEx+0xf0
02 0000002a`8b6ff4a0 00007ffe`e141693f     KERNELBASE!WaitForMultipleObjects+0xe
03 0000002a`8b6ff4e0 00007ffe`e14168a0     coreclr!ds_ipc_poll+0x7f
04 0000002a`8b6ff760 00007ffe`e1416784     coreclr!ds_ipc_stream_factory_get_next_available_stream+0x108
05 0000002a`8b6ff830 00007fff`400f53e0     coreclr!server_thread+0x54
06 0000002a`8b6ff8a0 00007fff`4160485b     kernel32!BaseThreadInitThunk+0x10
07 0000002a`8b6ff8d0 00000000`00000000     ntdll!RtlUserThreadStart+0x2b
```

```
   2  Id: 1370.860 Suspend: 0 Teb: 0000002a`8b0fb000 Unfrozen ".NET Debugger"
 # Child-SP          RetAddr               Call Site
00 0000002a`8b7ff3f8 00007fff`3f07dcb0     ntdll!NtWaitForMultipleObjects+0x14
01 0000002a`8b7ff400 00007ffe`e1407a9e     KERNELBASE!WaitForMultipleObjectsEx+0xf0
02 0000002a`8b7ff6f0 00007ffe`e1407e26     coreclr!DebuggerRCThread::MainLoop+0xee
03 0000002a`8b7ff7b0 00007ffe`e140785b     coreclr!DebuggerRCThread::ThreadProc+0x12e
04 0000002a`8b7ff810 00007fff`400f53e0     coreclr!DebuggerRCThread::ThreadProcStatic+0x5b
05 0000002a`8b7ff840 00007fff`4160485b     kernel32!BaseThreadInitThunk+0x10
06 0000002a`8b7ff870 00000000`00000000     ntdll!RtlUserThreadStart+0x2b
```

```
   3  Id: 1370.cd8 Suspend: 0 Teb: 0000002a`8b0fd000 Unfrozen ".NET Finalizer"
 # Child-SP          RetAddr               Call Site
00 0000002a`8b8ff4f8 00007fff`3f07dcb0     ntdll!NtWaitForMultipleObjects+0x14
01 0000002a`8b8ff500 00007ffe`e1408a90     KERNELBASE!WaitForMultipleObjectsEx+0xf0
02 0000002a`8b8ff7f0 00007ffe`e140889f     coreclr!FinalizerThread::WaitForFinalizerEvent+0x78
03 0000002a`8b8ff830 00007ffe`e13aef05     coreclr!FinalizerThread::FinalizerThreadWorker+0x4f
04 (Inline Function) --------`--------     coreclr!ManagedThreadBase_DispatchInner+0xd
05 0000002a`8b8ffa80 00007ffe`e13aee2d     coreclr!ManagedThreadBase_DispatchMiddle+0x79
06 0000002a`8b8ffb30 00007ffe`e13fe921     coreclr!ManagedThreadBase_DispatchOuter+0x8d
07 (Inline Function) --------`--------     coreclr!ManagedThreadBase_NoADTransition+0x28
08 (Inline Function) --------`--------     coreclr!ManagedThreadBase::FinalizerBase+0x28
09 0000002a`8b8ffba0 00007fff`400f53e0     coreclr!FinalizerThread::FinalizerThreadStart+0x91
0a 0000002a`8b8ffcb0 00007fff`4160485b     kernel32!BaseThreadInitThunk+0x10
0b 0000002a`8b8ffce0 00000000`00000000     ntdll!RtlUserThreadStart+0x2b

   4  Id: 1370.fac Suspend: 0 Teb: 0000002a`8b103000 Unfrozen ".NET TP Wait"
 # Child-SP          RetAddr               Call Site
00 0000002a`8afbf188 00007fff`3f0710ce     ntdll!NtWaitForSingleObject+0x14
01 0000002a`8afbf190 00007ffe`e142e230     KERNELBASE!WaitForSingleObjectEx+0x8e
02 (Inline Function) --------`--------     coreclr!GCEvent::Impl::Wait+0xf
03 (Inline Function) --------`--------     coreclr!GCEvent::Wait+0x16
04 0000002a`8afbf230 00007ffe`e13570b5     coreclr!WKS::GCHeap::WaitUntilGCComplete+0x30
05 0000002a`8afbf260 00007ffe`e12fe6f9     coreclr!Thread::RareDisablePreemptiveGC+0x9d
06 (Inline Function) --------`--------     coreclr!Thread::DisablePreemptiveGC+0x17e
07 (Inline Function) --------`--------     coreclr!GCHolderBase::PopInternal+0x18f
08 (Inline Function) --------`--------     coreclr!GCPreemp::{dtor}+0x18f
09 0000002a`8afbf2f0 00007ffe`e12fe35a     coreclr!Thread::DoAppropriateWaitWorker+0x351
0a 0000002a`8afbf3c0 00007ffe`e12fcd19     coreclr!Thread::DoAppropriateWait+0xa6
0b 0000002a`8afbf460 00007ffe`e0806fc3     coreclr!WaitHandleNative::CorWaitMultipleNative+0xf9
0c 0000002a`8afbf600 00007ffe`e0822dcc     System_Private_CoreLib!System.Threading.WaitHandle.WaitAnyMultiple+0xd3
0d 0000002a`8afbf690 00007ffe`e1442eb3     System_Private_CoreLib!System.Threading.PortableThreadPool.WaitThread.WaitThreadStart+0x8c
0e 0000002a`8afbf6f0 00007ffe`e13c1568     coreclr!CallDescrWorkerInternal+0x83
0f 0000002a`8afbf730 00007ffe`e14315a3     coreclr!DispatchCallSimple+0x60
10 0000002a`8afbf7c0 00007ffe`e13aef05     coreclr!ThreadNative::KickOffThread_Worker+0x63
11 (Inline Function) --------`--------     coreclr!ManagedThreadBase_DispatchInner+0xd
12 0000002a`8afbf820 00007ffe`e13aee2d     coreclr!ManagedThreadBase_DispatchMiddle+0x79
13 0000002a`8afbf8d0 00007ffe`e13aefbb     coreclr!ManagedThreadBase_DispatchOuter+0x8d
14 (Inline Function) --------`--------     coreclr!ManagedThreadBase_FullTransition+0x28
15 (Inline Function) --------`--------     coreclr!ManagedThreadBase::KickOff+0x28
16 0000002a`8afbf940 00007fff`400f53e0     coreclr!ThreadNative::KickOffThread+0x7b
17 0000002a`8afbf9a0 00007fff`4160485b     kernel32!BaseThreadInitThunk+0x10
18 0000002a`8afbf9d0 00000000`00000000     ntdll!RtlUserThreadStart+0x2b

   5  Id: 1370.ae0 Suspend: 0 Teb: 0000002a`8b107000 Unfrozen ".NET TP Gate"
 # Child-SP          RetAddr               Call Site
00 0000002a`8affef68 00007fff`3f07dcb0     ntdll!NtWaitForMultipleObjects+0x14
01 0000002a`8affef70 00007ffe`e12fe800     KERNELBASE!WaitForMultipleObjectsEx+0xf0
02 0000002a`8afff260 00007ffe`e12fe523     coreclr!Thread::DoAppropriateAptStateWait+0x5c
03 0000002a`8afff2a0 00007ffe`e12fe35a     coreclr!Thread::DoAppropriateWaitWorker+0x17b
04 0000002a`8afff370 00007ffe`e12fe24b     coreclr!Thread::DoAppropriateWait+0xa6
05 0000002a`8afff410 00007ffe`e0806653     coreclr!WaitHandleNative::CorWaitOneNative+0xdb
06 0000002a`8afff580 00007ffe`e08208ed     System_Private_CoreLib!System.Threading.WaitHandle.WaitOneNoCheck+0x83
07 0000002a`8afff5f0 00007ffe`e1442eb3     System_Private_CoreLib!System.Threading.PortableThreadPool.GateThread.GateThreadStart+0x18d
08 0000002a`8afff760 00007ffe`e13c1568     coreclr!CallDescrWorkerInternal+0x83
09 0000002a`8afff7a0 00007ffe`e14315a3     coreclr!DispatchCallSimple+0x60
0a 0000002a`8afff830 00007ffe`e13aef05     coreclr!ThreadNative::KickOffThread_Worker+0x63
0b (Inline Function) --------`--------     coreclr!ManagedThreadBase_DispatchInner+0xd
0c 0000002a`8afff890 00007ffe`e13aee2d     coreclr!ManagedThreadBase_DispatchMiddle+0x79
0d 0000002a`8afff940 00007ffe`e13aefbb     coreclr!ManagedThreadBase_DispatchOuter+0x8d
0e (Inline Function) --------`--------     coreclr!ManagedThreadBase_FullTransition+0x28
0f (Inline Function) --------`--------     coreclr!ManagedThreadBase::KickOff+0x28
10 0000002a`8afff9b0 00007fff`400f53e0     coreclr!ThreadNative::KickOffThread+0x7b
11 0000002a`8afffa10 00007fff`4160485b     kernel32!BaseThreadInitThunk+0x10
12 0000002a`8afffa40 00000000`00000000     ntdll!RtlUserThreadStart+0x2b

   6  Id: 1370.12a4 Suspend: 0 Teb: 0000002a`8b109000 Unfrozen
 # Child-SP          RetAddr               Call Site
00 0000002a`8bbff498 00007fff`3f07dcb0     ntdll!NtWaitForMultipleObjects+0x14
01 0000002a`8bbff4a0 00007fff`4130f598     KERNELBASE!WaitForMultipleObjectsEx+0xf0
02 0000002a`8bbff790 00007fff`4130f2d1     combase!WaitCoalesced+0xa4
03 0000002a`8bbffa20 00007fff`4130f189     combase!CRpcThread::WorkerLoop+0x11d
04 0000002a`8bbffa90 00007fff`400f53e0     combase!CRpcThreadCache::RpcWorkerThreadEntry+0x29
05 0000002a`8bbffac0 00007fff`4160485b     kernel32!BaseThreadInitThunk+0x10
06 0000002a`8bbffaf0 00000000`00000000     ntdll!RtlUserThreadStart+0x2b

   7  Id: 1370.6e0 Suspend: 0 Teb: 0000002a`8b10b000 Unfrozen
 # Child-SP          RetAddr               Call Site
00 0000002a`8bcff448 00007fff`41616cdf     ntdll!NtWaitForWorkViaWorkerFactory+0x14
01 0000002a`8bcff450 00007fff`400f53e0     ntdll!TppWorkerThread+0x2df
02 0000002a`8bcff740 00007fff`4160485b     kernel32!BaseThreadInitThunk+0x10
03 0000002a`8bcff770 00000000`00000000     ntdll!RtlUserThreadStart+0x2b

   8  Id: 1370.1e5c Suspend: 0 Teb: 0000002a`8b10d000 Unfrozen
 # Child-SP          RetAddr               Call Site
```

```
00 0000002a`8bdff938 00007fff`41616cdf     ntdll!NtWaitForWorkViaWorkerFactory+0x14
01 0000002a`8bdff940 00007fff`400f53e0     ntdll!TppWorkerThread+0x2df
02 0000002a`8bdffc30 00007fff`4160485b     kernel32!BaseThreadInitThunk+0x10
03 0000002a`8bdffc60 00000000`00000000     ntdll!RtlUserThreadStart+0x2b

   9  Id: 1370.1cf0 Suspend: 0 Teb: 0000002a`8b10f000 Unfrozen ".NET Timer"
 # Child-SP          RetAddr               Call Site
00 0000002a`8beff3a8 00007fff`3f07dcb0     ntdll!NtWaitForMultipleObjects+0x14
01 0000002a`8beff3b0 00007ffe`e12fe800     KERNELBASE!WaitForMultipleObjectsEx+0xf0
02 0000002a`8beff6a0 00007ffe`e12fe523     coreclr!Thread::DoAppropriateAptStateWait+0x5c
03 0000002a`8beff6e0 00007ffe`e12fe35a     coreclr!Thread::DoAppropriateWaitWorker+0x17b
04 0000002a`8beff7b0 00007ffe`e12fe24b     coreclr!Thread::DoAppropriateWait+0xa6
05 0000002a`8beff850 00007ffe`e0806653     coreclr!WaitHandleNative::CorWaitOneNative+0xdb
06 0000002a`8beff9c0 00007ffe`e081945f     System_Private_CoreLib!System.Threading.WaitHandle.WaitOneNoCheck+0x83
07 0000002a`8beffa30 00007ffe`e1442eb3     System_Private_CoreLib!System.Threading.TimerQueue.TimerThread+0x7f
08 0000002a`8beffac0 00007ffe`e13c1568     coreclr!CallDescrWorkerInternal+0x83
09 0000002a`8beffb00 00007ffe`e14315a3     coreclr!DispatchCallSimple+0x60
0a 0000002a`8beffb90 00007ffe`e13aef05     coreclr!ThreadNative::KickOffThread_Worker+0x63
0b (Inline Function) --------`--------     coreclr!ManagedThreadBase_DispatchInner+0xd
0c 0000002a`8beffbf0 00007ffe`e13aee2d     coreclr!ManagedThreadBase_DispatchMiddle+0x79
0d 0000002a`8beffca0 00007ffe`e13aefbb     coreclr!ManagedThreadBase_DispatchOuter+0x8d
0e (Inline Function) --------`--------     coreclr!ManagedThreadBase_FullTransition+0x28
0f (Inline Function) --------`--------     coreclr!ManagedThreadBase::KickOff+0x28
10 0000002a`8beffd10 00007fff`400f53e0     coreclr!ThreadNative::KickOffThread+0x7b
11 0000002a`8beffd70 00007fff`4160485b     kernel32!BaseThreadInitThunk+0x10
12 0000002a`8beffda0 00000000`00000000     ntdll!RtlUserThreadStart+0x2b

  10  Id: 1370.fec Suspend: 0 Teb: 0000002a`8b113000 Unfrozen
 # Child-SP          RetAddr               Call Site
00 0000002a`8c0ff468 00007fff`41616cdf     ntdll!NtWaitForWorkViaWorkerFactory+0x14
01 0000002a`8c0ff470 00007fff`400f53e0     ntdll!TppWorkerThread+0x2df
02 0000002a`8c0ff760 00007fff`4160485b     kernel32!BaseThreadInitThunk+0x10
03 0000002a`8c0ff790 00000000`00000000     ntdll!RtlUserThreadStart+0x2b

  11  Id: 1370.13a8 Suspend: 0 Teb: 0000002a`8b117000 Unfrozen ".NET Tiered Compilation Worker"
 # Child-SP          RetAddr               Call Site
00 0000002a`8b3ffb18 00007fff`4165b903     ntdll!NtDelayExecution+0x14
01 0000002a`8b3ffb20 00007fff`3f04d031     ntdll!RtlDelayExecution+0x43
02 0000002a`8b3ffb50 00007ffe`e1408715     KERNELBASE!SleepEx+0x71
03 (Inline Function) --------`--------     coreclr!ClrSleepEx+0xa
04 0000002a`8b3ffbd0 00007ffe`e1408645     coreclr!TieredCompilationManager::BackgroundWorkerStart+0x91
05 0000002a`8b3ffc20 00007ffe`e13aef05     coreclr!TieredCompilationManager::BackgroundWorkerBootstrapper1+0x55
06 (Inline Function) --------`--------     coreclr!ManagedThreadBase_DispatchInner+0xd
07 0000002a`8b3ffc60 00007ffe`e13aee2d     coreclr!ManagedThreadBase_DispatchMiddle+0x79
08 0000002a`8b3ffd10 00007ffe`e143c8da     coreclr!ManagedThreadBase_DispatchOuter+0x8d
09 (Inline Function) --------`--------     coreclr!ManagedThreadBase_FullTransition+0x24
0a (Inline Function) --------`--------     coreclr!ManagedThreadBase::KickOff+0x24
0b 0000002a`8b3ffd80 00007fff`400f53e0     coreclr!TieredCompilationManager::BackgroundWorkerBootstrapper0+0x3a
0c 0000002a`8b3ffdd0 00007fff`4160485b     kernel32!BaseThreadInitThunk+0x10
0d 0000002a`8b3ffe00 00000000`00000000     ntdll!RtlUserThreadStart+0x2b

  12  Id: 1370.950 Suspend: 0 Teb: 0000002a`8b119000 Unfrozen ".NET TP Worker"
 # Child-SP          RetAddr               Call Site
00 0000002a`8b4ff5b8 00007fff`3f07ebd3     ntdll!NtRemoveIoCompletion+0x14
01 0000002a`8b4ff5c0 00007ffe`e06d90e6     KERNELBASE!GetQueuedCompletionStatus+0x53
02 0000002a`8b4ff620 00007ffe`e08242bd     System_Private_CoreLib!Interop.Kernel32.GetQueuedCompletionStatus+0xa6
03 0000002a`8b4ff720 00007ffe`e0824256     System_Private_CoreLib!System.Threading.LowLevelLifoSemaphore.WaitForSignal+0x4d
04 0000002a`8b4ff790 00007ffe`e08235be     System_Private_CoreLib!System.Threading.LowLevelLifoSemaphore.Wait+0x1a6
05 0000002a`8b4ff7f0 00007ffe`e1442eb3
System_Private_CoreLib!System.Threading.PortableThreadPool.WorkerThread.WorkerThreadStart+0x12e
06 0000002a`8b4ff900 00007ffe`e13c1568     coreclr!CallDescrWorkerInternal+0x83
07 0000002a`8b4ff940 00007ffe`e14315a3     coreclr!DispatchCallSimple+0x60
08 0000002a`8b4ff9d0 00007ffe`e13aef05     coreclr!ThreadNative::KickOffThread_Worker+0x63
09 (Inline Function) --------`--------     coreclr!ManagedThreadBase_DispatchInner+0xd
0a 0000002a`8b4ffa30 00007ffe`e13aee2d     coreclr!ManagedThreadBase_DispatchMiddle+0x79
0b 0000002a`8b4ffae0 00007ffe`e13aefbb     coreclr!ManagedThreadBase_DispatchOuter+0x8d
0c (Inline Function) --------`--------     coreclr!ManagedThreadBase_FullTransition+0x28
0d (Inline Function) --------`--------     coreclr!ManagedThreadBase::KickOff+0x28
0e 0000002a`8b4ffb50 00007fff`400f53e0     coreclr!ThreadNative::KickOffThread+0x7b
0f 0000002a`8b4ffbb0 00007fff`4160485b     kernel32!BaseThreadInitThunk+0x10
10 0000002a`8b4ffbe0 00000000`00000000     ntdll!RtlUserThreadStart+0x2b

  13  Id: 1370.1f18 Suspend: 0 Teb: 0000002a`8b11b000 Unfrozen ".NET TP Worker"
 # Child-SP          RetAddr               Call Site
00 0000002a`8b5ff5b8 00007fff`3f07ebd3     ntdll!NtRemoveIoCompletion+0x14
01 0000002a`8b5ff5c0 00007ffe`e06d90e6     KERNELBASE!GetQueuedCompletionStatus+0x53
02 0000002a`8b5ff620 00007ffe`e08242bd     System_Private_CoreLib!Interop.Kernel32.GetQueuedCompletionStatus+0xa6
03 0000002a`8b5ff720 00007ffe`821a5c27     System_Private_CoreLib!System.Threading.LowLevelLifoSemaphore.WaitForSignal+0x4d
04 0000002a`8b5ff790 00007ffe`e08235be     System_Private_CoreLib!System.Threading.LowLevelLifoSemaphore.Wait+0x3e7
05 0000002a`8b5ff850 00007ffe`e1442eb3
System_Private_CoreLib!System.Threading.PortableThreadPool.WorkerThread.WorkerThreadStart+0x12e
06 0000002a`8b5ff960 00007ffe`e13c1568     coreclr!CallDescrWorkerInternal+0x83
07 0000002a`8b5ff9a0 00007ffe`e14315a3     coreclr!DispatchCallSimple+0x60
08 0000002a`8b5ffa30 00007ffe`e13aef05     coreclr!ThreadNative::KickOffThread_Worker+0x63
```

```
09 (Inline Function) --------`--------      coreclr!ManagedThreadBase_DispatchInner+0xd
0a 0000002a`8b5ffa90 00007ffe`e13aee2d      coreclr!ManagedThreadBase_DispatchMiddle+0x79
0b 0000002a`8b5ffb40 00007ffe`e13aefbb      coreclr!ManagedThreadBase_DispatchOuter+0x8d
0c (Inline Function) --------`--------      coreclr!ManagedThreadBase_FullTransition+0x28
0d (Inline Function) --------`--------      coreclr!ManagedThreadBase::KickOff+0x28
0e 0000002a`8b5ffbb0 00007fff`400f53e0      coreclr!ThreadNative::KickOffThread+0x7b
0f 0000002a`8b5ffc10 00007fff`4160485b      kernel32!BaseThreadInitThunk+0x10
10 0000002a`8b5ffc40 00000000`00000000      ntdll!RtlUserThreadStart+0x2b

  14  Id: 1370.1d04 Suspend: 0 Teb: 0000002a`8b11d000 Unfrozen ".NET TP Worker"
 # Child-SP          RetAddr               Call Site
00 0000002a`8b9ff818 00007fff`3f07ebd3      ntdll!NtRemoveIoCompletion+0x14
01 0000002a`8b9ff820 00007ffe`e06d90e6      KERNELBASE!GetQueuedCompletionStatus+0x53
02 0000002a`8b9ff880 00007ffe`e08242bd      System_Private_CoreLib!Interop.Kernel32.GetQueuedCompletionStatus+0xa6
03 0000002a`8b9ff980 00007ffe`821a5c27      System_Private_CoreLib!System.Threading.LowLevelLifoSemaphore.WaitForSignal+0x4d
04 0000002a`8b9ff9f0 00007ffe`e08235be      System_Private_CoreLib!System.Threading.LowLevelLifoSemaphore.Wait+0x3e7
05 0000002a`8b9ffab0 00007ffe`e1442eb3
System_Private_CoreLib!System.Threading.PortableThreadPool.WorkerThread.WorkerThreadStart+0x12e
06 0000002a`8b9ffbc0 00007ffe`e13c1568      coreclr!CallDescrWorkerInternal+0x83
07 0000002a`8b9ffc00 00007ffe`e14315a3      coreclr!DispatchCallSimple+0x60
08 0000002a`8b9ffc90 00007ffe`e13aef05      coreclr!ThreadNative::KickOffThread_Worker+0x63
09 (Inline Function) --------`--------      coreclr!ManagedThreadBase_DispatchInner+0xd
0a 0000002a`8b9ffcf0 00007ffe`e13aee2d      coreclr!ManagedThreadBase_DispatchMiddle+0x79
0b 0000002a`8b9ffda0 00007ffe`e13aefbb      coreclr!ManagedThreadBase_DispatchOuter+0x8d
0c (Inline Function) --------`--------      coreclr!ManagedThreadBase_FullTransition+0x28
0d (Inline Function) --------`--------      coreclr!ManagedThreadBase::KickOff+0x28
0e 0000002a`8b9ffe10 00007fff`400f53e0      coreclr!ThreadNative::KickOffThread+0x7b
0f 0000002a`8b9ffe70 00007fff`4160485b      kernel32!BaseThreadInitThunk+0x10
10 0000002a`8b9ffea0 00000000`00000000      ntdll!RtlUserThreadStart+0x2b

  15  Id: 1370.160c Suspend: 0 Teb: 0000002a`8b11f000 Unfrozen ".NET TP Worker"
 # Child-SP          RetAddr               Call Site
00 0000002a`8baff418 00007fff`3f07ebd3      ntdll!NtRemoveIoCompletion+0x14
01 0000002a`8baff420 00007ffe`e06d90e6      KERNELBASE!GetQueuedCompletionStatus+0x53
02 0000002a`8baff480 00007ffe`e08242bd      System_Private_CoreLib!Interop.Kernel32.GetQueuedCompletionStatus+0xa6
03 0000002a`8baff580 00007ffe`821a5c27      System_Private_CoreLib!System.Threading.LowLevelLifoSemaphore.WaitForSignal+0x4d
04 0000002a`8baff5f0 00007ffe`e08235be      System_Private_CoreLib!System.Threading.LowLevelLifoSemaphore.Wait+0x3e7
05 0000002a`8baff6b0 00007ffe`e1442eb3
System_Private_CoreLib!System.Threading.PortableThreadPool.WorkerThread.WorkerThreadStart+0x12e
06 0000002a`8baff7c0 00007ffe`e13c1568      coreclr!CallDescrWorkerInternal+0x83
07 0000002a`8baff800 00007ffe`e14315a3      coreclr!DispatchCallSimple+0x60
08 0000002a`8baff890 00007ffe`e13aef05      coreclr!ThreadNative::KickOffThread_Worker+0x63
09 (Inline Function) --------`--------      coreclr!ManagedThreadBase_DispatchInner+0xd
0a 0000002a`8baff8f0 00007ffe`e13aee2d      coreclr!ManagedThreadBase_DispatchMiddle+0x79
0b 0000002a`8baff9a0 00007ffe`e13aefbb      coreclr!ManagedThreadBase_DispatchOuter+0x8d
0c (Inline Function) --------`--------      coreclr!ManagedThreadBase_FullTransition+0x28
0d (Inline Function) --------`--------      coreclr!ManagedThreadBase::KickOff+0x28
0e 0000002a`8baffa10 00007fff`400f53e0      coreclr!ThreadNative::KickOffThread+0x7b
0f 0000002a`8baffa70 00007fff`4160485b      kernel32!BaseThreadInitThunk+0x10
10 0000002a`8baffaa0 00000000`00000000      ntdll!RtlUserThreadStart+0x2b

  16  Id: 1370.1fa4 Suspend: 0 Teb: 0000002a`8b121000 Unfrozen ".NET TP Worker"
 # Child-SP          RetAddr               Call Site
00 0000002a`8bfff758 00007fff`3f07ebd3      ntdll!NtRemoveIoCompletion+0x14
01 0000002a`8bfff760 00007ffe`e06d90e6      KERNELBASE!GetQueuedCompletionStatus+0x53
02 0000002a`8bfff7c0 00007ffe`e08242bd      System_Private_CoreLib!Interop.Kernel32.GetQueuedCompletionStatus+0xa6
03 0000002a`8bfff8c0 00007ffe`821a5c27      System_Private_CoreLib!System.Threading.LowLevelLifoSemaphore.WaitForSignal+0x4d
04 0000002a`8bfff930 00007ffe`e08235be      System_Private_CoreLib!System.Threading.LowLevelLifoSemaphore.Wait+0x3e7
05 0000002a`8bfff9f0 00007ffe`e1442eb3
System_Private_CoreLib!System.Threading.PortableThreadPool.WorkerThread.WorkerThreadStart+0x12e
06 0000002a`8bfffb00 00007ffe`e13c1568      coreclr!CallDescrWorkerInternal+0x83
07 0000002a`8bfffb40 00007ffe`e14315a3      coreclr!DispatchCallSimple+0x60
08 0000002a`8bfffbd0 00007ffe`e13aef05      coreclr!ThreadNative::KickOffThread_Worker+0x63
09 (Inline Function) --------`--------      coreclr!ManagedThreadBase_DispatchInner+0xd
0a 0000002a`8bfffc30 00007ffe`e13aee2d      coreclr!ManagedThreadBase_DispatchMiddle+0x79
0b 0000002a`8bfffce0 00007ffe`e13aefbb      coreclr!ManagedThreadBase_DispatchOuter+0x8d
0c (Inline Function) --------`--------      coreclr!ManagedThreadBase_FullTransition+0x28
0d (Inline Function) --------`--------      coreclr!ManagedThreadBase::KickOff+0x28
0e 0000002a`8bfffd50 00007fff`400f53e0      coreclr!ThreadNative::KickOffThread+0x7b
0f 0000002a`8bfffdb0 00007fff`4160485b      kernel32!BaseThreadInitThunk+0x10
10 0000002a`8bfffde0 00000000`00000000      ntdll!RtlUserThreadStart+0x2b
```

Note: We notice that the current thread #0 is active (not waiting) and doing garbage collection. However, looking at its stack trace top frame instruction pointer, we see an invalid pointer access violation. The invalid pointer itself contains regular UNICODE data:

```
0:000> r
rax=00000000002e0064 rbx=0000002a8b2fc770 rcx=0062007500670070
rdx=0000000000000000 rsi=0000002a8b2fbfd0 rdi=0000002a8b2fc280
```

```
rip=00007ffee135bd28 rsp=0000002a8b2fc9a0 rbp=0000002a8b2fcaa0
 r8=0000000000000001  r9=0000000000000000 r10=0000018a3e9f6420
r11=0000018a3e8915e8 r12=0000018a3e8915e8 r13=0000000000000000
r14=0000000000000001 r15=0000000000000000
iopl=0         nv up ei pl nz na pe nc
cs=0033  ss=002b  ds=002b  es=002b  fs=0053  gs=002b        efl=00010200
coreclr!MethodTable::GetFlag [inlined in coreclr!WKS::gc_heap::plan_phase+0x578]:
00007ffe`e135bd28 mov     eax,dword ptr [rcx]     ds:00620075`00670070=????????
```

```
0:000> .formats 00620075`00670070
Evaluate expression:
  Hex:      00620075`00670070
  Decimal:  27585050235568240
  Decimal (unsigned) : 27585050235568240
  Octal:    0001420007240031600160
  Binary:   00000000 01100010 00000000 01110101 00000000 01100111 00000000 01110000
  Chars:    .b.u.g.p
  Time:     Mon May 31 04:23:43.556 1688 (UTC + 1:00)
  Float:    low 9.45921e-039 high 9.00004e-039
  Double:   8.01106e-307
```

5.   We verify the managed heap (**!VerifyHeap** SOS extension command):

```
0:000> !VerifyHeap
The GC heap is not in a valid state for traversal.  (Use -ignoreGCState to override.)
```

```
0:000> !VerifyHeap -ignoreGCState
Segment      Object       Failure                      Reason
01ca503ff228 018a3e802210 InvalidObjectReference       Object 18a3e802210 has a bad member at offset 30: fdf8
01ca503ff228 018a3e813258 ObjectReferenceNotPointerAligned Object 18a3e813258 has an unaligned member at offset 28: is not pointer aligned
01ca503ff228 018a3e8355b8 InvalidObjectReference       Object 18a3e8355b8 has a bad member at offset 1d0: 22378
01ca503ff228 018a3e8464b8 InvalidMethodTable           Object 18a3e8464b8 has an invalid method table 3ba332
01ca503ff228 018a3e847088 InvalidObjectReference       Object 18a3e847088 has a bad member at offset 1d8: 460
01ca503ff228 018a3e868df0 InvalidMethodTable           Object 18a3e868df0 has an invalid method table 21b60
01ca503ff228 018a3e868e48 InvalidMethodTable           Object 18a3e868e48 has an invalid method table 40
01ca503ff228 018a3e86e9c8 InvalidMethodTable           Object 18a3e86e9c8 has an invalid method table 39248a
01ca503ff228 018a3e877ac8 InvalidMethodTable           Object 18a3e877ac8 has an invalid method table 38c940
01ca503ff228 018a3e87a980 InvalidMethodTable           Object 18a3e87a980 has an invalid method table 20
01ca503ff228 018a3e87a9f8 ObjectReferenceNotPointerAligned Object 18a3e87a9f8 has an unaligned member at offset 30: is not pointer aligned
01ca503ff228 018a3e87b2c8 InvalidObjectReference       Object 18a3e87b2c8 has a bad member at offset 30: 18a3e87b3f0
01ca503ff228 018a3e87b3f0 InvalidMethodTable           Object 18a3e87b3f0 has an invalid method table 6f8
01ca503ff228 018a3e87b738 InvalidMethodTable           Object 18a3e87b738 has an invalid method table 38c148
01ca503ff228 018a3e87bb38 ObjectReferenceNotPointerAligned Object 18a3e87bb38 has an unaligned member at offset 30: is not pointer aligned
01ca503ff228 018a3e87be10 InvalidObjectReference       Object 18a3e87be10 has a bad member at offset 8: 18a3e87be28
01ca503ff228 018a3e87be28 InvalidMethodTable           Object 18a3e87be28 has an invalid method table 38bdfa
01ca503ff228 018a3e87c058 InvalidObjectReference       Object 18a3e87c058 has a bad member at offset 8: 1f8
01ca503ff228 018a3e87c0f8 InvalidObjectReference       Object 18a3e87c0f8 has a bad member at offset 40: 88
01ca503ff228 018a3e87c710 InvalidObjectReference       Object 18a3e87c710 has a bad member at offset 30: 90
01ca503ff228 018a3e8831a0 InvalidObjectReference       Object 18a3e8831a0 has a bad member at offset 8: 6a28
01ca503ff228 018a3e885938 InvalidMethodTable           Object 18a3e885938 has an invalid method table 11
01ca503ff228 018a3e885af8 InvalidObjectReference       Object 18a3e885af8 has a bad member at offset 80: a0
01ca503ff228 018a3e885bc8 InvalidMethodTable           Object 18a3e885bc8 has an invalid method table 20
01ca503ff228 018a3e886c10 InvalidMethodTable           Object 18a3e886c10 has an invalid method table 6500730055005c
01ca503ff228 018a3e8871b0 InvalidObjectReference       Object 18a3e8871b0 has a bad member at offset 20: 40
01ca503ff228 018a3e8888f8 InvalidObjectReference       Object 18a3e8888f8 has a bad member at offset 10: 18a3e888960
01ca503ff228 018a3e888960 InvalidMethodTable           Object 18a3e888960 has an invalid method table 88
01ca503ff228 018a3e8889f8 InvalidObjectReference       Object 18a3e8889f8 has a bad member at offset 8: 78
01ca503ff228 018a3e888a38 InvalidObjectReference       Object 18a3e888a38 has a bad member at offset 8: 28
01ca503ff228 018a3e888a78 InvalidObjectReference       Object 18a3e888a78 has a bad member at offset 8: 28
01ca503ff228 018a3e888ab8 InvalidObjectReference       Object 18a3e888ab8 has a bad member at offset 8: 28
01ca503ff228 018a3e888af8 InvalidObjectReference       Object 18a3e888af8 has a bad member at offset 8: 28
01ca503ff228 018a3e888b38 InvalidObjectReference       Object 18a3e888b38 has a bad member at offset 8: 28
[...]
```

```
0:000> !DumpObj 018a3e802210
Name:        System.IO.MemoryStream
MethodTable: 00007ffe81ac89f8
Canonical MethodTable: 00007ffe81ac89f8
Tracked Type: false
Size:        64(0x40) bytes
File:        C:\Program Files\dotnet\shared\Microsoft.NETCore.App\9.0.4\System.Private.CoreLib.dll
Fields:
              MT    Field   Offset                 Type VT     Attr            Value Name
0000000000000000 4001da2        8 ...ing.SemaphoreSlim  0 instance 0000000000000000 _asyncActiveSemaphore
00007ffe81ac8198 4001da1        8     System.IO.Stream  0   static 0000000000000000 Null
```

```
00007ffe8194dea0   4001d48   10        System.Byte[]   0 instance   0000018a3f12a2c0  _buffer
00007ffe81827408   4001d49   18        System.Int32    1 instance                 0  _origin
00007ffe81827408   4001d4a   1c        System.Int32    1 instance            633272  _position
00007ffe81827408   4001d4b   20        System.Int32    1 instance                64  _length
00007ffe81827408   4001d4c   24        System.Int32    1 instance                 0  _capacity
00007ffe81822f78   4001d4d   28      System.Boolean    1 instance               234  _expandable
00007ffe81822f78   4001d4e   29      System.Boolean    1 instance               225  _writable
00007ffe81822f78   4001d4f   2a      System.Boolean    1 instance                63  _exposable
00007ffe81822f78   4001d50   2b      System.Boolean    1 instance                 0  _isOpen
00007ffe81ac8960   4001d51   30 ...ompletedInt32Task   1 instance   0000018a3e802240  _lastReadTask
```

```
0:000> !DumpObj 0000018a3e802240
<Note: this object has an invalid CLASS field>
The garbage collector data structures are not in a valid state for traversal.
It is either in the "plan phase," where objects are being moved around, or
we are at the initialization or shutdown of the gc heap. Commands related to
displaying, finding or traversing objects as well as gc heap segments may not
work properly. !dumpheap and !verifyheap may incorrectly complain of heap
consistency errors.
Invalid object
```

6.   We can also inspect raw memory for possible symbolic (**dps, dpp**) and string (**dpa, dpu, s-sa, s-su**) references and traces, if any (some suspicious pointers may also be interpreted using **!IP2MD**), and list nearest objects:

```
0:000> dps 018a3e802210 L100
0000018a`3e802210   00007ffe`81ac89f8
0000018a`3e802218   00000000`00000000
0000018a`3e802220   0000018a`3f12a2c0
0000018a`3e802228   0009a9b8`00000000
0000018a`3e802230   00000000`00000040
0000018a`3e802238   00000000`003fe1ea
0000018a`3e802240   00000000`0000fdf8
0000018a`3e802248   00000000`00000000
0000018a`3e802250   00007ffe`8195f8b0
0000018a`3e802258   00000000`00000000
0000018a`3e802260   00000000`00000000
0000018a`3e802268   00000000`00000000
[...]
```

```
0:000> !ListNearObj 018a3e802210
Before:        018a3e802048 456 (0x1c8)
System.Buffers.SharedArrayPoolThreadLocalArray[]
Current:       018a3e802210 64 (0x40)                    System.IO.MemoryStream
Error Detected: Object 18a3e802210 has a bad member at offset 30: fdf8 [verify heap]
Next:          018a3e802250 48 (0x30)                    System.Reflection.RuntimeAssembly
Heap local consistency not confirmed.
```

7.   We close logging before exiting WinDbg:

```
0:000> .logclose
Closing open log file C:\ANETMDA-Dumps\Windows\x64\LINQPadE.log
```

Exercise PN7 (Linux)

◉ **Goal:** Learn how to recognize and analyze heap corruption

◉ **Patterns:** Regular Data; Dynamic Memory Corruption (Managed Heap)

◉ **Commands:** print/c, verifyheap, listnearobj

◉ \ANETMDA-Dumps\Exercise-PN7-Linux.pdf

Exercise PN7 (Linux)

Goal: Learn how to recognize and analyze heap corruption.

Patterns: Regular Data; Dynamic Memory Corruption (Managed Heap).

Commands: print/c, verifyheap, listnearobj

1.   Open \ANETMDA-Dumps\Linux\ApplicationL\core.ApplicationL.946.dmp in LLDB:

```
/mnt/c/ANETMDA-Dumps/Linux/ApplicationL$ lldb -c core.ApplicationL.946.dmp
bin/Release/net9.0/ApplicationL
Current symbol store settings:
-> Cache: /home/coredump/.dotnet/symbolcache
-> Server: https://msdl.microsoft.com/download/symbols/ Timeout: 4 RetryCount: 0
(lldb) target create "bin/Release/net9.0/ApplicationL" --core "core.ApplicationL.946.dmp"
```

Core file '/mnt/c/ANETMDA-Dumps/Linux/ApplicationL/core.ApplicationL.946.dmp' (x86_64) was
loaded.

2.   Verify all stack traces:

```
(lldb) bt all
```

```
* thread #1, name = 'ApplicationL', stop reason = signal SIGSEGV
  * frame #0: 0x00007f1a6720e0ca libpthread.so.0`__waitpid(pid=956, stat_loc=0x00007f1a6722dd24, options=0) at waitpid.c:30
    frame #1: 0x00007f1a66b82d97 libcoreclr.so`PROCCreateCrashDump(std::vector<char const*, std::allocator<char const*> >&, char*, int, bool) + 647
    frame #2: 0x00007f1a66b8424b libcoreclr.so`PROCCreateCrashDumpIfEnabled + 3227
    frame #3: 0x00007f1a66b5726e libcoreclr.so`invoke_previous_action(sigaction*, int, siginfo_t*, void*, bool) + 270
    frame #4: 0x00007f1a66b56715 libcoreclr.so`sigsegv_handler(int, siginfo_t*, void*) + 469
    frame #5: 0x00007f1a6720e730 libpthread.so.0`___lldb_unnamed_symbol1$$libpthread.so.0 + 1
    frame #6: 0x00007f1a669a44f0 libcoreclr.so`WKS::gc_heap::plan_phase(int) + 7104
    frame #7: 0x00007f1a66699de60 libcoreclr.so`WKS::gc_heap::gc1() + 1024
    frame #8: 0x00007f1a669ab17b libcoreclr.so`WKS::gc_heap::garbage_collect(int) + 1739
    frame #9: 0x00007f1a66998e59 libcoreclr.so`WKS::GCHeap::GarbageCollectGeneration(unsigned int, gc_reason) + 1033
    frame #10: 0x00007f1a669caf35 libcoreclr.so`WKS::GCHeap::GarbageCollect(int, bool, int) + 485
    frame #11: 0x00007f1a6682c594 libcoreclr.so`GCInterface_Collect + 164
    frame #12: 0x00007f19e76bc8db
    frame #13: 0x00007f19e85119fb
    frame #14: 0x00007f19e851189b
    frame #15: 0x00007f1a669d2e04 libcoreclr.so`CallDescrWorkerInternal + 124
    frame #16: 0x00007f1a6681111c libcoreclr.so`MethodDescCallSite::CallTargetWorker(unsigned long const*, unsigned long*, int) + 1708
    frame #17: 0x00007f1a666f80c4 libcoreclr.so`RunMain(MethodDesc*, short, int*, PtrArray**) + 836
    frame #18: 0x00007f1a666f853c libcoreclr.so`Assembly::ExecuteMainMethod(PtrArray**, int) + 460
    frame #19: 0x00007f1a66721b34 libcoreclr.so`CorHost2::ExecuteAssembly(unsigned int, char16_t const*, int, char16_t const**, unsigned int*) + 740
    frame #20: 0x00007f1a666e4340 libcoreclr.so`coreclr_execute_assembly + 144
    frame #21: 0x00007f1a66cac301 libhostpolicy.so`run_app_for_context(hostpolicy_context_t const&, int, char const**) + 1089
    frame #22: 0x00007f1a66cad3f9 libhostpolicy.so`corehost_main + 345
    frame #23: 0x00007f1a66cec685 libhostfxr.so`fx_muxer_t::handle_exec_host_command(std::__cxx11::basic_string<char, std::char_traits<char>,
std::allocator<char> > const&, host_startup_info_t const&, std::__cxx11::basic_string<char, std::char_traits<char>, std::allocator<char> > const&,
std::unordered_map<known_options, std::vector<std::__cxx11::basic_string<char, std::char_traits<char>, std::allocator<char> >,
std::allocator<std::__cxx11::basic_string<char, std::char_traits<char>, std::allocator<char> > > >, known_options_hash, std::equal_to<known_options>,
std::allocator<std::pair<known_options const, std::vector<std::__cxx11::basic_string<char, std::char_traits<char>, std::allocator<char> >,
std::allocator<std::__cxx11::basic_string<char, std::char_traits<char>, std::allocator<char> > > > > > const&, int, char const**, int, host_mode_t, bool,
char*, int, int*) + 1477
    frame #24: 0x00007f1a66ceb67d libhostfxr.so`fx_muxer_t::execute(std::__cxx11::basic_string<char, std::char_traits<char>, std::allocator<char> >, int, char
const**, host_startup_info_t const&, char*, int, int*) + 765
    frame #25: 0x00007f1a66ce55f2 libhostfxr.so`hostfxr_main_startupinfo + 242
    frame #26: 0x000055f86092b21b ApplicationL`exe_start(int, char const**) + 1131
    frame #27: 0x000055f86092b53f ApplicationL`main + 175
```

```
    frame #28: 0x00007f1a66d3f09b libc.so.6`__libc_start_main(main=(ApplicationL`main), argc=1, argv=0x00007ffeebaf9ab8, init=<unavailable>,
fini=<unavailable>, rtld_fini=<unavailable>, stack_end=0x00007ffeebaf9aa8) at libc-start.c:308
    frame #29: 0x000055f86092a399 ApplicationL`_start + 41
  thread #2, stop reason = signal 0
    frame #0: 0x00007f1a66e096f9 libc.so.6`__GI___poll(fds=0x00007f1a66504d98, nfds=1, timeout=-1) at poll.c:29
    frame #1: 0x00007f1a66b7c800 libcoreclr.so`CorUnix::CPalSynchronizationManager::ReadBytesFromProcessPipe(int, unsigned char*, int) + 288
    frame #2: 0x00007f1a66b7be63 libcoreclr.so`CorUnix::CPalSynchronizationManager::WorkerThread(void*) + 147
    frame #3: 0x00007f1a66b859ae libcoreclr.so`CorUnix::CPalThread::ThreadEntry(void*) + 510
    frame #4: 0x00007f1a67203fa3 libpthread.so.0`start_thread(arg=<unavailable>) at pthread_create.c:486
    frame #5: 0x00007f1a66e1406f libc.so.6`__GI___clone at clone.S:95
  thread #3, stop reason = signal 0
    frame #0: 0x00007f1a66e096f9 libc.so.6`__GI___poll(fds=0x00007f19d8000f20, nfds=1, timeout=-1) at poll.c:29
    frame #1: 0x00007f1a66a83d5c libcoreclr.so`ds_ipc_poll(_DiagnosticsIpcPollHandle*, unsigned long, unsigned int, void (*)(char const*, unsigned int)) + 172
    frame #2: 0x00007f1a669fdf4b libcoreclr.so`ds_ipc_stream_factory_get_next_available_stream(void (*)(char const*, unsigned int)) + 731
    frame #3: 0x00007f1a66a02ca6 libcoreclr.so`server_thread(void*) + 198
    frame #4: 0x00007f1a66b859ae libcoreclr.so`CorUnix::CPalThread::ThreadEntry(void*) + 510
    frame #5: 0x00007f1a67203fa3 libpthread.so.0`start_thread(arg=<unavailable>) at pthread_create.c:486
    frame #6: 0x00007f1a66e1406f libc.so.6`__GI___clone at clone.S:95
  thread #4, stop reason = signal 0
    frame #0: 0x00007f1a6720dd0e libpthread.so.0`__libc_open64(file="/tmp/clr-debug-pipe-946-1550598-in", oflag=0) at open64.c:48
    frame #1: 0x00007f1a66a8377f libcoreclr.so`TwoWayPipe::WaitForConnection() + 31
    frame #2: 0x00007f1a66a7e797 libcoreclr.so`DbgTransportSession::TransportWorker() + 183
    frame #3: 0x00007f1a66a7d905 libcoreclr.so`DbgTransportSession::TransportWorkerStatic(void*) + 37
    frame #4: 0x00007f1a66b859ae libcoreclr.so`CorUnix::CPalThread::ThreadEntry(void*) + 510
    frame #5: 0x00007f1a67203fa3 libpthread.so.0`start_thread(arg=<unavailable>) at pthread_create.c:486
    frame #6: 0x00007f1a66e1406f libc.so.6`__GI___clone at clone.S:95
  thread #5, stop reason = signal 0
    frame #0: 0x00007f1a6720a00c libpthread.so.0`__pthread_cond_wait at futex-internal.h:88
    frame #1: 0x00007f1a67209ff1 libpthread.so.0`__pthread_cond_wait at pthread_cond_wait.c:502
    frame #2: 0x00007f1a67209f30 libpthread.so.0`__pthread_cond_wait(cond=0x000055f887bc6ed8, mutex=0x000055f887bc6eb0) at pthread_cond_wait.c:655
    frame #3: 0x00007f1a66b7a172 libcoreclr.so`CorUnix::CPalSynchronizationManager::ThreadNativeWait(CorUnix::_ThreadNativeWaitData*, unsigned int,
CorUnix::ThreadWakeupReason*, unsigned int*) + 354
    frame #4: 0x00007f1a66b79d7a libcoreclr.so`CorUnix::CPalSynchronizationManager::BlockThread(CorUnix::CPalThread*, unsigned int, bool, bool,
CorUnix::ThreadWakeupReason*, unsigned int*) + 378
    frame #5: 0x00007f1a66b7e952 libcoreclr.so`CorUnix::InternalWaitForMultipleObjectsEx(CorUnix::CPalThread*, unsigned int, void* const*, int, unsigned int,
int, int) + 1906
    frame #6: 0x00007f1a66b7ec03 libcoreclr.so`WaitForMultipleObjectsEx + 83
    frame #7: 0x00007f1a66a7c0ad libcoreclr.so`DebuggerRCThread::MainLoop() + 269
    frame #8: 0x00007f1a66a7bf28 libcoreclr.so`DebuggerRCThread::ThreadProc() + 312
    frame #9: 0x00007f1a66a7bc25 libcoreclr.so`DebuggerRCThread::ThreadProcStatic(void*) + 53
    frame #10: 0x00007f1a66b859ae libcoreclr.so`CorUnix::CPalThread::ThreadEntry(void*) + 510
    frame #11: 0x00007f1a67203fa3 libpthread.so.0`start_thread(arg=<unavailable>) at pthread_create.c:486
    frame #12: 0x00007f1a66e1406f libc.so.6`__GI___clone at clone.S:95
  thread #6, stop reason = signal 0
    frame #0: 0x00007f1a6720a3f9 libpthread.so.0`__pthread_cond_timedwait at futex-internal.h:142
    frame #1: 0x00007f1a6720a3da libpthread.so.0`__pthread_cond_timedwait at pthread_cond_wait.c:533
    frame #2: 0x00007f1a6720a2c0 libpthread.so.0`__pthread_cond_timedwait(cond=0x000055f887bd25c8, mutex=0x000055f887bd25a0, abstime=0x00007f1a643ad7d0) at
pthread_cond_wait.c:667
    frame #3: 0x00007f1a66b7a115 libcoreclr.so`CorUnix::CPalSynchronizationManager::ThreadNativeWait(CorUnix::_ThreadNativeWaitData*, unsigned int,
CorUnix::ThreadWakeupReason*, unsigned int*) + 261
    frame #4: 0x00007f1a66b79d7a libcoreclr.so`CorUnix::CPalSynchronizationManager::BlockThread(CorUnix::CPalThread*, unsigned int, bool, bool,
CorUnix::ThreadWakeupReason*, unsigned int*) + 378
    frame #5: 0x00007f1a66b7e952 libcoreclr.so`CorUnix::InternalWaitForMultipleObjectsEx(CorUnix::CPalThread*, unsigned int, void* const*, int, unsigned int,
int, int) + 1906
    frame #6: 0x00007f1a66b7ec03 libcoreclr.so`WaitForMultipleObjectsEx + 83
    frame #7: 0x00007f1a6684d111 libcoreclr.so`FinalizerThread::WaitForFinalizerEvent(CLREvent*) + 177
    frame #8: 0x00007f1a6684d27f libcoreclr.so`FinalizerThread::FinalizerThreadWorker(void*) + 239
    frame #9: 0x00007f1a667dec08 libcoreclr.so`ManagedThreadBase_DispatchOuter(ManagedThreadCallState*) + 344
    frame #10: 0x00007f1a667df10d libcoreclr.so`ManagedThreadBase::FinalizerBase(void (*)(void*)) + 45
    frame #11: 0x00007f1a6684d4b8 libcoreclr.so`FinalizerThread::FinalizerThreadStart(void*) + 88
    frame #12: 0x00007f1a66b859ae libcoreclr.so`CorUnix::CPalThread::ThreadEntry(void*) + 510
    frame #13: 0x00007f1a67203fa3 libpthread.so.0`start_thread(arg=<unavailable>) at pthread_create.c:486
    frame #14: 0x00007f1a66e1406f libc.so.6`__GI___clone at clone.S:95
  thread #7, stop reason = signal 0
    frame #0: 0x00007f1a6720a3f9 libpthread.so.0`__pthread_cond_timedwait at futex-internal.h:142
    frame #1: 0x00007f1a6720a3da libpthread.so.0`__pthread_cond_timedwait at pthread_cond_wait.c:533
    frame #2: 0x00007f1a6720a2c0 libpthread.so.0`__pthread_cond_timedwait(cond=0x00007ed934004fd8, mutex=0x00007ed934004fb0, abstime=0x00007f1a61d44b50) at
pthread_cond_wait.c:667
    frame #3: 0x00007f1a66b7a115 libcoreclr.so`CorUnix::CPalSynchronizationManager::ThreadNativeWait(CorUnix::_ThreadNativeWaitData*, unsigned int,
CorUnix::ThreadWakeupReason*, unsigned int*) + 261
    frame #4: 0x00007f1a66b79d7a libcoreclr.so`CorUnix::CPalSynchronizationManager::BlockThread(CorUnix::CPalThread*, unsigned int, bool, bool,
CorUnix::ThreadWakeupReason*, unsigned int*) + 378
    frame #5: 0x00007f1a66b7f089 libcoreclr.so`SleepEx + 153
    frame #6: 0x00007f1a667e24aa libcoreclr.so`TieredCompilationManager::BackgroundWorkerStart() + 186
    frame #7: 0x00007f1a667e2368 libcoreclr.so`TieredCompilationManager::BackgroundWorkerBootstrapper1(void*) + 104
    frame #8: 0x00007f1a667dec08 libcoreclr.so`ManagedThreadBase_DispatchOuter(ManagedThreadCallState*) + 344
    frame #9: 0x00007f1a667df0bd libcoreclr.so`ManagedThreadBase::KickOff(void (*)(void*), void*) + 45
    frame #10: 0x00007f1a667e2290 libcoreclr.so`TieredCompilationManager::BackgroundWorkerBootstrapper0(void*) + 32
    frame #11: 0x00007f1a66b859ae libcoreclr.so`CorUnix::CPalThread::ThreadEntry(void*) + 510
    frame #12: 0x00007f1a67203fa3 libpthread.so.0`start_thread(arg=<unavailable>) at pthread_create.c:486
    frame #13: 0x00007f1a66e1406f libc.so.6`__GI___clone at clone.S:95
```

Note: We noticed that the current thread #0 was doing garbage collection, and it received a segmentation fault signal. Also, frame #6 shows an invalid pointer that contains regular UNICODE-16 data:

```
(lldb) frame select 6
frame #6: 0x00007f1a669a44f0 libcoreclr.so`WKS::gc_heap::plan_phase(int) + 7104
libcoreclr.so`WKS::gc_heap::plan_phase:
    0x7f1a669a44f0 <+7104>: movl   (%rcx), %edx
    0x7f1a669a44f2 <+7106>: movl   0x4(%rcx), %ecx
    0x7f1a669a44f5 <+7109>: testl  %edx, %edx
```

```
     0x7f1a669a44f7 <+7111>: js       0x7f1a669a4480                    ; <+6992>

(lldb) register read $rcx
     rcx = 0x0062007500670070

(lldb) p/c $rcx
(unsigned long) $3 = p\0g\0u\0b\0
```

3.   We verify the managed heap:

```
(lldb) verifyheap
The GC heap is not in a valid state for traversal.  (Use -ignoreGCState to override.)

(lldb) verifyheap -ignoreGCState
Segment        Object          Failure                         Reason
7ed94f57f6d0   7ed9d28003c0    InvalidMethodTable              Object 7ed9d28003c0 has an invalid method table ffffffffff7fff9a
7ed94f57f6d0   7ed9d28009f0    ObjectReferenceNotPointerAligned Object 7ed9d28009f0 has an unaligned member at offset 8: is not pointer aligned
7ed94f57f6d0   7ed9d2800a08    InvalidMethodTable              Object 7ed9d2800a08 has an invalid method table 0
7ed94f57f6d0   7ed9d2800b70    InvalidMethodTable              Object 7ed9d2800b70 has an invalid method table 0
7ed94f57f6d0   7ed9d2800df8    InvalidMethodTable              Object 7ed9d2800df8 has an invalid method table 0
7ed94f57f6d0   7ed9d2800e58    InvalidMethodTable              Object 7ed9d2800e58 has an invalid method table 0
7ed94f57f6d0   7ed9d2801800    InvalidMethodTable              Object 7ed9d2801800 has an invalid method table ffffffffff7fff98
7ed94f57f6d0   7ed9d2808690    InvalidMethodTable              Object 7ed9d2808690 has an invalid method table 20
7ed94f57f6d0   7ed9d2808750    InvalidObjectReference          Object 7ed9d2808750 has a bad member at offset 40: 88
7ed94f57f6d0   7ed9d2809400    InvalidObjectReference          Object 7ed9d2809400 has a bad member at offset 20: 40
7ed94f57f6d0   7ed9d280ac80    InvalidObjectReference          Object 7ed9d280ac80 has a bad member at offset 8: 28
7ed94f57f6d0   7ed9d280acc0    InvalidObjectReference          Object 7ed9d280acc0 has a bad member at offset 8: 28
7ed94f57f6d0   7ed9d280ad00    InvalidObjectReference          Object 7ed9d280ad00 has a bad member at offset 8: 28
7ed94f57f6d0   7ed9d280ad40    InvalidObjectReference          Object 7ed9d280ad40 has a bad member at offset 8: 28
7ed94f57f6d0   7ed9d280ad80    InvalidObjectReference          Object 7ed9d280ad80 has a bad member at offset 8: 28
[...]
7ed94f57f6d0   7ed9d280fdb0    InvalidObjectReference          Object 7ed9d280fdb0 has a bad member at offset 8: 28
7ed94f57f6d0   7ed9d280fdf8    InvalidObjectReference          Object 7ed9d280fdf8 has a bad member at offset 8: 28
7ed94f57f6d0   7ed9d280fe40    InvalidObjectReference          Object 7ed9d280fe40 has a bad member at offset 8: 28
7ed94f57f6d0   7ed9d280feb0    InvalidMethodTable              Object 7ed9d280feb0 has an invalid method table ffffffffff7fc90a
7ed94f57f6d0   7ed9d280fee8    InvalidObjectReference          Object 7ed9d280fee8 has a bad member at offset 8: 28
7ed94f57f6d0   7ed9d280ff30    InvalidObjectReference          Object 7ed9d280ff30 has a bad member at offset 8: 28
7ed94f57f6d0   7ed9d280ff78    InvalidObjectReference          Object 7ed9d280ff78 has a bad member at offset 8: 28
7ed94f57f6d0   7ed9d280ffc0    InvalidObjectReference          Object 7ed9d280ffc0 has a bad member at offset 8: 28
7ed94f57f6d0   7ed9d2810008    InvalidObjectReference          Object 7ed9d2810008 has a bad member at offset 8: 28
7ed94f57f6d0   7ed9d2810050    InvalidObjectReference          Object 7ed9d2810050 has a bad member at offset 8: 28
7ed94f57f6d0   7ed9d28138c0    InvalidObjectReference          Object 7ed9d28138c0 has a bad member at offset 8: 7ed9d28138e8
7ed94f57f6d0   7ed9d28138e8    InvalidMethodTable              Object 7ed9d28138e8 has an invalid method table 3870
7ed94f57f6d0   7ed9d2813950    InvalidObjectReference          Object 7ed9d2813950 has a bad member at offset 10: 7ed9d2813908

2,201 objects verified, 312 errors.

(lldb) dumpobj 7ed9d2809400
Name:        System.Threading.Thread+StartHelper
MethodTable: 00007f19e85bb668
Canonical MethodTable: 00007f19e85bb668
Tracked Type: false
Size:        64(0x40) bytes
File:        /usr/share/dotnet/shared/Microsoft.NETCore.App/9.0.4/System.Private.CoreLib.dll
Fields:
              MT    Field   Offset                 Type VT     Attr            Value Name
00007f19e84a74f0  4000c14       30        System.Int32  1 instance                0 _maxStackSize
00007f19e84f82d0  4000c15        8     System.Delegate  0 instance 0000000000000000 _start
00007f19e7564910  4000c16       10       System.Object  0 instance 0000000000000000 _startArg
0000000000000000  4000c17       18 ...ation.CultureInfo  0 instance 0000000000000000 _culture
0000000000000000  4000c18       20 ...ation.CultureInfo  0 instance 0000000000000040 _uiCulture
00007f19e85bbae0  4000c19       28 ....ExecutionContext  0 instance ffffffffff7ffee0 _executionContext
0000000000000000  4000c1a        8 ...g.ContextCallback  0   static                  s_threadStartContextCallback
```

4.   We can also inspect raw memory for possible symbolic (x/a) and string references (x/s) and list the nearest objects:

```
(lldb) listnearobj 7ed9d2809400
Before:       7ed9d28093b8 72 (0x48)                         System.Threading.Thread
Current:      7ed9d2809400 64 (0x40)                         System.Threading.Thread+StartHelper
Error Detected: Object 7ed9d2809400 has a bad member at offset 20: 40
Next:         7ed9d2809440 104 (0x68)                        System.Object[]
Heap local consistency not confirmed.
```

Mechanisms (Heap Corruption)

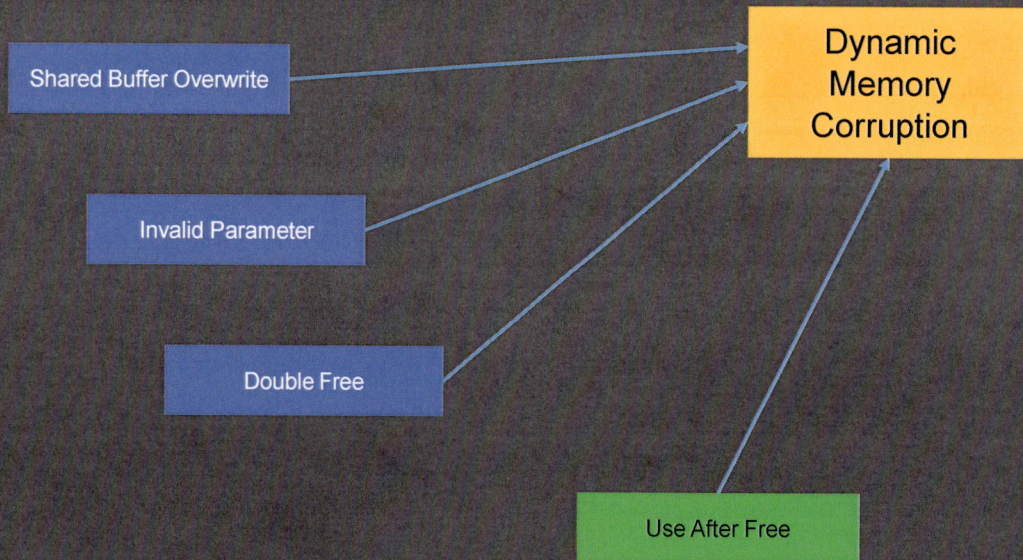

Exercise PN8 (Windows)

- **Goal:** Learn how to navigate virtual memory, search stack traces and memory for data and objects

- **Patterns:** Stack Overflow (Managed Space); Stack Trace Set; Context Pointer

- **Commands:** .kframes, !VMMap, !address, !uniqstack, !findstack, !ObjSize, !DumpArray, du, dpa, dpu, s

- \ANETMDA-Dumps\Exercise-PN8-Windows.pdf

Exercise PN8 (Windows)

Goal: Learn how to navigate virtual memory, search stack traces and memory for data and objects.

Patterns: Stack Overflow (Managed Space); Stack Trace Set; Context Pointer.

Commands: .kframes, !VMMap, !address, !uniqstack, !findstack, !ObjSize, !DumpArray, du, dpa, dpu, s.

1.   Launch WinDbg.

2.   Open \ANETMDA-Dumps\Windows\x64\LINQPad8.exe.3540.dmp

3.   We get the dump file loaded:

```
Microsoft (R) Windows Debugger Version 10.0.27829.1001 AMD64
Copyright (c) Microsoft Corporation. All rights reserved.


Loading Dump File [C:\ANETMDA-Dumps\Windows\x64\LINQPad8.exe.3540.dmp]
User Mini Dump File with Full Memory: Only application data is available


************* Path validation summary **************
Response                      Time (ms)     Location
Deferred                                    srv*
Symbol search path is: srv*
Executable search path is:
Windows 10 Version 22000 MP (4 procs) Free x64
Product: WinNt, suite: SingleUserTS
Edition build lab: 22000.1.amd64fre.co_release.210604-1628
Debug session time: Tue Apr 29 08:30:58.000 2025 (UTC + 1:00)
System Uptime: 0 days 0:37:54.968
Process Uptime: 0 days 0:02:54.000
.........................................................
.........................................................

This dump file has an exception of interest stored in it.
The stored exception information can be accessed via .ecxr
```
(dd4.2134): Stack overflow - code c00000fd (first/second chance not available)
```
For analysis of this file, run !analyze -v
*** WARNING: Unable to verify checksum for LINQPadQuery.dll
LINQPadQuery!UserQuery.<Main>g__foo|4_1+0x1:
00007ffe`82479081 push    rdi
```

5.   Open a log file using **.logopen** command and load the SOS extension if necessary:

```
0:000> .logopen C:\ANETMDA-Dumps\Windows\x64\LINQPadF.log
Opened log file 'C:\ANETMDA-Dumps\Windows\x64\LINQPadF.log'

0:000> .unload sos
Unloading sos extension DLL

0:000> .load C:\Users\dmitr\.dotnet\sos\sos.dll
```

Note: The WinDbg output may be slightly different on your system if you have a different WinDbg version, a different SOS extension version, you don't have .NET 9 installed, or you have a .NET version different from version 9.0.4 that was on a virtual machine where the dump was saved.

4.   Limit the number of frames to show for each stack trace:

```
0:000> .kframes ff
Default stack trace depth is 0n255 frames
```

5.   Verify the correctness of all stack traces:

```
0:000> ~*kL

.  0  Id: dd4.2134 Suspend: 0 Teb: 00000086`341f5000 Unfrozen
 # Child-SP          RetAddr               Call Site
00 00000086`34206000 00007ffe`824790a0    LINQPadQuery!UserQuery.<Main>g__foo|4_1+0x1
01 00000086`34206010 00007ffe`824790a0    LINQPadQuery!UserQuery.<Main>g__foo|4_1+0x20
02 00000086`34206050 00007ffe`824790a0    LINQPadQuery!UserQuery.<Main>g__foo|4_1+0x20
03 00000086`34206090 00007ffe`824790a0    LINQPadQuery!UserQuery.<Main>g__foo|4_1+0x20
04 00000086`342060d0 00007ffe`824790a0    LINQPadQuery!UserQuery.<Main>g__foo|4_1+0x20
05 00000086`34206110 00007ffe`824790a0    LINQPadQuery!UserQuery.<Main>g__foo|4_1+0x20
06 00000086`34206150 00007ffe`824790a0    LINQPadQuery!UserQuery.<Main>g__foo|4_1+0x20
07 00000086`34206190 00007ffe`824790a0    LINQPadQuery!UserQuery.<Main>g__foo|4_1+0x20
08 00000086`342061d0 00007ffe`824790a0    LINQPadQuery!UserQuery.<Main>g__foo|4_1+0x20
09 00000086`34206210 00007ffe`824790a0    LINQPadQuery!UserQuery.<Main>g__foo|4_1+0x20
0a 00000086`34206250 00007ffe`824790a0    LINQPadQuery!UserQuery.<Main>g__foo|4_1+0x20
0b 00000086`34206290 00007ffe`824790a0    LINQPadQuery!UserQuery.<Main>g__foo|4_1+0x20
0c 00000086`342062d0 00007ffe`824790a0    LINQPadQuery!UserQuery.<Main>g__foo|4_1+0x20
0d 00000086`34206310 00007ffe`824790a0    LINQPadQuery!UserQuery.<Main>g__foo|4_1+0x20
0e 00000086`34206350 00007ffe`824790a0    LINQPadQuery!UserQuery.<Main>g__foo|4_1+0x20
0f 00000086`34206390 00007ffe`824790a0    LINQPadQuery!UserQuery.<Main>g__foo|4_1+0x20
10 00000086`342063d0 00007ffe`824790a0    LINQPadQuery!UserQuery.<Main>g__foo|4_1+0x20
11 00000086`34206410 00007ffe`824790a0    LINQPadQuery!UserQuery.<Main>g__foo|4_1+0x20
12 00000086`34206450 00007ffe`824790a0    LINQPadQuery!UserQuery.<Main>g__foo|4_1+0x20
13 00000086`34206490 00007ffe`824790a0    LINQPadQuery!UserQuery.<Main>g__foo|4_1+0x20
14 00000086`342064d0 00007ffe`824790a0    LINQPadQuery!UserQuery.<Main>g__foo|4_1+0x20
15 00000086`34206510 00007ffe`824790a0    LINQPadQuery!UserQuery.<Main>g__foo|4_1+0x20
16 00000086`34206550 00007ffe`824790a0    LINQPadQuery!UserQuery.<Main>g__foo|4_1+0x20
17 00000086`34206590 00007ffe`824790a0    LINQPadQuery!UserQuery.<Main>g__foo|4_1+0x20
18 00000086`342065d0 00007ffe`824790a0    LINQPadQuery!UserQuery.<Main>g__foo|4_1+0x20
19 00000086`34206610 00007ffe`824790a0    LINQPadQuery!UserQuery.<Main>g__foo|4_1+0x20
1a 00000086`34206650 00007ffe`824790a0    LINQPadQuery!UserQuery.<Main>g__foo|4_1+0x20
1b 00000086`34206690 00007ffe`824790a0    LINQPadQuery!UserQuery.<Main>g__foo|4_1+0x20
1c 00000086`342066d0 00007ffe`824790a0    LINQPadQuery!UserQuery.<Main>g__foo|4_1+0x20
1d 00000086`34206710 00007ffe`824790a0    LINQPadQuery!UserQuery.<Main>g__foo|4_1+0x20
1e 00000086`34206750 00007ffe`824790a0    LINQPadQuery!UserQuery.<Main>g__foo|4_1+0x20
1f 00000086`34206790 00007ffe`824790a0    LINQPadQuery!UserQuery.<Main>g__foo|4_1+0x20
20 00000086`342067d0 00007ffe`824790a0    LINQPadQuery!UserQuery.<Main>g__foo|4_1+0x20
21 00000086`34206810 00007ffe`824790a0    LINQPadQuery!UserQuery.<Main>g__foo|4_1+0x20
22 00000086`34206850 00007ffe`824790a0    LINQPadQuery!UserQuery.<Main>g__foo|4_1+0x20
23 00000086`34206890 00007ffe`824790a0    LINQPadQuery!UserQuery.<Main>g__foo|4_1+0x20
24 00000086`342068d0 00007ffe`824790a0    LINQPadQuery!UserQuery.<Main>g__foo|4_1+0x20
25 00000086`34206910 00007ffe`824790a0    LINQPadQuery!UserQuery.<Main>g__foo|4_1+0x20
26 00000086`34206950 00007ffe`824790a0    LINQPadQuery!UserQuery.<Main>g__foo|4_1+0x20
27 00000086`34206990 00007ffe`824790a0    LINQPadQuery!UserQuery.<Main>g__foo|4_1+0x20
28 00000086`342069d0 00007ffe`824790a0    LINQPadQuery!UserQuery.<Main>g__foo|4_1+0x20
29 00000086`34206a10 00007ffe`824790a0    LINQPadQuery!UserQuery.<Main>g__foo|4_1+0x20
2a 00000086`34206a50 00007ffe`824790a0    LINQPadQuery!UserQuery.<Main>g__foo|4_1+0x20
2b 00000086`34206a90 00007ffe`824790a0    LINQPadQuery!UserQuery.<Main>g__foo|4_1+0x20
2c 00000086`34206ad0 00007ffe`824790a0    LINQPadQuery!UserQuery.<Main>g__foo|4_1+0x20
2d 00000086`34206b10 00007ffe`824790a0    LINQPadQuery!UserQuery.<Main>g__foo|4_1+0x20
2e 00000086`34206b50 00007ffe`824790a0    LINQPadQuery!UserQuery.<Main>g__foo|4_1+0x20
2f 00000086`34206b90 00007ffe`824790a0    LINQPadQuery!UserQuery.<Main>g__foo|4_1+0x20
30 00000086`34206bd0 00007ffe`824790a0    LINQPadQuery!UserQuery.<Main>g__foo|4_1+0x20
31 00000086`34206c10 00007ffe`824790a0    LINQPadQuery!UserQuery.<Main>g__foo|4_1+0x20
32 00000086`34206c50 00007ffe`824790a0    LINQPadQuery!UserQuery.<Main>g__foo|4_1+0x20
33 00000086`34206c90 00007ffe`824790a0    LINQPadQuery!UserQuery.<Main>g__foo|4_1+0x20
34 00000086`34206cd0 00007ffe`824790a0    LINQPadQuery!UserQuery.<Main>g__foo|4_1+0x20
35 00000086`34206d10 00007ffe`824790a0    LINQPadQuery!UserQuery.<Main>g__foo|4_1+0x20
36 00000086`34206d50 00007ffe`824790a0    LINQPadQuery!UserQuery.<Main>g__foo|4_1+0x20
37 00000086`34206d90 00007ffe`824790a0    LINQPadQuery!UserQuery.<Main>g__foo|4_1+0x20
38 00000086`34206dd0 00007ffe`824790a0    LINQPadQuery!UserQuery.<Main>g__foo|4_1+0x20
39 00000086`34206e10 00007ffe`824790a0    LINQPadQuery!UserQuery.<Main>g__foo|4_1+0x20
3a 00000086`34206e50 00007ffe`824790a0    LINQPadQuery!UserQuery.<Main>g__foo|4_1+0x20
3b 00000086`34206e90 00007ffe`824790a0    LINQPadQuery!UserQuery.<Main>g__foo|4_1+0x20
3c 00000086`34206ed0 00007ffe`824790a0    LINQPadQuery!UserQuery.<Main>g__foo|4_1+0x20
3d 00000086`34206f10 00007ffe`824790a0    LINQPadQuery!UserQuery.<Main>g__foo|4_1+0x20
3e 00000086`34206f50 00007ffe`824790a0    LINQPadQuery!UserQuery.<Main>g__foo|4_1+0x20
3f 00000086`34206f90 00007ffe`824790a0    LINQPadQuery!UserQuery.<Main>g__foo|4_1+0x20
40 00000086`34206fd0 00007ffe`824790a0    LINQPadQuery!UserQuery.<Main>g__foo|4_1+0x20
41 00000086`34207010 00007ffe`824790a0    LINQPadQuery!UserQuery.<Main>g__foo|4_1+0x20
42 00000086`34207050 00007ffe`824790a0    LINQPadQuery!UserQuery.<Main>g__foo|4_1+0x20
43 00000086`34207090 00007ffe`824790a0    LINQPadQuery!UserQuery.<Main>g__foo|4_1+0x20
44 00000086`342070d0 00007ffe`824790a0    LINQPadQuery!UserQuery.<Main>g__foo|4_1+0x20
45 00000086`34207110 00007ffe`824790a0    LINQPadQuery!UserQuery.<Main>g__foo|4_1+0x20
46 00000086`34207150 00007ffe`824790a0    LINQPadQuery!UserQuery.<Main>g__foo|4_1+0x20
47 00000086`34207190 00007ffe`824790a0    LINQPadQuery!UserQuery.<Main>g__foo|4_1+0x20
48 00000086`342071d0 00007ffe`824790a0    LINQPadQuery!UserQuery.<Main>g__foo|4_1+0x20
```

```
49 00000086`34207210 00007ffe`824790a0   LINQPadQuery!UserQuery.<Main>g__foo|4_1+0x20
4a 00000086`34207250 00007ffe`824790a0   LINQPadQuery!UserQuery.<Main>g__foo|4_1+0x20
4b 00000086`34207290 00007ffe`824790a0   LINQPadQuery!UserQuery.<Main>g__foo|4_1+0x20
4c 00000086`342072d0 00007ffe`824790a0   LINQPadQuery!UserQuery.<Main>g__foo|4_1+0x20
4d 00000086`34207310 00007ffe`824790a0   LINQPadQuery!UserQuery.<Main>g__foo|4_1+0x20
4e 00000086`34207350 00007ffe`824790a0   LINQPadQuery!UserQuery.<Main>g__foo|4_1+0x20
4f 00000086`34207390 00007ffe`824790a0   LINQPadQuery!UserQuery.<Main>g__foo|4_1+0x20
50 00000086`342073d0 00007ffe`824790a0   LINQPadQuery!UserQuery.<Main>g__foo|4_1+0x20
51 00000086`34207410 00007ffe`824790a0   LINQPadQuery!UserQuery.<Main>g__foo|4_1+0x20
52 00000086`34207450 00007ffe`824790a0   LINQPadQuery!UserQuery.<Main>g__foo|4_1+0x20
53 00000086`34207490 00007ffe`824790a0   LINQPadQuery!UserQuery.<Main>g__foo|4_1+0x20
54 00000086`342074d0 00007ffe`824790a0   LINQPadQuery!UserQuery.<Main>g__foo|4_1+0x20
55 00000086`34207510 00007ffe`824790a0   LINQPadQuery!UserQuery.<Main>g__foo|4_1+0x20
56 00000086`34207550 00007ffe`824790a0   LINQPadQuery!UserQuery.<Main>g__foo|4_1+0x20
57 00000086`34207590 00007ffe`824790a0   LINQPadQuery!UserQuery.<Main>g__foo|4_1+0x20
58 00000086`342075d0 00007ffe`824790a0   LINQPadQuery!UserQuery.<Main>g__foo|4_1+0x20
59 00000086`34207610 00007ffe`824790a0   LINQPadQuery!UserQuery.<Main>g__foo|4_1+0x20
5a 00000086`34207650 00007ffe`824790a0   LINQPadQuery!UserQuery.<Main>g__foo|4_1+0x20
5b 00000086`34207690 00007ffe`824790a0   LINQPadQuery!UserQuery.<Main>g__foo|4_1+0x20
5c 00000086`342076d0 00007ffe`824790a0   LINQPadQuery!UserQuery.<Main>g__foo|4_1+0x20
5d 00000086`34207710 00007ffe`824790a0   LINQPadQuery!UserQuery.<Main>g__foo|4_1+0x20
5e 00000086`34207750 00007ffe`824790a0   LINQPadQuery!UserQuery.<Main>g__foo|4_1+0x20
5f 00000086`34207790 00007ffe`824790a0   LINQPadQuery!UserQuery.<Main>g__foo|4_1+0x20
60 00000086`342077d0 00007ffe`824790a0   LINQPadQuery!UserQuery.<Main>g__foo|4_1+0x20
61 00000086`34207810 00007ffe`824790a0   LINQPadQuery!UserQuery.<Main>g__foo|4_1+0x20
62 00000086`34207850 00007ffe`824790a0   LINQPadQuery!UserQuery.<Main>g__foo|4_1+0x20
63 00000086`34207890 00007ffe`824790a0   LINQPadQuery!UserQuery.<Main>g__foo|4_1+0x20
64 00000086`342078d0 00007ffe`824790a0   LINQPadQuery!UserQuery.<Main>g__foo|4_1+0x20
65 00000086`34207910 00007ffe`824790a0   LINQPadQuery!UserQuery.<Main>g__foo|4_1+0x20
66 00000086`34207950 00007ffe`824790a0   LINQPadQuery!UserQuery.<Main>g__foo|4_1+0x20
67 00000086`34207990 00007ffe`824790a0   LINQPadQuery!UserQuery.<Main>g__foo|4_1+0x20
68 00000086`342079d0 00007ffe`824790a0   LINQPadQuery!UserQuery.<Main>g__foo|4_1+0x20
69 00000086`34207a10 00007ffe`824790a0   LINQPadQuery!UserQuery.<Main>g__foo|4_1+0x20
6a 00000086`34207a50 00007ffe`824790a0   LINQPadQuery!UserQuery.<Main>g__foo|4_1+0x20
6b 00000086`34207a90 00007ffe`824790a0   LINQPadQuery!UserQuery.<Main>g__foo|4_1+0x20
6c 00000086`34207ad0 00007ffe`824790a0   LINQPadQuery!UserQuery.<Main>g__foo|4_1+0x20
6d 00000086`34207b10 00007ffe`824790a0   LINQPadQuery!UserQuery.<Main>g__foo|4_1+0x20
6e 00000086`34207b50 00007ffe`824790a0   LINQPadQuery!UserQuery.<Main>g__foo|4_1+0x20
6f 00000086`34207b90 00007ffe`824790a0   LINQPadQuery!UserQuery.<Main>g__foo|4_1+0x20
70 00000086`34207bd0 00007ffe`824790a0   LINQPadQuery!UserQuery.<Main>g__foo|4_1+0x20
71 00000086`34207c10 00007ffe`824790a0   LINQPadQuery!UserQuery.<Main>g__foo|4_1+0x20
72 00000086`34207c50 00007ffe`824790a0   LINQPadQuery!UserQuery.<Main>g__foo|4_1+0x20
73 00000086`34207c90 00007ffe`824790a0   LINQPadQuery!UserQuery.<Main>g__foo|4_1+0x20
74 00000086`34207cd0 00007ffe`824790a0   LINQPadQuery!UserQuery.<Main>g__foo|4_1+0x20
75 00000086`34207d10 00007ffe`824790a0   LINQPadQuery!UserQuery.<Main>g__foo|4_1+0x20
76 00000086`34207d50 00007ffe`824790a0   LINQPadQuery!UserQuery.<Main>g__foo|4_1+0x20
77 00000086`34207d90 00007ffe`824790a0   LINQPadQuery!UserQuery.<Main>g__foo|4_1+0x20
78 00000086`34207dd0 00007ffe`824790a0   LINQPadQuery!UserQuery.<Main>g__foo|4_1+0x20
79 00000086`34207e10 00007ffe`824790a0   LINQPadQuery!UserQuery.<Main>g__foo|4_1+0x20
7a 00000086`34207e50 00007ffe`824790a0   LINQPadQuery!UserQuery.<Main>g__foo|4_1+0x20
7b 00000086`34207e90 00007ffe`824790a0   LINQPadQuery!UserQuery.<Main>g__foo|4_1+0x20
7c 00000086`34207ed0 00007ffe`824790a0   LINQPadQuery!UserQuery.<Main>g__foo|4_1+0x20
7d 00000086`34207f10 00007ffe`824790a0   LINQPadQuery!UserQuery.<Main>g__foo|4_1+0x20
7e 00000086`34207f50 00007ffe`824790a0   LINQPadQuery!UserQuery.<Main>g__foo|4_1+0x20
7f 00000086`34207f90 00007ffe`824790a0   LINQPadQuery!UserQuery.<Main>g__foo|4_1+0x20
80 00000086`34207fd0 00007ffe`824790a0   LINQPadQuery!UserQuery.<Main>g__foo|4_1+0x20
81 00000086`34208010 00007ffe`824790a0   LINQPadQuery!UserQuery.<Main>g__foo|4_1+0x20
82 00000086`34208050 00007ffe`824790a0   LINQPadQuery!UserQuery.<Main>g__foo|4_1+0x20
83 00000086`34208090 00007ffe`824790a0   LINQPadQuery!UserQuery.<Main>g__foo|4_1+0x20
84 00000086`342080d0 00007ffe`824790a0   LINQPadQuery!UserQuery.<Main>g__foo|4_1+0x20
85 00000086`34208110 00007ffe`824790a0   LINQPadQuery!UserQuery.<Main>g__foo|4_1+0x20
86 00000086`34208150 00007ffe`824790a0   LINQPadQuery!UserQuery.<Main>g__foo|4_1+0x20
87 00000086`34208190 00007ffe`824790a0   LINQPadQuery!UserQuery.<Main>g__foo|4_1+0x20
88 00000086`342081d0 00007ffe`824790a0   LINQPadQuery!UserQuery.<Main>g__foo|4_1+0x20
89 00000086`34208210 00007ffe`824790a0   LINQPadQuery!UserQuery.<Main>g__foo|4_1+0x20
8a 00000086`34208250 00007ffe`824790a0   LINQPadQuery!UserQuery.<Main>g__foo|4_1+0x20
8b 00000086`34208290 00007ffe`824790a0   LINQPadQuery!UserQuery.<Main>g__foo|4_1+0x20
8c 00000086`342082d0 00007ffe`824790a0   LINQPadQuery!UserQuery.<Main>g__foo|4_1+0x20
8d 00000086`34208310 00007ffe`824790a0   LINQPadQuery!UserQuery.<Main>g__foo|4_1+0x20
8e 00000086`34208350 00007ffe`824790a0   LINQPadQuery!UserQuery.<Main>g__foo|4_1+0x20
8f 00000086`34208390 00007ffe`824790a0   LINQPadQuery!UserQuery.<Main>g__foo|4_1+0x20
90 00000086`342083d0 00007ffe`824790a0   LINQPadQuery!UserQuery.<Main>g__foo|4_1+0x20
91 00000086`34208410 00007ffe`824790a0   LINQPadQuery!UserQuery.<Main>g__foo|4_1+0x20
92 00000086`34208450 00007ffe`824790a0   LINQPadQuery!UserQuery.<Main>g__foo|4_1+0x20
93 00000086`34208490 00007ffe`824790a0   LINQPadQuery!UserQuery.<Main>g__foo|4_1+0x20
94 00000086`342084d0 00007ffe`824790a0   LINQPadQuery!UserQuery.<Main>g__foo|4_1+0x20
95 00000086`34208510 00007ffe`824790a0   LINQPadQuery!UserQuery.<Main>g__foo|4_1+0x20
96 00000086`34208550 00007ffe`824790a0   LINQPadQuery!UserQuery.<Main>g__foo|4_1+0x20
97 00000086`34208590 00007ffe`824790a0   LINQPadQuery!UserQuery.<Main>g__foo|4_1+0x20
98 00000086`342085d0 00007ffe`824790a0   LINQPadQuery!UserQuery.<Main>g__foo|4_1+0x20
99 00000086`34208610 00007ffe`824790a0   LINQPadQuery!UserQuery.<Main>g__foo|4_1+0x20
9a 00000086`34208650 00007ffe`824790a0   LINQPadQuery!UserQuery.<Main>g__foo|4_1+0x20
9b 00000086`34208690 00007ffe`824790a0   LINQPadQuery!UserQuery.<Main>g__foo|4_1+0x20
9c 00000086`342086d0 00007ffe`824790a0   LINQPadQuery!UserQuery.<Main>g__foo|4_1+0x20
9d 00000086`34208710 00007ffe`824790a0   LINQPadQuery!UserQuery.<Main>g__foo|4_1+0x20
9e 00000086`34208750 00007ffe`824790a0   LINQPadQuery!UserQuery.<Main>g__foo|4_1+0x20
9f 00000086`34208790 00007ffe`824790a0   LINQPadQuery!UserQuery.<Main>g__foo|4_1+0x20
a0 00000086`342087d0 00007ffe`824790a0   LINQPadQuery!UserQuery.<Main>g__foo|4_1+0x20
a1 00000086`34208810 00007ffe`824790a0   LINQPadQuery!UserQuery.<Main>g__foo|4_1+0x20
a2 00000086`34208850 00007ffe`824790a0   LINQPadQuery!UserQuery.<Main>g__foo|4_1+0x20
a3 00000086`34208890 00007ffe`824790a0   LINQPadQuery!UserQuery.<Main>g__foo|4_1+0x20
a4 00000086`342088d0 00007ffe`824790a0   LINQPadQuery!UserQuery.<Main>g__foo|4_1+0x20
a5 00000086`34208910 00007ffe`824790a0   LINQPadQuery!UserQuery.<Main>g__foo|4_1+0x20
a6 00000086`34208950 00007ffe`824790a0   LINQPadQuery!UserQuery.<Main>g__foo|4_1+0x20
a7 00000086`34208990 00007ffe`824790a0   LINQPadQuery!UserQuery.<Main>g__foo|4_1+0x20
a8 00000086`342089d0 00007ffe`824790a0   LINQPadQuery!UserQuery.<Main>g__foo|4_1+0x20
a9 00000086`34208a10 00007ffe`824790a0   LINQPadQuery!UserQuery.<Main>g__foo|4_1+0x20
aa 00000086`34208a50 00007ffe`824790a0   LINQPadQuery!UserQuery.<Main>g__foo|4_1+0x20
```

```
ab 00000086`34208a90 00007ffe`824790a0     LINQPadQuery!UserQuery.<Main>g__foo|4_1+0x20
ac 00000086`34208ad0 00007ffe`824790a0     LINQPadQuery!UserQuery.<Main>g__foo|4_1+0x20
ad 00000086`34208b10 00007ffe`824790a0     LINQPadQuery!UserQuery.<Main>g__foo|4_1+0x20
ae 00000086`34208b50 00007ffe`824790a0     LINQPadQuery!UserQuery.<Main>g__foo|4_1+0x20
af 00000086`34208b90 00007ffe`824790a0     LINQPadQuery!UserQuery.<Main>g__foo|4_1+0x20
b0 00000086`34208bd0 00007ffe`824790a0     LINQPadQuery!UserQuery.<Main>g__foo|4_1+0x20
b1 00000086`34208c10 00007ffe`824790a0     LINQPadQuery!UserQuery.<Main>g__foo|4_1+0x20
b2 00000086`34208c50 00007ffe`824790a0     LINQPadQuery!UserQuery.<Main>g__foo|4_1+0x20
b3 00000086`34208c90 00007ffe`824790a0     LINQPadQuery!UserQuery.<Main>g__foo|4_1+0x20
b4 00000086`34208cd0 00007ffe`824790a0     LINQPadQuery!UserQuery.<Main>g__foo|4_1+0x20
b5 00000086`34208d10 00007ffe`824790a0     LINQPadQuery!UserQuery.<Main>g__foo|4_1+0x20
b6 00000086`34208d50 00007ffe`824790a0     LINQPadQuery!UserQuery.<Main>g__foo|4_1+0x20
b7 00000086`34208d90 00007ffe`824790a0     LINQPadQuery!UserQuery.<Main>g__foo|4_1+0x20
b8 00000086`34208dd0 00007ffe`824790a0     LINQPadQuery!UserQuery.<Main>g__foo|4_1+0x20
b9 00000086`34208e10 00007ffe`824790a0     LINQPadQuery!UserQuery.<Main>g__foo|4_1+0x20
ba 00000086`34208e50 00007ffe`824790a0     LINQPadQuery!UserQuery.<Main>g__foo|4_1+0x20
bb 00000086`34208e90 00007ffe`824790a0     LINQPadQuery!UserQuery.<Main>g__foo|4_1+0x20
bc 00000086`34208ed0 00007ffe`824790a0     LINQPadQuery!UserQuery.<Main>g__foo|4_1+0x20
bd 00000086`34208f10 00007ffe`824790a0     LINQPadQuery!UserQuery.<Main>g__foo|4_1+0x20
be 00000086`34208f50 00007ffe`824790a0     LINQPadQuery!UserQuery.<Main>g__foo|4_1+0x20
bf 00000086`34208f90 00007ffe`824790a0     LINQPadQuery!UserQuery.<Main>g__foo|4_1+0x20
c0 00000086`34208fd0 00007ffe`824790a0     LINQPadQuery!UserQuery.<Main>g__foo|4_1+0x20
c1 00000086`34209010 00007ffe`824790a0     LINQPadQuery!UserQuery.<Main>g__foo|4_1+0x20
c2 00000086`34209050 00007ffe`824790a0     LINQPadQuery!UserQuery.<Main>g__foo|4_1+0x20
c3 00000086`34209090 00007ffe`824790a0     LINQPadQuery!UserQuery.<Main>g__foo|4_1+0x20
c4 00000086`342090d0 00007ffe`824790a0     LINQPadQuery!UserQuery.<Main>g__foo|4_1+0x20
c5 00000086`34209110 00007ffe`824790a0     LINQPadQuery!UserQuery.<Main>g__foo|4_1+0x20
c6 00000086`34209150 00007ffe`824790a0     LINQPadQuery!UserQuery.<Main>g__foo|4_1+0x20
c7 00000086`34209190 00007ffe`824790a0     LINQPadQuery!UserQuery.<Main>g__foo|4_1+0x20
c8 00000086`342091d0 00007ffe`824790a0     LINQPadQuery!UserQuery.<Main>g__foo|4_1+0x20
c9 00000086`34209210 00007ffe`824790a0     LINQPadQuery!UserQuery.<Main>g__foo|4_1+0x20
ca 00000086`34209250 00007ffe`824790a0     LINQPadQuery!UserQuery.<Main>g__foo|4_1+0x20
cb 00000086`34209290 00007ffe`824790a0     LINQPadQuery!UserQuery.<Main>g__foo|4_1+0x20
cc 00000086`342092d0 00007ffe`824790a0     LINQPadQuery!UserQuery.<Main>g__foo|4_1+0x20
cd 00000086`34209310 00007ffe`824790a0     LINQPadQuery!UserQuery.<Main>g__foo|4_1+0x20
ce 00000086`34209350 00007ffe`824790a0     LINQPadQuery!UserQuery.<Main>g__foo|4_1+0x20
cf 00000086`34209390 00007ffe`824790a0     LINQPadQuery!UserQuery.<Main>g__foo|4_1+0x20
d0 00000086`342093d0 00007ffe`824790a0     LINQPadQuery!UserQuery.<Main>g__foo|4_1+0x20
d1 00000086`34209410 00007ffe`824790a0     LINQPadQuery!UserQuery.<Main>g__foo|4_1+0x20
d2 00000086`34209450 00007ffe`824790a0     LINQPadQuery!UserQuery.<Main>g__foo|4_1+0x20
d3 00000086`34209490 00007ffe`824790a0     LINQPadQuery!UserQuery.<Main>g__foo|4_1+0x20
d4 00000086`342094d0 00007ffe`824790a0     LINQPadQuery!UserQuery.<Main>g__foo|4_1+0x20
d5 00000086`34209510 00007ffe`824790a0     LINQPadQuery!UserQuery.<Main>g__foo|4_1+0x20
d6 00000086`34209550 00007ffe`824790a0     LINQPadQuery!UserQuery.<Main>g__foo|4_1+0x20
d7 00000086`34209590 00007ffe`824790a0     LINQPadQuery!UserQuery.<Main>g__foo|4_1+0x20
d8 00000086`342095d0 00007ffe`824790a0     LINQPadQuery!UserQuery.<Main>g__foo|4_1+0x20
d9 00000086`34209610 00007ffe`824790a0     LINQPadQuery!UserQuery.<Main>g__foo|4_1+0x20
da 00000086`34209650 00007ffe`824790a0     LINQPadQuery!UserQuery.<Main>g__foo|4_1+0x20
db 00000086`34209690 00007ffe`824790a0     LINQPadQuery!UserQuery.<Main>g__foo|4_1+0x20
dc 00000086`342096d0 00007ffe`824790a0     LINQPadQuery!UserQuery.<Main>g__foo|4_1+0x20
dd 00000086`34209710 00007ffe`824790a0     LINQPadQuery!UserQuery.<Main>g__foo|4_1+0x20
de 00000086`34209750 00007ffe`824790a0     LINQPadQuery!UserQuery.<Main>g__foo|4_1+0x20
df 00000086`34209790 00007ffe`824790a0     LINQPadQuery!UserQuery.<Main>g__foo|4_1+0x20
e0 00000086`342097d0 00007ffe`824790a0     LINQPadQuery!UserQuery.<Main>g__foo|4_1+0x20
e1 00000086`34209810 00007ffe`824790a0     LINQPadQuery!UserQuery.<Main>g__foo|4_1+0x20
e2 00000086`34209850 00007ffe`824790a0     LINQPadQuery!UserQuery.<Main>g__foo|4_1+0x20
e3 00000086`34209890 00007ffe`824790a0     LINQPadQuery!UserQuery.<Main>g__foo|4_1+0x20
e4 00000086`342098d0 00007ffe`824790a0     LINQPadQuery!UserQuery.<Main>g__foo|4_1+0x20
e5 00000086`34209910 00007ffe`824790a0     LINQPadQuery!UserQuery.<Main>g__foo|4_1+0x20
e6 00000086`34209950 00007ffe`824790a0     LINQPadQuery!UserQuery.<Main>g__foo|4_1+0x20
e7 00000086`34209990 00007ffe`824790a0     LINQPadQuery!UserQuery.<Main>g__foo|4_1+0x20
e8 00000086`342099d0 00007ffe`824790a0     LINQPadQuery!UserQuery.<Main>g__foo|4_1+0x20
e9 00000086`34209a10 00007ffe`824790a0     LINQPadQuery!UserQuery.<Main>g__foo|4_1+0x20
ea 00000086`34209a50 00007ffe`824790a0     LINQPadQuery!UserQuery.<Main>g__foo|4_1+0x20
eb 00000086`34209a90 00007ffe`824790a0     LINQPadQuery!UserQuery.<Main>g__foo|4_1+0x20
ec 00000086`34209ad0 00007ffe`824790a0     LINQPadQuery!UserQuery.<Main>g__foo|4_1+0x20
ed 00000086`34209b10 00007ffe`824790a0     LINQPadQuery!UserQuery.<Main>g__foo|4_1+0x20
ee 00000086`34209b50 00007ffe`824790a0     LINQPadQuery!UserQuery.<Main>g__foo|4_1+0x20
ef 00000086`34209b90 00007ffe`824790a0     LINQPadQuery!UserQuery.<Main>g__foo|4_1+0x20
f0 00000086`34209bd0 00007ffe`824790a0     LINQPadQuery!UserQuery.<Main>g__foo|4_1+0x20
f1 00000086`34209c10 00007ffe`824790a0     LINQPadQuery!UserQuery.<Main>g__foo|4_1+0x20
f2 00000086`34209c50 00007ffe`824790a0     LINQPadQuery!UserQuery.<Main>g__foo|4_1+0x20
f3 00000086`34209c90 00007ffe`824790a0     LINQPadQuery!UserQuery.<Main>g__foo|4_1+0x20
f4 00000086`34209cd0 00007ffe`824790a0     LINQPadQuery!UserQuery.<Main>g__foo|4_1+0x20
f5 00000086`34209d10 00007ffe`824790a0     LINQPadQuery!UserQuery.<Main>g__foo|4_1+0x20
f6 00000086`34209d50 00007ffe`824790a0     LINQPadQuery!UserQuery.<Main>g__foo|4_1+0x20
f7 00000086`34209d90 00007ffe`824790a0     LINQPadQuery!UserQuery.<Main>g__foo|4_1+0x20
f8 00000086`34209dd0 00007ffe`824790a0     LINQPadQuery!UserQuery.<Main>g__foo|4_1+0x20
f9 00000086`34209e10 00007ffe`824790a0     LINQPadQuery!UserQuery.<Main>g__foo|4_1+0x20
fa 00000086`34209e50 00007ffe`824790a0     LINQPadQuery!UserQuery.<Main>g__foo|4_1+0x20
fb 00000086`34209e90 00007ffe`824790a0     LINQPadQuery!UserQuery.<Main>g__foo|4_1+0x20
fc 00000086`34209ed0 00007ffe`824790a0     LINQPadQuery!UserQuery.<Main>g__foo|4_1+0x20
fd 00000086`34209f10 00007ffe`824790a0     LINQPadQuery!UserQuery.<Main>g__foo|4_1+0x20
fe 00000086`34209f50 00007ffe`824790a0     LINQPadQuery!UserQuery.<Main>g__foo|4_1+0x20

   1  Id: dd4.1a54 Suspend: 0 Teb: 00000086`341fd000 Unfrozen ".NET EventPipe"
 # Child-SP          RetAddr               Call Site
00 00000086`346ff4c8 00007fff`3f07dcb0     ntdll!NtWaitForMultipleObjects+0x14
01 00000086`346ff4d0 00007fff`3f07dbae     KERNELBASE!WaitForMultipleObjectsEx+0xf0
02 00000086`346ff7c0 00007ffe`e171693f     KERNELBASE!WaitForMultipleObjects+0xe
03 00000086`346ff800 00007ffe`e17168a0     coreclr!ds_ipc_poll+0x7f
04 00000086`346ffa80 00007ffe`e1716784     coreclr!ds_ipc_stream_factory_get_next_available_stream+0x108
05 00000086`346ffb50 00007fff`400f53e0     coreclr!server_thread+0x54
06 00000086`346ffbc0 00007fff`4160485b     kernel32!BaseThreadInitThunk+0x10
07 00000086`346ffbf0 00000000`00000000     ntdll!RtlUserThreadStart+0x2b

   2  Id: dd4.1550 Suspend: 0 Teb: 00000086`34000000 Unfrozen ".NET Debugger"
 # Child-SP          RetAddr               Call Site
```

```
00 00000086`347ff3d8 00007fff`3f07dcb0   ntdll!NtWaitForMultipleObjects+0x14
01 00000086`347ff3e0 00007ffe`e1707a9e   KERNELBASE!WaitForMultipleObjectsEx+0xf0
02 00000086`347ff6d0 00007ffe`e1707e26   coreclr!DebuggerRCThread::MainLoop+0xee
03 00000086`347ff790 00007ffe`e170785b   coreclr!DebuggerRCThread::ThreadProc+0x12e
04 00000086`347ff7f0 00007fff`400f53e0   coreclr!DebuggerRCThread::ThreadProcStatic+0x5b
05 00000086`347ff820 00007fff`4160485b   kernel32!BaseThreadInitThunk+0x10
06 00000086`347ff850 00000000`00000000   ntdll!RtlUserThreadStart+0x2b

   3  Id: dd4.1714 Suspend: 0 Teb: 00000086`34002000 Unfrozen ".NET Finalizer"
 # Child-SP          RetAddr               Call Site
00 00000086`348ff6b8 00007fff`3f0710ce   ntdll!NtWaitForSingleObject+0x14
01 00000086`348ff6c0 00007ffe`e17093a3   KERNELBASE!WaitForSingleObjectEx+0x8e
02 (Inline Function) --------`--------   coreclr!CLREventWaitHelper2+0x6
03 00000086`348ff760 00007ffe`e1708a39   coreclr!CLREventWaitHelper+0xf
04 (Inline Function) --------`--------   coreclr!CLREventBase::WaitEx+0x10
05 (Inline Function) --------`--------   coreclr!CLREventBase::Wait+0x10
06 00000086`348ff7b0 00007ffe`e170889f   coreclr!FinalizerThread::WaitForFinalizerEvent+0x21
07 00000086`348ff7f0 00007ffe`e16aef05   coreclr!FinalizerThread::FinalizerThreadWorker+0x4f
08 (Inline Function) --------`--------   coreclr!ManagedThreadBase_DispatchInner+0xd
09 00000086`348ffa40 00007ffe`e16aee2d   coreclr!ManagedThreadBase_DispatchMiddle+0x79
0a 00000086`348ffaf0 00007ffe`e16fe921   coreclr!ManagedThreadBase_DispatchOuter+0x8d
0b (Inline Function) --------`--------   coreclr!ManagedThreadBase_NoADTransition+0x28
0c (Inline Function) --------`--------   coreclr!ManagedThreadBase::FinalizerBase+0x28
0d 00000086`348ffb60 00007fff`400f53e0   coreclr!FinalizerThread::FinalizerThreadStart+0x91
0e 00000086`348ffc70 00007fff`4160485b   kernel32!BaseThreadInitThunk+0x10
0f 00000086`348ffca0 00000000`00000000   ntdll!RtlUserThreadStart+0x2b

   4  Id: dd4.20cc Suspend: 0 Teb: 00000086`34008000 Unfrozen ".NET TP Wait"
 # Child-SP          RetAddr               Call Site
00 00000086`33f6f078 00007fff`3f07dcb0   ntdll!NtWaitForMultipleObjects+0x14
01 00000086`33f6f080 00007ffe`e15fe800   KERNELBASE!WaitForMultipleObjectsEx+0xf0
02 00000086`33f6f370 00007ffe`e15fe523   coreclr!Thread::DoAppropriateAptStateWait+0x5c
03 00000086`33f6f3b0 00007ffe`e15fe35a   coreclr!Thread::DoAppropriateWaitWorker+0x17b
04 00000086`33f6f480 00007ffe`e15fcd19   coreclr!Thread::DoAppropriateWait+0xa6
05 00000086`33f6f520 00007ffe`e0b06fc3   coreclr!WaitHandleNative::CorWaitMultipleNative+0xf9
06 00000086`33f6f6c0 00007ffe`e0b22dcc   System_Private_CoreLib!System.Threading.WaitHandle.WaitAnyMultiple+0xd3
07 00000086`33f6f750 00007ffe`e1742eb3   System_Private_CoreLib!System.Threading.PortableThreadPool.WaitThread.WaitThreadStart+0x8c
08 00000086`33f6f7b0 00007ffe`e16c1568   coreclr!CallDescrWorkerInternal+0x83
09 00000086`33f6f7f0 00007ffe`e17315a3   coreclr!DispatchCallSimple+0x60
0a 00000086`33f6f880 00007ffe`e16aef05   coreclr!ThreadNative::KickOffThread_Worker+0x63
0b (Inline Function) --------`--------   coreclr!ManagedThreadBase_DispatchInner+0xd
0c 00000086`33f6f8e0 00007ffe`e16aee2d   coreclr!ManagedThreadBase_DispatchMiddle+0x79
0d 00000086`33f6f990 00007ffe`e16aefbb   coreclr!ManagedThreadBase_DispatchOuter+0x8d
0e (Inline Function) --------`--------   coreclr!ManagedThreadBase_FullTransition+0x28
0f (Inline Function) --------`--------   coreclr!ManagedThreadBase::KickOff+0x28
10 00000086`33f6fa00 00007fff`400f53e0   coreclr!ThreadNative::KickOffThread+0x7b
11 00000086`33f6fa60 00007fff`4160485b   kernel32!BaseThreadInitThunk+0x10
12 00000086`33f6fa90 00000000`00000000   ntdll!RtlUserThreadStart+0x2b

   5  Id: dd4.a10 Suspend: 0 Teb: 00000086`3400c000 Unfrozen ".NET TP Gate"
 # Child-SP          RetAddr               Call Site
00 00000086`33faf088 00007fff`3f07dcb0   ntdll!NtWaitForMultipleObjects+0x14
01 00000086`33faf090 00007ffe`e15fe800   KERNELBASE!WaitForMultipleObjectsEx+0xf0
02 00000086`33faf380 00007ffe`e15fe523   coreclr!Thread::DoAppropriateAptStateWait+0x5c
03 00000086`33faf3c0 00007ffe`e15fe35a   coreclr!Thread::DoAppropriateWaitWorker+0x17b
04 00000086`33faf490 00007ffe`e15fe24b   coreclr!Thread::DoAppropriateWait+0xa6
05 00000086`33faf530 00007ffe`e0b06653   coreclr!WaitHandleNative::CorWaitOneNative+0xdb
06 00000086`33faf6a0 00007ffe`e0b208ed   System_Private_CoreLib!System.Threading.WaitHandle.WaitOneNoCheck+0x83
07 00000086`33faf710 00007ffe`e1742eb3   System_Private_CoreLib!System.Threading.PortableThreadPool.GateThread.GateThreadStart+0x18d
08 00000086`33faf880 00007ffe`e16c1568   coreclr!CallDescrWorkerInternal+0x83
09 00000086`33faf8c0 00007ffe`e17315a3   coreclr!DispatchCallSimple+0x60
0a 00000086`33faf950 00007ffe`e16aef05   coreclr!ThreadNative::KickOffThread_Worker+0x63
0b (Inline Function) --------`--------   coreclr!ManagedThreadBase_DispatchInner+0xd
0c 00000086`33faf9b0 00007ffe`e16aee2d   coreclr!ManagedThreadBase_DispatchMiddle+0x79
0d 00000086`33fafa60 00007ffe`e16aefbb   coreclr!ManagedThreadBase_DispatchOuter+0x8d
0e (Inline Function) --------`--------   coreclr!ManagedThreadBase_FullTransition+0x28
0f (Inline Function) --------`--------   coreclr!ManagedThreadBase::KickOff+0x28
10 00000086`33fafad0 00007fff`400f53e0   coreclr!ThreadNative::KickOffThread+0x7b
11 00000086`33fafb30 00007fff`4160485b   kernel32!BaseThreadInitThunk+0x10
12 00000086`33fafb60 00000000`00000000   ntdll!RtlUserThreadStart+0x2b

   6  Id: dd4.fec Suspend: 0 Teb: 00000086`34014000 Unfrozen ".NET Timer"
 # Child-SP          RetAddr               Call Site
00 00000086`34eff3d8 00007fff`3f07dcb0   ntdll!NtWaitForMultipleObjects+0x14
01 00000086`34eff3e0 00007ffe`e15fe800   KERNELBASE!WaitForMultipleObjectsEx+0xf0
02 00000086`34eff6d0 00007ffe`e15fe523   coreclr!Thread::DoAppropriateAptStateWait+0x5c
03 00000086`34eff710 00007ffe`e15fe35a   coreclr!Thread::DoAppropriateWaitWorker+0x17b
04 00000086`34eff7e0 00007ffe`e15fe24b   coreclr!Thread::DoAppropriateWait+0xa6
05 00000086`34eff880 00007ffe`e0b06653   coreclr!WaitHandleNative::CorWaitOneNative+0xdb
06 00000086`34eff9f0 00007fff`e0b1945f   System_Private_CoreLib!System.Threading.WaitHandle.WaitOneNoCheck+0x83
07 00000086`34effa60 00007ffe`e1742eb3   System_Private_CoreLib!System.Threading.TimerQueue.TimerThread+0x7f
08 00000086`34effaf0 00007ffe`e16c1568   coreclr!CallDescrWorkerInternal+0x83
09 00000086`34effb30 00007ffe`e17315a3   coreclr!DispatchCallSimple+0x60
0a 00000086`34effbc0 00007ffe`e16aef05   coreclr!ThreadNative::KickOffThread_Worker+0x63
0b (Inline Function) --------`--------   coreclr!ManagedThreadBase_DispatchInner+0xd
0c 00000086`34effc20 00007ffe`e16aee2d   coreclr!ManagedThreadBase_DispatchMiddle+0x79
0d 00000086`34effcd0 00007ffe`e16aefbb   coreclr!ManagedThreadBase_DispatchOuter+0x8d
0e (Inline Function) --------`--------   coreclr!ManagedThreadBase_FullTransition+0x28
0f (Inline Function) --------`--------   coreclr!ManagedThreadBase::KickOff+0x28
10 00000086`34effd40 00007fff`400f53e0   coreclr!ThreadNative::KickOffThread+0x7b
11 00000086`34effda0 00007fff`4160485b   kernel32!BaseThreadInitThunk+0x10
12 00000086`34effdd0 00000000`00000000   ntdll!RtlUserThreadStart+0x2b

   7  Id: dd4.1608 Suspend: 0 Teb: 00000086`34018000 Unfrozen
 # Child-SP          RetAddr               Call Site
00 00000086`350ff8d8 00007fff`41616cdf   ntdll!NtWaitForWorkViaWorkerFactory+0x14
01 00000086`350ff8e0 00007fff`400f53e0   ntdll!TppWorkerThread+0x2df
02 00000086`350ffbd0 00007fff`4160485b   kernel32!BaseThreadInitThunk+0x10
```

```
03 00000086`350ffc00 00000000`00000000     ntdll!RtlUserThreadStart+0x2b

   8  Id: dd4.1628 Suspend: 0 Teb: 00000086`3401e000 Unfrozen ".NET Tiered Compilation Worker"
 # Child-SP          RetAddr               Call Site
00 00000086`343ff568 00007fff`4165b903     ntdll!NtDelayExecution+0x14
01 00000086`343ff570 00007fff`3f04d031     ntdll!RtlDelayExecution+0x43
02 00000086`343ff5a0 00007ffe`e1708715     KERNELBASE!SleepEx+0x71
03 (Inline Function) --------`--------     coreclr!ClrSleepEx+0xa
04 00000086`343ff620 00007ffe`e1708645     coreclr!TieredCompilationManager::BackgroundWorkerStart+0x91
05 00000086`343ff670 00007ffe`e16aef05     coreclr!TieredCompilationManager::BackgroundWorkerBootstrapper1+0x55
06 (Inline Function) --------`--------     coreclr!ManagedThreadBase_DispatchInner+0xd
07 00000086`343ff6b0 00007ffe`e16aee2d     coreclr!ManagedThreadBase_DispatchMiddle+0x79
08 00000086`343ff760 00007ffe`e173c8da     coreclr!ManagedThreadBase_DispatchOuter+0x8d
09 (Inline Function) --------`--------     coreclr!ManagedThreadBase_FullTransition+0x24
0a (Inline Function) --------`--------     coreclr!ManagedThreadBase::KickOff+0x24
0b 00000086`343ff7d0 00007fff`400f53e0     coreclr!TieredCompilationManager::BackgroundWorkerBootstrapper0+0x3a
0c 00000086`343ff820 00007fff`4160485b     kernel32!BaseThreadInitThunk+0x10
0d 00000086`343ff850 00000000`00000000     ntdll!RtlUserThreadStart+0x2b

   9  Id: dd4.df4 Suspend: 0 Teb: 00000086`34020000 Unfrozen ".NET TP Worker"
 # Child-SP          RetAddr               Call Site
00 00000086`344ff538 00007fff`3f07ebd3     ntdll!NtRemoveIoCompletion+0x14
01 00000086`344ff540 00007ffe`e09d90e6     KERNELBASE!GetQueuedCompletionStatus+0x53
02 00000086`344ff6a0 00007ffe`e0b242bd     System_Private_CoreLib!Interop.Kernel32.GetQueuedCompletionStatus+0xa6
03 00000086`344ff6a0 00007ffe`e0b24256     System_Private_CoreLib!System.Threading.LowLevelLifoSemaphore.WaitForSignal+0x4d
04 00000086`344ff710 00007ffe`e0b235be     System_Private_CoreLib!System.Threading.LowLevelLifoSemaphore.Wait+0x1a6
05 00000086`344ff770 00007ffe`e1742eb3     System_Private_CoreLib!System.Threading.PortableThreadPool.WorkerThread.WorkerThreadStart+0x12e
06 00000086`344ff880 00007ffe`e16c1568     coreclr!CallDescrWorkerInternal+0x83
07 00000086`344ff8c0 00007ffe`e17315a3     coreclr!DispatchCallSimple+0x60
08 00000086`344ff950 00007ffe`e16aef05     coreclr!ThreadNative::KickOffThread_Worker+0x63
09 (Inline Function) --------`--------     coreclr!ManagedThreadBase_DispatchInner+0xd
0a 00000086`344ff9b0 00007ffe`e16aee2d     coreclr!ManagedThreadBase_DispatchMiddle+0x79
0b 00000086`344ffa60 00007ffe`e16aefbb     coreclr!ManagedThreadBase_DispatchOuter+0x8d
0c (Inline Function) --------`--------     coreclr!ManagedThreadBase_FullTransition+0x28
0d (Inline Function) --------`--------     coreclr!ManagedThreadBase::KickOff+0x28
0e 00000086`344ffad0 00007fff`400f53e0     coreclr!ThreadNative::KickOffThread+0x7b
0f 00000086`344ffb30 00007fff`4160485b     kernel32!BaseThreadInitThunk+0x10
10 00000086`344ffb60 00000000`00000000     ntdll!RtlUserThreadStart+0x2b

  10  Id: dd4.bfc Suspend: 0 Teb: 00000086`34022000 Unfrozen ".NET TP Worker"
 # Child-SP          RetAddr               Call Site
00 00000086`345ff628 00007fff`3f07ebd3     ntdll!NtRemoveIoCompletion+0x14
01 00000086`345ff630 00007ffe`e09d90e6     KERNELBASE!GetQueuedCompletionStatus+0x53
02 00000086`345ff690 00007ffe`e0b242bd     System_Private_CoreLib!Interop.Kernel32.GetQueuedCompletionStatus+0xa6
03 00000086`345ff790 00007ffe`e0b24256     System_Private_CoreLib!System.Threading.LowLevelLifoSemaphore.WaitForSignal+0x4d
04 00000086`345ff800 00007ffe`e0b235be     System_Private_CoreLib!System.Threading.LowLevelLifoSemaphore.Wait+0x1a6
05 00000086`345ff860 00007ffe`e1742eb3     System_Private_CoreLib!System.Threading.PortableThreadPool.WorkerThread.WorkerThreadStart+0x12e
06 00000086`345ff970 00007ffe`e16c1568     coreclr!CallDescrWorkerInternal+0x83
07 00000086`345ff9b0 00007ffe`e17315a3     coreclr!DispatchCallSimple+0x60
08 00000086`345ffa40 00007ffe`e16aef05     coreclr!ThreadNative::KickOffThread_Worker+0x63
09 (Inline Function) --------`--------     coreclr!ManagedThreadBase_DispatchInner+0xd
0a 00000086`345ffaa0 00007ffe`e16aee2d     coreclr!ManagedThreadBase_DispatchMiddle+0x79
0b 00000086`345ffb50 00007ffe`e16aefbb     coreclr!ManagedThreadBase_DispatchOuter+0x8d
0c (Inline Function) --------`--------     coreclr!ManagedThreadBase_FullTransition+0x28
0d (Inline Function) --------`--------     coreclr!ManagedThreadBase::KickOff+0x28
0e 00000086`345ffbc0 00007fff`400f53e0     coreclr!ThreadNative::KickOffThread+0x7b
0f 00000086`345ffc20 00007fff`4160485b     kernel32!BaseThreadInitThunk+0x10
10 00000086`345ffc50 00000000`00000000     ntdll!RtlUserThreadStart+0x2b

  11  Id: dd4.1b20 Suspend: 0 Teb: 00000086`34024000 Unfrozen ".NET TP Worker"
 # Child-SP          RetAddr               Call Site
00 00000086`349ff6a8 00007fff`3f07ebd3     ntdll!NtRemoveIoCompletion+0x14
01 00000086`349ff6b0 00007ffe`e09d90e6     KERNELBASE!GetQueuedCompletionStatus+0x53
02 00000086`349ff710 00007ffe`e0b242bd     System_Private_CoreLib!Interop.Kernel32.GetQueuedCompletionStatus+0xa6
03 00000086`349ff810 00007ffe`e0b24256     System_Private_CoreLib!System.Threading.LowLevelLifoSemaphore.WaitForSignal+0x4d
04 00000086`349ff880 00007ffe`e0b235be     System_Private_CoreLib!System.Threading.LowLevelLifoSemaphore.Wait+0x1a6
05 00000086`349ff8e0 00007ffe`e1742eb3     System_Private_CoreLib!System.Threading.PortableThreadPool.WorkerThread.WorkerThreadStart+0x12e
06 00000086`349ff9f0 00007ffe`e16c1568     coreclr!CallDescrWorkerInternal+0x83
07 00000086`349ffa30 00007ffe`e17315a3     coreclr!DispatchCallSimple+0x60
08 00000086`349ffac0 00007ffe`e16aef05     coreclr!ThreadNative::KickOffThread_Worker+0x63
09 (Inline Function) --------`--------     coreclr!ManagedThreadBase_DispatchInner+0xd
0a 00000086`349ffb20 00007ffe`e16aee2d     coreclr!ManagedThreadBase_DispatchMiddle+0x79
0b 00000086`349ffbd0 00007ffe`e16aefbb     coreclr!ManagedThreadBase_DispatchOuter+0x8d
0c (Inline Function) --------`--------     coreclr!ManagedThreadBase_FullTransition+0x28
0d (Inline Function) --------`--------     coreclr!ManagedThreadBase::KickOff+0x28
0e 00000086`349ffc40 00007fff`400f53e0     coreclr!ThreadNative::KickOffThread+0x7b
0f 00000086`349ffca0 00007fff`4160485b     kernel32!BaseThreadInitThunk+0x10
10 00000086`349ffcd0 00000000`00000000     ntdll!RtlUserThreadStart+0x2b

  12  Id: dd4.1030 Suspend: 0 Teb: 00000086`34026000 Unfrozen ".NET TP Worker"
 # Child-SP          RetAddr               Call Site
00 00000086`34aff758 00007fff`3f07ebd3     ntdll!NtRemoveIoCompletion+0x14
01 00000086`34aff760 00007ffe`e09d90e6     KERNELBASE!GetQueuedCompletionStatus+0x53
02 00000086`34aff7c0 00007ffe`e0b242bd     System_Private_CoreLib!Interop.Kernel32.GetQueuedCompletionStatus+0xa6
03 00000086`34aff8c0 00007ffe`e0b24256     System_Private_CoreLib!System.Threading.LowLevelLifoSemaphore.WaitForSignal+0x4d
04 00000086`34aff930 00007ffe`e0b2355b     System_Private_CoreLib!System.Threading.LowLevelLifoSemaphore.Wait+0x1a6
05 00000086`34aff990 00007ffe`e1742eb3     System_Private_CoreLib!System.Threading.PortableThreadPool.WorkerThread.WorkerThreadStart+0xcb
06 00000086`34affaa0 00007ffe`e16c1568     coreclr!CallDescrWorkerInternal+0x83
07 00000086`34affae0 00007ffe`e17315a3     coreclr!DispatchCallSimple+0x60
08 00000086`34affb70 00007ffe`e16aef05     coreclr!ThreadNative::KickOffThread_Worker+0x63
09 (Inline Function) --------`--------     coreclr!ManagedThreadBase_DispatchInner+0xd
0a 00000086`34affbd0 00007ffe`e16aee2d     coreclr!ManagedThreadBase_DispatchMiddle+0x79
0b 00000086`34affc80 00007ffe`e16aefbb     coreclr!ManagedThreadBase_DispatchOuter+0x8d
0c (Inline Function) --------`--------     coreclr!ManagedThreadBase_FullTransition+0x28
0d (Inline Function) --------`--------     coreclr!ManagedThreadBase::KickOff+0x28
0e 00000086`34affcf0 00007fff`400f53e0     coreclr!ThreadNative::KickOffThread+0x7b
0f 00000086`34affd50 00007fff`4160485b     kernel32!BaseThreadInitThunk+0x10
10 00000086`34affd80 00000000`00000000     ntdll!RtlUserThreadStart+0x2b
```

Note: We notice that the current thread #0 is active and is doing recursive calls. We suspect stack overflow. Let's compare the current thread stack pointer with the thread stack region limit value:

```
0:000> r rsp
rsp=0000008634206000
```

```
0:000> !teb
TEB at 00000086341f5000
    ExceptionList:          0000000000000000
    StackBase:              0000008634300000
    StackLimit:             0000008634201000
    SubSystemTib:           0000000000000000
    FiberData:              0000000000001e00
    ArbitraryUserPointer:   0000000000000000
    Self:                   00000086341f5000
    EnvironmentPointer:     0000000000000000
    ClientId:               0000000000000dd4 . 0000000000002134
    RpcHandle:              0000000000000000
    Tls Storage:            000002336e5b42e0
    PEB Address:            00000086341f4000
    LastErrorValue:         0
    LastStatusValue:        c0000034
    Count Owned Locks:      0
    HardErrorMode:          0
```

Note: We notice it is very close to the limit. We check the last calls and also try to get a managed stack trace (time-consuming operation):

```
0:000> k 3
 # Child-SP          RetAddr           Call Site
00 00000086`34206000 00007ffe`824790a0 LINQPadQuery!UserQuery.<Main>g__foo|4_1+0x1
01 00000086`34206010 00007ffe`824790a0 LINQPadQuery!UserQuery.<Main>g__foo|4_1+0x20
02 00000086`34206050 00007ffe`824790a0 LINQPadQuery!UserQuery.<Main>g__foo|4_1+0x20
```

```
0:000> !IP2MD 00007ffe`824790a0
MethodDesc:     00007ffe82506118
Method Name:            UserQuery.<Main>g__foo|4_1()
Class:                  00007ffe82506150
MethodTable:            00007ffe82506150
mdToken:                0000000006000007
Module:                 00007ffe8245eb98
IsJitted:               yes
Current CodeAddr:       00007ffe82479080
Version History:
  ILCodeVersion:        0000000000000000
  ReJIT ID:             0
  IL Addr:              000001f2d99620f2
     CodeAddr:              00007ffe82479080  (MinOptJitted)
     NativeCodeVersion:    0000000000000000
```

```
0:000> !DumpIL 00007ffe82506118
ilAddr is 000001F2D99620F2 pImport is 000001AAB34FF6D0
ilAddr = 000001F2D99620F2
IL_0000: nop
IL_0001: call void UserQuery::<Main>g__foo|4_1()
IL_0006: nop
IL_0007: ret
```

```
0:000> !U 00007ffe82506118
Normal JIT generated code
UserQuery.<Main>g__foo|4_1()
ilAddr is 000001F2D99620F2 pImport is 000002425BCC0B90
Begin 00007FFE82479080, size 29
00007ffe`82479080 push    rbp
00007ffe`82479081 push    rdi
00007ffe`82479082 sub     rsp,28h
00007ffe`82479086 lea     rbp,[rsp+30h]
00007ffe`8247908b cmp     dword ptr [00007ffe`8245ede0],0
00007ffe`82479092 je      LINQPadQuery!UserQuery.<Main>g__foo|4_1+0x19 (00007ffe`82479099)
00007ffe`82479094 call    coreclr!JIT_DbgIsJustMyCode (00007ffe`e18533c0)
00007ffe`82479099 nop
00007ffe`8247909a call    qword ptr [CLRStub[MethodDescPrestub]@00007FFE8241C498 (00007ffe`8241c498)]
00007ffe`824790a0 nop
00007ffe`824790a1 nop
00007ffe`824790a2 add     rsp,28h
00007ffe`824790a6 pop     rdi
00007ffe`824790a7 pop     rbp
00007ffe`824790a8 ret


0:000> dps 00007ffe`8241c498 L1
00007ffe`8241c498  00007ffe`82479080 LINQPadQuery!UserQuery.<Main>g__foo|4_1


0:000> !CLRStack
OS Thread Id: 0x2134 (0)
        Child SP               IP Call Site
0000008634206000 00007ffe82479081 UserQuery.g__foo|4_1()
0000008634206010 00007ffe824790a0 UserQuery.g__foo|4_1()
0000008634206050 00007ffe824790a0 UserQuery.g__foo|4_1()
0000008634206090 00007ffe824790a0 UserQuery.g__foo|4_1()
00000086342060D0 00007ffe824790a0 UserQuery.g__foo|4_1()
0000008634206110 00007ffe824790a0 UserQuery.g__foo|4_1()
0000008634206150 00007ffe824790a0 UserQuery.g__foo|4_1()
0000008634206190 00007ffe824790a0 UserQuery.g__foo|4_1()
00000086342061D0 00007ffe824790a0 UserQuery.g__foo|4_1()
0000008634206210 00007ffe824790a0 UserQuery.g__foo|4_1()
0000008634206250 00007ffe824790a0 UserQuery.g__foo|4_1()
0000008634206290 00007ffe824790a0 UserQuery.g__foo|4_1()
[...]
0000008634228AD0 00007ffe824790a0 UserQuery.g__foo|4_1()
0000008634228B10 00007ffe824790a0 UserQuery.g__foo|4_1()
0000008634228B50 00007ffe824790a0 UserQuery.g__foo|4_1()
0000008634228B90 00007ffe824790a0 UserQuery.g__foo|4_1()
0000008634228BD0 00007ffe824790a0 UserQuery.g__foo|4_1()
0000008634228C10 00007ffe824790a0 UserQuery.g__foo|4_1()
0000008634228C50 00007ffe824790a0 UserQuery.g__foo|4_1()
0000008634228C90 00007ffe824790a0 UserQuery.g__foo|4_1()
<failed>
Stack Walk failed. Reported stack incomplete.
```

Note: It was far too long that we had to use Debug / Break (Ctrl+Break) to stop it. We now try to dump the unmanaged stack trace, where the output completes much faster.

```
0:000> .kframes 0xFFFF
Default stack trace depth is 0n65535 frames


0:000> kL
 # Child-SP          RetAddr           Call Site
00 00000086`34206000 00007ffe`824790a0 LINQPadQuery!UserQuery.<Main>g__foo|4_1+0x1
01 00000086`34206010 00007ffe`824790a0 LINQPadQuery!UserQuery.<Main>g__foo|4_1+0x20
```

```
02 00000086`34206050 00007ffe`824790a0    LINQPadQuery!UserQuery.<Main>g__foo|4_1+0x20
03 00000086`34206090 00007ffe`824790a0    LINQPadQuery!UserQuery.<Main>g__foo|4_1+0x20
04 00000086`342060d0 00007ffe`824790a0    LINQPadQuery!UserQuery.<Main>g__foo|4_1+0x20
05 00000086`34206110 00007ffe`824790a0    LINQPadQuery!UserQuery.<Main>g__foo|4_1+0x20
06 00000086`34206150 00007ffe`824790a0    LINQPadQuery!UserQuery.<Main>g__foo|4_1+0x20
[...]
3dae 00000086`342fcb50 00007ffe`824790a0    LINQPadQuery!UserQuery.<Main>g__foo|4_1+0x20
3daf 00000086`342fcb90 00007ffe`824790a0    LINQPadQuery!UserQuery.<Main>g__foo|4_1+0x20
3db0 00000086`342fcbd0 00007ffe`824790a0    LINQPadQuery!UserQuery.<Main>g__foo|4_1+0x20
3db1 00000086`342fcc10 00007ffe`824790a0    LINQPadQuery!UserQuery.<Main>g__foo|4_1+0x20
3db2 00000086`342fcc50 00007ffe`824790a0    LINQPadQuery!UserQuery.<Main>g__foo|4_1+0x20
3db3 00000086`342fcc90 00007ffe`824790a0    LINQPadQuery!UserQuery.<Main>g__foo|4_1+0x20
3db4 00000086`342fccd0 00007ffe`824790a0    LINQPadQuery!UserQuery.<Main>g__foo|4_1+0x20
3db5 00000086`342fcd10 00007ffe`824790a0    LINQPadQuery!UserQuery.<Main>g__foo|4_1+0x20
3db6 00000086`342fcd50 00007ffe`824790a0    LINQPadQuery!UserQuery.<Main>g__foo|4_1+0x20
3db7 00000086`342fcd90 00007ffe`824790a0    LINQPadQuery!UserQuery.<Main>g__foo|4_1+0x20
3db8 00000086`342fcdd0 00007ffe`82479050    LINQPadQuery!UserQuery.<Main>g__foo|4_1+0x20
3db9 00000086`342fce10 00007ffe`82479006    LINQPadQuery!UserQuery.<Main>g__bar|4_0+0x20
3dba 00000086`342fce50 00007ffe`8247492b    LINQPadQuery!UserQuery.Main+0x26
3dbb 00000086`342fce90 00007ffe`82470f2f    LINQPad_Runtime!LINQPad.ExecutionModel.ClrQueryRunner.Run+0x1deb
3dbc 00000086`342fd7e0 00007ffe`81c04479    LINQPad_Runtime!LINQPad.ExecutionModel.Server.RunQuery+0x21f
3dbd 00000086`342fdac0 00007ffe`81c03fa2    LINQPad_Runtime!LINQPad.ExecutionModel.Server.PrepareAndRunQuery+0x3e9
3dbe 00000086`342fdc00 00007ffe`81c03ecc    LINQPad_Runtime!LINQPad.ExecutionModel.Server.<ExecuteClrQuery>b__147_0+0x52
3dbf 00000086`342fdc40 00007ffe`81badc60    LINQPad_Runtime!LINQPad.ExecutionModel.SyncPCQ.<>c__DisplayClass14_0.<Enqueue>b__0+0x4c
3dc0 00000086`342fdc90 00007ffe`81bad9ae    LINQPad_Runtime!LINQPad.ExecutionModel.SyncPCQ.Consume+0x100
3dc1 00000086`342fdd10 00007ffe`81ba659f    LINQPad_Runtime!LINQPad.ExecutionModel.SyncPCQ.Start+0x2ee
3dc2 00000086`342fde10 00007ffe`81ba604b    LINQPad_Runtime!LINQPad.ExecutionModel.ProcessServer.TryRun+0x4cf
3dc3 00000086`342fdfd0 00007ffe`81ba5fd4    LINQPad_Runtime!LINQPad.ExecutionModel.ProcessServer.Run+0x3b
3dc4 00000086`342fe020 00007ffe`81ba56f3    LINQPad_Runtime!LINQPad.RuntimeLoader.Run+0x84
3dc5 00000086`342fe070 00007ffe`81ba566c    LINQPad_Runtime!LINQPad.RuntimeLoader.Start+0x43
3dc6 00000086`342fe0f0 00007ffe`e1742eb3    LINQPad_Runtime!LINQPad.EntryPoint.Main+0x4c
3dc7 00000086`342fe140 00007ffe`e1625559    coreclr!CallDescrWorkerInternal+0x83
3dc8 00000086`342fe180 00007ffe`e0b8e325    coreclr!RuntimeMethodHandle::InvokeMethod+0x3a9
3dc9 00000086`342fe4b0 00007ffe`e0b8dc2b    System_Private_CoreLib!System.Reflection.MethodBaseInvoker.InvokeDirectByRefWithFewArgs+0xb5
3dca 00000086`342fe530 00007ffe`e0b9f910    System_Private_CoreLib!System.Reflection.MethodBaseInvoker.InvokeWithOneArg+0x1bb
3dcb 00000086`342fe610 00007ffe`e0b8d203    System_Private_CoreLib!System.Reflection.RuntimeMethodInfo.Invoke+0x1b0
3dcc 00000086`342fe680 00007ffe`81ba19ff    System_Private_CoreLib!System.Reflection.MethodBase.Invoke+0x23
3dcd 00000086`342fe6c0 00007ffe`e1742eb3    LINQPad_Query!LINQPad.ProcessServer.ProcessServerProgram.Main+0x19f
3dce 00000086`342fe790 00007ffe`e16c180c    coreclr!CallDescrWorkerInternal+0x83
3dcf 00000086`342fe7d0 00007ffe`e16aba54    coreclr!MethodDescCallSite::CallTargetWorker+0x208
3dd0 (Inline Function) --------`--------    coreclr!MethodDescCallSite::Call_RetArgSlot+0xd
3dd1 00000086`342fe910 00007ffe`e16acc19    coreclr!RunMainInternal+0xb8
3dd2 00000086`342fea30 00007ffe`e16acf2d    coreclr!RunMain+0xd1
3dd3 00000086`342feac0 00007ffe`e16ac1bb    coreclr!Assembly::ExecuteMainMethod+0x199
3dd4 00000086`342fed90 00007ffe`e16a704c    coreclr!CorHost2::ExecuteAssembly+0x1cb
3dd5 00000086`342feea0 00007ffe`e1abe8ec    coreclr!coreclr_execute_assembly+0xcc
3dd6 (Inline Function) --------`--------    hostpolicy!coreclr_t::execute_assembly+0x2d
3dd7 00000086`342fef40 00007ffe`e1abebbc    hostpolicy!run_app_for_context+0x58c
3dd8 00000086`342ff070 00007ffe`e76c1be9    hostpolicy!run_app+0x3c
3dd9 00000086`342ff0b0 00007ff7`4a677377    hostfxr!fx_muxer_t::run_app+0x109
3dda 00000086`342ff120 00007ff7`4a685a72    LINQPad8+0x17377
3ddb 00000086`342ffa70 00007fff`400f53e0    LINQPad8+0x25a72
3ddc 00000086`342ffab0 00007fff`4160485b    kernel32!BaseThreadInitThunk+0x10
3ddd 00000086`342ffae0 00000000`00000000    ntdll!RtlUserThreadStart+0x2b
```

6.   We check the managed exception:

```
0:000> !pe
Exception object: 000001f2de800100
Exception type:    System.StackOverflowException
Message:           <none>
InnerException:    <none>
StackTrace (generated):
<none>
StackTraceString: <none>
HResult: 800703e9
```

7.   Now, for the rest of this exercise, we look at various ways to navigate process virtual space memory and search for objects and data. The following stack trace collection commands **!uniqstack** and **!findstack** also list unmanaged stack traces from threads but without duplicate stack traces and with filtered frames, respectively:

```
0:000> !uniqstack
Processing 13 threads, please wait

.  0  Id: dd4.2134 Suspend: 0 Teb: 00000086`341f5000 Unfrozen
      Start: LINQPad8+0x25ae0 (00007ff7`4a685ae0)
      Priority: 0  Priority class: 32  Affinity: f
 # Child-SP          RetAddr               Call Site
00 00000086`34206000 00007ffe`824790a0    LINQPadQuery!UserQuery.<Main>g__foo|4_1+0x1
01 00000086`34206010 00007ffe`824790a0    LINQPadQuery!UserQuery.<Main>g__foo|4_1+0x20
02 00000086`34206050 00007ffe`824790a0    LINQPadQuery!UserQuery.<Main>g__foo|4_1+0x20
03 00000086`34206090 00007ffe`824790a0    LINQPadQuery!UserQuery.<Main>g__foo|4_1+0x20
04 00000086`342060d0 00007ffe`824790a0    LINQPadQuery!UserQuery.<Main>g__foo|4_1+0x20
05 00000086`34206110 00007ffe`824790a0    LINQPadQuery!UserQuery.<Main>g__foo|4_1+0x20
```

```
06 00000086`34206150 00007ffe`824790a0     LINQPadQuery!UserQuery.<Main>g__foo|4_1+0x20
07 00000086`34206190 00007ffe`824790a0     LINQPadQuery!UserQuery.<Main>g__foo|4_1+0x20
08 00000086`342061d0 00007ffe`824790a0     LINQPadQuery!UserQuery.<Main>g__foo|4_1+0x20
09 00000086`34206210 00007ffe`824790a0     LINQPadQuery!UserQuery.<Main>g__foo|4_1+0x20
0a 00000086`34206250 00007ffe`824790a0     LINQPadQuery!UserQuery.<Main>g__foo|4_1+0x20
0b 00000086`34206290 00007ffe`824790a0     LINQPadQuery!UserQuery.<Main>g__foo|4_1+0x20
0c 00000086`342062d0 00007ffe`824790a0     LINQPadQuery!UserQuery.<Main>g__foo|4_1+0x20
0d 00000086`34206310 00007ffe`824790a0     LINQPadQuery!UserQuery.<Main>g__foo|4_1+0x20
0e 00000086`34206350 00007ffe`824790a0     LINQPadQuery!UserQuery.<Main>g__foo|4_1+0x20
[...]

.  1  Id: dd4.1a54 Suspend: 0 Teb: 00000086`341fd000 Unfrozen ".NET EventPipe"
      Start: coreclr!server_thread (00007ffe`e1716730)
      Priority: 0  Priority class: 32  Affinity: f
 # Child-SP          RetAddr               Call Site
00 00000086`346ff4c8 00007fff`3f07dcb0     ntdll!NtWaitForMultipleObjects+0x14
01 00000086`346ff4d0 00007fff`3f07dbae     KERNELBASE!WaitForMultipleObjectsEx+0xf0
02 00000086`346ff7c0 00007ffe`e171693f     KERNELBASE!WaitForMultipleObjects+0xe
03 00000086`346ff800 00007ffe`e17168a8     coreclr!ds_ipc_poll+0x7f [D:\a\_work\1\s\src\native\eventpipe\ds-ipc-pal-namedpipe.c @ 263]
04 00000086`346ffa80 00007ffe`e1716784     coreclr!ds_ipc_stream_factory_get_next_available_stream+0x108 [D:\a\_work\1\s\src\native\eventpipe\ds-ipc.c @ 402]
05 00000086`346ffb50 00007fff`400f53e0     coreclr!server_thread+0x54 [D:\a\_work\1\s\src\native\eventpipe\ds-server.c @ 129]
06 00000086`346ffbc0 00007fff`4160485b     kernel32!BaseThreadInitThunk+0x10
07 00000086`346ffbf0 00000000`00000000     ntdll!RtlUserThreadStart+0x2b

.  2  Id: dd4.1550 Suspend: 0 Teb: 00000086`34000000 Unfrozen ".NET Debugger"
      Start: coreclr!DebuggerRCThread::ThreadProcStatic (00007ffe`e1707800)
      Priority: 0  Priority class: 32  Affinity: f
 # Child-SP          RetAddr               Call Site
00 00000086`347ff3d8 00007fff`3f07dcb0     ntdll!NtWaitForMultipleObjects+0x14
01 00000086`347ff3e0 00007ffe`e1707a9e     KERNELBASE!WaitForMultipleObjectsEx+0xf0
02 00000086`347ff6d0 00007ffe`e1707e26     coreclr!DebuggerRCThread::MainLoop+0xee [D:\a\_work\1\s\src\coreclr\debug\ee\rcthread.cpp @ 927]
03 00000086`347ff790 00007ffe`e170785b     coreclr!DebuggerRCThread::ThreadProc+0x12e [D:\a\_work\1\s\src\coreclr\debug\ee\rcthread.cpp @ 730]
04 00000086`347ff7f0 00007fff`400f53e0     coreclr!DebuggerRCThread::ThreadProcStatic+0x5b [D:\a\_work\1\s\src\coreclr\debug\ee\rcthread.cpp @ 1321]
05 00000086`347ff820 00007fff`4160485b     kernel32!BaseThreadInitThunk+0x10
06 00000086`347ff850 00000000`00000000     ntdll!RtlUserThreadStart+0x2b

.  3  Id: dd4.1714 Suspend: 0 Teb: 00000086`34002000 Unfrozen ".NET Finalizer"
      Start: coreclr!FinalizerThread::FinalizerThreadStart (00007ffe`e16fe890)
      Priority: 2  Priority class: 32  Affinity: f
 # Child-SP          RetAddr               Call Site
00 00000086`348ff6b8 00007fff`3f0710ce     ntdll!NtWaitForSingleObject+0x14
01 00000086`348ff6c0 00007ffe`e17093a3     KERNELBASE!WaitForSingleObjectEx+0x8e
02 (Inline Function) --------`--------     coreclr!CLREventWaitHelper2+0x6 [D:\a\_work\1\s\src\coreclr\vm\synch.cpp @ 372]
03 00000086`348ff760 00007ffe`e1708a39     coreclr!CLREventWaitHelper+0xf [D:\a\_work\1\s\src\coreclr\vm\synch.cpp @ 397]
04 (Inline Function) --------`--------     coreclr!CLREventBase::WaitEx+0x10 [D:\a\_work\1\s\src\coreclr\vm\synch.cpp @ 466]
05 (Inline Function) --------`--------     coreclr!CLREventBase::Wait+0x10 [D:\a\_work\1\s\src\coreclr\vm\synch.cpp @ 412]
06 00000086`348ff7b0 00007ffe`e170889f     coreclr!FinalizerThread::WaitForFinalizerEvent+0x21 [D:\a\_work\1\s\src\coreclr\vm\finalizerthread.cpp @ 189]
07 00000086`348ff7f0 00007ffe`e16aef05     coreclr!FinalizerThread::FinalizerThreadWorker+0x4f [D:\a\_work\1\s\src\coreclr\vm\finalizerthread.cpp @ 321]
08 (Inline Function) --------`--------     coreclr!ManagedThreadBase_DispatchInner+0xd [D:\a\_work\1\s\src\coreclr\vm\threads.cpp @ 7110]
09 00000086`348ffa40 00007ffe`e16aee2d     coreclr!ManagedThreadBase_DispatchMiddle+0x79 [D:\a\_work\1\s\src\coreclr\vm\threads.cpp @ 7154]
0a 00000086`348ffaf0 00007ffe`e16fe921     coreclr!ManagedThreadBase_DispatchOuter+0x8d [D:\a\_work\1\s\src\coreclr\vm\threads.cpp @ 7313]
0b (Inline Function) --------`--------     coreclr!ManagedThreadBase_NoADTransition+0x28 [D:\a\_work\1\s\src\coreclr\vm\threads.cpp @ 7382]
0c (Inline Function) --------`--------     coreclr!ManagedThreadBase::FinalizerBase+0x28 [D:\a\_work\1\s\src\coreclr\vm\threads.cpp @ 7401]
0d 00000086`348ffb60 00007fff`400f53e0     coreclr!FinalizerThread::FinalizerThreadStart+0x91 [D:\a\_work\1\s\src\coreclr\vm\finalizerthread.cpp @ 464]
0e 00000086`348ffc70 00007fff`4160485b     kernel32!BaseThreadInitThunk+0x10
0f 00000086`348ffca0 00000000`00000000     ntdll!RtlUserThreadStart+0x2b

.  4  Id: dd4.20cc Suspend: 0 Teb: 00000086`34008000 Unfrozen ".NET TP Wait"
      Start: coreclr!ThreadNative::KickOffThread (00007ffe`e16aef40)
      Priority: 0  Priority class: 32  Affinity: f
 # Child-SP          RetAddr               Call Site
00 00000086`33f6f078 00007fff`3f07dcb0     ntdll!NtWaitForMultipleObjects+0x14
01 00000086`33f6f080 00007ffe`e15fe800     KERNELBASE!WaitForMultipleObjectsEx+0xf0
02 00000086`33f6f370 00007ffe`e15fe523     coreclr!Thread::DoAppropriateAptStateWait+0x5c [D:\a\_work\1\s\src\coreclr\vm\threads.cpp @ 3184]
03 00000086`33f6f3b0 00007ffe`e15fe35a     coreclr!Thread::DoAppropriateWaitWorker+0x17b [D:\a\_work\1\s\src\coreclr\vm\threads.cpp @ 3363]
04 00000086`33f6f480 00007ffe`e15fcd19     coreclr!Thread::DoAppropriateWait+0xa6 [D:\a\_work\1\s\src\coreclr\vm\threads.cpp @ 3032]
05 00000086`33f6f520 00007ffe`e0b06fc3     coreclr!WaitHandleNative::CorWaitMultipleNative+0xf9 [D:\a\_work\1\s\src\coreclr\vm\comwaithandle.cpp @ 76]
06 00000086`33f6f6c0 00007ffe`e0b22dcc     System_Private_CoreLib!System.Threading.WaitHandle.WaitAnyMultiple+0xd3
[/_/src/libraries/System.Private.CoreLib/src/System/Threading/WaitHandle.cs @ 393]
07 00000086`33f6f750 00007ffe`e1742eb3     System_Private_CoreLib!System.Threading.PortableThreadPool.WaitThread.WaitThreadStart+0x8c
[/_/src/libraries/System.Private.CoreLib/src/System/Threading/PortableThreadPool.WaitThread.cs @ 246]
08 00000086`33f6f7b0 00007ffe`e16c1568     coreclr!CallDescrWorkerInternal+0x83 [D:\a\_work\1\s\src\coreclr\vm\amd64\CallDescrWorkerAMD64.asm @ 74]
09 00000086`33f6f7f0 00007ffe`e17315a3     coreclr!DispatchCallSimple+0x60 [D:\a\_work\1\s\src\coreclr\vm\callhelpers.cpp @ 248]
0a 00000086`33f6f880 00007ffe`e16aef05     coreclr!ThreadNative::KickOffThread_Worker+0x63 [D:\a\_work\1\s\src\coreclr\vm\comsynchronizable.cpp @ 158]
0b (Inline Function) --------`--------     coreclr!ManagedThreadBase_DispatchInner+0xd [D:\a\_work\1\s\src\coreclr\vm\threads.cpp @ 7110]
0c 00000086`33f6f8e0 00007ffe`e16aee2d     coreclr!ManagedThreadBase_DispatchMiddle+0x79 [D:\a\_work\1\s\src\coreclr\vm\threads.cpp @ 7154]
0d 00000086`33f6f990 00007ffe`e16aefbb     coreclr!ManagedThreadBase_DispatchOuter+0x8d [D:\a\_work\1\s\src\coreclr\vm\threads.cpp @ 7313]
0e (Inline Function) --------`--------     coreclr!ManagedThreadBase_FullTransition+0x28 [D:\a\_work\1\s\src\coreclr\vm\threads.cpp @ 7358]
0f (Inline Function) --------`--------     coreclr!ManagedThreadBase::KickOff+0x28 [D:\a\_work\1\s\src\coreclr\vm\threads.cpp @ 7393]
10 00000086`33f6fa00 00007fff`400f53e0     coreclr!ThreadNative::KickOffThread+0x7b [D:\a\_work\1\s\src\coreclr\vm\comsynchronizable.cpp @ 230]
11 00000086`33f6fa60 00007fff`4160485b     kernel32!BaseThreadInitThunk+0x10
12 00000086`33f6fa90 00000000`00000000     ntdll!RtlUserThreadStart+0x2b

.  5  Id: dd4.a10 Suspend: 0 Teb: 00000086`3400c000 Unfrozen ".NET TP Gate"
      Start: coreclr!ThreadNative::KickOffThread (00007ffe`e16aef40)
      Priority: 0  Priority class: 32  Affinity: f
 # Child-SP          RetAddr               Call Site
00 00000086`33faf088 00007fff`3f07dcb0     ntdll!NtWaitForMultipleObjects+0x14
01 00000086`33faf090 00007ffe`e15fe800     KERNELBASE!WaitForMultipleObjectsEx+0xf0
02 00000086`33faf380 00007ffe`e15fe523     coreclr!Thread::DoAppropriateAptStateWait+0x5c [D:\a\_work\1\s\src\coreclr\vm\threads.cpp @ 3184]
03 00000086`33faf3c0 00007ffe`e15fe35a     coreclr!Thread::DoAppropriateWaitWorker+0x17b [D:\a\_work\1\s\src\coreclr\vm\threads.cpp @ 3363]
04 00000086`33faf490 00007ffe`e15fe24b     coreclr!Thread::DoAppropriateWait+0xa6 [D:\a\_work\1\s\src\coreclr\vm\threads.cpp @ 3032]
05 00000086`33faf530 00007ffe`e0b06653     coreclr!WaitHandleNative::CorWaitOneNative+0xdb [D:\a\_work\1\s\src\coreclr\vm\comwaithandle.cpp @ 32]
06 00000086`33faf6a0 00007ffe`e0b208ed     System_Private_CoreLib!System.Threading.WaitHandle.WaitOneNoCheck+0x83
[/_/src/libraries/System.Private.CoreLib/src/System/Threading/WaitHandle.cs @ 183]
07 00000086`33faf710 00007ffe`e1742eb3     System_Private_CoreLib!System.Threading.PortableThreadPool.GateThread.GateThreadStart+0x18d
[/_/src/libraries/System.Private.CoreLib/src/System/Threading/PortableThreadPool.GateThread.cs @ 70]
08 00000086`33faf880 00007ffe`e16c1568     coreclr!CallDescrWorkerInternal+0x83 [D:\a\_work\1\s\src\coreclr\vm\amd64\CallDescrWorkerAMD64.asm @ 74]
```

```
09 00000086`33faf8c0 00007ffe`e17315a3     coreclr!DispatchCallSimple+0x60 [D:\a\_work\1\s\src\coreclr\vm\callhelpers.cpp @ 248]
0a 00000086`33faf950 00007ffe`e16aef05     coreclr!ThreadNative::KickOffThread_Worker+0x63 [D:\a\_work\1\s\src\coreclr\vm\comsynchronizable.cpp @ 158]
0b (Inline Function) --------`--------     coreclr!ManagedThreadBase_DispatchInner+0xd [D:\a\_work\1\s\src\coreclr\vm\threads.cpp @ 7110]
0c 00000086`33faf9b0 00007ffe`e16aee2d     coreclr!ManagedThreadBase_DispatchMiddle+0x79 [D:\a\_work\1\s\src\coreclr\vm\threads.cpp @ 7154]
0d 00000086`33fafa60 00007ffe`e16aefbb     coreclr!ManagedThreadBase_DispatchOuter+0x8d [D:\a\_work\1\s\src\coreclr\vm\threads.cpp @ 7313]
0e (Inline Function) --------`--------     coreclr!ManagedThreadBase_FullTransition+0x28 [D:\a\_work\1\s\src\coreclr\vm\threads.cpp @ 7358]
0f (Inline Function) --------`--------     coreclr!ManagedThreadBase::KickOff+0x28 [D:\a\_work\1\s\src\coreclr\vm\threads.cpp @ 7393]
10 00000086`33fafad0 00007fff`400f53e0     coreclr!ThreadNative::KickOffThread+0x7b [D:\a\_work\1\s\src\coreclr\vm\comsynchronizable.cpp @ 230]
11 00000086`33fafb30 00007fff`4160485b     kernel32!BaseThreadInitThunk+0x10
12 00000086`33fafb60 00000000`00000000     ntdll!RtlUserThreadStart+0x2b

.  6  Id: dd4.fec Suspend: 0 Teb: 00000086`34014000 Unfrozen ".NET Timer"
      Start: coreclr!ThreadNative::KickOffThread (00007ffe`e16aef40)
      Priority: 0  Priority class: 32  Affinity: f
 # Child-SP          RetAddr               Call Site
00 00000086`34eff3d8 00007fff`3f07dcb0     ntdll!NtWaitForMultipleObjects+0x14
01 00000086`34eff3e0 00007ffe`e15fe800     KERNELBASE!WaitForMultipleObjectsEx+0xf0
02 00000086`34eff6d0 00007ffe`e15fe523     coreclr!Thread::DoAppropriateAptStateWait+0x5c [D:\a\_work\1\s\src\coreclr\vm\threads.cpp @ 3184]
03 00000086`34eff710 00007ffe`e15fe35a     coreclr!Thread::DoAppropriateWaitWorker+0x17b [D:\a\_work\1\s\src\coreclr\vm\threads.cpp @ 3363]
04 00000086`34eff7e0 00007ffe`e15fe24b     coreclr!Thread::DoAppropriateWait+0xa6 [D:\a\_work\1\s\src\coreclr\vm\threads.cpp @ 3032]
05 00000086`34eff880 00007ffe`e0b06653     coreclr!WaitHandleNative::CorWaitOneNative+0xdb [D:\a\_work\1\s\src\coreclr\vm\comwaithandle.cpp @ 32]
06 00000086`34eff9f0 00007ffe`e0b1945f     System_Private_CoreLib!System.Threading.WaitHandle.WaitOneNoCheck+0x83
[/_/src/libraries/System.Private.CoreLib/src/System/Threading/WaitHandle.cs @ 183]
07 00000086`34effa20 00007ffe`e1742eb3     System_Private_CoreLib!System.Threading.TimerQueue.TimerThread+0x7f
[/_/src/libraries/System.Private.CoreLib/src/System/Threading/TimerQueue.Portable.cs @ 95]
08 00000086`34effaf0 00007ffe`e16c1568     coreclr!CallDescrWorkerInternal+0x83 [D:\a\_work\1\s\src\coreclr\vm\amd64\CallDescrWorkerAMD64.asm @ 74]
09 00000086`34effb30 00007ffe`e17315a3     coreclr!DispatchCallSimple+0x60 [D:\a\_work\1\s\src\coreclr\vm\callhelpers.cpp @ 248]
0a 00000086`34effbc0 00007ffe`e16aef05     coreclr!ThreadNative::KickOffThread_Worker+0x63 [D:\a\_work\1\s\src\coreclr\vm\comsynchronizable.cpp @ 158]
0b (Inline Function) --------`--------     coreclr!ManagedThreadBase_DispatchInner+0xd [D:\a\_work\1\s\src\coreclr\vm\threads.cpp @ 7110]
0c 00000086`34effc20 00007ffe`e16aee2d     coreclr!ManagedThreadBase_DispatchMiddle+0x79 [D:\a\_work\1\s\src\coreclr\vm\threads.cpp @ 7154]
0d 00000086`34effcd0 00007ffe`e16aefbb     coreclr!ManagedThreadBase_DispatchOuter+0x8d [D:\a\_work\1\s\src\coreclr\vm\threads.cpp @ 7313]
0e (Inline Function) --------`--------     coreclr!ManagedThreadBase_FullTransition+0x28 [D:\a\_work\1\s\src\coreclr\vm\threads.cpp @ 7358]
0f (Inline Function) --------`--------     coreclr!ManagedThreadBase::KickOff+0x28 [D:\a\_work\1\s\src\coreclr\vm\threads.cpp @ 7393]
10 00000086`34effd40 00007fff`400f53e0     coreclr!ThreadNative::KickOffThread+0x7b [D:\a\_work\1\s\src\coreclr\vm\comsynchronizable.cpp @ 230]
11 00000086`34effda0 00007fff`4160485b     kernel32!BaseThreadInitThunk+0x10
12 00000086`34effdd0 00000000`00000000     ntdll!RtlUserThreadStart+0x2b

.  7  Id: dd4.1608 Suspend: 0 Teb: 00000086`34018000 Unfrozen
      Start: ntdll!TppWorkerThread (00007fff`41616a00)
      Priority: 0  Priority class: 32  Affinity: f
 # Child-SP          RetAddr               Call Site
00 00000086`350ff8d8 00007fff`41616cdf     ntdll!NtWaitForWorkViaWorkerFactory+0x14
01 00000086`350ff8e0 00007fff`400f53e0     ntdll!TppWorkerThread+0x2df
02 00000086`350ffbd0 00007fff`4160485b     kernel32!BaseThreadInitThunk+0x10
03 00000086`350ffc00 00000000`00000000     ntdll!RtlUserThreadStart+0x2b

.  8  Id: dd4.1628 Suspend: 0 Teb: 00000086`3401e000 Unfrozen ".NET Tiered Compilation Worker"
      Start: coreclr!TieredCompilationManager::BackgroundWorkerBootstrapper0 (00007ffe`e173c8a0)
      Priority: 0  Priority class: 32  Affinity: f
 # Child-SP          RetAddr               Call Site
00 00000086`343ff568 00007fff`4165b903     ntdll!NtDelayExecution+0x14
01 00000086`343ff570 00007fff`3f04d031     ntdll!RtlDelayExecution+0x43
02 00000086`343ff5a0 00007ffe`e1708715     KERNELBASE!SleepEx+0x71
03 (Inline Function) --------`--------     coreclr!ClrSleepEx+0xa [D:\a\_work\1\s\src\coreclr\vm\hosting.cpp @ 216]
04 00000086`343ff620 00007ffe`e1708645     coreclr!TieredCompilationManager::BackgroundWorkerStart+0x91 [D:\a\_work\1\s\src\coreclr\vm\tieredcompilation.cpp @ 520]
05 00000086`343ff670 00007ffe`e16aef05     coreclr!TieredCompilationManager::BackgroundWorkerBootstrapper1+0x55
[D:\a\_work\1\s\src\coreclr\vm\tieredcompilation.cpp @ 482]
06 (Inline Function) --------`--------     coreclr!ManagedThreadBase_DispatchInner+0xd [D:\a\_work\1\s\src\coreclr\vm\threads.cpp @ 7110]
07 00000086`343ff6b0 00007ffe`e16aee2d     coreclr!ManagedThreadBase_DispatchMiddle+0x79 [D:\a\_work\1\s\src\coreclr\vm\threads.cpp @ 7154]
08 00000086`343ff760 00007ffe`e173c8da     coreclr!ManagedThreadBase_DispatchOuter+0x8d [D:\a\_work\1\s\src\coreclr\vm\threads.cpp @ 7313]
09 (Inline Function) --------`--------     coreclr!ManagedThreadBase_FullTransition+0x24 [D:\a\_work\1\s\src\coreclr\vm\threads.cpp @ 7358]
0a (Inline Function) --------`--------     coreclr!ManagedThreadBase::KickOff+0x24 [D:\a\_work\1\s\src\coreclr\vm\threads.cpp @ 7393]
0b 00000086`343ff7d0 00007fff`400f53e0     coreclr!TieredCompilationManager::BackgroundWorkerBootstrapper0+0x3a
[D:\a\_work\1\s\src\coreclr\vm\tieredcompilation.cpp @ 465]
0c 00000086`343ff820 00007fff`4160485b     kernel32!BaseThreadInitThunk+0x10
0d 00000086`343ff850 00000000`00000000     ntdll!RtlUserThreadStart+0x2b

.  9  Id: dd4.df4 Suspend: 0 Teb: 00000086`34020000 Unfrozen ".NET TP Worker"
      Start: coreclr!ThreadNative::KickOffThread (00007ffe`e16aef40)
      Priority: 0  Priority class: 32  Affinity: f
 # Child-SP          RetAddr               Call Site
00 00000086`344ff538 00007fff`3f07ebd3     ntdll!NtRemoveIoCompletion+0x14
01 00000086`344ff540 00007ffe`e09d90e6     KERNELBASE!GetQueuedCompletionStatus+0x53
02 00000086`344ff5a0 00007ffe`e0b242bd     System_Private_CoreLib!Interop.Kernel32.GetQueuedCompletionStatus+0xa6
[/_/artifacts/obj/coreclr/System.Private.CoreLib/windows.x64.Release/generated/Microsoft.Interop.LibraryImportGenerator/Microsoft.Interop.LibraryImportGenerator/LibraryImports.g.cs @ 6290]
03 00000086`344ff6a0 00007ffe`e0b24256     System_Private_CoreLib!System.Threading.LowLevelLifoSemaphore.WaitForSignal+0x4d
[/_/src/libraries/System.Private.CoreLib/src/System/Threading/LowLevelLifoSemaphore.cs @ 160]
04 00000086`344ff710 00007ffe`e0b235be     System_Private_CoreLib!System.Threading.LowLevelLifoSemaphore.Wait+0x1a6
[/_/src/libraries/System.Private.CoreLib/src/System/Threading/LowLevelLifoSemaphore.cs @ 85]
05 00000086`344ff770 00007ffe`e1742eb3     System_Private_CoreLib!System.Threading.PortableThreadPool.WorkerThread.WorkerThreadStart+0x12e
[/_/src/libraries/System.Private.CoreLib/src/System/Threading/PortableThreadPool.WorkerThread.cs @ 126]
06 00000086`344ff880 00007ffe`e16c1568     coreclr!CallDescrWorkerInternal+0x83 [D:\a\_work\1\s\src\coreclr\vm\amd64\CallDescrWorkerAMD64.asm @ 74]
07 00000086`344ff8c0 00007ffe`e17315a3     coreclr!DispatchCallSimple+0x60 [D:\a\_work\1\s\src\coreclr\vm\callhelpers.cpp @ 248]
08 00000086`344ff950 00007ffe`e16aef05     coreclr!ThreadNative::KickOffThread_Worker+0x63 [D:\a\_work\1\s\src\coreclr\vm\comsynchronizable.cpp @ 158]
09 (Inline Function) --------`--------     coreclr!ManagedThreadBase_DispatchInner+0xd [D:\a\_work\1\s\src\coreclr\vm\threads.cpp @ 7110]
0a 00000086`344ff9b0 00007ffe`e16aee2d     coreclr!ManagedThreadBase_DispatchMiddle+0x79 [D:\a\_work\1\s\src\coreclr\vm\threads.cpp @ 7154]
0b 00000086`344ffa60 00007ffe`e16aefbb     coreclr!ManagedThreadBase_DispatchOuter+0x8d [D:\a\_work\1\s\src\coreclr\vm\threads.cpp @ 7313]
0c (Inline Function) --------`--------     coreclr!ManagedThreadBase_FullTransition+0x28 [D:\a\_work\1\s\src\coreclr\vm\threads.cpp @ 7358]
0d (Inline Function) --------`--------     coreclr!ManagedThreadBase::KickOff+0x28 [D:\a\_work\1\s\src\coreclr\vm\threads.cpp @ 7393]
0e 00000086`344ffad0 00007fff`400f53e0     coreclr!ThreadNative::KickOffThread+0x7b [D:\a\_work\1\s\src\coreclr\vm\comsynchronizable.cpp @ 230]
0f 00000086`344ffb30 00007fff`4160485b     kernel32!BaseThreadInitThunk+0x10
10 00000086`344ffb60 00000000`00000000     ntdll!RtlUserThreadStart+0x2b

. 12  Id: dd4.1030 Suspend: 0 Teb: 00000086`34026000 Unfrozen ".NET TP Worker"
      Start: coreclr!ThreadNative::KickOffThread (00007ffe`e16aef40)
      Priority: 0  Priority class: 32  Affinity: f
```

```
 # Child-SP          RetAddr           Call Site
00 00000086`34aff758 00007fff`3f07ebd3 ntdll!NtRemoveIoCompletion+0x14
01 00000086`34aff760 00007ffe`e09d90e6 KERNELBASE!GetQueuedCompletionStatus+0x53
02 00000086`34aff7c0 00007ffe`e0b242bd System_Private_CoreLib!Interop.Kernel32.GetQueuedCompletionStatus+0xa6
[/_/artifacts/obj/coreclr/System.Private.CoreLib/windows.x64.Release/generated/Microsoft.Interop.LibraryImportGenerator/Microsoft.Interop.LibraryImportGenerat
or/LibraryImports.g.cs @ 6290]
03 00000086`34aff8c0 00007ffe`e0b24256 System_Private_CoreLib!System.Threading.LowLevelLifoSemaphore.WaitForSignal+0x4d
[/_/src/libraries/System.Private.CoreLib/src/System/Threading/LowLevelLifoSemaphore.cs @ 160]
04 00000086`34aff930 00007ffe`e0b2355b System_Private_CoreLib!System.Threading.LowLevelLifoSemaphore.Wait+0x1a6
[/_/src/libraries/System.Private.CoreLib/src/System/Threading/LowLevelLifoSemaphore.cs @ 85]
05 00000086`34aff990 00007ffe`e1742eb3 System_Private_CoreLib!System.Threading.PortableThreadPool.WorkerThread.WorkerThreadStart+0xcb
[/_/src/libraries/System.Private.CoreLib/src/System/Threading/PortableThreadPool.WorkerThread.cs @ 125]
06 00000086`34affaa0 00007ffe`e16c1568 coreclr!CallDescrWorkerInternal+0x83 [D:\a\_work\1\s\src\coreclr\vm\amd64\CallDescrWorkerAMD64.asm @ 74]
07 00000086`34affae0 00007ffe`e17315a3 coreclr!DispatchCallSimple+0x60 [D:\a\_work\1\s\src\coreclr\vm\callhelpers.cpp @ 248]
08 00000086`34affb70 00007ffe`e16aef05 coreclr!ThreadNative::KickOffThread_Worker+0x63 [D:\a\_work\1\s\src\coreclr\vm\comsynchronizable.cpp @ 158]
09 (Inline Function) --------`-------- coreclr!ManagedThreadBase_DispatchInner+0xd [D:\a\_work\1\s\src\coreclr\vm\threads.cpp @ 7110]
0a 00000086`34affbd0 00007ffe`e16aee2d coreclr!ManagedThreadBase_DispatchMiddle+0x79 [D:\a\_work\1\s\src\coreclr\vm\threads.cpp @ 7154]
0b 00000086`34affc80 00007ffe`e16aefbb coreclr!ManagedThreadBase_DispatchOuter+0x8d [D:\a\_work\1\s\src\coreclr\vm\threads.cpp @ 7313]
0c (Inline Function) --------`-------- coreclr!ManagedThreadBase_FullTransition+0x28 [D:\a\_work\1\s\src\coreclr\vm\threads.cpp @ 7358]
0d (Inline Function) --------`-------- coreclr!ManagedThreadBase::KickOff+0x28 [D:\a\_work\1\s\src\coreclr\vm\threads.cpp @ 7393]
0e 00000086`34affcf0 00007fff`400f53e0 coreclr!ThreadNative::KickOffThread+0x7b [D:\a\_work\1\s\src\coreclr\vm\comsynchronizable.cpp @ 230]
0f 00000086`34affd50 00007fff`4160485b kernel32!BaseThreadInitThunk+0x10
10 00000086`34affd80 00000000`00000000 ntdll!RtlUserThreadStart+0x2b


Total threads: 13
Duplicate callstacks: 2 (windbg thread #s follow):
10, 11


0:000> !findstack coreclr
Thread 001, 3 frame(s) match
      * 03 000001f2d7e300e0 00007ffee17168a0 coreclr!ds_ipc_poll+0x7f
      * 04 00000086346ffae9 00007ffee1716784 coreclr!ds_ipc_stream_factory_get_next_available_stream+0x108
      * 05 00000086346ffbb0 00007fff400f53e0 coreclr!server_thread+0x54


Thread 002, 3 frame(s) match
      * 02 00000086347ff729 00007ffee1707e26 coreclr!DebuggerRCThread::MainLoop+0xee
      * 03 00000086347ff7d0 00007ffee170785b coreclr!DebuggerRCThread::ThreadProc+0x12e
      * 04 0000000000000000 00007fff400f53e0 coreclr!DebuggerRCThread::ThreadProcStatic+0x5b


Thread 003, 6 frame(s) match
      * 02 0000000000000000 00007ffee1708a39 coreclr!CLREventWaitHelper+0xf
      * 03 0000000000000000 00007ffee170889f coreclr!FinalizerThread::WaitForFinalizerEvent+0x21
      * 04 0000000000000000 00007ffee16aef05 coreclr!FinalizerThread::FinalizerThreadWorker+0x4f
      * 05 0000000000000000 00007ffee16aee2d coreclr!ManagedThreadBase_DispatchMiddle+0x79
      * 06 0000000000000000 00007ffee16fe921 coreclr!ManagedThreadBase_DispatchOuter+0x8d
      * 07 0000000000000000 00007fff400f53e0 coreclr!FinalizerThread::FinalizerThreadStart+0x91


Thread 004, 10 frame(s) match
      * 02 0000000000000003 00007ffee15fe523 coreclr!Thread::DoAppropriateAptStateWait+0x5c
      * 03 0000008633f6f431 00007ffee15fe35a coreclr!Thread::DoAppropriateWaitWorker+0x17b
      * 04 0000008633f6f700 00007ffee15fcd19 coreclr!Thread::DoAppropriateWait+0xa6
      * 05 0000008633f6f700 00007ffee0b06fc3 coreclr!WaitHandleNative::CorWaitMultipleNative+0xf9
      * 08 0000008633f6f7d0 00007ffee16c1568 coreclr!CallDescrWorkerInternal+0x83
      * 09 0000000000000004 00007ffee17315a3 coreclr!DispatchCallSimple+0x60
      * 10 0000000000000000 00007ffee16aef05 coreclr!ThreadNative::KickOffThread_Worker+0x63
      * 11 0000000000000000 00007ffee16aee2d coreclr!ManagedThreadBase_DispatchMiddle+0x79
      * 12 0000000000000000 00007ffee16aefbb coreclr!ManagedThreadBase_DispatchOuter+0x8d
      * 13 0000000000000000 00007fff400f53e0 coreclr!ThreadNative::KickOffThread+0x7b


Thread 005, 10 frame(s) match
      * 02 0000000000000001 00007ffee15fe523 coreclr!Thread::DoAppropriateAptStateWait+0x5c
      * 03 0000008633faf441 00007ffee15fe35a coreclr!Thread::DoAppropriateWaitWorker+0x17b
      * 04 0000008633faf700 00007ffee15fe24b coreclr!Thread::DoAppropriateWait+0xa6
      * 05 0000008633faf700 00007ffee0b06653 coreclr!WaitHandleNative::CorWaitOneNative+0xdb
      * 08 0000008633faf8a0 00007ffee16c1568 coreclr!CallDescrWorkerInternal+0x83
      * 09 0000000000000004 00007ffee17315a3 coreclr!DispatchCallSimple+0x60
      * 10 0000000000000000 00007ffee16aef05 coreclr!ThreadNative::KickOffThread_Worker+0x63
      * 11 0000000000000000 00007ffee16aee2d coreclr!ManagedThreadBase_DispatchMiddle+0x79
      * 12 0000000000000000 00007ffee16aefbb coreclr!ManagedThreadBase_DispatchOuter+0x8d
      * 13 0000000000000000 00007fff400f53e0 coreclr!ThreadNative::KickOffThread+0x7b


Thread 006, 10 frame(s) match
      * 02 0000000000000001 00007ffee15fe523 coreclr!Thread::DoAppropriateAptStateWait+0x5c
      * 03 0000008634eff791 00007ffee15fe35a coreclr!Thread::DoAppropriateWaitWorker+0x17b
      * 04 0000008634effa50 00007ffee15fe24b coreclr!Thread::DoAppropriateWait+0xa6
      * 05 0000008634effa50 00007ffee0b06653 coreclr!WaitHandleNative::CorWaitOneNative+0xdb
      * 08 0000008634effb10 00007ffee16c1568 coreclr!CallDescrWorkerInternal+0x83
      * 09 0000000000000004 00007ffee17315a3 coreclr!DispatchCallSimple+0x60
      * 10 0000000000000000 00007ffee16aef05 coreclr!ThreadNative::KickOffThread_Worker+0x63
      * 11 0000000000000000 00007ffee16aee2d coreclr!ManagedThreadBase_DispatchMiddle+0x79
```

265

```
          * 12 0000000000000000 00007ffee16aefbb coreclr!ManagedThreadBase_DispatchOuter+0x8d
          * 13 0000000000000000 00007fff400f53e0 coreclr!ThreadNative::KickOffThread+0x7b

  Thread 008, 5 frame(s) match
          * 03 0000000000000064 00007ffee1708645 coreclr!TieredCompilationManager::BackgroundWorkerStart+0x91
          * 04 0000000000000000 00007ffee16aef05 coreclr!TieredCompilationManager::BackgroundWorkerBootstrapper1+0x55
          * 05 0000000000000000 00007ffee16aee2d coreclr!ManagedThreadBase_DispatchMiddle+0x79
          * 06 0000000000000000 00007ffee173c8da coreclr!ManagedThreadBase_DispatchOuter+0x8d
          * 07 0000000000000000 00007fff400f53e0 coreclr!TieredCompilationManager::BackgroundWorkerBootstrapper0+0x3a

  Thread 009, 6 frame(s) match
          * 06 00000086344ff8a0 00007ffee16c1568 coreclr!CallDescrWorkerInternal+0x83
          * 07 0000000000000004 00007ffee17315a3 coreclr!DispatchCallSimple+0x60
          * 08 0000000000000000 00007ffee16aef05 coreclr!ThreadNative::KickOffThread_Worker+0x63
          * 09 0000000000000000 00007ffee16aee2d coreclr!ManagedThreadBase_DispatchMiddle+0x79
          * 10 0000000000000000 00007ffee16aefbb coreclr!ManagedThreadBase_DispatchOuter+0x8d
          * 11 0000000000000000 00007fff400f53e0 coreclr!ThreadNative::KickOffThread+0x7b

  Thread 010, 6 frame(s) match
          * 06 00000086345ff990 00007ffee16c1568 coreclr!CallDescrWorkerInternal+0x83
          * 07 0000000000000004 00007ffee17315a3 coreclr!DispatchCallSimple+0x60
          * 08 0000000000000000 00007ffee16aef05 coreclr!ThreadNative::KickOffThread_Worker+0x63
          * 09 0000000000000000 00007ffee16aee2d coreclr!ManagedThreadBase_DispatchMiddle+0x79
          * 10 0000000000000000 00007ffee16aefbb coreclr!ManagedThreadBase_DispatchOuter+0x8d
          * 11 0000000000000000 00007fff400f53e0 coreclr!ThreadNative::KickOffThread+0x7b

  Thread 011, 6 frame(s) match
          * 06 00000086349ffa10 00007ffee16c1568 coreclr!CallDescrWorkerInternal+0x83
          * 07 0000000000000004 00007ffee17315a3 coreclr!DispatchCallSimple+0x60
          * 08 0000000000000000 00007ffee16aef05 coreclr!ThreadNative::KickOffThread_Worker+0x63
          * 09 0000000000000000 00007ffee16aee2d coreclr!ManagedThreadBase_DispatchMiddle+0x79
          * 10 0000000000000000 00007ffee16aefbb coreclr!ManagedThreadBase_DispatchOuter+0x8d
          * 11 0000000000000000 00007fff400f53e0 coreclr!ThreadNative::KickOffThread+0x7b

  Thread 012, 6 frame(s) match
          * 06 0000008634affac0 00007ffee16c1568 coreclr!CallDescrWorkerInternal+0x83
          * 07 0000000000000004 00007ffee17315a3 coreclr!DispatchCallSimple+0x60
          * 08 0000000000000000 00007ffee16aef05 coreclr!ThreadNative::KickOffThread_Worker+0x63
          * 09 0000000000000000 00007ffee16aee2d coreclr!ManagedThreadBase_DispatchMiddle+0x79
          * 10 0000000000000000 00007ffee16aefbb coreclr!ManagedThreadBase_DispatchOuter+0x8d
          * 11 0000000000000000 00007fff400f53e0 coreclr!ThreadNative::KickOffThread+0x7b
```

Note: It missed thread #0 frames due to an insufficient default number of frames per stack trace.

8.   **!VMMap** SOS extension command briefly shows various memory regions and their protection and state attributes but is much less informative than the **!address** command we used previously. The latter command output includes region descriptions, mapped DLLs, and even the first data bytes:

```
0:000> !VMMap
Start            Stop             Length           AllocProtect Protect   State    Type
0000000000000000-000000007FFDFFFF 000000007FFE0000              NA        Free
000000007FFE0000-000000007FFE0FFF 0000000000001000 Rd           Rd        Commit   Private
000000007FFE1000-000000007FFE1FFF 0000000000001000 Rd           Rd        Commit   Private
000000007FFE2000-0000008633F2FFFF 00000085B3F4E000              NA        Free
0000008633F30000-0000008633F68FFF 0000000000039000 RdWr                   Reserve  Private
0000008633F69000-0000008633F6BFFF 0000000000003000 RdWr         G|RdWr    Commit   Private
0000008633F6C000-0000008633F6FFFF 0000000000004000 RdWr         RdWr      Commit   Private
0000008633F70000-0000008633FA7FFF 0000000000038000 RdWr                   Reserve  Private
0000008633FA8000-0000008633FAAFFF 0000000000003000 RdWr         G|RdWr    Commit   Private
0000008633FAB000-0000008633FAFFFF 0000000000005000 RdWr         RdWr      Commit   Private
0000008633FB0000-0000008633FFFFFF 0000000000050000              NA        Free
0000008634000000-0000008634003FFF 0000000000004000 RdWr         RdWr      Commit   Private
0000008634004000-0000008634007FFF 0000000000004000 RdWr                   Reserve  Private
0000008634008000-0000008634009FFF 0000000000002000 RdWr         RdWr      Commit   Private
000000863400A000-000000863400BFFF 0000000000002000 RdWr                   Reserve  Private
000000863400C000-000000863400DFFF 0000000000002000 RdWr         RdWr      Commit   Private
000000863400E000-0000008634013FFF 0000000000006000 RdWr                   Reserve  Private
```

```
0000008634014000-0000008634015FFF 0000000000002000  RdWr        RdWr        Commit   Private
0000008634016000-0000008634017FFF 0000000000002000  RdWr                    Reserve  Private
0000008634018000-0000008634019FFF 0000000000002000  RdWr        RdWr        Commit   Private
000000863401A000-000000863401DFFF 0000000000004000  RdWr                    Reserve  Private
000000863401E000-0000008634027FFF 000000000000A000  RdWr        RdWr        Commit   Private
0000008634028000-00000086341F3FFF 00000000001CC000  RdWr                    Reserve  Private
00000086341F4000-00000086341F6FFF 0000000000003000  RdWr        RdWr        Commit   Private
00000086341F7000-00000086341FCFFF 0000000000006000  RdWr                    Reserve  Private
[...]
```

```
0:000> !address
```

```
Mapping file section regions...
Mapping module regions...
Mapping PEB regions...
Mapping TEB and stack regions...
Mapping heap regions...
Mapping page heap regions...
Mapping other regions...
Mapping stack trace database regions...
Mapping activation context regions...

        BaseAddress      EndAddress+1        RegionSize     Type       State                 Protect             Usage
-----------------------------------------------------------------------------------------------------------------------
+        0`00000000        0`7ffe0000        0`7ffe0000             MEM_FREE    PAGE_NOACCESS                      Free
+        0`7ffe0000        0`7ffe1000        0`00001000 MEM_PRIVATE MEM_COMMIT  PAGE_READONLY                      Other      [User Shared Data]
+        0`7ffe1000        0`7ffe2000        0`00001000 MEM_PRIVATE MEM_COMMIT  PAGE_READONLY                      <unknown>  [.............M6.]
+        0`7ffe2000       86`33f30000       85`b3f4e000             MEM_FREE    PAGE_NOACCESS                      Free
+       86`33f30000       86`33f69000        0`00039000 MEM_PRIVATE MEM_RESERVE                                    Stack      [~4; dd4.20cc]
        86`33f69000       86`33f6c000        0`00003000 MEM_PRIVATE MEM_COMMIT  PAGE_READWRITE | PAGE_GUARD        Stack      [~4; dd4.20cc]
        86`33f6c000       86`33f70000        0`00004000 MEM_PRIVATE MEM_COMMIT  PAGE_READWRITE                     Stack      [~4; dd4.20cc]
+       86`33f70000       86`33fa8000        0`00038000 MEM_PRIVATE MEM_RESERVE                                    Stack      [~5; dd4.a10]
        86`33fa8000       86`33fab000        0`00003000 MEM_PRIVATE MEM_COMMIT  PAGE_READWRITE | PAGE_GUARD        Stack      [~5; dd4.a10]
        86`33fab000       86`33fb0000        0`00005000 MEM_PRIVATE MEM_COMMIT  PAGE_READWRITE                     Stack      [~5; dd4.a10]
+       86`33fb0000       86`34000000        0`00050000             MEM_FREE    PAGE_NOACCESS                      Free
+       86`34000000       86`34002000        0`00002000 MEM_PRIVATE MEM_COMMIT  PAGE_READWRITE                     TEB        [~2; dd4.1550]
        86`34002000       86`34004000        0`00002000 MEM_PRIVATE MEM_COMMIT  PAGE_READWRITE                     TEB        [~3; dd4.1714]
        86`34004000       86`34008000        0`00004000 MEM_PRIVATE MEM_RESERVE                                    <unknown>
        86`34008000       86`3400a000        0`00002000 MEM_PRIVATE MEM_COMMIT  PAGE_READWRITE                     TEB        [~4; dd4.20cc]
        86`3400a000       86`3400c000        0`00002000 MEM_PRIVATE MEM_RESERVE                                    <unknown>
        86`3400c000       86`3400e000        0`00002000 MEM_PRIVATE MEM_COMMIT  PAGE_READWRITE                     TEB        [~5; dd4.a10]
        86`3400e000       86`34014000        0`00006000 MEM_PRIVATE MEM_RESERVE                                    <unknown>
        86`34014000       86`34016000        0`00002000 MEM_PRIVATE MEM_COMMIT  PAGE_READWRITE                     TEB        [~6; dd4.fec]
        86`34016000       86`34018000        0`00002000 MEM_PRIVATE MEM_RESERVE                                    <unknown>
        86`34018000       86`3401a000        0`00002000 MEM_PRIVATE MEM_COMMIT  PAGE_READWRITE                     TEB        [~7; dd4.1608]
        86`3401a000       86`3401e000        0`00004000 MEM_PRIVATE MEM_RESERVE                                    <unknown>
        86`3401e000       86`34020000        0`00002000 MEM_PRIVATE MEM_COMMIT  PAGE_READWRITE                     TEB        [~8; dd4.1628]
        86`34020000       86`34022000        0`00002000 MEM_PRIVATE MEM_COMMIT  PAGE_READWRITE                     TEB        [~9; dd4.df4]
        86`34022000       86`34024000        0`00002000 MEM_PRIVATE MEM_COMMIT  PAGE_READWRITE                     TEB        [~10; dd4.bfc]
        86`34024000       86`34026000        0`00002000 MEM_PRIVATE MEM_COMMIT  PAGE_READWRITE                     TEB        [~11; dd4.1b20]
        86`34026000       86`34028000        0`00002000 MEM_PRIVATE MEM_COMMIT  PAGE_READWRITE                     TEB        [~12; dd4.1030]
        86`34028000       86`341f4000        0`001cc000 MEM_PRIVATE MEM_RESERVE                                    <unknown>
        86`341f4000       86`341f5000        0`00001000 MEM_PRIVATE MEM_COMMIT  PAGE_READWRITE                     PEB        [dd4]
        86`341f5000       86`341f7000        0`00002000 MEM_PRIVATE MEM_COMMIT  PAGE_READWRITE                     TEB        [~0; dd4.2134]
        86`341f7000       86`341fd000        0`00006000 MEM_PRIVATE MEM_RESERVE                                    <unknown>
        86`341fd000       86`341ff000        0`00002000 MEM_PRIVATE MEM_COMMIT  PAGE_READWRITE                     TEB        [~1; dd4.1a54]
        86`341ff000       86`34200000        0`00001000 MEM_PRIVATE MEM_RESERVE                                    <unknown>
+       86`34200000       86`34201000        0`00001000 MEM_PRIVATE MEM_RESERVE                                    Stack      [~0; dd4.2134]
        86`34201000       86`34300000        0`000ff000 MEM_PRIVATE MEM_COMMIT  PAGE_READWRITE                     Stack      [~0; dd4.2134]
+       86`34300000       86`343fb000        0`000fb000 MEM_PRIVATE MEM_RESERVE                                    Stack      [~8; dd4.1628]
        86`343fb000       86`343fe000        0`00003000 MEM_PRIVATE MEM_COMMIT  PAGE_READWRITE | PAGE_GUARD        Stack      [~8; dd4.1628]
        86`343fe000       86`34400000        0`00002000 MEM_PRIVATE MEM_COMMIT  PAGE_READWRITE                     Stack      [~8; dd4.1628]
+       86`34400000       86`344f2000        0`000f2000 MEM_PRIVATE MEM_RESERVE                                    Stack      [~9; dd4.df4]
        86`344f2000       86`344f5000        0`00003000 MEM_PRIVATE MEM_COMMIT  PAGE_READWRITE | PAGE_GUARD        Stack      [~9; dd4.df4]
        86`344f5000       86`34500000        0`0000b000 MEM_PRIVATE MEM_COMMIT  PAGE_READWRITE                     Stack      [~9; dd4.df4]
+       86`34500000       86`345f5000        0`000f5000 MEM_PRIVATE MEM_RESERVE                                    Stack      [~10; dd4.bfc]
        86`345f5000       86`345f8000        0`00003000 MEM_PRIVATE MEM_COMMIT  PAGE_READWRITE | PAGE_GUARD        Stack      [~10; dd4.bfc]
        86`345f8000       86`34600000        0`00008000 MEM_PRIVATE MEM_COMMIT  PAGE_READWRITE                     Stack      [~10; dd4.bfc]
+       86`34600000       86`346fb000        0`000fb000 MEM_PRIVATE MEM_RESERVE                                    Stack      [~1; dd4.1a54]
        86`346fb000       86`346fe000        0`00003000 MEM_PRIVATE MEM_COMMIT  PAGE_READWRITE | PAGE_GUARD        Stack      [~1; dd4.1a54]
        86`346fe000       86`34700000        0`00002000 MEM_PRIVATE MEM_COMMIT  PAGE_READWRITE                     Stack      [~1; dd4.1a54]
+       86`34700000       86`347fb000        0`000fb000 MEM_PRIVATE MEM_RESERVE                                    Stack      [~2; dd4.1550]
        86`347fb000       86`347fe000        0`00003000 MEM_PRIVATE MEM_COMMIT  PAGE_READWRITE | PAGE_GUARD        Stack      [~2; dd4.1550]
        86`347fe000       86`34800000        0`00002000 MEM_PRIVATE MEM_COMMIT  PAGE_READWRITE                     Stack      [~2; dd4.1550]
+       86`34800000       86`348f6000        0`000f6000 MEM_PRIVATE MEM_RESERVE                                    Stack      [~3; dd4.1714]
        86`348f6000       86`348f9000        0`00003000 MEM_PRIVATE MEM_COMMIT  PAGE_READWRITE | PAGE_GUARD        Stack      [~3; dd4.1714]
        86`348f9000       86`34900000        0`00007000 MEM_PRIVATE MEM_COMMIT  PAGE_READWRITE                     Stack      [~3; dd4.1714]
+       86`34900000       86`349f6000        0`000f6000 MEM_PRIVATE MEM_RESERVE                                    Stack      [~11; dd4.1b20]
        86`349f6000       86`349f9000        0`00003000 MEM_PRIVATE MEM_COMMIT  PAGE_READWRITE | PAGE_GUARD        Stack      [~11; dd4.1b20]
        86`349f9000       86`34a00000        0`00007000 MEM_PRIVATE MEM_COMMIT  PAGE_READWRITE                     Stack      [~11; dd4.1b20]
+       86`34a00000       86`34afb000        0`000fb000 MEM_PRIVATE MEM_RESERVE                                    Stack      [~12; dd4.1030]
        86`34afb000       86`34afe000        0`00003000 MEM_PRIVATE MEM_COMMIT  PAGE_READWRITE | PAGE_GUARD        Stack      [~12; dd4.1030]
        86`34afe000       86`34b00000        0`00002000 MEM_PRIVATE MEM_COMMIT  PAGE_READWRITE                     Stack      [~12; dd4.1030]
+       86`34b00000       86`34e00000        0`00300000             MEM_FREE    PAGE_NOACCESS                      Free
+       86`34e00000       86`34ef6000        0`000f6000 MEM_PRIVATE MEM_RESERVE                                    Stack      [~6; dd4.fec]
        86`34ef6000       86`34ef9000        0`00003000 MEM_PRIVATE MEM_COMMIT  PAGE_READWRITE | PAGE_GUARD        Stack      [~6; dd4.fec]
        86`34ef9000       86`34f00000        0`00007000 MEM_PRIVATE MEM_COMMIT  PAGE_READWRITE                     Stack      [~6; dd4.fec]
+       86`34f00000       86`35000000        0`00100000             MEM_FREE    PAGE_NOACCESS                      Free
+       86`35000000       86`350fb000        0`000fb000 MEM_PRIVATE MEM_RESERVE                                    Stack      [~7; dd4.1608]
        86`350fb000       86`350fe000        0`00003000 MEM_PRIVATE MEM_COMMIT  PAGE_READWRITE | PAGE_GUARD        Stack      [~7; dd4.1608]
        86`350fe000       86`35100000        0`00002000 MEM_PRIVATE MEM_COMMIT  PAGE_READWRITE                     Stack      [~7; dd4.1608]
+       86`35100000      1f2`d7bb0000      16c`a2ab0000             MEM_FREE    PAGE_NOACCESS                      Free
+      1f2`d7bb0000      1f2`d7bc0000        0`00010000 MEM_MAPPED  MEM_COMMIT  PAGE_READWRITE                     Heap       [ID: 1; Handle: 000001f2d7bb0000; Type: Segment]
+      1f2`d7bc0000      1f2`d7bc3000        0`00003000 MEM_MAPPED  MEM_COMMIT  PAGE_READONLY                      <unknown>  [........0...P...]
+      1f2`d7bc3000      1f2`d7bd0000        0`0000d000             MEM_FREE    PAGE_NOACCESS                      Free
+      1f2`d7bd0000      1f2`d7bef000        0`0001f000 MEM_MAPPED  MEM_COMMIT  PAGE_READONLY                      Other      [API Set Map]
+      1f2`d7bef000      1f2`d7bf0000        0`00001000             MEM_FREE    PAGE_NOACCESS                      Free
+      1f2`d7bf0000      1f2`d7bf4000        0`00004000 MEM_MAPPED  MEM_COMMIT  PAGE_READONLY                      Other      [System Default Activation Context Data]
+      1f2`d7bf4000      1f2`d7c00000        0`0000c000             MEM_FREE    PAGE_NOACCESS                      Free
+      1f2`d7c00000      1f2`d7c03000        0`00003000 MEM_MAPPED  MEM_COMMIT  PAGE_READONLY                      Other      [Activation Context Data]
+      1f2`d7c03000      1f2`d7c10000        0`0000d000             MEM_FREE    PAGE_NOACCESS                      Free
+      1f2`d7c10000      1f2`d7c12000        0`00002000 MEM_PRIVATE MEM_COMMIT  PAGE_READWRITE                     <unknown>  [................]
+      1f2`d7c12000      1f2`d7c20000        0`0000e000             MEM_FREE    PAGE_NOACCESS                      Free
+      1f2`d7c20000      1f2`d7c31000        0`00011000 MEM_MAPPED  MEM_COMMIT  PAGE_READONLY                      <unknown>  [................]
+      1f2`d7c31000      1f2`d7c40000        0`0000f000             MEM_FREE    PAGE_NOACCESS                      Free
+      1f2`d7c40000      1f2`d7c51000        0`00011000 MEM_MAPPED  MEM_COMMIT  PAGE_READONLY                      <unknown>  [................]
+      1f2`d7c51000      1f2`d7c60000        0`0000f000             MEM_FREE    PAGE_NOACCESS                      Free
+      1f2`d7c60000      1f2`d7c63000        0`00003000 MEM_MAPPED  MEM_COMMIT  PAGE_READONLY                      <unknown>  [........0...P...]
+      1f2`d7c63000      1f2`d7c70000        0`0000d000             MEM_FREE    PAGE_NOACCESS                      Free
+      1f2`d7c70000      1f2`d7c74000        0`00004000 MEM_PRIVATE MEM_COMMIT  PAGE_READWRITE                     Heap       [ID: 0; Handle: 000001f2d7d60000; Type: Front End]
       1f2`d7c74000      1f2`d7c77000        0`00003000 MEM_PRIVATE MEM_RESERVE                                    Heap       [ID: 0; Handle: 000001f2d7d60000; Type: Front End]
+      1f2`d7c77000      1f2`d7c80000        0`00009000             MEM_FREE    PAGE_NOACCESS                      Free
+      1f2`d7c80000      1f2`d7d4e000        0`000ce000 MEM_MAPPED  MEM_COMMIT  PAGE_READONLY                      <unknown>  [................]
+      1f2`d7d4e000      1f2`d7d50000        0`00002000             MEM_FREE    PAGE_NOACCESS                      Free
+      1f2`d7d50000      1f2`d7d51000        0`00001000 MEM_PRIVATE MEM_COMMIT  PAGE_READWRITE                     Heap       [ID: 2; Handle: 000001f2d8000000; Type: Front End]
       1f2`d7d51000      1f2`d7d57000        0`00006000 MEM_PRIVATE MEM_RESERVE                                    Heap       [ID: 2; Handle: 000001f2d8000000; Type: Front End]
+      1f2`d7d57000      1f2`d7d60000        0`00009000             MEM_FREE    PAGE_NOACCESS                      Free
+      1f2`d7d60000      1f2`d7e5f000        0`000ff000 MEM_PRIVATE MEM_COMMIT  PAGE_READWRITE                     Heap       [ID: 0; Handle: 000001f2d7d60000; Type: Segment]
       1f2`d7e5f000      1f2`d7e60000        0`00001000 MEM_PRIVATE MEM_RESERVE                                    <unknown>
+      1f2`d7e60000      1f2`d7e71000        0`00011000 MEM_MAPPED  MEM_COMMIT  PAGE_READONLY                      <unknown>  [................]
+      1f2`d7e71000      1f2`d7e80000        0`0000f000             MEM_FREE    PAGE_NOACCESS                      Free
+      1f2`d7e80000      1f2`d7e91000        0`00011000 MEM_MAPPED  MEM_COMMIT  PAGE_READONLY                      <unknown>  [................]
+      1f2`d7e91000      1f2`d7ea0000        0`0000f000             MEM_FREE    PAGE_NOACCESS                      Free
+      1f2`d7ea0000      1f2`d7ea4000        0`00004000 MEM_MAPPED  MEM_COMMIT  PAGE_READONLY                      <unknown>  [........G...C...]
       1f2`d7ea4000      1f2`d7ea8000        0`00004000 MEM_MAPPED  MEM_RESERVE                                    <unknown>
+      1f2`d7ea8000      1f2`d7eb0000        0`00008000             MEM_FREE    PAGE_NOACCESS                      Free
+      1f2`d7eb0000      1f2`d7eb1000        0`00001000 MEM_MAPPED  MEM_COMMIT  PAGE_READONLY                      <unknown>  [.....8..d.......]
+      1f2`d7eb1000      1f2`d7ec0000        0`0000f000             MEM_FREE    PAGE_NOACCESS                      Free
+      1f2`d7ec0000      1f2`d7ec1000        0`00001000 MEM_MAPPED  MEM_COMMIT  PAGE_READONLY                      <unknown>  [.....8..d.......]
+      1f2`d7ec1000      1f2`d7ed0000        0`0000f000             MEM_FREE    PAGE_NOACCESS                      Free
+      1f2`d7ed0000      1f2`d7ed1000        0`00001000 MEM_MAPPED  MEM_COMMIT  PAGE_READONLY                      <unknown>  [p....8......u...]
+      1f2`d7ed1000      1f2`d7ee0000        0`0000f000             MEM_FREE    PAGE_NOACCESS                      Free
```

```
+       1f2`d7ee0000      1f2`d7fdf000        0`000ff000 MEM_PRIVATE MEM_COMMIT  PAGE_READWRITE
        1f2`d7fdf000      1f2`d7fe0000        0`00001000 MEM_PRIVATE MEM_RESERVE
+       1f2`d7fe0000      1f2`d7fe2000        0`00002000 MEM_PRIVATE MEM_COMMIT  PAGE_READWRITE
        1f2`d7fe2000      1f2`d7fef000        0`0000d000 MEM_PRIVATE MEM_RESERVE
        1f2`d7fef000      1f2`d7ff0000        0`00001000 MEM_PRIVATE MEM_RESERVE
+       1f2`d7ff0000      1f2`d7ff1000        0`00001000 MEM_IMAGE   MEM_COMMIT  PAGE_READONLY
        1f2`d7ff1000      1f2`d7ff2000        0`00001000 MEM_IMAGE   MEM_RESERVE
        1f2`d7ff2000      1f2`d7ff3000        0`00001000 MEM_IMAGE   MEM_COMMIT  PAGE_READONLY
        1f2`d7ff3000      1f2`d7ff4000        0`00001000 MEM_IMAGE   MEM_RESERVE
        1f2`d7ff4000      1f2`d7ff5000        0`00001000 MEM_IMAGE   MEM_COMMIT  PAGE_READONLY
        1f2`d7ff5000      1f2`d7ff6000        0`00001000 MEM_IMAGE   MEM_RESERVE
        1f2`d7ff6000      1f2`d7ff7000        0`00001000 MEM_IMAGE   MEM_COMMIT  PAGE_READONLY
        1f2`d7ff7000      1f2`d7ff8000        0`00001000 MEM_IMAGE   MEM_RESERVE
+       1f2`d7ff8000      1f2`d8000000        0`00008000             MEM_FREE    PAGE_NOACCESS
+       1f2`d8000000      1f2`d8009000        0`00009000 MEM_PRIVATE MEM_COMMIT  PAGE_READWRITE
        1f2`d8009000      1f2`d800f000        0`00006000 MEM_PRIVATE MEM_RESERVE
        1f2`d800f000      1f2`d8010000        0`00001000 MEM_PRIVATE MEM_RESERVE
+       1f2`d8010000      1f2`d8020000        0`00010000 MEM_MAPPED  MEM_COMMIT  PAGE_READONLY
        1f2`d8020000      1f2`d8210000        0`001f0000 MEM_MAPPED  MEM_RESERVE
+       1f2`d8210000      1f2`d8391000        0`00181000 MEM_MAPPED  MEM_COMMIT  PAGE_READONLY
+       1f2`d8391000      1f2`d83a0000        0`0000f000             MEM_FREE    PAGE_NOACCESS
+       1f2`d83a0000      1f2`d841e000        0`0007e000 MEM_MAPPED  MEM_COMMIT  PAGE_READONLY
        1f2`d841e000      1f2`d97a1000        0`01383000 MEM_MAPPED  MEM_RESERVE
+       1f2`d97a1000      1f2`d97b0000        0`0000f000             MEM_FREE    PAGE_NOACCESS
+       1f2`d97b0000      1f2`d97b3000        0`00003000 MEM_PRIVATE MEM_COMMIT  PAGE_READWRITE
        1f2`d97b3000      1f2`d97c0000        0`0000d000 MEM_PRIVATE MEM_RESERVE
+       1f2`d97c0000      1f2`d97c1000        0`00001000 MEM_PRIVATE MEM_COMMIT  PAGE_READWRITE
+       1f2`d97c1000      1f2`d97d0000        0`0000f000             MEM_FREE    PAGE_NOACCESS
+       1f2`d97d0000      1f2`d97d1000        0`00001000 MEM_PRIVATE MEM_COMMIT  PAGE_READWRITE
+       1f2`d97d1000      1f2`d97e0000        0`0000f000             MEM_FREE    PAGE_NOACCESS
+       1f2`d97e0000      1f2`d97f0000        0`00010000 MEM_PRIVATE MEM_COMMIT  PAGE_READWRITE
+       1f2`d97f0000      1f2`d97f1000        0`00001000 MEM_MAPPED  MEM_COMMIT  PAGE_READONLY
+       1f2`d97f1000      1f2`d9800000        0`0000f000             MEM_FREE    PAGE_NOACCESS
+       1f2`d9800000      1f2`d9801000        0`00001000 MEM_IMAGE   MEM_COMMIT  PAGE_READONLY
Files\dotnet\shared\Microsoft.NETCore.App\9.0.4\System.Text.Encoding.Extensions.dll"]
        1f2`d9801000      1f2`d9802000        0`00001000 MEM_IMAGE   MEM_RESERVE
Files\dotnet\shared\Microsoft.NETCore.App\9.0.4\System.Text.Encoding.Extensions.dll"]
        1f2`d9802000      1f2`d9803000        0`00001000 MEM_IMAGE   MEM_COMMIT  PAGE_READONLY
Files\dotnet\shared\Microsoft.NETCore.App\9.0.4\System.Text.Encoding.Extensions.dll"]
        1f2`d9803000      1f2`d9804000        0`00001000 MEM_IMAGE   MEM_RESERVE
Files\dotnet\shared\Microsoft.NETCore.App\9.0.4\System.Text.Encoding.Extensions.dll"]
        1f2`d9804000      1f2`d9805000        0`00001000 MEM_IMAGE   MEM_COMMIT  PAGE_READONLY
Files\dotnet\shared\Microsoft.NETCore.App\9.0.4\System.Text.Encoding.Extensions.dll"]
        1f2`d9805000      1f2`d9806000        0`00001000 MEM_IMAGE   MEM_RESERVE
Files\dotnet\shared\Microsoft.NETCore.App\9.0.4\System.Text.Encoding.Extensions.dll"]
        1f2`d9806000      1f2`d9807000        0`00001000 MEM_IMAGE   MEM_COMMIT  PAGE_READONLY
Files\dotnet\shared\Microsoft.NETCore.App\9.0.4\System.Text.Encoding.Extensions.dll"]
        1f2`d9807000      1f2`d9808000        0`00001000 MEM_IMAGE   MEM_RESERVE
Files\dotnet\shared\Microsoft.NETCore.App\9.0.4\System.Text.Encoding.Extensions.dll"]
+       1f2`d9808000      1f2`d9810000        0`00008000             MEM_FREE    PAGE_NOACCESS
+       1f2`d9810000      1f2`d9811000        0`00001000 MEM_IMAGE   MEM_COMMIT  PAGE_READONLY
        1f2`d9811000      1f2`d9812000        0`00001000 MEM_IMAGE   MEM_RESERVE
        1f2`d9812000      1f2`d9821000        0`0000f000 MEM_IMAGE   MEM_COMMIT  PAGE_READONLY
        1f2`d9821000      1f2`d9822000        0`00001000 MEM_IMAGE   MEM_RESERVE
        1f2`d9822000      1f2`d9823000        0`00001000 MEM_IMAGE   MEM_COMMIT  PAGE_READONLY
        1f2`d9823000      1f2`d9824000        0`00001000 MEM_IMAGE   MEM_RESERVE
+       1f2`d9824000      1f2`d9830000        0`0000c000             MEM_FREE    PAGE_NOACCESS
+       1f2`d9830000      1f2`d9831000        0`00001000 MEM_IMAGE   MEM_COMMIT  PAGE_READONLY
        1f2`d9831000      1f2`d9832000        0`00001000 MEM_IMAGE   MEM_RESERVE
        1f2`d9832000      1f2`d983b000        0`00009000 MEM_IMAGE   MEM_COMMIT  PAGE_READONLY
        1f2`d983b000      1f2`d983c000        0`00001000 MEM_IMAGE   MEM_RESERVE
        1f2`d983c000      1f2`d983d000        0`00001000 MEM_IMAGE   MEM_COMMIT  PAGE_READONLY
        1f2`d983d000      1f2`d983e000        0`00001000 MEM_IMAGE   MEM_RESERVE
+       1f2`d983e000      1f2`d9840000        0`00002000             MEM_FREE    PAGE_NOACCESS
+       1f2`d9840000      1f2`d9842000        0`00002000 MEM_MAPPED  MEM_COMMIT  PAGE_READONLY
+       1f2`d9842000      1f2`d9850000        0`0000e000             MEM_FREE    PAGE_NOACCESS
+       1f2`d9850000      1f2`d9851000        0`00001000 MEM_IMAGE   MEM_COMMIT  PAGE_READONLY
        1f2`d9851000      1f2`d9852000        0`00001000 MEM_IMAGE   MEM_RESERVE
        1f2`d9852000      1f2`d9853000        0`00001000 MEM_IMAGE   MEM_COMMIT  PAGE_READONLY
        1f2`d9853000      1f2`d9854000        0`00001000 MEM_IMAGE   MEM_RESERVE
        1f2`d9854000      1f2`d9855000        0`00001000 MEM_IMAGE   MEM_COMMIT  PAGE_READONLY
        1f2`d9855000      1f2`d9856000        0`00001000 MEM_IMAGE   MEM_RESERVE
        1f2`d9856000      1f2`d9857000        0`00001000 MEM_IMAGE   MEM_COMMIT  PAGE_READONLY
        1f2`d9857000      1f2`d9858000        0`00001000 MEM_IMAGE   MEM_RESERVE
+       1f2`d9858000      1f2`d9860000        0`00008000             MEM_FREE    PAGE_NOACCESS
+       1f2`d9860000      1f2`d9864000        0`00004000 MEM_PRIVATE MEM_COMMIT  PAGE_READWRITE
        1f2`d9864000      1f2`d986f000        0`0000b000 MEM_PRIVATE MEM_RESERVE
        1f2`d986f000      1f2`d9870000        0`00001000 MEM_PRIVATE MEM_RESERVE
+       1f2`d9870000      1f2`d9871000        0`00001000 MEM_IMAGE   MEM_COMMIT  PAGE_READONLY
Files\dotnet\shared\Microsoft.NETCore.App\9.0.4\System.Runtime.Extensions.dll"]
        1f2`d9871000      1f2`d9872000        0`00001000 MEM_IMAGE   MEM_RESERVE
Files\dotnet\shared\Microsoft.NETCore.App\9.0.4\System.Runtime.Extensions.dll"]
        1f2`d9872000      1f2`d9875000        0`00003000 MEM_IMAGE   MEM_COMMIT  PAGE_READONLY
Files\dotnet\shared\Microsoft.NETCore.App\9.0.4\System.Runtime.Extensions.dll"]
        1f2`d9875000      1f2`d9876000        0`00001000 MEM_IMAGE   MEM_RESERVE
Files\dotnet\shared\Microsoft.NETCore.App\9.0.4\System.Runtime.Extensions.dll"]
        1f2`d9876000      1f2`d9877000        0`00001000 MEM_IMAGE   MEM_COMMIT  PAGE_READONLY
Files\dotnet\shared\Microsoft.NETCore.App\9.0.4\System.Runtime.Extensions.dll"]
        1f2`d9877000      1f2`d9878000        0`00001000 MEM_IMAGE   MEM_RESERVE
Files\dotnet\shared\Microsoft.NETCore.App\9.0.4\System.Runtime.Extensions.dll"]
+       1f2`d9878000      1f2`d9880000        0`00008000             MEM_FREE    PAGE_NOACCESS
+       1f2`d9880000      1f2`d9882000        0`00002000 MEM_MAPPED  MEM_COMMIT  PAGE_READONLY
+       1f2`d9882000      1f2`d9890000        0`0000e000             MEM_FREE    PAGE_NOACCESS
+       1f2`d9890000      1f2`d9891000        0`00001000 MEM_IMAGE   MEM_COMMIT  PAGE_READONLY
        1f2`d9891000      1f2`d9892000        0`00001000 MEM_IMAGE   MEM_RESERVE
        1f2`d9892000      1f2`d9893000        0`00001000 MEM_IMAGE   MEM_COMMIT  PAGE_READONLY
        1f2`d9893000      1f2`d9894000        0`00001000 MEM_IMAGE   MEM_RESERVE
        1f2`d9894000      1f2`d9895000        0`00001000 MEM_IMAGE   MEM_COMMIT  PAGE_READONLY
        1f2`d9895000      1f2`d9896000        0`00001000 MEM_IMAGE   MEM_RESERVE
        1f2`d9896000      1f2`d9897000        0`00001000 MEM_IMAGE   MEM_COMMIT  PAGE_READONLY
        1f2`d9897000      1f2`d9898000        0`00001000 MEM_IMAGE   MEM_RESERVE
+       1f2`d9898000      1f2`d98a0000        0`00008000             MEM_FREE    PAGE_NOACCESS
+       1f2`d98a0000      1f2`d98a1000        0`00001000 MEM_MAPPED  MEM_COMMIT  PAGE_READWRITE
+       1f2`d98a1000      1f2`d98b0000        0`0000f000             MEM_FREE    PAGE_NOACCESS
+       1f2`d98b0000      1f2`d98b1000        0`00001000 MEM_IMAGE   MEM_COMMIT  PAGE_READONLY
Files\dotnet\shared\Microsoft.NETCore.App\9.0.4\System.Threading.Tasks.dll"]
        1f2`d98b1000      1f2`d98b2000        0`00001000 MEM_IMAGE   MEM_RESERVE
Files\dotnet\shared\Microsoft.NETCore.App\9.0.4\System.Threading.Tasks.dll"]
        1f2`d98b2000      1f2`d98b3000        0`00001000 MEM_IMAGE   MEM_COMMIT  PAGE_READONLY
Files\dotnet\shared\Microsoft.NETCore.App\9.0.4\System.Threading.Tasks.dll"]
        1f2`d98b3000      1f2`d98b4000        0`00001000 MEM_IMAGE   MEM_RESERVE
Files\dotnet\shared\Microsoft.NETCore.App\9.0.4\System.Threading.Tasks.dll"]
        1f2`d98b4000      1f2`d98b5000        0`00001000 MEM_IMAGE   MEM_COMMIT  PAGE_READONLY
Files\dotnet\shared\Microsoft.NETCore.App\9.0.4\System.Threading.Tasks.dll"]
        1f2`d98b5000      1f2`d98b6000        0`00001000 MEM_IMAGE   MEM_RESERVE
Files\dotnet\shared\Microsoft.NETCore.App\9.0.4\System.Threading.Tasks.dll"]
        1f2`d98b6000      1f2`d98b7000        0`00001000 MEM_IMAGE   MEM_COMMIT  PAGE_READONLY
Files\dotnet\shared\Microsoft.NETCore.App\9.0.4\System.Threading.Tasks.dll"]
        1f2`d98b7000      1f2`d98b8000        0`00001000 MEM_IMAGE   MEM_RESERVE
Files\dotnet\shared\Microsoft.NETCore.App\9.0.4\System.Threading.Tasks.dll"]
+       1f2`d98b8000      1f2`d98c0000        0`00008000             MEM_FREE    PAGE_NOACCESS
+       1f2`d98c0000      1f2`d98d0000        0`00010000 MEM_MAPPED  MEM_COMMIT  PAGE_READWRITE
+       1f2`d98d0000      1f2`d98e0000        0`00010000 MEM_MAPPED  MEM_COMMIT  PAGE_READWRITE
+       1f2`d98e0000      1f2`d98e1000        0`00001000 MEM_IMAGE   MEM_COMMIT  PAGE_READONLY
Files\dotnet\shared\Microsoft.NETCore.App\9.0.4\System.Threading.ThreadPool.dll"]
        1f2`d98e1000      1f2`d98e2000        0`00001000 MEM_IMAGE   MEM_RESERVE
Files\dotnet\shared\Microsoft.NETCore.App\9.0.4\System.Threading.ThreadPool.dll"]
        1f2`d98e2000      1f2`d98e3000        0`00001000 MEM_IMAGE   MEM_COMMIT  PAGE_READONLY
Files\dotnet\shared\Microsoft.NETCore.App\9.0.4\System.Threading.ThreadPool.dll"]
        1f2`d98e3000      1f2`d98e4000        0`00001000 MEM_IMAGE   MEM_RESERVE
Files\dotnet\shared\Microsoft.NETCore.App\9.0.4\System.Threading.ThreadPool.dll"]
        1f2`d98e4000      1f2`d98e5000        0`00001000 MEM_IMAGE   MEM_COMMIT  PAGE_READONLY
Files\dotnet\shared\Microsoft.NETCore.App\9.0.4\System.Threading.ThreadPool.dll"]
        1f2`d98e5000      1f2`d98e6000        0`00001000 MEM_IMAGE   MEM_RESERVE
Files\dotnet\shared\Microsoft.NETCore.App\9.0.4\System.Threading.ThreadPool.dll"]
        1f2`d98e6000      1f2`d98e7000        0`00001000 MEM_IMAGE   MEM_COMMIT  PAGE_READONLY
Files\dotnet\shared\Microsoft.NETCore.App\9.0.4\System.Threading.ThreadPool.dll"]
        1f2`d98e7000      1f2`d98e8000        0`00001000 MEM_IMAGE   MEM_RESERVE
Files\dotnet\shared\Microsoft.NETCore.App\9.0.4\System.Threading.ThreadPool.dll"]
+       1f2`d98e8000      1f2`d98f0000        0`00008000             MEM_FREE    PAGE_NOACCESS
+       1f2`d98f0000      1f2`d98f1000        0`00001000 MEM_IMAGE   MEM_COMMIT  PAGE_READONLY
Files\dotnet\shared\Microsoft.NETCore.App\9.0.4\System.Threading.Thread.dll"]
        1f2`d98f1000      1f2`d98f2000        0`00001000 MEM_IMAGE   MEM_RESERVE
Files\dotnet\shared\Microsoft.NETCore.App\9.0.4\System.Threading.Thread.dll"]
        1f2`d98f2000      1f2`d98f3000        0`00001000 MEM_IMAGE   MEM_COMMIT  PAGE_READONLY
Files\dotnet\shared\Microsoft.NETCore.App\9.0.4\System.Threading.Thread.dll"]
        1f2`d98f3000      1f2`d98f4000        0`00001000 MEM_IMAGE   MEM_RESERVE
Files\dotnet\shared\Microsoft.NETCore.App\9.0.4\System.Threading.Thread.dll"]
```

```
Heap       [ID: 0; Handle: 000001f2d7d60000; Type: Segment]
<unknown>
Heap       [ID: 3; Handle: 000001f2d7fe0000; Type: Segment]
Heap       [ID: 3; Handle: 000001f2d7fe0000; Type: Segment]
<unknown>
Image      [System_Xml_XDocument; "C:\Program Files\dotnet\shared\Microsoft.NETCore.App\9.0.4\System.Xml.XDocument.dll"]
Image      [System_Xml_XDocument; "C:\Program Files\dotnet\shared\Microsoft.NETCore.App\9.0.4\System.Xml.XDocument.dll"]
Image      [System_Xml_XDocument; "C:\Program Files\dotnet\shared\Microsoft.NETCore.App\9.0.4\System.Xml.XDocument.dll"]
Image      [System_Xml_XDocument; "C:\Program Files\dotnet\shared\Microsoft.NETCore.App\9.0.4\System.Xml.XDocument.dll"]
Image      [System_Xml_XDocument; "C:\Program Files\dotnet\shared\Microsoft.NETCore.App\9.0.4\System.Xml.XDocument.dll"]
Image      [System_Xml_XDocument; "C:\Program Files\dotnet\shared\Microsoft.NETCore.App\9.0.4\System.Xml.XDocument.dll"]
Image      [System_Xml_XDocument; "C:\Program Files\dotnet\shared\Microsoft.NETCore.App\9.0.4\System.Xml.XDocument.dll"]
Image      [System_Xml_XDocument; "C:\Program Files\dotnet\shared\Microsoft.NETCore.App\9.0.4\System.Xml.XDocument.dll"]
Free
Heap       [ID: 2; Handle: 000001f2d8000000; Type: Segment]
Heap       [ID: 2; Handle: 000001f2d8000000; Type: Segment]
<unknown>
<unknown>  [................]
<unknown>
Other      [GDI Shared Handle Table]
Free
<unknown>  [........w...C...]
<unknown>
Free
<unknown>  [................]
<unknown>
Other      [WER Registration Data]
Free
<unknown>  [................]
Free
<unknown>  [................]
Other      [Activation Context Data]
Free
Image      [System_Text_Encoding_Extensions; "C:\Program

Image      [System_Text_Encoding_Extensions; "C:\Program

Image      [System_Text_Encoding_Extensions; "C:\Program

Image      [System_Text_Encoding_Extensions; "C:\Program

Image      [System_Text_Encoding_Extensions; "C:\Program

Image      [System_Text_Encoding_Extensions; "C:\Program

Image      [System_Text_Encoding_Extensions; "C:\Program

Image      [System_Text_Encoding_Extensions; "C:\Program

Free
Image      [LINQPad_Query; "C:\Users\User\AppData\Local\LINQPad\8.8.9\ProcessServer\9.0.4\LINQPad.Query.dll"]
Image      [LINQPad_Query; "C:\Users\User\AppData\Local\LINQPad\8.8.9\ProcessServer\9.0.4\LINQPad.Query.dll"]
Image      [LINQPad_Query; "C:\Users\User\AppData\Local\LINQPad\8.8.9\ProcessServer\9.0.4\LINQPad.Query.dll"]
Image      [LINQPad_Query; "C:\Users\User\AppData\Local\LINQPad\8.8.9\ProcessServer\9.0.4\LINQPad.Query.dll"]
Image      [LINQPad_Query; "C:\Users\User\AppData\Local\LINQPad\8.8.9\ProcessServer\9.0.4\LINQPad.Query.dll"]
Image      [LINQPad_Query; "C:\Users\User\AppData\Local\LINQPad\8.8.9\ProcessServer\9.0.4\LINQPad.Query.dll"]
Free
Image      [System_Runtime; "C:\Program Files\dotnet\shared\Microsoft.NETCore.App\9.0.4\System.Runtime.dll"]
Image      [System_Runtime; "C:\Program Files\dotnet\shared\Microsoft.NETCore.App\9.0.4\System.Runtime.dll"]
Image      [System_Runtime; "C:\Program Files\dotnet\shared\Microsoft.NETCore.App\9.0.4\System.Runtime.dll"]
Image      [System_Runtime; "C:\Program Files\dotnet\shared\Microsoft.NETCore.App\9.0.4\System.Runtime.dll"]
Image      [System_Runtime; "C:\Program Files\dotnet\shared\Microsoft.NETCore.App\9.0.4\System.Runtime.dll"]
Image      [System_Runtime; "C:\Program Files\dotnet\shared\Microsoft.NETCore.App\9.0.4\System.Runtime.dll"]
Free
Other      [Activation Context Data]
Free
Image      [System_Runtime_Loader; "C:\Program Files\dotnet\shared\Microsoft.NETCore.App\9.0.4\System.Runtime.Loader.dll"]
Image      [System_Runtime_Loader; "C:\Program Files\dotnet\shared\Microsoft.NETCore.App\9.0.4\System.Runtime.Loader.dll"]
Image      [System_Runtime_Loader; "C:\Program Files\dotnet\shared\Microsoft.NETCore.App\9.0.4\System.Runtime.Loader.dll"]
Image      [System_Runtime_Loader; "C:\Program Files\dotnet\shared\Microsoft.NETCore.App\9.0.4\System.Runtime.Loader.dll"]
Image      [System_Runtime_Loader; "C:\Program Files\dotnet\shared\Microsoft.NETCore.App\9.0.4\System.Runtime.Loader.dll"]
Image      [System_Runtime_Loader; "C:\Program Files\dotnet\shared\Microsoft.NETCore.App\9.0.4\System.Runtime.Loader.dll"]
Image      [System_Runtime_Loader; "C:\Program Files\dotnet\shared\Microsoft.NETCore.App\9.0.4\System.Runtime.Loader.dll"]
Image      [System_Runtime_Loader; "C:\Program Files\dotnet\shared\Microsoft.NETCore.App\9.0.4\System.Runtime.Loader.dll"]
Free
Heap       [ID: 4; Handle: 000001f2d9860000; Type: Segment]
Heap       [ID: 4; Handle: 000001f2d9860000; Type: Segment]
<unknown>
Image      [System_Runtime_Extensions; "C:\Program

Image      [System_Runtime_Extensions; "C:\Program

Image      [System_Runtime_Extensions; "C:\Program

Image      [System_Runtime_Extensions; "C:\Program

Image      [System_Runtime_Extensions; "C:\Program

Image      [System_Runtime_Extensions; "C:\Program

Free
Other      [Activation Context Data]
Free
Image      [System_IO_FileSystem; "C:\Program Files\dotnet\shared\Microsoft.NETCore.App\9.0.4\System.IO.FileSystem.dll"]
Image      [System_IO_FileSystem; "C:\Program Files\dotnet\shared\Microsoft.NETCore.App\9.0.4\System.IO.FileSystem.dll"]
Image      [System_IO_FileSystem; "C:\Program Files\dotnet\shared\Microsoft.NETCore.App\9.0.4\System.IO.FileSystem.dll"]
Image      [System_IO_FileSystem; "C:\Program Files\dotnet\shared\Microsoft.NETCore.App\9.0.4\System.IO.FileSystem.dll"]
Image      [System_IO_FileSystem; "C:\Program Files\dotnet\shared\Microsoft.NETCore.App\9.0.4\System.IO.FileSystem.dll"]
Image      [System_IO_FileSystem; "C:\Program Files\dotnet\shared\Microsoft.NETCore.App\9.0.4\System.IO.FileSystem.dll"]
Image      [System_IO_FileSystem; "C:\Program Files\dotnet\shared\Microsoft.NETCore.App\9.0.4\System.IO.FileSystem.dll"]
Image      [System_IO_FileSystem; "C:\Program Files\dotnet\shared\Microsoft.NETCore.App\9.0.4\System.IO.FileSystem.dll"]
Free
<unknown>  [................]
Free
Image      [System_Threading_Tasks; "C:\Program

Image      [System_Threading_Tasks; "C:\Program

Image      [System_Threading_Tasks; "C:\Program

Image      [System_Threading_Tasks; "C:\Program

Image      [System_Threading_Tasks; "C:\Program

Image      [System_Threading_Tasks; "C:\Program

Image      [System_Threading_Tasks; "C:\Program

Image      [System_Threading_Tasks; "C:\Program

Free
<unknown>  [................]
<unknown>  [................]
Image      [System_Threading_ThreadPool; "C:\Program

Image      [System_Threading_ThreadPool; "C:\Program

Image      [System_Threading_ThreadPool; "C:\Program

Image      [System_Threading_ThreadPool; "C:\Program

Image      [System_Threading_ThreadPool; "C:\Program

Image      [System_Threading_ThreadPool; "C:\Program

Image      [System_Threading_ThreadPool; "C:\Program

Image      [System_Threading_ThreadPool; "C:\Program

Free
Image      [System_Threading_Thread; "C:\Program

Image      [System_Threading_Thread; "C:\Program

Image      [System_Threading_Thread; "C:\Program

Image      [System_Threading_Thread; "C:\Program
```

```
    1f2`d98f4000    1f2`d98f5000    0`00001000 MEM_IMAGE   MEM_COMMIT  PAGE_READONLY              Image    [System_Threading_Thread; "C:\Program
Files\dotnet\shared\Microsoft.NETCore.App\9.0.4\System.Threading.Thread.dll"]
    1f2`d98f5000    1f2`d98f6000    0`00001000 MEM_IMAGE   MEM_RESERVE                            Image    [System_Threading_Thread; "C:\Program
Files\dotnet\shared\Microsoft.NETCore.App\9.0.4\System.Threading.Thread.dll"]
    1f2`d98f6000    1f2`d98f7000    0`00001000 MEM_IMAGE   MEM_COMMIT  PAGE_READONLY              Image    [System_Threading_Thread; "C:\Program
Files\dotnet\shared\Microsoft.NETCore.App\9.0.4\System.Threading.Thread.dll"]
    1f2`d98f7000    1f2`d98f8000    0`00001000 MEM_IMAGE   MEM_RESERVE                            Image    [System_Threading_Thread; "C:\Program
Files\dotnet\shared\Microsoft.NETCore.App\9.0.4\System.Threading.Thread.dll"]
+   1f2`d98f8000    1f2`d9900000    0`00008000             MEM_FREE    PAGE_NOACCESS              Free
+   1f2`d9900000    1f2`d9901000    0`00001000 MEM_IMAGE   MEM_COMMIT  PAGE_READONLY              Image    [System_Diagnostics_Debug; "C:\Program
Files\dotnet\shared\Microsoft.NETCore.App\9.0.4\System.Diagnostics.Debug.dll"]
    1f2`d9901000    1f2`d9902000    0`00001000 MEM_IMAGE   MEM_RESERVE                            Image    [System_Diagnostics_Debug; "C:\Program
Files\dotnet\shared\Microsoft.NETCore.App\9.0.4\System.Diagnostics.Debug.dll"]
    1f2`d9902000    1f2`d9903000    0`00001000 MEM_IMAGE   MEM_COMMIT  PAGE_READONLY              Image    [System_Diagnostics_Debug; "C:\Program
Files\dotnet\shared\Microsoft.NETCore.App\9.0.4\System.Diagnostics.Debug.dll"]
    1f2`d9903000    1f2`d9904000    0`00001000 MEM_IMAGE   MEM_COMMIT                             Image    [System_Diagnostics_Debug; "C:\Program
Files\dotnet\shared\Microsoft.NETCore.App\9.0.4\System.Diagnostics.Debug.dll"]
    1f2`d9904000    1f2`d9905000    0`00001000 MEM_IMAGE   MEM_COMMIT  PAGE_READONLY              Image    [System_Diagnostics_Debug; "C:\Program
Files\dotnet\shared\Microsoft.NETCore.App\9.0.4\System.Diagnostics.Debug.dll"]
    1f2`d9905000    1f2`d9906000    0`00001000 MEM_IMAGE   MEM_RESERVE                            Image    [System_Diagnostics_Debug; "C:\Program
Files\dotnet\shared\Microsoft.NETCore.App\9.0.4\System.Diagnostics.Debug.dll"]
    1f2`d9906000    1f2`d9907000    0`00001000 MEM_IMAGE   MEM_COMMIT  PAGE_READONLY              Image    [System_Diagnostics_Debug; "C:\Program
Files\dotnet\shared\Microsoft.NETCore.App\9.0.4\System.Diagnostics.Debug.dll"]
    1f2`d9907000    1f2`d9908000    0`00001000 MEM_IMAGE   MEM_RESERVE                            Image    [System_Diagnostics_Debug; "C:\Program
Files\dotnet\shared\Microsoft.NETCore.App\9.0.4\System.Diagnostics.Debug.dll"]
+   1f2`d9908000    1f2`d9910000    0`00008000             MEM_FREE    PAGE_NOACCESS              Free
+   1f2`d9910000    1f2`d9911000    0`00001000 MEM_IMAGE   MEM_COMMIT  PAGE_READONLY              Image    [System_Runtime_InteropServices_RuntimeInformation; "C:\Program
Files\dotnet\shared\Microsoft.NETCore.App\9.0.4\System.Runtime.InteropServices.RuntimeInformation.dll"]
    1f2`d9911000    1f2`d9912000    0`00001000 MEM_IMAGE   MEM_RESERVE                            Image    [System_Runtime_InteropServices_RuntimeInformation; "C:\Program
Files\dotnet\shared\Microsoft.NETCore.App\9.0.4\System.Runtime.InteropServices.RuntimeInformation.dll"]
    1f2`d9912000    1f2`d9913000    0`00001000 MEM_IMAGE   MEM_COMMIT  PAGE_READONLY              Image    [System_Runtime_InteropServices_RuntimeInformation; "C:\Program
Files\dotnet\shared\Microsoft.NETCore.App\9.0.4\System.Runtime.InteropServices.RuntimeInformation.dll"]
    1f2`d9913000    1f2`d9914000    0`00001000 MEM_IMAGE   MEM_RESERVE                            Image    [System_Runtime_InteropServices_RuntimeInformation; "C:\Program
Files\dotnet\shared\Microsoft.NETCore.App\9.0.4\System.Runtime.InteropServices.RuntimeInformation.dll"]
    1f2`d9914000    1f2`d9915000    0`00001000 MEM_IMAGE   MEM_COMMIT  PAGE_READONLY              Image    [System_Runtime_InteropServices_RuntimeInformation; "C:\Program
Files\dotnet\shared\Microsoft.NETCore.App\9.0.4\System.Runtime.InteropServices.RuntimeInformation.dll"]
    1f2`d9915000    1f2`d9916000    0`00001000 MEM_IMAGE   MEM_RESERVE                            Image    [System_Runtime_InteropServices_RuntimeInformation; "C:\Program
Files\dotnet\shared\Microsoft.NETCore.App\9.0.4\System.Runtime.InteropServices.RuntimeInformation.dll"]
    1f2`d9916000    1f2`d9917000    0`00001000 MEM_IMAGE   MEM_COMMIT  PAGE_READONLY              Image    [System_Runtime_InteropServices_RuntimeInformation; "C:\Program
Files\dotnet\shared\Microsoft.NETCore.App\9.0.4\System.Runtime.InteropServices.RuntimeInformation.dll"]
    1f2`d9917000    1f2`d9918000    0`00001000 MEM_IMAGE   MEM_RESERVE                            Image    [System_Runtime_InteropServices_RuntimeInformation; "C:\Program
Files\dotnet\shared\Microsoft.NETCore.App\9.0.4\System.Runtime.InteropServices.RuntimeInformation.dll"]
+   1f2`d9918000    1f2`d9920000    0`00008000             MEM_FREE    PAGE_NOACCESS              Free
+   1f2`d9920000    1f2`d9921000    0`00001000 MEM_IMAGE   MEM_COMMIT  PAGE_READONLY              Image    [Microsoft_Win32_Primitives; "C:\Program
Files\dotnet\shared\Microsoft.NETCore.App\9.0.4\Microsoft.Win32.Primitives.dll"]
    1f2`d9921000    1f2`d9922000    0`00001000 MEM_IMAGE   MEM_RESERVE                            Image    [Microsoft_Win32_Primitives; "C:\Program
Files\dotnet\shared\Microsoft.NETCore.App\9.0.4\Microsoft.Win32.Primitives.dll"]
    1f2`d9922000    1f2`d9923000    0`00001000 MEM_IMAGE   MEM_COMMIT  PAGE_READONLY              Image    [Microsoft_Win32_Primitives; "C:\Program
Files\dotnet\shared\Microsoft.NETCore.App\9.0.4\Microsoft.Win32.Primitives.dll"]
    1f2`d9923000    1f2`d9924000    0`00001000 MEM_IMAGE   MEM_COMMIT  PAGE_READONLY              Image    [Microsoft_Win32_Primitives; "C:\Program
Files\dotnet\shared\Microsoft.NETCore.App\9.0.4\Microsoft.Win32.Primitives.dll"]
    1f2`d9924000    1f2`d9925000    0`00001000 MEM_IMAGE   MEM_COMMIT  PAGE_READONLY              Image    [Microsoft_Win32_Primitives; "C:\Program
Files\dotnet\shared\Microsoft.NETCore.App\9.0.4\Microsoft.Win32.Primitives.dll"]
    1f2`d9925000    1f2`d9926000    0`00001000 MEM_IMAGE   MEM_RESERVE                            Image    [Microsoft_Win32_Primitives; "C:\Program
Files\dotnet\shared\Microsoft.NETCore.App\9.0.4\Microsoft.Win32.Primitives.dll"]
    1f2`d9926000    1f2`d9927000    0`00001000 MEM_IMAGE   MEM_COMMIT  PAGE_READONLY              Image    [Microsoft_Win32_Primitives; "C:\Program
Files\dotnet\shared\Microsoft.NETCore.App\9.0.4\Microsoft.Win32.Primitives.dll"]
    1f2`d9927000    1f2`d9928000    0`00001000 MEM_IMAGE   MEM_RESERVE                            Image    [Microsoft_Win32_Primitives; "C:\Program
Files\dotnet\shared\Microsoft.NETCore.App\9.0.4\Microsoft.Win32.Primitives.dll"]
+   1f2`d9928000    1f2`d9930000    0`00008000             MEM_FREE    PAGE_NOACCESS              Free
+   1f2`d9930000    1f2`d9931000    0`00001000 MEM_IMAGE   MEM_COMMIT  PAGE_READONLY              Image    [System_Reflection_Emit_Lightweight; "C:\Program
Files\dotnet\shared\Microsoft.NETCore.App\9.0.4\System.Reflection.Emit.Lightweight.dll"]
    1f2`d9931000    1f2`d9932000    0`00001000 MEM_IMAGE   MEM_RESERVE                            Image    [System_Reflection_Emit_Lightweight; "C:\Program
Files\dotnet\shared\Microsoft.NETCore.App\9.0.4\System.Reflection.Emit.Lightweight.dll"]
    1f2`d9932000    1f2`d9933000    0`00001000 MEM_IMAGE   MEM_COMMIT  PAGE_READONLY              Image    [System_Reflection_Emit_Lightweight; "C:\Program
Files\dotnet\shared\Microsoft.NETCore.App\9.0.4\System.Reflection.Emit.Lightweight.dll"]
    1f2`d9933000    1f2`d9934000    0`00001000 MEM_IMAGE   MEM_RESERVE                            Image    [System_Reflection_Emit_Lightweight; "C:\Program
Files\dotnet\shared\Microsoft.NETCore.App\9.0.4\System.Reflection.Emit.Lightweight.dll"]
    1f2`d9934000    1f2`d9935000    0`00001000 MEM_IMAGE   MEM_COMMIT  PAGE_READONLY              Image    [System_Reflection_Emit_Lightweight; "C:\Program
Files\dotnet\shared\Microsoft.NETCore.App\9.0.4\System.Reflection.Emit.Lightweight.dll"]
    1f2`d9935000    1f2`d9936000    0`00001000 MEM_IMAGE   MEM_RESERVE                            Image    [System_Reflection_Emit_Lightweight; "C:\Program
Files\dotnet\shared\Microsoft.NETCore.App\9.0.4\System.Reflection.Emit.Lightweight.dll"]
    1f2`d9936000    1f2`d9937000    0`00001000 MEM_IMAGE   MEM_COMMIT  PAGE_READONLY              Image    [System_Reflection_Emit_Lightweight; "C:\Program
Files\dotnet\shared\Microsoft.NETCore.App\9.0.4\System.Reflection.Emit.Lightweight.dll"]
    1f2`d9937000    1f2`d9938000    0`00001000 MEM_IMAGE   MEM_RESERVE                            Image    [System_Reflection_Emit_Lightweight; "C:\Program
Files\dotnet\shared\Microsoft.NETCore.App\9.0.4\System.Reflection.Emit.Lightweight.dll"]
+   1f2`d9938000    1f2`d9940000    0`00008000             MEM_FREE    PAGE_NOACCESS              Free
+   1f2`d9940000    1f2`d9941000    0`00001000 MEM_IMAGE   MEM_COMMIT  PAGE_READONLY              Image    [System_Reflection_Emit_ILGeneration; "C:\Program
Files\dotnet\shared\Microsoft.NETCore.App\9.0.4\System.Reflection.Emit.ILGeneration.dll"]
    1f2`d9941000    1f2`d9942000    0`00001000 MEM_IMAGE   MEM_RESERVE                            Image    [System_Reflection_Emit_ILGeneration; "C:\Program
Files\dotnet\shared\Microsoft.NETCore.App\9.0.4\System.Reflection.Emit.ILGeneration.dll"]
    1f2`d9942000    1f2`d9943000    0`00001000 MEM_IMAGE   MEM_COMMIT  PAGE_READONLY              Image    [System_Reflection_Emit_ILGeneration; "C:\Program
Files\dotnet\shared\Microsoft.NETCore.App\9.0.4\System.Reflection.Emit.ILGeneration.dll"]
    1f2`d9943000    1f2`d9944000    0`00001000 MEM_IMAGE   MEM_RESERVE                            Image    [System_Reflection_Emit_ILGeneration; "C:\Program
Files\dotnet\shared\Microsoft.NETCore.App\9.0.4\System.Reflection.Emit.ILGeneration.dll"]
    1f2`d9944000    1f2`d9945000    0`00001000 MEM_IMAGE   MEM_COMMIT  PAGE_READONLY              Image    [System_Reflection_Emit_ILGeneration; "C:\Program
Files\dotnet\shared\Microsoft.NETCore.App\9.0.4\System.Reflection.Emit.ILGeneration.dll"]
    1f2`d9945000    1f2`d9946000    0`00001000 MEM_IMAGE   MEM_COMMIT                             Image    [System_Reflection_Emit_ILGeneration; "C:\Program
Files\dotnet\shared\Microsoft.NETCore.App\9.0.4\System.Reflection.Emit.ILGeneration.dll"]
    1f2`d9946000    1f2`d9947000    0`00001000 MEM_IMAGE   MEM_COMMIT                             Image    [System_Reflection_Emit_ILGeneration; "C:\Program
Files\dotnet\shared\Microsoft.NETCore.App\9.0.4\System.Reflection.Emit.ILGeneration.dll"]
    1f2`d9947000    1f2`d9948000    0`00001000 MEM_IMAGE   MEM_COMMIT                             Image    [System_Reflection_Emit_ILGeneration; "C:\Program
Files\dotnet\shared\Microsoft.NETCore.App\9.0.4\System.Reflection.Emit.ILGeneration.dll"]
+   1f2`d9948000    1f2`d9950000    0`00008000             MEM_FREE    PAGE_NOACCESS              Free
+   1f2`d9950000    1f2`d9951000    0`00001000 MEM_IMAGE   MEM_COMMIT  PAGE_READONLY              Image    [System_Reflection_Primitives; "C:\Program
Files\dotnet\shared\Microsoft.NETCore.App\9.0.4\System.Reflection.Primitives.dll"]
    1f2`d9951000    1f2`d9952000    0`00001000 MEM_IMAGE   MEM_RESERVE                            Image    [System_Reflection_Primitives; "C:\Program
Files\dotnet\shared\Microsoft.NETCore.App\9.0.4\System.Reflection.Primitives.dll"]
    1f2`d9952000    1f2`d9953000    0`00001000 MEM_IMAGE   MEM_COMMIT  PAGE_READONLY              Image    [System_Reflection_Primitives; "C:\Program
Files\dotnet\shared\Microsoft.NETCore.App\9.0.4\System.Reflection.Primitives.dll"]
    1f2`d9953000    1f2`d9954000    0`00001000 MEM_IMAGE   MEM_RESERVE                            Image    [System_Reflection_Primitives; "C:\Program
Files\dotnet\shared\Microsoft.NETCore.App\9.0.4\System.Reflection.Primitives.dll"]
    1f2`d9954000    1f2`d9955000    0`00001000 MEM_IMAGE   MEM_COMMIT  PAGE_READONLY              Image    [System_Reflection_Primitives; "C:\Program
Files\dotnet\shared\Microsoft.NETCore.App\9.0.4\System.Reflection.Primitives.dll"]
    1f2`d9955000    1f2`d9956000    0`00001000 MEM_IMAGE   MEM_RESERVE                            Image    [System_Reflection_Primitives; "C:\Program
Files\dotnet\shared\Microsoft.NETCore.App\9.0.4\System.Reflection.Primitives.dll"]
    1f2`d9956000    1f2`d9957000    0`00001000 MEM_IMAGE   MEM_COMMIT  PAGE_READONLY              Image    [System_Reflection_Primitives; "C:\Program
Files\dotnet\shared\Microsoft.NETCore.App\9.0.4\System.Reflection.Primitives.dll"]
    1f2`d9957000    1f2`d9958000    0`00001000 MEM_IMAGE   MEM_RESERVE                            Image    [System_Reflection_Primitives; "C:\Program
Files\dotnet\shared\Microsoft.NETCore.App\9.0.4\System.Reflection.Primitives.dll"]
+   1f2`d9958000    1f2`d9960000    0`00008000             MEM_FREE    PAGE_NOACCESS              Free
+   1f2`d9960000    1f2`d9961000    0`00001000 MEM_IMAGE   MEM_COMMIT  PAGE_READONLY              Image    [LINQPadQuery; "C:\Users\User\AppData\Local\Temp\LINQPad8\_ctfuegif\ynycvo\LINQPadQuery.dll"]
    1f2`d9961000    1f2`d9962000    0`00001000 MEM_IMAGE   MEM_RESERVE                            Image    [LINQPadQuery; "C:\Users\User\AppData\Local\Temp\LINQPad8\_ctfuegif\ynycvo\LINQPadQuery.dll"]
    1f2`d9962000    1f2`d9963000    0`00001000 MEM_IMAGE   MEM_COMMIT  PAGE_READONLY              Image    [LINQPadQuery; "C:\Users\User\AppData\Local\Temp\LINQPad8\_ctfuegif\ynycvo\LINQPadQuery.dll"]
    1f2`d9963000    1f2`d9964000    0`00001000 MEM_IMAGE   MEM_RESERVE                            Image    [LINQPadQuery; "C:\Users\User\AppData\Local\Temp\LINQPad8\_ctfuegif\ynycvo\LINQPadQuery.dll"]
    1f2`d9964000    1f2`d9965000    0`00001000 MEM_IMAGE   MEM_COMMIT  PAGE_READONLY              Image    [LINQPadQuery; "C:\Users\User\AppData\Local\Temp\LINQPad8\_ctfuegif\ynycvo\LINQPadQuery.dll"]
    1f2`d9965000    1f2`d9966000    0`00001000 MEM_IMAGE   MEM_COMMIT                             Image    [LINQPadQuery; "C:\Users\User\AppData\Local\Temp\LINQPad8\_ctfuegif\ynycvo\LINQPadQuery.dll"]
+   1f2`d9966000    1f2`d9970000    0`0000a000             MEM_FREE    PAGE_NOACCESS              Free
+   1f2`d9970000    1f2`d997fbb8    0`0000fbb8 MEM_MAPPED  MEM_COMMIT  PAGE_READWRITE             Image    [NuGet_Versioning; "NuGet.Versioning.dll"]
    1f2`d997fbb8    1f2`d9980000    0`00000448 MEM_MAPPED  MEM_COMMIT  PAGE_READWRITE             <unknown> [..............]
+   1f2`d9980000    1f2`d9981000    0`00001000 MEM_IMAGE   MEM_COMMIT  PAGE_READONLY              Image    [System_Xml_ReaderWriter; "C:\Program
Files\dotnet\shared\Microsoft.NETCore.App\9.0.4\System.Xml.ReaderWriter.dll"]
    1f2`d9981000    1f2`d9982000    0`00001000 MEM_IMAGE   MEM_RESERVE                            Image    [System_Xml_ReaderWriter; "C:\Program
Files\dotnet\shared\Microsoft.NETCore.App\9.0.4\System.Xml.ReaderWriter.dll"]
    1f2`d9982000    1f2`d9985000    0`00003000 MEM_IMAGE   MEM_COMMIT  PAGE_READONLY              Image    [System_Xml_ReaderWriter; "C:\Program
Files\dotnet\shared\Microsoft.NETCore.App\9.0.4\System.Xml.ReaderWriter.dll"]
    1f2`d9985000    1f2`d9986000    0`00001000 MEM_IMAGE   MEM_RESERVE                            Image    [System_Xml_ReaderWriter; "C:\Program
Files\dotnet\shared\Microsoft.NETCore.App\9.0.4\System.Xml.ReaderWriter.dll"]
    1f2`d9986000    1f2`d9987000    0`00001000 MEM_IMAGE   MEM_COMMIT  PAGE_READONLY              Image    [System_Xml_ReaderWriter; "C:\Program
Files\dotnet\shared\Microsoft.NETCore.App\9.0.4\System.Xml.ReaderWriter.dll"]
    1f2`d9987000    1f2`d9988000    0`00001000 MEM_IMAGE   MEM_RESERVE                            Image    [System_Xml_ReaderWriter; "C:\Program
Files\dotnet\shared\Microsoft.NETCore.App\9.0.4\System.Xml.ReaderWriter.dll"]
    1f2`d9988000    1f2`d9989000    0`00001000 MEM_IMAGE   MEM_COMMIT  PAGE_READONLY              Image    [System_Xml_ReaderWriter; "C:\Program
Files\dotnet\shared\Microsoft.NETCore.App\9.0.4\System.Xml.ReaderWriter.dll"]
    1f2`d9989000    1f2`d998a000    0`00001000 MEM_IMAGE   MEM_COMMIT                             Image    [System_Xml_ReaderWriter; "C:\Program
Files\dotnet\shared\Microsoft.NETCore.App\9.0.4\System.Xml.ReaderWriter.dll"]
+   1f2`d998a000    1f2`d9990000    0`00006000             MEM_FREE    PAGE_NOACCESS              Free
+   1f2`d9990000    1f2`d9997000    0`00007000 MEM_MAPPED  MEM_COMMIT  PAGE_READONLY              <unknown> [MZ..............]
+   1f2`d9997000    1f2`d99a0000    0`00009000             MEM_FREE    PAGE_NOACCESS              Free
+   1f2`d99a0000    1f2`d99b0000    0`00010000 MEM_MAPPED  MEM_COMMIT  PAGE_READWRITE             <unknown> [MZ..............]
+   1f2`d99b0000    1f2`d99c0000    0`00010000 MEM_MAPPED  MEM_COMMIT  PAGE_READWRITE             <unknown> [..............]
+   1f2`d99c0000    1f2`d99d8000    0`00018000 MEM_MAPPED  MEM_COMMIT  PAGE_READWRITE             <unknown> [H..d4......au..H]
    1f2`d99d8000    1f2`d99e0000    0`00008000 MEM_MAPPED  MEM_RESERVE                            <unknown>
+   1f2`d99e0000    1f2`d99e1000    0`00001000 MEM_MAPPED  MEM_COMMIT  PAGE_READONLY              Other    [Activation Context Data]
+   1f2`d99e1000    1f2`d99f0000    0`0000f000             MEM_FREE    PAGE_NOACCESS              Free
+   1f2`d99f0000    1f2`d9a03000    0`00013000 MEM_MAPPED  MEM_COMMIT  PAGE_READONLY              Image    [Hyperlinq; "Hyperlinq.dll"]
    1f2`d9a03000    1f2`d9a10000    0`0000d000             MEM_FREE    PAGE_NOACCESS              Free
+   1f2`d9a10000    1f2`d9a11000    0`00001000 MEM_MAPPED  MEM_COMMIT  PAGE_READWRITE             <unknown> [..............]
```

```
+       1f2`d9a11000      1f2`d9a20000        0`0000f000              MEM_FREE    PAGE_NOACCESS                  Free
+       1f2`d9a20000      1f2`d9a22000        0`00002000 MEM_PRIVATE MEM_COMMIT  PAGE_EXECUTE_READWRITE         Heap       [ID: 5; Handle: 000001f2d9a20000; Type: Segment]
        1f2`d9a22000      1f2`d9a2f000        0`0000d000 MEM_PRIVATE MEM_RESERVE                                Heap       [ID: 5; Handle: 000001f2d9a20000; Type: Segment]
        1f2`d9a2f000      1f2`d9a30000        0`00001000 MEM_PRIVATE MEM_RESERVE                                <unknown>
+       1f2`d9a30000      1f2`d9c00000        0`001d0000 MEM_PRIVATE MEM_RESERVE                                <unknown>
        1f2`d9c00000      1f2`d9c11000        0`00011000 MEM_PRIVATE MEM_COMMIT  PAGE_READWRITE                 <unknown>  [................]
        1f2`d9c11000      1f2`dbc00000        0`01fef000 MEM_PRIVATE MEM_RESERVE                                <unknown>
        1f2`dbc00000      1f2`dbc61000        0`00061000 MEM_PRIVATE MEM_COMMIT  PAGE_READWRITE                 <unknown>  [................]
        1f2`dbc61000      1f2`dc000000        0`0039f000 MEM_PRIVATE MEM_RESERVE                                <unknown>
        1f2`dc000000      1f2`dc2b2000        0`002b2000 MEM_PRIVATE MEM_COMMIT  PAGE_READWRITE                 <unknown>  [................]
        1f2`dc2b2000      1f2`dc400000        0`0014e000 MEM_PRIVATE MEM_RESERVE                                <unknown>
        1f2`dc400000      1f2`dc491000        0`00091000 MEM_PRIVATE MEM_COMMIT  PAGE_READWRITE                 <unknown>  [................]
        1f2`dc491000      1f2`dc800000        0`0036f000 MEM_PRIVATE MEM_RESERVE                                <unknown>
        1f2`dc800000      1f2`dcb86000        0`00386000 MEM_PRIVATE MEM_COMMIT  PAGE_READWRITE                 <unknown>  [................]
        1f2`dcb86000      1f2`de800000        0`01c7a000 MEM_PRIVATE MEM_RESERVE                                <unknown>
        1f2`de800000      1f2`de851000        0`00051000 MEM_PRIVATE MEM_COMMIT  PAGE_READWRITE                 <unknown>  [................]
        1f2`de851000      232`d9a30000       3f`fb1df000 MEM_PRIVATE MEM_RESERVE                                <unknown>
+       232`d9a30000      232`d9a44000        0`00014000 MEM_PRIVATE MEM_COMMIT  PAGE_READWRITE                 <unknown>  [.........p......]
        232`d9a44000      232`e1a2f000        0`07feb000 MEM_PRIVATE MEM_RESERVE                                <unknown>
        232`e1a2f000      232`e1a43000        0`00014000 MEM_PRIVATE MEM_COMMIT  PAGE_READWRITE                 <unknown>  [................]
        232`e1a43000      232`e9a2f000        0`07fec000 MEM_PRIVATE MEM_RESERVE                                <unknown>
        232`e9a2f000      232`e9a30000        0`00001000 MEM_PRIVATE MEM_COMMIT  PAGE_READWRITE                 <unknown>  [................]
        232`e9a30000      232`e9a4f000        0`0001f000 MEM_PRIVATE MEM_RESERVE                                <unknown>
        232`e9a4f000      232`e9a59000        0`0000a000 MEM_PRIVATE MEM_COMMIT  PAGE_READWRITE                 <unknown>  [................]
        232`e9a59000      232`eda4e000        0`03ff5000 MEM_PRIVATE MEM_RESERVE                                <unknown>
        232`eda4e000      232`eda4f000        0`00001000 MEM_PRIVATE MEM_COMMIT  PAGE_READWRITE                 <unknown>  [................]
        232`eda4f000      232`eda5e000        0`0000f000 MEM_PRIVATE MEM_RESERVE                                <unknown>
        232`eda5e000      232`eda61000        0`00003000 MEM_PRIVATE MEM_COMMIT  PAGE_READWRITE                 <unknown>  [................]
        232`eda61000      233`6e4d7000        0`80a76000 MEM_PRIVATE MEM_RESERVE                                <unknown>
+       233`6e4d7000      233`6e4e0000        0`00009000              MEM_FREE    PAGE_NOACCESS                  Free
+       233`6e4e0000      233`6e4e1000        0`00001000 MEM_PRIVATE MEM_COMMIT  PAGE_READWRITE                 Heap       [ID: 0; Handle: 000001f2d7d60000; Type: Segment]
        233`6e4e1000      233`6e5a8000        0`000c7000 MEM_PRIVATE MEM_RESERVE                                Heap       [ID: 0; Handle: 000001f2d7d60000; Type: Segment]
        233`6e5a8000      233`6e60d000        0`00065000 MEM_PRIVATE MEM_COMMIT  PAGE_READWRITE                 Heap       [ID: 0; Handle: 000001f2d7d60000; Type: Segment]
        233`6e60d000      233`6e60e000        0`00001000 MEM_PRIVATE MEM_COMMIT  PAGE_NOACCESS                  Heap       [ID: 0; Handle: 000001f2d7d60000; Type: Segment]
        233`6e60e000      233`6e6df000        0`000d1000 MEM_PRIVATE MEM_COMMIT  PAGE_READWRITE                 Heap       [ID: 0; Handle: 000001f2d7d60000; Type: Segment]
        233`6e6df000      233`6e6e0000        0`00001000 MEM_PRIVATE MEM_RESERVE                                <unknown>
+       233`6e6e0000      233`6e710000        0`00030000 MEM_PRIVATE MEM_COMMIT  PAGE_READWRITE                 <unknown>  [................]
        233`6e710000      233`6eae0000        0`003d0000 MEM_PRIVATE MEM_RESERVE                                <unknown>
+       233`6eae0000      233`6ee1a000        0`0033a000 MEM_MAPPED  MEM_COMMIT  PAGE_READONLY                  <unknown>  [........hl..x...]
+       233`6ee1a000      233`6ee20000        0`00006000              MEM_FREE    PAGE_NOACCESS                  Free
+       233`6ee20000      233`6ee21000        0`00001000 MEM_IMAGE   MEM_COMMIT  PAGE_READONLY                  Image      [LINQPad_Runtime; "C:\Program Files\LINQPad8\LINQPad.Runtime.dll"]
        233`6ee21000      233`6ee22000        0`00001000 MEM_IMAGE   MEM_RESERVE                                Image      [LINQPad_Runtime; "C:\Program Files\LINQPad8\LINQPad.Runtime.dll"]
        233`6ee22000      233`70f57000        0`02135000 MEM_IMAGE   MEM_COMMIT  PAGE_READONLY                  Image      [LINQPad_Runtime; "C:\Program Files\LINQPad8\LINQPad.Runtime.dll"]
        233`70f57000      233`70f58000        0`00001000 MEM_IMAGE   MEM_RESERVE                                Image      [LINQPad_Runtime; "C:\Program Files\LINQPad8\LINQPad.Runtime.dll"]
        233`70f58000      233`70f59000        0`00001000 MEM_IMAGE   MEM_COMMIT  PAGE_READONLY                  Image      [LINQPad_Runtime; "C:\Program Files\LINQPad8\LINQPad.Runtime.dll"]
        233`70f59000      233`70f5a000        0`00001000 MEM_IMAGE   MEM_RESERVE                                Image      [LINQPad_Runtime; "C:\Program Files\LINQPad8\LINQPad.Runtime.dll"]
        233`70f5a000      233`70f5b000        0`00001000 MEM_IMAGE   MEM_COMMIT  PAGE_READONLY                  Image      [LINQPad_Runtime; "C:\Program Files\LINQPad8\LINQPad.Runtime.dll"]
        233`70f5b000      233`70f5c000        0`00001000 MEM_IMAGE   MEM_RESERVE                                Image      [LINQPad_Runtime; "C:\Program Files\LINQPad8\LINQPad.Runtime.dll"]
+       233`70f5c000      233`70f60000        0`00004000              MEM_FREE    PAGE_NOACCESS                  Free
+       233`70f60000      233`72a62000        0`01b02000 MEM_MAPPED  MEM_COMMIT  PAGE_READONLY                  <unknown>  [............CmnD]
+       233`72a62000      233`72a70000        0`0000e000              MEM_FREE    PAGE_NOACCESS                  Free
+       233`72a70000      233`72b94000        0`00124000 MEM_PRIVATE MEM_COMMIT  PAGE_READWRITE                 Heap       [ID: 0; Handle: 000001f2d7d60000; Type: Segment]
        233`72b94000      233`72c93000        0`000ff000 MEM_PRIVATE MEM_RESERVE                                Heap       [ID: 0; Handle: 000001f2d7d60000; Type: Segment]
        233`72c93000      233`72d9f000        0`0010c000 MEM_PRIVATE MEM_COMMIT  PAGE_READWRITE                 Heap       [ID: 0; Handle: 000001f2d7d60000; Type: Segment]
        233`72d9f000      233`72e6f000        0`000d0000 MEM_PRIVATE MEM_RESERVE                                Heap       [ID: 0; Handle: 000001f2d7d60000; Type: Segment]
        233`72e6f000      233`72e70000        0`00001000 MEM_PRIVATE MEM_RESERVE                                <unknown>
+       233`72e70000      233`72e71000        0`00001000 MEM_IMAGE   MEM_COMMIT  PAGE_READONLY                  Image      [netstandard; "C:\Program Files\dotnet\shared\Microsoft.NETCore.App\9.0.4\netstandard.dll"]
        233`72e71000      233`72e72000        0`00001000 MEM_IMAGE   MEM_RESERVE                                Image      [netstandard; "C:\Program Files\dotnet\shared\Microsoft.NETCore.App\9.0.4\netstandard.dll"]
        233`72e72000      233`72e89000        0`00017000 MEM_IMAGE   MEM_COMMIT  PAGE_READONLY                  Image      [netstandard; "C:\Program Files\dotnet\shared\Microsoft.NETCore.App\9.0.4\netstandard.dll"]
        233`72e89000      233`72e8a000        0`00001000 MEM_IMAGE   MEM_RESERVE                                Image      [netstandard; "C:\Program Files\dotnet\shared\Microsoft.NETCore.App\9.0.4\netstandard.dll"]
        233`72e8a000      233`72e8b000        0`00001000 MEM_IMAGE   MEM_COMMIT  PAGE_READONLY                  Image      [netstandard; "C:\Program Files\dotnet\shared\Microsoft.NETCore.App\9.0.4\netstandard.dll"]
        233`72e8b000      233`72e8c000        0`00001000 MEM_IMAGE   MEM_RESERVE                                Image      [netstandard; "C:\Program Files\dotnet\shared\Microsoft.NETCore.App\9.0.4\netstandard.dll"]
+       233`72e8c000      233`72e90000        0`00004000              MEM_FREE    PAGE_NOACCESS                  Free
+       233`72e90000      233`72f32290        0`000a2290 MEM_MAPPED  MEM_COMMIT  PAGE_READWRITE                 Image      [LINQPad_Runtime_UI; "LINQPad.Runtime.UI.dll"]
        233`72f32290      233`72f33000        0`00000d70 MEM_MAPPED  MEM_COMMIT  PAGE_READWRITE                 <unknown>  [................]
+       233`72f33000      233`72f50000        0`0001d000              MEM_FREE    PAGE_NOACCESS                  Free
+       233`72f50000      233`72fea9b8        0`0009a9b8 MEM_MAPPED  MEM_COMMIT  PAGE_READWRITE                 Image      [NuGet_Packaging; "NuGet.Packaging.dll"]
        233`72fea9b8      233`72feb000        0`00000648 MEM_MAPPED  MEM_COMMIT  PAGE_READWRITE                 <unknown>  [................]
+       233`72feb000      233`72ff0000        0`00005000              MEM_FREE    PAGE_NOACCESS                  Free
+       233`72ff0000      233`72ffa000        0`0000a000 MEM_MAPPED  MEM_COMMIT  PAGE_READWRITE                 <unknown>  [H.0U............]
        233`72ffa000      233`73000000        0`00006000 MEM_MAPPED  MEM_RESERVE                                <unknown>
+       233`73000000      233`73003000        0`00003000 MEM_MAPPED  MEM_COMMIT  PAGE_READWRITE                 <unknown>  [................]
        233`73003000      233`73004000        0`00001000 MEM_MAPPED  MEM_RESERVE                                <unknown>
        233`73004000      233`7300c000        0`00008000 MEM_MAPPED  MEM_COMMIT  PAGE_READWRITE                 <unknown>  [................]
        233`7300c000      233`7300d000        0`00001000 MEM_MAPPED  MEM_RESERVE                                <unknown>
        233`7300d000      233`7300e000        0`00001000 MEM_MAPPED  MEM_COMMIT  PAGE_READWRITE                 <unknown>  [................]
        233`7300e000      233`73010000        0`00002000 MEM_MAPPED  MEM_RESERVE                                <unknown>
+       233`73010000      233`73032000        0`00022000 MEM_MAPPED  MEM_COMMIT  PAGE_READONLY                  <unknown>  [MZ..............]
+       233`73032000      7ff4`51dd0000    7dc0`ded9e000              MEM_FREE    PAGE_NOACCESS                  Free
+      7ff4`51dd0000      7ff4`51dd5000        0`00005000 MEM_MAPPED  MEM_COMMIT  PAGE_READONLY                  Other      [Read Only Shared Memory]
       7ff4`51dd5000      7ff4`51ed0000        0`000fb000 MEM_MAPPED  MEM_RESERVE                                <unknown>
+      7ff4`51ed0000      7ff5`51ef0000        1`00020000 MEM_PRIVATE MEM_RESERVE                                <unknown>
+      7ff5`51ef0000      7ff5`53ef0000        0`02000000 MEM_PRIVATE MEM_RESERVE                                <unknown>
       7ff5`53ef0000      7ff5`53ef1000        0`00001000 MEM_PRIVATE MEM_COMMIT  PAGE_READWRITE                 <unknown>  [................]
+      7ff5`53ef1000      7ff5`53f00000        0`0000f000              MEM_FREE    PAGE_NOACCESS                  Free
+      7ff5`53f00000      7ff5`53f01000        0`00001000 MEM_MAPPED  MEM_COMMIT  PAGE_READONLY                  <unknown>  [................]
+      7ff5`53f01000      7ff7`4a660000        1`f675f000              MEM_FREE    PAGE_NOACCESS                  Free
+      7ff7`4a660000      7ff7`4a661000        0`00001000 MEM_IMAGE   MEM_COMMIT  PAGE_READONLY                  Image      [LINQPad8; "C:\Program Files\LINQPad8\LINQPad8.exe"]
       7ff7`4a661000      7ff7`4a6ae000        0`0004d000 MEM_IMAGE   MEM_COMMIT  PAGE_EXECUTE_READ              Image      [LINQPad8; "C:\Program Files\LINQPad8\LINQPad8.exe"]
       7ff7`4a6ae000      7ff7`4a6dd000        0`0002f000 MEM_IMAGE   MEM_COMMIT  PAGE_READONLY                  Image      [LINQPad8; "C:\Program Files\LINQPad8\LINQPad8.exe"]
       7ff7`4a6dd000      7ff7`4a6e1000        0`00004000 MEM_IMAGE   MEM_COMMIT  PAGE_READWRITE                 Image      [LINQPad8; "C:\Program Files\LINQPad8\LINQPad8.exe"]
       7ff7`4a6e1000      7ff7`4a707000        0`00026000 MEM_IMAGE   MEM_COMMIT  PAGE_READONLY                  Image      [LINQPad8; "C:\Program Files\LINQPad8\LINQPad8.exe"]
+      7ff7`4a707000      7ffe`81a50000        7`37349000              MEM_FREE    PAGE_NOACCESS                  Free
+      7ffe`81a50000      7ffe`81a60000        0`00010000 MEM_MAPPED  MEM_COMMIT  PAGE_EXECUTE_READ              <unknown>  [.fffffff........]
+      7ffe`81a60000      7ffe`81a63000        0`00003000 MEM_MAPPED  MEM_COMMIT  PAGE_READWRITE                 <unknown>  [................]
       7ffe`81a63000      7ffe`81a64000        0`00001000 MEM_MAPPED  MEM_RESERVE                                <unknown>
       7ffe`81a64000      7ffe`81a6c000        0`00008000 MEM_MAPPED  MEM_COMMIT  PAGE_READWRITE                 <unknown>  [................]
       7ffe`81a6c000      7ffe`81a6d000        0`00001000 MEM_MAPPED  MEM_RESERVE                                <unknown>
       7ffe`81a6d000      7ffe`81a6e000        0`00001000 MEM_MAPPED  MEM_COMMIT  PAGE_EXECUTE_READ              <unknown>  [................]
       7ffe`81a6e000      7ffe`81a70000        0`00002000 MEM_MAPPED  MEM_RESERVE                                <unknown>
+      7ffe`81a70000      7ffe`81a71000        0`00001000 MEM_MAPPED  MEM_COMMIT  PAGE_READWRITE                 <unknown>  [................]
       7ffe`81a71000      7ffe`81a76000        0`00005000 MEM_MAPPED  MEM_RESERVE                                <unknown>
       7ffe`81a76000      7ffe`81a77000        0`00001000 MEM_MAPPED  MEM_COMMIT  PAGE_READWRITE                 <unknown>  [.h..............]
       7ffe`81a77000      7ffe`81a80000        0`00009000 MEM_MAPPED  MEM_RESERVE                                <unknown>
+      7ffe`81a80000      7ffe`81b00000        0`00080000 MEM_MAPPED  MEM_COMMIT  PAGE_READWRITE                 <unknown>  [................]
+      7ffe`81b00000      7ffe`81b04000        0`00004000 MEM_MAPPED  MEM_COMMIT  PAGE_EXECUTE_READ              <unknown>  [L.............f.]
       7ffe`81b04000      7ffe`81b08000        0`00004000 MEM_MAPPED  MEM_COMMIT  PAGE_READWRITE                 <unknown>  [.H........t.....]
       7ffe`81b08000      7ffe`81b0c000        0`00004000 MEM_MAPPED  MEM_COMMIT  PAGE_EXECUTE_READ              <unknown>  [L.............f.]
       7ffe`81b0c000      7ffe`81b10000        0`00004000 MEM_MAPPED  MEM_COMMIT  PAGE_READWRITE                 <unknown>  [..........t.....]
+      7ffe`81b10000      7ffe`81b14000        0`00004000 MEM_MAPPED  MEM_COMMIT  PAGE_EXECUTE_READ              <unknown>  [......L.........]
       7ffe`81b14000      7ffe`81b18000        0`00004000 MEM_MAPPED  MEM_COMMIT  PAGE_READWRITE                 <unknown>  [.........F......]
       7ffe`81b18000      7ffe`81b1c000        0`00004000 MEM_MAPPED  MEM_COMMIT  PAGE_EXECUTE_READ              <unknown>  [......L.........]
       7ffe`81b1c000      7ffe`81b20000        0`00004000 MEM_MAPPED  MEM_COMMIT  PAGE_READWRITE                 <unknown>  [................]
+      7ffe`81b20000      7ffe`81b30000        0`00010000 MEM_MAPPED  MEM_COMMIT  PAGE_READWRITE                 <unknown>  [................]
+      7ffe`81b30000      7ffe`81b40000        0`00010000 MEM_MAPPED  MEM_COMMIT  PAGE_READWRITE                 <unknown>  [................]
+      7ffe`81b40000      7ffe`81b50000        0`00010000 MEM_MAPPED  MEM_COMMIT  PAGE_READWRITE                 <unknown>  [................]
+      7ffe`81b50000      7ffe`81b60000        0`00010000 MEM_MAPPED  MEM_COMMIT  PAGE_READWRITE                 <unknown>  [................]
+      7ffe`81b60000      7ffe`81b70000        0`00010000 MEM_MAPPED  MEM_COMMIT  PAGE_READWRITE                 <unknown>  [H...............]
+      7ffe`81b70000      7ffe`81b80000        0`00010000 MEM_MAPPED  MEM_COMMIT  PAGE_READWRITE                 <unknown>  [................]
+      7ffe`81b80000      7ffe`81b90000        0`00010000 MEM_MAPPED  MEM_COMMIT  PAGE_READWRITE                 <unknown>  [................]
+      7ffe`81b90000      7ffe`81ba0000        0`00010000 MEM_MAPPED  MEM_COMMIT  PAGE_READWRITE                 <unknown>  [................]
+      7ffe`81ba0000      7ffe`81c08000        0`00068000 MEM_MAPPED  MEM_COMMIT  PAGE_EXECUTE_READ              <unknown>  [H.0U............]
       7ffe`81c08000      7ffe`81c20000        0`00018000 MEM_MAPPED  MEM_RESERVE                                <unknown>
+      7ffe`81c20000      7ffe`81c30000        0`00010000 MEM_MAPPED  MEM_COMMIT  PAGE_READWRITE                 <unknown>  [................]
+      7ffe`81c30000      7ffe`81c40000        0`00010000 MEM_MAPPED  MEM_COMMIT  PAGE_READWRITE                 <unknown>  [.........v......]
+      7ffe`81c40000      7ffe`81c50000        0`00010000 MEM_MAPPED  MEM_COMMIT  PAGE_READWRITE                 <unknown>  [................]
+      7ffe`81c50000      7ffe`81c60000        0`00010000 MEM_MAPPED  MEM_COMMIT  PAGE_READWRITE                 <unknown>  [................]
+      7ffe`81c60000      7ffe`81c6e000        0`0000e000 MEM_MAPPED  MEM_COMMIT  PAGE_READWRITE                 <unknown>  [................]
       7ffe`81c6e000      7ffe`81c70000        0`00002000 MEM_MAPPED  MEM_RESERVE                                <unknown>
+      7ffe`81c70000      7ffe`81cd0000        0`00060000 MEM_MAPPED  MEM_COMMIT  PAGE_READWRITE                 <unknown>  [................]
+      7ffe`81cd0000      7ffe`81cd1000        0`00001000 MEM_MAPPED  MEM_COMMIT  PAGE_READWRITE                 <unknown>  [W...............]
       7ffe`81cd1000      7ffe`81ce0000        0`0000f000 MEM_MAPPED  MEM_RESERVE                                <unknown>
+      7ffe`81ce0000      7ffe`81d03000        0`00023000 MEM_MAPPED  MEM_COMMIT  PAGE_READWRITE                 <unknown>  [................]
       7ffe`81d03000      7ffe`81d10000        0`0000d000 MEM_MAPPED  MEM_RESERVE                                <unknown>
+      7ffe`81d10000      7ffe`81d20000        0`00010000 MEM_MAPPED  MEM_COMMIT  PAGE_READWRITE                 <unknown>  [................]
+      7ffe`81d20000      7ffe`81d5f000        0`0003f000 MEM_MAPPED  MEM_COMMIT  PAGE_READWRITE                 <unknown>  [................]
       7ffe`81d5f000      7ffe`81d60000        0`00001000 MEM_MAPPED  MEM_RESERVE                                <unknown>
+      7ffe`81d60000      7ffe`81d70000        0`00010000 MEM_MAPPED  MEM_COMMIT  PAGE_READWRITE                 <unknown>  [................]
+      7ffe`81d70000      7ffe`81d80000        0`00010000 MEM_MAPPED  MEM_COMMIT  PAGE_READWRITE                 <unknown>  [................]
+      7ffe`81d80000      7ffe`81d90000        0`00010000 MEM_MAPPED  MEM_COMMIT  PAGE_READWRITE                 <unknown>  [................]
+      7ffe`81d90000      7ffe`81da0000        0`00010000 MEM_MAPPED  MEM_COMMIT  PAGE_READWRITE                 <unknown>  [................]
+      7ffe`81da0000      7ffe`81da7000        0`00007000 MEM_MAPPED  MEM_COMMIT  PAGE_READWRITE                 <unknown>  [................]
       7ffe`81da7000      7ffe`81db0000        0`00009000 MEM_MAPPED  MEM_RESERVE                                <unknown>
+      7ffe`81db0000      7ffe`81dc0000        0`00010000 MEM_MAPPED  MEM_COMMIT  PAGE_READWRITE                 <unknown>  [................]
+      7ffe`81dc0000      7ffe`81dd0000        0`00010000 MEM_MAPPED  MEM_COMMIT  PAGE_READWRITE                 <unknown>  [................]
+      7ffe`81dd0000      7ffe`81e10000        0`00040000 MEM_MAPPED  MEM_COMMIT  PAGE_READWRITE                 <unknown>  [................]
+      7ffe`81e10000      7ffe`81e20000        0`00010000 MEM_MAPPED  MEM_COMMIT  PAGE_READWRITE                 <unknown>  [................]
+      7ffe`81e20000      7ffe`81e30000        0`00010000 MEM_MAPPED  MEM_COMMIT  PAGE_READWRITE                 <unknown>  [................]
```

```
+     7ffe`81e30000     7ffe`81e40000        0`00010000 MEM_MAPPED  MEM_COMMIT  PAGE_READWRITE              <unknown>  [................]
+     7ffe`81e40000     7ffe`81e4f000        0`0000f000 MEM_MAPPED  MEM_COMMIT  PAGE_READWRITE              <unknown>  [................]
      7ffe`81e4f000     7ffe`81e50000        0`00001000 MEM_MAPPED  MEM_RESERVE                             <unknown>
+     7ffe`81e50000     7ffe`81e54000        0`00004000 MEM_MAPPED  MEM_COMMIT  PAGE_EXECUTE_READ           <unknown>  [......L.........]
      7ffe`81e54000     7ffe`81e58000        0`00004000 MEM_MAPPED  MEM_COMMIT  PAGE_READWRITE              <unknown>  [................]
      7ffe`81e58000     7ffe`81e5c000        0`00004000 MEM_MAPPED  MEM_COMMIT  PAGE_EXECUTE_READ           <unknown>  [......L.........]
      7ffe`81e5c000     7ffe`81e60000        0`00004000 MEM_MAPPED  MEM_COMMIT  PAGE_READWRITE              <unknown>  [.2..............]
+     7ffe`81e60000     7ffe`81e70000        0`00010000 MEM_MAPPED  MEM_COMMIT  PAGE_READWRITE              <unknown>  [................]
+     7ffe`81e70000     7ffe`81e80000        0`00010000 MEM_MAPPED  MEM_COMMIT  PAGE_READWRITE              <unknown>  [................]
+     7ffe`81e80000     7ffe`81e90000        0`00010000 MEM_MAPPED  MEM_COMMIT  PAGE_READWRITE              <unknown>  [................]
+     7ffe`81e90000     7ffe`81ea0000        0`00010000 MEM_MAPPED  MEM_COMMIT  PAGE_READWRITE              <unknown>  [........h.......]
+     7ffe`81ea0000     7ffe`81eb0000        0`00010000 MEM_MAPPED  MEM_COMMIT  PAGE_READWRITE              <unknown>  [................]
+     7ffe`81eb0000     7ffe`81ec0000        0`00010000 MEM_MAPPED  MEM_COMMIT  PAGE_READWRITE              <unknown>  [................]
+     7ffe`81ec0000     7ffe`81ed0000        0`00010000 MEM_MAPPED  MEM_COMMIT  PAGE_READWRITE              <unknown>  [................]
+     7ffe`81ed0000     7ffe`81edf000        0`0000f000 MEM_MAPPED  MEM_COMMIT  PAGE_READWRITE              <unknown>  [................]
      7ffe`81edf000     7ffe`81ee0000        0`00001000 MEM_MAPPED  MEM_RESERVE                             <unknown>
+     7ffe`81ee0000     7ffe`81ef0000        0`00010000 MEM_MAPPED  MEM_COMMIT  PAGE_READWRITE              <unknown>  [................]
+     7ffe`81ef0000     7ffe`81f00000        0`00010000 MEM_MAPPED  MEM_COMMIT  PAGE_READWRITE              <unknown>  [.........R......]
+     7ffe`81f00000     7ffe`81f10000        0`00010000 MEM_MAPPED  MEM_COMMIT  PAGE_READWRITE              <unknown>  [x...............]
+     7ffe`81f10000     7ffe`81f1f000        0`0000f000 MEM_MAPPED  MEM_COMMIT  PAGE_READWRITE              <unknown>  [................]
      7ffe`81f1f000     7ffe`81f20000        0`00001000 MEM_MAPPED  MEM_RESERVE                             <unknown>
+     7ffe`81f20000     7ffe`81f30000        0`00010000 MEM_MAPPED  MEM_COMMIT  PAGE_READWRITE              <unknown>  [.........f......]
+     7ffe`81f30000     7ffe`81f34000        0`00004000 MEM_MAPPED  MEM_COMMIT  PAGE_EXECUTE_READ           <unknown>  [......L.........]
      7ffe`81f34000     7ffe`81f38000        0`00004000 MEM_MAPPED  MEM_COMMIT  PAGE_READWRITE              <unknown>  [................]
      7ffe`81f38000     7ffe`81f3c000        0`00004000 MEM_MAPPED  MEM_COMMIT  PAGE_EXECUTE_READ           <unknown>  [......L.........]
      7ffe`81f3c000     7ffe`81f40000        0`00004000 MEM_MAPPED  MEM_COMMIT  PAGE_READWRITE              <unknown>  [p.......X.......]
+     7ffe`81f40000     7ffe`81f50000        0`00010000 MEM_MAPPED  MEM_COMMIT  PAGE_READWRITE              <unknown>  [X...............]
+     7ffe`81f50000     7ffe`81f60000        0`00010000 MEM_MAPPED  MEM_COMMIT  PAGE_READWRITE              <unknown>  [................]
+     7ffe`81f60000     7ffe`81f70000        0`00010000 MEM_MAPPED  MEM_COMMIT  PAGE_READWRITE              <unknown>  [................]
+     7ffe`81f70000     7ffe`81f80000        0`00010000 MEM_MAPPED  MEM_COMMIT  PAGE_READWRITE              <unknown>  [................]
+     7ffe`81f80000     7ffe`81f90000        0`00010000 MEM_MAPPED  MEM_COMMIT  PAGE_READWRITE              <unknown>  [................]
+     7ffe`81f90000     7ffe`81fa0000        0`00010000 MEM_MAPPED  MEM_COMMIT  PAGE_READWRITE              <unknown>  [................]
+     7ffe`81fa0000     7ffe`81fb0000        0`00010000 MEM_MAPPED  MEM_COMMIT  PAGE_READWRITE              <unknown>  [................]
+     7ffe`81fb0000     7ffe`81fc0000        0`00010000 MEM_MAPPED  MEM_COMMIT  PAGE_READWRITE              <unknown>  [................]
+     7ffe`81fc0000     7ffe`81fc4000        0`00004000 MEM_MAPPED  MEM_COMMIT  PAGE_EXECUTE_READ           <unknown>  [......L.........]
      7ffe`81fc4000     7ffe`81fc8000        0`00004000 MEM_MAPPED  MEM_COMMIT  PAGE_READWRITE              <unknown>  [........P.......]
      7ffe`81fc8000     7ffe`81fcc000        0`00004000 MEM_MAPPED  MEM_COMMIT  PAGE_EXECUTE_READ           <unknown>  [......L.........]
      7ffe`81fcc000     7ffe`81fd0000        0`00004000 MEM_MAPPED  MEM_COMMIT  PAGE_READWRITE              <unknown>  [................]
+     7ffe`81fd0000     7ffe`81fdc000        0`0000c000 MEM_MAPPED  MEM_COMMIT  PAGE_READWRITE              <unknown>  [................]
      7ffe`81fdc000     7ffe`81fe0000        0`00004000 MEM_MAPPED  MEM_RESERVE                             <unknown>
+     7ffe`81fe0000     7ffe`81ff0000        0`00010000 MEM_MAPPED  MEM_COMMIT  PAGE_READWRITE              <unknown>  [................]
+     7ffe`81ff0000     7ffe`82000000        0`00010000 MEM_MAPPED  MEM_COMMIT  PAGE_READWRITE              <unknown>  [................]
+     7ffe`82000000     7ffe`8200e000        0`0000e000 MEM_MAPPED  MEM_COMMIT  PAGE_READWRITE              <unknown>  [................]
      7ffe`8200e000     7ffe`82010000        0`00002000 MEM_MAPPED  MEM_RESERVE                             <unknown>
+     7ffe`82010000     7ffe`82020000        0`00010000 MEM_MAPPED  MEM_COMMIT  PAGE_READWRITE              <unknown>  [h..........0....]
+     7ffe`82020000     7ffe`82060000        0`00040000 MEM_MAPPED  MEM_COMMIT  PAGE_READWRITE              <unknown>  [................]
+     7ffe`82060000     7ffe`82070000        0`00010000 MEM_MAPPED  MEM_COMMIT  PAGE_READWRITE              <unknown>  [......3...2....4]
+     7ffe`82070000     7ffe`82080000        0`00010000 MEM_MAPPED  MEM_COMMIT  PAGE_READWRITE              <unknown>  [.........9......]
+     7ffe`82080000     7ffe`82090000        0`00010000 MEM_MAPPED  MEM_COMMIT  PAGE_READWRITE              <unknown>  [................]
+     7ffe`82090000     7ffe`820a0000        0`00010000 MEM_MAPPED  MEM_COMMIT  PAGE_READWRITE              <unknown>  [h...............]
+     7ffe`820a0000     7ffe`820a6000        0`00006000 MEM_MAPPED  MEM_COMMIT  PAGE_READWRITE              <unknown>  [................]
      7ffe`820a6000     7ffe`820b0000        0`0000a000 MEM_MAPPED  MEM_RESERVE                             <unknown>
+     7ffe`820b0000     7ffe`820c0000        0`00010000 MEM_MAPPED  MEM_COMMIT  PAGE_READWRITE              <unknown>  [................]
+     7ffe`820c0000     7ffe`820e0000        0`00020000 MEM_MAPPED  MEM_COMMIT  PAGE_READWRITE              <unknown>  [................]
+     7ffe`820e0000     7ffe`820e8000        0`00008000 MEM_MAPPED  MEM_COMMIT  PAGE_READWRITE              <unknown>  [................]
      7ffe`820e8000     7ffe`820f0000        0`00008000 MEM_MAPPED  MEM_RESERVE                             <unknown>
+     7ffe`820f0000     7ffe`82100000        0`00010000 MEM_MAPPED  MEM_COMMIT  PAGE_READWRITE              <unknown>  [................]
+     7ffe`82100000     7ffe`82104000        0`00004000 MEM_MAPPED  MEM_COMMIT  PAGE_EXECUTE_READ           <unknown>  [......L.........]
      7ffe`82104000     7ffe`82108000        0`00004000 MEM_MAPPED  MEM_COMMIT  PAGE_READWRITE              <unknown>  [................]
      7ffe`82108000     7ffe`8210c000        0`00004000 MEM_MAPPED  MEM_COMMIT  PAGE_EXECUTE_READ           <unknown>  [......L.........]
      7ffe`8210c000     7ffe`82110000        0`00004000 MEM_MAPPED  MEM_COMMIT  PAGE_READWRITE              <unknown>  [........h.......]
+     7ffe`82110000     7ffe`82124000        0`00014000 MEM_MAPPED  MEM_COMMIT  PAGE_READWRITE              <unknown>  [................]
      7ffe`82124000     7ffe`82130000        0`0000c000 MEM_MAPPED  MEM_RESERVE                             <unknown>
+     7ffe`82130000     7ffe`82140000        0`00010000 MEM_MAPPED  MEM_COMMIT  PAGE_READWRITE              <unknown>  [................]
+     7ffe`82140000     7ffe`82160000        0`00020000 MEM_MAPPED  MEM_COMMIT  PAGE_READWRITE              <unknown>  [................]
+     7ffe`82160000     7ffe`82170000        0`00010000 MEM_MAPPED  MEM_COMMIT  PAGE_READWRITE              <unknown>  [................]
+     7ffe`82170000     7ffe`8217a000        0`0000a000 MEM_MAPPED  MEM_COMMIT  PAGE_READWRITE              <unknown>  [........X.......]
      7ffe`8217a000     7ffe`82180000        0`00006000 MEM_MAPPED  MEM_RESERVE                             <unknown>
+     7ffe`82180000     7ffe`82190000        0`00010000 MEM_MAPPED  MEM_COMMIT  PAGE_READWRITE              <unknown>  [................]
+     7ffe`82190000     7ffe`821a0000        0`00010000 MEM_MAPPED  MEM_COMMIT  PAGE_READWRITE              <unknown>  [.........k......]
+     7ffe`821a0000     7ffe`821b0000        0`00010000 MEM_MAPPED  MEM_COMMIT  PAGE_READWRITE              <unknown>  [................]
+     7ffe`821b0000     7ffe`821c0000        0`00010000 MEM_MAPPED  MEM_COMMIT  PAGE_READWRITE              <unknown>  [........X.......]
+     7ffe`821c0000     7ffe`821d0000        0`00010000 MEM_MAPPED  MEM_COMMIT  PAGE_READWRITE              <unknown>  [................]
+     7ffe`821d0000     7ffe`821e0000        0`00010000 MEM_MAPPED  MEM_COMMIT  PAGE_READWRITE              <unknown>  [..........l.i...]
+     7ffe`821e0000     7ffe`821e4000        0`00004000 MEM_MAPPED  MEM_COMMIT  PAGE_EXECUTE_READ           <unknown>  [H......f..t.....]
      7ffe`821e4000     7ffe`821e8000        0`00004000 MEM_MAPPED  MEM_COMMIT  PAGE_READWRITE              <unknown>  [X.hn3...........]
      7ffe`821e8000     7ffe`821ec000        0`00004000 MEM_MAPPED  MEM_COMMIT  PAGE_EXECUTE_READ           <unknown>  [H......f..t.....]
      7ffe`821ec000     7ffe`821f0000        0`00004000 MEM_MAPPED  MEM_COMMIT  PAGE_READWRITE              <unknown>  [.P.r3...........]
+     7ffe`821f0000     7ffe`821f4000        0`00004000 MEM_MAPPED  MEM_COMMIT  PAGE_EXECUTE_READ           <unknown>  [H......f..t.....]
      7ffe`821f4000     7ffe`821f8000        0`00004000 MEM_MAPPED  MEM_COMMIT  PAGE_READWRITE              <unknown>  [.f.r3...........]
      7ffe`821f8000     7ffe`821fc000        0`00004000 MEM_MAPPED  MEM_COMMIT  PAGE_EXECUTE_READ           <unknown>  [H......f..t.....]
      7ffe`821fc000     7ffe`82200000        0`00004000 MEM_MAPPED  MEM_COMMIT  PAGE_READWRITE              <unknown>  [x..r3...........]
+     7ffe`82200000     7ffe`82204000        0`00004000 MEM_MAPPED  MEM_COMMIT  PAGE_EXECUTE_READ           <unknown>  [......L.........]
      7ffe`82204000     7ffe`82208000        0`00004000 MEM_MAPPED  MEM_COMMIT  PAGE_READWRITE              <unknown>  [................]
      7ffe`82208000     7ffe`8220c000        0`00004000 MEM_MAPPED  MEM_COMMIT  PAGE_EXECUTE_READ           <unknown>  [......L.........]
      7ffe`8220c000     7ffe`82210000        0`00004000 MEM_MAPPED  MEM_COMMIT  PAGE_READWRITE              <unknown>  [.a..............]
+     7ffe`82210000     7ffe`82220000        0`00010000 MEM_MAPPED  MEM_COMMIT  PAGE_READWRITE              <unknown>  [Y...............]
+     7ffe`82220000     7ffe`82230000        0`00010000 MEM_MAPPED  MEM_COMMIT  PAGE_READWRITE              <unknown>  [................]
+     7ffe`82230000     7ffe`82240000        0`00010000 MEM_MAPPED  MEM_COMMIT  PAGE_READWRITE              <unknown>  [................]
+     7ffe`82240000     7ffe`82250000        0`00010000 MEM_MAPPED  MEM_COMMIT  PAGE_READWRITE              <unknown>  [B.B.............]
+     7ffe`82250000     7ffe`82260000        0`00010000 MEM_MAPPED  MEM_COMMIT  PAGE_READWRITE              <unknown>  [................]
+     7ffe`82260000     7ffe`82261000        0`00001000 MEM_MAPPED  MEM_COMMIT  PAGE_EXECUTE_READ           <unknown>  [.9.r3...........]
      7ffe`82261000     7ffe`82270000        0`0000f000 MEM_MAPPED  MEM_RESERVE                             <unknown>
+     7ffe`82270000     7ffe`82280000        0`00010000 MEM_MAPPED  MEM_COMMIT  PAGE_READWRITE              <unknown>  [................]
+     7ffe`82280000     7ffe`82290000        0`00010000 MEM_MAPPED  MEM_COMMIT  PAGE_READWRITE              <unknown>  [................]
+     7ffe`82290000     7ffe`822a0000        0`00010000 MEM_MAPPED  MEM_COMMIT  PAGE_READWRITE              <unknown>  [................]
+     7ffe`822a0000     7ffe`822b0000        0`00010000 MEM_MAPPED  MEM_COMMIT  PAGE_READWRITE              <unknown>  [................]
+     7ffe`822b0000     7ffe`822c0000        0`00010000 MEM_MAPPED  MEM_COMMIT  PAGE_READWRITE              <unknown>  [................]
+     7ffe`822c0000     7ffe`822c5000        0`00005000 MEM_MAPPED  MEM_COMMIT  PAGE_READWRITE              <unknown>  [................]
      7ffe`822c5000     7ffe`822d0000        0`0000b000 MEM_MAPPED  MEM_RESERVE                             <unknown>
+     7ffe`822d0000     7ffe`822e0000        0`00010000 MEM_MAPPED  MEM_COMMIT  PAGE_READWRITE              <unknown>  [................]
+     7ffe`822e0000     7ffe`822f0000        0`00010000 MEM_MAPPED  MEM_COMMIT  PAGE_READWRITE              <unknown>  [................]
+     7ffe`822f0000     7ffe`82300000        0`00010000 MEM_MAPPED  MEM_COMMIT  PAGE_READWRITE              <unknown>  [................]
+     7ffe`82300000     7ffe`82304000        0`00004000 MEM_MAPPED  MEM_COMMIT  PAGE_EXECUTE_READ           <unknown>  [......L.........]
      7ffe`82304000     7ffe`82308000        0`00004000 MEM_MAPPED  MEM_COMMIT  PAGE_READWRITE              <unknown>  [..0.............]
      7ffe`82308000     7ffe`8230c000        0`00004000 MEM_MAPPED  MEM_COMMIT  PAGE_EXECUTE_READ           <unknown>  [......L.........]
      7ffe`8230c000     7ffe`82310000        0`00004000 MEM_MAPPED  MEM_COMMIT  PAGE_READWRITE              <unknown>  [..0.....H.3.....]
+     7ffe`82310000     7ffe`82320000        0`00010000 MEM_MAPPED  MEM_COMMIT  PAGE_READWRITE              <unknown>  [................]
+     7ffe`82320000     7ffe`82330000        0`00010000 MEM_MAPPED  MEM_COMMIT  PAGE_READWRITE              <unknown>  [..2.............]
+     7ffe`82330000     7ffe`82340000        0`00010000 MEM_MAPPED  MEM_COMMIT  PAGE_READWRITE              <unknown>  [................]
+     7ffe`82340000     7ffe`82350000        0`00010000 MEM_MAPPED  MEM_COMMIT  PAGE_READWRITE              <unknown>  [................]
+     7ffe`82350000     7ffe`82360000        0`00010000 MEM_MAPPED  MEM_COMMIT  PAGE_READWRITE              <unknown>  [.........x......]
+     7ffe`82360000     7ffe`82370000        0`00010000 MEM_MAPPED  MEM_COMMIT  PAGE_READWRITE              <unknown>  [..6.............]
+     7ffe`82370000     7ffe`82380000        0`00010000 MEM_MAPPED  MEM_COMMIT  PAGE_READWRITE              <unknown>  [..........7.....]
+     7ffe`82380000     7ffe`82390000        0`00010000 MEM_MAPPED  MEM_COMMIT  PAGE_READWRITE              <unknown>  [..8.............]
+     7ffe`82390000     7ffe`823a0000        0`00010000 MEM_MAPPED  MEM_COMMIT  PAGE_READWRITE              <unknown>  [................]
+     7ffe`823a0000     7ffe`823a4000        0`00004000 MEM_MAPPED  MEM_COMMIT  PAGE_EXECUTE_READ           <unknown>  [......L.........]
      7ffe`823a4000     7ffe`823a8000        0`00004000 MEM_MAPPED  MEM_COMMIT  PAGE_READWRITE              <unknown>  [........p.9.....]
      7ffe`823a8000     7ffe`823ac000        0`00004000 MEM_MAPPED  MEM_COMMIT  PAGE_EXECUTE_READ           <unknown>  [......L.........]
      7ffe`823ac000     7ffe`823b0000        0`00004000 MEM_MAPPED  MEM_COMMIT  PAGE_READWRITE              <unknown>  [........Hn......]
+     7ffe`823b0000     7ffe`823c0000        0`00010000 MEM_MAPPED  MEM_COMMIT  PAGE_READWRITE              <unknown>  [................]
+     7ffe`823c0000     7ffe`823d0000        0`00010000 MEM_MAPPED  MEM_COMMIT  PAGE_READWRITE              <unknown>  [................]
+     7ffe`823d0000     7ffe`823e0000        0`00010000 MEM_MAPPED  MEM_COMMIT  PAGE_READWRITE              <unknown>  [p...............]
+     7ffe`823e0000     7ffe`823f0000        0`00010000 MEM_MAPPED  MEM_COMMIT  PAGE_READWRITE              <unknown>  [................]
+     7ffe`823f0000     7ffe`82400000        0`00010000 MEM_MAPPED  MEM_COMMIT  PAGE_READWRITE              <unknown>  [................]
+     7ffe`82400000     7ffe`82410000        0`00010000 MEM_MAPPED  MEM_COMMIT  PAGE_READWRITE              <unknown>  [................]
+     7ffe`82410000     7ffe`82414000        0`00004000 MEM_MAPPED  MEM_COMMIT  PAGE_EXECUTE_READ           <unknown>  [......L.........]
      7ffe`82414000     7ffe`82418000        0`00004000 MEM_MAPPED  MEM_COMMIT  PAGE_READWRITE              <unknown>  [..A.............]
      7ffe`82418000     7ffe`8241c000        0`00004000 MEM_MAPPED  MEM_COMMIT  PAGE_EXECUTE_READ           <unknown>  [......L.........]
      7ffe`8241c000     7ffe`82420000        0`00004000 MEM_MAPPED  MEM_COMMIT  PAGE_READWRITE              <unknown>  [..A......JP.....]
+     7ffe`82420000     7ffe`82423000        0`00003000 MEM_MAPPED  MEM_COMMIT  PAGE_READWRITE              <unknown>  [..B.............]
      7ffe`82423000     7ffe`82430000        0`0000d000 MEM_MAPPED  MEM_RESERVE                             <unknown>
+     7ffe`82430000     7ffe`8244f000        0`0001f000 MEM_MAPPED  MEM_COMMIT  PAGE_READWRITE              <unknown>  [................]
      7ffe`8244f000     7ffe`82450000        0`00001000 MEM_MAPPED  MEM_RESERVE                             <unknown>
+     7ffe`82450000     7ffe`82460000        0`00010000 MEM_MAPPED  MEM_COMMIT  PAGE_READWRITE              <unknown>  [..E.............]
+     7ffe`82460000     7ffe`82464000        0`00004000 MEM_MAPPED  MEM_COMMIT  PAGE_EXECUTE_READ           <unknown>  [L.............f.]
      7ffe`82464000     7ffe`82468000        0`00004000 MEM_MAPPED  MEM_COMMIT  PAGE_READWRITE              <unknown>  [..E.......t.....]
      7ffe`82468000     7ffe`82470000        0`00008000 MEM_MAPPED  MEM_RESERVE                             <unknown>
+     7ffe`82470000     7ffe`8247a000        0`0000a000 MEM_MAPPED  MEM_COMMIT  PAGE_EXECUTE_READ           <unknown>  [H.0U............]
      7ffe`8247a000     7ffe`824f0000        0`00076000 MEM_MAPPED  MEM_RESERVE                             <unknown>
+     7ffe`824f0000     7ffe`824fc000        0`0000c000 MEM_MAPPED  MEM_COMMIT  PAGE_READWRITE              <unknown>  [................]
      7ffe`824fc000     7ffe`82500000        0`00004000 MEM_MAPPED  MEM_RESERVE                             <unknown>
+     7ffe`82500000     7ffe`82508000        0`00008000 MEM_MAPPED  MEM_COMMIT  PAGE_READWRITE              <unknown>  [..P........0....]
      7ffe`82508000     7ffe`82510000        0`00008000 MEM_MAPPED  MEM_RESERVE                             <unknown>
+     7ffe`82510000     7ffe`dbdf0000        0`598e0000             MEM_FREE    PAGE_NOACCESS               Free
+     7ffe`dbdf0000     7ffe`dbdf1000        0`00001000 MEM_IMAGE   MEM_COMMIT  PAGE_READONLY               Image      [Microsoft_CSharp; "C:\Program Files\dotnet\shared\Microsoft.NETCore.App\9.0.4\Microsoft.CSharp.dll"]
      7ffe`dbdf1000     7ffe`dbed0000        0`000df000 MEM_IMAGE   MEM_COMMIT  PAGE_EXECUTE_READ           Image      [Microsoft_CSharp; "C:\Program Files\dotnet\shared\Microsoft.NETCore.App\9.0.4\Microsoft.CSharp.dll"]
      7ffe`dbed0000     7ffe`dbed7000        0`00007000 MEM_IMAGE   MEM_COMMIT  PAGE_READWRITE              Image      [Microsoft_CSharp; "C:\Program Files\dotnet\shared\Microsoft.NETCore.App\9.0.4\Microsoft.CSharp.dll"]
```

```
7ffe`dbed7000   7ffe`dbede000   0`00007000 MEM_IMAGE    MEM_COMMIT  PAGE_WRITECOPY       Image   [Microsoft_CSharp; "C:\Program Files\dotnet\shared\Microsoft.NETCore.App\9.0.4\Microsoft.CSharp.dll"]
7ffe`dbede000   7ffe`dbee0000   0`00002000 MEM_IMAGE    MEM_COMMIT  PAGE_READONLY        Image   [Microsoft_CSharp; "C:\Program Files\dotnet\shared\Microsoft.NETCore.App\9.0.4\Microsoft.CSharp.dll"]
+ 7ffe`dbee0000 7ffe`dbee1000   0`00001000 MEM_IMAGE    MEM_COMMIT  PAGE_READONLY        Image   [System_Text_Json; "C:\Program Files\dotnet\shared\Microsoft.NETCore.App\9.0.4\System.Text.Json.dll"]
7ffe`dbee1000   7ffe`dc074000   0`00193000 MEM_IMAGE    MEM_COMMIT  PAGE_EXECUTE_READ    Image   [System_Text_Json; "C:\Program Files\dotnet\shared\Microsoft.NETCore.App\9.0.4\System.Text.Json.dll"]
7ffe`dc074000   7ffe`dc075000   0`00001000 MEM_IMAGE    MEM_COMMIT  PAGE_WRITECOPY       Image   [System_Text_Json; "C:\Program Files\dotnet\shared\Microsoft.NETCore.App\9.0.4\System.Text.Json.dll"]
7ffe`dc075000   7ffe`dc076000   0`00001000 MEM_IMAGE    MEM_COMMIT  PAGE_READWRITE       Image   [System_Text_Json; "C:\Program Files\dotnet\shared\Microsoft.NETCore.App\9.0.4\System.Text.Json.dll"]
7ffe`dc076000   7ffe`dc091000   0`0001b000 MEM_IMAGE    MEM_COMMIT  PAGE_WRITECOPY       Image   [System_Text_Json; "C:\Program Files\dotnet\shared\Microsoft.NETCore.App\9.0.4\System.Text.Json.dll"]
7ffe`dc091000   7ffe`dc094000   0`00003000 MEM_IMAGE    MEM_COMMIT  PAGE_READONLY        Image   [System_Text_Json; "C:\Program Files\dotnet\shared\Microsoft.NETCore.App\9.0.4\System.Text.Json.dll"]
+ 7ffe`dc094000 7ffe`dc0a0000   0`0000c000              MEM_FREE     PAGE_NOACCESS        Free
+ 7ffe`dc0a0000 7ffe`dc0a1000   0`00001000 MEM_IMAGE    MEM_COMMIT  PAGE_READONLY        Image   [System_Collections_Immutable; "C:\Program
Files\dotnet\shared\Microsoft.NETCore.App\9.0.4\System.Collections.Immutable.dll"]
7ffe`dc0a1000   7ffe`dc160000   0`000bf000 MEM_IMAGE    MEM_COMMIT  PAGE_EXECUTE_READ    Image   [System_Collections_Immutable; "C:\Program
Files\dotnet\shared\Microsoft.NETCore.App\9.0.4\System.Collections.Immutable.dll"]
7ffe`dc160000   7ffe`dc161000   0`00001000 MEM_IMAGE    MEM_COMMIT  PAGE_READWRITE       Image   [System_Collections_Immutable; "C:\Program
Files\dotnet\shared\Microsoft.NETCore.App\9.0.4\System.Collections.Immutable.dll"]
7ffe`dc161000   7ffe`dc178000   0`00017000 MEM_IMAGE    MEM_COMMIT  PAGE_WRITECOPY       Image   [System_Collections_Immutable; "C:\Program
Files\dotnet\shared\Microsoft.NETCore.App\9.0.4\System.Collections.Immutable.dll"]
7ffe`dc178000   7ffe`dc17a000   0`00002000 MEM_IMAGE    MEM_COMMIT  PAGE_READONLY        Image   [System_Collections_Immutable; "C:\Program
Files\dotnet\shared\Microsoft.NETCore.App\9.0.4\System.Collections.Immutable.dll"]
+ 7ffe`dc17a000 7ffe`dc180000   0`00006000              MEM_FREE     PAGE_NOACCESS        Free
+ 7ffe`dc180000 7ffe`dc181000   0`00001000 MEM_IMAGE    MEM_COMMIT  PAGE_READONLY        Image   [System_Linq_Expressions; "C:\Program
Files\dotnet\shared\Microsoft.NETCore.App\9.0.4\System.Linq.Expressions.dll"]
7ffe`dc181000   7ffe`dc494000   0`00313000 MEM_IMAGE    MEM_COMMIT  PAGE_EXECUTE_READ    Image   [System_Linq_Expressions; "C:\Program
Files\dotnet\shared\Microsoft.NETCore.App\9.0.4\System.Linq.Expressions.dll"]
7ffe`dc494000   7ffe`dc49a000   0`00006000 MEM_IMAGE    MEM_COMMIT  PAGE_READWRITE       Image   [System_Linq_Expressions; "C:\Program
Files\dotnet\shared\Microsoft.NETCore.App\9.0.4\System.Linq.Expressions.dll"]
7ffe`dc49a000   7ffe`dc49e000   0`00004000 MEM_IMAGE    MEM_COMMIT  PAGE_WRITECOPY       Image   [System_Linq_Expressions; "C:\Program
Files\dotnet\shared\Microsoft.NETCore.App\9.0.4\System.Linq.Expressions.dll"]
7ffe`dc49e000   7ffe`dc49f000   0`00001000 MEM_IMAGE    MEM_COMMIT  PAGE_READWRITE       Image   [System_Linq_Expressions; "C:\Program
Files\dotnet\shared\Microsoft.NETCore.App\9.0.4\System.Linq.Expressions.dll"]
7ffe`dc49f000   7ffe`dc4a2000   0`00003000 MEM_IMAGE    MEM_COMMIT  PAGE_WRITECOPY       Image   [System_Linq_Expressions; "C:\Program
Files\dotnet\shared\Microsoft.NETCore.App\9.0.4\System.Linq.Expressions.dll"]
7ffe`dc4a2000   7ffe`dc4a8000   0`00006000 MEM_IMAGE    MEM_COMMIT  PAGE_READWRITE       Image   [System_Linq_Expressions; "C:\Program
Files\dotnet\shared\Microsoft.NETCore.App\9.0.4\System.Linq.Expressions.dll"]
7ffe`dc4a8000   7ffe`dc4ac000   0`00004000 MEM_IMAGE    MEM_COMMIT  PAGE_WRITECOPY       Image   [System_Linq_Expressions; "C:\Program
Files\dotnet\shared\Microsoft.NETCore.App\9.0.4\System.Linq.Expressions.dll"]
7ffe`dc4ac000   7ffe`dc4ba000   0`0000e000 MEM_IMAGE    MEM_COMMIT  PAGE_READWRITE       Image   [System_Linq_Expressions; "C:\Program
Files\dotnet\shared\Microsoft.NETCore.App\9.0.4\System.Linq.Expressions.dll"]
7ffe`dc4ba000   7ffe`dc4f6000   0`0003c000 MEM_IMAGE    MEM_COMMIT  PAGE_WRITECOPY       Image   [System_Linq_Expressions; "C:\Program
Files\dotnet\shared\Microsoft.NETCore.App\9.0.4\System.Linq.Expressions.dll"]
7ffe`dc4f6000   7ffe`dc4fd000   0`00007000 MEM_IMAGE    MEM_COMMIT  PAGE_READONLY        Image   [System_Linq_Expressions; "C:\Program
Files\dotnet\shared\Microsoft.NETCore.App\9.0.4\System.Linq.Expressions.dll"]
+ 7ffe`dc4fd000 7ffe`dc500000   0`00003000              MEM_FREE     PAGE_NOACCESS        Free
+ 7ffe`dc500000 7ffe`dc501000   0`00001000 MEM_IMAGE    MEM_COMMIT  PAGE_READONLY        Image   [System_Data_Common; "C:\Program Files\dotnet\shared\Microsoft.NETCore.App\9.0.4\System.Data.Common.dll"]
7ffe`dc501000   7ffe`dc792000   0`00291000 MEM_IMAGE    MEM_COMMIT  PAGE_EXECUTE_READ    Image   [System_Data_Common; "C:\Program Files\dotnet\shared\Microsoft.NETCore.App\9.0.4\System.Data.Common.dll"]
7ffe`dc792000   7ffe`dc794000   0`00002000 MEM_IMAGE    MEM_COMMIT  PAGE_WRITECOPY       Image   [System_Data_Common; "C:\Program Files\dotnet\shared\Microsoft.NETCore.App\9.0.4\System.Data.Common.dll"]
7ffe`dc794000   7ffe`dc795000   0`00001000 MEM_IMAGE    MEM_COMMIT  PAGE_READWRITE       Image   [System_Data_Common; "C:\Program Files\dotnet\shared\Microsoft.NETCore.App\9.0.4\System.Data.Common.dll"]
7ffe`dc795000   7ffe`dc7b2000   0`0001d000 MEM_IMAGE    MEM_COMMIT  PAGE_WRITECOPY       Image   [System_Data_Common; "C:\Program Files\dotnet\shared\Microsoft.NETCore.App\9.0.4\System.Data.Common.dll"]
7ffe`dc7b2000   7ffe`dc7b5000   0`00003000 MEM_IMAGE    MEM_COMMIT  PAGE_READONLY        Image   [System_Data_Common; "C:\Program Files\dotnet\shared\Microsoft.NETCore.App\9.0.4\System.Data.Common.dll"]
+ 7ffe`dc7b5000 7ffe`dca00000   0`0024b000              MEM_FREE     PAGE_NOACCESS        Free
+ 7ffe`dca00000 7ffe`dca01000   0`00001000 MEM_IMAGE    MEM_COMMIT  PAGE_READONLY        Image   [System_Reflection_Metadata; "C:\Program
Files\dotnet\shared\Microsoft.NETCore.App\9.0.4\System.Reflection.Metadata.dll"]
7ffe`dca01000   7ffe`dcb0b000   0`0010a000 MEM_IMAGE    MEM_COMMIT  PAGE_EXECUTE_READ    Image   [System_Reflection_Metadata; "C:\Program
Files\dotnet\shared\Microsoft.NETCore.App\9.0.4\System.Reflection.Metadata.dll"]
7ffe`dcb0b000   7ffe`dcb12000   0`00007000 MEM_IMAGE    MEM_COMMIT  PAGE_READWRITE       Image   [System_Reflection_Metadata; "C:\Program
Files\dotnet\shared\Microsoft.NETCore.App\9.0.4\System.Reflection.Metadata.dll"]
7ffe`dcb12000   7ffe`dcb1a000   0`00008000 MEM_IMAGE    MEM_COMMIT  PAGE_WRITECOPY       Image   [System_Reflection_Metadata; "C:\Program
Files\dotnet\shared\Microsoft.NETCore.App\9.0.4\System.Reflection.Metadata.dll"]
7ffe`dcb1a000   7ffe`dcb1c000   0`00002000 MEM_IMAGE    MEM_COMMIT  PAGE_READONLY        Image   [System_Reflection_Metadata; "C:\Program
Files\dotnet\shared\Microsoft.NETCore.App\9.0.4\System.Reflection.Metadata.dll"]
+ 7ffe`dcb1c000 7ffe`dd310000   0`007f4000              MEM_FREE     PAGE_NOACCESS        Free
+ 7ffe`dd310000 7ffe`dd311000   0`00001000 MEM_IMAGE    MEM_COMMIT  PAGE_READONLY        Image   [System_Runtime_Serialization_Formatters; "C:\Program
Files\dotnet\shared\Microsoft.NETCore.App\9.0.4\System.Runtime.Serialization.Formatters.dll"]
7ffe`dd311000   7ffe`dd329000   0`00018000 MEM_IMAGE    MEM_COMMIT  PAGE_EXECUTE_READ    Image   [System_Runtime_Serialization_Formatters; "C:\Program
Files\dotnet\shared\Microsoft.NETCore.App\9.0.4\System.Runtime.Serialization.Formatters.dll"]
7ffe`dd329000   7ffe`dd32a000   0`00001000 MEM_IMAGE    MEM_COMMIT  PAGE_READWRITE       Image   [System_Runtime_Serialization_Formatters; "C:\Program
Files\dotnet\shared\Microsoft.NETCore.App\9.0.4\System.Runtime.Serialization.Formatters.dll"]
7ffe`dd32a000   7ffe`dd32b000   0`00001000 MEM_IMAGE    MEM_COMMIT  PAGE_WRITECOPY       Image   [System_Runtime_Serialization_Formatters; "C:\Program
Files\dotnet\shared\Microsoft.NETCore.App\9.0.4\System.Runtime.Serialization.Formatters.dll"]
7ffe`dd32b000   7ffe`dd32c000   0`00001000 MEM_IMAGE    MEM_COMMIT  PAGE_READONLY        Image   [System_Runtime_Serialization_Formatters; "C:\Program
Files\dotnet\shared\Microsoft.NETCore.App\9.0.4\System.Runtime.Serialization.Formatters.dll"]
+ 7ffe`dd32c000 7ffe`dd330000   0`00004000              MEM_FREE     PAGE_NOACCESS        Free
+ 7ffe`dd330000 7ffe`dd331000   0`00001000 MEM_IMAGE    MEM_COMMIT  PAGE_READONLY        Image   [System_Private_Xml; "C:\Program Files\dotnet\shared\Microsoft.NETCore.App\9.0.4\System.Private.Xml.dll"]
7ffe`dd331000   7ffe`dda5e000   0`0072d000 MEM_IMAGE    MEM_COMMIT  PAGE_EXECUTE_READ    Image   [System_Private_Xml; "C:\Program Files\dotnet\shared\Microsoft.NETCore.App\9.0.4\System.Private.Xml.dll"]
7ffe`dda5e000   7ffe`dda61000   0`00003000 MEM_IMAGE    MEM_COMMIT  PAGE_WRITECOPY       Image   [System_Private_Xml; "C:\Program Files\dotnet\shared\Microsoft.NETCore.App\9.0.4\System.Private.Xml.dll"]
7ffe`dda61000   7ffe`dda63000   0`00002000 MEM_IMAGE    MEM_COMMIT  PAGE_READWRITE       Image   [System_Private_Xml; "C:\Program Files\dotnet\shared\Microsoft.NETCore.App\9.0.4\System.Private.Xml.dll"]
7ffe`dda63000   7ffe`dda67000   0`00004000 MEM_IMAGE    MEM_COMMIT  PAGE_WRITECOPY       Image   [System_Private_Xml; "C:\Program Files\dotnet\shared\Microsoft.NETCore.App\9.0.4\System.Private.Xml.dll"]
7ffe`dda67000   7ffe`dda69000   0`00002000 MEM_IMAGE    MEM_COMMIT  PAGE_READWRITE       Image   [System_Private_Xml; "C:\Program Files\dotnet\shared\Microsoft.NETCore.App\9.0.4\System.Private.Xml.dll"]
7ffe`dda69000   7ffe`dda78000   0`0000f000 MEM_IMAGE    MEM_COMMIT  PAGE_WRITECOPY       Image   [System_Private_Xml; "C:\Program Files\dotnet\shared\Microsoft.NETCore.App\9.0.4\System.Private.Xml.dll"]
7ffe`dda78000   7ffe`dda79000   0`00001000 MEM_IMAGE    MEM_COMMIT  PAGE_READWRITE       Image   [System_Private_Xml; "C:\Program Files\dotnet\shared\Microsoft.NETCore.App\9.0.4\System.Private.Xml.dll"]
7ffe`dda79000   7ffe`dda7a000   0`00001000 MEM_IMAGE    MEM_COMMIT  PAGE_READONLY        Image   [System_Private_Xml; "C:\Program Files\dotnet\shared\Microsoft.NETCore.App\9.0.4\System.Private.Xml.dll"]
7ffe`dda7a000   7ffe`dda7b000   0`00001000 MEM_IMAGE    MEM_COMMIT  PAGE_WRITECOPY       Image   [System_Private_Xml; "C:\Program Files\dotnet\shared\Microsoft.NETCore.App\9.0.4\System.Private.Xml.dll"]
7ffe`dda7b000   7ffe`dda7c000   0`00001000 MEM_IMAGE    MEM_COMMIT  PAGE_READWRITE       Image   [System_Private_Xml; "C:\Program Files\dotnet\shared\Microsoft.NETCore.App\9.0.4\System.Private.Xml.dll"]
7ffe`dda7c000   7ffe`dda80000   0`00004000 MEM_IMAGE    MEM_COMMIT  PAGE_WRITECOPY       Image   [System_Private_Xml; "C:\Program Files\dotnet\shared\Microsoft.NETCore.App\9.0.4\System.Private.Xml.dll"]
7ffe`dda80000   7ffe`dda81000   0`00003000 MEM_IMAGE    MEM_COMMIT  PAGE_READWRITE       Image   [System_Private_Xml; "C:\Program Files\dotnet\shared\Microsoft.NETCore.App\9.0.4\System.Private.Xml.dll"]
7ffe`dda81000   7ffe`ddab4000   0`00033000 MEM_IMAGE    MEM_COMMIT  PAGE_WRITECOPY       Image   [System_Private_Xml; "C:\Program Files\dotnet\shared\Microsoft.NETCore.App\9.0.4\System.Private.Xml.dll"]
7ffe`ddab4000   7ffe`ddabb000   0`00007000 MEM_IMAGE    MEM_COMMIT  PAGE_READONLY        Image   [System_Private_Xml; "C:\Program Files\dotnet\shared\Microsoft.NETCore.App\9.0.4\System.Private.Xml.dll"]
+ 7ffe`ddabb000 7ffe`ddb90000   0`000d5000              MEM_FREE     PAGE_NOACCESS        Free
+ 7ffe`ddb90000 7ffe`ddb91000   0`00001000 MEM_IMAGE    MEM_COMMIT  PAGE_READONLY        Image   [System_ObjectModel; "C:\Program Files\dotnet\shared\Microsoft.NETCore.App\9.0.4\System.ObjectModel.dll"]
7ffe`ddb91000   7ffe`ddb9f000   0`0000e000 MEM_IMAGE    MEM_COMMIT  PAGE_EXECUTE_READ    Image   [System_ObjectModel; "C:\Program Files\dotnet\shared\Microsoft.NETCore.App\9.0.4\System.ObjectModel.dll"]
7ffe`ddb9f000   7ffe`ddba0000   0`00001000 MEM_IMAGE    MEM_COMMIT  PAGE_READWRITE       Image   [System_ObjectModel; "C:\Program Files\dotnet\shared\Microsoft.NETCore.App\9.0.4\System.ObjectModel.dll"]
7ffe`ddba0000   7ffe`ddba1000   0`00001000 MEM_IMAGE    MEM_COMMIT  PAGE_WRITECOPY       Image   [System_ObjectModel; "C:\Program Files\dotnet\shared\Microsoft.NETCore.App\9.0.4\System.ObjectModel.dll"]
7ffe`ddba1000   7ffe`ddba2000   0`00001000 MEM_IMAGE    MEM_COMMIT  PAGE_READONLY        Image   [System_ObjectModel; "C:\Program Files\dotnet\shared\Microsoft.NETCore.App\9.0.4\System.ObjectModel.dll"]
+ 7ffe`ddba2000 7ffe`ddbd0000   0`0002e000              MEM_FREE     PAGE_NOACCESS        Free
+ 7ffe`ddbd0000 7ffe`ddbd1000   0`00001000 MEM_IMAGE    MEM_COMMIT  PAGE_READONLY        Image   [System_IO_Compression_Native; "C:\Program
Files\dotnet\shared\Microsoft.NETCore.App\9.0.4\System.IO.Compression.Native.dll"]
7ffe`ddbd1000   7ffe`ddc36000   0`00065000 MEM_IMAGE    MEM_COMMIT  PAGE_EXECUTE_READ    Image   [System_IO_Compression_Native; "C:\Program
Files\dotnet\shared\Microsoft.NETCore.App\9.0.4\System.IO.Compression.Native.dll"]
7ffe`ddc36000   7ffe`ddcaf000   0`00079000 MEM_IMAGE    MEM_COMMIT  PAGE_READONLY        Image   [System_IO_Compression_Native; "C:\Program
Files\dotnet\shared\Microsoft.NETCore.App\9.0.4\System.IO.Compression.Native.dll"]
7ffe`ddcaf000   7ffe`ddcb0000   0`00001000 MEM_IMAGE    MEM_COMMIT  PAGE_READWRITE       Image   [System_IO_Compression_Native; "C:\Program
Files\dotnet\shared\Microsoft.NETCore.App\9.0.4\System.IO.Compression.Native.dll"]
7ffe`ddcb0000   7ffe`ddcb5000   0`00005000 MEM_IMAGE    MEM_COMMIT  PAGE_READONLY        Image   [System_IO_Compression_Native; "C:\Program
Files\dotnet\shared\Microsoft.NETCore.App\9.0.4\System.IO.Compression.Native.dll"]
+ 7ffe`ddcb5000 7ffe`ddd40000   0`0008b000              MEM_FREE     PAGE_NOACCESS        Free
+ 7ffe`ddd40000 7ffe`ddd41000   0`00001000 MEM_IMAGE    MEM_COMMIT  PAGE_READONLY        Image   [System_ComponentModel_TypeConverter; "C:\Program
Files\dotnet\shared\Microsoft.NETCore.App\9.0.4\System.ComponentModel.TypeConverter.dll"]
7ffe`ddd41000   7ffe`ddea0000   0`000a9000 MEM_IMAGE    MEM_COMMIT  PAGE_EXECUTE_READ    Image   [System_ComponentModel_TypeConverter; "C:\Program
Files\dotnet\shared\Microsoft.NETCore.App\9.0.4\System.ComponentModel.TypeConverter.dll"]
7ffe`ddea0000   7ffe`ddeae000   0`00001000 MEM_IMAGE    MEM_COMMIT  PAGE_WRITECOPY       Image   [System_ComponentModel_TypeConverter; "C:\Program
Files\dotnet\shared\Microsoft.NETCore.App\9.0.4\System.ComponentModel.TypeConverter.dll"]
7ffe`ddeab000   7ffe`ddeac000   0`00001000 MEM_IMAGE    MEM_COMMIT  PAGE_READWRITE       Image   [System_ComponentModel_TypeConverter; "C:\Program
Files\dotnet\shared\Microsoft.NETCore.App\9.0.4\System.ComponentModel.TypeConverter.dll"]
7ffe`ddeac000   7ffe`dddf8000   0`0000c000 MEM_IMAGE    MEM_COMMIT  PAGE_WRITECOPY       Image   [System_ComponentModel_TypeConverter; "C:\Program
Files\dotnet\shared\Microsoft.NETCore.App\9.0.4\System.ComponentModel.TypeConverter.dll"]
7ffe`dddf8000   7ffe`dddfa000   0`00002000 MEM_IMAGE    MEM_COMMIT  PAGE_READONLY        Image   [System_ComponentModel_TypeConverter; "C:\Program
Files\dotnet\shared\Microsoft.NETCore.App\9.0.4\System.ComponentModel.TypeConverter.dll"]
+ 7ffe`dddfa000 7ffe`de310000   0`00516000              MEM_FREE     PAGE_NOACCESS        Free
+ 7ffe`de310000 7ffe`de311000   0`00001000 MEM_IMAGE    MEM_COMMIT  PAGE_READONLY        Image   [System_Collections_Concurrent; "C:\Program
Files\dotnet\shared\Microsoft.NETCore.App\9.0.4\System.Collections.Concurrent.dll"]
7ffe`de311000   7ffe`de34f000   0`0003e000 MEM_IMAGE    MEM_COMMIT  PAGE_EXECUTE_READ    Image   [System_Collections_Concurrent; "C:\Program
Files\dotnet\shared\Microsoft.NETCore.App\9.0.4\System.Collections.Concurrent.dll"]
7ffe`de34f000   7ffe`de351000   0`00002000 MEM_IMAGE    MEM_COMMIT  PAGE_READWRITE       Image   [System_Collections_Concurrent; "C:\Program
Files\dotnet\shared\Microsoft.NETCore.App\9.0.4\System.Collections.Concurrent.dll"]
7ffe`de351000   7ffe`de354000   0`00003000 MEM_IMAGE    MEM_COMMIT  PAGE_WRITECOPY       Image   [System_Collections_Concurrent; "C:\Program
Files\dotnet\shared\Microsoft.NETCore.App\9.0.4\System.Collections.Concurrent.dll"]
7ffe`de354000   7ffe`de355000   0`00001000 MEM_IMAGE    MEM_COMMIT  PAGE_READONLY        Image   [System_Collections_Concurrent; "C:\Program
Files\dotnet\shared\Microsoft.NETCore.App\9.0.4\System.Collections.Concurrent.dll"]
+ 7ffe`de355000 7ffe`deaf0000   0`0079b000              MEM_FREE     PAGE_NOACCESS        Free
+ 7ffe`deaf0000 7ffe`deaf1000   0`00001000 MEM_IMAGE    MEM_COMMIT  PAGE_READONLY        Image   [System_Text_RegularExpressions; "C:\Program
Files\dotnet\shared\Microsoft.NETCore.App\9.0.4\System.Text.RegularExpressions.dll"]
7ffe`deaf1000   7ffe`debd2000   0`000e1000 MEM_IMAGE    MEM_COMMIT  PAGE_EXECUTE_READ    Image   [System_Text_RegularExpressions; "C:\Program
Files\dotnet\shared\Microsoft.NETCore.App\9.0.4\System.Text.RegularExpressions.dll"]
7ffe`debd2000   7ffe`debda000   0`00008000 MEM_IMAGE    MEM_COMMIT  PAGE_READWRITE       Image   [System_Text_RegularExpressions; "C:\Program
Files\dotnet\shared\Microsoft.NETCore.App\9.0.4\System.Text.RegularExpressions.dll"]
7ffe`debda000   7ffe`debe5000   0`0000b000 MEM_IMAGE    MEM_COMMIT  PAGE_WRITECOPY       Image   [System_Text_RegularExpressions; "C:\Program
Files\dotnet\shared\Microsoft.NETCore.App\9.0.4\System.Text.RegularExpressions.dll"]
7ffe`debe5000   7ffe`debe7000   0`00002000 MEM_IMAGE    MEM_COMMIT  PAGE_READONLY        Image   [System_Text_RegularExpressions; "C:\Program
Files\dotnet\shared\Microsoft.NETCore.App\9.0.4\System.Text.RegularExpressions.dll"]
+ 7ffe`debe7000 7ffe`decc0000   0`000d9000              MEM_FREE     PAGE_NOACCESS        Free
+ 7ffe`decc0000 7ffe`decc1000   0`00001000 MEM_IMAGE    MEM_COMMIT  PAGE_READONLY        Image   [System_Private_Xml_Linq; "C:\Program
Files\dotnet\shared\Microsoft.NETCore.App\9.0.4\System.Private.Xml.Linq.dll"]
7ffe`decc1000   7ffe`ded17000   0`00056000 MEM_IMAGE    MEM_COMMIT  PAGE_EXECUTE_READ    Image   [System_Private_Xml_Linq; "C:\Program
Files\dotnet\shared\Microsoft.NETCore.App\9.0.4\System.Private.Xml.Linq.dll"]
7ffe`ded17000   7ffe`ded18000   0`00001000 MEM_IMAGE    MEM_COMMIT  PAGE_READWRITE       Image   [System_Private_Xml_Linq; "C:\Program
Files\dotnet\shared\Microsoft.NETCore.App\9.0.4\System.Private.Xml.Linq.dll"]
```

272

```
      7ffe`ded18000      7ffe`ded1e000        0`00006000 MEM_IMAGE   MEM_COMMIT  PAGE_WRITECOPY      Image      [System_Private_Xml_Linq; "C:\Program
Files\dotnet\shared\Microsoft.NETCore.App\9.0.4\System.Private.Xml.Linq.dll"]
      7ffe`ded1e000      7ffe`ded1f000        0`00001000 MEM_IMAGE   MEM_COMMIT  PAGE_READONLY       Image      [System_Private_Xml_Linq; "C:\Program
Files\dotnet\shared\Microsoft.NETCore.App\9.0.4\System.Private.Xml.Linq.dll"]
+     7ffe`ded1f000      7ffe`ded70000        0`00051000             MEM_FREE    PAGE_NOACCESS       Free
+     7ffe`ded70000      7ffe`ded71000        0`00001000 MEM_IMAGE   MEM_COMMIT  PAGE_READONLY       Image      [System_Private_Uri; "C:\Program Files\dotnet\shared\Microsoft.NETCore.App\9.0.4\System.Private.Uri.dll"]
      7ffe`ded71000      7ffe`deda9000        0`00038000 MEM_IMAGE   MEM_COMMIT  PAGE_EXECUTE_READ   Image      [System_Private_Uri; "C:\Program Files\dotnet\shared\Microsoft.NETCore.App\9.0.4\System.Private.Uri.dll"]
      7ffe`deda9000      7ffe`dedab000        0`00002000 MEM_IMAGE   MEM_COMMIT  PAGE_READWRITE      Image      [System_Private_Uri; "C:\Program Files\dotnet\shared\Microsoft.NETCore.App\9.0.4\System.Private.Uri.dll"]
      7ffe`dedab000      7ffe`dedac000        0`00001000 MEM_IMAGE   MEM_COMMIT  PAGE_WRITECOPY      Image      [System_Private_Uri; "C:\Program Files\dotnet\shared\Microsoft.NETCore.App\9.0.4\System.Private.Uri.dll"]
      7ffe`dedac000      7ffe`dedad000        0`00001000 MEM_IMAGE   MEM_COMMIT  PAGE_READONLY       Image      [System_Private_Uri; "C:\Program Files\dotnet\shared\Microsoft.NETCore.App\9.0.4\System.Private.Uri.dll"]
+     7ffe`dedad000      7ffe`def90000        0`001e3000             MEM_FREE    PAGE_NOACCESS       Free
+     7ffe`def90000      7ffe`def91000        0`00001000 MEM_IMAGE   MEM_COMMIT  PAGE_READONLY       Image      [System_IO_Pipes; "C:\Program Files\dotnet\shared\Microsoft.NETCore.App\9.0.4\System.IO.Pipes.dll"]
      7ffe`def91000      7ffe`defb3000        0`00022000 MEM_IMAGE   MEM_COMMIT  PAGE_EXECUTE_READ   Image      [System_IO_Pipes; "C:\Program Files\dotnet\shared\Microsoft.NETCore.App\9.0.4\System.IO.Pipes.dll"]
      7ffe`defb3000      7ffe`defb4000        0`00001000 MEM_IMAGE   MEM_COMMIT  PAGE_READWRITE      Image      [System_IO_Pipes; "C:\Program Files\dotnet\shared\Microsoft.NETCore.App\9.0.4\System.IO.Pipes.dll"]
      7ffe`defb4000      7ffe`defb6000        0`00002000 MEM_IMAGE   MEM_COMMIT  PAGE_WRITECOPY      Image      [System_IO_Pipes; "C:\Program Files\dotnet\shared\Microsoft.NETCore.App\9.0.4\System.IO.Pipes.dll"]
      7ffe`defb6000      7ffe`defb7000        0`00001000 MEM_IMAGE   MEM_COMMIT  PAGE_READONLY       Image      [System_IO_Pipes; "C:\Program Files\dotnet\shared\Microsoft.NETCore.App\9.0.4\System.IO.Pipes.dll"]
+     7ffe`defb7000      7ffe`defc0000        0`00009000             MEM_FREE    PAGE_NOACCESS       Free
+     7ffe`defc0000      7ffe`defc1000        0`00001000 MEM_IMAGE   MEM_COMMIT  PAGE_READONLY       Image      [System_Memory; "C:\Program Files\dotnet\shared\Microsoft.NETCore.App\9.0.4\System.Memory.dll"]
      7ffe`defc1000      7ffe`defe1000        0`00020000 MEM_IMAGE   MEM_COMMIT  PAGE_EXECUTE_READ   Image      [System_Memory; "C:\Program Files\dotnet\shared\Microsoft.NETCore.App\9.0.4\System.Memory.dll"]
      7ffe`defe1000      7ffe`defe2000        0`00001000 MEM_IMAGE   MEM_COMMIT  PAGE_READWRITE      Image      [System_Memory; "C:\Program Files\dotnet\shared\Microsoft.NETCore.App\9.0.4\System.Memory.dll"]
      7ffe`defe2000      7ffe`defe4000        0`00002000 MEM_IMAGE   MEM_COMMIT  PAGE_WRITECOPY      Image      [System_Memory; "C:\Program Files\dotnet\shared\Microsoft.NETCore.App\9.0.4\System.Memory.dll"]
      7ffe`defe4000      7ffe`defe5000        0`00001000 MEM_IMAGE   MEM_COMMIT  PAGE_READONLY       Image      [System_Memory; "C:\Program Files\dotnet\shared\Microsoft.NETCore.App\9.0.4\System.Memory.dll"]
+     7ffe`defe5000      7ffe`df0c0000        0`000db000             MEM_FREE    PAGE_NOACCESS       Free
+     7ffe`df0c0000      7ffe`df0c1000        0`00001000 MEM_IMAGE   MEM_COMMIT  PAGE_READONLY       Image      [System_Transactions_Local; "C:\Program
Files\dotnet\shared\Microsoft.NETCore.App\9.0.4\System.Transactions.Local.dll"]
      7ffe`df0c1000      7ffe`df153000        0`00092000 MEM_IMAGE   MEM_COMMIT  PAGE_EXECUTE_READ   Image      [System_Transactions_Local; "C:\Program
Files\dotnet\shared\Microsoft.NETCore.App\9.0.4\System.Transactions.Local.dll"]
      7ffe`df153000      7ffe`df154000        0`00001000 MEM_IMAGE   MEM_COMMIT  PAGE_READWRITE      Image      [System_Transactions_Local; "C:\Program
Files\dotnet\shared\Microsoft.NETCore.App\9.0.4\System.Transactions.Local.dll"]
      7ffe`df154000      7ffe`df15c000        0`00008000 MEM_IMAGE   MEM_COMMIT  PAGE_WRITECOPY      Image      [System_Transactions_Local; "C:\Program
Files\dotnet\shared\Microsoft.NETCore.App\9.0.4\System.Transactions.Local.dll"]
      7ffe`df15c000      7ffe`df15d000        0`00001000 MEM_IMAGE   MEM_COMMIT  PAGE_READONLY       Image      [System_Transactions_Local; "C:\Program
Files\dotnet\shared\Microsoft.NETCore.App\9.0.4\System.Transactions.Local.dll"]
+     7ffe`df15d000      7ffe`df160000        0`00003000             MEM_FREE    PAGE_NOACCESS       Free
+     7ffe`df160000      7ffe`df161000        0`00001000 MEM_IMAGE   MEM_COMMIT  PAGE_READONLY       Image      [System_Diagnostics_Process; "C:\Program
Files\dotnet\shared\Microsoft.NETCore.App\9.0.4\System.Diagnostics.Process.dll"]
      7ffe`df161000      7ffe`df1a9000        0`00048000 MEM_IMAGE   MEM_COMMIT  PAGE_EXECUTE_READ   Image      [System_Diagnostics_Process; "C:\Program
Files\dotnet\shared\Microsoft.NETCore.App\9.0.4\System.Diagnostics.Process.dll"]
      7ffe`df1a9000      7ffe`df1ac000        0`00003000 MEM_IMAGE   MEM_COMMIT  PAGE_READWRITE      Image      [System_Diagnostics_Process; "C:\Program
Files\dotnet\shared\Microsoft.NETCore.App\9.0.4\System.Diagnostics.Process.dll"]
      7ffe`df1ac000      7ffe`df1af000        0`00003000 MEM_IMAGE   MEM_COMMIT  PAGE_WRITECOPY      Image      [System_Diagnostics_Process; "C:\Program
Files\dotnet\shared\Microsoft.NETCore.App\9.0.4\System.Diagnostics.Process.dll"]
      7ffe`df1af000      7ffe`df1b0000        0`00001000 MEM_IMAGE   MEM_COMMIT  PAGE_READONLY       Image      [System_Diagnostics_Process; "C:\Program
Files\dotnet\shared\Microsoft.NETCore.App\9.0.4\System.Diagnostics.Process.dll"]
+     7ffe`df1b0000      7ffe`df270000        0`000c0000             MEM_FREE    PAGE_NOACCESS       Free
+     7ffe`df270000      7ffe`df271000        0`00001000 MEM_IMAGE   MEM_COMMIT  PAGE_READONLY       Image      [System_Linq; "C:\Program Files\dotnet\shared\Microsoft.NETCore.App\9.0.4\System.Linq.dll"]
      7ffe`df271000      7ffe`df2fc000        0`0008b000 MEM_IMAGE   MEM_COMMIT  PAGE_EXECUTE_READ   Image      [System_Linq; "C:\Program Files\dotnet\shared\Microsoft.NETCore.App\9.0.4\System.Linq.dll"]
      7ffe`df2fc000      7ffe`df302000        0`00006000 MEM_IMAGE   MEM_COMMIT  PAGE_READWRITE      Image      [System_Linq; "C:\Program Files\dotnet\shared\Microsoft.NETCore.App\9.0.4\System.Linq.dll"]
      7ffe`df302000      7ffe`df30c000        0`0000a000 MEM_IMAGE   MEM_COMMIT  PAGE_WRITECOPY      Image      [System_Linq; "C:\Program Files\dotnet\shared\Microsoft.NETCore.App\9.0.4\System.Linq.dll"]
      7ffe`df30c000      7ffe`df30e000        0`00002000 MEM_IMAGE   MEM_COMMIT  PAGE_READONLY       Image      [System_Linq; "C:\Program Files\dotnet\shared\Microsoft.NETCore.App\9.0.4\System.Linq.dll"]
+     7ffe`df30e000      7ffe`df310000        0`00002000             MEM_FREE    PAGE_NOACCESS       Free
+     7ffe`df310000      7ffe`df311000        0`00001000 MEM_IMAGE   MEM_COMMIT  PAGE_READONLY       Image      [System_Collections; "C:\Program Files\dotnet\shared\Microsoft.NETCore.App\9.0.4\System.Collections.dll"]
      7ffe`df311000      7ffe`df357000        0`00046000 MEM_IMAGE   MEM_COMMIT  PAGE_EXECUTE_READ   Image      [System_Collections; "C:\Program Files\dotnet\shared\Microsoft.NETCore.App\9.0.4\System.Collections.dll"]
      7ffe`df357000      7ffe`df35a000        0`00003000 MEM_IMAGE   MEM_COMMIT  PAGE_READWRITE      Image      [System_Collections; "C:\Program Files\dotnet\shared\Microsoft.NETCore.App\9.0.4\System.Collections.dll"]
      7ffe`df35a000      7ffe`df35e000        0`00004000 MEM_IMAGE   MEM_COMMIT  PAGE_WRITECOPY      Image      [System_Collections; "C:\Program Files\dotnet\shared\Microsoft.NETCore.App\9.0.4\System.Collections.dll"]
      7ffe`df35e000      7ffe`df35f000        0`00001000 MEM_IMAGE   MEM_COMMIT  PAGE_READONLY       Image      [System_Collections; "C:\Program Files\dotnet\shared\Microsoft.NETCore.App\9.0.4\System.Collections.dll"]
+     7ffe`df35f000      7ffe`df360000        0`00001000             MEM_FREE    PAGE_NOACCESS       Free
+     7ffe`df360000      7ffe`df361000        0`00001000 MEM_IMAGE   MEM_COMMIT  PAGE_READONLY       Image      [System_Windows_Forms_Primitives; "C:\Program
Files\dotnet\shared\Microsoft.WindowsDesktop.App\9.0.4\System.Windows.Forms.Primitives.dll"]
      7ffe`df361000      7ffe`df700000        0`0039f000 MEM_IMAGE   MEM_COMMIT  PAGE_EXECUTE_READ   Image      [System_Windows_Forms_Primitives; "C:\Program
Files\dotnet\shared\Microsoft.WindowsDesktop.App\9.0.4\System.Windows.Forms.Primitives.dll"]
      7ffe`df700000      7ffe`df705000        0`00005000 MEM_IMAGE   MEM_COMMIT  PAGE_WRITECOPY      Image      [System_Windows_Forms_Primitives; "C:\Program
Files\dotnet\shared\Microsoft.WindowsDesktop.App\9.0.4\System.Windows.Forms.Primitives.dll"]
      7ffe`df705000      7ffe`df709000        0`00004000 MEM_IMAGE   MEM_COMMIT  PAGE_READWRITE      Image      [System_Windows_Forms_Primitives; "C:\Program
Files\dotnet\shared\Microsoft.WindowsDesktop.App\9.0.4\System.Windows.Forms.Primitives.dll"]
      7ffe`df709000      7ffe`df70d000        0`00004000 MEM_IMAGE   MEM_COMMIT  PAGE_WRITECOPY      Image      [System_Windows_Forms_Primitives; "C:\Program
Files\dotnet\shared\Microsoft.WindowsDesktop.App\9.0.4\System.Windows.Forms.Primitives.dll"]
      7ffe`df70d000      7ffe`df710000        0`00003000 MEM_IMAGE   MEM_COMMIT  PAGE_READWRITE      Image      [System_Windows_Forms_Primitives; "C:\Program
Files\dotnet\shared\Microsoft.WindowsDesktop.App\9.0.4\System.Windows.Forms.Primitives.dll"]
      7ffe`df710000      7ffe`df722000        0`00012000 MEM_IMAGE   MEM_COMMIT  PAGE_WRITECOPY      Image      [System_Windows_Forms_Primitives; "C:\Program
Files\dotnet\shared\Microsoft.WindowsDesktop.App\9.0.4\System.Windows.Forms.Primitives.dll"]
      7ffe`df722000      7ffe`df725000        0`00003000 MEM_IMAGE   MEM_COMMIT  PAGE_READONLY       Image      [System_Windows_Forms_Primitives; "C:\Program
Files\dotnet\shared\Microsoft.WindowsDesktop.App\9.0.4\System.Windows.Forms.Primitives.dll"]
+     7ffe`df725000      7ffe`df730000        0`0000b000             MEM_FREE    PAGE_NOACCESS       Free
+     7ffe`df730000      7ffe`df731000        0`00001000 MEM_IMAGE   MEM_COMMIT  PAGE_READONLY       Image      [System_Private_Windows_Core; "C:\Program
Files\dotnet\shared\Microsoft.WindowsDesktop.App\9.0.4\System.Private.Windows.Core.dll"]
      7ffe`df731000      7ffe`df84d000        0`0011c000 MEM_IMAGE   MEM_COMMIT  PAGE_EXECUTE_READ   Image      [System_Private_Windows_Core; "C:\Program
Files\dotnet\shared\Microsoft.WindowsDesktop.App\9.0.4\System.Private.Windows.Core.dll"]
      7ffe`df84d000      7ffe`df851000        0`00004000 MEM_IMAGE   MEM_COMMIT  PAGE_READWRITE      Image      [System_Private_Windows_Core; "C:\Program
Files\dotnet\shared\Microsoft.WindowsDesktop.App\9.0.4\System.Private.Windows.Core.dll"]
      7ffe`df851000      7ffe`df856000        0`00005000 MEM_IMAGE   MEM_COMMIT  PAGE_WRITECOPY      Image      [System_Private_Windows_Core; "C:\Program
Files\dotnet\shared\Microsoft.WindowsDesktop.App\9.0.4\System.Private.Windows.Core.dll"]
      7ffe`df856000      7ffe`df857000        0`00001000 MEM_IMAGE   MEM_COMMIT  PAGE_READONLY       Image      [System_Private_Windows_Core; "C:\Program
Files\dotnet\shared\Microsoft.WindowsDesktop.App\9.0.4\System.Private.Windows.Core.dll"]
+     7ffe`df857000      7ffe`df860000        0`00009000             MEM_FREE    PAGE_NOACCESS       Free
+     7ffe`df860000      7ffe`df861000        0`00001000 MEM_IMAGE   MEM_COMMIT  PAGE_READONLY       Image      [System_Windows_Forms; "C:\Program
Files\dotnet\shared\Microsoft.WindowsDesktop.App\9.0.4\System.Windows.Forms.dll"]
      7ffe`df861000      7ffe`e0504000        0`00ca3000 MEM_IMAGE   MEM_COMMIT  PAGE_EXECUTE_READ   Image      [System_Windows_Forms; "C:\Program
Files\dotnet\shared\Microsoft.WindowsDesktop.App\9.0.4\System.Windows.Forms.dll"]
      7ffe`e0504000      7ffe`e0505000        0`00001000 MEM_IMAGE   MEM_COMMIT  PAGE_WRITECOPY      Image      [System_Windows_Forms; "C:\Program
Files\dotnet\shared\Microsoft.WindowsDesktop.App\9.0.4\System.Windows.Forms.dll"]
      7ffe`e0505000      7ffe`e0506000        0`00001000 MEM_IMAGE   MEM_COMMIT  PAGE_READWRITE      Image      [System_Windows_Forms; "C:\Program
Files\dotnet\shared\Microsoft.WindowsDesktop.App\9.0.4\System.Windows.Forms.dll"]
      7ffe`e0506000      7ffe`e050b000        0`00005000 MEM_IMAGE   MEM_COMMIT  PAGE_WRITECOPY      Image      [System_Windows_Forms; "C:\Program
Files\dotnet\shared\Microsoft.WindowsDesktop.App\9.0.4\System.Windows.Forms.dll"]
      7ffe`e050b000      7ffe`e050d000        0`00002000 MEM_IMAGE   MEM_COMMIT  PAGE_READWRITE      Image      [System_Windows_Forms; "C:\Program
Files\dotnet\shared\Microsoft.WindowsDesktop.App\9.0.4\System.Windows.Forms.dll"]
      7ffe`e050d000      7ffe`e050e000        0`00001000 MEM_IMAGE   MEM_COMMIT  PAGE_WRITECOPY      Image      [System_Windows_Forms; "C:\Program
Files\dotnet\shared\Microsoft.WindowsDesktop.App\9.0.4\System.Windows.Forms.dll"]
      7ffe`e050e000      7ffe`e050f000        0`00001000 MEM_IMAGE   MEM_COMMIT  PAGE_READWRITE      Image      [System_Windows_Forms; "C:\Program
Files\dotnet\shared\Microsoft.WindowsDesktop.App\9.0.4\System.Windows.Forms.dll"]
      7ffe`e050f000      7ffe`e0510000        0`00001000 MEM_IMAGE   MEM_COMMIT  PAGE_WRITECOPY      Image      [System_Windows_Forms; "C:\Program
Files\dotnet\shared\Microsoft.WindowsDesktop.App\9.0.4\System.Windows.Forms.dll"]
      7ffe`e0510000      7ffe`e0514000        0`00004000 MEM_IMAGE   MEM_COMMIT  PAGE_READWRITE      Image      [System_Windows_Forms; "C:\Program
Files\dotnet\shared\Microsoft.WindowsDesktop.App\9.0.4\System.Windows.Forms.dll"]
      7ffe`e0514000      7ffe`e052a000        0`00016000 MEM_IMAGE   MEM_COMMIT  PAGE_WRITECOPY      Image      [System_Windows_Forms; "C:\Program
Files\dotnet\shared\Microsoft.WindowsDesktop.App\9.0.4\System.Windows.Forms.dll"]
      7ffe`e052a000      7ffe`e052b000        0`00001000 MEM_IMAGE   MEM_COMMIT  PAGE_READWRITE      Image      [System_Windows_Forms; "C:\Program
Files\dotnet\shared\Microsoft.WindowsDesktop.App\9.0.4\System.Windows.Forms.dll"]
      7ffe`e052b000      7ffe`e052c000        0`00001000 MEM_IMAGE   MEM_COMMIT  PAGE_WRITECOPY      Image      [System_Windows_Forms; "C:\Program
Files\dotnet\shared\Microsoft.WindowsDesktop.App\9.0.4\System.Windows.Forms.dll"]
      7ffe`e052c000      7ffe`e052e000        0`00002000 MEM_IMAGE   MEM_COMMIT  PAGE_READWRITE      Image      [System_Windows_Forms; "C:\Program
Files\dotnet\shared\Microsoft.WindowsDesktop.App\9.0.4\System.Windows.Forms.dll"]
      7ffe`e052e000      7ffe`e052f000        0`00001000 MEM_IMAGE   MEM_COMMIT  PAGE_WRITECOPY      Image      [System_Windows_Forms; "C:\Program
Files\dotnet\shared\Microsoft.WindowsDesktop.App\9.0.4\System.Windows.Forms.dll"]
      7ffe`e052f000      7ffe`e0530000        0`00001000 MEM_IMAGE   MEM_COMMIT  PAGE_READWRITE      Image      [System_Windows_Forms; "C:\Program
Files\dotnet\shared\Microsoft.WindowsDesktop.App\9.0.4\System.Windows.Forms.dll"]
      7ffe`e0530000      7ffe`e0534000        0`00004000 MEM_IMAGE   MEM_COMMIT  PAGE_WRITECOPY      Image      [System_Windows_Forms; "C:\Program
Files\dotnet\shared\Microsoft.WindowsDesktop.App\9.0.4\System.Windows.Forms.dll"]
      7ffe`e0534000      7ffe`e0535000        0`00001000 MEM_IMAGE   MEM_COMMIT  PAGE_READWRITE      Image      [System_Windows_Forms; "C:\Program
Files\dotnet\shared\Microsoft.WindowsDesktop.App\9.0.4\System.Windows.Forms.dll"]
      7ffe`e0535000      7ffe`e0539000        0`00004000 MEM_IMAGE   MEM_COMMIT  PAGE_WRITECOPY      Image      [System_Windows_Forms; "C:\Program
Files\dotnet\shared\Microsoft.WindowsDesktop.App\9.0.4\System.Windows.Forms.dll"]
      7ffe`e0539000      7ffe`e053a000        0`00001000 MEM_IMAGE   MEM_COMMIT  PAGE_READWRITE      Image      [System_Windows_Forms; "C:\Program
Files\dotnet\shared\Microsoft.WindowsDesktop.App\9.0.4\System.Windows.Forms.dll"]
      7ffe`e053a000      7ffe`e0576000        0`0003c000 MEM_IMAGE   MEM_COMMIT  PAGE_WRITECOPY      Image      [System_Windows_Forms; "C:\Program
Files\dotnet\shared\Microsoft.WindowsDesktop.App\9.0.4\System.Windows.Forms.dll"]
      7ffe`e0576000      7ffe`e0580000        0`0000a000 MEM_IMAGE   MEM_COMMIT  PAGE_READONLY       Image      [System_Windows_Forms; "C:\Program
Files\dotnet\shared\Microsoft.WindowsDesktop.App\9.0.4\System.Windows.Forms.dll"]
+     7ffe`e0580000      7ffe`e0581000        0`00001000 MEM_IMAGE   MEM_COMMIT  PAGE_READONLY       Image      [clrjit; "C:\Program Files\dotnet\shared\Microsoft.NETCore.App\9.0.4\clrjit.dll"]
      7ffe`e0581000      7ffe`e070b000        0`0018a000 MEM_IMAGE   MEM_COMMIT  PAGE_EXECUTE_READ   Image      [clrjit; "C:\Program Files\dotnet\shared\Microsoft.NETCore.App\9.0.4\clrjit.dll"]
      7ffe`e070b000      7ffe`e0748000        0`0003d000 MEM_IMAGE   MEM_COMMIT  PAGE_READONLY       Image      [clrjit; "C:\Program Files\dotnet\shared\Microsoft.NETCore.App\9.0.4\clrjit.dll"]
      7ffe`e0748000      7ffe`e074c000        0`00004000 MEM_IMAGE   MEM_COMMIT  PAGE_READWRITE      Image      [clrjit; "C:\Program Files\dotnet\shared\Microsoft.NETCore.App\9.0.4\clrjit.dll"]
      7ffe`e074c000      7ffe`e075f000        0`00013000 MEM_IMAGE   MEM_COMMIT  PAGE_READONLY       Image      [clrjit; "C:\Program Files\dotnet\shared\Microsoft.NETCore.App\9.0.4\clrjit.dll"]
+     7ffe`e075f000      7ffe`e0760000        0`00001000             MEM_FREE    PAGE_NOACCESS       Free
+     7ffe`e0760000      7ffe`e0761000        0`00001000 MEM_IMAGE   MEM_COMMIT  PAGE_READONLY       Image      [System_Private_CoreLib; "C:\Program
Files\dotnet\shared\Microsoft.NETCore.App\9.0.4\System.Private.CoreLib.dll"]
      7ffe`e0761000      7ffe`e154e000        0`00ded000 MEM_IMAGE   MEM_COMMIT  PAGE_EXECUTE_READ   Image      [System_Private_CoreLib; "C:\Program
Files\dotnet\shared\Microsoft.NETCore.App\9.0.4\System.Private.CoreLib.dll"]
      7ffe`e154e000      7ffe`e1565000        0`00017000 MEM_IMAGE   MEM_COMMIT  PAGE_READWRITE      Image      [System_Private_CoreLib; "C:\Program
Files\dotnet\shared\Microsoft.NETCore.App\9.0.4\System.Private.CoreLib.dll"]
      7ffe`e1565000      7ffe`e1566000        0`00001000 MEM_IMAGE   MEM_COMMIT  PAGE_WRITECOPY      Image      [System_Private_CoreLib; "C:\Program
Files\dotnet\shared\Microsoft.NETCore.App\9.0.4\System.Private.CoreLib.dll"]
      7ffe`e1566000      7ffe`e1589000        0`00023000 MEM_IMAGE   MEM_COMMIT  PAGE_READWRITE      Image      [System_Private_CoreLib; "C:\Program
Files\dotnet\shared\Microsoft.NETCore.App\9.0.4\System.Private.CoreLib.dll"]
      7ffe`e1589000      7ffe`e15e0000        0`00057000 MEM_IMAGE   MEM_COMMIT  PAGE_WRITECOPY      Image      [System_Private_CoreLib; "C:\Program
Files\dotnet\shared\Microsoft.NETCore.App\9.0.4\System.Private.CoreLib.dll"]
```

```
     7ffe`e15e0000     7ffe`e15ec000        0`0000c000 MEM_IMAGE   MEM_COMMIT  PAGE_READONLY       Image      [System_Private_CoreLib; "C:\Program
Files\dotnet\shared\Microsoft.NETCore.App\9.0.4\System.Private.CoreLib.dll"]
+    7ffe`e15ec000     7ffe`e15f0000        0`00004000             MEM_FREE    PAGE_NOACCESS       Free
+    7ffe`e15f0000     7ffe`e15f1000        0`00001000 MEM_IMAGE   MEM_COMMIT  PAGE_READONLY       Image      [coreclr; "C:\Program Files\dotnet\shared\Microsoft.NETCore.App\9.0.4\coreclr.dll"]
     7ffe`e15f1000     7ffe`e1981000        0`00390000 MEM_IMAGE   MEM_COMMIT  PAGE_EXECUTE_READ   Image      [coreclr; "C:\Program Files\dotnet\shared\Microsoft.NETCore.App\9.0.4\coreclr.dll"]
     7ffe`e1981000     7ffe`e1a4b000        0`000ca000 MEM_IMAGE   MEM_COMMIT  PAGE_READONLY       Image      [coreclr; "C:\Program Files\dotnet\shared\Microsoft.NETCore.App\9.0.4\coreclr.dll"]
     7ffe`e1a4b000     7ffe`e1a4d000        0`00002000 MEM_IMAGE   MEM_COMMIT  PAGE_READWRITE      Image      [coreclr; "C:\Program Files\dotnet\shared\Microsoft.NETCore.App\9.0.4\coreclr.dll"]
     7ffe`e1a4d000     7ffe`e1a4e000        0`00001000 MEM_IMAGE   MEM_COMMIT  PAGE_WRITECOPY      Image      [coreclr; "C:\Program Files\dotnet\shared\Microsoft.NETCore.App\9.0.4\coreclr.dll"]
     7ffe`e1a4e000     7ffe`e1a52000        0`00004000 MEM_IMAGE   MEM_COMMIT  PAGE_READWRITE      Image      [coreclr; "C:\Program Files\dotnet\shared\Microsoft.NETCore.App\9.0.4\coreclr.dll"]
     7ffe`e1a52000     7ffe`e1a54000        0`00002000 MEM_IMAGE   MEM_COMMIT  PAGE_WRITECOPY      Image      [coreclr; "C:\Program Files\dotnet\shared\Microsoft.NETCore.App\9.0.4\coreclr.dll"]
     7ffe`e1a54000     7ffe`e1a62000        0`0000e000 MEM_IMAGE   MEM_COMMIT  PAGE_READWRITE      Image      [coreclr; "C:\Program Files\dotnet\shared\Microsoft.NETCore.App\9.0.4\coreclr.dll"]
     7ffe`e1a62000     7ffe`e1a92000        0`00030000 MEM_IMAGE   MEM_COMMIT  PAGE_READONLY       Image      [coreclr; "C:\Program Files\dotnet\shared\Microsoft.NETCore.App\9.0.4\coreclr.dll"]
     7ffe`e1a92000     7ffe`e1a93000        0`00001000 MEM_IMAGE   MEM_COMMIT  PAGE_READWRITE      Image      [coreclr; "C:\Program Files\dotnet\shared\Microsoft.NETCore.App\9.0.4\coreclr.dll"]
     7ffe`e1a93000     7ffe`e1a9a000        0`00007000 MEM_IMAGE   MEM_COMMIT  PAGE_READONLY       Image      [coreclr; "C:\Program Files\dotnet\shared\Microsoft.NETCore.App\9.0.4\coreclr.dll"]
+    7ffe`e1a9a000     7ffe`e1aa0000        0`00006000             MEM_FREE    PAGE_NOACCESS       Free
+    7ffe`e1aa0000     7ffe`e1aa1000        0`00001000 MEM_IMAGE   MEM_COMMIT  PAGE_READONLY       Image      [hostpolicy; "C:\Program Files\dotnet\shared\Microsoft.NETCore.App\9.0.4\hostpolicy.dll"]
     7ffe`e1aa1000     7ffe`e1ae1000        0`00040000 MEM_IMAGE   MEM_COMMIT  PAGE_EXECUTE_READ   Image      [hostpolicy; "C:\Program Files\dotnet\shared\Microsoft.NETCore.App\9.0.4\hostpolicy.dll"]
     7ffe`e1ae1000     7ffe`e1af6000        0`00015000 MEM_IMAGE   MEM_COMMIT  PAGE_READONLY       Image      [hostpolicy; "C:\Program Files\dotnet\shared\Microsoft.NETCore.App\9.0.4\hostpolicy.dll"]
     7ffe`e1af6000     7ffe`e1af8000        0`00002000 MEM_IMAGE   MEM_COMMIT  PAGE_READWRITE      Image      [hostpolicy; "C:\Program Files\dotnet\shared\Microsoft.NETCore.App\9.0.4\hostpolicy.dll"]
     7ffe`e1af8000     7ffe`e1afe000        0`00006000 MEM_IMAGE   MEM_COMMIT  PAGE_READONLY       Image      [hostpolicy; "C:\Program Files\dotnet\shared\Microsoft.NETCore.App\9.0.4\hostpolicy.dll"]
+    7ffe`e1afe000     7ffe`e7370000        0`05872000             MEM_FREE    PAGE_NOACCESS       Free
+    7ffe`e7370000     7ffe`e7371000        0`00001000 MEM_IMAGE   MEM_COMMIT  PAGE_READONLY       Image      [System_Diagnostics_TextWriterTraceListener; "C:\Program
Files\dotnet\shared\Microsoft.NETCore.App\9.0.4\System.Diagnostics.TextWriterTraceListener.dll"]
     7ffe`e7371000     7ffe`e737c000        0`0000b000 MEM_IMAGE   MEM_COMMIT  PAGE_EXECUTE_READ   Image      [System_Diagnostics_TextWriterTraceListener; "C:\Program
Files\dotnet\shared\Microsoft.NETCore.App\9.0.4\System.Diagnostics.TextWriterTraceListener.dll"]
     7ffe`e737c000     7ffe`e737d000        0`00001000 MEM_IMAGE   MEM_COMMIT  PAGE_READWRITE      Image      [System_Diagnostics_TextWriterTraceListener; "C:\Program
Files\dotnet\shared\Microsoft.NETCore.App\9.0.4\System.Diagnostics.TextWriterTraceListener.dll"]
     7ffe`e737d000     7ffe`e737e000        0`00001000 MEM_IMAGE   MEM_COMMIT  PAGE_READONLY       Image      [System_Diagnostics_TextWriterTraceListener; "C:\Program
Files\dotnet\shared\Microsoft.NETCore.App\9.0.4\System.Diagnostics.TextWriterTraceListener.dll"]
+    7ffe`e737e000     7ffe`e7380000        0`00002000             MEM_FREE    PAGE_NOACCESS       Free
+    7ffe`e7380000     7ffe`e7381000        0`00001000 MEM_IMAGE   MEM_COMMIT  PAGE_READONLY       Image      [System_Diagnostics_TraceSource; "C:\Program
Files\dotnet\shared\Microsoft.NETCore.App\9.0.4\System.Diagnostics.TraceSource.dll"]
     7ffe`e7381000     7ffe`e739e000        0`0001d000 MEM_IMAGE   MEM_COMMIT  PAGE_EXECUTE_READ   Image      [System_Diagnostics_TraceSource; "C:\Program
Files\dotnet\shared\Microsoft.NETCore.App\9.0.4\System.Diagnostics.TraceSource.dll"]
     7ffe`e739e000     7ffe`e739f000        0`00001000 MEM_IMAGE   MEM_COMMIT  PAGE_READWRITE      Image      [System_Diagnostics_TraceSource; "C:\Program
Files\dotnet\shared\Microsoft.NETCore.App\9.0.4\System.Diagnostics.TraceSource.dll"]
     7ffe`e739f000     7ffe`e73a0000        0`00001000 MEM_IMAGE   MEM_COMMIT  PAGE_WRITECOPY      Image      [System_Diagnostics_TraceSource; "C:\Program
Files\dotnet\shared\Microsoft.NETCore.App\9.0.4\System.Diagnostics.TraceSource.dll"]
     7ffe`e73a0000     7ffe`e73a1000        0`00001000 MEM_IMAGE   MEM_COMMIT  PAGE_READONLY       Image      [System_Diagnostics_TraceSource; "C:\Program
Files\dotnet\shared\Microsoft.NETCore.App\9.0.4\System.Diagnostics.TraceSource.dll"]
+    7ffe`e73a1000     7ffe`e74b0000        0`0010f000             MEM_FREE    PAGE_NOACCESS       Free
+    7ffe`e74b0000     7ffe`e74b1000        0`00001000 MEM_IMAGE   MEM_COMMIT  PAGE_READONLY       Image      [System_IO_MemoryMappedFiles; "C:\Program
Files\dotnet\shared\Microsoft.NETCore.App\9.0.4\System.IO.MemoryMappedFiles.dll"]
     7ffe`e74b1000     7ffe`e74bf000        0`0000e000 MEM_IMAGE   MEM_COMMIT  PAGE_EXECUTE_READ   Image      [System_IO_MemoryMappedFiles; "C:\Program
Files\dotnet\shared\Microsoft.NETCore.App\9.0.4\System.IO.MemoryMappedFiles.dll"]
     7ffe`e74bf000     7ffe`e74c0000        0`00001000 MEM_IMAGE   MEM_COMMIT  PAGE_READWRITE      Image      [System_IO_MemoryMappedFiles; "C:\Program
Files\dotnet\shared\Microsoft.NETCore.App\9.0.4\System.IO.MemoryMappedFiles.dll"]
     7ffe`e74c0000     7ffe`e74c1000        0`00001000 MEM_IMAGE   MEM_COMMIT  PAGE_WRITECOPY      Image      [System_IO_MemoryMappedFiles; "C:\Program
Files\dotnet\shared\Microsoft.NETCore.App\9.0.4\System.IO.MemoryMappedFiles.dll"]
     7ffe`e74c1000     7ffe`e74c2000        0`00001000 MEM_IMAGE   MEM_COMMIT  PAGE_READONLY       Image      [System_IO_MemoryMappedFiles; "C:\Program
Files\dotnet\shared\Microsoft.NETCore.App\9.0.4\System.IO.MemoryMappedFiles.dll"]
+    7ffe`e74c2000     7ffe`e76b0000        0`001ee000             MEM_FREE    PAGE_NOACCESS       Free
+    7ffe`e76b0000     7ffe`e76b1000        0`00001000 MEM_IMAGE   MEM_COMMIT  PAGE_READONLY       Image      [hostfxr; "C:\Program Files\dotnet\host\fxr\9.0.4\hostfxr.dll"]
     7ffe`e76b1000     7ffe`e76ec000        0`0003b000 MEM_IMAGE   MEM_COMMIT  PAGE_EXECUTE_READ   Image      [hostfxr; "C:\Program Files\dotnet\host\fxr\9.0.4\hostfxr.dll"]
     7ffe`e76ec000     7ffe`e7702000        0`00016000 MEM_IMAGE   MEM_COMMIT  PAGE_READONLY       Image      [hostfxr; "C:\Program Files\dotnet\host\fxr\9.0.4\hostfxr.dll"]
     7ffe`e7702000     7ffe`e7704000        0`00002000 MEM_IMAGE   MEM_COMMIT  PAGE_READWRITE      Image      [hostfxr; "C:\Program Files\dotnet\host\fxr\9.0.4\hostfxr.dll"]
     7ffe`e7704000     7ffe`e7709000        0`00005000 MEM_IMAGE   MEM_COMMIT  PAGE_READONLY       Image      [hostfxr; "C:\Program Files\dotnet\host\fxr\9.0.4\hostfxr.dll"]
+    7ffe`e7709000     7fff`000d0000        0`189c7000             MEM_FREE    PAGE_NOACCESS       Free
+    7fff`000d0000     7fff`000d1000        0`00001000 MEM_IMAGE   MEM_COMMIT  PAGE_READONLY       Image      [System_Diagnostics_FileVersionInfo; "C:\Program
Files\dotnet\shared\Microsoft.NETCore.App\9.0.4\System.Diagnostics.FileVersionInfo.dll"]
     7fff`000d1000     7fff`000d7000        0`00006000 MEM_IMAGE   MEM_COMMIT  PAGE_EXECUTE_READ   Image      [System_Diagnostics_FileVersionInfo; "C:\Program
Files\dotnet\shared\Microsoft.NETCore.App\9.0.4\System.Diagnostics.FileVersionInfo.dll"]
     7fff`000d7000     7fff`000d8000        0`00001000 MEM_IMAGE   MEM_COMMIT  PAGE_READWRITE      Image      [System_Diagnostics_FileVersionInfo; "C:\Program
Files\dotnet\shared\Microsoft.NETCore.App\9.0.4\System.Diagnostics.FileVersionInfo.dll"]
     7fff`000d8000     7fff`000d9000        0`00001000 MEM_IMAGE   MEM_COMMIT  PAGE_READONLY       Image      [System_Diagnostics_FileVersionInfo; "C:\Program
Files\dotnet\shared\Microsoft.NETCore.App\9.0.4\System.Diagnostics.FileVersionInfo.dll"]
+    7fff`000d9000     7fff`09590000        0`094b7000             MEM_FREE    PAGE_NOACCESS       Free
+    7fff`09590000     7fff`09591000        0`00001000 MEM_IMAGE   MEM_COMMIT  PAGE_READONLY       Image      [System_IO_Compression; "C:\Program Files\dotnet\shared\Microsoft.NETCore.App\9.0.4\System.IO.Compression.dll"]
     7fff`09591000     7fff`095ca000        0`00039000 MEM_IMAGE   MEM_COMMIT  PAGE_EXECUTE_READ   Image      [System_IO_Compression; "C:\Program Files\dotnet\shared\Microsoft.NETCore.App\9.0.4\System.IO.Compression.dll"]
     7fff`095ca000     7fff`095cc000        0`00002000 MEM_IMAGE   MEM_COMMIT  PAGE_READWRITE      Image      [System_IO_Compression; "C:\Program Files\dotnet\shared\Microsoft.NETCore.App\9.0.4\System.IO.Compression.dll"]
     7fff`095cc000     7fff`095ce000        0`00002000 MEM_IMAGE   MEM_COMMIT  PAGE_WRITECOPY      Image      [System_IO_Compression; "C:\Program Files\dotnet\shared\Microsoft.NETCore.App\9.0.4\System.IO.Compression.dll"]
     7fff`095ce000     7fff`095cf000        0`00001000 MEM_IMAGE   MEM_COMMIT  PAGE_READONLY       Image      [System_IO_Compression; "C:\Program Files\dotnet\shared\Microsoft.NETCore.App\9.0.4\System.IO.Compression.dll"]
+    7fff`095cf000     7fff`15b60000        0`0c591000             MEM_FREE    PAGE_NOACCESS       Free
+    7fff`15b60000     7fff`15b61000        0`00001000 MEM_IMAGE   MEM_COMMIT  PAGE_READONLY       Image      [System_Drawing_Primitives; "C:\Program
Files\dotnet\shared\Microsoft.NETCore.App\9.0.4\System.Drawing.Primitives.dll"]
     7fff`15b61000     7fff`15b7c000        0`0001b000 MEM_IMAGE   MEM_COMMIT  PAGE_EXECUTE_READ   Image      [System_Drawing_Primitives; "C:\Program
Files\dotnet\shared\Microsoft.NETCore.App\9.0.4\System.Drawing.Primitives.dll"]
     7fff`15b7c000     7fff`15b7d000        0`00001000 MEM_IMAGE   MEM_COMMIT  PAGE_READWRITE      Image      [System_Drawing_Primitives; "C:\Program
Files\dotnet\shared\Microsoft.NETCore.App\9.0.4\System.Drawing.Primitives.dll"]
     7fff`15b7d000     7fff`15b7e000        0`00001000 MEM_IMAGE   MEM_COMMIT  PAGE_WRITECOPY      Image      [System_Drawing_Primitives; "C:\Program
Files\dotnet\shared\Microsoft.NETCore.App\9.0.4\System.Drawing.Primitives.dll"]
     7fff`15b7e000     7fff`15b7f000        0`00001000 MEM_IMAGE   MEM_COMMIT  PAGE_READONLY       Image      [System_Drawing_Primitives; "C:\Program
Files\dotnet\shared\Microsoft.NETCore.App\9.0.4\System.Drawing.Primitives.dll"]
+    7fff`15b7f000     7fff`175d0000        0`01a51000             MEM_FREE    PAGE_NOACCESS       Free
+    7fff`175d0000     7fff`175d1000        0`00001000 MEM_IMAGE   MEM_COMMIT  PAGE_READONLY       Image      [System_ComponentModel; "C:\Program Files\dotnet\shared\Microsoft.NETCore.App\9.0.4\System.ComponentModel.dll"]
     7fff`175d1000     7fff`175d3000        0`00002000 MEM_IMAGE   MEM_COMMIT  PAGE_EXECUTE_READ   Image      [System_ComponentModel; "C:\Program Files\dotnet\shared\Microsoft.NETCore.App\9.0.4\System.ComponentModel.dll"]
     7fff`175d3000     7fff`175d4000        0`00001000 MEM_IMAGE   MEM_COMMIT  PAGE_READWRITE      Image      [System_ComponentModel; "C:\Program Files\dotnet\shared\Microsoft.NETCore.App\9.0.4\System.ComponentModel.dll"]
     7fff`175d4000     7fff`175d5000        0`00001000 MEM_IMAGE   MEM_COMMIT  PAGE_READONLY       Image      [System_ComponentModel; "C:\Program Files\dotnet\shared\Microsoft.NETCore.App\9.0.4\System.ComponentModel.dll"]
+    7fff`175d5000     7fff`17890000        0`002bb000             MEM_FREE    PAGE_NOACCESS       Free
+    7fff`17890000     7fff`17891000        0`00001000 MEM_IMAGE   MEM_COMMIT  PAGE_READONLY       Image      [System_ComponentModel_Primitives; "C:\Program
Files\dotnet\shared\Microsoft.NETCore.App\9.0.4\System.ComponentModel.Primitives.dll"]
     7fff`17891000     7fff`1789f000        0`0000e000 MEM_IMAGE   MEM_COMMIT  PAGE_EXECUTE_READ   Image      [System_ComponentModel_Primitives; "C:\Program
Files\dotnet\shared\Microsoft.NETCore.App\9.0.4\System.ComponentModel.Primitives.dll"]
     7fff`1789f000     7fff`178a0000        0`00001000 MEM_IMAGE   MEM_COMMIT  PAGE_READWRITE      Image      [System_ComponentModel_Primitives; "C:\Program
Files\dotnet\shared\Microsoft.NETCore.App\9.0.4\System.ComponentModel.Primitives.dll"]
     7fff`178a0000     7fff`178a1000        0`00001000 MEM_IMAGE   MEM_COMMIT  PAGE_READONLY       Image      [System_ComponentModel_Primitives; "C:\Program
Files\dotnet\shared\Microsoft.NETCore.App\9.0.4\System.ComponentModel.Primitives.dll"]
+    7fff`178a1000     7fff`179b0000        0`0010f000             MEM_FREE    PAGE_NOACCESS       Free
+    7fff`179b0000     7fff`179b1000        0`00001000 MEM_IMAGE   MEM_COMMIT  PAGE_READONLY       Image      [System_Threading; "C:\Program Files\dotnet\shared\Microsoft.NETCore.App\9.0.4\System.Threading.dll"]
     7fff`179b1000     7fff`179c0000        0`0000f000 MEM_IMAGE   MEM_COMMIT  PAGE_EXECUTE_READ   Image      [System_Threading; "C:\Program Files\dotnet\shared\Microsoft.NETCore.App\9.0.4\System.Threading.dll"]
     7fff`179c0000     7fff`179c1000        0`00001000 MEM_IMAGE   MEM_COMMIT  PAGE_READWRITE      Image      [System_Threading; "C:\Program Files\dotnet\shared\Microsoft.NETCore.App\9.0.4\System.Threading.dll"]
     7fff`179c1000     7fff`179c2000        0`00001000 MEM_IMAGE   MEM_COMMIT  PAGE_READONLY       Image      [System_Threading; "C:\Program Files\dotnet\shared\Microsoft.NETCore.App\9.0.4\System.Threading.dll"]
+    7fff`179c2000     7fff`179d0000        0`0000e000             MEM_FREE    PAGE_NOACCESS       Free
+    7fff`179d0000     7fff`179d1000        0`00001000 MEM_IMAGE   MEM_COMMIT  PAGE_READONLY       Image      [System_Console; "C:\Program Files\dotnet\shared\Microsoft.NETCore.App\9.0.4\System.Console.dll"]
     7fff`179d1000     7fff`179f4000        0`00023000 MEM_IMAGE   MEM_COMMIT  PAGE_EXECUTE_READ   Image      [System_Console; "C:\Program Files\dotnet\shared\Microsoft.NETCore.App\9.0.4\System.Console.dll"]
     7fff`179f4000     7fff`179f6000        0`00002000 MEM_IMAGE   MEM_COMMIT  PAGE_READWRITE      Image      [System_Console; "C:\Program Files\dotnet\shared\Microsoft.NETCore.App\9.0.4\System.Console.dll"]
     7fff`179f6000     7fff`179f7000        0`00001000 MEM_IMAGE   MEM_COMMIT  PAGE_WRITECOPY      Image      [System_Console; "C:\Program Files\dotnet\shared\Microsoft.NETCore.App\9.0.4\System.Console.dll"]
     7fff`179f7000     7fff`179f8000        0`00001000 MEM_IMAGE   MEM_COMMIT  PAGE_READONLY       Image      [System_Console; "C:\Program Files\dotnet\shared\Microsoft.NETCore.App\9.0.4\System.Console.dll"]
+    7fff`179f8000     7fff`180e0000        0`006e8000             MEM_FREE    PAGE_NOACCESS       Free
+    7fff`180e0000     7fff`180e1000        0`00001000 MEM_IMAGE   MEM_COMMIT  PAGE_READONLY       Image      [System_Runtime_InteropServices; "C:\Program
Files\dotnet\shared\Microsoft.NETCore.App\9.0.4\System.Runtime.InteropServices.dll"]
     7fff`180e1000     7fff`180f6000        0`00015000 MEM_IMAGE   MEM_COMMIT  PAGE_EXECUTE_READ   Image      [System_Runtime_InteropServices; "C:\Program
Files\dotnet\shared\Microsoft.NETCore.App\9.0.4\System.Runtime.InteropServices.dll"]
     7fff`180f6000     7fff`180f7000        0`00001000 MEM_IMAGE   MEM_COMMIT  PAGE_READWRITE      Image      [System_Runtime_InteropServices; "C:\Program
Files\dotnet\shared\Microsoft.NETCore.App\9.0.4\System.Runtime.InteropServices.dll"]
     7fff`180f7000     7fff`180f8000        0`00001000 MEM_IMAGE   MEM_COMMIT  PAGE_WRITECOPY      Image      [System_Runtime_InteropServices; "C:\Program
Files\dotnet\shared\Microsoft.NETCore.App\9.0.4\System.Runtime.InteropServices.dll"]
     7fff`180f8000     7fff`180f9000        0`00001000 MEM_IMAGE   MEM_COMMIT  PAGE_READONLY       Image      [System_Runtime_InteropServices; "C:\Program
Files\dotnet\shared\Microsoft.NETCore.App\9.0.4\System.Runtime.InteropServices.dll"]
+    7fff`180f9000     7fff`2f720000        0`17627000             MEM_FREE    PAGE_NOACCESS       Free
+    7fff`2f720000     7fff`2f721000        0`00001000 MEM_IMAGE   MEM_COMMIT  PAGE_READONLY       Image      [MpClient; "C:\ProgramData\Microsoft\Windows Defender\Platform\4.18.25030.2-0\MpClient.dll"]
     7fff`2f721000     7fff`2f830000        0`0010f000 MEM_IMAGE   MEM_COMMIT  PAGE_EXECUTE_READ   Image      [MpClient; "C:\ProgramData\Microsoft\Windows Defender\Platform\4.18.25030.2-0\MpClient.dll"]
     7fff`2f830000     7fff`2f88d000        0`0005d000 MEM_IMAGE   MEM_COMMIT  PAGE_READONLY       Image      [MpClient; "C:\ProgramData\Microsoft\Windows Defender\Platform\4.18.25030.2-0\MpClient.dll"]
     7fff`2f88d000     7fff`2f88e000        0`00001000 MEM_IMAGE   MEM_COMMIT  PAGE_READWRITE      Image      [MpClient; "C:\ProgramData\Microsoft\Windows Defender\Platform\4.18.25030.2-0\MpClient.dll"]
     7fff`2f88e000     7fff`2f896000        0`00008000 MEM_IMAGE   MEM_COMMIT  PAGE_WRITECOPY      Image      [MpClient; "C:\ProgramData\Microsoft\Windows Defender\Platform\4.18.25030.2-0\MpClient.dll"]
     7fff`2f896000     7fff`2f89a000        0`00004000 MEM_IMAGE   MEM_COMMIT  PAGE_READWRITE      Image      [MpClient; "C:\ProgramData\Microsoft\Windows Defender\Platform\4.18.25030.2-0\MpClient.dll"]
     7fff`2f89a000     7fff`2f89c000        0`00002000 MEM_IMAGE   MEM_COMMIT  PAGE_WRITECOPY      Image      [MpClient; "C:\ProgramData\Microsoft\Windows Defender\Platform\4.18.25030.2-0\MpClient.dll"]
     7fff`2f89c000     7fff`2f89d000        0`00001000 MEM_IMAGE   MEM_COMMIT  PAGE_READWRITE      Image      [MpClient; "C:\ProgramData\Microsoft\Windows Defender\Platform\4.18.25030.2-0\MpClient.dll"]
     7fff`2f89d000     7fff`2f8af000        0`00012000 MEM_IMAGE   MEM_COMMIT  PAGE_READONLY       Image      [MpClient; "C:\ProgramData\Microsoft\Windows Defender\Platform\4.18.25030.2-0\MpClient.dll"]
+    7fff`2f8af000     7fff`31050000        0`017a1000             MEM_FREE    PAGE_NOACCESS       Free
+    7fff`31050000     7fff`31051000        0`00001000 MEM_IMAGE   MEM_COMMIT  PAGE_READONLY       Image      [icu; "C:\Windows\System32\icu.dll"]
     7fff`31051000     7fff`311f9000        0`001a8000 MEM_IMAGE   MEM_COMMIT  PAGE_EXECUTE_READ   Image      [icu; "C:\Windows\System32\icu.dll"]
     7fff`311f9000     7fff`31295000        0`0009c000 MEM_IMAGE   MEM_COMMIT  PAGE_READONLY       Image      [icu; "C:\Windows\System32\icu.dll"]
     7fff`31295000     7fff`31296000        0`00001000 MEM_IMAGE   MEM_COMMIT  PAGE_READWRITE      Image      [icu; "C:\Windows\System32\icu.dll"]
     7fff`31296000     7fff`31297000        0`00001000 MEM_IMAGE   MEM_COMMIT  PAGE_WRITECOPY      Image      [icu; "C:\Windows\System32\icu.dll"]
     7fff`31297000     7fff`31298000        0`00001000 MEM_IMAGE   MEM_COMMIT  PAGE_READWRITE      Image      [icu; "C:\Windows\System32\icu.dll"]
     7fff`31298000     7fff`3129c000        0`00004000 MEM_IMAGE   MEM_COMMIT  PAGE_WRITECOPY      Image      [icu; "C:\Windows\System32\icu.dll"]
     7fff`3129c000     7fff`3129f000        0`00003000 MEM_IMAGE   MEM_COMMIT  PAGE_READWRITE      Image      [icu; "C:\Windows\System32\icu.dll"]
     7fff`3129f000     7fff`312a0000        0`00001000 MEM_IMAGE   MEM_COMMIT  PAGE_WRITECOPY      Image      [icu; "C:\Windows\System32\icu.dll"]
     7fff`312a0000     7fff`312ba000        0`0001a000 MEM_IMAGE   MEM_COMMIT  PAGE_READONLY       Image      [icu; "C:\Windows\System32\icu.dll"]
+    7fff`312ba000     7fff`38520000        0`07266000             MEM_FREE    PAGE_NOACCESS       Free
+    7fff`38520000     7fff`38521000        0`00001000 MEM_IMAGE   MEM_COMMIT  PAGE_READONLY       Image      [version; "C:\Windows\System32\version.dll"]
     7fff`38521000     7fff`38524000        0`00003000 MEM_IMAGE   MEM_COMMIT  PAGE_EXECUTE_READ   Image      [version; "C:\Windows\System32\version.dll"]
     7fff`38524000     7fff`38526000        0`00002000 MEM_IMAGE   MEM_COMMIT  PAGE_READONLY       Image      [version; "C:\Windows\System32\version.dll"]
     7fff`38526000     7fff`38527000        0`00001000 MEM_IMAGE   MEM_COMMIT  PAGE_READWRITE      Image      [version; "C:\Windows\System32\version.dll"]
     7fff`38527000     7fff`3852a000        0`00003000 MEM_IMAGE   MEM_COMMIT  PAGE_READONLY       Image      [version; "C:\Windows\System32\version.dll"]
+    7fff`3852a000     7fff`38570000        0`00046000             MEM_FREE    PAGE_NOACCESS       Free
+    7fff`38570000     7fff`38571000        0`00001000 MEM_IMAGE   MEM_COMMIT  PAGE_READONLY       Image      [MpOAV; "C:\ProgramData\Microsoft\Windows Defender\Platform\4.18.25030.2-0\MpOAV.dll"]
```

```
    7fff`38571000   7fff`385b7000   0`00046000 MEM_IMAGE  MEM_COMMIT  PAGE_EXECUTE_READ   Image   [MpOAV; "C:\ProgramData\Microsoft\Windows Defender\Platform\4.18.25030.2-0\MpOAV.dll"]
    7fff`385b7000   7fff`385d1000   0`0001a000 MEM_IMAGE  MEM_COMMIT  PAGE_READONLY       Image   [MpOAV; "C:\ProgramData\Microsoft\Windows Defender\Platform\4.18.25030.2-0\MpOAV.dll"]
    7fff`385d1000   7fff`385d2000   0`00001000 MEM_IMAGE  MEM_COMMIT  PAGE_READWRITE      Image   [MpOAV; "C:\ProgramData\Microsoft\Windows Defender\Platform\4.18.25030.2-0\MpOAV.dll"]
    7fff`385d2000   7fff`385d4000   0`00002000 MEM_IMAGE  MEM_COMMIT  PAGE_WRITECOPY      Image   [MpOAV; "C:\ProgramData\Microsoft\Windows Defender\Platform\4.18.25030.2-0\MpOAV.dll"]
    7fff`385d4000   7fff`385d7000   0`00003000 MEM_IMAGE  MEM_COMMIT  PAGE_READWRITE      Image   [MpOAV; "C:\ProgramData\Microsoft\Windows Defender\Platform\4.18.25030.2-0\MpOAV.dll"]
    7fff`385d7000   7fff`3860b000   0`00034000 MEM_IMAGE  MEM_COMMIT  PAGE_READONLY       Image   [MpOAV; "C:\ProgramData\Microsoft\Windows Defender\Platform\4.18.25030.2-0\MpOAV.dll"]
+   7fff`3860b000   7fff`38830000   0`00225000            MEM_FREE    PAGE_NOACCESS       Free
+   7fff`38830000   7fff`38831000   0`00001000 MEM_IMAGE  MEM_COMMIT  PAGE_READONLY       Image   [amsi; "C:\Windows\System32\amsi.dll"]
    7fff`38831000   7fff`38843000   0`00012000 MEM_IMAGE  MEM_COMMIT  PAGE_EXECUTE_READ   Image   [amsi; "C:\Windows\System32\amsi.dll"]
    7fff`38843000   7fff`3884b000   0`00008000 MEM_IMAGE  MEM_COMMIT  PAGE_READONLY       Image   [amsi; "C:\Windows\System32\amsi.dll"]
    7fff`3884b000   7fff`3884d000   0`00002000 MEM_IMAGE  MEM_COMMIT  PAGE_READWRITE      Image   [amsi; "C:\Windows\System32\amsi.dll"]
    7fff`3884d000   7fff`38853000   0`00006000 MEM_IMAGE  MEM_COMMIT  PAGE_READONLY       Image   [amsi; "C:\Windows\System32\amsi.dll"]
+   7fff`38853000   7fff`3be90000   0`0363d000            MEM_FREE    PAGE_NOACCESS       Free
+   7fff`3be90000   7fff`3be91000   0`00001000 MEM_IMAGE  MEM_COMMIT  PAGE_READONLY       Image   [System_Diagnostics_StackTrace; "C:\Program
Files\dotnet\shared\Microsoft.NETCore.App\9.0.4\System.Diagnostics.StackTrace.dll"]
    7fff`3be91000   7fff`3be97000   0`00006000 MEM_IMAGE  MEM_COMMIT  PAGE_EXECUTE_READ   Image   [System_Diagnostics_StackTrace; "C:\Program
Files\dotnet\shared\Microsoft.NETCore.App\9.0.4\System.Diagnostics.StackTrace.dll"]
    7fff`3be97000   7fff`3be98000   0`00001000 MEM_IMAGE  MEM_COMMIT  PAGE_READWRITE      Image   [System_Diagnostics_StackTrace; "C:\Program
Files\dotnet\shared\Microsoft.NETCore.App\9.0.4\System.Diagnostics.StackTrace.dll"]
    7fff`3be98000   7fff`3be99000   0`00001000 MEM_IMAGE  MEM_COMMIT  PAGE_READONLY       Image   [System_Diagnostics_StackTrace; "C:\Program
Files\dotnet\shared\Microsoft.NETCore.App\9.0.4\System.Diagnostics.StackTrace.dll"]
+   7fff`3be99000   7fff`3c0e0000   0`00247000            MEM_FREE    PAGE_NOACCESS       Free
+   7fff`3c0e0000   7fff`3c0e1000   0`00001000 MEM_IMAGE  MEM_COMMIT  PAGE_READONLY       Image   [uxtheme; "C:\Windows\System32\uxtheme.dll"]
    7fff`3c0e1000   7fff`3c149000   0`00068000 MEM_IMAGE  MEM_COMMIT  PAGE_EXECUTE_READ   Image   [uxtheme; "C:\Windows\System32\uxtheme.dll"]
    7fff`3c149000   7fff`3c17e000   0`00035000 MEM_IMAGE  MEM_COMMIT  PAGE_READONLY       Image   [uxtheme; "C:\Windows\System32\uxtheme.dll"]
    7fff`3c17e000   7fff`3c180000   0`00002000 MEM_IMAGE  MEM_COMMIT  PAGE_READWRITE      Image   [uxtheme; "C:\Windows\System32\uxtheme.dll"]
    7fff`3c180000   7fff`3c181000   0`00001000 MEM_IMAGE  MEM_COMMIT  PAGE_WRITECOPY      Image   [uxtheme; "C:\Windows\System32\uxtheme.dll"]
    7fff`3c181000   7fff`3c18c000   0`0000b000 MEM_IMAGE  MEM_COMMIT  PAGE_READONLY       Image   [uxtheme; "C:\Windows\System32\uxtheme.dll"]
+   7fff`3c18c000   7fff`3c9d0000   0`00844000            MEM_FREE    PAGE_NOACCESS       Free
+   7fff`3c9d0000   7fff`3c9d1000   0`00001000 MEM_IMAGE  MEM_COMMIT  PAGE_READONLY       Image   [WinTypes; "C:\Windows\System32\WinTypes.dll"]
    7fff`3c9d1000   7fff`3ca55000   0`00084000 MEM_IMAGE  MEM_COMMIT  PAGE_EXECUTE_READ   Image   [WinTypes; "C:\Windows\System32\WinTypes.dll"]
    7fff`3ca55000   7fff`3cb11000   0`000bc000 MEM_IMAGE  MEM_COMMIT  PAGE_READONLY       Image   [WinTypes; "C:\Windows\System32\WinTypes.dll"]
    7fff`3cb11000   7fff`3cb13000   0`00002000 MEM_IMAGE  MEM_COMMIT  PAGE_READWRITE      Image   [WinTypes; "C:\Windows\System32\WinTypes.dll"]
    7fff`3cb13000   7fff`3cb37000   0`00024000 MEM_IMAGE  MEM_COMMIT  PAGE_READONLY       Image   [WinTypes; "C:\Windows\System32\WinTypes.dll"]
+   7fff`3cb37000   7fff`3cb40000   0`00009000            MEM_FREE    PAGE_NOACCESS       Free
+   7fff`3cb40000   7fff`3cb41000   0`00001000 MEM_IMAGE  MEM_COMMIT  PAGE_READONLY       Image   [windows_storage; "C:\Windows\System32\windows.storage.dll"]
    7fff`3cb41000   7fff`3d184000   0`00643000 MEM_IMAGE  MEM_COMMIT  PAGE_EXECUTE_READ   Image   [windows_storage; "C:\Windows\System32\windows.storage.dll"]
    7fff`3d184000   7fff`3d31a000   0`00196000 MEM_IMAGE  MEM_COMMIT  PAGE_READONLY       Image   [windows_storage; "C:\Windows\System32\windows.storage.dll"]
    7fff`3d31a000   7fff`3d321000   0`00007000 MEM_IMAGE  MEM_COMMIT  PAGE_READWRITE      Image   [windows_storage; "C:\Windows\System32\windows.storage.dll"]
    7fff`3d321000   7fff`3d322000   0`00001000 MEM_IMAGE  MEM_COMMIT  PAGE_WRITECOPY      Image   [windows_storage; "C:\Windows\System32\windows.storage.dll"]
    7fff`3d322000   7fff`3d3a4000   0`00082000 MEM_IMAGE  MEM_COMMIT  PAGE_READONLY       Image   [windows_storage; "C:\Windows\System32\windows.storage.dll"]
+   7fff`3d3a4000   7fff`3dad0000   0`0072c000            MEM_FREE    PAGE_NOACCESS       Free
+   7fff`3dad0000   7fff`3dad1000   0`00001000 MEM_IMAGE  MEM_COMMIT  PAGE_READONLY       Image   [kernel_appcore; "C:\Windows\System32\kernel.appcore.dll"]
    7fff`3dad1000   7fff`3dada000   0`00009000 MEM_IMAGE  MEM_COMMIT  PAGE_EXECUTE_READ   Image   [kernel_appcore; "C:\Windows\System32\kernel.appcore.dll"]
    7fff`3dada000   7fff`3dae3000   0`00009000 MEM_IMAGE  MEM_COMMIT  PAGE_READONLY       Image   [kernel_appcore; "C:\Windows\System32\kernel.appcore.dll"]
    7fff`3dae3000   7fff`3dae4000   0`00001000 MEM_IMAGE  MEM_COMMIT  PAGE_READWRITE      Image   [kernel_appcore; "C:\Windows\System32\kernel.appcore.dll"]
    7fff`3dae4000   7fff`3dae8000   0`00004000 MEM_IMAGE  MEM_COMMIT  PAGE_READONLY       Image   [kernel_appcore; "C:\Windows\System32\kernel.appcore.dll"]
+   7fff`3dae8000   7fff`3dfc0000   0`004d8000            MEM_FREE    PAGE_NOACCESS       Free
+   7fff`3dfc0000   7fff`3dfc1000   0`00001000 MEM_IMAGE  MEM_COMMIT  PAGE_READONLY       Image   [gpapi; "C:\Windows\System32\gpapi.dll"]
    7fff`3dfc1000   7fff`3dfd3000   0`00012000 MEM_IMAGE  MEM_COMMIT  PAGE_EXECUTE_READ   Image   [gpapi; "C:\Windows\System32\gpapi.dll"]
    7fff`3dfd3000   7fff`3dfde000   0`0000b000 MEM_IMAGE  MEM_COMMIT  PAGE_READONLY       Image   [gpapi; "C:\Windows\System32\gpapi.dll"]
    7fff`3dfde000   7fff`3dfe0000   0`00002000 MEM_IMAGE  MEM_COMMIT  PAGE_READWRITE      Image   [gpapi; "C:\Windows\System32\gpapi.dll"]
    7fff`3dfe0000   7fff`3dfe4000   0`00004000 MEM_IMAGE  MEM_COMMIT  PAGE_READONLY       Image   [gpapi; "C:\Windows\System32\gpapi.dll"]
+   7fff`3dfe4000   7fff`3dff0000   0`0000c000            MEM_FREE    PAGE_NOACCESS       Free
+   7fff`3dff0000   7fff`3dff1000   0`00001000 MEM_IMAGE  MEM_COMMIT  PAGE_READONLY       Image   [userenv; "C:\Windows\System32\userenv.dll"]
    7fff`3dff1000   7fff`3e007000   0`00016000 MEM_IMAGE  MEM_COMMIT  PAGE_EXECUTE_READ   Image   [userenv; "C:\Windows\System32\userenv.dll"]
    7fff`3e007000   7fff`3e011000   0`0000a000 MEM_IMAGE  MEM_COMMIT  PAGE_READONLY       Image   [userenv; "C:\Windows\System32\userenv.dll"]
    7fff`3e011000   7fff`3e012000   0`00001000 MEM_IMAGE  MEM_COMMIT  PAGE_READWRITE      Image   [userenv; "C:\Windows\System32\userenv.dll"]
    7fff`3e012000   7fff`3e019000   0`00007000 MEM_IMAGE  MEM_COMMIT  PAGE_READONLY       Image   [userenv; "C:\Windows\System32\userenv.dll"]
+   7fff`3e019000   7fff`3e270000   0`00257000            MEM_FREE    PAGE_NOACCESS       Free
+   7fff`3e270000   7fff`3e271000   0`00001000 MEM_IMAGE  MEM_COMMIT  PAGE_READONLY       Image   [msasn1; "C:\Windows\System32\msasn1.dll"]
    7fff`3e271000   7fff`3e27a000   0`00009000 MEM_IMAGE  MEM_COMMIT  PAGE_EXECUTE_READ   Image   [msasn1; "C:\Windows\System32\msasn1.dll"]
    7fff`3e27a000   7fff`3e27e000   0`00004000 MEM_IMAGE  MEM_COMMIT  PAGE_READONLY       Image   [msasn1; "C:\Windows\System32\msasn1.dll"]
    7fff`3e27e000   7fff`3e27f000   0`00001000 MEM_IMAGE  MEM_COMMIT  PAGE_READWRITE      Image   [msasn1; "C:\Windows\System32\msasn1.dll"]
    7fff`3e27f000   7fff`3e282000   0`00003000 MEM_IMAGE  MEM_COMMIT  PAGE_READONLY       Image   [msasn1; "C:\Windows\System32\msasn1.dll"]
+   7fff`3e282000   7fff`3e990000   0`0070e000            MEM_FREE    PAGE_NOACCESS       Free
+   7fff`3e990000   7fff`3e991000   0`00001000 MEM_IMAGE  MEM_COMMIT  PAGE_READONLY       Image   [profapi; "C:\Windows\System32\profapi.dll"]
    7fff`3e991000   7fff`3e9a3000   0`00012000 MEM_IMAGE  MEM_COMMIT  PAGE_EXECUTE_READ   Image   [profapi; "C:\Windows\System32\profapi.dll"]
    7fff`3e9a3000   7fff`3e9ab000   0`00008000 MEM_IMAGE  MEM_COMMIT  PAGE_READONLY       Image   [profapi; "C:\Windows\System32\profapi.dll"]
    7fff`3e9ab000   7fff`3e9ac000   0`00001000 MEM_IMAGE  MEM_COMMIT  PAGE_READWRITE      Image   [profapi; "C:\Windows\System32\profapi.dll"]
    7fff`3e9ac000   7fff`3e9b1000   0`00005000 MEM_IMAGE  MEM_COMMIT  PAGE_READONLY       Image   [profapi; "C:\Windows\System32\profapi.dll"]
+   7fff`3e9b1000   7fff`3ea60000   0`000af000            MEM_FREE    PAGE_NOACCESS       Free
+   7fff`3ea60000   7fff`3ea61000   0`00001000 MEM_IMAGE  MEM_COMMIT  PAGE_READONLY       Image   [wintrust; "C:\Windows\System32\wintrust.dll"]
    7fff`3ea61000   7fff`3eaa9000   0`00048000 MEM_IMAGE  MEM_COMMIT  PAGE_EXECUTE_READ   Image   [wintrust; "C:\Windows\System32\wintrust.dll"]
    7fff`3eaa9000   7fff`3eabd000   0`00014000 MEM_IMAGE  MEM_COMMIT  PAGE_READONLY       Image   [wintrust; "C:\Windows\System32\wintrust.dll"]
    7fff`3eabd000   7fff`3eabf000   0`00002000 MEM_IMAGE  MEM_COMMIT  PAGE_READWRITE      Image   [wintrust; "C:\Windows\System32\wintrust.dll"]
    7fff`3eabf000   7fff`3eac7000   0`00008000 MEM_IMAGE  MEM_COMMIT  PAGE_READONLY       Image   [wintrust; "C:\Windows\System32\wintrust.dll"]
+   7fff`3eac7000   7fff`3eb90000   0`000c9000            MEM_FREE    PAGE_NOACCESS       Free
+   7fff`3eb90000   7fff`3eb91000   0`00001000 MEM_IMAGE  MEM_COMMIT  PAGE_READONLY       Image   [bcrypt; "C:\Windows\System32\bcrypt.dll"]
    7fff`3eb91000   7fff`3ebab000   0`0001a000 MEM_IMAGE  MEM_COMMIT  PAGE_EXECUTE_READ   Image   [bcrypt; "C:\Windows\System32\bcrypt.dll"]
    7fff`3ebab000   7fff`3ebb1000   0`00006000 MEM_IMAGE  MEM_COMMIT  PAGE_READONLY       Image   [bcrypt; "C:\Windows\System32\bcrypt.dll"]
    7fff`3ebb1000   7fff`3ebb2000   0`00001000 MEM_IMAGE  MEM_COMMIT  PAGE_READWRITE      Image   [bcrypt; "C:\Windows\System32\bcrypt.dll"]
    7fff`3ebb2000   7fff`3ebb7000   0`00005000 MEM_IMAGE  MEM_COMMIT  PAGE_READONLY       Image   [bcrypt; "C:\Windows\System32\bcrypt.dll"]
+   7fff`3ebb7000   7fff`3ebc0000   0`00009000            MEM_FREE    PAGE_NOACCESS       Free
+   7fff`3ebc0000   7fff`3ebc1000   0`00001000 MEM_IMAGE  MEM_COMMIT  PAGE_READONLY       Image   [ucrtbase; "C:\Windows\System32\ucrtbase.dll"]
    7fff`3ebc1000   7fff`3ec84000   0`000c3000 MEM_IMAGE  MEM_COMMIT  PAGE_EXECUTE_READ   Image   [ucrtbase; "C:\Windows\System32\ucrtbase.dll"]
    7fff`3ec84000   7fff`3ecbf000   0`0003b000 MEM_IMAGE  MEM_COMMIT  PAGE_READONLY       Image   [ucrtbase; "C:\Windows\System32\ucrtbase.dll"]
    7fff`3ecbf000   7fff`3ecc2000   0`00003000 MEM_IMAGE  MEM_COMMIT  PAGE_READWRITE      Image   [ucrtbase; "C:\Windows\System32\ucrtbase.dll"]
    7fff`3ecc2000   7fff`3ecd1000   0`0000f000 MEM_IMAGE  MEM_COMMIT  PAGE_READONLY       Image   [ucrtbase; "C:\Windows\System32\ucrtbase.dll"]
+   7fff`3ecd1000   7fff`3ece0000   0`0000f000            MEM_FREE    PAGE_NOACCESS       Free
+   7fff`3ece0000   7fff`3ece1000   0`00001000 MEM_IMAGE  MEM_COMMIT  PAGE_READONLY       Image   [bcryptPrimitives; "C:\Windows\System32\bcryptPrimitives.dll"]
    7fff`3ece1000   7fff`3ed42000   0`00061000 MEM_IMAGE  MEM_COMMIT  PAGE_EXECUTE_READ   Image   [bcryptPrimitives; "C:\Windows\System32\bcryptPrimitives.dll"]
    7fff`3ed42000   7fff`3ed58000   0`00016000 MEM_IMAGE  MEM_COMMIT  PAGE_READONLY       Image   [bcryptPrimitives; "C:\Windows\System32\bcryptPrimitives.dll"]
    7fff`3ed58000   7fff`3ed59000   0`00001000 MEM_IMAGE  MEM_COMMIT  PAGE_READWRITE      Image   [bcryptPrimitives; "C:\Windows\System32\bcryptPrimitives.dll"]
    7fff`3ed59000   7fff`3ed5f000   0`00006000 MEM_IMAGE  MEM_COMMIT  PAGE_READONLY       Image   [bcryptPrimitives; "C:\Windows\System32\bcryptPrimitives.dll"]
+   7fff`3ed5f000   7fff`3ed60000   0`00001000            MEM_FREE    PAGE_NOACCESS       Free
+   7fff`3ed60000   7fff`3ed61000   0`00001000 MEM_IMAGE  MEM_COMMIT  PAGE_READONLY       Image   [gdi32full; "C:\Windows\System32\gdi32full.dll"]
    7fff`3ed61000   7fff`3ee0a000   0`000a9000 MEM_IMAGE  MEM_COMMIT  PAGE_EXECUTE_READ   Image   [gdi32full; "C:\Windows\System32\gdi32full.dll"]
    7fff`3ee0a000   7fff`3ee5a000   0`00050000 MEM_IMAGE  MEM_COMMIT  PAGE_READONLY       Image   [gdi32full; "C:\Windows\System32\gdi32full.dll"]
    7fff`3ee5a000   7fff`3ee5f000   0`00005000 MEM_IMAGE  MEM_COMMIT  PAGE_READWRITE      Image   [gdi32full; "C:\Windows\System32\gdi32full.dll"]
    7fff`3ee5f000   7fff`3ee7c000   0`0001d000 MEM_IMAGE  MEM_COMMIT  PAGE_READONLY       Image   [gdi32full; "C:\Windows\System32\gdi32full.dll"]
+   7fff`3ee7c000   7fff`3ee80000   0`00004000            MEM_FREE    PAGE_NOACCESS       Free
+   7fff`3ee80000   7fff`3ee81000   0`00001000 MEM_IMAGE  MEM_COMMIT  PAGE_READONLY       Image   [crypt32; "C:\Windows\System32\crypt32.dll"]
    7fff`3ee81000   7fff`3ef94000   0`00113000 MEM_IMAGE  MEM_COMMIT  PAGE_EXECUTE_READ   Image   [crypt32; "C:\Windows\System32\crypt32.dll"]
    7fff`3ef94000   7fff`3efca000   0`00036000 MEM_IMAGE  MEM_COMMIT  PAGE_READONLY       Image   [crypt32; "C:\Windows\System32\crypt32.dll"]
    7fff`3efca000   7fff`3efd1000   0`00007000 MEM_IMAGE  MEM_COMMIT  PAGE_READWRITE      Image   [crypt32; "C:\Windows\System32\crypt32.dll"]
    7fff`3efd1000   7fff`3efe2000   0`00011000 MEM_IMAGE  MEM_COMMIT  PAGE_READONLY       Image   [crypt32; "C:\Windows\System32\crypt32.dll"]
+   7fff`3efe2000   7fff`3eff0000   0`0000e000            MEM_FREE    PAGE_NOACCESS       Free
+   7fff`3eff0000   7fff`3eff1000   0`00001000 MEM_IMAGE  MEM_COMMIT  PAGE_READONLY       Image   [win32u; "C:\Windows\System32\win32u.dll"]
    7fff`3eff1000   7fff`3effd000   0`0000c000 MEM_IMAGE  MEM_COMMIT  PAGE_EXECUTE_READ   Image   [win32u; "C:\Windows\System32\win32u.dll"]
    7fff`3effd000   7fff`3f00e000   0`00011000 MEM_IMAGE  MEM_COMMIT  PAGE_READONLY       Image   [win32u; "C:\Windows\System32\win32u.dll"]
    7fff`3f00e000   7fff`3f00f000   0`00001000 MEM_IMAGE  MEM_COMMIT  PAGE_READWRITE      Image   [win32u; "C:\Windows\System32\win32u.dll"]
    7fff`3f00f000   7fff`3f016000   0`00007000 MEM_IMAGE  MEM_COMMIT  PAGE_READONLY       Image   [win32u; "C:\Windows\System32\win32u.dll"]
+   7fff`3f016000   7fff`3f020000   0`0000a000            MEM_FREE    PAGE_NOACCESS       Free
+   7fff`3f020000   7fff`3f021000   0`00001000 MEM_IMAGE  MEM_COMMIT  PAGE_READONLY       Image   [KERNELBASE; "C:\Windows\System32\KERNELBASE.dll"]
    7fff`3f021000   7fff`3f1a1000   0`00180000 MEM_IMAGE  MEM_COMMIT  PAGE_EXECUTE_READ   Image   [KERNELBASE; "C:\Windows\System32\KERNELBASE.dll"]
    7fff`3f1a1000   7fff`3f357000   0`001b6000 MEM_IMAGE  MEM_COMMIT  PAGE_READONLY       Image   [KERNELBASE; "C:\Windows\System32\KERNELBASE.dll"]
    7fff`3f357000   7fff`3f35c000   0`00005000 MEM_IMAGE  MEM_COMMIT  PAGE_READWRITE      Image   [KERNELBASE; "C:\Windows\System32\KERNELBASE.dll"]
    7fff`3f35c000   7fff`3f3a5000   0`00049000 MEM_IMAGE  MEM_COMMIT  PAGE_READONLY       Image   [KERNELBASE; "C:\Windows\System32\KERNELBASE.dll"]
+   7fff`3f3a5000   7fff`3f3b0000   0`0000b000            MEM_FREE    PAGE_NOACCESS       Free
+   7fff`3f3b0000   7fff`3f3b1000   0`00001000 MEM_IMAGE  MEM_COMMIT  PAGE_READONLY       Image   [msvcp_win; "C:\Windows\System32\msvcp_win.dll"]
    7fff`3f3b1000   7fff`3f406000   0`00055000 MEM_IMAGE  MEM_COMMIT  PAGE_EXECUTE_READ   Image   [msvcp_win; "C:\Windows\System32\msvcp_win.dll"]
    7fff`3f406000   7fff`3f441000   0`0003b000 MEM_IMAGE  MEM_COMMIT  PAGE_READONLY       Image   [msvcp_win; "C:\Windows\System32\msvcp_win.dll"]
    7fff`3f441000   7fff`3f442000   0`00001000 MEM_IMAGE  MEM_COMMIT  PAGE_WRITECOPY      Image   [msvcp_win; "C:\Windows\System32\msvcp_win.dll"]
    7fff`3f442000   7fff`3f445000   0`00003000 MEM_IMAGE  MEM_COMMIT  PAGE_READWRITE      Image   [msvcp_win; "C:\Windows\System32\msvcp_win.dll"]
    7fff`3f445000   7fff`3f44d000   0`00008000 MEM_IMAGE  MEM_COMMIT  PAGE_READONLY       Image   [msvcp_win; "C:\Windows\System32\msvcp_win.dll"]
+   7fff`3f44d000   7fff`3f450000   0`00003000            MEM_FREE    PAGE_NOACCESS       Free
+   7fff`3f450000   7fff`3f451000   0`00001000 MEM_IMAGE  MEM_COMMIT  PAGE_READONLY       Image   [msvcrt; "C:\Windows\System32\msvcrt.dll"]
    7fff`3f451000   7fff`3f4ca000   0`00079000 MEM_IMAGE  MEM_COMMIT  PAGE_EXECUTE_READ   Image   [msvcrt; "C:\Windows\System32\msvcrt.dll"]
    7fff`3f4ca000   7fff`3f4e4000   0`0001a000 MEM_IMAGE  MEM_COMMIT  PAGE_READONLY       Image   [msvcrt; "C:\Windows\System32\msvcrt.dll"]
    7fff`3f4e4000   7fff`3f4e7000   0`00003000 MEM_IMAGE  MEM_COMMIT  PAGE_READWRITE      Image   [msvcrt; "C:\Windows\System32\msvcrt.dll"]
    7fff`3f4e7000   7fff`3f4e9000   0`00002000 MEM_IMAGE  MEM_COMMIT  PAGE_WRITECOPY      Image   [msvcrt; "C:\Windows\System32\msvcrt.dll"]
    7fff`3f4e9000   7fff`3f4ec000   0`00003000 MEM_IMAGE  MEM_COMMIT  PAGE_READWRITE      Image   [msvcrt; "C:\Windows\System32\msvcrt.dll"]
    7fff`3f4ec000   7fff`3f4f3000   0`00007000 MEM_IMAGE  MEM_COMMIT  PAGE_READONLY       Image   [msvcrt; "C:\Windows\System32\msvcrt.dll"]
+   7fff`3f4f3000   7fff`3f500000   0`0000d000            MEM_FREE    PAGE_NOACCESS       Free
+   7fff`3f500000   7fff`3f501000   0`00001000 MEM_IMAGE  MEM_COMMIT  PAGE_READONLY       Image   [ole32; "C:\Windows\System32\ole32.dll"]
    7fff`3f501000   7fff`3f5db000   0`000da000 MEM_IMAGE  MEM_COMMIT  PAGE_EXECUTE_READ   Image   [ole32; "C:\Windows\System32\ole32.dll"]
    7fff`3f5db000   7fff`3f60c000   0`00031000 MEM_IMAGE  MEM_COMMIT  PAGE_READONLY       Image   [ole32; "C:\Windows\System32\ole32.dll"]
    7fff`3f60c000   7fff`3f60e000   0`00002000 MEM_IMAGE  MEM_COMMIT  PAGE_READWRITE      Image   [ole32; "C:\Windows\System32\ole32.dll"]
    7fff`3f60e000   7fff`3f60f000   0`00001000 MEM_IMAGE  MEM_COMMIT  PAGE_WRITECOPY      Image   [ole32; "C:\Windows\System32\ole32.dll"]
    7fff`3f60f000   7fff`3f69a000   0`0008b000 MEM_IMAGE  MEM_COMMIT  PAGE_READONLY       Image   [ole32; "C:\Windows\System32\ole32.dll"]
+   7fff`3f69a000   7fff`3f6a0000   0`00006000            MEM_FREE    PAGE_NOACCESS       Free
+   7fff`3f6a0000   7fff`3f6a1000   0`00001000 MEM_IMAGE  MEM_COMMIT  PAGE_READONLY       Image   [shell32; "C:\Windows\System32\shell32.dll"]
    7fff`3f6a1000   7fff`3fcae000   0`0060d000 MEM_IMAGE  MEM_COMMIT  PAGE_EXECUTE_READ   Image   [shell32; "C:\Windows\System32\shell32.dll"]
    7fff`3fcae000   7fff`3fdf4000   0`00146000 MEM_IMAGE  MEM_COMMIT  PAGE_READONLY       Image   [shell32; "C:\Windows\System32\shell32.dll"]
    7fff`3fdf4000   7fff`3fdfd000   0`00009000 MEM_IMAGE  MEM_COMMIT  PAGE_READWRITE      Image   [shell32; "C:\Windows\System32\shell32.dll"]
    7fff`3fdfd000   7fff`3fdfe000   0`00001000 MEM_IMAGE  MEM_COMMIT  PAGE_WRITECOPY      Image   [shell32; "C:\Windows\System32\shell32.dll"]
    7fff`3fdfe000   7fff`3fe66000   0`00068000 MEM_IMAGE  MEM_COMMIT  PAGE_READONLY       Image   [shell32; "C:\Windows\System32\shell32.dll"]
```

```
  +    7fff`3fe66000   7fff`400e0000   0`0027a000              MEM_FREE    PAGE_NOACCESS      Free
  +    7fff`400e0000   7fff`400e1000   0`00001000 MEM_IMAGE   MEM_COMMIT  PAGE_READONLY       Image  [kernel32; "C:\Windows\System32\kernel32.dll"]
       7fff`400e1000   7fff`4015e000   0`0007d000 MEM_IMAGE   MEM_COMMIT  PAGE_EXECUTE_READ   Image  [kernel32; "C:\Windows\System32\kernel32.dll"]
       7fff`4015e000   7fff`40192000   0`00034000 MEM_IMAGE   MEM_COMMIT  PAGE_READONLY       Image  [kernel32; "C:\Windows\System32\kernel32.dll"]
       7fff`40192000   7fff`40193000   0`00001000 MEM_IMAGE   MEM_COMMIT  PAGE_READWRITE      Image  [kernel32; "C:\Windows\System32\kernel32.dll"]
       7fff`40193000   7fff`40194000   0`00001000 MEM_IMAGE   MEM_COMMIT  PAGE_WRITECOPY      Image  [kernel32; "C:\Windows\System32\kernel32.dll"]
       7fff`40194000   7fff`4019d000   0`00009000 MEM_IMAGE   MEM_COMMIT  PAGE_READONLY       Image  [kernel32; "C:\Windows\System32\kernel32.dll"]
  +    7fff`4019d000   7fff`401b0000   0`00013000              MEM_FREE    PAGE_NOACCESS      Free
  +    7fff`401b0000   7fff`401b1000   0`00001000 MEM_IMAGE   MEM_COMMIT  PAGE_READONLY       Image  [imm32; "C:\Windows\System32\imm32.dll"]
       7fff`401b1000   7fff`401d0000   0`0001f000 MEM_IMAGE   MEM_COMMIT  PAGE_EXECUTE_READ   Image  [imm32; "C:\Windows\System32\imm32.dll"]
       7fff`401d0000   7fff`401d7000   0`00007000 MEM_IMAGE   MEM_COMMIT  PAGE_READONLY       Image  [imm32; "C:\Windows\System32\imm32.dll"]
       7fff`401d7000   7fff`401d8000   0`00001000 MEM_IMAGE   MEM_COMMIT  PAGE_READWRITE      Image  [imm32; "C:\Windows\System32\imm32.dll"]
       7fff`401d8000   7fff`401e1000   0`00009000 MEM_IMAGE   MEM_COMMIT  PAGE_READONLY       Image  [imm32; "C:\Windows\System32\imm32.dll"]
  +    7fff`401e1000   7fff`401f0000   0`0000f000              MEM_FREE    PAGE_NOACCESS      Free
  +    7fff`401f0000   7fff`401f1000   0`00001000 MEM_IMAGE   MEM_COMMIT  PAGE_READONLY       Image  [gdi32; "C:\Windows\System32\gdi32.dll"]
       7fff`401f1000   7fff`401ff000   0`0000e000 MEM_IMAGE   MEM_COMMIT  PAGE_EXECUTE_READ   Image  [gdi32; "C:\Windows\System32\gdi32.dll"]
       7fff`401ff000   7fff`40213000   0`00014000 MEM_IMAGE   MEM_COMMIT  PAGE_READONLY       Image  [gdi32; "C:\Windows\System32\gdi32.dll"]
       7fff`40213000   7fff`40214000   0`00001000 MEM_IMAGE   MEM_COMMIT  PAGE_READWRITE      Image  [gdi32; "C:\Windows\System32\gdi32.dll"]
       7fff`40214000   7fff`40219000   0`00005000 MEM_IMAGE   MEM_COMMIT  PAGE_READONLY       Image  [gdi32; "C:\Windows\System32\gdi32.dll"]
  +    7fff`40219000   7fff`40220000   0`00007000              MEM_FREE    PAGE_NOACCESS      Free
  +    7fff`40220000   7fff`40221000   0`00001000 MEM_IMAGE   MEM_COMMIT  PAGE_READONLY       Image  [advapi32; "C:\Windows\System32\advapi32.dll"]
       7fff`40221000   7fff`4028b000   0`0006a000 MEM_IMAGE   MEM_COMMIT  PAGE_EXECUTE_READ   Image  [advapi32; "C:\Windows\System32\advapi32.dll"]
       7fff`4028b000   7fff`402c3000   0`00038000 MEM_IMAGE   MEM_COMMIT  PAGE_READONLY       Image  [advapi32; "C:\Windows\System32\advapi32.dll"]
       7fff`402c3000   7fff`402c4000   0`00001000 MEM_IMAGE   MEM_COMMIT  PAGE_READWRITE      Image  [advapi32; "C:\Windows\System32\advapi32.dll"]
       7fff`402c4000   7fff`402c5000   0`00001000 MEM_IMAGE   MEM_COMMIT  PAGE_WRITECOPY      Image  [advapi32; "C:\Windows\System32\advapi32.dll"]
       7fff`402c5000   7fff`402c7000   0`00002000 MEM_IMAGE   MEM_COMMIT  PAGE_READWRITE      Image  [advapi32; "C:\Windows\System32\advapi32.dll"]
       7fff`402c7000   7fff`402c8000   0`00001000 MEM_IMAGE   MEM_COMMIT  PAGE_WRITECOPY      Image  [advapi32; "C:\Windows\System32\advapi32.dll"]
       7fff`402c8000   7fff`402d1000   0`00009000 MEM_IMAGE   MEM_COMMIT  PAGE_READONLY       Image  [advapi32; "C:\Windows\System32\advapi32.dll"]
  +    7fff`402d1000   7fff`40370000   0`0009f000              MEM_FREE    PAGE_NOACCESS      Free
  +    7fff`40370000   7fff`40371000   0`00001000 MEM_IMAGE   MEM_COMMIT  PAGE_READONLY       Image  [user32; "C:\Windows\System32\user32.dll"]
       7fff`40371000   7fff`40405000   0`00094000 MEM_IMAGE   MEM_COMMIT  PAGE_EXECUTE_READ   Image  [user32; "C:\Windows\System32\user32.dll"]
       7fff`40405000   7fff`40427000   0`00022000 MEM_IMAGE   MEM_COMMIT  PAGE_READONLY       Image  [user32; "C:\Windows\System32\user32.dll"]
       7fff`40427000   7fff`40429000   0`00002000 MEM_IMAGE   MEM_COMMIT  PAGE_READWRITE      Image  [user32; "C:\Windows\System32\user32.dll"]
       7fff`40429000   7fff`4051c000   0`000f3000 MEM_IMAGE   MEM_COMMIT  PAGE_READONLY       Image  [user32; "C:\Windows\System32\user32.dll"]
  +    7fff`4051c000   7fff`40610000   0`000f4000              MEM_FREE    PAGE_NOACCESS      Free
  +    7fff`40610000   7fff`40611000   0`00001000 MEM_IMAGE   MEM_COMMIT  PAGE_READONLY       Image  [SHCore; "C:\Windows\System32\SHCore.dll"]
       7fff`40611000   7fff`406b3000   0`000a2000 MEM_IMAGE   MEM_COMMIT  PAGE_EXECUTE_READ   Image  [SHCore; "C:\Windows\System32\SHCore.dll"]
       7fff`406b3000   7fff`406e7000   0`00034000 MEM_IMAGE   MEM_COMMIT  PAGE_READONLY       Image  [SHCore; "C:\Windows\System32\SHCore.dll"]
       7fff`406e7000   7fff`406e9000   0`00002000 MEM_IMAGE   MEM_COMMIT  PAGE_READWRITE      Image  [SHCore; "C:\Windows\System32\SHCore.dll"]
       7fff`406e9000   7fff`406fa000   0`00011000 MEM_IMAGE   MEM_COMMIT  PAGE_READONLY       Image  [SHCore; "C:\Windows\System32\SHCore.dll"]
  +    7fff`406fa000   7fff`40700000   0`00006000              MEM_FREE    PAGE_NOACCESS      Free
  +    7fff`40700000   7fff`40701000   0`00001000 MEM_IMAGE   MEM_COMMIT  PAGE_READONLY       Image  [shlwapi; "C:\Windows\System32\shlwapi.dll"]
       7fff`40701000   7fff`40735000   0`00034000 MEM_IMAGE   MEM_COMMIT  PAGE_EXECUTE_READ   Image  [shlwapi; "C:\Windows\System32\shlwapi.dll"]
       7fff`40735000   7fff`40755000   0`00020000 MEM_IMAGE   MEM_COMMIT  PAGE_READONLY       Image  [shlwapi; "C:\Windows\System32\shlwapi.dll"]
       7fff`40755000   7fff`40757000   0`00002000 MEM_IMAGE   MEM_COMMIT  PAGE_READWRITE      Image  [shlwapi; "C:\Windows\System32\shlwapi.dll"]
       7fff`40757000   7fff`4075d000   0`00006000 MEM_IMAGE   MEM_COMMIT  PAGE_READONLY       Image  [shlwapi; "C:\Windows\System32\shlwapi.dll"]
  +    7fff`4075d000   7fff`40770000   0`00013000              MEM_FREE    PAGE_NOACCESS      Free
  +    7fff`40770000   7fff`40771000   0`00001000 MEM_IMAGE   MEM_COMMIT  PAGE_READONLY       Image  [rpcrt4; "C:\Windows\System32\rpcrt4.dll"]
       7fff`40771000   7fff`40851000   0`000e0000 MEM_IMAGE   MEM_COMMIT  PAGE_EXECUTE_READ   Image  [rpcrt4; "C:\Windows\System32\rpcrt4.dll"]
       7fff`40851000   7fff`4087a000   0`00029000 MEM_IMAGE   MEM_COMMIT  PAGE_READONLY       Image  [rpcrt4; "C:\Windows\System32\rpcrt4.dll"]
       7fff`4087a000   7fff`4087c000   0`00002000 MEM_IMAGE   MEM_COMMIT  PAGE_READWRITE      Image  [rpcrt4; "C:\Windows\System32\rpcrt4.dll"]
       7fff`4087c000   7fff`40891000   0`00015000 MEM_IMAGE   MEM_COMMIT  PAGE_READONLY       Image  [rpcrt4; "C:\Windows\System32\rpcrt4.dll"]
  +    7fff`40891000   7fff`40eb0000   0`0061f000              MEM_FREE    PAGE_NOACCESS      Free
  +    7fff`40eb0000   7fff`40eb1000   0`00001000 MEM_IMAGE   MEM_COMMIT  PAGE_READONLY       Image  [sechost; "C:\Windows\System32\sechost.dll"]
       7fff`40eb1000   7fff`40f1a000   0`00069000 MEM_IMAGE   MEM_COMMIT  PAGE_EXECUTE_READ   Image  [sechost; "C:\Windows\System32\sechost.dll"]
       7fff`40f1a000   7fff`40f43000   0`00029000 MEM_IMAGE   MEM_COMMIT  PAGE_READONLY       Image  [sechost; "C:\Windows\System32\sechost.dll"]
       7fff`40f43000   7fff`40f44000   0`00001000 MEM_IMAGE   MEM_COMMIT  PAGE_READWRITE      Image  [sechost; "C:\Windows\System32\sechost.dll"]
       7fff`40f44000   7fff`40f45000   0`00001000 MEM_IMAGE   MEM_COMMIT  PAGE_WRITECOPY      Image  [sechost; "C:\Windows\System32\sechost.dll"]
       7fff`40f45000   7fff`40f47000   0`00002000 MEM_IMAGE   MEM_COMMIT  PAGE_READWRITE      Image  [sechost; "C:\Windows\System32\sechost.dll"]
       7fff`40f47000   7fff`40f51000   0`0000a000 MEM_IMAGE   MEM_COMMIT  PAGE_READONLY       Image  [sechost; "C:\Windows\System32\sechost.dll"]
  +    7fff`40f51000   7fff`41130000   0`001df000              MEM_FREE    PAGE_NOACCESS      Free
  +    7fff`41130000   7fff`41131000   0`00001000 MEM_IMAGE   MEM_COMMIT  PAGE_READONLY       Image  [oleaut32; "C:\Windows\System32\oleaut32.dll"]
       7fff`41131000   7fff`411ce000   0`0009d000 MEM_IMAGE   MEM_COMMIT  PAGE_EXECUTE_READ   Image  [oleaut32; "C:\Windows\System32\oleaut32.dll"]
       7fff`411ce000   7fff`411f4000   0`00026000 MEM_IMAGE   MEM_COMMIT  PAGE_READONLY       Image  [oleaut32; "C:\Windows\System32\oleaut32.dll"]
       7fff`411f4000   7fff`411f7000   0`00003000 MEM_IMAGE   MEM_COMMIT  PAGE_READWRITE      Image  [oleaut32; "C:\Windows\System32\oleaut32.dll"]
       7fff`411f7000   7fff`41206000   0`0000f000 MEM_IMAGE   MEM_COMMIT  PAGE_READONLY       Image  [oleaut32; "C:\Windows\System32\oleaut32.dll"]
  +    7fff`41206000   7fff`41240000   0`0003a000              MEM_FREE    PAGE_NOACCESS      Free
  +    7fff`41240000   7fff`41241000   0`00001000 MEM_IMAGE   MEM_COMMIT  PAGE_READONLY       Image  [combase; "C:\Windows\System32\combase.dll"]
       7fff`41241000   7fff`414a0000   0`0025f000 MEM_IMAGE   MEM_COMMIT  PAGE_EXECUTE_READ   Image  [combase; "C:\Windows\System32\combase.dll"]
       7fff`414a0000   7fff`41562000   0`000c2000 MEM_IMAGE   MEM_COMMIT  PAGE_READONLY       Image  [combase; "C:\Windows\System32\combase.dll"]
       7fff`41562000   7fff`41568000   0`00006000 MEM_IMAGE   MEM_COMMIT  PAGE_READWRITE      Image  [combase; "C:\Windows\System32\combase.dll"]
       7fff`41568000   7fff`415b6000   0`0004e000 MEM_IMAGE   MEM_COMMIT  PAGE_READONLY       Image  [combase; "C:\Windows\System32\combase.dll"]
  +    7fff`415b6000   7fff`41600000   0`0004a000              MEM_FREE    PAGE_NOACCESS      Free
  +    7fff`41600000   7fff`41601000   0`00001000 MEM_IMAGE   MEM_COMMIT  PAGE_READONLY       Image  [ntdll; "C:\Windows\System32\ntdll.dll"]
       7fff`41601000   7fff`4172c000   0`0012b000 MEM_IMAGE   MEM_COMMIT  PAGE_EXECUTE_READ   Image  [ntdll; "C:\Windows\System32\ntdll.dll"]
       7fff`4172c000   7fff`41774000   0`00048000 MEM_IMAGE   MEM_COMMIT  PAGE_READONLY       Image  [ntdll; "C:\Windows\System32\ntdll.dll"]
       7fff`41774000   7fff`41775000   0`00001000 MEM_IMAGE   MEM_COMMIT  PAGE_READWRITE      Image  [ntdll; "C:\Windows\System32\ntdll.dll"]
       7fff`41775000   7fff`41777000   0`00002000 MEM_IMAGE   MEM_COMMIT  PAGE_WRITECOPY      Image  [ntdll; "C:\Windows\System32\ntdll.dll"]
       7fff`41777000   7fff`4177f000   0`00008000 MEM_IMAGE   MEM_COMMIT  PAGE_READWRITE      Image  [ntdll; "C:\Windows\System32\ntdll.dll"]
       7fff`4177f000   7fff`41780000   0`00001000 MEM_IMAGE   MEM_COMMIT  PAGE_WRITECOPY      Image  [ntdll; "C:\Windows\System32\ntdll.dll"]
       7fff`41780000   7fff`4180a000   0`0008a000 MEM_IMAGE   MEM_COMMIT  PAGE_READONLY       Image  [ntdll; "C:\Windows\System32\ntdll.dll"]
  +    7fff`4180a000   7fff`ffff0000   0`be7e6000              MEM_FREE    PAGE_NOACCESS      Free
```

9. The !dso (!DumpStackObjects) command we used previously also interprets the current CPU register values if they are pointers to objects:

```
0:000> !dso
OS Thread Id: 0x2134 (0)
         SP/REG          Object Name
           rcx    01f2dc091128 UserQuery
           rdx    01f2dc091f38 System.Action
            r8    01f2dc091f38 System.Action
    0086342f3b50    02336e6f84f0 System.String
    0086342f5250    01f2dc090da8 System.String
    0086342f52e8    01f2dc090d68 System.Int32
    0086342f5310    01f2dc090d80 System.String
    0086342f5318    01f2dc090d68 System.Int32
    0086342f5320    01f2dc090d10 System.String
    0086342f5da0    01f2dc090c08 System.String
[...]
    0086342fe750    01f2de80c8b0 LINQPad.ProcessServer.LINQPadRuntimeLoadContext
    0086342fe758    01f2de80bb10 System.String
    0086342fe778    01f2de80ca10 System.Reflection.RuntimeAssembly
    0086342fe790    01f2de80b7d0 System.String[]
    0086342fea30    01f2de80b7d0 System.String[]
    0086342fedb8    01f2de80b7d0 System.String[]
```

10. The following command dumps all dependent objects with their overall size information:

```
0:000> !ObjSize 01f2dc091128
Objects which 1f2dc091128 (UserQuery) transitively keep alive:

        Address           MT        Size
   01f2dc091128    7ffe82506150          24
   01f2dc0911c8    7ffe82501d80          40
   01f2dc0911f0    7ffe81e9f978          32
   01f2dc091188    7ffe82503d50          64
```

01f2dc07c008	7ffe82501a90	56
01f2dc473580	7ffe8240c300	40
01f2dc07c040	7ffe82502258	24
01f2dc404468	7ffe820ba258	384
01f2dc07ace8	7ffe81c5f8b0	48
01f2dc07a808	7ffe82452da0	72
01f2dc4045e8	7ffe81a64730	24
01f2dc404600	7ffe81a64730	24
01f2dc4098e8	7ffe822d6fd8	72
01f2dc409948	7ffe822d7348	72
01f2dc472fe0	7ffe82407058	96
01f2dc0463e8	7ffe81eb9218	128
01f2de8230d0	7ffe81b7fda0	72
01f2dc404618	7ffe81c20950	40
01f2dc404640	7ffe81ec3de8	56
01f2dc4046b8	7ffe822a63b0	32
01f2dc4046f0	7ffe822a6940	32
01f2dc404728	7ffe822a6940	32
01f2dc046ce0	7ffe81f4b528	32
01f2dc404748	7ffe81eb5648	48
01f2dc046370	7ffe821cd0d8	40
01f2dc0463b0	7ffe821cc628	32
01f2dc046ba8	7ffe81f47568	152
01f2dc071e28	7ffe81f47568	152
01f2dc4098d0	7ffe822d6ab8	24
01f2dc409b18	7ffe820ba638	160
01f2dc4099a8	7ffe81b7bf40	172
01f2dc404778	7ffe81dc1928	64
01f2dc4047b8	7ffe822a6ec8	32
01f2de826e60	7ffe81d108f0	28
02336e6e6b50	7ffe81b7bf40	26
01f2dc409930	7ffe81a64730	24
01f2de821858	7ffe81e7dda8	120
02336e6fb028	7ffe81a6a038	40
01f2dc409990	7ffe81a64730	24
02336e6fb050	7ffe81a6a038	40
01f2dc473088	7ffe81a64730	24
01f2dc4730a0	7ffe81eb4d68	40
01f2dc473140	7ffe81eb5648	48
01f2dc473040	7ffe81eba800	40
01f2dc473170	7ffe81ec0c90	56
01f2dc40bc78	7ffe81b7bf40	52
01f2dc0464d0	7ffe81a64730	24
01f2dc0464e8	7ffe81eb4d68	40
01f2dc046588	7ffe81eb5648	48
01f2dc40bce0	7ffe81b7bf40	74
01f2dc046a50	7ffe81ebb280	24
01f2dc0466d8	7ffe81eb9538	80
01f2dc046468	7ffe81a64730	24
01f2dc046480	7ffe81eb9648	32
01f2dc013360	7ffe81eca860	40
01f2dc404678	7ffe81a64730	24
01f2dc404690	7ffe81ec4b18	40
01f2dc4046d8	7ffe822a6fa8	24
01f2dc404710	7ffe81f44518	24
01f2de826e80	7ffe81f4bfd8	24
01f2dc046398	7ffe81a64730	24
01f2dc0463d0	7ffe82453900	24
01f2dc046c40	7ffe81a64730	24
01f2dc046b60	7ffe82452da0	72
01f2dc046c58	7ffe81f49c50	48
01f2dc046cc0	7ffe81f48770	32
01f2dc06e9e0	7ffe81b7bf40	13,312
02336e6f4508	7ffe81b7bf40	54
01f2dc071ec0	7ffe81a64730	24
01f2dc071de0	7ffe82452da0	72
01f2dc071ed8	7ffe81f49c50	48
01f2dc071f40	7ffe81f48770	32
01f2dc077ae0	7ffe81b7bf40	11,558
01f2dc40bd60	7ffe81b7bf40	58
01f2dc40bdd0	7ffe81b7bf40	58
01f2dc40be58	7ffe81b7bf40	32
01f2dc40c458	7ffe81c55328	24
01f2dc40c4d0	7ffe81b7bf40	204
01f2dc40c5d0	7ffe81b7bf40	32
01f2de800440	7ffe81c24890	24
01f2dc4047d8	7ffe81a64730	24
01f2de8212e8	7ffe81e7c1f8	72
01f2de821a48	7ffe81a64730	24
01f2de821a60	7ffe81eb4d68	40
01f2de821b00	7ffe81eb5648	48
01f2de821c40	7ffe81eb9218	128
01f2de822130	7ffe81ec3b80	112
01f2de8218d0	7ffe81a64730	24
01f2de8218e8	7ffe81eb1c20	80
01f2de821938	7ffe81eb2b10	80
01f2de8219a0	7ffe81eb36e8	80
01f2de821bb0	7ffe81eb48b8	56
01f2de821a08	7ffe81eb3f10	64
01f2dc4730c8	7ffe81a64730	24
01f2dc4730e0	7ffe81eb5d78	24
01f2dc473068	7ffe81ebea68	32
01f2dc4731a8	7ffe81ec1168	40
01f2dc4731d0	7ffe81ec2880	48
01f2dc046510	7ffe81a64730	24
01f2dc046528	7ffe81eb5d78	24
01f2dc046b40	7ffe81ec3718	32
01f2dc046728	7ffe81a64730	24

277

01f2dc046740	7ffe81eb4d68	40
01f2dc0467e0	7ffe81eb5648	48
01f2dc0465b8	7ffe81eba800	40
01f2dc046810	7ffe81ec0c90	56
01f2de821cf8	7ffe81eb9bf8	24
01f2dc013328	7ffe8240f7f8	32
01f2de822578	7ffe81ec62e0	24
01f2dc046c88	7ffe81d108f0	56
01f2dc071f08	7ffe81d108f0	56
01f2dc071f60	7ffe81f4b528	32
01f2de800428	7ffe81c218a8	24
01f2de821a88	7ffe81a64730	24
01f2de821aa0	7ffe81eb5d78	24
01f2de821d40	7ffe81a64730	24
01f2de821d58	7ffe81eb4d68	40
01f2de821df8	7ffe81eb5648	48
01f2de821be8	7ffe81b7bf40	86
01f2de822060	7ffe81ebb280	24
01f2de821e98	7ffe81eb9538	80
01f2de821cc0	7ffe81a64730	24
01f2de821cd8	7ffe81eb9648	32
01f2de8221d0	7ffe81a64730	24
01f2de8221e8	7ffe81eb4d68	40
01f2de822288	7ffe81eb5648	48
01f2de822098	7ffe81b7bf40	86
01f2de8224c8	7ffe81ebb280	24
01f2de822300	7ffe81eb9538	80
01f2de8221a0	7ffe81eb5648	48
01f2de8220f0	7ffe81eb3f10	64
01f2de822500	7ffe81ec3de8	56
01f2dc404198	7ffe81b78e48	36
01f2dc4041c0	7ffe8228d258	96
01f2dc404220	7ffe81b78e48	36
01f2dc404248	7ffe8228d528	96
01f2de821988	7ffe81c22710	24
01f2dc408bd0	7ffe81b78e48	36
01f2dc408bf8	7ffe822d22e0	96
01f2de80d808	7ffe81c5e7a0	40
01f2de8219f0	7ffe81eb3e60	24
01f2dc4730f8	7ffe81eb69e8	72
01f2dc046540	7ffe81eb69e8	72
01f2dc046768	7ffe81a64730	24
01f2dc046780	7ffe81eb5d78	24
01f2dc0466b8	7ffe81ebea68	32
01f2dc046920	7ffe81ec1168	40
01f2dc0469c8	7ffe81ec2880	48
01f2dc013310	7ffe8240f558	24
01f2dc406ee0	7ffe822ab558	128
01f2de821ab8	7ffe81eb69e8	72
01f2de821d80	7ffe81a64730	24
01f2de821d98	7ffe81eb5d78	24
01f2de822078	7ffe81ec3718	32
01f2de821ee8	7ffe81a64730	24
01f2de821f00	7ffe81eb4d68	40
01f2de821fa0	7ffe81eb5648	48
01f2de821e28	7ffe81eba800	40
01f2de821fd0	7ffe81ec0c90	56
01f2de822210	7ffe81a64730	24
01f2de822228	7ffe81eb5d78	24
01f2de8224e0	7ffe81ec3718	32
01f2de822350	7ffe81a64730	24
01f2de822368	7ffe81eb4d68	40
01f2de822408	7ffe81eb5648	48
01f2de8222b8	7ffe81eba800	40
01f2de822438	7ffe81ec0c90	56
01f2de824430	7ffe81ee5980	64
01f2de822538	7ffe81a64730	24
01f2de822550	7ffe81ec4b18	40
01f2de823140	7ffe81ec6010	120
01f2dc404138	7ffe8228bb20	72
01f2dc404808	7ffe822a6200	72
01f2de80ca10	7ffe81c5f8b0	48
01f2dc046798	7ffe81eb69e8	72
01f2dc407048	7ffe81a64730	24
02336e6fa858	7ffe81b7bf40	168
01f2dc406f60	7ffe81a64730	24
01f2dc406cf8	7ffe822a4900	120
01f2dc406f78	7ffe822acaa8	80
01f2dc406fc8	7ffe81dc1928	64
01f2dc407008	7ffe81dc1928	64
01f2de821db0	7ffe81eb69e8	72
01f2de821f28	7ffe81a64730	24
01f2de821f40	7ffe81eb5d78	24
01f2de821e78	7ffe81ebea68	32
01f2de822008	7ffe81ec1168	40
01f2de822030	7ffe81ec2880	48
01f2de822240	7ffe81eb69e8	72
01f2de822390	7ffe81a64730	24
01f2de8223a8	7ffe81eb5d78	24
01f2de8222e0	7ffe81ebea68	32
01f2de822470	7ffe81ec1168	40
01f2de822498	7ffe81ec2880	48
01f2dc4043d0	7ffe81ee5ad0	80
01f2de824470	7ffe81ee5ad0	80
01f2de8243a0	7ffe81ec62e0	56
01f2de823088	7ffe81eca420	40
01f2de8234b8	7ffe81ecb118	56
01f2dc404180	7ffe81a64730	24

```
01f2dc404120    7ffe81e74b38          24
01f2dc4042e8    7ffe81e71f58          64
01f2dc404850    7ffe81a64730          24
01f2dc4048a8    7ffe81e71f58          64
01f2dc402238    7ffe81b7bf40         186
01f2dc406df0    7ffe81c55328          24
01f2dc406e20    7ffe81c55328          24
01f2dc406e08    7ffe81c55328          24
01f2dc406e38    7ffe81b7bf40         142
01f2dc07c650    7ffe81dcdc80          80
01f2dc406d70    7ffe81dc1928          64
01f2dc406db0    7ffe81dc1928          64
01f2de800488    7ffe81c24ae8          24
01f2de821f58    7ffe81eb69e8          72
01f2de8223c0    7ffe81eb69e8          72
01f2de8243f0    7ffe81ec69c0          64
01f2dc08ec90    7ffe81e71f58          64
01f2de823118    7ffe81eca860          40
01f2dc08ec10    7ffe81eb5d78          24
01f2de822590    7ffe81ec51c0          64
01f2de8234f0    7ffe81ecb3f8         528
01f2de823700    7ffe81ecb4b8         536
01f2de823918    7ffe81ecb3f8         528
01f2de823b28    7ffe81ecb1f0          24
01f2dc4042c8    7ffe8228cf28          32
01f2dc404888    7ffe8228cf28          32
01f2de8004a0    7ffe81c258f0          24
01f2de8243d8    7ffe81ee56f8          24
01f2dc08ebf8    7ffe81ee5060          24
01f2dc08ec28    7ffe81eb69e8          72
01f2de8265f8    7ffe81ec6010         120
01f2de823b40    7ffe81ec3718          32
01f2de826570    7ffe81ec3718          32
01f2dc4042a8    7ffe8228ce38          32
01f2dc404868    7ffe8228ce38          32
01f2dc08eea8    7ffe81ee86b8          32
01f2de8265d0    7ffe81eca420          40
01f2dc08eec8    7ffe81b22170          56
01f2de826590    7ffe81ec51c0          64
01f2de826538    7ffe81f2e7a0          24
01f2dc08ed58    7ffe81ee60f8          40
01f2dc08ee80    7ffe81ee60f8          40
01f2de826418    7ffe81e7a588         288
01f2dc08ed10    7ffe81ee5e70          72
01f2de823bc8    7ffe81ecc008          24
01f2dc08ee38    7ffe81ee81a0          72
01f2de826550    7ffe81f2e500          32
02336e6e2b10    7ffe81b7bf40          24
01f2de826688    7ffe81d66548          64
01f2dc08ecd0    7ffe81ee54f8          64
01f2dc08edf8    7ffe81e91120          64
01f2de826670    7ffe81e90d20          24
01f2dc08ec70    7ffe81ee5468          32
01f2dc08ed80    7ffe81ee6588          24
01f2dc08ed98    7ffe81ee72e0          24
01f2dc08edb0    7ffe81e7c1f8          72
01f2dc08f010    7ffe81ee60f8          40
01f2dc08efc8    7ffe81eea338          72
01f2dc08ef88    7ffe81ee96e0          64
01f2dc08ef00    7ffe81ee9240          40
01f2de8244f0    7ffe81ee8da0          64
01f2dc08ef28    7ffe81ee72e0          24
01f2de8244d8    7ffe81ee8cc8          24
01f2dc08ef40    7ffe81e7c1f8          72
01f2dc08f0f8    7ffe81e71f58          64
01f2dc08f0d0    7ffe82502828          40
01f2dc08f090    7ffe82502580          64
01f2dc08f038    7ffe81e71f58          64
01f2dc08f078    7ffe825026d0          24
01f2de824530    7ffe81eed108          80
01f2de824308    7ffe81ee1cf8         104
```

Statistics:
```
      MT Count TotalSize Class Name
7ffe82506150    1        24 UserQuery
7ffe82502258    1        24 LINQPad.Extensibility.DataContext.QueryExecutionManager
7ffe822d6ab8    1        24 LINQPad.UI.RuntimeUIServices
7ffe822a6fa8    1        24 System.Action<System.Object>[]
7ffe81f44518    1        24 System.Action[]
7ffe81f4bfd8    1        24 LINQPad.ObjectGraph.Formatters.Explorable[]
7ffe82453900    1        24 System.IDisposable[]
7ffe81c24890    1        24 System.Collections.Generic.NonRandomizedStringEqualityComparer+OrdinalComparer
7ffe81eb9bf8    1        24 LINQPad.ExecutionModel.MMFileWrapper[]
7ffe81c218a8    1        24 System.Collections.Generic.StringEqualityComparer
7ffe81c22710    1        24 System.Collections.Generic.ObjectEqualityComparer<System.Object>
7ffe81eb3e60    1        24 LINQPad.ExecutionModel.FastChannel+<>c
7ffe8240f558    1        24 System.Threading.AsyncLocal<System.Runtime.Loader.AssemblyLoadContext>
7ffe81e74b38    1        24 LINQPad.ExecutionModel.ProcessServer
7ffe81c24ae8    1        24 System.Collections.Generic.NonRandomizedStringEqualityComparer+OrdinalIgnoreCaseComparer
7ffe81ecb1f0    1        24 System.Threading.AutoResetEvent
7ffe81c258f0    1        24 System.OrdinalIgnoreCaseComparer
7ffe81ee56f8    1        24 System.Threading.CancellationToken+<>c
7ffe81ee5060    1        24 LINQPad.Threading.AsyncAutoResetEvent+<>c__DisplayClass8_0
7ffe81f2e7a0    1        24 Interop+Kernel32+ProcessWaitHandle
7ffe81ecc008    1        24 System.Threading.Tasks.ThreadPoolTaskScheduler
7ffe81e90d20    1        24 LINQPad.ExecutionModel.ProcessServer+<>c
7ffe81ee6588    1        24 LINQPad.TaskExtensions+<>c__DisplayClass5_0<System.Boolean>
7ffe81ee8cc8    1        24 LINQPad.TaskExtensions+<>c__15<System.Boolean>
```

```
7ffe825026d0    1     24 System.Runtime.CompilerServices.TaskAwaiter+<>c
7ffe81e9f978    1     32 System.LazyHelper
7ffe822a63b0    1     32 System.Collections.Generic.List<System.Action<System.Object>>
7ffe821cc628    1     32 System.Collections.Generic.List<System.IDisposable>
7ffe822a6ec8    1     32 LINQPad.Threading.PCQ
7ffe8240f7f8    1     32 System.Threading.AsyncLocalValueMap+OneElementAsyncLocalValueMap
7ffe81ee86b8    1     32 System.Collections.Generic.List<System.Object>
7ffe81f2e500    1     32 Microsoft.Win32.SafeHandles.SafeProcessHandle
7ffe81ee5468    1     32 LINQPad.Threading.AsyncAutoResetEvent+<>c__DisplayClass8_1
7ffe82501d80    1     40 System.Lazy<System.Threading.CancellationToken>
7ffe8240c300    1     40 LINQPad.ExecutionModel.ClrQueryRunner
7ffe81c20950    1     40 System.Diagnostics.Stopwatch
7ffe821cd0d8    1     40 LINQPad.Threading.Countdown
7ffe81c5e7a0    1     40 System.Reflection.RuntimeModule
7ffe81ee9240    1     40 LINQPad.TaskExtensions+<>c__DisplayClass11_0<System.Boolean>
7ffe82502828    1     40 System.Runtime.CompilerServices.AsyncMethodBuilderCore+ContinuationWrapper
7ffe81ee72e0    2     48 System.Threading.Tasks.TaskCompletionSource<System.Boolean>
7ffe82501a90    1     56 LINQPad.ExecutionModel.ClrQueryRunner+<>c__DisplayClass11_0
7ffe81eb48b8    1     56 LINQPad.ExecutionModel.FastSerializer
7ffe81ecb118    1     56 System.Threading.PortableThreadPool+WaitThread
7ffe81b22170    1     56 System.Object[]
7ffe82503d50    1     64 System.Func<System.Threading.CancellationToken>
7ffe822a6940    2     64 System.Collections.Generic.List<System.Action>
7ffe81f4b528    2     64 System.Collections.Generic.List<LINQPad.ObjectGraph.Formatters.Explorable>
7ffe81eb9648    2     64 System.Collections.Generic.List<LINQPad.ExecutionModel.MMFileWrapper>
7ffe81f48770    1     64 LINQPad.ObjectGraph.Formatters.HHtmlFormatter
7ffe81ee5980    1     64 System.Threading.CancellationTokenSource+Registrations
7ffe81ec69c0    1     64 System.Action<System.Object>
7ffe8228cf28    2     64 LINQPad.ExecutionModel.FastChannel+<>c__DisplayClass28_1
7ffe8228ce38    2     64 LINQPad.ExecutionModel.FastChannel+<>c__DisplayClass28_0
7ffe81d66548    1     64 System.EventHandler
7ffe81ee54f8    1     64 System.Action<System.Threading.Tasks.Task<System.Object>>
7ffe81e91120    1     64 System.Action<System.Threading.Tasks.Task>
7ffe81ee96e0    1     64 System.Action<System.Threading.Tasks.Task<System.Boolean>>
7ffe81ee8da0    1     64 System.Func<System.Exception, System.Boolean>
7ffe82502580    1     64 System.Action<System.Action, System.Threading.Tasks.Task>
7ffe822d6fd8    1     72 LINQPad.ExecutionModel.Proxy<LINQPad.ExecutionModel.IClient>
7ffe822d7348    1     72 LINQPad.ExecutionModel.Proxy<LINQPad.ExecutionModel.IPluginWindowClient>
7ffe81b7fda0    1     72 System.Threading.Thread
7ffe81ebb280    3     72 System.Threading.EventWaitHandle
7ffe8228bb20    1     72 LINQPad.ExecutionModel.Proxy<LINQPad.ExecutionModel.ProcessServer>
7ffe822a6200    1     72 LINQPad.ExecutionModel.Proxy<LINQPad.ExecutionModel.IServer>
7ffe81ee5e70    1     72 System.Threading.Tasks.ContinuationTaskFromResultTask<System.Object>
7ffe81ee81a0    1     72 System.Threading.Tasks.ContinuationTaskFromTask
7ffe81eea338    1     72 System.Threading.Tasks.ContinuationTaskFromResultTask<System.Boolean>
7ffe81a6a038    2     80 System.RuntimeType
7ffe81eca860    2     80 System.Threading.ExecutionContext
7ffe81ec4b18    2     80 System.Collections.Generic.Queue<System.Threading.Tasks.TaskCompletionSource<System.Object>>
7ffe81eb1c20    1     80 System.Collections.Generic.Dictionary<System.Int32, LINQPad.ExecutionModel.IProxy>
7ffe81eb2b10    1     80 System.Collections.Generic.Dictionary<System.Object, LINQPad.ExecutionModel.IProxy>
7ffe81eb36e8    1     80 System.Collections.Generic.Dictionary<System.Int32, System.Action<LINQPad.ExecutionModel.FastChannel+MessageType, System.Object>>
7ffe81ec62e0    2     80 System.Threading.Tasks.TaskCompletionSource<System.Object>[]
7ffe822acaa8    1     80 System.Collections.Generic.Dictionary<System.String, System.Reflection.Assembly>
7ffe81eca420    2     80 System.Threading._ThreadPoolWaitOrTimerCallback
7ffe81dcdc80    1     80 System.Collections.Generic.Dictionary<System.String, System.String>
7ffe81eed108    1     80
System.Runtime.CompilerServices.AsyncTaskMethodBuilder<System.Threading.Tasks.VoidTaskResult>+AsyncStateMachineBox<LINQPad.ExecutionModel.InPipe+<Go>d__6>
7ffe81c5f8b0    2     96 System.Reflection.RuntimeAssembly
7ffe82407058    1     96 LINQPad.ExecutionModel.SharedMemoryValueWrapper<LINQPad.ExecutionModel.LockFreeExecutionInfo>
7ffe81f49c50    2     96 System.Text.StringBuilder
7ffe81c55328    4     96 System.String[]
7ffe8228d258    1     96 System.Collections.Generic.Dictionary<System.Int32, LINQPad.ExecutionModel.IProxy>+Entry[]
7ffe8228d528    1     96 System.Collections.Generic.Dictionary<System.Object, LINQPad.ExecutionModel.IProxy>+Entry[]
7ffe822d22e0    1     96 System.Collections.Generic.Dictionary<System.Int32, System.Action<LINQPad.ExecutionModel.FastChannel+MessageType,
System.Object>>+Entry[]
7ffe81ee1cf8    1    104 LINQPad.ExecutionModel.InPipe+<Go>d__6
7ffe81b78e48    3    108 System.Int32[]
7ffe81ec3de8    2    112 LINQPad.Threading.AsyncAutoResetEvent
7ffe81ec3b80    1    112 LINQPad.ExecutionModel.InPipe
7ffe81e7dda8    1    120 LINQPad.ExecutionModel.FastChannel
7ffe822a4900    1    120 LINQPad.ExecutionModel.ProbingSet
7ffe81ee60f8    3    120 System.Threading.Tasks.ContinueWithTaskContinuation
7ffe81eb3f10    2    128 System.Action<System.Byte[]>
7ffe81ebea68    4    128 Microsoft.Win32.SafeHandles.SafeMemoryMappedFileHandle
7ffe822ab558    1    128 LINQPad.ExecutionModel.UserLoadContext
7ffe81ec51c0    2    128 System.Threading.WaitOrTimerCallback
7ffe81d108f0    3    140 System.Char[]
7ffe820ba638    1    160 LINQPad.ExecutionModel.ExecutionStartInfo
7ffe81eba800    4    160 System.IO.MemoryMappedFiles.MemoryMappedFile
7ffe81ec1168    4    160 Microsoft.Win32.SafeHandles.SafeMemoryMappedViewHandle
7ffe81ec3718    5    160 Microsoft.Win32.SafeHandles.SafeWaitHandle
7ffe81ee5ad0    2    160 System.Threading.CancellationTokenSource+CallbackNode
7ffe81ec2880    2    192 System.IO.MemoryMappedFiles.MemoryMappedView
7ffe82452da0    3    216 LINQPad.ObjectGraph.Formatters.FastChannelResultsWriter
7ffe81e7c1f8    3    216 System.Threading.Tasks.Task<System.Boolean>
7ffe81eb5d78    9    216 System.Threading.Tasks.TaskCompletionSource<System.Object>
7ffe81ec0c90    4    224 System.IO.MemoryMappedFiles.MemoryMappedViewAccessor
7ffe81eb9538    3    240 LINQPad.ExecutionModel.MMFileWrapper
7ffe81ec6010    2    240 System.Threading.RegisteredWaitHandle
7ffe81eb9218    2    256 LINQPad.ExecutionModel.OutPipe
7ffe81e7a588    1    288 System.Diagnostics.Process
7ffe81f47568    2    304 LINQPad.ObjectGraph.Formatters.HtmlWriter
7ffe81dc1928    5    320 System.Collections.Generic.HashSet<System.String>
7ffe81eb4d68    8    320 LINQPad.Threading.AsyncCountdownEvent
7ffe81e71f58    5    320 System.Action
7ffe820ba258    1    384 LINQPad.ExecutionModel.Server
7ffe81eb5648   10    480 System.Threading.CancellationTokenSource
7ffe81ecb4b8    1    536 Microsoft.Win32.SafeHandles.SafeWaitHandle[]
```

```
7ffe81eb69e8      9       648 System.Threading.Tasks.Task<System.Object>
7ffe81a64730     33       792 System.Object
7ffe81ecb3f8      2     1,056 System.Threading.RegisteredWaitHandle[]
7ffe81b7bf40     18    26,324 System.String
Total 271 objects, 40,388 bytes
```

11.   If you have an array, you can list all its objects with details (we take one of String[] arrays from the output of the **!dso** command):

```
0:000> !DumpObj 01f2de80b7d0
Name:         System.String[]
MethodTable: 00007ffe81c55328
Canonical MethodTable: 00007ffe81b22170
Tracked Type: false
Size:         136(0x88) bytes
Array:        Rank 1, Number of elements 14, Type CLASS (Print Array)
Fields:
None


0:000> !DumpArray 01f2de80b7d0
Name:         System.String[]
MethodTable: 00007ffe81c55328
EEClass:      00007ffe81b22170
Size:         136(0x88) bytes
Array:        Rank 1, Number of elements 14, Type CLASS
Element Methodtable: 00007ffe81b7bf40
[0] 000001f2de80b910
[1] 000001f2de80b930
[2] 000001f2de80b9b8
[3] 000001f2de80ba38
[4] 000001f2de80ba80
[5] 000001f2de80c840
[6] 000001f2de80bb80
[7] 000001f2de80bbc8
[8] 000001f2de80bc20
[9] 000001f2de80bc48
[10] 000001f2de80bc68
[11] 000001f2de80bc88
[12] 000001f2de80bca8
[13] 000001f2de80bcc8


0:000> !DumpArray -details 01f2de80b7d0
Name:         System.String[]
MethodTable: 00007ffe81c55328
EEClass:      00007ffe81b22170
Size:         136(0x88) bytes
Array:        Rank 1, Number of elements 14, Type CLASS
Element Methodtable: 00007ffe81b7bf40
[0] 000001f2de80b910
    Name:         System.String
    MethodTable: 00007ffe81b7bf40
    Canonical MethodTable: 00007ffe81b7bf40
    Tracked Type: false
    Size:         30(0x1e) bytes
    File:         C:\Program Files\dotnet\shared\Microsoft.NETCore.App\9.0.4\System.Private.CoreLib.dll
    String:       *:PS
    Fields:
                    MT    Field   Offset                 Type VT    Attr            Value Name
        00007ffe81b27408  4000355        8         System.Int32  1  instance                4 _stringLength
        00007ffe81b42f60  4000356        c         System.Char   1  instance               2a _firstChar
        00007ffe81b7bf40  4000354        8       System.String   0    static  000002336e6e0008 Empty
[1] 000001f2de80b930
    Name:         System.String
    MethodTable: 00007ffe81b7bf40
    Canonical MethodTable: 00007ffe81b7bf40
    Tracked Type: false
    Size:         134(0x86) bytes
```

281

```
        File:            C:\Program Files\dotnet\shared\Microsoft.NETCore.App\9.0.4\System.Private.CoreLib.dll
        String:          DataContext Driver: LINQPad.Drivers.EFCore.DynamicDriver
        Fields:
                      MT    Field   Offset              Type VT     Attr            Value Name
        00007ffe81b27408  4000355       8         System.Int32  1     instance               56    _stringLength
        00007ffe81b42f60  4000356       c         System.Char   1     instance               44    _firstChar
        00007ffe81b7bf40  4000354       8       System.String   0       static   000002336e6e0008    Empty
[2] 000001f2de80b9b8
        Name:            System.String
        MethodTable: 00007ffe81b7bf40
        Canonical MethodTable: 00007ffe81b7bf40
        Tracked Type: false
        Size:            122(0x7a) bytes
        File:            C:\Program Files\dotnet\shared\Microsoft.NETCore.App\9.0.4\System.Private.CoreLib.dll
        String:          C:/Program Files/dotnet/host/fxr/9.0.4/hostfxr.dll
        Fields:
                      MT    Field   Offset              Type VT     Attr            Value Name
        00007ffe81b27408  4000355       8         System.Int32  1     instance               50    _stringLength
        00007ffe81b42f60  4000356       c         System.Char   1     instance               43    _firstChar
        00007ffe81b7bf40  4000354       8       System.String   0       static   000002336e6e0008    Empty
[3] 000001f2de80ba38
        Name:            System.String
        MethodTable: 00007ffe81b7bf40
        Canonical MethodTable: 00007ffe81b7bf40
        Tracked Type: false
        Size:            68(0x44) bytes
        File:            C:\Program Files\dotnet\shared\Microsoft.NETCore.App\9.0.4\System.Private.CoreLib.dll
        String:          C:/Program Files/dotnet
        Fields:
                      MT    Field   Offset              Type VT     Attr            Value Name
        00007ffe81b27408  4000355       8         System.Int32  1     instance               23    _stringLength
        00007ffe81b42f60  4000356       c         System.Char   1     instance               43    _firstChar
        00007ffe81b7bf40  4000354       8       System.String   0       static   000002336e6e0008    Empty
[4] 000001f2de80ba80
        Name:            System.String
        MethodTable: 00007ffe81b7bf40
        Canonical MethodTable: 00007ffe81b7bf40
        Tracked Type: false
        Size:            144(0x90) bytes
        File:            C:\Program Files\dotnet\shared\Microsoft.NETCore.App\9.0.4\System.Private.CoreLib.dll
        String:          C:/Users/User/AppData/Local/LINQPad/8.8.9/ProcessServer/9.0.4
        Fields:
                      MT    Field   Offset              Type VT     Attr            Value Name
        00007ffe81b27408  4000355       8         System.Int32  1     instance               61    _stringLength
        00007ffe81b42f60  4000356       c         System.Char   1     instance               43    _firstChar
        00007ffe81b7bf40  4000354       8       System.String   0       static   000002336e6e0008    Empty
[5] 000001f2de80c840
        Name:            System.String
        MethodTable: 00007ffe81b7bf40
        Canonical MethodTable: 00007ffe81b7bf40
        Tracked Type: false
        Size:            112(0x70) bytes
        File:            C:\Program Files\dotnet\shared\Microsoft.NETCore.App\9.0.4\System.Private.CoreLib.dll
        String:          C:\Program Files\LINQPad8\LINQPad.Runtime.dll
        Fields:
                      MT    Field   Offset              Type VT     Attr            Value Name
        00007ffe81b27408  4000355       8         System.Int32  1     instance               45    _stringLength
        00007ffe81b42f60  4000356       c         System.Char   1     instance               43    _firstChar
        00007ffe81b7bf40  4000354       8       System.String   0       static   000002336e6e0008    Empty
[6] 000001f2de80bb80
        Name:            System.String
        MethodTable: 00007ffe81b7bf40
        Canonical MethodTable: 00007ffe81b7bf40
        Tracked Type: false
        Size:            72(0x48) bytes
        File:            C:\Program Files\dotnet\shared\Microsoft.NETCore.App\9.0.4\System.Private.CoreLib.dll
        String:          C:/Program Files/LINQPad8
        Fields:
                      MT    Field   Offset              Type VT     Attr            Value Name
        00007ffe81b27408  4000355       8         System.Int32  1     instance               25    _stringLength
        00007ffe81b42f60  4000356       c         System.Char   1     instance               43    _firstChar
        00007ffe81b7bf40  4000354       8       System.String   0       static   000002336e6e0008    Empty
[7] 000001f2de80bbc8
        Name:            System.String
        MethodTable: 00007ffe81b7bf40
        Canonical MethodTable: 00007ffe81b7bf40
        Tracked Type: false
        Size:            82(0x52) bytes
        File:            C:\Program Files\dotnet\shared\Microsoft.NETCore.App\9.0.4\System.Private.CoreLib.dll
        String:          LINQPad8.ctfuegif.zkvvqpnmmo.2
        Fields:
                      MT    Field   Offset              Type VT     Attr            Value Name
        00007ffe81b27408  4000355       8         System.Int32  1     instance               30    _stringLength
        00007ffe81b42f60  4000356       c         System.Char   1     instance               4c    _firstChar
```

```
          00007ffe81b7bf40  4000354         8           System.String    0      static     000002336e6e0008   Empty
[8] 000001f2de80bc20
    Name:        System.String
    MethodTable: 00007ffe81b7bf40
    Canonical MethodTable: 00007ffe81b7bf40
    Tracked Type: false
    Size:        38(0x26) bytes
    File:        C:\Program Files\dotnet\shared\Microsoft.NETCore.App\9.0.4\System.Private.CoreLib.dll
    String:      ctfuegif
    Fields:
                     MT     Field    Offset              Type VT      Attr          Value Name
          00007ffe81b27408  4000355         8           System.Int32   1     instance           8   _stringLength
          00007ffe81b42f60  4000356         c           System.Char    1     instance          63   _firstChar
          00007ffe81b7bf40  4000354         8           System.String  0       static   000002336e6e0008   Empty
[9] 000001f2de80bc48
    Name:        System.String
    MethodTable: 00007ffe81b7bf40
    Canonical MethodTable: 00007ffe81b7bf40
    Tracked Type: false
    Size:        30(0x1e) bytes
    File:        C:\Program Files\dotnet\shared\Microsoft.NETCore.App\9.0.4\System.Private.CoreLib.dll
    String:      8864
    Fields:
                     MT     Field    Offset              Type VT      Attr          Value Name
          00007ffe81b27408  4000355         8           System.Int32   1     instance           4   _stringLength
          00007ffe81b42f60  4000356         c           System.Char    1     instance          38   _firstChar
          00007ffe81b7bf40  4000354         8           System.String  0       static   000002336e6e0008   Empty
[10] 000001f2de80bc68
    Name:        System.String
    MethodTable: 00007ffe81b7bf40
    Canonical MethodTable: 00007ffe81b7bf40
    Tracked Type: false
    Size:        30(0x1e) bytes
    File:        C:\Program Files\dotnet\shared\Microsoft.NETCore.App\9.0.4\System.Private.CoreLib.dll
    String:      True
    Fields:
                     MT     Field    Offset              Type VT      Attr          Value Name
          00007ffe81b27408  4000355         8           System.Int32   1     instance           4   _stringLength
          00007ffe81b42f60  4000356         c           System.Char    1     instance          54   _firstChar
          00007ffe81b7bf40  4000354         8           System.String  0       static   000002336e6e0008   Empty
[11] 000001f2de80bc88
    Name:        System.String
    MethodTable: 00007ffe81b7bf40
    Canonical MethodTable: 00007ffe81b7bf40
    Tracked Type: false
    Size:        32(0x20) bytes
    File:        C:\Program Files\dotnet\shared\Microsoft.NETCore.App\9.0.4\System.Private.CoreLib.dll
    String:      False
    Fields:
                     MT     Field    Offset              Type VT      Attr          Value Name
          00007ffe81b27408  4000355         8           System.Int32   1     instance           5   _stringLength
          00007ffe81b42f60  4000356         c           System.Char    1     instance          46   _firstChar
          00007ffe81b7bf40  4000354         8           System.String  0       static   000002336e6e0008   Empty
[12] 000001f2de80bca8
    Name:        System.String
    MethodTable: 00007ffe81b7bf40
    Canonical MethodTable: 00007ffe81b7bf40
    Tracked Type: false
    Size:        32(0x20) bytes
    File:        C:\Program Files\dotnet\shared\Microsoft.NETCore.App\9.0.4\System.Private.CoreLib.dll
    String:      False
    Fields:
                     MT     Field    Offset              Type VT      Attr          Value Name
          00007ffe81b27408  4000355         8           System.Int32   1     instance           5   _stringLength
          00007ffe81b42f60  4000356         c           System.Char    1     instance          46   _firstChar
          00007ffe81b7bf40  4000354         8           System.String  0       static   000002336e6e0008   Empty
[13] 000001f2de80bcc8
    Name:        System.String
    MethodTable: 00007ffe81b7bf40
    Canonical MethodTable: 00007ffe81b7bf40
    Tracked Type: false
    Size:        36(0x24) bytes
    File:        C:\Program Files\dotnet\shared\Microsoft.NETCore.App\9.0.4\System.Private.CoreLib.dll
    String:      9.0.4.0
    Fields:
                     MT     Field    Offset              Type VT      Attr          Value Name
          00007ffe81b27408  4000355         8           System.Int32   1     instance           7   _stringLength
          00007ffe81b42f60  4000356         c           System.Char    1     instance          39   _firstChar
          00007ffe81b7bf40  4000354         8           System.String  0       static   000002336e6e0008   Empty
```

12.   Finally, we can search in memory (including stack regions and managed heap) using **s** command (for example, for UNICODE strings) and interpret values as pointers to ASCII and UNICODE character sequences using **dpa** and **dpu** commands:

```
0:000> s-u 01f2de80b7d0 L1000 "LINQPad"
000001f2`de80b89c  004c 0049 004e 0051 0050 0061 0064 005c  L.I.N.Q.P.a.d.\.
000001f2`de80b8e0  004c 0049 004e 0051 0050 0061 0064 002e  L.I.N.Q.P.a.d...
000001f2`de80b964  004c 0049 004e 0051 0050 0061 0064 002e  L.I.N.Q.P.a.d...
000001f2`de80bac4  004c 0049 004e 0051 0050 0061 0064 002f  L.I.N.Q.P.a.d./.
000001f2`de80bb3e  004c 0049 004e 0051 0050 0061 0064 0038  L.I.N.Q.P.a.d.8.
000001f2`de80bb50  004c 0049 004e 0051 0050 0061 0064 002e  L.I.N.Q.P.a.d...
000001f2`de80bbae  004c 0049 004e 0051 0050 0061 0064 0038  L.I.N.Q.P.a.d.8.
000001f2`de80bbd4  004c 0049 004e 0051 0050 0061 0064 0038  L.I.N.Q.P.a.d.8.
000001f2`de80c86e  004c 0049 004e 0051 0050 0061 0064 0038  L.I.N.Q.P.a.d.8.
000001f2`de80c880  004c 0049 004e 0051 0050 0061 0064 002e  L.I.N.Q.P.a.d...

0:000> du 000001f2`de80b89c
000001f2`de80b89c  "LINQPad\8.8.9\ProcessServer\9.0."
000001f2`de80b8dc  "4\LINQPad.Query.dll"

0:000> !teb
    ExceptionList:         0000000000000000
    StackBase:             0000008634300000
    StackLimit:            0000008634201000
    SubSystemTib:          0000000000000000
    FiberData:             0000000000001e00
    ArbitraryUserPointer:  0000000000000000
    Self:                  00000086341f5000
    EnvironmentPointer:    0000000000000000
    ClientId:              0000000000000dd4 . 0000000000002134
    RpcHandle:             0000000000000000
    Tls Storage:           000002336e5b42e0
    PEB Address:           00000086341f4000
    LastErrorValue:        0
    LastStatusValue:       c0000034
    Count Owned Locks:     0
    HardErrorMode:         0

0:000> dpa 0000008634201000 0000008634300000
[...]
00000086`342fefd8  000001f2`d7e2c1d0 "C:\Users\User\AppData\Local\LINQPad\8.8.9\ProcessServer"
[...]

0:000> dpu 0000008634201000 0000008634300000
[...]
00000086`342ffa00  000001f2`d7d66f84 "Winsta0\Default"
00000086`342ffa08  000001f2`d7d66f36 "C:\Program Files\LINQPad8\LINQPad8.exe"
[...]
```

13.   We close logging before exiting WinDbg:

```
0:000> .logclose
Closing open log file C:\ANETMDA-Dumps\Windows\x64\LINQPadF.log
```

Exercise PN8 (Linux)

- **Goal:** Learn how to recognize and analyze a stack overflow

- **Patterns:** Stack Overflow (Managed Space)

- **Commands:** memory region

- \ANETMDA-Dumps\Exercise-PN8-Linux.pdf

Exercise PN8 (Linux)

Goal: Learn how to recognize and analyze a stack overflow.

Patterns: Stack Overflow (Managed Space).

Commands: memory region

1.   Open \ANETMDA-Dumps\Linux\ApplicationM\core.ApplicationM.1487.dmp in LLDB:

```
/mnt/c/ANETMDA-Dumps/Linux/ApplicationM$ lldb -c core.ApplicationM.1487.dmp
bin/Release/net9.0/ApplicationM
Current symbol store settings:
-> Cache: /home/coredump/.dotnet/symbolcache
-> Server: https://msdl.microsoft.com/download/symbols/ Timeout: 4 RetryCount: 0
(lldb) target create "bin/Release/net9.0/ApplicationM" --core "core.ApplicationM.1487.dmp"
warning: (x86_64) /usr/share/dotnet/host/fxr/9.0.4/libhostfxr.so unsupported DW_FORM values:
0x1b 0x21 0x22 0x23 0x25 0x26 0x64
warning: (x86_64) /usr/share/dotnet/shared/Microsoft.NETCore.App/9.0.4/libhostpolicy.so
unsupported DW_FORM values: 0x1b 0x21 0x22 0x23 0x25 0x26 0x64
warning: (x86_64) /usr/share/dotnet/shared/Microsoft.NETCore.App/9.0.4/libcoreclr.so
unsupported DW_FORM values: 0x1b 0x21 0x22 0x23 0x25 0x26 0x64
warning: (x86_64) /usr/share/dotnet/shared/Microsoft.NETCore.App/9.0.4/libSystem.Native.so
unsupported DW_FORM values: 0x1b 0x21 0x22 0x23 0x25 0x26
warning: (x86_64) /usr/share/dotnet/shared/Microsoft.NETCore.App/9.0.4/libclrjit.so unsupported
DW_FORM values: 0x1b 0x21 0x22 0x23 0x25 0x26 0x64
warning: (x86_64) /mnt/c/ANETMDA-Dumps/Linux/ApplicationM/bin/Release/net9.0/ApplicationM
unsupported DW_FORM values: 0x1b 0x21 0x22 0x23 0x25 0x26 0x64
Core file '/mnt/c/ANETMDA-Dumps/Linux/ApplicationM/core.ApplicationM.1487.dmp' (x86_64) was
loaded.
```

2.   Verify all stack traces:

```
(lldb) bt all
* thread #1, name = 'ApplicationM', stop reason = signal SIGABRT
  * frame #0: 0x00007fb030ff20ca libpthread.so.0`__waitpid(pid=1495, stat_loc=0x00007fb02fae3a14, options=0) at waitpid.c:30
    frame #1: 0x00007fb030966d97 libcoreclr.so`PROCCreateCrashDump(std::vector<char const*, std::allocator<char const*> >&, char*, int, bool) + 647
    frame #2: 0x00007fb03096824b libcoreclr.so`PROCCreateCrashDumpIfEnabled + 3227
    frame #3: 0x00007fb03096597d libcoreclr.so`PROCAbort + 45
    frame #4: 0x00007fb0309658a9 libcoreclr.so`TerminateProcess + 137
    frame #5: 0x00007fb030625726 libcoreclr.so`EEPolicy::HandleFatalStackOverflow(_EXCEPTION_POINTERS*, int) + 902
    frame #6: 0x00007fb0306e660b libcoreclr.so`HandleHardwareException(PAL_SEHException*) + 603
    frame #7: 0x00007fb03093945c libcoreclr.so`SEHProcessException(PAL_SEHException*) + 316
    frame #8: 0x00007fb03093b000 libcoreclr.so`common_signal_handler(int, siginfo_t*, void*, int, ...) + 656
    frame #9: 0x00007fb03093ad06 libcoreclr.so`signal_handler_worker + 118
    frame #10: 0x00007fb03096bcb2 libcoreclr.so`CallSignalHandlerWrapper0 + 6
    frame #11: 0x00007fafb230191d
    frame #12: 0x00007fafb2301967
    frame #13: 0x00007fafb2301967
    frame #14: 0x00007fafb2301967
    frame #15: 0x00007fafb2301967
    frame #16: 0x00007fafb2301967
    frame #17: 0x00007fafb2301967
    frame #18: 0x00007fafb2301967
    frame #19: 0x00007fafb2301967
    frame #20: 0x00007fafb2301967
    frame #21: 0x00007fafb2301967
[...]
    frame #2017: 0x00007fafb2301967
    frame #2018: 0x00007fafb2301967
    frame #2019: 0x00007fafb2301967
    frame #2020: 0x00007fafb2301967
    frame #2021: 0x00007fafb2301967
    frame #2022: 0x00007fafb2301967
    frame #2023: 0x00007fafb2301967
    frame #2024: 0x00007fafb2301967
    frame #2025: 0x00007fafb2301967
    frame #2026: 0x00007fafb23018ca
    frame #2027: 0x00007fafb230189a
    frame #2028: 0x00007fafb2301874
    frame #2029: 0x00007fb0307b6e04 libcoreclr.so`CallDescrWorkerInternal + 124
```

```
    frame #2030: 0x00007fb0305f511c libcoreclr.so`MethodDescCallSite::CallTargetWorker(unsigned long const*, unsigned long*, int) + 1708
    frame #2031: 0x00007fb0304dc0c4 libcoreclr.so`RunMain(MethodDesc*, short, int*, PtrArray**) + 836
    frame #2032: 0x00007fb0304dc53c libcoreclr.so`Assembly::ExecuteMainMethod(PtrArray**, int) + 460
    frame #2033: 0x00007fb030505b34 libcoreclr.so`CorHost2::ExecuteAssembly(unsigned int, char16_t const*, int, char16_t const**, unsigned int*) + 740
    frame #2034: 0x00007fb0304c8340 libcoreclr.so`coreclr_execute_assembly + 144
    frame #2035: 0x00007fb030a90301 libhostpolicy.so`run_app_for_context(hostpolicy_context_t const&, int, char const**) + 1089
    frame #2036: 0x00007fb030a913f9 libhostpolicy.so`corehost_main + 345
    frame #2037: 0x00007fb030ad0685 libhostfxr.so`fx_muxer_t::handle_exec_host_command(std::__cxx11::basic_string<char, std::char_traits<char>,
std::allocator<char> > const&, host_startup_info_t const&, std::__cxx11::basic_string<char, std::char_traits<char>, std::allocator<char> > const&,
std::unordered_map<known_options, std::vector<std::__cxx11::basic_string<char, std::char_traits<char>, std::allocator<char> >,
std::allocator<std::__cxx11::basic_string<char, std::char_traits<char>, std::allocator<char> > >, known_options_hash, std::equal_to<known_options>,
std::allocator<std::pair<known_options const, std::vector<std::__cxx11::basic_string<char, std::char_traits<char>, std::allocator<char> >,
std::allocator<std::__cxx11::basic_string<char, std::char_traits<char>, std::allocator<char> > > > > > const&, int, char const**, int, host_mode_t, bool,
char*, int, int*) + 1477
    frame #2038: 0x00007fb030acf67d libhostfxr.so`fx_muxer_t::execute(std::__cxx11::basic_string<char, std::char_traits<char>, std::allocator<char> >, int,
char const**, host_startup_info_t const&, char*, int, int*) + 765
    frame #2039: 0x00007fb030ac95f2 libhostfxr.so`hostfxr_main_startupinfo + 242
    frame #2040: 0x0000561c10f7221b ApplicationM`exe_start(int, char const**) + 1131
    frame #2041: 0x0000561c10f7253f ApplicationM`main + 175
    frame #2042: 0x00007fb030b2309b libc.so.6`__libc_start_main(main=(ApplicationM`main), argc=1, argv=0x00007ffcf6368b78, init=<unavailable>,
fini=<unavailable>, rtld_fini=<unavailable>, stack_end=0x00007ffcf6368b68) at libc-start.c:308
    frame #2043: 0x0000561c10f71399 ApplicationM`_start + 41
  thread #2, stop reason = signal 0
    frame #0: 0x00007fb030bed6f9 libc.so.6`__GI___poll(fds=0x0000000000000000, nfds=0, timeout=-1) at poll.c:29
    frame #1: 0x00007fb03096018e libcoreclr.so`CorUnix::CPalSynchronizationManager::WorkerThread(void*) + 958
    frame #2: 0x00007fb0309699ae libcoreclr.so`CorUnix::CPalThread::ThreadEntry(void*) + 510
    frame #3: 0x00007fb030fe7fa3 libpthread.so.0`start_thread(arg=<unavailable>) at pthread_create.c:486
    frame #4: 0x00007fb030bf806f libc.so.6`__GI___clone at clone.S:95
  thread #3, stop reason = signal 0
    frame #0: 0x00007fb030bed6f9 libc.so.6`__GI___poll(fds=0x00007fafa4000f20, nfds=1, timeout=-1) at poll.c:29
    frame #1: 0x00007fb0308867d5c libcoreclr.so`ds_ipc_poll(_DiagnosticsIpcPollHandle*, unsigned long, unsigned int, void (*)(char const*, unsigned int)) + 172
    frame #2: 0x00007fb0307e1f4b libcoreclr.so`ds_ipc_stream_factory_get_next_available_stream(void (*)(char const*, unsigned int)) + 731
    frame #3: 0x00007fb0307e6ca6 libcoreclr.so`server_thread(void*) + 198
    frame #4: 0x00007fb0309699ae libcoreclr.so`CorUnix::CPalThread::ThreadEntry(void*) + 510
    frame #5: 0x00007fb030fe7fa3 libpthread.so.0`start_thread(arg=<unavailable>) at pthread_create.c:486
    frame #6: 0x00007fb030bf806f libc.so.6`__GI___clone at clone.S:95
  thread #4, stop reason = signal 0
    frame #0: 0x00007fb030ff1d0e libpthread.so.0`__libc_open64(file="/tmp/clr-debug-pipe-1487-1799063-in", oflag=0) at open64.c:48
    frame #1: 0x00007fb030806777f libcoreclr.so`TwoWayPipe::WaitForConnection() + 31
    frame #2: 0x00007fb030862797 libcoreclr.so`DbgTransportSession::TransportWorker() + 183
    frame #3: 0x00007fb030861905 libcoreclr.so`DbgTransportSession::TransportWorkerStatic(void*) + 37
    frame #4: 0x00007fb0309699ae libcoreclr.so`CorUnix::CPalThread::ThreadEntry(void*) + 510
    frame #5: 0x00007fb030fe7fa3 libpthread.so.0`start_thread(arg=<unavailable>) at pthread_create.c:486
    frame #6: 0x00007fb030bf806f libc.so.6`__GI___clone at clone.S:95
  thread #5, stop reason = signal 0
    frame #0: 0x00007fb030fee00c libpthread.so.0`__pthread_cond_wait at futex-internal.h:88
    frame #1: 0x00007fb030fedff1 libpthread.so.0`__pthread_cond_wait at pthread_cond_wait.c:502
    frame #2: 0x00007fb030fedf30 libpthread.so.0`__pthread_cond_wait(cond=0x0000561c235fef38, mutex=0x0000561c235fef10) at pthread_cond_wait.c:655
    frame #3: 0x00007fb03095e172 libcoreclr.so`CorUnix::CPalSynchronizationManager::ThreadNativeWait(CorUnix::_ThreadNativeWaitData*, unsigned int,
CorUnix::ThreadWakeupReason*, unsigned int*) + 354
    frame #4: 0x00007fb03095dd7a libcoreclr.so`CorUnix::CPalSynchronizationManager::BlockThread(CorUnix::CPalThread*, unsigned int, bool, bool,
CorUnix::ThreadWakeupReason*, unsigned int*) + 378
    frame #5: 0x00007fb030962952 libcoreclr.so`CorUnix::InternalWaitForMultipleObjectsEx(CorUnix::CPalThread*, unsigned int, void* const*, int, unsigned int,
int, int) + 1906
    frame #6: 0x00007fb030962c03 libcoreclr.so`WaitForMultipleObjectsEx + 83
    frame #7: 0x00007fb0308600ad libcoreclr.so`DebuggerRCThread::MainLoop() + 269
    frame #8: 0x00007fb03085ff28 libcoreclr.so`DebuggerRCThread::ThreadProc() + 312
    frame #9: 0x00007fb03085fc25 libcoreclr.so`DebuggerRCThread::ThreadProcStatic(void*) + 53
    frame #10: 0x00007fb0309699ae libcoreclr.so`CorUnix::CPalThread::ThreadEntry(void*) + 510
    frame #11: 0x00007fb030fe7fa3 libpthread.so.0`start_thread(arg=<unavailable>) at pthread_create.c:486
    frame #12: 0x00007fb030bf806f libc.so.6`__GI___clone at clone.S:95
  thread #6, stop reason = signal 0
    frame #0: 0x00007fb030fee3f9 libpthread.so.0`__pthread_cond_timedwait at futex-internal.h:142
    frame #1: 0x00007fb030fee3da libpthread.so.0`__pthread_cond_timedwait at pthread_cond_wait.c:533
    frame #2: 0x00007fb030fee2c0 libpthread.so.0`__pthread_cond_timedwait(cond=0x0000561c2360a628, mutex=0x0000561c2360a600, abstime=0x00007fb02e18d730) at
pthread_cond_wait.c:667
    frame #3: 0x00007fb03095e115 libcoreclr.so`CorUnix::CPalSynchronizationManager::ThreadNativeWait(CorUnix::_ThreadNativeWaitData*, unsigned int,
CorUnix::ThreadWakeupReason*, unsigned int*) + 261
    frame #4: 0x00007fb03095dd7a libcoreclr.so`CorUnix::CPalSynchronizationManager::BlockThread(CorUnix::CPalThread*, unsigned int, bool, bool,
CorUnix::ThreadWakeupReason*, unsigned int*) + 378
    frame #5: 0x00007fb030962952 libcoreclr.so`CorUnix::InternalWaitForMultipleObjectsEx(CorUnix::CPalThread*, unsigned int, void* const*, int, unsigned int,
int, int) + 1906
    frame #6: 0x00007fb030962b29 libcoreclr.so`WaitForSingleObjectEx + 89
    frame #7: 0x00007fb0306beefe libcoreclr.so`CLREventBase::WaitEx(unsigned int, WaitMode, PendingSync*) + 238
    frame #8: 0x00007fb03063107f libcoreclr.so`FinalizerThread::WaitForFinalizerEvent(CLREvent*) + 31
    frame #9: 0x00007fb03063127f libcoreclr.so`FinalizerThread::FinalizerThreadWorker(void*) + 239
    frame #10: 0x00007fb0305c2c08 libcoreclr.so`ManagedThreadBase_DispatchOuter(ManagedThreadCallState*) + 344
    frame #11: 0x00007fb0305c310d libcoreclr.so`ManagedThreadBase::FinalizerBase(void (*)(void*)) + 45
    frame #12: 0x00007fb0306314b8 libcoreclr.so`FinalizerThread::FinalizerThreadStart(void*) + 88
    frame #13: 0x00007fb0309699ae libcoreclr.so`CorUnix::CPalThread::ThreadEntry(void*) + 510
    frame #14: 0x00007fb030fe7fa3 libpthread.so.0`start_thread(arg=<unavailable>) at pthread_create.c:486
    frame #15: 0x00007fb030bf806f libc.so.6`__GI___clone at clone.S:95
  thread #7, stop reason = signal 0
    frame #0: 0x00007fb030fee3f9 libpthread.so.0`__pthread_cond_timedwait at futex-internal.h:142
    frame #1: 0x00007fb030fee3da libpthread.so.0`__pthread_cond_timedwait at pthread_cond_wait.c:533
    frame #2: 0x00007fb030fee2c0 libpthread.so.0`__pthread_cond_timedwait(cond=0x0000561c236134b8, mutex=0x0000561c23613490, abstime=0x00007fb02c755b50) at
pthread_cond_wait.c:667
    frame #3: 0x00007fb03095e115 libcoreclr.so`CorUnix::CPalSynchronizationManager::ThreadNativeWait(CorUnix::_ThreadNativeWaitData*, unsigned int,
CorUnix::ThreadWakeupReason*, unsigned int*) + 261
    frame #4: 0x00007fb03095dd7a libcoreclr.so`CorUnix::CPalSynchronizationManager::BlockThread(CorUnix::CPalThread*, unsigned int, bool, bool,
CorUnix::ThreadWakeupReason*, unsigned int*) + 378
    frame #5: 0x00007fb030963089 libcoreclr.so`SleepEx + 153
    frame #6: 0x00007fb0305c64aa libcoreclr.so`TieredCompilationManager::BackgroundWorkerStart() + 186
    frame #7: 0x00007fb0305c6368 libcoreclr.so`TieredCompilationManager::BackgroundWorkerBootstrapper1(void*) + 104
    frame #8: 0x00007fb0305c2c08 libcoreclr.so`ManagedThreadBase_DispatchOuter(ManagedThreadCallState*) + 344
    frame #9: 0x00007fb0305c30bd libcoreclr.so`ManagedThreadBase::KickOff(void (*)(void*), void*) + 45
    frame #10: 0x00007fb0305c6290 libcoreclr.so`TieredCompilationManager::BackgroundWorkerBootstrapper0(void*) + 32
    frame #11: 0x00007fb0309699ae libcoreclr.so`CorUnix::CPalThread::ThreadEntry(void*) + 510
```

```
frame #12: 0x00007fb030fe7fa3 libpthread.so.0`start_thread(arg=<unavailable>) at pthread_create.c:486
frame #13: 0x00007fb030bf806f libc.so.6`__GI___clone at clone.S:95
```

Note: We noticed that the current thread #0 was doing recursive calls. We suspect stack overflow. Let's compare the current thread stack pointer with the thread stack region limit value:

```
(lldb) ip2md 0x00007fafb230191d
MethodDesc:     00007fafb23a97a0
Method Name:            Program.<<Main>$>g__foo|0_2()
Class:                  00007fafb23a97c0
MethodTable:            00007fafb23a97c0
mdToken:                0000000006000005
Module:                 00007fafb23a7038
IsJitted:               yes
Current CodeAddr:       00007fafb23018f0
Version History:
  ILCodeVersion:        0000000000000000
  ReJIT ID:             0
  IL Addr:              00007fb02f2d0270
     CodeAddr:              00007fafb23018f0  (QuickJitted)
     NativeCodeVersion:  0000000000000000
Source file:    /mnt/c/ANETMDA-Examples/ApplicationM/Program.cs @ 12

(lldb) ip2md 0x00007fafb2301967
MethodDesc:     00007fafb23a97a0
Method Name:            Program.<<Main>$>g__foo|0_2()
Class:                  00007fafb23a97c0
MethodTable:            00007fafb23a97c0
mdToken:                0000000006000005
Module:                 00007fafb23a7038
IsJitted:               yes
Current CodeAddr:       00007fafb23018f0
Version History:
  ILCodeVersion:        0000000000000000
  ReJIT ID:             0
  IL Addr:              00007fb02f2d0270
     CodeAddr:              00007fafb23018f0  (QuickJitted)
     NativeCodeVersion:  0000000000000000
Source file:    /mnt/c/ANETMDA-Examples/ApplicationM/Program.cs @ 14

(lldb) frame select 11
frame #11: 0x00007fafb230191d
    0x7fafb230191d: testl  %esp, (%rsp)
    0x7fafb2301920: subq   $0x1000, %rsp            ; imm = 0x1000
    0x7fafb2301927: cmpq   %rax, %rsp
    0x7fafb230192a: jae    0x7fafb230191d

(lldb) register read $rsp
    rsp = 0x00007fb02fae9080

(lldb) memory region $rsp
[0x00007fb02fae9080-0x00007fb02faea000) ---

(lldb) frame select 12
frame #12: 0x00007fafb2301967
    0x7fafb2301967: cmpq   $0x1128451, -0x20(%rbp)  ; imm = 0x1128451
    0x7fafb230196f: je     0x7fafb2301976
    0x7fafb2301971: callq  0x7fb030654f90           ; JIT_FailFast
    0x7fafb2301976: nop
```

```
(lldb) register read $rsp
      rsp = 0x00007ffcf5b6a450

(lldb) memory region $rsp
[0x00007ffcf5b6a000-0x00007ffcf636a000) rw-

(lldb) memory region 0x00007ffcf5b6a000-1
[0x00007ffcf5b69fff-0x00007ffcf5b6a000) ---
```

Note: We notice that stack pointer value belongs to an inaccessible page and the next frame stack pointer is very close to the stack region limit. We also get managed stack trace (time-consuming operation):

```
(lldb) clrstack
OS Thread Id: 0x5cf (1)
        Child SP            IP Call Site
00007FB02FAE3B70 00007fb030ff20ca [FaultingExceptionFrame: 00007fb02fae3b70]
00007FFCF5B69410 00007FAFB230191D Program.<<Main>$>g__foo|0_2() [/mnt/c/ANETMDA-Examples/ApplicationM/Program.cs @ 12]
00007FFCF5B6A450 00007FAFB2301967 Program.<<Main>$>g__foo|0_2() [/mnt/c/ANETMDA-Examples/ApplicationM/Program.cs @ 13]
00007FFCF5B6B490 00007FAFB2301967 Program.<<Main>$>g__foo|0_2() [/mnt/c/ANETMDA-Examples/ApplicationM/Program.cs @ 13]
00007FFCF5B6C4D0 00007FAFB2301967 Program.<<Main>$>g__foo|0_2() [/mnt/c/ANETMDA-Examples/ApplicationM/Program.cs @ 13]
00007FFCF5B6D510 00007FAFB2301967 Program.<<Main>$>g__foo|0_2() [/mnt/c/ANETMDA-Examples/ApplicationM/Program.cs @ 13]
00007FFCF5B6E550 00007FAFB2301967 Program.<<Main>$>g__foo|0_2() [/mnt/c/ANETMDA-Examples/ApplicationM/Program.cs @ 13]
00007FFCF5B6F590 00007FAFB2301967 Program.<<Main>$>g__foo|0_2() [/mnt/c/ANETMDA-Examples/ApplicationM/Program.cs @ 13]
[...]
00007FFCF6360A10 00007FAFB2301967 Program.<<Main>$>g__foo|0_2() [/mnt/c/ANETMDA-Examples/ApplicationM/Program.cs @ 13]
00007FFCF6361A50 00007FAFB2301967 Program.<<Main>$>g__foo|0_2() [/mnt/c/ANETMDA-Examples/ApplicationM/Program.cs @ 13]
00007FFCF6362A90 00007FAFB2301967 Program.<<Main>$>g__foo|0_2() [/mnt/c/ANETMDA-Examples/ApplicationM/Program.cs @ 13]
00007FFCF6363AD0 00007FAFB2301967 Program.<<Main>$>g__foo|0_2() [/mnt/c/ANETMDA-Examples/ApplicationM/Program.cs @ 13]
00007FFCF6364B10 00007FAFB2301967 Program.<<Main>$>g__foo|0_2() [/mnt/c/ANETMDA-Examples/ApplicationM/Program.cs @ 13]
00007FFCF6365B50 00007FAFB2301967 Program.<<Main>$>g__foo|0_2() [/mnt/c/ANETMDA-Examples/ApplicationM/Program.cs @ 13]
00007FFCF6366B90 00007FAFB2301967 Program.<<Main>$>g__foo|0_2() [/mnt/c/ANETMDA-Examples/ApplicationM/Program.cs @ 13]
00007FFCF6367BD0 00007FAFB23018CA Program.<<Main>$>g__bar|0_1() [/mnt/c/ANETMDA-Examples/ApplicationM/Program.cs @ 7]
00007FFCF6367BE0 00007FAFB230189A Program.<<Main>$>g__Main|0_0() [/mnt/c/ANETMDA-Examples/ApplicationM/Program.cs @ 16]
00007FFCF6367BF0 00007FAFB2301874 Program.<Main>$(System.String[]) [/mnt/c/ANETMDA-Examples/ApplicationM/Program.cs @ 1]
```

3.   We check the managed exception:

```
(lldb) pe
Exception object: 00007f6f9e800100
Exception type:    System.StackOverflowException
Message:           <none>
InnerException:    <none>
StackTrace (generated):
<none>
StackTraceString: <none>
HResult: 800703e9
```

Mechanisms (Stack Overflow)

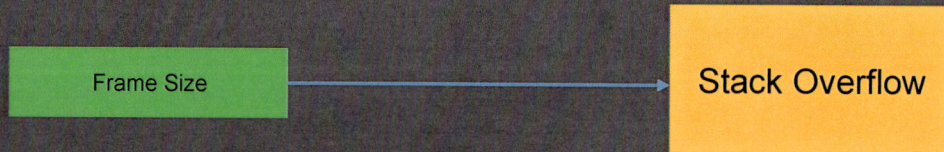

Frame Size → Stack Overflow

Conclusion

Pattern Links

CLR Thread
Managed Code Exception
Stack Trace Collection
Memory Leak
JIT Code
Managed Stack Trace
Multiple Exceptions
Caller-n-Callee
Deadlock
Hidden Exception
Mixed Exception

Technology-Specific Subtrace
Stack Overflow
Dynamic Memory Corruption
Special Thread
Execution Residue
Handled Exception
Annotated Disassembly
Wait Chain
Context Pointer
Object Distribution Anomaly
Nested Exceptions

CLR-related and managed (full list)

Incorrect Stack Trace   Execution Residue   Stack Trace
NULL Pointer (Data)   Handle Leak   Exception Stack Trace
Software Exception   Platform-Specific Debugger
Spiking Thread   Hidden Exception   Regular Data
Coincidental Symbolic Information   Active Thread
Truncated Stack Trace   Value References   Manual Dump
Stack Trace Set   Rough Stack Trace   Stack Trace Collection
Distributed Spike   Paratext

Unmanaged user space

Here are links to pattern descriptions and additional examples:

CLR Thread:
http://www.dumpanalysis.org/blog/index.php/2009/12/07/crash-dump-analysis-patterns-part-95/

Deadlock (Managed Space):
http://www.dumpanalysis.org/blog/index.php/2011/10/17/crash-dump-analysis-patterns-part-9g/

Managed Code Exception:
http://www.dumpanalysis.org/blog/index.php/2007/07/20/crash-dump-analysis-patterns-part-17/

Stack Trace Collection (Managed Space):
http://www.dumpanalysis.org/blog/index.php/2011/10/24/crash-dump-analysis-patterns-part-27b/

Dynamic Memory Corruption (Managed Heap):
http://www.dumpanalysis.org/blog/index.php/2011/10/24/crash-dump-analysis-patterns-part-2c/

Memory Leak (Managed Heap):
http://www.dumpanalysis.org/blog/index.php/2007/08/19/crash-dump-analysis-patterns-part-20b/

JIT Code:

http://www.dumpanalysis.org/blog/index.php/2009/05/15/crash-dump-analysis-patterns-part-84/

Execution Residue (Managed Space):

http://www.dumpanalysis.org/blog/index.php/2011/10/17/crash-dump-analysis-patterns-part-60b/

Managed Stack Trace:

http://www.dumpanalysis.org/blog/index.php/2011/06/17/crash-dump-analysis-patterns-part-139/

Handled Exception (.NET CLR):

http://www.dumpanalysis.org/blog/index.php/2011/10/17/crash-dump-analysis-patterns-part-152b/

Multiple Exceptions (Managed Space):

http://www.dumpanalysis.org/blog/index.php/2011/06/28/crash-dump-analysis-patterns-part-1c/

Annotated Disassembly (JIT .NET Code):

http://www.dumpanalysis.org/blog/index.php/2011/10/13/crash-dump-analysis-patterns-part-151/

Technology-Specific Subtrace (JIT .NET Code):

http://www.dumpanalysis.org/blog/index.php/2011/10/10/crash-dump-analysis-patterns-part-127c/

Caller-n-Callee:

http://www.dumpanalysis.org/blog/index.php/2011/10/10/crash-dump-analysis-patterns-part-150/

Special Thread (.NET CLR):

http://www.dumpanalysis.org/blog/index.php/2011/10/27/crash-dump-analysis-patterns-part-154a/

Wait Chain (CLR Monitors):

http://www.dumpanalysis.org/blog/index.php/2014/04/09/crash-dump-analysis-patterns-part-42l/

Hidden Exception (Managed Space):

http://www.dumpanalysis.org/blog/index.php/2018/08/11/crash-dump-analysis-patterns-part-8c/

Object Distribution Anomaly (.NET Heap):

http://www.dumpanalysis.org/blog/index.php/2015/09/12/crash-dump-analysis-patterns-part-35b/

Stack Overflow (Managed Space):

https://www.dumpanalysis.org/blog/index.php/2022/02/04/crash-dump-analysis-patterns-part-16e/

Mixed Exception:

https://www.dumpanalysis.org/blog/index.php/2009/10/28/crash-dump-analysis-patterns-part-90/

Nested Exceptions:

https://www.dumpanalysis.org/blog/index.php/2008/06/25/crash-dump-analysis-patterns-part-67b/

Context Pointer:

https://www.dumpanalysis.org/blog/index.php/2020/06/15/crash-dump-analysis-patterns-part-269/

The full list of .NET / CLR / Managed Space patterns:

https://www.dumpanalysis.org/blog/index.php/2011/04/22/net-clr-managed-space-patterns/

Incorrect Stack Trace:

http://www.dumpanalysis.org/blog/index.php/2007/04/03/crash-dump-analysis-patterns-part-11/

NULL Pointer (Data):

http://www.dumpanalysis.org/blog/index.php/2009/04/14/crash-dump-analysis-patterns-part-6b/

Handle Leak:

http://www.dumpanalysis.org/blog/index.php/2012/12/23/crash-dump-analysis-patterns-part-189/

Spiking Thread:

http://www.dumpanalysis.org/blog/index.php/2007/05/11/crash-dump-analysis-patterns-part-14/

Hidden Exception (User Space):

http://www.dumpanalysis.org/blog/index.php/2007/02/02/crash-dump-analysis-patterns-part-8/

Execution Residue (Unmanaged Space):

http://www.dumpanalysis.org/blog/index.php/2008/04/29/crash-dump-analysis-patterns-part-60/

Exception Stack Trace:

http://www.dumpanalysis.org/blog/index.php/2010/08/05/crash-dump-analysis-patterns-part-105/

Software Exception:

http://www.dumpanalysis.org/blog/index.php/2015/02/28/crash-dump-analysis-patterns-part-222/

Platform-Specific Debugger:

http://www.dumpanalysis.org/blog/index.php/2009/11/24/crash-dump-analysis-patterns-part-93/

Regular Data:

http://www.dumpanalysis.org/blog/index.php/2012/02/12/crash-dump-analysis-patterns-part-167/

Coincidental Symbolic Information:

http://www.dumpanalysis.org/blog/index.php/2007/08/30/crash-dump-analysis-patterns-part-24/

Active Thread:

https://www.dumpanalysis.org/blog/index.php/2015/10/31/crash-dump-analysis-patterns-part-232/

Truncated Stack Trace:

https://www.dumpanalysis.org/blog/index.php/2011/03/20/crash-dump-analysis-patterns-part-133/

Value References:

https://www.dumpanalysis.org/blog/index.php/2011/12/05/crash-dump-analysis-patterns-part-159/

Manual Dump:

https://www.dumpanalysis.org/blog/index.php/2007/12/17/crash-dump-analysis-patterns-part-41b/

Stack Trace Set:

https://www.dumpanalysis.org/blog/index.php/2011/09/07/crash-dump-analysis-patterns-part-148/

Rough Stack Trace (Unmanaged Space):

https://www.dumpanalysis.org/blog/index.php/2014/10/07/crash-dump-analysis-patterns-part-213/

Stack Trace:

https://www.dumpanalysis.org/blog/index.php/2007/09/10/crash-dump-analysis-patterns-part-25/

Stack Trace Collection (Unmanaged Space):

https://www.dumpanalysis.org/blog/index.php/2007/09/14/crash-dump-analysis-patterns-part-27/

Distributed Spike:

https://www.dumpanalysis.org/blog/index.php/2010/09/19/crash-dump-analysis-patterns-part-106/

Paratext:

https://www.dumpanalysis.org/blog/index.php/2015/12/14/crash-dump-analysis-patterns-part-180-linux/

Note: all these patterns (and hundreds of others) are also available in **Memory Dump Analysis Anthology (Diagnomicon)** volumes or **Encyclopedia of Crash Dump Analysis Patterns** (see the **References** slide).

SOS Checklist (Windows)

- CLR module and SOS extension versions (lmv and .chain)
- Managed exceptions (~*e !pe -nested)
- Managed threads (!Threads -special)
- Managed stack traces (!CLRStack -all)
- Managed execution residue (~*e !DumpStackObjects)
- Managed heap (!VerifyHeap, !DumpHeap -stat, and !eeheap -gc)
- GC handles (!GCHandles)
- Finalizer queue (!FinalizeQueue)
- Sync blocks (!syncblk)

SOS Checklist (Linux)

- Managed exceptions (thread select and pe -nested)
- Managed threads (clrthreads)
- Managed stack traces (thread select and clrthread)
- Managed execution residue (thread select and dso)
- Managed heap (verifyheap, dumpheap -stat, and eeheap -gc)
- GC handles (gchandles)
- Finalizer queue (finalizequeue)
- Sync blocks (syncblk)

Useful Reference Links

- SOS commands https://learn.microsoft.com/en-us/dotnet/core/diagnostics/sos-debugging-extension

- dotnet-sos https://learn.microsoft.com/en-us/dotnet/core/diagnostics/dotnet-sos

- dotnet-symbol https://learn.microsoft.com/en-us/dotnet/core/diagnostics/dotnet-symbol

- dumps on crash https://learn.microsoft.com/en-us/dotnet/core/diagnostics/collect-dumps-crash

SOS commands
https://learn.microsoft.com/en-us/dotnet/core/diagnostics/sos-debugging-extension

dotnet-sos
https://learn.microsoft.com/en-us/dotnet/core/diagnostics/dotnet-sos

dotnet-symbol
https://learn.microsoft.com/en-us/dotnet/core/diagnostics/dotnet-symbol

dumps on crash
https://learn.microsoft.com/en-us/dotnet/core/diagnostics/collect-dumps-crash

Resources

- WinDbg Help / WinDbg.org (quick links)
- DumpAnalysis.org / PatternDiagnostics.com
- Debugging.TV / YouTube.com/DebuggingTV / YouTube.com/PatternDiagnostics
- .NET Runtime https://github.com/dotnet/runtime
- Pro .NET Memory Management: For Better Code, Performance, and Scalability
- Expert .NET 2.0 IL Assembler
- Accelerated Windows Memory Dump Analysis, 6th Edition, Part 1: Process User Space
- Encyclopedia of Crash Dump Analysis Patterns, 3rd Edition
- Memory Dump Analysis Anthology (Diagnomicon)

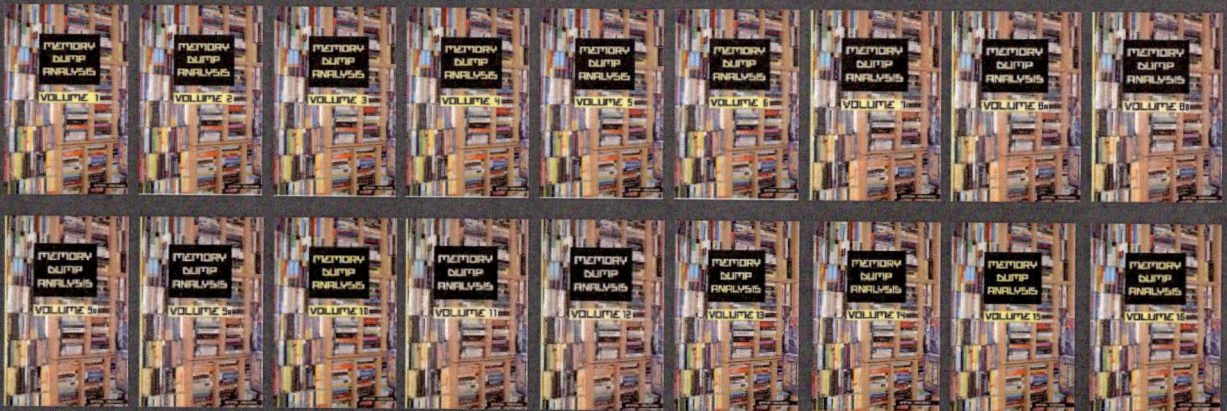

Additional learning and reference resources:

WinDbg quick links
http://WinDbg.org

Software Diagnostics Institute
http://www.dumpanalysis.org

Debugging.TV
http://debugging.tv

Pattern Diagnostics Seminars
https://www.youtube.com/PatternDiagnostics

Software Diagnostics Services
http://www.patterndiagnostics.com

Accelerated Windows Memory Dump Analysis, 6th Edition, Part 1: Process User Space
https://www.patterndiagnostics.com/accelerated-windows-memory-dump-analysis-book-part1

Encyclopedia of Crash Dump Analysis Patterns, 3rd Edition
https://www.patterndiagnostics.com/encyclopedia-crash-dump-analysis-patterns

Memory Dump Analysis Anthology (Diagnomicon)
https://www.patterndiagnostics.com/mdaa-volumes

Application Source Code

```csharp
namespace ApplicationA
{
    public partial class ApplicationA : Form
    {
        public ApplicationA()
        {
            InitializeComponent();
        }

        private void CrashButton_Click(object sender, EventArgs e)
        {
            unsafe
            {
                int* p = (int*)0;
                *p = 1;
            }
        }
    }
}
```

LinqB

```
<Query Kind="Program" />

void Main()
{
    new ClassMain().Main();
}

// Define other methods and classes here

public class ClassMain
{
    public bool time2stop = false;

    public void Main()
    {
        while (!time2stop)
        {
            DoWork();
        }
    }

    volatile int inSensor, outSensor;

    void DoWork()
    {
        outSensor ^= inSensor;
    }
}
```

```
<Query Kind="Program" />

void Main()
{
    new ClassMain().Main();
}

public class ClassMain
{
    static string cs1 = "critical section 1";
    static string cs2 = "critical section 2";

    static volatile int inSensor, outSensor;

    static void DoWork()
    {
        outSensor ^= inSensor;
    }

    static void thread_proc_1()
    {
        try
        {
            Monitor.Enter(cs1);
            {
                DoWork();
                unsafe
                {
                    int* p = (int *)0;
                    *p = 1;
                }
            }
            Monitor.Exit(cs1);
        }
        catch (Exception e)
        {
            Console.WriteLine("We caught an exception.");
        }

        Thread.Sleep(2000);

        Monitor.Enter(cs2);
        {
            DoWork();
        }
        Monitor.Exit(cs2);

        Console.WriteLine("Thread 1 has finished.");
    }
```

```csharp
static void thread_proc_2()
{
    Monitor.Enter(cs2);
    {
        DoWork();
        Monitor.Enter(cs1);
        {
            DoWork();
            Thread.Sleep(3000);
            DoWork();
        }
        Monitor.Exit(cs1);
        DoWork();
    }
    Monitor.Exit(cs2);

    Console.WriteLine("Thread 2 has finished.");
}

public void Main()
{
    Thread t1 = new Thread(thread_proc_1);
    t1.Start();
    Thread.Sleep(1000);
    Thread t2 = new Thread(thread_proc_2);
    t2.Start();
    t1.Join();
    t2.Join();
}
}
```

```csharp
// ApplicationD.linq
// Copyright (c) 2011-2025 Software Diagnostics Technology and Services
// GNU GENERAL PUBLIC LICENSE
// http://www.gnu.org/licenses/gpl-3.0.txt

using System;
using System.Threading;
using System.IO;

namespace ApplicationD
{
    public class CustomException : Exception
    {
        public string description;
        public int code;

        public CustomException(string _description, int _code)
        {
            description = _description;
            code = _code;
        }
    }

    public class SmallObject
    {
        private static void thread_proc() { }
        private int[] buffer;
        private Thread thread;

        public SmallObject()
        {
            thread = new Thread(thread_proc);
            thread.Start();
            buffer = new int[4096];
        }

        ~SmallObject()
        {
            unsafe
            {
                int* p = (int*)0;
                *p = 1;
            }
            ;
        }
    }
}
```

```csharp
public class ClassMain
{
    public static void Main(string[] args)
    {
        new ClassMain().Main();
    }

    void thread_proc_1()
    {
        throw new FileNotFoundException();
    }

    void thread_proc_2()
    {
        int max = 50000;
        for (int i = 0; i < max; ++i)
            new SmallObject();
    }

    void thread_proc_3()
    {
        try
        {
            throw new FileNotFoundException();
        }
        catch (Exception)
        {
            throw new CustomException("File Not Found", 5);
        }
    }

    public void Main()
    {
        Thread t1 = new Thread(thread_proc_1);
        t1.Start();
        Thread t2 = new Thread(thread_proc_2);
        t2.Start();
        Thread t3 = new Thread(thread_proc_3);
        t3.Start();

        GC.Collect();

        t1.Join();
        t2.Join();
        t3.Join();
    }
}
```

LinqD

```csharp
<Query Kind="Program" />

void Main()
{
    new ClassMain().Main();
}

public class CustomException : Exception
{
    public string description;
    public int code;

    public CustomException (string _description, int _code)
    {
        description = _description;
        code = _code;
    }
}

public class SmallObject
{
    static void thread_proc() {}
    public int[] buffer;
    public Thread thread;

    public SmallObject ()
    {
        thread = new Thread(thread_proc);
        thread.Start();
        buffer = new int[4096];
    }

    ~SmallObject ()
    {
        unsafe
        {
            int *p = (int *)0;
            *p = 1;
        };
    }
}
```

```csharp
public class ClassMain
{
        void thread_proc_1()
        {
                throw new FileNotFoundException();
        }

        void thread_proc_2()
        {
                int max = 50000;
                for (int i = 0; i < max; ++i)
                        new SmallObject();
        }

        void thread_proc_3()
        {
                try
                {
                        throw new FileNotFoundException();
                }
                catch (Exception e)
                {
                        throw new CustomException ("File Not Found", 5);
                }
        }

        public void Main()
        {
                Thread t1 = new Thread(thread_proc_1);
                t1.Start();
                Thread t2 = new Thread(thread_proc_2);
                t2.Start();
                Thread t3 = new Thread(thread_proc_3);
                t3.Start();
                t1.Join();
                t2.Join();
                t3.Join();
        }
}
```

LinqE

```
<Query Kind="Program" />

void Main()
{
        new ClassMain().Main();
}

public class SomeObject
{
        int id;
        String data;
        SomeObject prev;

        public SomeObject (int _id, SomeObject _prev)
        {
                id = _id;
                data = id.ToString();
                prev = _prev;
        }

        public SomeObject Prev
        {
           get { return prev; }
        }

        unsafe public int * idptr ()
        {
                fixed ( int *p = &id ) { return p; }
        }
}

public class ClassMain
{
        static int id;
        static SomeObject sobjRoot = new SomeObject (0, null);
        static SomeObject sobjLast;

        void thread_proc_1()
        {
                SomeObject sobj = sobjRoot;
                for (id = 1; id < 1000; ++id)
                {
                        sobj = new SomeObject (id, sobj);
                }
                sobjLast = sobj;
        }
}
```

```csharp
void thread_proc_2()
{
        SomeObject sobj = sobjLast;
        for (id = 1; id < 500; ++id)
        {
                sobj = sobj.Prev;
        }
        unsafe
        {
            char[] b = {'b', 'u', 'g', 's', '.', 'd', 'l', 'l', ' ',
                        'b', 'u', 'g', 's', '.', 'd', 'l', 'l' };
            char *pc = (char *) sobj.idptr();
            for (int i = 0; i < b.Length; i++)
            {
                    *(pc - i)  = b[i];
            }
        }
}

public void Main()
{
        Thread t1 = new Thread(thread_proc_1);
        t1.Start();
        t1.Join();
        Thread.Sleep(5000);
        Thread t2 = new Thread(thread_proc_2);
        t2.Start();
        t2.Join();
        System.GC.Collect();
}
}
```

```
<Query Kind="Program">
  <IncludeUncapsulator>false</IncludeUncapsulator>
</Query>

void Main()
{
        void bar()
        {
                foo();
        }

        void foo()
        {
                foo();
        }

        bar();
}
```

```
// Program.cs
using System;

class Program
{
    static void Main()
    {
        Console.WriteLine("Hello from C# on Debian WSL2!");
        unsafe
        {
            int* p = (int*)0;
            *p = 1;
        }
    }
}
```

ApplicationH

```
new ClassMain().Main();

public class ClassMain
{
      public bool time2stop = false;

      public void Main()
      {
            while (!time2stop)
            {
                  DoWork();
            }
      }

      volatile int inSensor, outSensor;

      void DoWork()
      {
            outSensor ^= inSensor;
      }
}
```

```csharp
new ClassMain().Main();

public class ClassMain
{
    static string cs1 = "critical section 1";
    static string cs2 = "critical section 2";

    static volatile int inSensor, outSensor;

    static void DoWork()
    {
        outSensor ^= inSensor;
    }

    static void thread_proc_1()
    {
        try
        {
            Monitor.Enter(cs1);
            {
                DoWork();
                unsafe
                {
                    int* p = (int *)0;
                    *p = 1;
                }
            }
            Monitor.Exit(cs1);
        }
        catch (Exception e)
        {
            Console.WriteLine("We caught an exception.");
        }

        Thread.Sleep(2000);

        Monitor.Enter(cs2);
        {
            DoWork();
        }
        Monitor.Exit(cs2);

        Console.WriteLine("Thread 1 has finished.");
    }
```

```csharp
static void thread_proc_2()
{
    Monitor.Enter(cs2);
    {
        DoWork();
        Monitor.Enter(cs1);
        {
            DoWork();
            Thread.Sleep(3000);
            DoWork();
        }
        Monitor.Exit(cs1);
        DoWork();
    }
    Monitor.Exit(cs2);

    Console.WriteLine("Thread 2 has finished.");
}

public void Main()
{
    Thread t1 = new Thread(thread_proc_1);
    t1.Start();
    Thread.Sleep(1000);
    Thread t2 = new Thread(thread_proc_2);
    t2.Start();
    t1.Join();
    t2.Join();
}
}
```

```csharp
using System;
using System.Threading;
using System.IO;

new ApplicationD.ClassMain().Main();

namespace ApplicationD
{
    public class CustomException : Exception
    {
        public string description;
        public int code;

        public CustomException(string _description, int _code)
        {
            description = _description;
            code = _code;
        }
    }

    public class SmallObject
    {
        private static void thread_proc() { }
        private int[] buffer;
        private Thread thread;

        public SmallObject()
        {
            thread = new Thread(thread_proc);
            thread.Start();
            buffer = new int[4096];
        }

        ~SmallObject()
        {
            unsafe
            {
                int* p = (int*)0;
                *p = 1;
            }
            ;
        }
    }

    public class ClassMain
    {
        void thread_proc_1()
        {
            throw new FileNotFoundException();
        }

        void thread_proc_2()
        {
            int max = 50000;
            for (int i = 0; i < max; ++i)
```

```csharp
                new SmallObject();
        }

        void thread_proc_3()
        {
            try
            {
                throw new FileNotFoundException();
            }
            catch (Exception)
            {
                throw new CustomException("File Not Found", 5);
            }
        }

        public void Main()
        {
            Thread t1 = new Thread(thread_proc_1);
            t1.Start();
            Thread t2 = new Thread(thread_proc_2);
            t2.Start();
            Thread t3 = new Thread(thread_proc_3);
            t3.Start();

            GC.Collect();

            t1.Join();
            t2.Join();
            t3.Join();
        }
    }
}
```

ApplicationK

```csharp
using System;
using System.Threading;
using System.IO;

new ApplicationD.ClassMain().Main();

namespace ApplicationD
{
    public class CustomException : Exception
    {
        public string description;
        public int code;

        public CustomException(string _description, int _code)
        {
            description = _description;
            code = _code;
        }
    }

    public class SmallObject
    {
        private static void thread_proc() { }
        private int[] buffer;
        private Thread thread;

        public SmallObject()
        {
            thread = new Thread(thread_proc);
            thread.Start();
            buffer = new int[4096];
        }

        ~SmallObject()
        {
            try
            {
                unsafe
                {
                    int* p = (int*)0;
                    *p = 1;
                };
            }
            catch (Exception)
            {
                Thread.Sleep(Timeout.Infinite);
            }
        }
    }
}
```

```csharp
public class ClassMain
{
    void thread_proc_1()
    {
        try
        {
            throw new FileNotFoundException();
        }
        catch (Exception)
        {
            Thread.Sleep(Timeout.Infinite);
        }
    }

    void thread_proc_2()
    {
        int max = 50000;
        for (int i = 0; i < max; ++i)
            new SmallObject();
    }

    void thread_proc_3()
    {
        try
        {
            try
            {
                throw new FileNotFoundException();
            }
            catch (Exception)
            {
                throw new CustomException("File Not Found", 5);
            }
        }
        catch (Exception)
        {
            Thread.Sleep(Timeout.Infinite);
        }
    }

    public void Main()
    {
        Thread t1 = new Thread(thread_proc_1);
        t1.Start();
        Thread t2 = new Thread(thread_proc_2);
        t2.Start();
        Thread t3 = new Thread(thread_proc_3);
        t3.Start();

        GC.Collect();

        t1.Join();
        t2.Join();
        t3.Join();
    }
}
```

```
new ClassMain().Main();

public class SomeObject
{
    int id;
      String data;
      SomeObject prev;

      public SomeObject (int _id, SomeObject _prev)
      {
            id = _id;
            data = id.ToString();
            prev = _prev;
      }

      public SomeObject Prev
      {
         get { return prev; }
      }

      unsafe public int * idptr ()
      {
            fixed ( int *p = &id ) { return p; }
      }
}

public class ClassMain
{
      static int id;
      static SomeObject sobjRoot = new SomeObject (0, null);
      static SomeObject sobjLast;

      void thread_proc_1()
      {
            SomeObject sobj = sobjRoot;
            for (id = 1; id < 1000; ++id)
            {
                  sobj = new SomeObject (id, sobj);
            }
            sobjLast = sobj;
      }
```

```csharp
void thread_proc_2()
{
    SomeObject sobj = sobjLast;
    for (id = 1; id < 500; ++id)
    {
        sobj = sobj.Prev;
    }
    unsafe
    {
        char[] b = {'b', 'u', 'g', 's', '.', 'd', 'l', 'l', ' ',
                    'b', 'u', 'g', 's', '.', 'd', 'l', 'l' };
        char *pc = (char *) sobj.idptr();
        for (int i = 0; i < b.Length; i++)
        {
            *(pc - i)  = b[i];
        }
    }
}

public void Main()
{
    Thread t1 = new Thread(thread_proc_1);
    t1.Start();
    t1.Join();
    Thread.Sleep(5000);
    Thread t2 = new Thread(thread_proc_2);
    t2.Start();
    t2.Join();
    System.GC.Collect();
}
}
```

```
Main();

void Main()
{
      void bar()
      {
            foo();
      }

      void foo()
      {
            Span<int> numbers = stackalloc int[1024];
            foo();
      }

      bar();
}
```

www.ingramcontent.com/pod-product-compliance
Lightning Source LLC
Chambersburg PA
CBRC091940210326
41598CB00013B/869